MORALITY
AND THE
GOOD LIFE

Edited by
Thomas L. Carson and Paul K. Moser

New York   Oxford
OXFORD UNIVERSITY PRESS
1997

OXFORD UNIVERSITY PRESS

Oxford   New York
Athens Auckland Bangkok Bogota Bombay
Buenos Aires Calcutta Cape Town Dar es Salaam Delhi
Florence Hong Kong Istanbul Karachi
Kuala Lumpur Madras Madrid Melbourne
Mexico City Nairobi Paris Singapore
Taipei Tokyo Toronto

and associated companies in

Berlin Ibadan

Library of Congress Cataloging-in-Publication Data
Morality and the good life
/ edited by Thomas L. Carson and Paul K. Moser.
p.   cm.
Includes bibliographical references and index.
ISBN 0-19-510537-0 (cloth).   ISBN 0-19-510538-9 (pbk.)
1. Ethics, Modern—20th century—Sources.   2. Ethics.
I. Carson, Thomas L., 1950–   .   II. Moser, Paul K., 1957–   .
BJ319.M665   1996
170—dc21   96-44810 CIP

Printing (last digit): 9   8   7   6   5   4   3   2

Printed in the United States of America
on acid-free paper

For Our Parents

Contents

PART I. CONCEPTS OF GOODNESS

Cognitivist Approaches

Noncognitivist Approaches: Defense and Criticism

Kinds of Goodness

PART II. WHAT THINGS ARE GOOD?

Hedonism: Defense and Criticism

The Desire-Satisfaction Theory: Defense and Criticism

Preface

This book includes thirty-four selections on morality and the theory of value. Its selections are essentially nontechnical and thus accessible to a wide range of readers, including advanced undergraduates, from various disciplines. The book's selections fall under six main topics: (I) Concepts of Goodness, (II) What Things are Good?, (III) Virtues and Ethics, (IV) Realism vs. Anti-Realism, (V) Value and Obligation, and (VI) The Value and Meaning of Life.

Given the philosophical breadth and prominence of its topics, the book can serve as the main text for undergraduate and graduate courses on contemporary ethical theory, moral philosophy, or theory of value. To enhance its pedagogical and research value, the book includes a substantial general introduction and an extensive topical bibliography on morality and the theory of value. Nonacademic readers curious about contemporary ethical theory should consult the introduction; it includes explanatory summaries of all the book's selections.

Many people have aided our work on the book. We thank Robert Miller, senior editor at Oxford University Press, for his help and encouragement in various ways, and several anonymous referees for Oxford. We also thank Marcia Baron, John Deigh, Tom Hurka, Noah Lemos, Julie Ward, and Tom Wren for helpful suggestions. We have benefited from the help of several philosophy graduate students at Loyola University of Chicago: Jason Beyer, Gregg Clark, Carmella Epright, Daniel Lorca, Chris Meyers, Colleen Sweeney, Jason Silverman, and especially Dwayne Mulder. We are grateful for their fine services. Loyola University of Chicago has provided an excellent environment for work on the book.

Chicago
March 20, 1996

T.L.C.
P.K.M.

Introduction

Twentieth-century moral philosophers have produced an enormous amount of published work, perhaps more than all the ethical work in the entire history of Western philosophy prior to the twentieth century. Much contemporary ethical work is more specialized than the ethical work of earlier philosophers. Twentieth-century moral philosophers in the Anglo-American tradition have been preoccupied with questions about the status of ethical judgments, but they have not neglected substantive ethical issues about what is right or wrong and what is good or bad. This book's selections illustrate the richness and variety of twentieth-century ethical theory in the Anglo-American philosophical tradition.

Ethical theory, broadly construed, includes virtually all the issues falling within the scope of ethics and moral philosophy. First-order ethical questions of *normative ethics* (e.g., "What things are good or bad?" and "What standards determine whether something is good or bad?") differ from second-order ethical questions of *metaethics* (e.g., "What does it mean to say that something is good or bad?" and "Are moral judgments true or false independent of what anyone thinks or prefers?"). The main questions of normative ethics concern what things are good or bad and what actions are right or wrong. The selections in Parts II, V, and VI of this volume address mainly first-order ethical questions of normative ethics; the selections in Parts I and IV address mainly second-order ethical questions of metaethics. The selections in Part III resist such easy categorization.

I. Concepts of Goodness

Cognitivist Approaches

1/G. E. Moore

Moore claims that "good" is indefinable and denotes a simple indefinable quality just as the word "yellow" does. We can give synonyms of "good" and "yellow" and explain how they are used in language, but these terms are indefinable in that they cannot be analyzed into component properties. Moore asks us to suppose that we have an acceptable definition of "good"—say, "good" means the same as "X" (where "X" is any term denoting a property). It makes sense to ask "Is X good?" but the question "Is X X?" makes no sense. So, the terms "good" and "X" do not mean the same thing. We can thus intelligibly ask the question "Is pleasure good?" but the question "Is pleasure pleasure?" lacks sense—it is self-contradictory to deny that pleasure is pleasure. So, "good" and "pleasure" do not mean the same thing.

Moore distinguishes between being good as a means and being good as an end. He claims that the concepts of right and wrong can be defined in terms of "good" and "bad": "to assert that a certain line of conduct is, at a given time, absolutely right or obligatory, is obviously to assert that more good or less evil will exist in the world, if it be adopted than if anything else be done instead." This makes a consequentialist theory of right and wrong true in virtue of the meaning of the words "right" and "obligatory."[1] Moore also defends the "principle of organic unities," which implies that value is not summative, that is, that the value of a given situation is not necessarily the same as the sum of the values of its parts taken in isolation. For example, beauty has very little value in itself (when it is unperceived), but it can contribute greatly to the value of certain wider states of affairs (e.g., aesthetic pleasure).

Moore's argument against naturalism is one of the most influential and widely discussed arguments in the entire history of philosophy. Many twentieth-century philosophers have accepted Moore's arguments to show that "good" does not refer to a complex property capable of being analyzed into constituent properties. Many of the same philosophers, however, believe that there are serious metaphysical and epistemological problems with Moore's view that "good" refers to a simple unanalyzable property that is directly intuited. Noncognitivist ethical theories,[2] such as emotivism and prescriptivism, arose in a context of philosophical debate in which it was generally assumed that (a) Moore has shown that "good" is not definable in the way that "horse" is, and (b) Moore's own positive view is untenable—"good" does not refer to a simple property of things that we can intuit. Many philosophers concluded that such words as "good" and "bad" do not refer to any properties at all.

2/Roderick Firth

In "Ethical Absolutism and the Ideal Observer," Roderick Firth offers a version of what Moore calls naturalism. Firth analyzes the meaning of moral concepts in terms of the notion of an ideal observer. According to Firth, moral judgments of the form "X is ———" (where "———" is a moral predicate such as "good" or "bad" or "right" or "wrong") are to be analyzed along the following lines: "All ideal observers would react in such and such ways to X." This means, roughly, that to make a favorable moral judgment about something (e.g., to say that it is good or right) is to say that all ideal observers would feel moral approval for it; to make an unfavorable moral judgment about something is to say that all ideal observers would feel moral disapproval for it. According to Firth, moral approval and disapproval are felt experiences or felt properties of experiences that are specifiable independent of our moral beliefs.

Firth ascribes the following characteristics to an ideal observer: (a) omniscience with respect to all nonmoral facts; (b) omnipercipience, or the ability to imagine vividly any events or states of affairs, including the experiences of others; (c) disinterestedness, or not having any interests or desires that involve essential reference to particular persons or things (for example, an ideal observer cannot desire his own happiness; he can desire only such things as the happiness of all human beings); (d) dispassionateness, or not having any emotions that are directed upon objects because they are believed to have essentially particular features (an ideal observer could not love a person only because the latter person is her own child); (e) consistency; and (f) normality "in other respects."

According to Firth, questions about the objectivity of morals are to be answered by determining the extent to which ideal observers would agree in their attitudes about moral questions. Firth would accept roughly the following as a criterion for the objective truth of moral judgments: A favorable (unfavorable) moral judgment about X is objectively true or correct if and only if all possible ideal observers would feel moral approval (disapproval) toward X. Firth thinks that ideal observers would all agree in their "morally significant attitudes" (moral approval and disapproval) about all possible moral questions. Given this, and given his version of the ideal-observer theory, all moral judgments must be either objectively true or objectively false. If ideal observers could disagree in their morally relevant attitudes about some or all ethical issues, then the ideal-observer theory commits us to relativism of some sort.[3]

Noncognitivist Approaches: Defense and Criticism

3/A. J. Ayer

According to A. J. Ayer's "Critique of Ethics," value judgments "are simply expressions of emotion which can neither be true nor false." He adds that ethical judgments not only express emotions but also arouse emotions in others or stimulate them to act in certain ways. Ayer distinguishes his view from "subjectivism," the view that ethical judgments are *statements* about one's emotions or attitudes. Subjectivists claim that "Lincoln was a good man" (as said by me) means roughly "I like Lincoln." On Ayer's theory, "Lincoln was a good man" means something more like "Yea Lincoln!" Some critics contend that emotivism cannot account for the obvious and pervasive phenomenon of *disagreement* about ethical questions. Suppose you say that Stalin was a good man and I say that he was a bad man. According to Ayer's theory, we are not making statements that contradict each other. In what sense, then, are we disagreeing? In this selection from the first edition of *Language, Truth and Logic*, Ayer denies that people ever really disagree about questions of value.

4/W. D. Ross

In selection 4, "Critique of Ayer," Ross criticizes A. J. Ayer's claim that people never disagree about questions of value. Ayer tries to show that (apparent) disagreements about value are really disagreements about questions of fact. Ross agrees that disagreements about value are often resolvable if the parties can agree about factual matters, but he claims that sometimes disagreements about value persist even if people agree about the relevant factual matters. Disagreement can persist even if the parties have exhausted any basis for arguing or justifying their views, for example, by showing that the other person is mistaken about the relevant facts. Ross claims that, on Ayer's view, it is puzzling that people should debate questions of value or be concerned to alter the attitudes of others. Debates about value are more than expressions of like or dislike for things. In such debates, people try to show each other that certain attitudes toward things are *justified*, that certain things deserve to be liked or disliked.

5/A. J. Ayer

In selection 5, from the introduction to the second edition of *Language, Truth, and Logic*, Ayer softens his earlier claims about the impossibility of disagreement about value. He claims that his view allows that there can be significant disagreements about questions of value, even though value judgments are not statements or propositions that can be true or false. Similarly, people can disagree about matters of taste, even if they do not disagree about the truth of any particular proposition. According to Ayer, such disagreements consist, in part, in the fact that each party is attempting to change the other person's attitudes. Ayer claims that disagreements about matters of basic ethical principle are not subject to rational resolution. Ethical reasoning and argumentation can take the form of disputing about relevant factual issues and pointing to inconsistencies in another person's views, but it can neither establish nor disprove basic attitudes or principles that are consistently held.

6/Allan Gibbard

Allan Gibbard's theory, called "expressivism," resembles emotivism. According to Gibbard, to say that something (an act, belief, or feeling) is rational, in the sense of "being apt" or "making sense," is to express one's acceptance of norms permitting it.

Gibbard analyzes moral judgments in terms of the aptness or rationality of feelings of guilt and anger. As a first approximation, Gibbard proposes the following analysis of "moral wrong": What a person does is *morally wrong* if and only if it is rational for the person to feel guilty for having done it and for others to be angry at that person for having done it. Refining this view, Gibbard distinguishes between "objective" and "subjective" wrongness. He also proposes an analysis of "blameworthy" and "reprehensible." Gibbard does not appeal to "the meaning" of moral concepts; he claims that recent developments in the philosophy of language and Quine's attack on the analytic-synthetic distinction have discredited the idea that conceptual analysis in philosophy should seek to explicate "the meanings" of concepts. Gibbard takes his conceptual scheme to be a proposal about how to use normative concepts. He claims that his proposals allow us to raise important questions and do not foreclose or answer substantive questions by appeal to the meaning of concepts.

Evidently, not every society has a normative system that includes norms for guilt and anger. Thus, on Gibbard's narrow construal of "morality," not every society has a morality. Gibbard asks us to consider whether we would be better off without morality narrowly construed, that is, without a normative system in which norms for guilt and resentment play a large role. Gibbard says very little about the concept of value or intrinsic goodness in selection 6 (or anywhere else in the book from which the selection derives). In a subsequent publication, Gibbard speaks briefly to questions about how he would analyze the concept of intrinsic value: "[G]ood means desirable. Something is intrinsically good if an intrinsic desire for it is warranted. This, of course, needs refinement."[4]

7/R. M. Hare

Hare claims that moral judgments are universalizable prescriptions. To say that moral judgments are universalizable, on Hare's view, means that if one makes a moral judgment about something, one is committed to making exactly the same judgment about anything similar to it in the relevant respects. A descriptive term such as "red" is universalizable in that way. If you call something "red," you are committed to saying that anything like it in the relevant respects is also red. Prescriptions are commands, or imperatives (e.g., "Don't lie!"). Hare claims elsewhere that a necessary condition of one's accepting a prescription is that one actually follow it or try to follow it if one is able to do so.[5] This is tantamount to a denial of the existence of moral weakness, or *akrasia*. Hare uses his theory of meaning as the basis of a theory of moral reasoning, proposing that we can criticize a person's moral judgments by asking whether that person would be willing to universalize those judgments. For example, suppose a Nazi says that it is permissible to kill Jews. On pain of inconsistency, the Nazi must say that it would be right for others to kill *him* if he were Jewish.[6]

In his later book *Moral Thinking*, Hare modifies his view. There he claims that moral judgments are universalizable prescriptions that the speaker takes to be "overriding." Hare's earlier theory had difficulty distinguishing moral judgments from other kinds of universalizable prescriptions, for example, "Don't bet on a lame horse!"[7] His later view enables us to explain why "Don't bet on a lame horse!" is not a moral judgment in ordinary contexts. "Don't bet on a lame horse!," as uttered by me, is not a moral judgment, because I don't think that it should be overriding.

8/Philippa Foot

According to Foot, both emotivism and prescriptivism imply that for someone to say that something is good/bad or right/wrong is just for her to have a certain sort of attitude about it. There are, according to these theories, no limits to the kinds of things that can be *objects* of our attitudes. One can consistently call *anything* good or bad. In "Moral Beliefs," Foot claims that this is a mistake; she contends that there are limits to the things to which "good" can be consistently ascribed. Something can be called a "good action" only if it satisfies one of the following conditions: (a) It is the fulfillment of a special duty derived from a role or promise, or (b) it exemplifies a virtue. It follows that we can't say that twiddling one's thumbs, for instance, is a morally good action in the absence of special reasons for thinking that it serves some purpose.

Foot claims that sometimes facts about things entail evaluative conclusions. For example, the fact that something is injurious to one suggests that one has prima facie reason to avoid it. Foot claims that we have reason to be virtuous only if being virtuous is advantageous for us: "[I]f justice is not a good to the just man, moralists who recommend it as a virtue are perpetuating a fraud." Foot argues that the virtues, including justice, are generally advantageous to those who possess them.

Kinds of Goodness

9/Christine Korsgaard

Christine Korsgaard's paper, "Two Distinctions in Goodness," does not speak to the same conceptual issues addressed by the other selections in Part I. Instead, it attempts to clarify distinctions between different kinds of value. Many philosophers distinguish between things "intrinsically good" and things "instrumentally good." Korsgaard argues that this way of speaking obscures the fact that these terms require us to make *two* distinctions between different kinds of goodness. Being intrinsically good (possessing value in itself or in isolation) is not the same as being good as an end. The distinction between intrinsic and extrinsic goodness is not the same as the distinction between being good as an end and being good as a means. There is no reason to think that everything that has noncausal or noninstrumental value possesses value in isolation, and there is no reason to think that things having value in isolation always possess noncausal value when they occur as parts of wider states of affairs. (Moore makes the same point with his concept of the "organic unity of value"—the value of a whole is not simply the sum of values of its parts taken in isolation.)

According to Korsgaard, things good as ends can be either conditionally or unconditionally good (she claims that this distinction can be found in Kant). Things that are conditionally good are good and make the world a better place, but only if certain conditions hold. Unconditionally good things make the world a better place regardless of what other conditions hold. According to Kant, happiness is a conditionally good end. It is good on the condition that the person possessing it is morally good and thus worthy of being happy. Kant thinks that a "good will" is the only thing that is unconditionally good.[8]

II. What Things Are Good?

Hedonistic theories of value imply that pleasure is the only thing good as an end and that pain is the only thing bad as an end; they also imply that all pleasure is good as an end and that all pain is bad as an end. According to such a theory, pleasure is the only thing ultimately constitutive of a good life; other things make for a good life only insofar as they promote pleasure or prevent pain. Classical utilitarians (e.g., Bentham, Mill, and Sidgwick) defended a hedonistic theory of value.

Many contemporary utilitarians defend a desire-satisfaction theory of value (welfare). A desire-satisfaction theory is usually presented as a theory of personal welfare, rather than as a theory of value. Roughly, a desire-satisfaction theory of welfare implies that one's welfare is determined (solely) by the satisfaction of one's (actual or ideal) desires. Such a theory implies that what makes something good (as an end) is that it is desired by someone as an end (or would be desired as an end by someone who was rational). Selections 12 and 13, by von Wright and Kraut, construe a desire-satisfaction theory as a theory of welfare.

"Objectivist" theories imply that things other than pleasure and pain are good and bad as ends and that some things are good or bad independent of one's desiring them, even one's desiring them if one were rational. Some objectivist theories of value, such as Hurka's, are based on the notion of human nature. Roughly, they say that to have a good life is to develop to a high degree those capacities essential for being human. Other objectivist theories, such as those defended by Moore and Ross, imply that a number of different things are ultimately good or bad.

Hedonism: Defense and Criticism

10/Henry Sidgwick

Henry Sidgwick defends a (quantitative) hedonistic theory of value. In several passages from *The Methods of Ethics*, not included here, Sidgwick defines pleasure as a feeling one apprehends to be "desirable":

> Let, then, pleasure be defined as feeling which the sentient individual at the time of feeling it implicitly or explicitly apprehends to be desirable;—desirable, that is, when considered merely as feeling, and not in respect of its objective conditions or consequences, or of any facts that come directly within the cognisance and judgment of others besides the sentient individual.[9]

Few would deny that pleasure is good. Critics of hedonism, however, generally deny that pleasure is the only thing good as an end. In "Ultimate Good," Sidgwick attempts to answer this objection by asking us to consider some of the things other than pleasure that nonhedonists have regarded as part of the ultimate good: being virtuous, possessing a good will (being the kind of person who does what he thinks is right), and having talent. He argues that none of these is good in itself.

The outlines of Sidgwick's main positive argument for the truth of hedonism are as follows. Nothing can be good apart from entering into or helping to bring about desirable conscious states; a universe without conscious beings would possess no value. Therefore, the ultimate good consists in desirable states of consciousness. Conscious states include feelings, volitions, and cognitions, but volitions and cognitions are not intrinsically valuable. So, the ultimate good consists in desirable feelings. This conclusion, taken together with Sidgwick's definition of "pleasure" as any feeling experienced as desirable and his claim that the desirability of feelings is directly cognizable by those having them (a feeling's being desirable is just its being experienced as desirable), implies that pleasure alone is the ultimate good.[10] Sidgwick also argues that only a hedonistic theory of value enables us to "systematize" our common sense beliefs about what things are good or bad. He claims that the things valued by common sense are all productive of pleasure and esteemed by us roughly in proportion as they tend to produce pleasure.

11/Robert Nozick

In "Value and Pleasure," Robert Nozick imagines a machine that could give us any kind of experience we desire. Nozick uses this thought experiment to assess the following question: "What else can matter to us, other than how our lives feel from the inside?" Nozick claims that three other kinds of things matter to us and that, in consequence, we will find the idea of living in an experience machine unappealing in three respects. First, according to Nozick, we want to *do* certain things and not just to have the experience of doing them. Second, we want to be persons of a certain sort. A brain passively undergoing experiences as a result of electrode stimulation cannot properly be characterized as courageous, kind, or loving. We care not only about what kinds of experiences we have but also about what kinds of people we are. Third, in an experience machine we are not in contact with reality. Nozick imagines further variations of the experience machine, for instance, a result machine that will give you any result you want. Snap your fingers and become a talented virtuous person, if you so desire. Nozick asks whether the results in question would matter much to us if we didn't have to strive to achieve them. Even if Nozick is correct in claiming that most people care about things other than pleasure and the absence of pain, defenders of a hedonistic theory of value might argue that we are *mistaken* in caring about anything other than pleasure and the absence of pain.[11]

The Desire-Satisfaction Theory: Defense and Criticism

12/G. H. von Wright

In "The Good of Man," G.H. von Wright defends a desire-satisfaction theory of personal welfare. The key notion is that of wanting something in itself. I want something in itself provided that, if offered it, I would take it rather than leave it (abstracting from all considerations about its causal prerequisites and consequences). Von Wright defends the ideal-desire (rather than the actual-desire) version of the theory. According to von Wright, the question whether it would enhance one's welfare to have X cannot be answered simply by determining whether one actually wants X in itself. Acquiring X would enhance one's welfare provided that, *if one were informed*, one *would prefer* the whole consisting of X and its causal requirements and consequences to the whole consisting of not-X and its causal requirements and consequences. Von Wright also proposes an analysis of "happiness" in terms of being pleased with one's life as a whole.

13/Richard Kraut

In "Desire and the Human Good," Richard Kraut objects to the desire-satisfaction theory of welfare. His main objection notes that a person might desire to harm or punish herself. Such a desire could be rational in any of the various senses of "rational" proposed by standard versions of the desire-satisfaction theory. It would be absurd, however, to think that the satisfaction of such a desire contributes to the *good* (welfare) of the person in question since, in such a case, one desires to do what is detrimental to one's own good (welfare). Proponents of the (ideal) desire-satisfaction theory must either (a) deny that it could be rational to desire to punish oneself or (b) deny Kraut's claim that it would be absurd to say that self-punishment promotes one's own welfare (even if one rationally desires to punish oneself).

Kraut takes "being good" to mean, roughly, "being worthy of being loved or cared about." According to Kraut, being wanted by someone does not confer desirability on things. The goodness of things consists in their having objective properties that make them worthy of being wanted. Kraut does not formulate a complete theory of value, but he suggests that the correct theory is a pluralistic theory according to which different kinds of things and lives are good.

Objectivist Theories

14/G. E. Moore

In "The Ideal," G. E. Moore rejects both hedonism and desire-satisfaction theories of value. He claims that by far the best things in the universe (with which we are acquainted) are "the pleasures of human intercourse and the enjoyment of beautiful objects." According to Moore, the three greatest evils are (a) the "enjoyment or admiring contemplation of things which are themselves evil or ugly," (b) "the hatred of what is good or beautiful," and (c) intense pain. Moore's theory is asymmetrical in that it regards intense pain by itself as a great evil but does not regard intense pleasure by itself as a great good. Moore defends the "principle of organic unities," which states that the value of concrete situations ("wholes") is not simply the sum of the values of their parts in isolation. Pleasure has little intrinsic value (Moore takes "intrinsic value" to mean value in isolation), but it can have great value as a part of the enjoyment of beauty. Pleasure sometimes detracts from the value of larger situations, as in cases of *schadenfreude*, or pleasure in the bad.

Moore denies that the ideal includes any evil and adds that it is better that the universe not include any evil, even if this makes it impossible for moral goodness to exist. (Moore's claim that moral goodness/virtue is not a great good is crucial here.) Moore rejects traditional attempts to solve the problem of evil by claiming that the existence of evil is necessary for (the greater good of) moral goodness. He concedes that it is *possible* that evil contributes to the value of some larger organic whole. He denies, however, that we have any reason to think that this is so.

Moore describes the nature of aesthetic experience and aesthetic pleasure. He defines "the beautiful" as "that of which the admiring contemplation is good in itself." He defines "the ugly" as "that of which the admiring contemplation is evil in itself."

15/W. D. Ross

In "What Things are Good?," W. D. Ross proposes that the only things that are intrinsically good are (a) morally virtuous actions and dispositions, (b) pleasures that are neither "undeserved" (undeserved pleasures are the pleasures of morally bad people) nor the result of bad dispositions, and (c) knowledge (and, to a lesser extent, true opinion). Ross claims that moral virtue is of incomparably greater value than either pleasure or knowledge. On his view, the value of *any* amount of moral virtue (however small) exceeds the value of *any* amount of pleasure or knowledge (however great). Ross also claims that knowledge is more valuable than pleasure.

Ross holds that the moral goodness of an action depends on the motives from which it springs. He distinguishes between the moral *rightness or wrongness* of an action and its moral *goodness or badness*. A morally right act can be morally bad, and a morally wrong act can be morally good. Ross holds that the desire to do one's duty is the morally best motive. The desire to bring about good states of affairs and the desire to give others pleasure and to save them from pain are also morally good motives. Ross mentions a case where a person does what is right and is motivated by both the desire to do what is right and the desire to give another person pleasure. On one interpretation, Kant holds that this act would have greater moral worth if it were motivated solely by the desire to do what is right. Ross objects, arguing that the best kind of person would have both kinds of motive.[12]

16/Thomas Hurka

In "Perfectionism," Thomas Hurka defends a perfectionist theory of value. As a first approximation, Hurka takes perfectionism, as a theory of value or the good life, to state that a good life develops to a high degree those properties central to human nature. Hurka identifies Plato, Aristotle, Marx, Nietzsche, Green, and Bosanquet as perfectionists. He gives three reasons to reject the view that a good life consists in the development of characteristics unique to human beings. First, not all uniquely human characteristics are good. The unique features of the human digestive system, for instance, have no normative significance; further, certain bad features of human beings—e.g., our ability to kill for fun—may be uniquely human. Second, the development of physical aspects of our nature that we share with animals is partly constitutive of our good. Third, whether the development of human capacities such as rationality is constitutive of the human good is independent of whether nonhuman creatures possess those capacities. Hurka claims that, according to Aristotle and Marx, a good life consists in the exercise of characteristics essential for and unique to being human. He rejects this view on the ground that it invites the second and third objections.

Hurka holds that a good life develops to a high degree those properties essential for being human[13] and claims that this view avoids the three objections. While such characteristics as lying and killing for fun may be unique to humans, they are not essential for being human. Hurka is not committed to saying that the development of such characteristics constitutes a good life. Since characteristics can be essential for being human even if they aren't unique to human beings, Hurka's theory avoids the second and third objections. Hurka argues that rationality (or the potential to be rational) is essential for being human and that, therefore, the perfection of our rational powers is a crucial element of the good life.

17/Derek Parfit

In "What Makes Someone's Life Go Best?," Derek Parfit discusses the notion of self-interest, or personal welfare—the notion of what is "good and bad for us." He examines three different kinds of theories: hedonistic theories, desire-fulfillment theories, and objective-list theories. Parfit makes additional distinctions within the first two categories. "Preference hedonism," for instance, combines a hedonistic theory of welfare with the view that pleasant experiences are those wanted for their own sake and unpleasant experiences are those unwanted for their own sake. The unrestricted version of the desire-fulfillment theory claims that the satisfaction of *any* of one's desires contributes to one's well-being. An alternative version of the desire-fulfillment theory, which Parfit calls the "success theory," holds that our welfare is determined by the satisfaction (or nonsatisfaction) of "our preferences about our own lives." Parfit argues that the success theory is more plausible than the unrestricted version of the desire-fulfillment theory, but he does not offer clear criteria for distinguishing between preferences "for our own lives" and other preferences.[14]

Parfit distinguishes between "summative" and "global" desire-fulfillment theories. Summative theories view one's overall welfare as a net sum of the satisfaction and nonsatisfaction of one's individual desires. Global theories, in contrast, make welfare a function of the satisfaction (or nonsatisfaction) of global desires for one's life as a whole (or significant parts of one's life). Parfit offers some arguments for preferring global theories to summative theories. While not making a clear distinction between the actual-desire and the ideal-desire versions of the desire-fulfillment theory, Parfit seems to prefer the latter. "Objective-list" theories imply that certain things are good or bad for people independent of whether they desire or would desire those things. These goods and bads might include such things as knowledge, moral goodness, and not being deceived. Parfit concludes by sketching a compromise between hedonism and the objective-list theory, for which he expresses considerable sympathy.

III. Virtues and Ethics

Late-twentieth-century moral philosophy has shown renewed interest in the virtues and the possibility of using a concept of virtue as a basis for ethical theories. Elizabeth Anscombe's paper "Modern Moral Philosophy" (selection 18) marks the beginning of this trend. Her paper also contributed to renewed interest in divine-command theories of morality. The selections by MacIntyre and Foot discuss the concept of virtue and certain specific virtues. Anscombe addresses the tenability of ethical theories based on a concept of virtue.

18/G. E. M. Anscombe

In "Modern Moral Philosophy," G. E. M. Anscombe contends that contemporary moral philosophy employs categories very different from the categories of Aristotle's moral philosophy. According to Anscombe, Aristotle has no notion of obligation or moral goodness corresponding to ours. She claims that the concepts of duty and obligation are legalistic notions deriving from Judaism and Christianity. A legalistic conception of morality makes no sense, according to Anscombe, unless we suppose that there is a lawgiver, that is, God. Theories of moral obligation make sense only within the context of a divine-law, or divine-command, theory.[15]

Much of modern moral philosophy is incoherent in that it retains the notions of moral duty and obligation while rejecting the religious beliefs they presuppose. Anscombe likens this to calling people "criminals" in a world where there are no criminal laws or criminal courts. Those who reject a divine lawgiver, according to Anscombe, should drop the notion of "morally ought." It will not do for them to try to substitute the laws or norms of actual societies as the source of moral law, because history shows that the laws and norms of actual societies can be dreadfully bad. The best option for atheists would be to adopt a system of morality based, like Aristotle's, on a notion of virtue. A notion of virtue and the kind of moral theory Aristotle offers need not presuppose the existence of God. Anscombe concludes with an attack on utilitarianism.

19/Philippa Foot

In "Virtues and Vices," Philippa Foot claims that the word "virtue" had a broader meaning in ancient Greece than it now has. The Greek word *arete* means "excellence," connoting any kind of excellence—including excellences of the speculative intellect. In modern English, the word "virtue" has a narrower meaning, connoting moral virtues. In a preliminary definition, Foot proposes that virtues are strengths or excellences of the will that are beneficial and needed for ourselves or others. Virtue is not just a function of what we do or try to do; it is also a function of feeling and how we are disposed to feel. Virtue concerns "what is wished for as well as what is sought." This needs to be qualified, since practical wisdom is a virtue but is not (exclusively) a quality of the will. Foot restricts her analysis to the moral virtues. She claims that the moral virtues are in some way beneficial to us, as we don't fare well without them. Some virtues, such as courage, temperance, and wisdom, benefit both ourselves and others. Some people think that such virtues as charity and justice benefit only others. Foot, however, thinks that people are better off, on the whole, if they are charitable and just and suggests that there are unusual circumstances where one must sacrifice everything for the sake of justice or charity.[16]

Foot considers the thesis that virtues are correctives, with "each one standing at a point at which there is some temptation to be resisted or deficiency of motivation to be made good." Such virtues as temperance, courage, humility, and industry are correctives. It is not clear, however, that justice and charity are correctives to anything in particular. Foot asks about the relation between virtuous action and difficult action. Suppose I have difficulty performing a virtuous act. Other things equal, does this difficulty make the act more or less virtuous? Foot also asks whether virtue can be exercised in the pursuit of bad actions. Can one, for example, display courage in committing a terrible crime? Foot holds that one can display courage in morally bad actions but that in such circumstance courage is not a virtue.

20/Alasdair MacIntyre

In "The Nature of the Virtues," Alasdair MacIntyre confronts problems raised by the diversity of historically important views about the virtues. Identification of the virtues varies significantly even among such key Western influences as Homer, Aristotle, and the New Testament. This prompts the question whether there is in fact a common, core notion of the virtues that people in these and other traditions aim to capture. MacIntyre emphasizes the diversity within the Western tradition by comparing ancient systems of virtues with those of two more recent authors, Jane Austen and Benjamin Franklin.

The most striking differences between the accounts of the virtues, according to MacIntyre, concern the preconditions for the virtues. In Homer, the notion of a virtue depends on the prior notion of a social role, as virtues are identified only in application to specified social roles. In Aristotle, the notion of a virtue depends on specification of a universal human nature, including specification of the *telos* of humans. The New Testament account of virtue also depends on claims about the good for humans, but it specifies a supernatural good in addition to a natural good for humans. Jane Austen combines the Christian morality of the New Testament with a distinct concern for social roles. Benjamin Franklin's account of the virtues is teleological (as is Aristotle's) but also utilitarian. These sources employ three very different conceptions of a virtue: (a) a virtue is a quality enabling one to fill a social role, (b) a virtue is a quality enabling one to achieve one's specifically human *telos*, either natural or supernatural, and (c) a virtue is a quality having utility in achieving success.

MacIntyre argues that there is a core concept of virtue common to the Western tradition. The application of a concept of a virtue always requires some prior account of social and moral life for its definition and explanation. Central to this account of social and moral life is the notion of a *practice*. MacIntyre defines a practice as "any coherent and complex form of socially established cooperative human activity through which goods internal to that form of activity are realized in the course of trying to

achieve those standards of excellence which are appropriate to, and partially definitive of, that form of activity." The goods internal to a practice can be adequately judged
only by those within the practice, those proficient to some degree in the practice. Such
goods set the standards of excellence. MacIntyre characterizes the core idea of a virtue
as "an acquired human quality the possession and exercise of which tends to enable
us to achieve those goods which are internal to practices and the lack of which effectively prevents us from achieving any such goods." In short, virtues are qualities
that contribute to excellence, the increase of internal rewards, in a practice.
Participation in a practice defines one's relationships with others in the practice, and
the virtues have a proper bearing on those relationships.

MacIntyre examines how closely his core conception of a virtue accords with the
traditional sources noted previously. He claims that it fits fairly well with some of
these views, especially Aristotle's, but clearly does not fit with any utilitarian conception of the virtues, such as Franklin's. A utilitarian concept defines "virtue" in
terms of external goods, whereas MacIntyre defines it only in terms of internal goods.
He claims that a utilitarian concept of virtue is fundamentally at odds with the ancient and medieval tradition.

IV. Realism vs. Antirealism

Contemporary debates about moral (or axiological) realism and antirealism concern
the ontological status of values. The key issue is whether, and if so in what manner,
values exist independent of human attitudes. Moral realists affirm the independent
existence of values; moral antirealists deny the independent existence of values. A
key issue of moral epistemology concerns how we can rationally adjudicate this long-
standing conflict. The selections in this section represent various perspectives on value
realism.

21/J. L. Mackie

In "The Subjectivity of Values," J. L. Mackie argues that there are no objective values.
Distinguishing his thesis from various first-order ethical views and claims about the
meanings of moral terms, Mackie emphasizes that his is a negative ontological claim.
He argues that the matter of objectivity in ethics has important implications for metaphysics, epistemology, philosophical psychology, practical reason, and moral argument.

The denial of objective values does not entail a denial of the objectivity of value
judgments relative to some given set of standards of evaluation. Mackie addresses
rather the objectivity of the standards themselves, claiming that his thesis can be understood via the familiar distinction between hypothetical and categorical imperatives. After clarifying this distinction, Mackie denies the objective validity of any categorical imperative and argues that objective validity attaches only to hypothetical
imperatives.

According to Mackie, the objectivity of values is presupposed in traditional ethical
theory and in ordinary, common-sense moral judgments. Mackie holds that the common claim to objectivity in moral discourse is nonetheless false. Thus, he holds an
"error theory" of morality, arguing that all moral judgments are false or mistaken in
that they purport to be objectively true, but aren't. Mackie uses arguments from rel-

ativity and queerness to support his theory. The claim that the variability of moral standards results from divergent perceptions of objective values is highly implausible, according to Mackie. The argument from queerness claims that if there were objective values "they would be entities or qualities or relations of a very strange sort, utterly different from anything else in the universe." If we are to have knowledge of objective values, furthermore, it must be through some very strange channels, quite unlike the familiar channels for acquiring knowledge. Another queer feature of objective values would be their relation to natural features, requiring a kind of dependence difficult to explicate.

Mackie explains how we came to think of values as objective. He identifies objectification of values as a type of projection and examines both the personal and the social pressures toward such projection. Mackie concedes, in conclusion, that if there were a God who authored moral imperatives, moral values could be considered objective. He does not, however, find theism defensible.

22/John McDowell

In "Values and Secondary Qualities," John McDowell argues that evaluative thought, or the experience of values, brings us into contact with an objective reality. McDowell takes values to be secondary qualities like colors. Following Locke, such philosophers as J. L. Mackie believe that only the experience of *primary* qualities brings us into contact with objective features of the objects of experience.

McDowell characterizes secondary-quality experience as experience of a genuine disposition, or power, in things to produce certain sorts of perceptual experiences under certain conditions. He criticizes Mackie's analysis of secondary-quality experience, which claims that it is a "projection error" to take such experience as being of some genuine aspect of the world. Mackie thinks that taking secondary-quality experience as genuine entails ascribing to the objects of experience the properties that they possess *as experienced*. To say, for example, that an experienced red object has an objective property of being red is, according to Mackie, to claim that it possesses the property of experienced redness, the identical qualitative redness of our perceptual experience. McDowell disagrees, arguing that Mackie's interpretation of secondary-quality experience is incoherent. Redness, on McDowell's account, is the genuine disposition in certain objects to produce in us under certain conditions qualitatively red experiences. He explains how secondary-quality experience is subjective in one sense but *not* in the sense that it cannot reveal genuine aspects of the world. McDowell's account of secondary-quality experience explains how value experience can reveal genuine aspects of the world.

McDowell criticizes arguments against the objective status of values based on considerations of the demands of explanation. The disposition to produce, for example, red sensations in us can be real even though it does not contribute to an explanation of why something looks red. Likewise, values can be real even if they do not contribute to explanations of value experience. McDowell notes one important distinguishing characteristic of values: They not only elicit certain attitudes but also merit certain attitudes. We make sense of moral attitudes by seeing them as responses to objects that merit such responses. McDowell claims, in opposition to Simon Blackburn, that the training of feelings of value experience is just the cultivation of an ability to spot objective fitnesses of things. He denies that his approach requires the codifiability of evaluative experience in a set of general principles.

23/Simon Blackburn

In "Errors and the Phenomenology of Value," Simon Blackburn defends his thesis of projectivism against some prominent criticisms. He notes a general problem faced by any error theory such as Mackie's. Mackie's error theory claims that normal moral discourse carries with it a commitment to an objectivist interpretation of moral claims and that this commitment is in fact in error. Our ordinary moral judgments, on this theory, are all in error because no objective moral values exist. Still, Mackie advocates preserving ordinary moral discourse, and he uses it extensively himself. This presents a problem, as one would expect defenders of an error theory to advocate elimination or revision of the relevant areas of erroneous discourse.

Blackburn examines arguments for the retention of the erroneous vocabulary, but he regards his "quasi-realism" as the best account of the function of moral discourse for a projectivist. He admits that the quasi-realist solution will leave some people uneasy about whether quasi-realists have good reason to take morality seriously. It may appear that quasi-realism undermines the felt forcefulness of moral directives, especially the force of moral obligations. Blackburn examines various attempts, compatible with projectivism, to preserve the phenomenological character of moral obligations, including their seeming to come from without. He finds no problem in maintaining the feeling of being bound by moral obligations that receive a subjective explanation.

Blackburn examines the moral realist's comparison of our knowledge of ethics with our knowledge of mathematics and secondary qualities. He claims that quasi-realism can be helpful here and emphasizes various disanalogies between secondary qualities and values or obligations. He concludes that the analogy with experience of secondary qualities does not support a realist theory of ethics. Analogies with mathematics also fail, as realist explanations of mathematical practice are no better than antirealist explanations. Blackburn rejects the "quietist" claim that we need no explanation of moral thinking, and he proposes that the projectivist explanation is the best. Blackburn notes that his view seems to recommend a type of consequentialism, "motive-consequentialism," as a first-order theory of ethics.

24/Nicholas Sturgeon

In "Moral Explanations," Nicholas Sturgeon responds to Gilbert Harman's argument that moral realism is untenable because reference to moral facts seems completely irrelevant to the explanation of our moral observations and moral beliefs. The explanatory irrelevance of moral facts allegedly shows that we are not justified in thinking that there are moral facts. Sturgeon aims to show that Harman's argument either rests on highly dubious assumptions or supports a general skeptical attitude that is not a problem unique to ethics. Sturgeon also intends to show that moral realism is defensible and, further, that ethical naturalism is plausible even in the absence of reductive naturalistic definitions for ethical terms.

The problem that Harman presents for ethics is not merely the verificationist worry about empirical testability. His charge is specifically that we need not assume that there are any moral facts in order to explain our moral observations or beliefs. We can explain them adequately with psychological descriptions of the agent making the observations or holding the beliefs. Sturgeon agrees that the explanatory role of alleged moral facts is relevant to the justification of belief in them, but he claims that appeals to alleged moral facts actually have an explanatory role that justifies our accepting them as genuine facts. In attacking Harman's argument, Sturgeon argues that, on the assumption that they exist, moral facts can be relevant to explanations of moral observations and beliefs. He defends this argumentative strategy by interpreting Harman's thesis as the claim that moral facts, even if we assume they exist, are explanatorily irrelevant. Sturgeon notes also that if there are naturalistic reductions of all moral terms, reference to moral facts will be eliminable from all explanations of moral observations and beliefs. He argues, however, not even an ethical naturalist need accept this reducibility thesis.

Sturgeon provides examples of moral explanations that rely on moral facts, such as facts about moral character. He argues that the reference to moral facts is not completely irrelevant to these explanations by pointing out that if the moral facts in question had not obtained, we would not expect the explained moral beliefs to have occurred. He criticizes a competing interpretation of Harman's thesis that would lead to a different counterfactual question: If all the nonmoral facts had been exactly the same but the moral facts in question had not obtained, would the agent's moral beliefs have been the same? Sturgeon claims that the antecedent of this counterfactual is necessarily false, because of the supervenience of moral facts on natural nonmoral facts. Sturgeon concludes by indicating why someone already attracted to moral skepticism or moral nihilism would find Harman's argument plausible. He notes that there remains a distinct, and more troubling, argument for moral skepticism based on the difficulty of settling disputed moral questions, and he claims that the moral realist should focus attention on that argument.

V. Value and Obligation

Questions about right and wrong or duty and obligation are centrally important in moral philosophy. Theories of right and wrong are either consequentialist or nonconsequentialist. Utilitarians, or consequentialists, hold that the rightness or wrongness of an action is determined solely by the goodness or badness of its results. More precisely, utilitarianism/consequentialism implies that an action is morally right if and only if no alternative course of action open to the agent would result in better consequences overall and suggests that an action is morally obligatory if and only if it results in better consequences overall than any alternative course of action open to the agent. Nonconsequentialists, in contrast, deny that the rightness or wrongness of actions depends solely on their consequences.

25/G. E. Moore

In "Results the Test of Right and Wrong," G. E. Moore claims that the rightness or wrongness of an action is determined solely by its consequences. It is always right and always one's duty to perform the action having the best consequences (of all possible alternative actions). According to Moore, it is "self-evident that knowingly to do an action that would make the world, on the whole, really and truly *worse* than if we had acted differently, must always be wrong." Departing from his earlier views, Moore does not take this to be true in virtue the meaning of the words "duty" and "right."[17] In answer to the objection that motives at least partly determine the rightness or wrongness of actions, Moore replies that, while motives are relevant to certain kinds of moral judgments (judgments about the praiseworthiness or blameworthiness of people), they are not relevant to determining the rightness or wrongness of actions.[18]

Sometimes it is difficult, if not impossible, for people to know the consequences of what they do. Suppose someone makes every possible effort to bring about the best consequences, but, for reasons she could not have foreseen, her action turns out not to have the best consequences. Moore's view implies that this action would be wrong. Some find this an objectionable implication of Moore's theory. As an alternative, one might suggest that the rightness or wrongness of an action depends on its *probable consequences* as opposed to its *actual consequences*. Moore thinks that this objection can be answered by invoking the distinction between what is *right* (wrong) and what is *praiseworthy* (blameworthy). In the imagined case, the action is wrong, but the person is not blameworthy for having performed it.

26/J. J. C. Smart

In "Act-Utilitarianism and Rule-Utilitarianism," J. J. C. Smart defines "act-utilitarianism" (AU) as the view that "the rightness or wrongness of an action is to be judged by the consequences, good or bad, of the action itself." He defines "rule-utilitarianism" (RU) as the view that "the rightness or wrongness of an action is to be judged by the goodness or badness of the consequences of a rule that everyone should perform the action in like circumstances." Smart defends AU over RU. Advocates of RU claim that the two theories yield different results in practice. If this is correct, then there will be cases where following the rules endorsed by RU will not permit the course of action producing the best possible outcome in a given situation.

According to Smart, the rule-utilitarian is guilty of irrational "rule worship." The rule-utilitarian endorses certain moral rules because they promote human happiness but insists on following them when they don't serve their intended purpose. Smart argues that, when properly construed, rule-utilitarianism is probably extensionally equivalent to act-utilitarianism. The set of rules that would produce the best consequences upon being followed by everyone "would in fact consist of one rule, only, the act-utilitarian one: 'maximize probable benefit.' "

27/Richard Brandt

In "The Real and Alleged Problems of Utilitarianism," Richard Brandt argues in favor of rule utilitarianism (RU). He defines RU as the view that "right actions are the kind permitted by the moral code optimal for the society of which the agent is a member. An optimal moral code is one designed to maximize welfare or what is good." Brandt claims that RU is not equivalent to act utilitarianism (AU), because it is possible that particular actions permitted by an optimal moral code would not maximize benefit. An optimal moral code includes not only rules but also the inculcation of "desires or aversions directed at certain kinds of actions, and the disposition to feel guilt about not conforming to these desires or aversions, as well as to disapprove of such failure to conform on the part of others when they have no excuse." In trying to determine the content of the optimal moral code for a society, we must weigh not only the benefits of discouraging objectionable actions (and encouraging desirable actions) by means of inculcating aversions or desires for those actions but also the "costs" of inculcating those aversions and desires (e.g., the distress produced by guilt). Brandt suggests that the optimal moral code for a given society might include special rules for members of subgroups, such as physicians. He argues that certain standard objections to utilitarianism are ill founded (including the objection that it does not yield an adequate theory of distributive justice). Brandt points to a number of issues and difficulties requiring that the theory be refined and developed. He thinks that rule-utilitarians need to say much more about issues of population control (the total amount of good might be maximized if people have as many children as possible) and issues of how the good of animals is to be weighed against the good of humans.

Brandt asks whether our obligation to help others is as strong as our obligation not to harm others. AU, as generally understood, denies the moral relevance of the distinction between harming others and failing to benefit them. Many philosophers find AU objectionable in this respect. Brandt expresses sympathy for this worry but observes that the implications of RU for this matter need further examination. Brandt here touches on a common objection to AU, namely, that the theory is "too demanding." According to AU, it is always one's obligation to perform the action that will produce the best consequences (best balance of good to bad consequences) of any alternative course of action open to one. In principle, there is no limit to the sacrifices one can be obligated to make. If giving away 60 percent of my income to famine relief would produce better consequences than spending that money on myself and my family, then AU implies that it is my moral duty to give it away.[19]

28/W. D. Ross

W. D. Ross's "What Makes Right Acts Right?" states his distinctive theory of moral obligation, based on the concept of a prima facie duty (obligation). A prima facie duty is a conditional duty; it is one's actual duty if it does not conflict with any more important prima facie duty. For example, to say that keeping promises is a prima facie duty means that one ought to keep a promise unless doing so conflicts with a more important duty. Ross proposes the following list of prima facie duties: (1) duties arising from one's own past actions (e.g., the duty to keep promises, the duty not to lie, and the duty to make reparations to those one has harmed); (2) duties of gratitude; (3) the duty to promote a just distribution of happiness according to merit; (4) the duty to do things that benefit others (i.e., give others pleasure or improve their intellects or characters); (5) the duty to improve one's own intellect and moral character; (6) the duty not to harm others. Ross claims that it is "self-evident" that these are prima facie duties.

Ross's theory agrees with utilitarianism in taking the consequences of actions to be relevant to their rightness or wrongness, but he recognizes a greater number of ultimate moral obligations than do typical utilitarians. He claims that utilitarianism "ignores or does not do justice to" the many ways in which personal relations can create moral obligations. Ross thinks that, on reflection, most "thoughtful and well-educated people" will find that his theory fits better with their moral convictions than does utilitarianism.[20] Ross considers a case where a person must choose between two actions that will produce equal amounts of good but one of which involves keeping a promise and the other of which involves breaking a promise (the actions don't differ in any other morally relevant respects). Surely, Ross claims, it is the person's moral duty to keep the promise.

29/William K. Frankena

In "Obligation and Motivation in Recent Moral Philosophy," William K. Frankena examines recent debates about whether it is possible for a person to have a moral obligation without having any motivation to fulfill that obligation. Frankena refers to the view that obligation entails motivation as "internalism," and he calls the thesis that obligation does not entail motivation "externalism." He defends the fundamental importance of the question but claims to find comparatively little discussion of it within ethics. Frankena favors externalism, but he does not claim to provide decisive support for externalism or a decisive refutation of internalism. Instead, he examines a number of arguments in the literature that have some bearing on the debate between internalists and externalists. He discusses intuitionism as a prominent version of externalism; intuitionism allows for an agent to intuit nonnatural moral features without feeling any motivation based on them.

Frankena examines a number of internalist criticisms of externalism, and in responding to them he offers many clarifying distinctions. The first important distinction is between *justifying* reasons and *motivating* reasons for performing an action to fulfill an obligation. Frankena uses this distinction in the first half of his article to dismiss a number of arguments against externalism. The second half uses the distinction between subjective and objective obligations, the distinction between having an obligation, assenting to an obligation, and saying that one has an obligation, and the distinction between what is logically implied and what is presupposed in some nonlogical sense by moral judgments. Claiming that there is no quick refutation of either externalism or internalism, Frankena contends that the discussion must move to a more fundamental level, as the dispute between externalism and internalism reflects fairly strongly opposed accounts of morality.

30/Robert M. Adams

The traditional divine-command theory implies that an action is morally obligatory (wrong) if and only if it is commanded (forbidden) by God. This theory invites two objections: (1) It implies that if God commanded us to perform acts of cruelty, we would be morally obligated to perform those acts, and (2) it implies that if God does not exist (or if God does not command or forbid anything), nothing is morally obligatory or morally wrong. (In the words of Ivan Karamazov, "if God is dead, then everything is permitted.") The point of the second objection is that some actions would be wrong or obligatory even if God did not exist. Adams proposes a modified divine-command theory according to which "X is ethically wrong" means "X is contrary to the commands of a *loving* God." He proposes this as an analysis of what at least some religious believers mean by "wrong." Adams's modified divine-command theory avoids the first objection, since it does not imply that we would be morally obligated to obey God's commands if God commanded cruelty. Adams says that his concept of moral wrongness would "break down" if God commanded cruelty. His theory does not, however, avoid the second objection; it implies that if a loving God does not exist, then no actions are morally wrong or obligatory.[21]

Adams defends the divine-command theory only as a theory of right and wrong. His theory allows that things can be good or bad independent of God's commands. It also allows that "God is good" means something other than that "God does what he wills." (Adams holds that God's goodness consists in part of his kindness and faithfulness.) Atheists who call certain acts right or wrong do not, of course, take "X is ethically wrong" to mean "X is contrary to the commands of (a loving) God." It seems, however, that atheists and religious believers engage in common moral discourse and sometimes agree about the rightness and wrongness of actions. Adams contends that his theory allows for a common moral discourse shared by believers and nonbelievers alike, but he also claims that there are ways in which moral judgments have different meanings for believers and nonbelievers.

VI. The Value and Meaning of Life

When talking about "the meaning of life," people have in mind various issues. Most of these issues fall under one or both of the following questions: (a) Is human life, including my life, worth living?, and (b) does human life, including my life, have a purpose? Much literature on this topic, including some of this section's selections, focuses on the question whether the existence of God and the existence of an afterlife are necessary for a meaningful life.

31/Leo Tolstoy

Selection 31 from Tolstoy's autobiographical work, *My Confession*, describes a prolonged spiritual crisis of Tolstoy's mid-life. Tolstoy despaired over the thought of his own death. Death, he thought, undermines everything we do and makes our life's efforts futile. In spite of his success as a writer, Tolstoy, like everyone else, would eventually die and be forgotten. Tolstoy gives a vivid account of his own fear of death and its paralyzing effect on him. He aims to do more than simply describe his own experiences; he claims that his reaction to the thought of his own death is *warranted*, at least on the assumption that there is no God and no afterlife. Tolstoy argues that science and reason cannot provide answers to questions about the meaning of life. Science tells us that life has no ultimate meaning. Tolstoy observes that common people are untroubled by the prospect of death and by questions about the meaning of life, since their religious beliefs enable them to answer questions about death and the meaning of life. Their faith gives them the only kind of meaning not destroyed by death.

32/Paul Edwards

Some people hold that human life cannot be meaningful or worth living unless one or both of the following is true: (a) God exists and our lives are part of a divine plan for the universe, and (b) there is an afterlife. In "Meaning and the Value of Life," Paul Edwards rejects this view, arguing that the rejection of belief in God and immortality does not warrant pessimism about the value of human life. Some people do report, of course, that the belief that there is no God and no afterlife has led them to conclude that everything is futile and nothing matters. Edwards argues that there is no reason to think that the nonexistence of God and an afterlife *warrants* pessimism.

Edwards claims that many pessimists have an arbitrary and indefensible preference to judge things from the perspective of the distant future rather than from the perspective of the present. Tolstoy, for example, asks us to consider our work and our lives from the perspective of the distant future, reasoning as follows: A thousand years from now, no one will remember me or what I have done; therefore, my life is futile and nothing matters. Edwards replies that things we do can matter very much *now* even if they will not matter in the distant future. He proposes criteria for a good life, distinguishing between objectively and subjectively worthwhile lives. If my life is subjectively worthwhile, I have goals that I care about, deem important, and am able to attain. My life is objectively worthwhile if it meets the foregoing conditions and my goals have positive value. The life of someone whose goals involve the service of an evil cause, such as Hitler, might be subjectively worthwhile but could not be objectively worthwhile.

33/Norman Dahl

In "Morality and the Meaning of Life: Some First Thoughts," Norman Dahl identifies some questions that seem to motivate inquiry about the meaning of life. These questions indicate what conditions must be satisfied by an adequate account of the meaning of life. Dahl examines these conditions in connection with an orthodox Christian approach to the meaningfulness of life and in connection with a familiar philosophical approach implying that our desires and choices create meaningfulness of life for us. He holds that asking whether life is meaningful is asking "whether there isn't a way of living one's life that in retrospect allows one to say that it was *good* that one lived it in that way, *better* than had one lived it in some other way, and *better* than had one not lived it at all." Accordingly, proponents of the Christian approach will note that a life is good to the extent that it fulfills the purpose of someone with the perfect credentials of the Christian God. Dahl claims that we have reason to question the Christian approach in the absence of an explanation of why the existence of evil does not challenge the goodness of God's character. In addition, he questions the aforementioned familiar philosophical approach on the ground that it neglects the requirement that the meaningfulness of a life not be a subjective matter in the way implied.

Dahl identifies several necessary conditions for a meaningful life: (a) The value that makes a life meaningful must be something that a person will want to realize upon understanding its nature; (b) the relevant value must be objective in that there is a single correct answer to disputes about it; (c) the value that makes a life meaningful must not depend on the particular desires of some person or subset of persons; (d) the meaningfulness of a life cannot hold necessarily of every life; (e) a meaningful life should be available to the ordinary person. Dahl considers the view that a moral life is itself a meaningful life, even apart from its fulfilling the purpose of a transcendent God. He sketches a theory of rationality-based morality that satisfies his necessary conditions for a meaningful life and suggests that a moral life is at least part of what makes a life meaningful. Dahl also examines whether his account of the moral life omits something important for the meaningfulness of life. He notes that his account of the moral life may neglect the importance of one's acting out of compassionate concern for others. Dahl thus acknowledges that his sketch of a moral life is tentative and in need of further examination.

34/Michael Slote

In "Goods and Lives," Michael Slote argues against theories of value that imply that value is temporally neutral—that the value of various goods and bads in one's life is independent of their temporal order and position in one's life as a whole. Other things being equal, having a good (or bad) at one time is no better (or no worse) than having the same good (or bad) at some other time in one's life. Slote claims that successes or failures in "the prime of life" are more important than successes or failures at other times.[22] Success or good fortune in the prime of life can "make up for" failure or bad luck in one's youth, but not vice versa. Slote also claims that a life that slowly progresses to some great achievement or good fortune is preferable to a life in which the same sort of achievement or good fortune comes early and is followed by decline.[23]

Notes

1. In a later work, reprinted as selection 25 in this book, Moore modifies his view. He still defends a consequentialist theory of right and wrong but does not claim that it is true in virtue of the meaning of the words "right" and "wrong."

2. Cognitivism is roughly the view that normative judgments are statements that are true or false; noncognitivism is the view that normative judgments are not statements that are true or false.

3. On the question whether ideal observers could disagree, see Charles Taliaferro, "Relativizing the Ideal Observer Theory," *Philosophy and Phenomenological Research* 49 (1989), 123–38; and Thomas Carson, "Could Ideal Observers Disagree?: A Reply to Taliaferro," *Philosophy and Phenomenological Research* 50 (1989): 115–124.

4. Gibbard, "Reply to Blackburn, Carson, Hill and Railton," *Philosophy and Phenomenological Research* 52 (1992): 980.

5. See Hare, *Freedom and Reason* (Oxford: Oxford University Press, 1963), chap. 5, and idem, *Moral Thinking* (Oxford: Oxford University Press, 1981), pp. 57–60.

6. See Hare, *Freedom and Reason*, chaps. 6–11, and idem, *Moral Thinking*, pp. 169–87.

7. See Hare, *Moral Thinking*, pp. 57–60.

8. See Kant, *Grounding for the Metaphysics of Morals*, 2d ed., trans. James W. Ellington (Indianapolis: Hackett, 1981), pp. 393–97.

9. Sidgwick, *The Methods of Ethics*, 7th ed. (London: Macmillan, 1907), p. 131; cf. p. 127.

10. This argument is criticized at length by G. E. Moore in chapter 3 of *Principia Ethica* (Cambridge: Cambridge University Press, 1903).

11. In "Fairness to Happiness," *Social Theory and Practice* 15 (1989), 33–58, Richard Brandt attempts to defend a hedonistic theory of value by arguing that it is likely that our desires for pleasant experiences are our only *rational* noninstrumental desires—i.e., that it is likely that they are the only noninstrumental desires that would survive maximal criticism on full information.

12. This criticism of Kant is discussed in the following papers: Richard Henson, "What Kant Might Have Said: Moral Worth and the Overdetermination of Dutiful Action," *Philosophical Review* 88 (1979): 39–54; Barbara Herman, "On the Value of Acting from the Motive of Duty," *Philosophical Review* 90 (1981): 359–82; and Marcia Baron, "The Alleged Moral Repugnance of Acting from Duty," *Journal of Philosophy* 81 (1984): 197–220.

13. Some commentators attribute such a view to Aristotle. See, for instance, Jennifer Whiting, "Aristotle's Function Argument: A Defense," *Ancient Philosophy* 8 (1988): 37–38, and C. D. C. Reeve, *Practices of Reason* (Oxford: Oxford University Press, 1992), pp. 125–26.

14. Mark Overvold has attempted to clarify this distinction in the following papers: "Self-Interest and the Concept of Self-Sacrifice," *Canadian Journal of Philosophy* 10 (1980): 105–18; "Self-Interest and Getting What You Want," in *The Limits of Utilitarianism*, ed. H. Miller and W. Williams (Minneapolis: University of Minnesota Press, 1982), pp. 186–94; and "Morality, Self-Interest, and Reasons for Being Moral," *Philosophy and Phenomenological Research* 44 (1984): 493–507.

15. Robert Adams's paper "A Modified Divine Command Theory of Ethical Wrongness" (selection 30) also defends a divine command theory.

16. In "Moral Beliefs" (selection 8), Foot argues that we have no reason to be just unless justice "pays" for the just person.

17. In chapter 1 of *Principia Ethica* (see selection 1), Moore claims that his consequentialist theory of right and wrong is true in virtue of the meaning of the words "right" and "wrong."

18. Moore here follows Mill's arguments in chapter 2 of *Utilitarianism* (Indianapolis: Hackett, 1979), in which Mill writes that "utilitarian moralists have gone beyond almost all others in affirming that the motive has nothing to do with the morality of the action, though much with the worth of the agent" (pp. 17–18).

19. For arguments that AU is too demanding, see Bernard Williams, "A Critique of Utilitarianism," in J. J. C. Smart and Bernard Williams, *Utilitarianism For and Against* (Cambridge: Cambridge University Press, 1973); Bernard Williams, *Moral Luck* (Cambridge: Cambridge University Press, 1991); Bernard Williams, *Ethics and the Limits of Philosophy* (Cambridge, Mass.: Harvard University Press, 1985); Samuel Scheffler, *The Rejection of Consequentialism* (Oxford: Oxford University Press, 1982); and Dan Brock, "Utilitarianism and Aiding Others," in *The Limits of Utilitarianism*, ed. H. Miller and W. Williams (Minneapolis: University of Minnesota Press, 1982), pp. 225–41. For defenses of AU against this objection, see R. M. Hare, *Moral Thinking* (Oxford: Oxford University Press, 1981), and Shelly Kagan, *The Limits of Morality* (Oxford: Oxford University Press, 1989). For discussions of the implications of RU for the issue of demandingness, see Richard Brandt, "Morality and Its Critics," in Brandt, *Morality, Utilitarianism, and Rights* (Cambridge: Cambridge University Press, 1992), pp. 73–92; Brad Hooker, "Rule Consequentialism," *Mind* 99 (1990): 67–77; and Hooker, "Rule Consequentialism and Demandingness: A Reply to Carson," *Mind* 100 (1991): 269–76. Brandt and Hooker argue that RU is substantially less demanding than AU.

20. Versions of act consequentialism that attach intrinsic value or disvalue to actions in virtue of their being of certain types (e.g., being an instance of lying or being an instance of breaking or fulfilling a promise) might be extensionally equivalent to Ross's theory. For a defense of such a version of consequentialism and a defense of the claim that it is extensionally equivalent to a Rossian theory, see A. C. Ewing, *The Definition of Good* (New York: Macmillan, 1947), chap. 6.

21. Adams acknowledges this in his later paper "Divine Command Metaethics Modified Again," in Adams, *The Virtue of Faith* (Oxford: Oxford University Press, 1987), p. 129. The latter paper incorporates further modifications to avoid the second objection. Adams writes: "If there is no loving God, then . . . ethical wrongness is the property with which it is identified by the best remaining alternative theory" (p. 141).

22. J. David Velleman has defended a similar view, with some modifications, in "Well-Being and Time," *Pacific Philosophical Quarterly* 72 (1991): 48–77.

23. Note the following passage from Brentano's *Foundation and Construction of Ethics*: "Let us think of a process which goes from good to bad or from a great good to a lesser good; then compare it with one which goes in the opposite direction. The latter shows itself as the one to be preferred. This holds even if the sum of the goods in the one process is equal to that in the other" (pp. 196–97). Roderick Chisholm writes as follows: "If *A* is a situation in which a certain amount of value *x* is increased to a larger amount *y*, and if *B* is like *A* except that in *B* there is a decrease from the larger amount of value *y* to the smaller amount *x*, then *A* is preferable to *B* (*Brentano and Intrinsic Value* [Cambridge: Cambridge University Press, 1986], p. 71). Noah Lemos has also defended this view, in *Intrinsic Value* (Cambridge: Cambridge University Press, 1994), pp. 37–40, 199–200.

PART I

CONCEPTS OF GOODNESS

Cognitivist Approaches

1 / G. E. MOORE

The Subject-Matter of Ethics

1. It is very easy to point out some among our every-day judgments, with the truth of which Ethics is undoubtedly concerned. Whenever we say, 'So and so is a good man,' or 'That fellow is a villain'; whenever we ask, 'What ought I to do?' or 'Is it wrong for me to do like this?'; whenever we hazard such remarks as 'Temperance is a virtue and drunkenness a vice'—it is undoubtedly the business of Ethics to discuss such questions and such statements; to argue what is the true answer when we ask what it is right to do, and to give reasons for thinking that our statements about the character of persons or the morality of actions are true or false. In the vast majority of cases, where we make statements involving any of the terms 'virtue,' 'vice,' 'duty,' 'right,' 'ought,' 'good,' 'bad,' we are making ethical judgments; and if we wish to discuss their truth, we shall be discussing a point of Ethics.

So much as this is not disputed; but it falls very far short of defining the province of Ethics. That province may indeed be defined as the whole truth about that which is at the same time common to all such judgments and peculiar to them. But we have still to ask the question: What is it that is thus common and peculiar? And this is a question to which very different answers have been given by ethical philosophers of

acknowledged reputation, and none of them, perhaps, completely satisfactory.

2. If we take such examples as those given above, we shall not be far wrong in saying that they are all of them concerned with the question of 'conduct'—with the question, what, in the conduct of us, human beings, is good, and what is bad, what is right, and what is wrong. For when we say that a man is good, we commonly mean that he acts rightly; when we say that drunkenness is a vice, we commonly mean that to get drunk is a wrong or wicked action. And this discussion of human conduct is, in fact, that with which the name 'Ethics' is most intimately associated. It is so associated by derivation; and conduct is undoubtedly by far the commonest and most generally interesting object of ethical judgments.

Accordingly, we find that many ethical philosophers are disposed to accept as an adequate definition of 'Ethics' the statement that it deals with the question what is good or bad in human conduct. They hold that its enquiries are properly confined to 'conduct' or to 'practice'; they hold that the name 'practical philosophy' covers all the matter with which it has to do. Now, without discussing the proper meaning of the word (for verbal questions are properly left to the writers of dictionaries and other persons interested in literature; philosophy, as we shall see, has no concern with them), I may say that I intend to use 'Ethics' to cover more than this—a usage, for which there is, I think, quite sufficient authority. I am using it to cover an enquiry for which,

Reprinted by permission of the publisher and copyright holder from G. E. Moore, *Principia Ethica* (Cambridge: Cambridge University Press, 1903), pp. 1–3, 5–30.

at all events, there is no other word: the general enquiry into what is good.

Ethics is undoubtedly concerned with the question what good conduct is; but, being concerned with this, it obviously does not start at the beginning, unless it is prepared to tell us what is good as well as what is conduct. For 'good conduct' is a complex notion: all conduct is not good; for some is certainly bad and some may be indifferent. And on the other hand, other things, beside conduct, may be good; and if they are so, then, 'good' denotes some property, that is common to them and conduct; and if we examine good conduct alone of all good things, then we shall be in danger of mistaking for this property, some property which is not shared by those other things: and thus we shall have made a mistake about Ethics even in this limited sense; for we shall not know what good conduct really is. This is a mistake which many writers have actually made, from limiting their enquiry to conduct. And hence I shall try to avoid it by considering first what is good in general; hoping, that if we can arrive at any certainty about this, it will be much easier to settle the question of good conduct: for we all know pretty well what 'conduct' is. This, then, is our first question: What is good? and What is bad? and to the discussion of this question (or these questions) I give the name of Ethics, since that science must, at all events, include it.

. . .

5. But our question 'What is good?' may have still another meaning. We may, in the third place, mean to ask, not what thing or things are good, but how 'good' is to be defined. This is an enquiry which belongs only to Ethics, not to Casuistry; and this is the enquiry which will occupy us first.

It is an enquiry to which most special attention should be directed; since this question, how 'good' is to be defined, is the most fundamental question in all Ethics. That which is meant by 'good' is, in fact, except its converse 'bad,' the *only* simple object of thought which is peculiar to Ethics. Its definition is, therefore, the most essential point

in the definition of Ethics; and moreover a mistake with regard to it entails a far larger number of erroneous ethical judgments than any other. Unless this first question be fully understood, and its true answer clearly recognised, the rest of Ethics is as good as useless from the point of view of systematic knowledge. True ethical judgments, of the two kinds last dealt with, may indeed be made by those who do not know the answer to this question as well as by those who do; and it goes without saying that the two classes of people may lead equally good lives. But it is extremely unlikely that the *most general* ethical judgments will be equally valid, in the absence of a true answer to this question: I shall presently try to shew that the gravest errors have been largely due to beliefs in a false answer. And, in any case, it is impossible that, till the answer to this question be known, any one should know *what is the evidence* for any ethical judgment whatsoever. But the main object of Ethics, as a systematic science, is to give correct *reasons* for thinking that this or that is good; and, unless this question be answered, such reasons cannot be given. Even, therefore, apart from the fact that a false answer leads to false conclusions, the present enquiry is a most necessary and important part of the science of Ethics.

6. What, then, is good? How is good to be defined? Now, it may be thought that this is a verbal question. A definition does indeed often mean the expressing of one word's meaning in other words. But this is not the sort of definition I am asking for. Such a definition can never be of ultimate importance in any study except lexicography. If I wanted that kind of definition I should have to consider in the first place how people generally used the word 'good'; but my business is not with its proper usage, as established by custom. I should, indeed, be foolish, if I tried to use it for something which it did not usually denote: if, for instance, I were to announce that, whenever I used the word 'good,' I must be understood to be thinking of that object which is usually denoted by the word 'table.' I shall, therefore, use the word

in the sense in which I think it is ordinarily used; but at the same time I am not anxious to discuss whether I am right in thinking that it is so used. My business is solely with that object or idea, which I hold, rightly or wrongly, that the word is generally used to stand for. What I want to discover is the nature of that object or idea, and about this I am extremely anxious to arrive at an agreement.

But, if we understand the question in this sense, my answer to it may seem a very disappointing one. If I am asked 'What is good?' my answer is that good is good, and that is the end of the matter. Or if I am asked 'How is good to be defined?' my answer is that it cannot be defined, and that is all I have to say about it. But disappointing as these answers may appear, they are of the very last importance. To readers who are familiar with philosophic terminology, I can express their importance by saying that they amount to this: That propositions about the good are all of them synthetic and never analytic; and that is plainly no trivial matter. And the same thing may be expressed more popularly, by saying that, if I am right, then nobody can foist upon us such an axiom as that 'Pleasure is the only good' or that 'The good is the desired' on the pretence that this is 'the very meaning of the word.'

7. Let us, then, consider this position. My point is that 'good' is a simple notion, just as 'yellow' is a simple notion; that, just as you cannot, by any manner of means, explain to any one who does not already know it, what yellow is, so you cannot explain what good is. Definitions of the kind that I was asking for, definitions which describe the real nature of the object or notion denoted by a word, and which do not merely tell us what the word is used to mean, are only possible when the object or notion in question is something complex. You can give a definition of a horse, because a horse has many different properties and qualities, all of which you can enumerate. But when you have enumerated them all, when you have reduced a horse to his simplest terms, then you can no

longer define those terms. They are simply something which you think of or perceive, and to any one who cannot think of or perceive them, you can never, by any definition, make their nature known. It may perhaps be objected to this that we are able to describe to others, objects which they have never seen or thought of. We can, for instance, make a man understand what a chimaera is, although he has never heard of one or seen one. You can tell him that it is an animal with a lioness's head and body, with a goat's head growing from the middle of its back, and with a snake in place of a tail. But here the object which you are describing is a complex object; it is entirely composed of parts, with which we are all perfectly familiar—a snake, a goat, a lioness; and we know, too, the manner in which those parts are to be put together, because we know what is meant by the middle of a lioness's back, and where her tail is wont to grow. And so it is with all objects, not previously known, which we are able to define: they are all complex; all composed of parts, which may themselves, in the first instance, be capable of similar definition, but which must in the end be reducible to simplest parts, which can no longer be defined. But yellow and good, we say, are not complex: they are notions of that simple kind, out of which definitions are composed and with which the power of further defining ceases.

8. When we say, as Webster says, 'The definition of horse is "A hoofed quadruped of the genus Equus,"' we may, in fact, mean three different things. (1) We may mean merely: 'When I say "horse," you are to understand that I am talking about a hoofed quadruped of the genus Equus.' This might be called the arbitrary verbal definition: and I do not mean that good is indefinable in that sense. (2) We may mean, as Webster ought to mean: 'When most English people say "horse," they mean a hoofed quadruped of the genus Equus.' This may be called the verbal definition proper, and I do not say that good is indefinable in this sense either; for it is certainly possible to discover how people use a

word: otherwise, we could never have known that 'good' may be translated by 'gut' in German and by 'bon' in French. But (3) we may, when we define horse, mean something much more important. We may mean that a certain object, which we all of us know, is composed in a certain manner: that it has four legs, a head, a heart, a liver, etc., etc., all of them arranged in definite relations to one another. It is in this sense that I deny good to be definable. I say that it is not composed of any parts, which we can substitute for it in our minds when we are thinking of it. We might think just as clearly and correctly about a horse, if we thought of all its parts and their arrangement instead of thinking of the whole: we could, I say, think how a horse differed from a donkey just as well, just as truly, in this way, as now we do, only not so easily; but there is nothing whatsoever which we could so substitute for good; and that is what I mean, when I say that good is indefinable.

9. But I am afraid I have still not removed the chief difficulty which may prevent acceptance of the proposition that good is indefinable. I do not mean to say that *the* good, that which is good, is thus indefinable; if I did think so, I should not be writing on Ethics, for my main object is to help towards discovering that definition. It is just because I think there will be less risk of error in our search for a definition of 'the good,' that I am now insisting that *good* is indefinable. I must try to explain the difference between these two. I suppose it may be granted that 'good' is an adjective. Well 'the good, 'that which is good,' must therefore be the substantive to which the adjective 'good' will apply: it must be the whole of that to which the adjective will apply, and the adjective must *always* truly apply to it. But if it is that to which the adjective will apply, it must be something different from that adjective itself; and the whole of that something different, whatever it is, will be our definition of *the* good. Now it may be that this something will have other adjectives, beside 'good,' that will apply to it. It may be full of pleasure, for example; it may be intelligent: and if

these two adjectives are really part of its definition, then it will certainly be true, that pleasure and intelligence are good. And many people appear to think that, if we say 'Pleasure and intelligence are good,' or if we say 'Only pleasure and intelligence are good,' we are defining 'good.' Well, I cannot deny that propositions of this nature may sometimes be called definitions; I do not know well enough how the word is generally used to decide upon this point. I only wish it to be understood that that is not what I mean when I say there is no possible definition of good, and that I shall not mean this if I use the word again. I do most fully believe that some true proposition of the form 'Intelligence is good and intelligence alone is good' can be found; if none could be found, our definition of *the* good would be impossible. As it is, I believe *the* good to be definable; and yet I still say that good itself is indefinable.

10. 'Good,' then, if we mean by it that quality which we assert to belong to a thing, when we say that the thing is good, is incapable of any definition, in the most important sense of that word. The most important sense of 'definition' is that in which a definition states what are the parts which invariably compose a certain whole; and in this sense 'good' has no definition because it is simple and has no parts. It is one of those innumerable objects of thought which are themselves incapable of definition, because they are the ultimate terms by reference to which whatever *is* capable of definition must be defined. That there must be an indefinite number of such terms is obvious, on reflection; since we cannot define anything except by an analysis, which, when carried as far as it will go, refers us to something, which is simply different from anything else, and which by that ultimate difference explains the peculiarity of the whole which we are defining: for every whole contains some parts which are common to other wholes also. There is, therefore, no intrinsic difficulty in the contention that 'good' denotes a simple and indefinable quality. There are many other instances of such qualities.

Consider yellow, for example. We may try to define it, by describing its physical equivalent; we may state what kind of light-vibrations must stimulate the normal eye, in order that we may perceive it. But a moment's reflection is sufficient to shew that those light-vibrations are not themselves what we mean by yellow. *They* are not what we perceive. Indeed we should never have been able to discover their existence, unless we had first been struck by the patent difference of quality between the different colours. The most we can be entitled to say of those vibrations is that they are what corresponds in space to the yellow which we actually perceive.

Yet a mistake of this simple kind has commonly been made about 'good.' It may be true that all things which are good are *also* something else, just as it is true that all things which are yellow produce a certain kind of vibration in the light. And it is a fact, that Ethics aims at discovering what are those other properties belonging to all things which are good. But far too many philosophers have thought that when they named those other properties they were actually defining good; that these properties, in fact, were simply not 'other,' but absolutely and entirely the same with goodness. This view I propose to call the 'naturalistic fallacy' and of it I shall now endeavour to dispose.

11. Let us consider what it is such philosophers say. And first it is to be noticed that they do not agree among themselves. They not only say that they are right as to what good is, but they endeavour to prove that other people who say that it is something else, are wrong. One, for instance, will affirm that good is pleasure, another, perhaps, that good is that which is desired; and each of these will argue eagerly to prove that the other is wrong. But how is that possible? One of them says that good is nothing but the object of desire, and at the same time tries to prove that it is not pleasure. But from his first assertion, that good just means the object of desire, one of two things must follow as regards his proof:

(1) He may be trying to prove that the object of desire is not pleasure. But, if this be all, where is his Ethics? The position he is maintaining is merely a psychological one. Desire is something which occurs in our minds, and pleasure is something else which so occurs; and our would-be ethical philosopher is merely holding that the latter is not the object of the former. But what has that to do with the question in dispute? His opponent held the ethical proposition that pleasure was the good, and although he should prove a million times over the psychological proposition that pleasure is not the object of desire, he is no nearer proving his opponent to be wrong. The position is like this. One man says a triangle is a circle: another replies 'A triangle is a straight line, and I will prove to you that I am right: *for*' (this is the only argument) 'a straight line is not a circle.' 'That is quite true,' the other may reply; 'but nevertheless a triangle is a circle, and you have said nothing whatever to prove the contrary. What is proved is that one of us is wrong, for we agree that a triangle cannot be both a straight line and a circle: but which is wrong, there can be no earthly means of proving, since you define triangle as straight line and I define it as circle'—Well, that is one alternative which any naturalistic Ethics has to face; if good is *defined* as something else, it is then impossible either to prove that any other definition is wrong or even to deny such definition.

(2) The other alternative will scarcely be more welcome. It is that the discussion is after all a verbal one. When A says 'Good means pleasant' and B says 'Good means desired,' they may merely wish to assert that most people have used the word for what is pleasant and for what is desired respectively. And this is quite an interesting subject for discussion: only it is not a whit more an ethical discussion than the last was. Nor do I think that any exponent of naturalistic Ethics would be willing to allow that this was all he meant. They are all so anxious to persuade us that what they call the good is what we really ought to do. 'Do, pray, act so, because the word "good"

is generally used to denote actions of this nature': such, on this view, would be the substance of their teaching. And in so far as they tell us how we ought to act, their teaching is truly ethical, as they mean it to be. But how perfectly absurd is the reason they would give for it! 'You are to do this, because most people use a certain word to denote conduct such as this.' 'You are to say the thing which is not, because most people call it lying.' That is an argument just as good!—My dear sirs, what we want to know from you as ethical teachers, is not how people use a word; it is not even, what kind of actions they approve, which the use of this word 'good' may certainly imply: what we want to know is simply what *is* good. We may indeed agree that what most people do think good, is actually so; we shall at all events be glad to know their opinions: but when we say their opinions about what *is* good, we do mean what we say; we do not care whether they call that thing which they mean 'horse' or 'table' or 'chair,' 'gut' or 'bon' or '*ἀγαθός*'; we want to know what it is that they so call. When they say 'Pleasure is good,' we cannot believe that they merely mean 'Pleasure is pleasure' and nothing more than that.

12. Suppose a man says 'I am pleased'; and suppose that is not a lie or a mistake but the truth. Well, if it is true, what does that mean? It means that his mind, a certain definite mind, distinguished by certain definite marks from all others, has at this moment a certain definite feeling called pleasure. 'Pleased' *means* nothing but having pleasure, and though we may be more pleased or less pleased, and even, we may admit for the present, have one or another kind of pleasure; yet in so far as it is pleasure we have, whether there be more or less of it, and whether it be of one kind or another, what we have is one definite thing, absolutely indefinable, some one thing that is the same in all the various degrees and in all the various kinds of it that there may be. We may be able to say how it is related to other things: that, for example, it is in the mind, that it causes desire, that we are conscious of it, etc., etc. We can, I say, de-

scribe its relations to other things, but define it we can *not*. And if anybody tried to define pleasure for us as being any other natural object; if anybody were to say, for instance, that pleasure *means* the sensation of red, and were to proceed to deduce from that that pleasure is a colour, we should be entitled to laugh at him and to distrust his future statements about pleasure. Well, that would be the same fallacy which I have called the naturalistic fallacy. That 'pleased' does not mean 'having the sensation of red,' or anything else whatever, does not prevent us from understanding what it does mean. It is enough for us to know that 'pleased' does mean 'having the sensation of pleasure,' and though pleasure is absolutely indefinable, though pleasure is pleasure and nothing else whatever, yet we feel no difficulty in saying that we are pleased. The reason is, of course, that when I say 'I am pleased,' I do *not* mean that 'I' am the same thing as 'having pleasure.' And similarly no difficulty need be found in my saying that 'pleasure is good' and yet not meaning that 'pleasure' is the same thing as 'good,' that pleasure *means* good, and that good *means* pleasure. If I were to imagine that when I said 'I am pleased,' I meant that I was exactly the same thing as 'pleased,' I should not indeed call that a naturalistic fallacy, although it would be the same fallacy as I have called naturalistic with reference to Ethics. The reason of this is obvious enough. When a man confuses two natural objects with one another, defining the one by the other, if for instance, he confuses himself, who is one natural object, with 'pleased' or with 'pleasure' which are others, then there is no reason to call the fallacy naturalistic. But if he confuses 'good,' which is not in the same sense a natural object, with any natural object whatever, then there is a reason for calling that a naturalistic fallacy; its being made with regard to 'good' marks it as something quite specific, and this specific mistake deserves a name because it is so common. As for the reasons why good is not to be considered a natural object, they may be reserved for discussion in another place. But, for the present, it is sufficient to notice this: Even if it were a natural object, that would not alter the nature of the fallacy nor diminish its importance one whit. All that I have said about it would remain quite equally true: only the name which I have called it would not be so appropriate as I think it is. And I do not care about the name: what I do care about is the fallacy. It does not matter what we call it, provided we recognise it when we meet with it. It is to be met with in almost every book on Ethics; and yet it is not recognised: and that is why it is necessary to multiply illustrations of it, and convenient to give it a name. It is a very simple fallacy indeed. When we say that an orange is yellow, we do not think our statement binds us to hold that 'orange' means nothing else than 'yellow,' or that nothing can be yellow but an orange. Supposing the orange is also sweet! Does that bind us to say that 'sweet' is exactly the same thing as 'yellow,' that 'sweet' must be defined as 'yellow'? And supposing it be recognised that 'yellow' just means 'yellow' and nothing else whatever, does that make it any more difficult to hold that oranges are yellow? Most certainly it does not: on the contrary, it would be absolutely meaningless to say that oranges were yellow, unless yellow did in the end mean just 'yellow' and nothing else whatever—unless it was absolutely indefinable. We should not get any very clear notion about things, which are yellow—we should not get very far with our science, if we were bound to hold that everything which was yellow, *meant* exactly the same thing as yellow. We should find we had to hold that an orange was exactly the same thing as a stool, a piece of paper, a lemon, anything you like. We could prove any number of absurdities; but should we be the nearer to the truth? Why, then, should it be different with 'good'? Why, if good is good and indefinable, should I be held to deny that pleasure is good? Is there any difficulty in holding both to be true at once? On the contrary, there is no meaning in saying that pleasure is good, unless good is something different from pleasure. It is ab-

solutely useless, so far as Ethics is concerned, to prove, as Mr Spencer tries to do, that increase of pleasure coincides with increase of life, unless good *means* something different from either life or pleasure. He might just as well try to prove that an orange is yellow by shewing that it always is wrapped up in paper.

13. In fact, if it is not the case that 'good' denotes something simple and indefinable, only two alternatives are possible: either it is a complex, a given whole, about the correct analysis of which there may be disagreement; or else it means nothing at all, and there is no such subject as Ethics. In general, however, ethical philosophers have attempted to define good, without recognising what such an attempt must mean. They actually use arguments which involve one or both of the absurdities considered in §11. We are, therefore, justified in concluding that the attempt to define good is chiefly due to want of clearness as to the possible nature of definition. There are, in fact, only two serious alternatives to be considered, in order to establish the conclusion that 'good' does denote a simple and indefinable notion. It might possibly denote a complex, as 'horse' does; or it might have no meaning at all. Neither of these possibilities has, however, been clearly conceived and seriously maintained, as such, by those who presume to define good; and both may be dismissed by a simple appeal to facts.

(1) The hypothesis that disagreement about the meaning of good is disagreement with regard to the correct analysis of a given whole, may be most plainly seen to be incorrect by consideration of the fact that, whatever definition be offered, it may be always asked, with significance, of the complex so defined, whether it is itself good. To take, for instance, one of the more plausible, because one of the more complicated, of such proposed definitions, it may easily be thought, at first sight, that to be good may mean to be that which we desire to desire. Thus if we apply this definition to a particular instance and say 'When we think that A is good, we are thinking that

A is one of the things which we desire to desire,' our proposition may seem quite plausible. But, if we carry the investigation further, and ask ourselves 'Is it good to desire to desire A?' it is apparent, on a little reflection, that this question is itself as intelligible, as the original question 'Is A good?'—that we are, in fact, now asking for exactly the same information about the desire to desire A, for which we formerly asked with regard to A itself. But it is also apparent that the meaning of this second question cannot be correctly analysed into 'Is the desire to desire A one of the things which we desire to desire?': we have not before our minds anything so complicated as the question 'Do we desire to desire to desire to desire A?' Moreover any one can easily convince himself by inspection that the predicate of this proposition—'good'—is positively different from the notion of 'desiring to desire' which enters into its subject: 'That we should desire to desire A is good' is *not* merely equivalent to 'That A should be good is good.' It may indeed be true that what we desire to desire is always also good; perhaps, even the converse may be true: but it is very doubtful whether this is the case, and the mere fact that we understand very well what is meant by doubting it, shews clearly that we have two different notions before our minds.

(2) And the same consideration is sufficient to dismiss the hypothesis that 'good' has no meaning whatsoever. It is very natural to make the mistake of supposing that what is universally true is of such a nature that its negation would be self-contradictory: the importance which has been assigned to analytic propositions in the history of philosophy shews how easy such a mistake is. And thus it is very easy to conclude that what seems to be a universal ethical principle is in fact an identical proposition; that, if, for example, whatever is called 'good' seems to be pleasant, the proposition 'Pleasure is the good' does not assert a connection between two different notions, but involves only one, that of pleasure, which is easily recognised as a distinct entity. But whoever will attentively

consider with himself what is actually before his mind when he asks the question 'Is pleasure (or whatever it may be) after all good?' can easily satisfy himself that he is not merely wondering whether pleasure is pleasant. And if he will try this experiment with each suggested definition in succession, he may become expert enough to recognise that in every case he has before his mind a unique object, with regard to the connection of which with any other object, a distinct question may be asked. Every one does in fact understand the question 'Is this good?' When he thinks of it, his state of mind is different from what it would be, were he asked 'Is this pleasant, or desired, or approved?' It has a distinct meaning for him, even though he may not recognise in what respect it is distinct. Whenever he thinks of 'intrinsic value,' or 'intrinsic worth,' or says that a thing 'ought to exist,' he has before his mind the unique object— the unique property of things—which I mean by 'good.' Everybody is constantly aware of this notion, although he may never become aware at all that it is different from other notions of which he is also aware. But, for correct ethical reasoning, it is extremely important that he should become aware of this fact; and, as soon as the nature of the problem is clearly understood, there should be little difficulty in advancing so far in analysis.

14. 'Good,' then, is indefinable; and yet, so far as I know, there is only one ethical writer, Prof. Henry Sidgwick, who has clearly recognised and stated this fact. We shall see, indeed, how far many of the most reputed ethical systems fall short of drawing the conclusions which follow from such a recognition. At present I will only quote one instance, which will serve to illustrate the meaning and importance of this principle that 'good' is indefinable, or, as Prof. Sidgwick says, an 'unanalysable notion.' It is an instance to which Prof. Sidgwick himself refers in a note on the passage, in which he argues that 'ought' is unanalysable[1].

'Bentham,' says Sidgwick, 'explains that his fundamental principle "states the greatest happiness of all those whose interest is in question as being the right and proper end of human action'"; and yet 'his language in other passages of the same chapter would seem to imply' that he *means* by the word "right" "conducive to the general happiness." Prof. Sidgwick sees that, if you take these two statements together, you get the absurd result that 'greatest happiness is the end of human action, which is conducive to the general happiness'; and so absurd does it seem to him to call this result, as Bentham calls it, 'the fundamental principle of a moral system,' that he suggests that Bentham cannot have meant it. Yet Prof. Sidgwick himself states elsewhere[2] that Psychological Hedonism is 'not seldom confounded with Egoistic Hedonism'; and that confusion, as we shall see, rests chiefly on that same fallacy, the naturalistic fallacy, which is implied in Bentham's statements. Prof. Sidgwick admits therefore that this fallacy is sometimes committed, absurd as it is; and I am inclined to think that Bentham may really have been one of those who committed it. Mill, as we shall see, certainly did commit it. In any case, whether Bentham committed it or not, his doctrine, as above quoted, will serve as a very good illustration of this fallacy, and of the importance of the contrary proposition that good is indefinable.

Let us consider this doctrine. Bentham seems to imply, so Prof. Sidgwick says, that the word 'right' *means* 'conducive to general happiness.' Now this, by itself, need not necessarily involve the naturalistic fallacy. For the word 'right' is very commonly appropriated to actions which lead to the attainment of what is good; which are regarded as *means* to the ideal and not as ends-in-themselves. This use of 'right,' as denoting what is good as a means, whether or not it be also good as an end, is indeed the use to which I shall confine the word. Had Bentham been using 'right' in this sense, it might be perfectly consistent for him to *define* right as 'conducive to the general happiness,' *provided only* (and notice this proviso) he had already proved, or laid down as an axiom, that general happiness was *the* good, or (what is equivalent to this)

that general happiness alone was good. For in that case he would have already defined *the* good as general happiness (a position perfectly consistent, as we have seen, with the contention that 'good' is indefinable), and, since right was to be defined as 'conducive to *the* good,' it would actually *mean* 'conducive to general happiness.' But this method of escape from the charge of having committed the naturalistic fallacy has been closed by Bentham himself. For his fundamental principle is, we see, that the greatest happiness of all concerned is the *right* and proper *end* of human action. He applies the word 'right,' therefore, to the end, as such, not only to the means which are conducive to it; and, that being so, right can no longer be defined as 'conducive to the general happiness,' without involving the fallacy in question. For now it is obvious that the definition of right as conducive to general happiness can be used by him in support of the fundamental principle that general happiness is the right end; instead of being itself derived from that principle. If right, by definition, means conducive to general happiness, then it is obvious that general happiness is the right end. It is not necessary now first to prove or assert that general happiness is the right end, before right is defined as conducive to general happiness—a perfectly valid procedure; but on the contrary the definition of right as conducive to general happiness proves general happiness to be the right end—a perfectly invalid procedure, since in this case the statement that 'general happiness is the right end of human action' is not an ethical principle at all, but either, as we have seen, a proposition about the meaning of words, or else a proposition about the *nature* of general happiness, not about its rightness or goodness.

Now, I do not wish the importance I assign to this fallacy to be misunderstood. The discovery of it does not at all refute Bentham's contention that greatest happiness is the proper end of human action, if that be understood as an ethical proposition, as he undoubtedly intended it. That principle may be true all the same; we shall consider whether it is so in succeeding chapters. Bentham might have maintained it, as Prof. Sidgwick does, even if the fallacy had been pointed out to him. What I am maintaining is that the *reasons* which he actually gives for his ethical proposition are fallacious ones so far as they consist in a definition of right. What I suggest is that he did not perceive them to be fallacious; that, if he had done so, he would have been led to seek for other reasons in support of his Utilitarianism; and that, had he sought for other reasons, he *might* have found none which he thought to be sufficient. In that case he would have changed his whole system—a most important consequence. It is undoubtedly also possible that he would have thought other reasons to be sufficient, and in that case his ethical system, in its main results, would still have stood. But, even in this latter case, his use of the fallacy would be a serious objection to him as an ethical philosopher. For it is the business of Ethics, I must insist, not only to obtain true results, but also to find valid reasons for them. The direct object of Ethics is knowledge and not practice; and any one who uses the naturalistic fallacy has certainly not fulfilled this first object, however correct his practical principles may be.

My objections to Naturalism are then, in the first place, that it offers no reason at all, far less any valid reason, for any ethical principle whatever; and in this it already fails to satisfy the requirements of Ethics, as a scientific study. But in the second place I contend that, though it gives a reason for no ethical principle, it is a *cause* of the acceptance of false principles—it deludes the mind into accepting ethical principles, which are false; and in this it is contrary to every aim of Ethics. It is easy to see that if we start with a definition of right conduct as conduct conducive to general happiness; then, knowing that right conduct is universally conduct conducive to the good, we very easily arrive at the result that the good is general happiness. If, on the other hand, we once recognise that we must start our Ethics without a definition, we shall be much more apt to look about us, before we

adopt any ethical principle whatever; and the more we look about us, the less likely are we to adopt a false one. It may be replied to this: Yes, but we shall look about us just as much, before we settle on our definition, and are therefore just as likely to be right. But I will try to shew that this is not the case. If we start with the conviction that a definition of good can be found, we start with the conviction that good *can mean* nothing else than some one property of things; and our only business will then be to discover what that property is. But if we recognise that, so far as the meaning of good goes, anything whatever may be good, we start with a much more open mind. Moreover, apart from the fact that, when we think we have a definition, we cannot logically defend our ethical principles in any way whatever, we shall also be much less apt to defend them well, even if illogically. For we shall start with the conviction that good must mean so and so, and shall therefore be inclined either to misunderstand our opponent's arguments or to cut them short with the reply, 'This is not an open question: the very meaning of the word decides it; no one can think otherwise except through confusion.'

15. Our first conclusion as to the subject-matter of Ethics is, then, that there is a simple, indefinable, unanalysable object of thought by reference to which it must be defined. By what name we call this unique object is a matter of indifference, so long as we clearly recognise what it is and that it does differ from other objects. The words which are commonly taken as the signs of ethical judgments all do refer to it; and they are expressions of ethical judgments solely because they do so refer. But they may refer to it in two different ways, which it is very important to distinguish, if we are to have a complete definition of the range of ethical judgments. Before I proceeded to argue that there was such an indefinable notion involved in ethical notions, I stated (§4) that it was necessary for Ethics to enumerate all true universal judgments, asserting that such and such a thing was good, whenever it occurred. But, although

all such judgments do refer to that unique notion which I have called 'good,' they do not all refer to it in the same way. They may either assert that this unique property does always attach to the thing in question, or else they may assert only that the thing in question is *a cause or necessary condition* for the existence of other things to which this unique property does attach. The nature of these two species of universal ethical judgments is extremely different; and a great part of the difficulties, which are met with in ordinary ethical speculation, are due to the failure to distinguish them clearly. Their difference has, indeed, received expression in ordinary language by the contrast between the terms 'good as means' and 'good in itself,' 'value as a means' and 'intrinsic value.' But these terms are apt to be applied correctly only in the more obvious instances; and this seems to be due to the fact that the distinction between the conceptions which they denote has not been made a separate object of investigation. This distinction may be briefly pointed out as follows.

16. Whenever we judge that a thing is 'good as a means,' we are making a judgment with regard to its causal relations: we judge *both* that it will have a particular kind of effect, *and* that that effect will be good in itself. But to find causal judgments that are universally true is notoriously a matter of extreme difficulty. The late date at which most of the physical sciences became exact, and the comparative fewness of the laws which they have succeeded in establishing even now, are sufficient proofs of this difficulty. With regard, then, to what are the most frequent objects of ethical judgments, namely actions, it is obvious that we cannot be satisfied that any of our universal causal judgments are true, even in the sense in which scientific laws are so. We cannot even discover hypothetical laws of the form 'Exactly this action will always, under these conditions, produce exactly that effect.' But for a correct ethical judgment with regard to the effects of certain actions we require more than this in two respects. (1) We require to know that a given action

will produce a certain effect, *under whatever circumstances it occurs.* But this is certainly impossible. It is certain that in different circumstances the same action may produce effects which are utterly different in all respects upon which the value of the effects depends. Hence we can never be entitled to more than a *generalisation*—to a proposition of the form 'This result *generally* follows this kind of action'; and even this generalisation will only be true, if the circumstances under which the action occurs are generally the same. This is in fact the case, to a great extent, within any one particular age and state of society. But, when we take other ages into account, in many most important cases the normal circumstances of a given kind of action will be so different, that the generalisation which is true for one will not be true for another. With regard then to ethical judgments which assert that a certain kind of action is good as a means to a certain kind of effect, none will be *universally* true; and many, though *generally* true at one period, will be generally false at others. But (2) we require to know not only that *one* good effect will be produced, but that, among all subsequent events affected by the action in question, the balance of good will be greater than if any other possible action had been performed. In other words, to judge that an action is generally a means to good is to judge not only that it generally does *some* good, but that it generally does the greatest good of which the circumstances admit. In this respect ethical judgments about the effects of action involve a difficulty and a complication far greater than that involved in the establishment of scientific laws. For the latter we need only consider a single effect; for the former it is essential to consider not only this, but the effects of that effect, and so on as far as our view into the future can reach. It is, indeed, obvious that our view can never reach far enough for us to be certain that any action will produce the best possible effects. We must be content, if the greatest possible balance of good seems to be produced within a limited period. But it is important to notice that the whole series of effects within a period of considerable length is actually taken account of in our common judgments that an action is good as a means; and that hence this additional complication, which makes ethical generalisations so far more difficult to establish than scientific laws, is one which is involved in actual ethical discussions, and is of practical importance. The commonest rules of conduct involve such considerations as the balancing of future bad health against immediate gains; and even if we can never settle with any certainty how we shall secure the greatest possible total of good, we try at least to assure ourselves that probable future evils will not be greater than the immediate good.

17. There are, then, judgments which state that certain kinds of things have good effects; and such judgments, for the reasons just given, have the important characteristics (1) that they are unlikely to be true, if they state that the kind of thing in question *always* has good effects, and (2) that, even if they only state that it *generally* has good effects, many of them will only be true of certain periods in the world's history. On the other hand there are judgments which state that certain kinds of things are themselves good; and these differ from the last in that, if true at all, they are all of them universally true. It is, therefore, extremely important to distinguish these two kinds of possible judgments. Both may be expressed in the same language: in both cases we commonly say 'Such and such a thing is good.' But in the one case 'good' will mean 'good as means,' *i.e.* merely that the thing is a means to good—will have good effects: in the other case it will mean 'good as end'—we shall be judging that the thing itself has the property which, in the first case, we asserted only to belong to its effects. It is plain that these are very different assertions to make about a thing; it is plain that either or both of them may be made, both truly and falsely, about all manner of things; and it is certain that unless we are clear as to which of the two we mean to assert, we shall have a very poor chance of deciding rightly whether our assertion is

true or false. It is precisely this clearness as to the meaning of the question asked which has hitherto been almost entirely lacking in ethical speculation. Ethics has always been predominantly concerned with the investigation of a limited class of actions. With regard to these we may ask *both* how far they are good in themselves *and* how far they have a general tendency to produce good results. And the arguments brought forward in ethical discussion have always been of both classes—both such as would prove the conduct in question to be good in itself and such as would prove it to be good as a means. But that these are the only questions which any ethical discussion can have to settle, and that to settle the one is *not* the same thing as to settle the other— these two fundamental facts have in general escaped the notice of ethical philosophers. Ethical questions are commonly asked in an ambiguous form. It is asked 'What is a man's duty under these circumstances?' or 'Is it right to act in this way?' or 'What ought we to aim at securing?' But all these questions are capable of further analysis; a correct answer to any of them involves both judgments of what is good in itself and causal judgments. This is implied even by those who maintain that we have a direct and immediate judgment of absolute rights and duties. Such a judgment can only mean that the course of action in question is *the* best thing to do; that, by acting so, every good that *can* be secured will have been secured. Now we are not concerned with the question whether such a judgment will ever be true. The question is: What does it imply, if it is true? And the only possible answer is that, whether true or false, it implies both a proposition as to the degree of goodness of the action in question, as compared with other things, and a number of causal propositions. For it cannot be denied that the action will have consequences: and to deny that the consequences matter is to make a judgment of their intrinsic value, as compared with the action itself. In asserting that the action is *the* best thing to do, we assert that it together with its consequences presents a greater sum of intrinsic value than any possible alternative. And this condition may be realised by any of the three cases:—(a) If the action itself has greater intrinsic value than any alternative, whereas both its consequences and those of the alternatives are absolutely devoid either of intrinsic merit or intrinsic demerit; or (b) if, though its consequences are intrinsically bad, the balance of intrinsic value is greater than would be produced by any alternative; or (c) if, its consequences being intrinsically good, the degree of value belonging to them and it conjointly is greater than that of any alternative series. In short, to assert that a certain line of conduct is, at a given time, absolutely right or obligatory, is obviously to assert that more good or less evil will exist in the world, if it be adopted than if anything else be done instead. But this implies a judgment as to the value both of its own consequences and of those of any possible alternative. And that an action will have such and such consequences involves a number of causal judgments.

Similarly, in answering the question 'What ought we to aim at securing?' causal judgments are again involved, but in a somewhat different way. We are liable to forget, because it is so obvious, that this question can never be answered correctly except by naming something which *can* be secured. Not everything can be secured; and, even if we judge that nothing which cannot be obtained would be of equal value with that which can, the possibility of the latter, as well as its value, is essential to its being a proper end of action. Accordingly neither our judgments as to what actions we ought to perform, nor even our judgments as to the ends which they ought to produce, are pure judgments of intrinsic value. With regard to the former, an action which is absolutely obligatory *may* have no intrinsic value whatsoever; that it is perfectly virtuous may mean merely that it causes the best possible effects. And with regard to the latter, these best possible results which justify our action can, in any case, have only so much of intrinsic value as the laws of nature allow us to secure;

and they in their turn *may* have no intrinsic value whatsoever, but may merely be a means to the attainment (in a still further future) of something that has such value. Whenever, therefore, we ask 'What ought we to do?' or 'What ought we to try to get?' we are asking questions which involve a correct answer to two others, completely different in kind from one another. We must know *both* what degree of intrinsic value different things have, *and* how these different things may be obtained. But the vast majority of questions which have actually been discussed in Ethics—*all* practical questions, indeed—involve this double knowledge; and they have been discussed without any clear separation of the two distinct questions involved. A great part of the vast disagreements prevalent in Ethics is to be attributed to this failure in analysis. By the use of conceptions which involve both that of intrinsic value and that of causal relation, as if they involved intrinsic value only, two different errors have been rendered almost universal. Either it is assumed that nothing has intrinsic value which is not possible, or else it is assumed that what is necessary must have intrinsic value. Hence the primary and peculiar business of Ethics, the determination what things have intrinsic value and in what degrees, has received no adequate treatment at all. And on the other hand a *thorough* discussion of means has been also largely neglected, owing to an obscure perception of the truth that it is perfectly irrelevant to the question of intrinsic values. But however this may be, and however strongly any particular reader may be convinced that some one of the mutually contradictory systems which hold the field has given a correct answer either to the question what has intrinsic value, or to the question what we ought to do, or to both, it must at least be admitted that the questions what is best in itself and what will bring about the best possible, are utterly distinct; that both belong to the actual subject-matter of Ethics; and that the more clearly distinct questions are distinguished, the better is our chance of answering both correctly.

18. There remains one point which must not be omitted in a complete description of the kind of questions which Ethics has to answer. The main division of those questions is, as I have said, into two; the question what things are good in themselves, and the question to what other things these are related as effects. The first of these, which is the primary ethical question and is presupposed by the other, includes a correct comparison of the various things which have intrinsic value (if there are many such) in respect of the degree of value which they have; and such comparison involves a difficulty of principle which has greatly aided the confusion of intrinsic value with mere 'goodness as a means.' It has been pointed out that one difference between a judgment which asserts that a thing is good in itself, and a judgment which asserts that it is a means to good, consists in the fact that the first, if true of one instance of the thing in question, is necessarily true of all; whereas a thing which has good effects under some circumstances may have bad ones under others. Now it is certainly true that all judgments of intrinsic value are in this sense universal; but the principle which I have now to enunciate may easily make it appear as if they were not so but resembled the judgment of means in being merely general. There is, as will presently be maintained, a vast number of different things, each of which has intrinsic value; there are also very many which are positively bad; and there is a still larger class of things, which appear to be indifferent. But a thing belonging to any of these three classes may occur as part of a whole, which includes among its other parts other things belonging both to the same and to the other two classes; and these wholes, as such, may also have intrinsic value. The paradox, to which it is necessary to call attention, is that *the value of such a whole bears no regular proportion to the sum of the values of its parts.* It is certain that a good thing may exist in such a relation to another good thing that the value of the whole thus formed is immensely greater than the sum of the values of the two good things. It is certain that a whole

formed of a good thing and an indifferent thing may have immensely greater value than that good thing itself possesses. It is certain that two bad things or a bad thing and an indifferent thing may form a whole much worse than the sum of badness of its parts. And it seems as if indifferent things may also be the sole constituents of a whole which has great value, either positive or negative. Whether the addition of a bad thing to a good whole may increase the positive value of the whole, or the addition of a bad thing to a bad may produce a whole having positive value, may seem more doubtful; but it is, at least, possible, and this possibility must be taken into account in our ethical investigations. However we may decide particular questions, the principle is clear. *The value of a whole must not be assumed to be the same as the sum of the values of its parts.*

A single instance will suffice to illustrate the kind of relation in question. It seems to be true that to be conscious of a beautiful object is a thing of great intrinsic value; whereas the same object, if no one be conscious of it, has certainly comparatively little value, and is commonly held to have none at all. But the consciousness of a beautiful object is certainly a whole of some sort in which we can distinguish as parts the object on the one hand and the being conscious on the other. Now this latter factor occurs as part of a different whole, whenever we are conscious of anything; and it would seem that some of these wholes have at all events very little value, and may even be indifferent or positively bad. Yet we cannot always attribute the slightness of their value to any positive demerit in the object which differentiates them from the consciousness of beauty; the object itself may approach as near as possible to absolute neutrality. Since, therefore, mere consciousness does not always confer great value upon the whole of which it forms a part, even though its object may have no great demerit, we cannot attribute the great superiority of the consciousness of a beautiful thing over the beautiful thing itself to the mere addition of the value of consciousness to that of the beautiful thing.

Whatever the intrinsic value of consciousness may be, it does not give to the whole of which it forms a part a value proportioned to the sum of its value and that of its object. If this be so, we have here an instance of a whole possessing a different intrinsic value from the sum of that of its parts; and whether it be so or not, what is meant by such a difference is illustrated by this case.

19. There are, then, wholes which possess the property that their value is different from the sum of the values of their parts; and the relations which subsist between such parts and the whole of which they form a part have not hitherto been distinctly recognised or received a separate name. Two points are especially worthy of notice. (1) It is plain that the existence of any such part is a necessary condition for the existence of that good which is constituted by the whole. And exactly the same language will also express the relation between a means and the good thing which is its effect. But yet there is a most important difference between the two cases, constituted by the fact that the part is, whereas the means is not, a part of the good thing for the existence of which its existence is a necessary condition. The necessity by which, if the good in question is to exist, the means to it must exist is merely a natural or causal necessity. If the laws of nature were different, exactly the same good might exist, although what is now a necessary condition of its existence did not exist. The existence of the means has no intrinsic value; and its utter annihilation would leave the value of that which it is now necessary to secure entirely unchanged. But in the case of a part of such a whole as we are now considering, it is otherwise. In this case the good in question cannot conceivably exist, unless the part exist also. The necessity which connects the two is quite independent of natural law. What is asserted to have intrinsic value is the existence of the whole; and the existence of the whole includes the existence of its part. Suppose the part removed, and what remains is *not* what was asserted to have intrinsic value; but if we suppose a

means removed, what remains is just what *was* asserted to have intrinsic value. And yet (2) the existence of the part may *itself* have no more intrinsic value than that of the means. It is this fact which constitutes the paradox of the relation which we are discussing. It has just been said that what has intrinsic value is the existence of the whole, and that this includes the existence of the part; and from this it would seem a natural inference that the existence of the part has intrinsic value. But the inference would be as false as if we were to conclude that, because the number of two stones was two, each of the stones was also two. The part of a valuable whole retains exactly the same value when it is, as when it is not, a part of that whole. If it had value under other circumstances, its value is not any greater, when it is part of a far more valuable whole; and if it had no value by itself, it has none still, however great be that of the whole of which it now forms a part. We are not then justified in asserting that one and the same thing is under some circumstances intrinsically good, and under others not so; as we are justified in asserting of a means that it sometimes does and sometimes does not produce good results. And yet we are justified in asserting that it is far more desirable that a certain thing should exist under some circumstances than under others; namely when other things will exist in such relations to it as to form a more valuable whole. *It* will not have more intrinsic value under these circumstances than under others; *it* will not necessarily even be a means to the existence of things having more intrinsic value: but it will, like a means, be a necessary condition for the existence of that which *has* greater intrinsic value, although, unlike a means, it will itself form a part of this more valuable existent.

Notes

1. *Methods of Ethics*, Bk. I, Chap. iii, § 1 (6th edition).

2. *Methods of Ethics*, Bk. I, Chap. iv, § 1.

2 / RODERICK FIRTH

ETHICAL ABSOLUTISM AND THE IDEAL OBSERVER

The moral philosophy of the first half of the twentieth century, at least in the English-speaking part of the world, has been largely devoted to problems concerning the analysis of ethical statements, and to correlative problems of an ontological or epistemological nature. This concentration of effort by many acute analytical minds has not produced any general agreement with respect to the solution of these problems; it seems likely, on the contrary, that the wealth of proposed solutions, each making some claim to plausibility, has resulted in greater disagreement than ever before, and in some cases disagreement about issues so fundamental that certain schools of thought now find it unrewarding, if not impossible, to communicate with one another. Moral philosophers of almost all schools seem to agree, however, that no major possibility has been neglected during this period, and that every proposed solution which can be adjudged at all plausible has been examined with considerable thoroughness. It is now common practice, for example, for the authors of books on moral philosophy to introduce their own theories by what purports to be a classification and review of all *possible* solutions to the basic problems of analysis; and in many cases, indeed, the primary defense of the author's own position seems to consist in the negative argument that his own position cannot fail to be correct because none of the others which he has mentioned is satisfactory.

Reprinted by permission of the publisher and copyright holder from *Philosophy and Phenomenological Research* 12 (1952): pp. 317–45.

There is one kind of analysis of ethical statements, however, which has certainly not been examined with the thoroughness that it deserves—the kind of analysis, namely, which construes ethical statements to be both absolutist and dispositional. In a paper entitled "Some Reflections on Moral-Sense Theories of Ethics,"[1] Broad has discussed a number of the most important features of this kind of analysis, and has even said that most competent persons would now agree that there are only two other theories about the meaning of ethical terms which are worth as much serious consideration. Yet there are many moral philosophers who leave no place for this kind of analysis in their classification of ethical theories, and many others who treat it unfairly by classifying it with less plausible proposals which are superficially similar. And what makes such carelessness especially unfortunate, is the fact that this kind of analysis seems to be capable of satisfying the major demands of certain schools of ethical thought which are ordinarily supposed to be diametrically opposed to one another. It is a kind of analysis, moreover, which may have been proposed and defended by several classical moralists;[2] and this is perhaps one good reason for giving it at least a small share of the attention which is now lavished on positions which are no more plausible.

The following discussion of absolutist dispositional analyses of ethical statements, is divided into two parts. In the first part I have discussed some of the important characteristics which are common to all analyses of this general form. In the second part I have discussed some of the problems which would have to be solved in working out a concrete analysis of this kind, and I have made certain proposals about the manner in which such an analysis can best be formulated.[3]

Part One: Characteristics of the Analysis

1. It Is Absolutist

To explain the precise sense in which a dispositional analysis of ethical statements may be absolutist rather than relativist, it is helpful to begin by defining the two terms "relative statement" and "relativist analysis."

Speaking first about statements, we may say that any statement is relative if its meaning cannot be expressed without using a word or other expression which is egocentric. And egocentric expressions may be described as expressions of which the meaning varies systematically with the speaker. They are expressions which are ambiguous in abstraction from their relation to a speaker, but their ambiguity is conventional and systematic. They include the personal pronouns ("I," "you," etc.), the corresponding possessive adjectives ("my," "your," etc.), words which refer directly but relatively to spatial and temporal location ("this," "that," "here," "there," "now," "then," "past," "present," "future"), reflexive expressions such as "the person who is speaking," and the various linguistic devices which are used to indicate the tense of verbs. All of these egocentric expressions can apparently be defined in terms of the word "this."[4]

A moral philosopher is commonly called a relativist, and his analysis of ethical statements is said to be a relativist analysis, if he construes ethical statements to be relative. We may thus say, derivatively, that an analysis of ethical statements is relativist if it includes an egocentric expression, and if it is incompatible with any alternative analysis which does not include an egocentric expression.

It follows, therefore, that relativist analyses, no matter how much they may differ from one another, can always be conveniently and positively identified by direct inspection of their constituent expressions. Thus, to give a few examples, a philosopher is an ethical relativist if he believes that the meaning of ethical statements of the form "Such and such a particular act (x) is right" can be expressed by other statements which have any of the following forms: "*I* like x as much as any alternative to it," "*I* should (in fact) feel ashamed of myself if *I* did not feel approval towards x, and *I* wish that *other people* would too," "Most people *now* living would feel approval towards x if they knew what they really wanted," "If *I* should perceive or think about x and its alternatives, x would seem to *me* to be demanding to be performed," "x is compatible with the mores of the social group to which *the speaker* gives his primary allegiance," and "x will satisfy a maximum of the interests of people *now* living or who *will* live *in the future*." Each one of these possible analyses contains an egocentric expression (which I have italicized). And it is evident that if any of these analyses were correct, it would be possible for one person to say that a certain act is right, and for another person (provided, in some cases, that he is not a member of the same social group, nor living at the same time) to say that that very same act is not right, without logically contradicting each other. This familiar characteristic of all relativist analyses is not *definitive* of relativism; it is, however, a necessary *consequence* of the fact that relativist analyses contain egocentric expressions.

We may now define an absolutist analysis of ethical statements as one which is not relativist.[6] The kind of analysis which I propose to discuss in this paper, therefore, is one which does not include an egocentric expression. It is a kind of analysis, I suspect, which is closely associated with relativism in the minds of many philosophers, but it is unquestionably absolutist and implies that ethical statements are true or false, and consistent or inconsistent with one another, without special reference to the people who happen to be asserting them.

2. It Is Dispositional

I shall say that a proposed analysis of ethical statements is dispositional if it construes ethical statements to assert that a certain being (or beings), either actual or hypothetical, is (or are) disposed to react to something in a certain way. To say that a certain being is disposed to react in a certain way is to say that the being in question would react in that way under certain specifiable conditions. Thus a dispositional analysis of an ethical statement may always be formulated as a hypothetical statement of the kind which is commonly called a "contrary-to-fact conditional." A dispositional analysis of statements of the form "x is right," for example, might have the form: "Such and such a being, if it existed, would react to x in such and such a way if such and such conditions were realized."

During the past fifty years moral philosophers have given a good deal of attention to the evaluation of dispositional analyses which are *relativist*, and a comprehensive defense of one such relativist analysis can be found in the writings of Westermarck.[6] Westermarck believes, if I understand him, that the meaning of statements of the form "x is wrong," can be expressed by other statements of the form "The speaker tends to feel towards x (i.e., *would* feel in the absence of specifiable inhibiting factors), an emotion of disinterested moral disapproval which would be experienced by him as a quality or dynamic tendency in x." Although this analysis is considerably more sophisticated than many of the analyses which relativists have proposed, it is typical of a position to which absolutists have raised a number of closely-related, and by now very familiar, objections.

A dispositional analysis of ethical statements which was *absolutist* would not, of course, be open to the same objections. It would construe ethical statements in one of

the following three ways: (1) as assertions about the dispositions of all *actual* (past, present, and future) beings of a certain kind; (2) as assertions about the dispositions of all *possible* beings of a certain kind (of which there might in fact exist only one or none at all), or (3) as assertions about the dispositions of a majority (or other fraction) of a number of beings (actual or possible) of a certain kind. It is evident that an analysis of any of these three types would include no egocentric expression, and would therefore construe ethical statements in such a way that they would be true or false, and consistent or inconsistent with one another, without special reference to the people who happen to be asserting them.

It is only the second of these three kinds of analysis which I propose to examine in this paper, for analyses of the other two types, it seems to me, are open to obvious and yet insuperable objections. An analysis of the first type would construe ethical statements to entail that there actually exists a being (perhaps God) whose dispositions are definitive of certain ethical terms. But this would mean that all ethical statements containing these ethical terms are necessarily false if such a being does *not* exist—a consequence which seems to be incompatible with what we intend to assert when we use ethical terms. And in my opinion an analysis of the third type would be even less plausible, because it would imply that ethical statements express judgments which can only be verified or refuted, at least theoretically, by statistical procedures. I shall not amplify these familiar arguments, however, since much of what I shall say about ethical analyses of the second type can be equally well applied to analyses of the other two types, and anyone who so wishes may easily make the necessary translations in reading the second part of this paper.

It will be convenient, throughout the following pages, to use the term "ideal observer" in speaking about a possible being of the kind referred to in an absolutist dispositional analysis. The adjective "ideal" is used here in approximately the same sense in which we speak of a perfect vacuum or a frictionless machine as ideal things; it is not intended to suggest that an ideal observer is necessarily *virtuous*, but merely that he is conceivable and that he has certain characteristics to an extreme degree. Perhaps it would seem more natural to call such a being an ideal *judge*, but this term could be quite misleading if it suggested that the function of an ideal observer is to pass judgment on ethical issues. As an ideal observer, of course, it is sufficient that he be capable of reacting in a manner which will determine by definition whether an ethical judgment is true or false. And it is even conceivable, indeed, that an ideal observer, according to some analyses, should lack some of the characteristics which would make it *possible* for him to pass judgment on ethical issues—which would mean, of course, simply that he would not be able to judge the nature of his own dispositions.

Using the term "ideal observer," then, the kind of analysis which I shall examine in this paper is the kind which would construe statements of the form "x is P," in which P is some particular ethical predicate, to be identical in meaning with statements of the form: "Any ideal observer would react to x in such and such a way under such and such conditions."[7]

This formulation may draw attention to the fact that a dispositional analysis which is absolutist may nevertheless be extensionally equivalent to one that is relativist. For the egocentric expression in a relativist analysis is often qualified by reference to ideal conditions (described in if-clauses), and it is evident that each of these qualifications limits the respects in which one speaker could differ from another if the reactions of each were relevant to the truth of his own ethical statement. Westermarck, for example, analyzes ethical statements not by reference simply to the feeling which the speaker would actually have if confronted with a particular act or situation, but by reference to the feelings which he would have *if* he were impartial and *if* certain inhibiting factors (e.g., fatigue)

were absent. And if a relativist were to continue to add such qualifications to his analysis, he might eventually reach a point at which *any* speaker who met all these qualifications would have all the characteristics which an absolutist might wish to attribute to an ideal observer. In that case ethical statements, when analyzed, would be contrary-to-fact conditionals of the form: "If I were an ideal observer I would react to x in such and such a way under such and such conditions." And if the specified characteristics of an ideal observer were sufficient to insure, in virtue of the laws of nature, that all ideal observers would react in the same way, it is evident that the truth value of ethical statements, so interpreted, would not differ from their truth value if interpreted absolutistically as statements about *any* ideal observer. Intensionally, however, the two analyses would still differ: the relativist, unlike the absolutist, would still maintain that the egocentric reference is essential, and by this he would imply, as we have seen, that two different speakers cannot make ethical assertions which are logically incompatible.

Let us now consider briefly some of the derivative characteristics of an analysis which is both absolutist and dispositional.

3. It Is Objectivist

The adjectives "subjectivist" and "objectivist" are often used in a *logical* sense, and as synonyms, respectively, of the terms "relativist" and "absolutist"; in this sense, as we have seen, an analysis of the kind that we are discussing is objectivist. To avoid duplication of meaning, however, I shall use the terms "subjectivist" and "objectivist" in a traditional *ontological* sense—in the sense in which Berkeley's analysis of all physical statements is subjectivist, and Descartes's analysis of some physical statements is objectivist. We may say, in this sense, that a proposed analysis of ethical statements is subjectivist if it construes ethical statements in such a way that they would all be false by definition if there existed no experiencing subjects (past, present, or future). An analysis may be called "objectivist," on the other hand, if it is not subjectivist. Thus it is evident that in this ontological sense, as well as in the logical sense, an analysis of the kind which we are discussing is objectivist: it construes ethical statements to be assertions about the reactions of an *ideal* observer—an observer who is conceivable but whose existence or non-existence is logically irrelevant to the truth or falsity of ethical statements.

This fact that a dispositional analysis is objectivist, is obviously a reflection of the fact that ethical statements, according to such an analysis, may always be formulated as conditional statements in the subjunctive mood; they may always be construed, in other words, as asserting that if such and such *were* the case, such and such *would* be the case. Hypothetical statements of this kind are commonly called "contrary-to-fact conditionals," but since they are sometimes used in such a way that they may be true even though they are not contrary to fact, they are perhaps more aptly referred to as "independent-of-fact conditionals." As used in an absolutist dispositional analysis, for example, such statements are not intended to imply *either* that there exists, *nor* that there does not exist, a being who satisfies the description of an ideal observer; they are intended to imply, on the contrary, that the existence or non-existence of such a being is *irrelevant* to the truth of the statement. Since the subjunctive conditional has exactly the same function whether the analysis is absolutist or relativist, it is evident that objectivism and absolutism are logically independent characteristics of an analysis of ethical statements; thus Westermarck's analysis is objectivist and relativist, whereas the one which we shall be examining is objectivist and absolutist.

The fact that an analysis of ethical statements is objectivist, moreover, is independent of all questions concerning the kinds of things to which ethical terms can be correctly applied. Thus it might in fact be true that the term "good" can be correctly applied only to conscious states, and hence

that all ethical statements of the form "x is good" would in fact be false if there existed no experiencing subjects. And similarly, it might in fact always be false to say that a given act is wrong if neither that act, nor any of its alternatives, has any effect on the experience of conscious beings. But such facts would be entirely compatible with an objectivist *analysis* of ethical statements, for to say that an analysis is objectivist is to say merely that the existence of experiencing subjects is not essential *by definition* to the truth of ethical statements. This distinction is important because the term "subjectivist" is sometimes applied to hedonism and to certain forms of pluralistic utilitarianism, on the ground that these theories attribute value only to states of consciousness, or that they regard actual productivity of these valuable states as the sole determinant of the rightness or wrongness of an act. It is evident, however, that philosophers who support these theories should not be said to accept a subjectivist analysis of ethical statements unless they believe—as some of them, of course, do not—that ethical terms must be *defined* by reference to the experience of actual beings.

4. It Is Relational

An analysis of ethical statements is *relational* if it construes ethical terms in such a way that to apply an ethical term to a particular thing (e.g., an act), is to assert that that thing is related in a certain way to some other thing, either actual or hypothetical. There is no doubt that an absolutist dispositional analysis is relational, since it construes ethical statements as asserting that a lawful relationship exists between certain reactions of an ideal observer and the acts or other things to which an ethical term may correctly be applied. But to avoid misunderstanding, this fact must be interpreted in the light of certain qualifying observations.

It should not be overlooked, in the first place, that if an absolutist dispositional analysis were correct, ethical statements would have the same form that statements about secondary qualities are often supposed to have. Not only phenomenalists and subjectivists, but many epistemological dualists, would agree that to say that a daffodil is yellow is to say something about the way the daffodil would appear to a certain kind of observer under certain conditions; and the analysis of ethical statements which we are considering is exactly analogous to this. Thus the sense in which an absolutist dispositional analysis is relational, is the very sense in which a great many philosophers believe that yellow is a relational property of physical objects; and to say that a statement of the form "x is right" is relational, therefore, is not necessarily to deny that the terms "right" and "yellow" designate equally simple properties.

But the analogy can be carried still further if a distinction is drawn between a relational and a non-relational sense of "yellow." Many philosophers believe that the adjective "yellow" has two meanings; they believe that it designates both a relational property of physical objects and a nonrelational property of sense-data—a distinction corresponding roughly to the popular use of the terms "really yellow" and "apparently yellow." And it is quite possible not only that the term "right" is similarly ambiguous, but also that in one of its senses it designates a characteristic of human experience (apparent rightness) which in some important respect is just as simple and unanalyzable as the property of apparent yellowness. And thus we might even decide by analogy with the case of "yellow," that "really right" must be defined in terms of "apparently right"—i.e., that the experiencing of apparent rightness is an essential part of any ethically-significant reaction of an ideal observer.

And finally, it must be remembered that to call an absolutist analysis "relational," is not to imply that it construes the ethical properties of one thing to be dependent by definition on the *existence* of any other thing, either natural or supernatural. Since an ideal observer is a *hypothetical* being, no changes in the relationships of existent things would require us, for logical reasons

alone, to attribute new ethical properties to any object, nor to revise any ethical judgment which we have previously made. For this reason an absolutist dispositional analysis is not open to one of the most familiar objections to relational analyses, namely, that such analyses construe the ethical properties of an object to be dependent on facts which seem quite clearly to be *accidental*—on the fact, for example, that certain actual people happen to have a certain attitude toward the object.[8]

5. It Is Empirical

If we define the term "empirical" liberally enough so that the dispositional concepts of the natural sciences may properly be called empirical, there is no doubt that an absolutist dispositional analysis of ethical statements *might* be empirical. Such an analysis would be empirical for example, if the defining characteristics of an ideal observer were psychological traits, and if the ethically-significant reactions of an ideal observer were feelings of desire, or emotions of approval and disapproval, or some other experiences accessible to psychological observation.

It might be somewhat less evident, however, that an absolutist dispositional analysis *must* be empirical. For most of the philosophers who maintain that ethical properties are non-natural, and that ethical truths are known by rational intuition, have admitted that ethical intuitions may be erroneous under certain unfavorable conditions, or else, if this is regarded as self-contradictory, that under certain conditions we may appear to be intuiting an ethical truth although in fact we are not.[9] And it might seem that to recognize the possibility of error in either of these two ways is to recognize a distinction between the property of apparent rightness and the property of real rightness—a distinction, as we have seen, which is sufficient to permit the formulation of an absolutist dispositional analysis.

On this issue, however, I think we must take the word of the rational intuitionists themselves, and if there is any one fact about which intuitionists agree, it is the fact that some ethical properties are neither introspectable nor analyzable. And from this fact it follows, necessarily, that their ethical theory is epistemologically dualist—i.e., that there is no formula, however complex, by which ethical statements can be translated into statements about experiences which confirm them. Intuitionists must admit, I believe, that they are able to assess the cognitive value of their ostensible intuitions by reference to the conditions under which these intuitions occur, and they must admit that they would not be able to do this unless they had some conception of an ideal observer. Thus Ewing lists[10] four factors which are responsible for false intuitions: (1) lack of experience, (2) intellectual confusions, (3) failure to attend adequately to certain aspects of the situation, (4) psychological causes "such as those with which the psychoanalyst deals." And the very fact that Ewing can compile such a list is proof that he has some conception of an ideal observer whose definition excludes these four factors. But this fact does not make intuitionism any less dualist, of course, for Ewing and other intuitionists will maintain that in formulating these ideal conditions they are merely formulating a *test* for the validity of an ethical statement, and not an analysis of the statement.[11]

Even though we conclude that an absolutist dispositional analysis must be empirical, however, there is still considerable room for disagreement about the precise nature of the ethically-significant reactions of an ideal observer. It seems clear that these reactions, if the analysis is to be at all plausible, must be defined in terms of the kind of moral experience which we take to be evidence, under ideal conditions, for the truth of our ethical judgments. It is important to observe that experiences of this kind—which we may properly call "moral data"—cannot be states of moral *belief.* An absolutist dispositional analysis, like any other analysis which grants cognitive meaning to ethical sentences, would per-

mit us to say that we *do* have moral beliefs, and even that moral consciousness is *ordinarily* a state of belief. But if the ethically-significant reaction of an ideal observer were the belief (or judgment) that a certain act is right or wrong, it is evident that an absolutist dispositional analysis would be circular: it would contain the very ethical terms which it is intended to define.

In order to define an absolutist dispositional analysis, therefore, it is necessary to maintain that moral data are the moral experiences to which we appeal when *in doubt* about the correct solution of a moral problem, or when attempting to *justify* a moral belief. For the epistemic function of moral data, when defined in this way, will correspond to the function of color sensations in determining or justifying the belief that a certain material object is "really yellow." And in that case moral data could play the same role in the analysis of "right" that color sensations play in the analysis of "really yellow."

Now there are many debatable questions concerning the nature of moral data, and until these questions are answered it will not be possible to explain precisely what is meant by the "ethically-significant reactions" of an ideal observer. These questions are primarily psychological, however, and can easily be separated from other questions concerning the content of an absolutist dispositional analysis. And if it is possible to provide a satisfactory formulation of the other components of an absolutist dispositional analysis (especially the definition of "ideal observer") this formulation will be compatible with *any* phenomenological description of moral data.

One of the most salient differences of opinion, for example, concerning the nature of moral data, is the difference of opinion concerning what we may call their "phenomenal location." There are many philosophers, on the one hand, who maintain that moral data are primarily feelings, or emotions, or other elements of experience which appear in the deliberative consciousness of the moral judge as ostensible states of the judge himself. There seems to be a growing number of philosophers, on the other hand, who are equally empirical in their epistemology, but who maintain that the typical moral datum is an obligatoriness or "demand quality" which appears in the deliberative consciousness of the moral judge as an ostensible property of an envisaged act or goal.[12] But however important this difference of opinion may be, it is a difference of opinion about the nature of moral data and not about the logical or epistemological relationships between moral data and ethical statements; both of these positions are compatible, therefore, with the theory that ethical statements are statements about the dispositions of an ideal observer to experience moral data (whatever they may be) under certain specifiable conditions.

Whatever conclusion we might reach concerning the phenomenal location of moral data, it will still be necessary to distinguish very carefully between moral data themselves, which, under ideal conditions, are the *evidence* for moral beliefs, and the very similar experiences which may be the *consequences* of moral beliefs. This distinction would not be difficult to make if we were content to say that moral data are simply feelings of desire (or, correlatively, that moral data are "demand qualities" of *all* kinds). For there seems to be little reason to doubt that feelings of desire may occur in the absence of moral beliefs. But if we should wish to maintain, as many philosophers have done, that moral data are the emotions of moral approval and disapproval, it would be much harder to make the necessary distinction. As Broad has pointed out, those emotions of approval and disapproval which we think of as specifically *moral* emotions, are the very ones "which appear *prima facie* to be felt towards persons or actions in respect of certain moral characteristics which they are believed to have."[13] So if these emotions are said to be the evidence for moral beliefs, there appears to be a vicious circle in the process by which moral beliefs are justified. And there appears to be a similar vicious circle in an absolutist dispositional analysis. For if moral emotions are experienced only as a consequence of moral beliefs or judgments, and if we refuse to attribute moral beliefs to an ideal observer in our analysis, then there is no reason to think that an ideal observer would experience any moral emotions at all. But if, on the other hand, we do attribute moral beliefs to an ideal observer, we should have to employ the very ethical terms (e.g., "right") which we are attempting to analyze. This fact, in one form or another, has provided the basis for many arguments in support of non-naturalist ethics.

But the difficulty, I believe, has been highly exaggerated. It cannot plausibly be denied that moral emotions are often (perhaps usually) felt as a consequence of moral beliefs—that we often feel approval, for example, toward those acts which we believe to be right. But this is merely to say, if an absolutist dispositional analysis is valid, that we often feel approval toward those acts which we think would produce approval in an ideal observer. The crucial question is whether it is possible to feel an emotion of moral approval toward an act when we are *in doubt* about whether it is right or wrong. And surely this *is* possible.[14] It is not uncommon, for example, to find ourselves feeling moral approval toward an act, and then to begin to wonder whether our reaction is *justified*: we might wonder, for example, whether we are sufficiently familiar with "the facts of the case" or whether our emotions are being unduly influenced by some selfish consideration. At such times we may continue to experience the emotion of moral approval although in doubt about the rightness of the act. We may even attempt to rationalize our emotion by persuading ourselves that the act is right. In rare cases, indeed, we may even continue to experience the emotion although convinced that our reaction is *not* justified. (This is sometimes the case, for example, when people feel approval toward an act of retribution.) Consequently, unless apparent facts of this kind can be discounted by subtle phenomenological analysis, there is no epistemological objec-

tion to defining the ethically significant reactions of an ideal observer in terms of
moral emotions.

Whether or not this is the correct way to
define these reactions, however, is a psychological question which I shall not consider in this paper. There are other, more
fundamental, questions concerning the
content of an absolutist dispositional
analysis, and it is these to which the remaining part of this paper will be devoted.

Part Two: The Content
of the Analysis

If it is possible to formulate a satisfactory
absolutist and dispositional analysis of ethical statements, it must be possible, as we
have seen, to express the meaning of statements of the form "x is right" in terms of
other statements which have the form:
"Any ideal observer would react to x in
such and such a way under such and such
conditions." Thus even if we are not to discuss the nature of the ethically-significant
reactions of an ideal observer in this paper,
it might seem that we are nevertheless
faced with two distinct questions: (1) What
are the defining characteristics of an ideal
observer? and (2) Under what conditions
do the reactions of an ideal observer determine the truth or falsity of ethical statements? I believe, however, that the second
of these questions can be treated as part of
the first. For it is evident that the conditions
under which the ethically-significant reactions of an ideal observer might occur,
could be relevant to the meaning of ethical
statements only if they could affect an ideal
observer in such a way as to influence his
ethically-significant reactions. And since
the influence of any such relevant conditions must therefore be *indirect*, it would always be possible to insure precisely the
same reactions by attributing suitable characteristics directly to the ideal observer. If,
for example, the absence of certain emotional stimuli is thought to be a relevant
and favorable condition, this fact could be
taken into account simply by specifying
that the ideal observer is by definition un-

responsive to such emotional stimuli. I
think it will soon become clear, moreover,
that this procedure yields a type of analysis which comes closer to expressing what
we actually intend to assert when we utter
ethical statements. But even if I am mistaken about this, it will not be prejudicial
to any basic problem if we assume, for simplicity, that the second question may be reduced to the first, namely, What are the
defining characteristics of an ideal observer?

Before attempting to answer this question, however, there are a few remarks
which I think should be made about the implications and methodology of any such attempt to define an ideal observer.

It is important, in the first place, to view
any attempt of this kind in proper perspective. It would undoubtedly be difficult
to arrive at a rational conclusion concerning the plausibility of absolutist dispositional analyses in general, without first
experimenting with various concrete formulations. At the present stage in the history of moral philosophy, however, it
would be especially unfortunate if the inadequacies of some particular formulation
were to prejudice philosophers against absolutist dispositional analyses in general.
Any plausible formulation is certain to be
very complex, and there is no reason to
suppose that philosophers could ever reach
complete agreement concerning all the details of an adequate analysis. But this in itself should not prevent philosophers from
agreeing that this general *form* of analysis
is valid. Nor would it necessarily be irrational for a philosopher to decide that this
general form is valid, although he is dissatisfied even with *his own* attempts to formulate a concrete analysis.[15]

Ethical words, moreover, like all other
words, are probably used by different people, even in similar contexts, to express
somewhat different meanings; and a
correct analysis of one particular ethical
statement, therefore, may not be a correct
analysis of another statement which is sym-
bolized in exactly the same way but asserted by a different person. This kind of
ambiguity is a familiar obstacle to all philo-

sophical analysis, but it causes unusual difficulties when we attempt to evaluate a proposed dispositional analysis of ethical statements. Any such analysis, if it is at all plausible, is certain to assign a number of complex characteristics to an ideal observer, and to refer to complex psychological phenomena in describing the nature of his ethically-significant reactions. And assuming that ethical statements *can* be analyzed in this manner, there is no good reason to believe that all human beings, no matter what the extent of their individual development, and no matter what their past social environment, could analyze their ethical statements correctly by reference to precisely the same kind of ideal observer and precisely the same psychological phenomena. If there *are* any irreducible differences in the intended meaning of ethical statements, some of these differences might not be discoverable, and most of them might be so slight that they could not be held responsible for differences of opinion concerning the proper analysis of ethical statements. Some of these differences in meaning, on the other hand, might be sufficiently large to be reflected in the formulation of philosophical analyses of ethical statements. And there is consequently a clear sense in which philosophers may appear to disagree about the analysis of ethical statements, although in fact, because ethical words are somewhat ambiguous, they are analyzing different statements and hence not disagreeing at all.

It would be a serious mistake, however, to confuse the kind of ambiguity to which I have just referred with the kind of ambiguity which is definitive of a relativist analysis. The ambiguity which is definitive of relativism, as we have seen, is conventional, systematic, and characteristic only of statements which contain an egocentric expression. The kind of ambiguity which we have just been discussing, on the other hand, is accidental, unsystematic, and characteristic in some degree of all symbols. Thus it is not ordinarily the intention of an ethical absolutist to maintain that the words which we use to express ethical statements have a unique semiotical capacity—the capacity, namely, to express exactly the same meaning no matter who utters them; in fact even those absolutists who believe that ethical words express simple, unanalyzable, concepts, could scarcely maintain that there is any conclusive evidence to show that an ethical word, no matter who employs it, always expresses the *same* unanalyzable concept. The thesis maintained by the absolutist as such, is simply that ethical statements are not *conventionally* ambiguous in a manner which would require them to be analyzed by means of an egocentric expression; and this thesis is quite consistent, of course, with the proposition that ethical statements are *accidentally* ambiguous—perhaps even more ambiguous, indeed, than most other statements.

In the light of this distinction, then, it seems clear that if two philosophers believe that they are in perfect agreement concerning the meaning of ethical statements—i.e., if they believe that their ability to communicate is not limited by accidental ambiguity—they may still be either relativists or absolutists. If they are relativists, and related to one another spatially, temporally, and socially in certain ways, they will believe that neither of them could assert an ethical statement which is logically inconsistent with any ethical statement asserted by the other. If they are absolutists, however, they will believe that they *can* contradict each other in their ethical statements. Thus the absolutist, unlike the relativist, believes that nothing stands in the way of the expression of cognitive disagreement about ethical matters except the accidental ambiguity which is characteristic of all symbols. And since the absolutist can consistently admit that this accidental ambiguity may be sufficiently great to prevent philosophers from agreeing on a concrete analysis of ethical statements, the apparent inadequacy of any particular analysis, such as the one which I shall propose, should not be considered as proof that the general form of an absolutist dispositional analysis is unsatisfactory.

It should also be kept in mind that the kind of analysis which we are seeking is one which would be an analysis of ethical statements in the sense (and probably only in the sense) in which hypothetical statements about the way a daffodil would appear to a "normal" observer are said to constitute an analysis of the material object statement "This daffodil is yellow." To attempt an analysis of this sense of the word "analysis" would lead to difficult problems far beyond the scope of this paper. But two points may be mentioned. First, an analysis in this sense of the word is not required to be *prima facie* or "intuitively" equivalent to the analyzandum, and for this reason the surprising complexity of a proposed analysis is not a sufficient reason for rejecting it: thus the fact that a proposed analysis of "This daffodil is yellow" happens to refer to white light, a transparent medium, a neutral background, and a variety of physiological conditions of an observer, is not ordinarily thought to make the analysis unsatisfactory. And second, an analysis in this sense of the word is an analysis of the so-called "cognitive meaning" of ethical statements, and thus is not required to have the same emotive meaning as the analyzandum. Even if we should find a satisfactory analysis of ethical statements, therefore, we should still have to supplement this analysis by a theory of emotive meaning if we wished to take account of all the functions of ethical statements in actual discourse.

The method employed in formulating dispositional analyses—whether of "soluble" or "yellow" or "right"—is the method most aptly described as "pragmatic." In analyzing ethical statements, for example, we must try to determine the characteristics of an ideal observer by examining the procedures which we actually regard, implicitly or explicitly, as the rational ones for *deciding* ethical questions. These procedures, to mention just a few, might include religious exercises, the acquisition of certain kinds of factual information, appeals to a moral authority, and attempts to suppress one's emotions if they are thought to be prejudicial. Each of these procedures will suggest certain characteristics of an ideal observer, and there is reason to believe that the char-

acteristics suggested by these various procedures will not be incompatible with one another: some of the characteristics which are likely to be attributed to a moral authority, for example, seem to be the very ones which we try to produce or to approximate in ourselves when we engage in religious exercises, or seek for factual information, or attempt to suppress emotions which we think are prejudicial.

This appeal to the procedures by which we judge or decide ethical questions, does not imply that the pragmatic method will force us to deny the important distinction, previously mentioned, between an ideal *observer* and an ideal *judge:* there is clearly no logical reason why a judge should have to *be* an ideal observer, or should even have to be closely similar to an ideal observer, in order to make correct judgments about the ethically-significant reactions of such a being. On the other hand, there cannot be much doubt that the ethically-significant reactions of an ideal observer must be psychological in nature, and that some of the evidence for the occurrence of these reactions could be directly accessible only to an ideal observer himself. It is for this epistemic reason that in practice we are likely to rate moral judges by reference to their similarity to an ideal observer. And it is to be expected, consequently, that any plausible description of an ideal observer will be a partial description of God, if God is conceived to be an infallible moral judge. But of course an ideal observer need not possess such characteristics as the power to create physical objects or even the power to reward and punish, if these characteristics appear to be irrelevant to God's capacities as a moral judge.

Characteristics of An Ideal Observer

1. He Is Omniscient With Respect to Non-Ethical Facts

We sometimes disqualify ourselves as judges of a particular ethical question on the ground that we are not sufficiently familiar with the facts of the case, and we regard one person as a better moral judge than another if, other things being equal, the one has a larger amount of relevant factual knowledge than the other. This suggests that an ideal observer must be characterized in part by reference to his knowledge of non-ethical facts. I say "non-ethical" because, as we have seen, the characteristics of an ideal observer must be determined by examining the procedures which we actually take to be the rational ones for deciding ethical questions; and there are many ethical questions (viz., questions about "ultimate ethical principles") which cannot be decided by inference from ethical premises. This does not mean, of course, that an ideal observer (e.g., God) *cannot* have knowledge of ethical facts (facts, that is to say, about his own dispositions); it means merely that such knowledge is not *essential* to an ideal observer.

A difficulty seems to arise from the fact that in practice we evaluate the factual knowledge of a moral judge by reference to some standard of relevance, and regard one judge as better than another if, other things being equal, the one has more complete knowledge of all the facts which are *relevant*. But it is evident that a concept of relevance cannot be employed in *defining* an ideal observer. To say that a certain body of factual knowledge is not relevant to the rightness or wrongness of a given act, is to say, assuming that an absolutist dispositional analysis is correct, that the dispositions of an ideal observer toward the given act would be the same *whether or not* he possessed that particular body of factual knowledge or any part of it. It follows, therefore, that in order to explain what we mean by "relevant knowledge," we should have to employ the very concept of ideal observer which we are attempting to define.

Fortunately, however, we do not seem to think that a person is to any extent disqualified as a moral judge merely because he possesses factual information which we take to be *superfluous*. Our difficulty would be overcome, therefore, if we were simply to stipulate that an ideal observer is *omni-*

scient with respect to non-ethical facts, and so far as I can see the term "omniscient," when employed in this way, is neither extravagant nor mysterious. We apparently believe not only that the "facts of the case" are relevant to the objective rightness or wrongness of a particular act, but also that there is no point at which we could be logically certain that further information about matters of fact (e.g., further information about the consequences of the act), would be irrelevant. A satisfactory ethical analysis must be so formulated, therefore, that no facts are irrelevant *by definition* to the rightness or wrongness of any particular act. And this is the intent of the term "omniscient," for to say that an ideal observer is omniscient is to insure that no limits are put on the kinds or the quality of factual information which are available to influence his ethically-significant reactions.

Since omniscience implies complete knowledge of the *past* as well as the future, it might be wondered whether we are not being unnecessarily generous in attributing omniscience to the ideal observer. And it might seem that one's answer to this question will depend on one's views concerning the factors which determine whether an act is in fact right or wrong. Thus a philosopher whose position is not purely utilitarian (i.e., teleological), but to some extent deontological, might be expected to take one position; he might be expected to believe that certain events prior to the performance of an act (e.g., the making of contracts) are directly relevant to the objective rightness or wrongness of an act, in which case he would naturally wish to stipulate that the knowledge of an ideal observer extend to the past as well as the future. The typical utilitarian, on the other hand, believing that the past events are relevant only in so far as they affect the future, might be expected to deny that an ideal observer must have any knowledge about events occurring prior to the act which is being judged.

It seems clear, however, that this difference of opinion would exist only if the utilitarian wished to define rightness and wrongness in such a way that the thesis of utilitarianism followed analytically from his definitions, and most contemporary utilitarians maintain, I believe, that the thesis of utilitarianism is a synthetic proposition. What they would wish to say, therefore, if they accepted an absolutist dispositional analysis of ethical statements, is that an ideal observer, although he *is* by definition fully cognizant of all past events, would nevertheless have precisely the same ethically-significant reactions to a present act if by definition he were *not* cognizant of past events. Thus there is no reason why the utilitarian and the deontologist must disagree at this point about the analysis of ethical statements.

2. He Is Omnipercipient

We sometimes disqualify ourselves as judges of certain ethical questions on the ground that we cannot satisfactorily imagine or visualize some of the relevant facts, and in general we regard one person as a better moral judge than another if, other things being equal, the one is better able to imagine or visualize the relevant facts. Practical moralists have often maintained that lack of imagination is responsible for many crimes, and some have suggested that our failure to treat strangers like brothers is in large part a result of our inability to imagine the joys and sorrows of strangers as vividly as those of our siblings. These facts seem to indicate that the ideal observer must be characterized by extraordinary powers of imagination.

The imaginal powers of the ideal observer, to be sure, are very closely related to his omniscience, and the word "omniscience" has sometimes been used to designate an unlimited imagination of perception. But however we may decide to use the word "omniscience," the important point is simply that it is not sufficient for an ideal observer to possess factual knowledge in a manner which will permit him to make true factual judgments. The ideal observer must be able, on the contrary, simultaneously to visualize all actual facts, and the consequences of all possible acts in any given situation, just as vividly as he would if he were actually perceiving them all. It is undoubtedly impossible for us to imagine the experience of a being capable of this kind of universal perception, but in making ethical decisions we sometimes attempt to visualize several alternative acts and their consequences in rapid succession, very much *as though* we wished our decision to be based on a simultaneous perception of the alternatives. And in view of this fact, and the others which I have mentioned, it seems necessary to attribute universal imagination to an ideal observer, thus guaranteeing that his ethically-significant reactions are forcefully and equitably stimulated.

3. He Is Disinterested

We sometimes disqualify ourselves as judges of certain ethical questions on the ground that we cannot make ourselves impartial, and we regard one person as a better moral judge than another if, other things being equal, the one is more impartial than the other. This suggests that one of the defining characteristics of an ideal observer must be complete impartiality. But it is difficult to define the term "impartial" in a manner which will not make our analysis circular or be otherwise inconsistent with our purpose.

It is important, in the first place, not to confuse the impartiality of an ideal observer with the *uniformity* of his ethically-significant reactions. We are likely to think of a judge who is impartial as a judge who arrives at similar decisions in similar cases, and we may be tempted, therefore, to define an ideal observer as an observer whose ethically-significant reactions to two acts would always be the same if the two acts were alike in all ethically-relevant respects. But this will not do. For even if we could find a way to avoid circularity in defining "ethically-relevant respects," the characteristic which we should have analyzed would be more appropriately called "consistency" than "impartiality." And the fact that it is not self-contradictory to say that a person (e.g., a magistrate) is consistently partial, indicates that consistency and impartiality are not identical characteristics. Consistency, as we shall later see, *is* one of the characteristics of an ideal observer. But to say that an ideal observer is consistent is to say something about the uniformity of his ethically-significant reactions, whereas to say that he is impartial is to say something about the factors which *influence* his reactions.

When we try, however, to specify the kinds of factors which do and do not influence the decisions of an impartial judge, it is difficult to avoid interpreting the term "impartial" too broadly. For impartiality is so closely associated with the capacity for correct moral judgment, that we are likely to conclude that a judge lacks impartiality only if we believe that his decisions have been influenced by factors which *pervert* them—by factors, that is to say, which cause them to be incorrect. And whatever the justification for such reasoning may be when we are evaluating a moral judge, our analysis would evidently be circular if the term "impartial," as applied to an ideal observer, involved some concealed reference to a standard of correct moral judgment. It is difficulties of this kind which may have led Broad to remark that a philosopher who attempts this kind of dispositional analysis "is on a very slippery slope, and scarcely ever manages to avoid inconsistency. In defining his ideal he nearly always unwittingly introduces some characteristic which is in fact ethical, and thus fails ... to define ethical characteristics in completely non-ethical terms."[16]

It is also difficult, on the other hand, to avoid interpreting the term "impartial" too narrowly. There is a familiar sense of this term, for example, which seems to be well represented by Bentham's maxim that every man should count for one and none for more than one. In this sense of the term a man would be impartial, in making a decision about his duty in a given situation, if he gave equal consideration to the welfare of each person who could be affected by his acts, regardless of how the person

happened to be related to him.[17] And the maxim that we should treat all men as our brothers, has likewise been interpreted to imply a rule of impartiality in this sense— i.e., to imply that there are no special relationships which justify giving more consideration to one person than to another. But to analyze ethical statements by reference to this kind of impartiality, would rule out, by very definition of the words "right" and "wrong," the moral theory (held by Ross and others) that the rightness or wrongness of an act is determined in part by irreducible obligations arising directly from certain personal relationships; such as analysis would entail, for example, that there is never any moral justification, other things (including the value of the consequences) being equal, for making a decision which favors one's mother or friend or creditor at the expense of a greater benefit to someone else. Most philosophers would probably agree, however, that a correct analysis of ethical statements would not entail any particular conclusions concerning material questions of this sort. The solutions to such questions, they would agree, are synthetic and must not be prejudiced by our definitions.

Now it seems to me that a large part of what we mean when we say that an ideal judge is impartial, is that such a judge will not be influenced by interests of the kind which are commonly described as "particular"—interests, that is to say, which are directed toward a particular person or or thing but not toward other persons or things of the same kind; and in so far as this is what we mean by "impartiality," we can define the term without falling into either of the errors which we have been considering. For to say that an ideal observer is not influenced by particular interests, is to attribute to him a certain psychological characteristic which does not refer, either explicitly or implicitly, to a moral standard. Nor does it logically entail, on the other hand, either that an ideal observer would react favorably, or that he would react unfavorably, to an act which benefits one person at the expense of a greater benefit to another.

The term "particular interest," to be sure, is a difficult one to define, and raises problems about the nature of particularity which are beyond the scope of this paper; but I think that for present purposes it is not unreasonable to pass over these problems. Since ethical judgments are concerned, directly or indirectly, with acts, let us use "x" to denote the performance of a certain act by a certain agent. Let us first draw a distinction between the "essentially general properties" of x and the "essentially particular properties" of x. The properties of x which are essentially particular are those properties which cannot be defined without the use of proper names (which we may understand, for present purposes, to include egocentric particulars such as "I," "here," "now," and "this"); thus one of the essentially particular properties of x might be its tendency to increase the happiness of the citizens of the U.S.A. All other properties are essentially general; thus one of the essentially general properties of x might be its tendency to increase happiness. We may then say that a person has a positive particular interest in x if (1) he desires x, (2) he believes that x has a certain essentially particular property P, and (3) he would not desire x, or would desire it less intensely, if, his other beliefs remaining constant, he did not believe that x had this property P.

It may seem that this definition makes a variety of logical and ontological assumptions, some of which can be questioned. But I think that the intent of the definition is clear enough, and that the distinctions which it requires must be made, in one form or another, by any adequate logic and ontology. The definition is intended to represent the characteristic which we have in mind when we say that a moral judge who lacks impartiality is one who is tempted to "sacrifice principle"—i.e., to judge one act in a manner in which he would not wish to judge other acts which he thought to be of the same kind. And the definition proposes, in effect, that to say in this context that two acts are thought to be "of the same kind," is to say that they are thought to

have the same essentially general properties. It is quite likely, of course, that we never actually believe that any two acts *do* have the same essentially general properties; it is for this reason, indeed, that we find it so easy to rationalize and "make exceptions" when judging acts which affect ourselves, our children, or our country. But this fact does not affect the usefulness of the definition, because part (3) is formulated hypothetically in the subjunctive mood: whether or not a person has a particular interest, is something to be decided by inferring, as best we can, how he *would* react *if* his beliefs were altered in certain ways.

It is important to observe that a person should not be said to have a particular interest in a certain act (x) merely because his interest in x is a result of his belief that x is related in a certain way to a *unique particular*. Let us suppose, for example, that Crito wanted Socrates to escape from prison because he thought that Socrates was the wisest man who would ever live. Let us suppose, for simplicity, that Crito did not want the wisest of men to be killed by his fellow human beings, and that this was his *sole* reason for wanting Socrates to escape. Now in this case it would surely be a mistake to maintain that Crito was necessarily influenced by a particular interest, for this would mean, if particular interests are excluded from an ideal observer, that the ethically-significant reactions of an ideal observer could *never* be influenced by the fact that a particular person or thing has a certain distinguishing property. And it is evident, I assume, that the ethical relevance or irrelevance of a fact of this sort cannot be decided merely by analyzing the meaning of ethical terms.

The crucial question about Crito's interest, therefore, is not whether it is an interest in the fate of a unique particular (Socrates), but whether the properties of Socrates which arouse this interest are essentially particular, i.e., properties which cannot be analyzed without the use of proper names. Two of the essentially particular properties which Crito might have attributed to Socrates are (A) being the wisest friend of Crito, and (B) being the most effective gad-fly in Athens. In a terminology suggested by Broad (following McTaggart), we may say that each of these is an "exclusive description" of Socrates. But Crito's interest, we are supposing, is a result of his belief that Socrates has the essentially general property (C) being wiser than any other man. In Broad's terminology this third property might also be an exclusive description of Socrates. But unlike the other two, this property is a "sufficient description," i.e., one which "refers to no merely designated particulars, but consists wholly of universals."[18] We may say, therefore, that Crito is interested in Socrates because of a certain sufficient description which he attributes to Socrates. For this reason his interest is not particular; it is an interest, so to speak, which he would have in *any* person whom he thought to be the wisest of all men. Interests of this kind, therefore, even though they are directed toward a particular person or thing, do not tend to make us impartial in our moral judgments.

Assuming now, that we have found a satisfactory definition of "particular interest," we must still decide how to use this term in our analysis. Shall we say that an ideal observer is completely lacking in particular interests? Or shall we say simply that his ethically-significant reactions are uninfluenced by such interests, leaving open the possibility, so far as our analysis is concerned, that such interests might be present but in some sense "suppressed"? At first thought the latter statement seems to be adequate to represent our concept of an impartial moral judge, for we often admire such a judge precisely because we believe that he does have particular interests but that his desire to be impartial has counteracted their influence. On further reflection it will be discovered, however, that we cannot explain what it means to say that a judge is uninfluenced by particular interests, except by reference, directly or indirectly, to the manner in which he *would* react *if* he had no particular interests. And this seems to imply that the first alterna-

tive is ultimately unavoidable if our analysis is to be complete. I think we must conclude, therefore, that an ideal observer is entirely lacking in particular interests—that he is, in this sense, *disinterested*.

4. He Is Dispassionate

The concept of impartiality cannot be exhaustively analyzed in terms of interests, for an impartial judge, as ordinarily conceived, is a judge whose decisions are unaffected not only by his interests, but also by his emotions. This suggests that an ideal observer must be defined as a person who is in some sense dispassionate as well as disinterested. It is possible, to be sure, that the supposed effects of an emotion on our ethically-significant reactions, are always the effects of an accompanying or constituent interest; and if this were proved to our satisfaction, our conception of an ideal observer might be somewhat simplified. For our present purpose, however, this is irrelevant so long as it is generally believed that moral nearsightedness or blindness can be caused by the typically passional features of an emotion. We are searching for an analysis of ordinary ethical statements, and it is not to be expected that such an analysis will reflect all those distinctions, or just those distinctions, which would be required for an adequate system of psychology.

It is possible to construct a definition of the term "dispassionate" which will correspond, point by point, with our definition of the term "disinterested." Thus we can define a "particular emotion" as one which is directed toward an object only because the object is thought to have one or more essentially particular properties. And we can say that an ideal observer is dispassionate in the sense that he is incapable of experiencing emotions of this kind—such emotions as jealousy, self-love, personal hatred, and others which are directed towards particular individuals as such. At present this seems to me to be the most satisfactory way of defining the term "dispassionate" as applied to an ideal observer.

It would also be possible, however, to go a good deal further and to say that an ideal observer is incapable of experiencing any emotions at all, thus bringing our conception of an ideal observer closer to Kant's conception of a "purely rational being." There is no corresponding alternative open to us for the definition of "disinterested," because it seems unlikely that an ideal observer who had no interests at all would ever have any ethically-significant reactions. But the issue is not so clear with respect to emotions, especially if the moral datum, and hence the ethically-significant reactions of an ideal observer, can be defined in terms of a non-emotional, ostensibly objective, "demand quality."[19] And even those who believe that the moral datum is emotional, could maintain that an exception needs to be made only for moral approval and disapproval, or other emotions constituting the ethically-significant reactions of an ideal observer.

It might be maintained, to be sure, that there are certain emotions which are essential to an ideal observer, not because they constitute his ethically-significant reactions, but because they will influence these reactions in certain ways. And it should be observed that if this is an error, it is not a *logical* error, for precisely how an ideal observer should be defined can be determined only by analyzing the meaning of ethical statements. In fact, provided that we base our analysis on a direct examination of the meaning of ethical statements, it would not even be a logical mistake to attribute *virtues* to an ideal observer—to say, for example, that he has love and compassion for all human beings. It is true that love and compassion, assuming that they are truly virtues, are virtues only because of their relationship to certain ethically-significant reactions of an ideal observer— to those reactions, namely, by reference to which the ethical term "virtue" is defined; but virtues may be attributed to an ideal observer without circularity, of course, provided that we do not have to justify their attribution by reference to the fact that

they are virtues. If, for example, the Christian conception of God has influenced our conception of an ideal observer, then, if an absolutist dispositional analysis is correct, it has influenced the very meaning of ethical statements. And if philosophers from a non-Christian culture have a somewhat different conception of an ideal observer, this fact implies nothing more surprising than that ethical statements possess the kind of ambiguity which I have called "accidental." Thus my reason for believing that it is not necessary to attribute such virtues as love and compassion to an ideal observer, is not that it would be a logical mistake to do so, but simply that I am not inclined to think that a man is necessarily a better moral judge, however superior as a person, merely because he possesses such virtues. The value of love and compassion to a judge, considered solely as a judge, seems to lie in the qualities of knowledge and disinterestedness which are so closely related to them; and these two qualities, as we have seen, can be independently attributed to an ideal observer.

5. He Is Consistent

Consistency is ordinarily regarded as one of the characteristics of a good judge, and this fact suggests that an ideal observer must be described in part as a being whose ethically-significant reactions are perfectly consistent with one another. But there are obstacles, as we shall see, to defining the relevant kind of consistency in a manner which avoids circularity and yet makes consistency an independent characteristic of an ideal observer.

When we say that the ethical decisions of a judge in two different cases are consistent with one another—or, correspondingly, that in two different situations the ethically-significant reactions of an ideal observer are consistent—we are evidently not passing judgment on the logic of any actual process of thought. There is an obvious sense, to be sure, in which a judge might accept consistent or inconsistent *premises* or use consistent or inconsistent *arguments* (either in reaching his decisions or in attempting to justify them); but when we assert that the two decisions of the judge are *themselves* consistent with one another, we intend to say something about a particular relationship between the two ethical statements which express the judge's final conclusions, and nothing, unless perhaps by insinuation, about the judge's processes of thought.

But it is also clear that we do not intend to say merely that these two ethical statements are *logically* consistent with one another. For since the two statements express ethical decisions about two different cases, they necessarily refer to different acts or events, and of course *any* two self-consistent statements are logically consistent with one another if they refer to different acts or events. Thus the kind of consistency which we have in mind must be "stronger" than logical consistency: we must mean to say that it is in some sense *possible* that the two statements are both true, but not merely that it is *logically* possible.

If this is so, however, the consistency or inconsistency of two ethical decisions must depend on the relationship of these decisions to certain general ethical principles which are conceived as restricting the "possible" combinations of ethical statements. And this conclusion is supported, I believe, by examination of the kind of reasoning which actually leads us to conclude that two decisions are consistent or inconsistent with one another. We might assert, for example, that a moral judge is inconsistent because in one case he decided in favor of act x rather than x', whereas in another case he decided in favor of y rather than y'; and if we assert this, an analysis of our reasoning would probably show that we are assuming that it is possible for x to be the right act only if a certain ethical principle (P) is true, whereas it is possible for y to be the right act only if P is false.[20] Our judgment that the two decisions are inconsistent, therefore, is based on the assumption that there is no *other* valid ethical principle

(a certain principle Q, for example) which could in some way take precedence over P in one of the two cases.[21] We are not, to be sure, committing ourselves either to the belief that P is true or to the belief that P is false. But we *are* assuming that the facts of the two cases are not different in some respect which is ethically crucial. And to assume even this is to presuppose at least one ethical proposition, namely, that there is no valid ethical principle (e.g., Q) which, together with P, could be used to justify *both* decisions.

I think we must conclude, therefore, that whenever we assert that the decisions of a moral judge in two different cases are consistent with one another, we are presupposing a certain amount of ethical knowledge. And this implies that our analysis would be circular if we made consistency of this kind one of the defining characteristics of an ideal observer.

There is, however, a much more limited kind of consistency which we might wish to attribute to an ideal observer. For if we agree that his ethically-significant reactions are stimulated by his imagination of a possible act, then, since an act may be imagined at any number of different times, there is nothing in our analysis up to this point which would logically require that an ideal observer always react in the same way even when he imagines one *particular* act (i.e., an act occurring at a particular time and place and hence having a certain particular set of alternatives). And if this appears to be a deficiency in our analysis, we could easily correct it by attributing a limited consistency to an ideal observer: we could define him, in part, as a being whose ethically-significant reactions to any particular act would always be exactly similar.

If we decide to do this, however, it is important to notice that consistency, when interpreted in this way, has a status very different from that of omniscience, disinterestedness, and the other defining characteristics of an ideal observer which we have so far considered. For according to the kind of absolutist analysis which we have been examining, ethical statements, as we have previously observed, are statements which depend for their truth or falsity on the existence of certain psychological laws; and if ethical statements are ever true, they are true only because we have defined an ideal observer in such a way that, in virtue of the relevant psychological laws, *any* ideal observer would react in the same way to a particular act. Thus in attributing omniscience, disinterestedness, and other such characteristics to an ideal observer, we are doing something of crucial importance for the kind of analysis which we are considering: we are eliminating from the personality of the ideal observer, so to speak, various factors which actually cause certain people to differ in their ethically-significant reactions from other people—such factors, for example, as selfish desires and ignorance of the facts of the case. And assuming that ethical statements *are* sometimes true, and absolutist dispositional analysis can be adequate only if such factors are completely eliminated from the personality of an ideal observer.

The characteristic of consistency, however, unlike omniscience, disinterestedness, and the others which we have discussed, does not eliminate some particular source of disagreement in ethical reactions. It is, on the contrary, a *consequence* of eliminating such disagreement, since any factor which could cause two different ideal observers to react in different ways to a particular act, could also cause one and the same ideal observer to react in different ways at different times. And this means, to put the matter bluntly, that if it is necessary to attribute consistency to an ideal observer in order to insure that he is psychologically incapable of reacting to the same act in different ways at different times, then we have simply failed to find all the *other* characteristics of an ideal observer which are necessary for the formulation of an adequate analysis. Thus an ideal observer will indeed be consistent if an adequate dispositional analysis can be formulated; but his consistency will be a derivative characteristic—a consequence of his other charac-

teristics together with certain psychological laws.

6. In Other Respects He Is Normal

An examination of the procedures by which we attempt to decide moral questions, reveals that there are a great many conditions which we recognize, though not always explicitly, to be favorable or unfavorable for making valid moral judgments. Mild bodily exercise such as walking, the presence of other people trying to make similar decisions, and certain kinds of esthetic stimuli, have all been regarded by some people as favorable conditions, whereas mental fatigue, distracting sensory stimuli, and lack of experience, are generally regarded as unfavorable. It seems likely, however, that our analysis will take all these special conditions into account if we attribute such general characteristics as omniscience and disinterestedness to an ideal observer.

It seems fairly clear, on the other hand, that no analysis in terms solely of such general, and highly ideal, characteristics, could be fully adequate to the meaning of ethical statements. For however ideal some of his characteristics may be, an ideal observer is, after all, a *person;* and whatever may be true of the future, our conception of the personality of an ideal observer has not yet undergone the refining processes which have enabled theologians, apparently with clear conscience, to employ the term "person" in exceedingly abstract ways. Most of us, indeed, can be said to have a conception of an ideal observer only in the sense that the characteristics of such a person are implicit in the procedures by which we compare and evaluate moral judges, and it seems doubtful, therefore, that an ideal observer can be said to lack any of the determinable properties of human beings.

The determinate properties of an ideal observer, however, except for the ideal characteristics which we have so far discussed, are apparently not capable of precise definition. We may employ the customary linguistic device, to be sure, and say that the properties of an ideal observer cannot vary beyond the limits of "normality," but there are a number of reasons why it does not seem to be possible to define these limits satisfactorily. It is evident, for example, that normality is a gestalt concept, and that a certain trait which in abstraction might properly be called abnormal, could nevertheless contribute to a total personality which falls within the bounds of normality. And this fact by itself is sufficient to destroy any hope of defining the term "normal" by continuing to add specific characteristics to the ones which we have already attributed to an ideal observer. This difficulty, however, and the others which prevent us from formulating a satisfactory definition of "normal," are practical rather than theoretical, and they do not tend in the slightest degree to disprove the thesis that ethical statements are statements about an ideal observer and his ethically-significant reactions. There are analogous difficulties, moreover, in formulating a dispositional analysis of the statement "This is (really) yellow"; and I have yet to find any convincing reason, indeed, for believing that "yellow" can be defined dispositionally although "right" cannot.

Notes

1. C. D. Broad, *Proceedings of the Aristotelian Society*, N.S. Vol. XLV, pp. 131–166.

2. Adam Smith comes immediately to mind, but Hume can likewise be interpreted as accepting an absolutist dispositional analysis of "right." (*Vide*, e.g., F. C. Sharp, "Hume's Ethical Theory," *Mind*, N.S. Vol. XXX, pp. 53–56. But for a different interpretation of Hume, *vide* Broad, *Five Types of Ethical Theory*, pp. 84–93.) It is even possible to make out a case for including Kant in this list. Sidgwick, although he denied that "right" is analyzable, seems not unwilling to accept an absolutist dispositional analysis of "good." (*Methods of Ethics*, 4th ed., p. 112, last sentence.)

3. In this connection I am much indebted to Professor R. B. Brandt, with whom I have discussed the problems of moral philosophy at great length. He is not, of course, responsible for my errors.

4. *Vide* Bertrand Russell, *An Enquiry Into Meaning and Truth*, p. 134, and *Human Knowledge, Its Scope and Its Limits*, p. 92.

5. It will be observed that according to these definitions a pure emotive theory of ethics is neither absolutist nor relativist. For absolutism and relativism are theories about the meaning of ethical *statements*, whereas a pure emotive theory denies, in effect, that there *are* any ethical statements (as contrasted with ethical exclamations, exhortations, etc.).

6. *Vide* especially *Ethical Relativity*, Ch. V. An equally interesting relativist dispositional analysis has been proposed by F. C. Sharp, *Ethics*, Appleton-Century, N. Y., 1928, Ch. VII.

7. Lewis has proposed that dispositional analyses of "objective statements" be formulated with a "probability qualification." (*Vide An Analysis of Knowledge and Valuation*, pp. 235–243.) If such a qualification were introduced into the analysis of ethical statements, an absolutist dispositional analysis would have the form: "Under such and such conditions an ideal observer would *in all probability* react in such and such a way." For simplicity I shall not consider this alternative, but none of the conclusions reached in this paper will be incompatible with the introduction of such a probability qualification.

8. Since, according to an absolutist dispositional analysis, the truth or falsity of ethical statements is dependent on the laws of nature, ethical statements are not intuitively or logically necessary; they are necessary, however, in whatever sense the laws of nature are necessary.

9. A. C. Ewing, for example, is willing to say that intuitions are sometimes false. (*Vide The Definition of Good*, pp. 27–9.) But Hastings Rashdall, for example, preferred to say that it is difficult to distinguish in-

tuitions from "mere feelings or aversions which may be only prejudices due to inheritance or environment or superstition." (*Vide The Theory of Good and Evil*, Vol. I, pp. 211–213.)

10. *Op. cit.*, p. 26.

11. An empiricist could be expected to ask how the intuitionist can *know* that one particular set of conditions is preferable to another; for, if the intuitionist's position is correct, it is surely not inconceivable that any given pathological condition (e.g., any of "those with which the psychoanalyst deals") is especially conducive to, or even absolutely necessary for, correct intuiting. (Cf. Brandt, "The Significance of Differences of Ethical Opinion for Ethical Rationalism," *Philosophy and Phenomenological Research*, Vol. IV, No. 4, pp. 488–490.) If this creates a problem for the intuitionist, however, it is a kind of problem which he shares with epistemological dualists in general.

12. *Vide, e. g.*, w. Köhler, *The Place of Value in a World of Facts*, Ch. III. Elsewhere ("Sense-data and the Percept Theory," *Mind*, Vol. LVIII, N.S., No. 232, and Vol. LIX, N.S., No. 233.) I have discussed in some detail the general philosophical significance of the view that such ostensible properties may be "objectively localized."

13. "Some of the Main Problems of Ethics," *Philosophy*, Vol. XXI, No. 79, p. 115.

14. I am assuming, of course, that an emotion of moral approval is not *defined* as an emotion of approval produced by a moral belief.

15. Cf. A. C. Ewing's statement (*The Definition of Good*, p. 43) that he can "see" in advance that nobody will ever be able to produce a satisfactory empirical analysis of ethical statements. Similarly a philosopher might "see" that *only* an empirical analysis which is absolutist and dispositional could be satisfactory.

16. *Five Types of Ethical Theory*, p. 263.

17. Impartiality in this sense has sometimes been equated with distributive justice, *Vide*, e.g., Rashdall, *The Theory of Good and Evil*, Vol. I, Ch. VIII.

18. Broad, *Examination of McTaggart's Philosophy*, Vol. I, p. 178.

19. *Vide supra*, Part I, Section 5.

20. We might reason, for example, that x could be right only if we have a special obligation toward those who have suffered for our sake, whereas y could be right only if we do *not* have such an obligation. In some cases, of course, the principle P might itself be a complex conjunction of ethical principles.

21. There are at least two kinds of cases in which a principle Q might be said to "take precedence over" a principle P: (1) Cases in which P and Q are conflicting principles, each representing a "claim" against the agent, and (2) cases in which P is simply an incomplete statement of a more completely qualified principle, Q.

NONCOGNITIVIST APPROACHES: DEFENSE AND CRITICISM

3 / A. J. AYER

CRITIQUE OF ETHICS

There is still one objection to be met before we can claim to have justified our view that all synthetic propositions are empirical hypotheses. This objection is based on the common supposition that our speculative knowledge is of two distinct kinds—that which relates to questions of empirical fact, and that which relates to questions of value. It will be said that "statements of value" are genuine synthetic propositions, but that they cannot with any show of justice be represented as hypotheses, which are used to predict the course of our sensations; and, accordingly, that the existence of ethics and æsthetics as branches of speculative knowledge presents an insuperable objection to our radical empiricist thesis.

In face of this objection, it is our business to give an account of "judgements of value" which is both satisfactory in itself and consistent with our general empiricist principles. We shall set ourselves to show that in so far as statements of value are significant, they are ordinary "scientific" statements; and that in so far as they are not scientific, they are not in the literal sense significant, but are simply expressions of emotion which can be neither true

Reprinted by permission of the publisher and copyright holder from A. J. Ayer, *Language, Truth and Logic*, 2d ed. (New York: Dover, 1946), pp. 102–14. The following three selections follow those in Sellars and Hospers, *Readings in Ethical Theory*, 2d ed. (Englewood Cliffs, N.J.: Prentice-Hall, 1970).

nor false. In maintaining this view, we may confine ourselves for the present to the case of ethical statements. What is said about them will be found to apply, *mutatis mutandis*, to the case of æsthetic statements also.[1]

The ordinary system of ethics, as elaborated in the works of ethical philosophers, is very far from being a homogeneous whole. Not only is it apt to contain pieces of metaphysics, and analyses of non-ethical concepts: its actual ethical contents are themselves of very different kinds. We may divide them, indeed, into four main classes. There are, first of all, propositions which express definitions of ethical terms, or judgements about the legitimacy or possibility of certain definitions. Secondly, there are propositions describing the phenomena of moral experience, and their causes. Thirdly, there are exhortations to moral virtue. And, lastly, there are actual ethical judgements. It is unfortunately the case that the distinction between these four classes, plain as it is, is commonly ignored by ethical philosophers; with the result that it is often very difficult to tell from their works what it is that they are seeking to discover or prove.

In fact, it is easy to see that only the first of our four classes, namely that which comprises the propositions relating to the definitions of ethical terms, can be said to constitute ethical philosophy. The propositions which describe the phenomena of moral experience, and their causes, must be assigned to the science of psychology, or sociology. The exhortations to moral virtue are not propositions at all, but ejaculations or commands which are designed to provoke the reader to action of a certain sort. Accordingly, they do not belong to any branch of philosophy or science. As for the expressions of ethical judgements, we have not yet determined how they should be classified. But inasmuch as they are certainly neither definitions nor comments upon definitions, nor quotations, we may say decisively that they do not belong to ethical philosophy. A strictly philosophical treatise on ethics should therefore make no ethical pronouncements. But it should, by giving an analysis of ethical terms, show what is the category to which all such pronouncements belong. And this is what we are now about to do.

A question which is often discussed by ethical philosophers is whether it is possible to find definitions which would reduce all ethical terms to one or two fundamental terms. But this question, though it undeniably belongs to ethical philosophy, is not relevant to our present enquiry. We are not now concerned to discover which term, within the sphere of ethical terms, is to be taken as fundamental; whether, for example, "good" can be defined in terms of "right" or "right" in terms of "good," or both in terms of "value." What we are interested in is the possibility of reducing the whole sphere of ethical terms to non-ethical terms. We are enquiring whether statements of ethical value can be translated into statements of empirical fact.

That they can be so translated is the contention of those ethical philosophers who are commonly called subjectivists, and of those who are known as utilitarians. For the utilitarian defines the rightness of actions, and the goodness of ends, in terms of the pleasure, or happiness, or satisfaction, to which they give rise; the subjectivist, in terms of the feelings of approval which a certain person, or group of people, has towards them. Each of these types of

definition makes moral judgements into a sub-class of psychological or sociological judgements; and for this reason they are very attractive to us. For, if either was correct, it would follow that ethical assertions were not generically different from the factual assertions which are ordinarily contrasted with them; and the account which we have already given of empirical hypotheses would apply to them also.

Nevertheless we shall not adopt either a subjectivist or a utilitarian analysis of ethical terms. We reject the subjectivist view that to call an action right, or a thing good, is to say that it is generally approved of, because it is not self-contradictory to assert that some actions which are generally approved of are not right, or that some things which are generally approved of are not good. And we reject the alternative subjectivist view that a man who asserts that a certain action is right, or that a certain thing is good, is saying that he himself approves of it, on the ground that a man who confessed that he sometimes approved of what was bad or wrong would not be contradicting himself. And a similar argument is fatal to utilitarianism. We cannot agree that to call an action right is to say that of all the actions possible in the circumstances it would cause, or be likely to cause, the greatest happiness, or the greatest balance of pleasure over pain, or the greatest balance of satisfied over unsatisfied desire, because we find that it is not self-contradictory to say that it is sometimes wrong to perform the action which would actually or probably cause the greatest happiness, or the greatest balance of pleasure over pain, or of satisfied over unsatisfied desire. And since it is not self-contradictory to say that some pleasant things are not good, or that some bad things are desired, it cannot be the case that the sentence "x is good" is equivalent to "x is pleasant," or to "x is desired." And to every other variant of utilitarianism with which I am acquainted the same objection can be made. And therefore we should, I think, conclude that the validity of ethical judgements is not determined by the felicific tendencies of actions, any more than by the nature of people's feelings; but that it must be regarded as "absolute" or "intrinsic," and not empirically calculable.

If we say this, we are not, of course, denying that it is possible to invent a language in which all ethical symbols are definable in non-ethical terms, or even that it is desirable to invent such a language and adopt it in place of our own; what we are denying is that the suggested reduction of ethical to non-ethical statements is consistent with the conventions of our actual language. That is, we reject utilitarianism and subjectivism, not as proposals to replace our existing ethical notions by new ones, but as analyses of our existing ethical notions. Our contention is simply that, in our language, sentences which contain normative ethical symbols are not equivalent to sentences which express psychological propositions, or indeed empirical propositions of any kind.

It is advisable here to make it plain that it is only normative ethical symbols, and not descriptive ethical symbols, that are held by us to be indefinable in factual terms. There is a danger of confusing these two types of symbols, because they are commonly constituted by signs of the same sensible form. Thus a complex sign of the form "x is wrong" may constitute a sentence which expresses a moral judgement concerning a certain type of conduct, or it may constitute a sentence which states that a certain type of conduct is repugnant to the moral sense of a particular society. In the latter case, the symbol "wrong" is a descriptive ethical symbol, and the sentence in which it occurs expresses an ordinary sociological proposition; in the former case, the symbol "wrong" is a normative ethical symbol, and the sentence in which it occurs does not, we maintain, express an empirical proposition at all. It is only with normative ethics that we are at present concerned; so that whenever ethical symbols are used in the course of this argument without qualification, they are always to be interpreted as symbols of the normative type.

In admitting that normative ethical concepts are irreducible to empirical concepts, we seem to be leaving the way clear for the "absolutist" view of ethics—that is, the view that statements of value are not controlled by observation, as ordinary empirical propositions are, but only by a mysterious "intellectual intuition." A feature of this theory, which is seldom recognized by its advocates, is that it makes statements of value unverifiable. For it is notorious that what seems intuitively certain to one person may seem doubtful, or even false, to another. So that unless it is possible to provide some criterion by which one may decide between conflicting intuitions, a mere appeal to intuition is worthless as a test of a proposition's validity. But in the case of moral judgements, no such criterion can be given. Some moralists claim to settle the matter by saying that they "know" that their own moral judgements are correct. But such an assertion is of purely psychological interest, and has not the slightest tendency to prove the validity of any moral judgement. For dissentient moralists may equally well "know" that their ethical views are correct. And, as far as subjective certainty goes, there will be nothing to choose between them. When such differences of opinion arise in connection with an ordinary empirical proposition, one may attempt to resolve them by referring to, or actually carrying out, some relevant empirical test. But with regard to ethical statements, there is, on the "absolutist" or "intuitionist" theory, no relevant empirical test. We are therefore justified in saying that on this theory ethical statements are held to be unverifiable. They are, of course, also held to be genuine synthetic propositions.

Considering the use which we have made of the principle that a synthetic proposition is significant only if it is empirically verifiable, it is clear that the acceptance of an "absolutist" theory of ethics would undermine the whole of our main argument. And as we have already rejected the "naturalistic" theories which are commonly supposed to provide the only alternative to "absolutism" in ethics, we seem to have reached a difficult position. We shall meet the difficulty by showing that the correct treatment of ethical statements is afforded by a third theory, which is wholly compatible with our radical empiricism.

We begin by admitting that the fundamental ethical concepts are unanalysable, inasmuch as there is no criterion by which one can test the validity of the judgements in which they occur. So far we are in agreement with the absolutists. But, unlike the absolutists, we are able to give an explanation of this fact about ethical concepts. We say that the reason why they are unanalysable is that they are mere pseudo-concepts. The presence of an ethical symbol in a proposition adds nothing to its factual content. Thus if I say to someone, "You acted wrongly in stealing that money," I am not stating anything more than if I had simply said, "You stole that money." In adding that this action is wrong I am not making any further statement about it. I am simply evincing my moral disapproval of it. It is as if I had said, "You stole that money," in a peculiar tone of horror, or written it with the addition of some special exclamation marks. The tone, or the exclamation marks, adds nothing to the literal meaning of the sentence. It merely serves to show that the expression of it is attended by certain feelings in the speaker.

If now I generalise my previous statement and say, "Stealing money is wrong," I produce a sentence which has no factual meaning—that is, expresses no proposition which can be either true or false. It is as if I had written "Stealing money!!"—where the shape and thickness of the exclamation marks show, by a suitable convention, that a special sort of moral disapproval is the feeling which is being expressed. It is clear that there is nothing said here which can be true or false. Another man may disagree with me about the wrongness of stealing, in the sense that he may not have the same feelings about stealing as I have, and he may quarrel with me on account of my moral sentiments. But he cannot, strictly

speaking, contradict me. For in saying that a certain type of action is right or wrong, I am not making any factual statement, not even a statement about my own state of mind. I am merely expressing certain moral sentiments. And the man who is ostensibly contradicting me is merely expressing his moral sentiments. So that there is plainly no sense in asking which of us is in the right. For neither of us is asserting a genuine proposition.

What we have just been saying about the symbol "wrong" applies to all normative ethical symbols. Sometimes they occur in sentences which record ordinary empirical facts besides expressing ethical feeling about those facts: sometimes they occur in sentences which simply express ethical feeling about a certain type of action, or situation, without making any statement of fact. But in every case in which one would commonly be said to be making an ethical judgement, the function of the relevant ethical word is purely "emotive." It is used to express feeling about certain objects, but not to make any assertion about them.

It is worth mentioning that ethical terms do not serve only to express feeling. They are calculated also to arouse feeling, and so to stimulate action. Indeed some of them are used in such a way as to give the sentences in which they occur the effect of commands. Thus the sentence "It is your duty to tell the truth" may be regarded both as the expression of a certain sort of ethical feeling about truthfulness and as the expression of the command "Tell the truth." The sentence "You ought to tell the truth" also involves the command "Tell the truth," but here the tone of the command is less emphatic. In the sentence "It is good to tell the truth" the command has become little more than a suggestion. And thus the "meaning" of the word "good," in its ethical usage, is differentiated from that of the word "duty" or the word "ought." In fact we may define the meaning of the various ethical words in terms both of the different feelings they are ordinarily taken to express, and also the different responses which they are calculated to provoke.

We can now see why it is impossible to find a criterion for determining the validity of ethical judgements. It is not because they have an "absolute" validity which is mysteriously independent of ordinary sense-experience, but because they have no objective validity whatsoever. If a sentence makes no statement at all, there is obviously no sense in asking whether what it says is true or false. And we have seen that sentences which simply express moral judgements do not say anything. They are pure expressions of feeling and as such do not come under the category of truth and falsehood. They are unverifiable for the same reason as a cry of pain or a word of command is unverifiable—because they do not express genuine propositions.

Thus, although our theory of ethics might fairly be said to be radically subjectivist, it differs in a very important respect from the orthodox subjectivist theory. For the orthodox subjectivist does not deny, as we do, that the <u>sentences of a moralizer express genuine propositions</u>. All he denies is that they express propositions of a unique non-empirical character. His own view is that they express propositions about the speaker's feelings. If this were so, ethical judgements clearly would be capable of being true or false. They would be true if the speaker had the relevant feelings, and false if he had not. And this is a matter which is, in principle, empirically verifiable. Furthermore they could be significantly contradicted. For if I say, "Tolerance is a virtue," and someone answers, "You don't approve of it," he would, on the ordinary subjectivist theory, be contradicting me. On our theory, he would not be contradicting me, because, in saying that tolerance was a virtue, I should not be making any statement about my own feelings or about anything else. I should simply be evincing my feelings, which is not at all the same thing as saying that I have them.

The distinction between the expression of feeling and the assertion of feeling is complicated by the fact that the assertion that one has a certain feeling often accompanies the expression of that feeling, and is

then, indeed, a factor in the expression of that feeling. Thus I may simultaneously express boredom and say that I am bored, and in that case my utterance of the words, "I am bored," is one of the circumstances which make it true to say that I am expressing or evincing boredom. But I can express boredom without actually saying that I am bored. I can express it by my tone and gestures, while making a statement about something wholly unconnected with it, or by an ejaculation, or without uttering any words at all. So that even if the assertion that one has a certain feeling always involves the expression of that feeling, the expression of a feeling assuredly does not always involve the assertion that one has it. And this is the important point to grasp in considering the distinction between our theory and the ordinary subjectivist theory. For whereas the subjectivist holds that ethical statements actually assert the existence of certain feelings, we hold that ethical statements are expressions and excitants of feeling which do not necessarily involve any assertions.

We have already remarked that the main objection to the ordinary subjectivist theory is that the validity of ethical judgements is not determined by the nature of their author's feelings. And this is an objection which our theory escapes. For it does not imply that the existence of any feelings is a necessary and sufficient condition of the validity of an ethical judgement. It implies, on the contrary, that ethical judgements have no validity.

There is, however, a celebrated argument against subjectivist theories which our theory does not escape. It has been pointed out by Moore that if ethical statements were simply statements about the speaker's feelings, it would be impossible to argue about questions of value.[2] To take a typical example: if a man said that thrift was a virtue, and another replied that it was a vice, they would not, on this theory, be disputing with one another. One would be saying that he approved of thrift, and the other that *he* didn't; and there is no reason why both these statements should not be true. Now Moore held it to be obvious that we do dispute about questions of value, and accordingly concluded that the particular form of subjectivism which he was discussing was false.

It is plain that the conclusion that it is impossible to dispute about questions of value follows from our theory also. For as we hold that such sentences as "Thrift is a virtue" and "Thrift is a vice" do not express propositions at all, we clearly cannot hold that they express incompatible propositions. We must therefore admit that if Moore's argument really refutes the ordinary subjectivist theory, it also refutes ours. But, in fact, we deny that it does refute even the ordinary subjectivist theory. For we hold that one really never does dispute about questions of value.

This may seem, at first sight, to be a very paradoxical assertion. For we certainly do engage in disputes which are ordinarily regarded as disputes about questions of value. But, in all such cases, we find, if we consider the matter closely, that the dispute is not really about a question of value, but about a question of fact. When someone disagrees with us about the moral value of a certain action or type of action, we do admittedly resort to argument in order to win him over to our way of thinking. But we do not attempt to show by our arguments that he has the "wrong" ethical feeling towards a situation whose nature he has correctly apprehended. What we attempt to show is that he is mistaken about the facts of the case. We argue that he has misconceived the agent's motive: or that he has misjudged the effects of the action, or its probable effects in view of the agent's knowledge; or that he has failed to take into account the special circumstances in which the agent was placed. Or else we employ more general arguments about the effects which actions of a certain type tend to produce, or the qualities which are usually manifested in their performance. We do this in the hope that we have only to get our opponent to agree with us about the nature of the empirical facts for him to adopt the same moral attitude towards

them as we do. And as the people with whom we argue have generally received the same moral education as ourselves, and live in the same social order, our expectation is usually justified. But if our opponent happens to have undergone a different process of moral "conditioning" from ourselves, so that, even when he acknowledges all the facts, he still disagrees with us about the moral value of the actions under discussion, then we abandon the attempt to convince him by argument. We say that it is impossible to argue with him because he has a distorted or undeveloped moral sense; which signifies merely that he employs a different set of values from our own. We feel that our own system of values is superior, and therefore speak in such derogatory terms of his. But we cannot bring forward any arguments to show that our system is superior. For our judgement that it is so is itself a judgement of value, and accordingly outside the scope of argument. It is because argument fails us when we come to deal with pure questions of value, as distinct from questions of fact, that we finally resort to mere abuse.

In short, we find that argument is possible on moral questions only if some system of values is presupposed. If our opponent concurs with us in expressing moral disapproval of all actions of a given type t, then we may get him to condemn a particular action A, by bringing forward arguments to show that A is of type t. For the question whether A does or does not belong to that type is a plain question of fact. Given that a man has certain moral principles, we argue that he must, in order to be consistent, react morally to certain things in a certain way. What we do not and cannot argue about is the validity of these moral principles. We merely praise or condemn them in the light of our own feelings.

If anyone doubts the accuracy of this account of moral disputes, let him try to construct even an imaginary argument on a question of value which does not reduce itself to an argument about a question of logic or about an empirical matter of fact. I am confident that he will not succeed in producing a single example. And if that is the case, he must allow that its involving the impossibility of purely ethical arguments is not, as Moore thought, a ground of objection to our theory, but rather a point in favour of it.

Having upheld our theory against the only criticism which appeared to threaten it, we may now use it to define the nature of all ethical enquiries. We find that ethical philosophy consists simply in saying that ethical concepts are pseudo-concepts and therefore unanalysable. The further task of describing the different feelings that the different ethical terms are used to express, and the different reactions that they customarily provoke, is a task for the psychologist. There cannot be such a thing as ethical science, if by ethical science one means the elaboration of a "true" system of morals. For we have seen that, as ethical judgements are mere expressions of feeling, there can be no way of determining the validity of any ethical system, and, indeed, no sense in asking whether any such system is true. All that one may legitimately enquire in this connection is, What are the moral habits of a given person or group of people, and what causes them to have precisely those habits and feelings? And this enquiry falls wholly within the scope of the existing social sciences.

It appears, then, that ethics, as a branch of knowledge, is nothing more than a department of psychology and sociology. And in case anyone thinks that we are overlooking the existence of casuistry, we may remark that casuistry is not a science, but is a purely analytical investigation of the structure of a given moral system. In other words, it is an exercise in formal logic.

When one comes to pursue the psychological enquiries which constitute ethical science, one is immediately enabled to account for the Kantian and hedonistic theories of morals. For one finds that one of the chief causes of moral behaviour is fear, both conscious and unconscious, of a god's displeasure, and fear of the enmity of society. And this, indeed, is the reason why moral precepts present themselves to some people as "categorical" commands. And one finds, also, that the moral code of a society is partly determined by the beliefs of that society concerning the conditions of its own happiness—or, in other words, that a society tends to encourage or discourage a given type of conduct by the use of moral sanctions according as it appears to promote or detract from the contentment of the society as a whole. And this is the reason why altruism is recommended in most moral codes and egotism condemned. It is from the observation of this connection between morality and happiness that hedonistic or eudæmonistic theories of morals ultimately spring, just as the moral theory of Kant is based on the fact, previously explained, that moral precepts have for some people the force of inexorable commands. As each of these theories ignores the fact which lies at the root of the other, both may be criticized as being one-sided; but this is not the main objection to either of them. Their essential defect is that they treat propositions which refer to the causes and attributes of our ethical feelings as if they were definitions of ethical concepts. And thus they fail to recognise that ethical concepts are pseudo-concepts and consequently indefinable.

As we have already said, our conclusions about the nature of ethics apply to æsthetics also. Æsthetic terms are used in exactly the same way as ethical terms. Such æsthetic words as "beautiful" and "hideous" are employed, as ethical words are employed, not to make statements of fact, but simply to express certain feelings and evoke a certain response. It follows, as in ethics, that there is no sense in attributing objective validity to æsthetic judgements, and no possibility of arguing about questions of value in æsthetics, but only about questions of fact. A scientific treatment of æsthetics would show us what in general were the causes of æsthetic feeling, why various societies produced and admired the works of art they did, why taste varies as it does within a given society, and so forth. And these are ordinary psychological or sociological questions. They have, of course, little or nothing to do with æsthetic criticism as we understand it. But that is because the purpose of æsthetic criticism is not so much to give knowledge as to communicate emotion. The critic, by calling attention to certain features of the work under review, and expressing his own feelings about them, endeavours to make us share his attitude towards the work as a whole. The only relevant propositions that he formulates are propositions describing the nature of the work. And these are plain records of fact. We conclude, therefore, that there is nothing in æsthetics, any more than there is in ethics, to justify the view that it embodies a unique type of knowledge.

It should now be clear that the only information which we can legitimately derive from the study of our æsthetic and moral experiences is information about our own mental and physical make-up. We take note of these experiences as providing data for our psychological and sociological generalisations. And this is the only way in which they serve to increase our knowledge. It follows that any attempt to make our use of ethical and æsthetic concepts the basis of a metaphysical theory concerning the existence of a world of values, as distinct from the world of facts, involves a false analysis of these concepts. Our own analysis has shown that the phenomena of moral experience cannot fairly be used to support any rationalist or metaphysical doctrine whatsoever. In particular, they cannot, as Kant hoped, be used to establish the existence of a transcendent god.

Notes

1. The argument that follows should be read in conjunction with the Introduction, pp. 20–2, of *Language, Truth, and Logic* [reprinted in this volume, pp. 71–72].

2. Cf. *Philosophical Studies*, "The Nature of Moral Philosophy."

4 / W. D. ROSS

CRITIQUE OF AYER

[T]here is one of the arguments put forward by the positivists which seems to me to provide, when reflected on, an argument in favour not only of the view that our ethical judgements are genuine judgements, but of the view that there are fundamental ethical judgements for which general agreement may be claimed. Mr. Ayer remarks[1] that, while his theory escapes many of the objections brought against subjectivistic theories in ethics, there is one which it does not escape. This is the argument[2] that such theories would make it impossible to argue about questions of value, which nevertheless we undoubtedly do. He admits that his own theory also would make it impossible to argue about questions of value; as he holds that such sentences as 'thrift is a virtue' and 'thrift is a vice' do not express propositions at all, he clearly cannot hold that they express incompatible propositions. If, then, he is to resist the argument in question, he must simply deny that in fact we ever do dispute about questions of value; for if we did dispute about things which on his theory we cannot dispute about, his theory would clearly be untrue. He boldly adopts the course to which he is logically forced, and denies that we ever do dispute about questions of value. And he justifies this by saying that apparent disputes about questions of value are really disputes about questions of fact. . . .

Reprinted by permission of the publisher and copyright holder from W. D. Ross, *The Foundations of Ethics* (Oxford: Oxford University Press, 1939), pp. 38–41.

It is perfectly true that, when we differ on a question of right or wrong, or of goodness or badness, it is by consideration of questions of fact—of the precise nature of the consequences or of the probable consequences, or of the motives involved—that we try to remove the difference of opinion on the moral question. And in doing so we betray the conviction that if we could get down to agreement about the facts of the case, we should find ourselves in agreement on the moral question; or in other words, that though we may differ in our moral judgements on some complicated case, we agree in our fundamental judgements as to what kinds of consequences ought to be aimed at and what kinds of motive are good. The more Mr. Ayer emphasizes this element in our discussion of moral questions, the more he pays tribute to the strength of this conviction; for unless we thought that if we could agree on the factual nature of the act we should probably agree on its rightness or wrongness, there would be no point in trying to reach agreement about its factual nature. And in the great majority of cases we find this confidence confirmed, by finding that we agree in our moral judgements when we agree about the facts. But no doubt we sometimes fail to find agreement even then. We do not find, however, as Mr. Ayer claims, that no subject of dispute remains. We find, indeed, that there is no room for further *argument*; when we have come to some premiss which to us seems axiomatic, and which the other person denies, we can argue no further. But we do not find that all *difference of opinion* has vanished, and that we are left only with different feelings, one liking certain consequences or motives and another disliking them. We find ourselves still saying 'this is good', and the person with whom we are speaking still saying 'this is bad'. And it is not by showing that *argument* ceases, but by showing that *difference of opinion* ceases, that Mr. Ayer could escape from Professor Moore's argument.

But indeed our adoption of the very practice which Mr. Ayer here describes is enough to refute his account of the nature of what are commonly called ethical judgements. He denies that they are judgements; he says they are mere expressions of liking or dislike. If that were all they are, why argue at all? What should we be trying to prove? Is *A* arguing to prove that he likes the given act, and *B* to prove that he

dislikes it? Clearly not. *A* does not doubt that *B* dislikes it, nor *B* that *A* likes it; and if they did doubt, they would adopt quite different means of convincing one another, e.g. *A* by consistently seeking to do similar acts and *B* by consistently avoiding them. What they are attempting to do by the process Mr. Ayer describes is to convince each other that the liking, or the dislike, is justified, in other words that the act has a character that *deserves* to be liked or disliked, is good or is bad.

Notes

1. A. J. Ayer. *Language, Truth and Logic*, p. 163.

2. Professor Moore's argument, in *Philosophical Studies*, 333–4.

5 / A. J. AYER

REPLY TO CRITICS

The emotive theory of values, which is developed in the sixth chapter of this book, has provoked a fair amount of criticism; but I find that this criticism has been directed more often against the positivistic principles on which the theory has been assumed to depend than against the theory itself.[1] Now I do not deny that in putting forward this theory I was concerned with maintaining the general consistency of my position; but it is not the only ethical theory that would have satisfied this requirement, nor does it actually entail any of the non-ethical statements which form the remainder of my argument. Consequently, even if it could be shown that these other statements were invalid, this would not in itself refute the emotive analysis of ethical judgements; and in fact I believe this analysis to be valid on its own account.

Having said this, I must acknowledge that the theory is here presented in a very summary way, and that it needs to be supported by a more detailed analysis of specimen ethical judgements than I make any attempt to give.[2] Thus, among other things, I fail to bring out the point that the common objects of moral approval or disapproval are not particular actions so much as classes of actions; by which I mean that if an action is labelled right or wrong, or good or bad, as the case may be, it is because it is thought to be an action of a certain type. And this point seems to me important, because I think that what seems to

be an ethical judgement is very often a factual classification of an action as belonging to some class of actions by which a certain moral attitude on the part of the speaker is habitually aroused. Thus, a man who is a convinced utilitarian may simply mean by calling an action right that it tends to promote, or more probably that it is the sort of action that tends to promote, the general happiness; and in that case the validity of his statement becomes an empirical matter of fact. Similarly, a man who bases his ethical upon his religious views may actually mean by calling an action right or wrong that it is the sort of action that is enjoined or forbidden by some ecclesiastical authority; and this also may be empirically verified. Now in these cases the form of words by which the factual statement is expressed is the same as that which would be used to express a normative statement; and this may to some extent explain why statements which are recognized to be normative are nevertheless often thought to be factual. Moreover, a great many ethical statements contain, as a factual element, some description of the action, or the situation, to which the ethical term in question is being applied. But although there may be a number of cases in which this ethical term is itself to be understood descriptively, I do not think that this is always so. I think that there are many statements in which an ethical term is used in a purely normative way, and it is to statements of this kind that the emotive theory of ethics is intended to apply.

The objection that if the emotive theory was correct it would be impossible for one person to contradict another on a question of value is here met by the answer that what seem to be disputes about questions of value are really disputes about questions of fact. I should, however, have made it clear that it does not follow from this that two persons cannot significantly disagree about a question of value, or that it is idle for them to attempt to convince one another. For a consideration of any dispute about a matter of taste will show that there can be disagreement without formal contradiction, and that in order to alter another man's opinions, in the sense of getting him to change his attitude, it is not necessary to contradict anything that he asserts. Thus, if one wishes to affect another person in such a way as to bring his sentiments on a given point into accordance with one's own, there are various ways in which one may proceed. One may, for example, call his attention to certain facts that one supposes him to have overlooked; and, as I have already remarked, I believe that much of what passes for ethical discussion is a proceeding of this type. It is, however, also possible to influence other people by a suitable choice of emotive language; and this is the practical justification for the use of norma-

tive expressions of value. At the same time, it must be admitted that if the other person persists in maintaining his contrary attitude, without however disputing any of the relevant facts, a point is reached at which the discussion can go no further. And in that case there is no sense in asking which of the conflicting views is true. For, since the expression of a value judgement is not a proposition, the question of truth or falsehood does not here arise.

Notes

1. Cf. Sir W. David Ross, *The Foundations of Ethics*, pp. 30–41.

2. I understand that this deficiency has been made good by C. L. Stevenson in his book, *Ethics and Language*, but the book was published in America and I have not yet been able to obtain it. There is a review of it by Austin Duncan-Jones in *Mind*, October, 1945, and a good indication of Stevenson's line of argument is to be found in his articles on "The Emotive Meaning of Ethical Terms," *Mind*, 1937, "Ethical Judgements and Avoidability," *Mind*, 1938, and "Persuasive Definitions," *Mind*, 1938.

6 / ALLAN GIBBARD

EXPRESSIVISM

Analysis

In popular lore and philosophic tradition, meanings are given by definitions—by analyses, as philosophers came to say. Noncognitivists like Ayer, Stevenson, and Hare broadened the tradition: an analysis need not say the same thing in other words. It can describe a use, saying directly what the person who uses a term is doing with it. Still, the tradition now seems dated. The problem is not just fashion; major developments in the philosophy of language seem to discredit analysis. Where do meanings and analyses fit in the best picture of thought and talk?

The naive reason for starting with analyses is, of course, to clarify what we are asking. We want to know what makes acts right or wrong, sensible or foolish. If we want good answers, it seems, we ought first to know what we are asking. When questions seem deeply problematical, part of the problem may lie in confusion over terms. We resolve the confusion if we say clearly what our questions mean, and meanings seem to call for definitions.

Recent philosophy of language throws this rationale into doubt. When a term is central to our conceptions, the lesson seems to be, a search for definitions is misguided. To expect analyses to do serious philosophical work is to succumb to a myth of meaning.

Reprinted by permission of the publisher and copyright holder from Allan Gibbard, *Wise Choices and Apt Feelings* (Cambridge, Mass.: Harvard University Press, 1990), pp. 30–54.

The myth may take the form of accepting a sharp analytic-synthetic distinction—a divide between truth in virtue of logic and meaning alone, and truth in virtue of the ways things substantively are. Quine challenged the myth in this form. He despaired of tying meanings straight to empirical tests, and suggested "It is nonsense, and the root of much nonsense, to speak of a linguistic component and a factual component in the truth of any individual statement. Science has its double dependence on language and experience; but this duality is not significantly traceable into the statements of science taken one by one" (1951, 39). Now, without a linguistic component, how can there be clear sense in asking what a term means? And if we cannot ask about the meanings of terms, one by one, how is there any room for non-cognitivism? Non-cognitivists think there is something special about normative language that makes it peculiarly resist straightforward definition. Language, they think, can be divided into expressions that are descriptive and expressions that are not—and normative language falls on the non-descriptive side. If Quine is right, though, and all philosophically interesting notions resist definition, then normative terms call for no special remedy.

Other writers attack a fact-value distinction by insisting that facts themselves are infused with values. The same would presumably go for a fact-norm distinction. Putnam writes, "The practices of scientific inquiry upon which we rely to decide what is and what is not a fact, presuppose values" (1981, 128). The terms that ground our

73

conception of rational acceptability—'coherent', 'simple', 'justified', and the like—"are often used as terms of *praise*," and they "have too many characteristics in common with the paradigmatic value terms" for us to deny that that is what they are (136).

Is there still, then, any important place for analysis in normative theory? In particular, if we treat thought and talk naturalistically, if we reject meanings as magic, can we still proceed by analysis? I cannot respond fully, especially at the outset. At this point, though, I should say a little.

An analysis must be judged by its fruits: How much does it explain? How much thought does it make intelligible, and how little would it have us dismiss as unintelligible? How good an explanation emerges of the role of a kind of language in human life? How, by these tests, do the alternatives compare? I claim that much of ordinary thought comes out as intelligible on the analyses I shall be giving. Important parts of human life are explained.

An analysis can be offered not as a bald statement of fact about what people mean, but as a proposal. Where a term is problematical, a new and clearer sense may serve its purposes—or some of them. No unique analysis need be correct; rather, we can expect some analyses to work better than others. There may be an analysis that is clearly best for certain purposes, and there may not. Even if not, trying out top candidates is bound to reveal something about the term.[1]

Any philosophical analysis strains its concept. We can learn about a concept by seeing what choice of strains it offers. When an analysis keeps us from saying things we want to say, then we have to think how important it is to go on saying them, and we have to think about costs. Analyses let us compare the strains of alternatives.

Of course, once our conception of analysis is loosened in this way, simple tests cannot settle matters. Descriptivistic analyses strain the concepts they analyze, but so, in all likelihood, will any analysis. What I shall be arguing is this: For an important

range of purposes—the purposes of fundamental inquiry into how to live—the norm-expressivistic analysis of 'rational' strains the concept less than do the alternatives. The analysis allows questions other analyses preclude, the questions that lie most deeply embedded in the inquiry. More broadly, the analysis can transform our view of what we are doing when we ponder fundamental normative questions, and allow us to proceed more effectively in our normative thinking because we now have a clear account of what we are doing. No sharp analytic-synthetic distinction, no myth of meaning is needed for claims like these.

What, though, of the special element that makes normative thought and language normative? There is such an element, I am claiming, and it involves a kind of endorsement—an endorsement that any descriptivistic analysis treats inadequately. The problem is not merely that every time one loophole in the analysis is closed, others remain. It is that a single loophole remains unpluggable by descriptivistic analysis.

In a community of stable, widely accepted norms, this element of endorsement might be carried by properties—the properties that, in everyone's mind, qualify a thing for this kind of endorsement. We might imagine a community where everyone condemns as wrong, say, whatever violates the Ten Commandments, and only that. Their use of this standard is confident, and their interpretations of the commandments are clear and agreed upon. Then there might be no fact of the matter whether 'wrong' means "violates the Ten Commandments" or something expressive.

This quiescent community, though, would not have language suited for philosophical inquiry. Philosophy is a child of leisure, but of leisure conjoined with turmoil and clashes of ways of life. If different ways of thinking seem open to us, we need a language in which to put the alternatives. We need to be able to ask whether it is ever right to violate one of the Ten

Commandments. Norm-expressivism, I claim, describes a coherent language for doing so.

A philosopher might hope to find an account of normative terms that transformed discussion, and thereby put us into the position of this quiescent community. Perhaps some property of the things it makes sense to do, to think, and to feel is so compelling, so obviously what matters once we see matters clearly, that the only thing left to discuss is what things have that property. In that case we can indifferently either use that property to define 'rational' or stick to an expressivistic analysis. We will be confident beyond all need for discussion that just those things that have that property are rational in the expressivistic sense.

No one, though, has found such a property, and so we still need a language fit for fundamental normative inquiry.[2] Moreover, suppose someone did. We might still want to examine our bases for the ways of thinking we now found undoubtedly right, and we would need a language that let us do so. We might want to explain what had happened since our days of basic puzzlement. What we now realize, we could say, is that something is rational precisely if it has property *P*—or at least that is what we could say if we still gave 'rational' an expressivistic sense.

Examples will not shatter an analysis. What examples can show is a kind of strain we might hope to avoid, a purpose the analysis serves inadequately. The examples of the last chapter showed that for normative terms, prime descriptivistic analyses rule out a use we need. They strain their concepts in ways we cannot afford for some purposes—for purposes of basic inquiry into how to live. They do this because they narrow too far the endorsement these terms carry. For other ends these may be the best analyses, but the examples identify ways we might hope to do better.

What, then, of Putnam's claim that norms infuse facts? With this I fully agree: the beliefs I am calling factual depend on epistemic norms—on norms for belief. That we continue to hold the beliefs we do depends on our thinking it makes sense to do so. It would be incoherent, then, to dismiss all normative judgments as merely subjective, while accepting some factual beliefs as firmly and objectively grounded. From the point of view of their justification, they are on a par; factual beliefs and normative judgments stand or fall together.

None of this means that epistemic norms themselves are facts, or that factual judgments themselves are normative. The justification of factual beliefs is a normative matter, but that does not turn factual beliefs into normative judgments. There remains the challenge to say what the difference is. I have suggested a simple linguistic test: a notion is normative if we can paraphrase it in terms of what it *makes sense* to do, to think, or to feel. Later I try for a more systematic account of the correspondence a factual judgment can have to fact, and the place of this correspondence in nature (see Chapter 6). I do this by developing a theory of natural and artificial representation.

The charge that norms infuse facts can be pushed further: Norms infuse meaning itself, it is widely held. Statements imputing meaning are normative; they invoke standards of *correctness*; they say what *commitments* accepting a statement brings. If nature contains no normative facts, it follows it contains no facts of meaning. Talk of meaning works on different "constitutive principles" from talk of nature, and so even though we can speak of ourselves as a part of nature, thoughts and meanings are no part of that talk. Naturalistic theorizing and imputations of meaning are both legitimate, but they are two different kinds of discourse that cannot be fused.[3]

I think, on the contrary, that we need something very much like meanings in an adequate naturalistic theory of talk and what lies behind it—and so in an adequate naturalistic theory of human interactions. Naturalistically conceived, we are immensely complex products of Darwinian selection. A naturalistic treatment of animals, *homo sapiens* included, requires stratagems: the patterns are not just in the details of the neurons, but in the shaping of brain mechanisms to promote inclusive fitness in a world of complex and subtle interactions among organisms. Try to understand how all this might work, I suggest, and we are led to patterns in nature that fit, roughly, the things we already believed about meanings.

This, of course, is far from the only way of trying to understand the place of meaning in nature, and other philosophers are at work on alternatives. We are part of nature, some agree, and yet our meanings are not; they then try to explain. My aim is not to assess these competing programs. I allude to them only occasionally, and then only to particular aspects of particular attempts. My goal, rather (or one of them), is to try out a way of conceiving meaning and normative life as a part of nature, and to see how much that might explain. . . .

What Is Appraised as Rational or Not

We appraise a wide variety of human attributes as rational or irrational. Not only can a person act rationally or irrationally, but he can believe rationally or irrationally, and he can be angry or grateful or envious rationally or irrationally. It is irrational, say, to be angry at the messenger who brings bad tidings, but rational to be angry at the miscreant who deliberately wrongs one. At least this is what we tend to think in the normal course of life. If the word 'rational' seems overly learned here, substitutes come with a more homely flavor: It "doesn't make sense" to be angry at the person who brings bad news he had no part in making. The anger "isn't warranted". You "shouldn't be grateful" to someone who benefited you only inadvertently in seeking his own gain.

It is this family of appraisals that I want to interpret. Do they make genuine sense, and if so, how are they to be understood? If the term 'rational' applies intelligibly to acts and beliefs and feelings, does it have the same meaning in all these uses?

It might be thought that for something to be rational is for it to be desirable or advantageous. Such a crude pragmatism, though, would leave ordinary thought about rationality mysterious: it may fit actions, but it fails with beliefs and attitudes.[4] Take the stock example of the man who has evidence his wife is unfaithful. Whether it is still rational for him to believe her faithful—whether such a belief would be warranted—depends on his evidence, and on his evidence alone. Whether it is desirable for him to believe her faithful, and whether his believing her faithful is good for him, depend as well on how his beliefs would affect his feelings toward her. The rationality of a belief and its desirability, then, are different, if ordinary thought is to be trusted. Likewise, it might be disadvantageous for one of Cleopatra's courtiers to be angry at her, even if she ordered an execution unjustly and it thus "made sense" to be angry at her. For the courtier might want to ingratiate himself with her, and he might rightly fear that anger would cloud his countenance and spoil his charm. In that case, he would have every reason to want not to be angry, and still, we seem to think, it would make sense for him to be angry. It did not, in contrast, make sense for Cleopatra to be angry at the bearer of bad tidings, however therapeutic or palliative her anger might have been. It would make sense for the courtier to be angry, and so for anger to make sense is not for it to be advantageous.

The point is not chiefly about how we use words. Perhaps we can call anger "irrational" for the courtier, just because of the bad consequences he knows it must bring. Perhaps we can say "it makes no sense" for him to be angry, because anger would be disastrous. That, however, is a different judgment from the one I want to pursue. The judgments I want us to consider are ones of warrant. It makes no sense, we judge, for Cleopatra to be angry at the messenger, in that her anger is ill founded. It would be rational for the courtier to be angry, in that his anger is well founded or warranted, because Cleopatra has acted outrageously and without excuse. I reserve 'rational' and 'make sense' for these uses.

If we understood the word 'rational' in this sense, we could put the distinction as follows. In the case of the courtier and the queen, even though it is *rational* for him *to be angry* with her for ordering an execution unjustly, it may also be *rational* for him *to want* to ingratiate himself with her, for his own good or for that of others. If anger would prevent that, then it may be rational for him *to want* not to be angry with her. In such a case it is rational *to be angry*, but also rational *to want not to be angry*. This pattern applies not only to emotion but also to belief. Take again the case of the deceived husband: his evidence may make it rational for him *to believe* his wife unfaithful, but the way the belief would affect his feelings toward her may make it rational for him *to want to believe* her faithful. Rationally *feeling* or *believing* something is distinct from rationally *wanting* to feel or believe it.

We must also distinguish saying that it makes sense *for* a person *to be* angry from saying that it makes sense *that* the person *is* angry. If I have had a bad day and now face a new disappointment, it "makes sense that I am angry"—we can expect me to be angry in the circumstances, for reasons we understand—even if it doesn't "make sense for me to be angry" because the new disappointment is no one's fault. Likewise, it makes sense *that* Cleopatra *was* angry at the messenger, but it made no sense *for* her *to be* angry at him. Misdirected anger in the circumstance was to be expected, but the bad news was not the messenger's fault.

Talk of emotions as "rational" or "irrational" will strike many as dubious. True, we may say the kinds of things I have been claiming we say: that it "makes sense to be angry" in certain cases and it "makes no sense to be angry" in others. It may still be asked, though, whether these judgments can bear scrutiny. It may well seem that we can appraise as rational or irrational only what is under a person's voluntary control. Emotions fail this test, since they are not under a person's direct voluntary control.

True, they can be nurtured or repressed, but a person cannot simply be angry at will, or grateful at will. Nor can a person refrain from any of these things simply at will. What can be appraised as rational or irrational is not an emotion itself, but taking measures to nurture or repress it.

Now I accept, of course, that emotions cannot be had or cast off at will. What I deny is the dictum "Only the voluntary can be appraised as rational or irrational." Beliefs seem prime examples of what we can appraise as rational or irrational, but beliefs, like emotions, cannot be had or cast off at will. We may be able to "make believe" at will, but that is not the same as really believing at will.

It is common enough, then, for states of mind to be appraised as rational or irrational, even though they cannot be had or cast off at will. Indeed I think that something stronger can be said: even in the case of actions, what is primarily appraised as rational or irrational is not the directly voluntary. What, after all, makes an action voluntary? It is presumably at least in part that the action is tied to wanting, in a certain familiar way. When an action is voluntary, wanting or preference has led in a familiar way to intention, and the intention has been carried out. What, then, makes a voluntary action rational? It is the rationality of the intention that stands behind the action—and that is a matter of whether the intention is suited to satisfying a rational set of preferences. To appraise a voluntary action as rational, then, is to appraise the preferences that stand behind it as rational, and to appraise the intention it carries out as rational as a means to satisfying those preferences. Whether a voluntary action is rational, then, is a matter of the rationality of preferences and intentions.

Now preferences and intentions are not themselves voluntary. In the case of preferences, that is clear enough. I might, for instance, be convinced that I will be happy if and only if I cease to want to be happy, but I cannot on that account stop wanting to be happy, simply at will. There may be things I can do to cultivate an indifference to happiness, but that is not the same as being indifferent at will. In the case of intentions, matters are less clear than with preferences, but to ask whether the forming of intentions is voluntary seems puzzling. The question appears misdirected; it smacks of a category mistake.[5] Whether or not, then, we should call intentions "involuntary", we can at least deny that they are, in the most straightforward sense, "voluntary". Thus even in the case of actions, appraisals of rationality depend at base on appraisals of things that are not straightforwardly voluntary.

It is widely accepted that beliefs can be appraised as rational or irrational, even though they are not voluntary. Emotions are more controversial: it is sometimes maintained that an emotion can be rational or irrational only inasmuch as a belief involved in it is rational or irrational.[6] If it didn't make sense for Cleopatra to be angry at the messenger, that must be because her anger involved thinking the slave had wronged her, and that belief was irrational.

It would be hard, though, to identify what the irrational belief involved is supposed to be. Most of us have experienced being angry and yet thinking that no wrong has been done, so that the anger is unjustified. In such cases, one *feels* as if a wrong had been done, but *thinks* that no wrong has been done. Where is the irrational belief? True, if the anger is indeed irrational, as one thinks, then there is a belief it *would* be irrational to have. It would be irrational to believe a wrong has been done. That, however, is precisely what one doesn't believe; that is why one considers one's own anger irrational in such cases.

Perhaps the belief is subconscious: one believes subconsciously that a wrong has been done, in the face of a conscious realization to the contrary. Why, though, might we think one really has this subconscious belief? Chiefly because one is angry: to be angry is for it to be as if one thought a wrong had been done, even if one consciously thinks otherwise. Does thinking subconsciously that a wrong has been done, then, consist in anything indepen-

dent of being angry? If we try to reduce talk of irrational anger to talk of irrational subconscious beliefs about wrongs, the beliefs are beliefs of a special kind. They are so parasitical on emotions that little has been gained by the reduction.

In short, then, we appraise as rational or irrational things that are clearly involuntary, like beliefs and attitudes—and there is no special reason to think we are mistaken. Even in the case of action, appraisals of rationality apply primarily to states of mind that are not straightforwardly voluntary. In itself, then, the fact that emotions are involuntary gives us no reason to think that they cannot be appraised as rational or not. When we do appraise the rationality of an emotion, moreover, it seems hard to make out that we are really appraising a belief. No independently identifiable kind of belief is always involved in a given kind of emotion.

None of this is to say that when we call something "rational"—an act, belief, or emotion—we are saying anything intelligible. That remains to be seen. I am saying that we talk and think as if such appraisals are intelligible. It may be worthwhile, then, to see if we can interpret them as intelligible.

Rationality and Morality

It would be good to know what the term 'rational' means, as applied to acts, beliefs, and emotions. Before hunting down an account of its meaning, though, I turn to morality and its tie to rationality. Suppose naively, for now, that we know what 'rational' means.

In the history of moral philosophy, there seem to be at least two sharply different conceptions of what morality is. On the broadest of conceptions, morality is simply practical rationality in the fullest sense: to say that an act is morally right is to say that it is rational. Sidgwick is a prime exponent of this broad conception, and perhaps Kant is; it is shared by many current writers.[7] On this conception, it makes no sense to ask

"Is it always rational to do what is morally right?" for "the morally right" simply means "the rational". On a narrow conception of morality, in contrast, moral considerations are just some of the considerations that bear on what it makes sense to do. Non-moral considerations matter too. On the narrow conception it is normally wrong, say, to injure others, to steal, or break one's word. It would normally not be morally wrong, though, to fritter away a day for which one had planned an enjoyable hike—however irrational that might be. On the broad conception of morality, morally right action simply is action that is truly rational, whereas on the narrow conception, an act may be truly irrational without being morally wrong. (Perhaps too an action can be morally wrong without being truly irrational.)

In chapter 5 of *Utilitarianism*, John Stuart Mill uses the term 'morality' in this narrow sense, and offers an account of what is distinctive about morality so taken. "Morality", he says, "pertains to what is wrong or not wrong, and to say that an act is wrong is to say that there ought to be a sanction against it, a sanction of law, of public opinion, or of conscience." The 'ought' here, Mill proposes, should be judged by the standards of the greatest happiness principle—but that is part of the normative theory Mill is giving, not a part of his analysis of the term 'morally wrong'. What I propose to do is to take over Mill's analysis of what morality is in the narrow sense, with various interpretations and modifications.[8]

When Mill says there "ought" to be a sanction, let us read him as saying that a sanction is rational—or, perhaps, rationally required. Let us also drop talk of legal sanctions. Suppose we think that people who overpark at parking meters ought to be fined, but that they ought not to feel guilty, and ought not to be resented by others for overparking. In that case, it seems to me, we do not think overparking morally wrong; we merely think that a price should be charged. That leaves sanctions of conscience and of public opinion: sanctions of

guilt and remorse on the one hand, and of blame, resentment, and moral outrage on the other. Thus, as the proposal now stands, what a person does is *morally wrong* if and only if it is rational for him to feel guilty for doing it, and for others to resent him for doing it.[9]

'Resent' here is in some ways the wrong term. It suggests a sense of personal injury, injury to oneself, whereas blame may well be impartial. Resentment, outrage, condemnation, indignation, blame—all these get roughly at the sentiment I want. Now all these terms suggest anger, perhaps along with a sense of justification. The sense of justification goes with my talk of rationality, and so what is left is anger of various kinds. Try this formulation, then: what a person does is *morally wrong* if and only if it is rational for him to feel guilty for having done it, and for others to be angry at him for having done it.

As the formulation stands, it is more plausible for 'blameworthy' than for 'morally wrong'. What is it, then, for an act to be morally wrong? The term 'wrong' is often said to have two distinct moral senses, the *objective* and the *subjective*. The difference between the two is displayed through stories like this: Yesterday, I had the brakes of my car checked. Today, I drive a friend to the supermarket, but on the way, my brakes fail and I kill a pedestrian. Driving my car, then, has turned out to be wrong in the objective sense, but not in the subjective sense—since I had every reason to think my brakes reliable, and my friend needed to get to the store. Thus an act is wrong in the objective sense if it is wrong in light of all the facts, knowable and unknowable, whereas it is wrong in the subjective sense if it is wrong in light of what the agent had good reason to believe. More precisely, an act is wrong in the subjective sense if it is wrong in light of the degrees of plausibility (or "subjective probabilities") the agent has reason to ascribe to relevant propositions.

Now the analysis I have proposed will clearly not work for 'wrong' in the objective sense. In the story, my driving my car turns out to be wrong in the objective sense, but it would not make sense for me to feel guilty over it, or for others to resent me for it. Thus an act may be wrong in the objective sense without being wrong on the proposed analysis. That in itself is no defect, for, as I shall argue, the objective sense is not the useful one. It will turn out, though, that even for the subjective sense, the analysis does not work as it stands.

It is clear enough why we should want a theory of what kinds of acts are right in the subjective sense. Such a theory offers moral guidance: even when we know we are ignorant of the relevant facts, we can use the theory, together with what we think we do know, to decide what acts to avoid on moral grounds. Why, though, should we want a theory of what kinds of acts are right in the objective sense? Such a theory offers no guidance when we know we are ignorant of relevant facts; in that case we need rules for acting without full information. To be sure, if I could place myself under the guidance of a reliable soothsayer, I would want him to tell me which of the things I might do is right in the objective rather than the subjective sense—but reliable soothsayers are hard to find. It might seem that a theory for the objective sense would at least be useful in those rare cases when I take myself to know all the relevant facts. Even then, however, the theory is superfluous if we have criteria for rightness in the subjective sense, for in the case of full knowledge, the subjective and the objective senses of 'wrong' coincide; thus to determine what is right in the objective sense, the agent with full knowledge need only determine what is right in the subjective sense. In short, then, for an agent who knows he is ignorant, standards for objective rightness are useless; what he needs is standards for subjective rightness; whereas for the agent with full knowledge, standards for objective rightness are superfluous so long as he has standards for rightness in the subjective sense. I see no need, then, for an account of what it means to call an act wrong in the objective sense. If no such account could be given, there would be no practical loss, since what we need for moral guidance is criteria for what kinds of acts are wrong in the subjective sense.[10] Henceforth, when I use the words 'right' and 'wrong', I intend the subjective sense.

Might the analysis I have proposed work as it stands, then, for 'wrong' in the subjective sense? Might an act be wrong in the subjective sense if and only if it fits the analysis—if and only if it is rational for the agent to feel guilty over the act and for others to resent him for it? The proposal seems most apt, as I have said, as an analysis of 'blameworthiness', and wrongness in the subjective sense is not the same as blameworthiness. To see the difference, imagine that in a paroxysm of grief I speak rudely to a friend who offers condolences, and so hurt his feelings. My rudeness is unprovoked, but understandable in the circumstances. I have thus acted wrongly, but because of my agitated state, it may not make sense to blame me. If it does not, then my act is wrong in the subjective sense, but not blameworthy.[11]

How, then, can the proposal be modified to serve as an analysis of 'wrong' in the subjective sense? We might first ask why we should need a distinct concept of wrong in the subjective sense, as opposed to blameworthy. The answer seems to be that the concepts of right and wrong are forward-looking in a way that the concept of blameworthiness is not. The morally conscientious agent is one who asks himself which of the acts open to him are right and which are wrong, and then rules out any act he judges wrong. That means, among other things, that the rightness or wrongness of an alternative does not depend on the agent's motives. Rather, conscientious motivation consists in trying to confine one's actions to what is right. Blame, in contrast, attaches to the agent in retrospect; the agent is blamed for acting with insufficient morally desirable motivation. Rightness is prospective; blame is retrospective.

How can we exploit this difference? Mill's proposal, as I have said, applies most plausibly to blame. Let us tentatively accept it, then, as an account of blamewor-thiness, so that to call an action *morally reprehensible* (or to say that an agent is *blameworthy* or *to be blamed* on account of that action) is to say this: it would be rational for the agent to feel guilt over having performed the action, and for others to feel angry at him for having performed it.

What, then, might it mean to call an act wrong? Roughly, we might say, the standards of right and wrong are the standards we demand an agent use to rule out certain alternatives. In assessing blame, we apply two kinds of tests. First, we ask whether the agent's level of morally desirable motivation was satisfactory. If not, we ask whether there are extenuating circumstances that render the agent not fully responsible. Standards of right and wrong pertain to the first part: an agent's motives are morally acceptable if he is sufficiently motivated to avoid wrong acts. Standards for wrongness, then, are the standards such that an agent is *prima facie* blameworthy if he does not use them to rule out acts that violate them. The reason the blameworthiness is only *prima facie* is that facts about the person's motivational state may be extenuating. Blame thus depends both on standards for wrongness in the subjective sense, and on standards for responsibility. Formally put, then, the definitions I propose are these: An act is *wrong* if and only if it violates standards for ruling out actions, such that if an agent in a normal frame of mind violated those standards because he was not substantially motivated to conform to them, he would be to blame. To say that he would *be to blame* is to say that it would be rational for him to feel guilty and for others to resent him.

An act can be seriously wrong or trivially wrong, and we can say something about this with the framework I have sketched. When a person violates a standard, how seriously wrong that is is a matter of the degree of motivation a person must normally have to abide by that standard, if he is not to be blamed for lack of sufficient motivation. Alternatively, we might say, it is the degree to which an agent

is normally to be blamed if he lacks all motivation to abide by that standard. (These two characterizations are logically distinct, but I cannot think of circumstances in which judgments on the two characterizations would significantly diverge.) Call what we have characterized the agent's *prima facie degree of blameworthiness*. A person has diminished responsibility, then, to the extent that his degree of blameworthiness for an action falls short of his degree of *prima facie* blameworthiness for it.

What I have done in this section is to suppose that we know what 'rational' means, and to propose a way of interpreting the relation between rationality and concepts that are "moral" in the narrow sense. In the next section, I propose in rough terms an analysis of 'rational', and plug it into the analyses I have given these moral concepts.

The Norm-Expressivistic Analysis

What does it mean to call something "rational"? One way of tackling such a question is to psychologize it. What, we may ask, is the psychological state of *regarding* something as rational, of *taking* it to be rational, of *believing* it rational? Put roughly and cryptically, my hypothesis is that to think something rational is to accept norms that permit it. Much of the book will consist of elucidation, refinement, and assessment of this rough hypothesis. I begin with some preliminary explanation.

By a *norm* here, I mean a possible norm: a possible rule or prescription, expressible by an imperative. The prescription need not actually be made by anyone, or accepted by anyone, to count as a "norm" as I am using the term. The main thing to be explained is not what a norm is, but what "accepting a norm" is—or, more precisely, what it is for something to be permitted or required by the norms a person "accepts". I mean these latter notions to be psychological: they are meant to figure in an explanatory theory of human experience and action.

Take next some schematic illustrations. Delilah, suppose, is pondering whether various of Samson's acts, beliefs, and feelings are rational. What is it for her to come to an opinion? It is to come to accept norms. When Samson destroys the Philistine temple, Delilah considers that rational if and only if she accepts norms that permit, for Samson's situation as she takes it to be, destroying the temple. Perhaps she accepts the norm "When in the hands of one's enemies with no hope of escape, kill as many of them as possible, even if you must kill yourself in the process." Then if she believes that Samson is in the hands of his enemies with no hope of escape, and that destroying the temple will kill as many as possible, she thinks his action rational. Earlier Samson believed Delilah loyal. Delilah thinks this belief to have been rational if and only if she accepts the right sorts of norms for belief. She must accept norms that, for Samson's situation at the time as she now conceives it, permit believing one's woman loyal. Samson hates the Philistines, and Delilah considers his hatred rational if and only if she accepts norms that, for his situation, permit such hatred.

Nothing I have said here, I stress, speaks to whether Samson's acts, beliefs, and emotions really *were* rational. I might have tried an analysis of quite a different form: that an act, belief, or attitude of a person *is* rational if someone—be it I, or he, or a commentator—accepts norms that prescribe it for that person's circumstances. My own analysis, though, is not directly a hypothesis about what it *is* for something to be rational at all. It is a hypothesis about what it is to *think* or *believe* something rational, to *regard* it as rational, to *consider* it rational. An observer *believes* an action, belief, or attitude A of mine to be rational if and only if he accepts norms that permit A for my circumstances. It follows that if we want to decide what really *is* rational, we shall have to settle what norms to accept ourselves—for that is what it is to form an opinion as to the rationality of something.

Return now to norms of morality. In an-

alyzing the narrowly moral notions "blameworthy" and "wrong", I took the term 'rational' as understood. If we now combine these analyses with our rough analysis of 'rational', we can derive an account of the distinction between moral norms and norms of rationality. All norms, in a sense, are norms of rationality, but moral norms in particular are norms for the rationality of guilt and resentment. Consider first what it is for an action to be "blameworthy". The analyses given so far tell us this: First, an observer thinks an act *blameworthy*, or *morally reprehensible*, if and only if he thinks it rational for the agent to feel guilty over the act, and for others to resent the agent for it. Second, to think something 'rational' is to accept norms that prescribe it. Therefore, we may conclude, to think an act *morally reprehensible* is to accept norms that prescribe, for such a situation, guilt on the part of the agent and resentment on the part of others.

Next consider the term 'morally wrong' (in the subjective sense). The standards for whether an act is wrong, we have said, are the standards such that guilt and resentment are *prima facie* rational if the agent is not disposed to rule out alternatives that violate them. Thus to think an act wrong is to accept norms for guilt and resentment that, *prima facie*, would sanction guilt and resentment if the act were performed. '*Prima facie*' here means before questions of the psychological peculiarities of the agent are raised—the psychological peculiarities, that is, that bear on whether the agent is to be considered fully responsible. Norms for wrongness are thus explained in terms of norms for guilt and resentment.

This proposal as it stands requires an independent account of responsibility. Now the psychic makeup of the agent has some bearing not only on whether the agent is responsible, but on what acts open to him are wrong. How do we separate the two? Suppose, for instance, that an act is the only one that is eligible, in the sense that all alternatives to it would leave the agent desperately unhappy. That fact may, in our opinion, tend to justify the act morally: it might be that even though the act would otherwise be wrong, this consideration turns it right. That, in any case, is what we might well think, and an analysis should allow for the possibility. In what ways, then, might psychological peculiarities of an agent bear on his degree of moral responsibility by itself, without bearing on the rightness and wrongness of the acts open to him?

Standards for responsibility, I might say, are standards for when an agent is to blame for acting on *prima facie* blameworthy motivations, and *prima facie* blameworthy motivations are motives for which an agent is to blame if he is fully responsible. If I say this, however, then even though the term 'blameworthy' itself has been defined independently, the terms '*prima facie* blameworthy' and 'responsible' will be defined only in terms of each other.

This circularity can be eliminated as follows. Consider an agent who has various psychological peculiarities, and an act for which I would consider the agent to blame if I thought him normal. Our problem is to untangle whether, because of his psychological peculiarities, I regard the act as right, or whether instead I consider the act to be wrong but the agent not to blame. The test I propose is this: Take an agent with psychological peculiarities, and imagine him for the moment rendered normal, but expecting to reacquire his psychological peculiarities once he had decided how to act on this occasion. He thus must take these psychological peculiarities into account in deciding what to do, though he is rid of them for the moment, apart from his belief that he has them. Whether I consider the act to be wrong, then, is a matter of whether I accept norms that would sanction guilt and anger if the agent, while temporarily rendered normal, were to perform that act.

Second Thoughts

'Rational' is in some ways the wrong word for my purposes. I treat calling something "rational" as a flat recommendation, but it has a special flavor—a flavor some do not like. Some people are irrationalists: they think rationality overrated; they prefer passion and spontaneity. The lover of reason disagrees. On the account I am giving, though, it seems both must mistake what is at issue. The irrationalist cannot be what he thinks himself to be, for whatever he endorses he thereby thinks rational. If that is implausible, perhaps that shows the term 'rational' does not mean what I say it does.

My real claim is not for the word 'rational', but for a meaning I want to exploit. Perhaps the word 'rational' rarely has this meaning, but when it does, then what it is rational to do settles what to do. Likewise, what it is rational to believe settles what to believe, and what it is rational to feel about something settles how to feel about it. Not that a person will always do what he thinks it rational to do, but settling what it is rational to do at least ends discussion. The person who agrees and then acts otherwise has not been effectively governed by what he himself has conceded. For this sense of 'rational', there is no such thing as a considered determination to do what one thinks irrational.

Other phrases may capture this notion better. I have freely substituted talk of what it "makes sense" to do, to think, and to feel about things; that might be my best canonical phrase. Alternatively, we might talk of what one "ought" to do, think, or feel, and explain that the 'ought' is not the moral one. With feelings and beliefs, we can talk of what states of mind are "warranted", "well grounded", or "apt"; with acts we can talk of the "best thing to do". We might talk simply of "the thing to do" or "the thing to feel" about something. If a flavorless recommendation on balance can be found in any of these terms, then that is what 'rational' shall mean in this book. My claim is that some phrase or other can be used in this sense, and that a wide range of important concepts can be paraphrased in terms of this one.

Still, what is the irrationalist rejecting as "rational", and what is the lover of reason embracing? The word 'rational' is connected with reasoning. Reasoning is a natural, psychological phenomenon, something we do at times and avoid at times. It involves thinking through the possibilities, drawing inferences, and the like. Now a person can reason and act on the basis of his reasoning, or he can act spontaneously without reasoning. He can act on his reasoning, or he can act from whim or unreasoned passion. In one sense, the word 'rational' just means "pertaining to reasoning". The irrationalist is against being guided in one's actions by reasoning, or by reasoning pressed too far. Reasoning is to be explained naturalistically, and one can intelligibly be against it.

In another sense, a person is rational only if he tends to be guided by reasoning that is good. This sense is normative, and so, I would claim, not straightforwardly naturalistic. A rational person in this sense is not only guided by reasoning; he reasons in ways it makes sense to reason—in ways it is "rational" in my own chief sense to reason. Can rationality in this normative sense be suspect?

One question is whether to reason well or badly, but another is how much to reason at all. We can ask how much to be guided even by our best reasoning. Being guided by good reasoning has advantages, but it has drawbacks too. It can detract from spontaneity; it can work against the free flow of feelings. Acting from feelings is part of what gives life its flavor, and reasoning can stifle that. The irrationalist does not favor being guided by reasoning he thinks bad; he is against being guided by reasoning of any kind. That is intelligible, and even when the wild irrationalist goes overboard, we can see what drove him. We too can appreciate the drawbacks of reasoned action. We can see being guided by good reasoning as competing with other goods, and in that sense, we think rationality simply one good that competes with others.[12]

All this is to talk of rational people: a person is rational if he guides himself by good reasoning. I have been talking about rational acts, beliefs, and feelings, and not di-rectly about rational people. Can one reject acts one thinks rational? It does seem so: "That would be the rational thing to do" can be said in a sour tone of voice.

A lover might say such a thing, when his prospects look bleak and we urge him to turn elsewhere. Perhaps his opinions are simply at odds with his feelings, and he speaks from his feelings. He might, though, want to praise his feelings, and have a rationale. He might agree that it makes sense to turn elsewhere, but think, nevertheless, it makes sense to want to be the sort of person who will not. One whose loves are too much guided by reasoning, he may think—even the best of reasoning—will never truly kiss. It makes sense to give up, he agrees, but it makes sense to want to be someone who would not.

Alternatively, the rational act may not be the best one given what one knows, but the one good reasoning would select. The two might differ, for perhaps in some realms even the best of reasoning is not the best guide. The best reasoning is best for the things reasoning can promote, but perhaps that leaves out some aspects of life. In some realms, perhaps, faith does better, though good reasoning will not endorse it. The thing to do, then, is what faith picks out, and not what reasoning would pick out—even the best of reasoning.

That is what someone might mean by 'rational', but it is not what I mean. When we settle the thing to do, then in my sense we have thereby made up our minds that it is the rational thing to do.

So much for the irrationalist. What now of the moralist with special views, the moralist who rejects guilt and anger? The morality of guilt and anger alone is morality very narrowly understood. Guilt and anger are bleakly negative, and even morality tightly construed seems to take in positive feelings of moral approbation. Then too, other cultures may lack guilt altogether, or may give it no great play in their norms of social control. Could there not be shame moralities, or fear moralities?

The question is really one of stipulation. The term 'moral' has no sharp boundaries in normal thought, and I am proposing one reading among others. Morality, construed narrowly in this way, concerns what is blameworthy and what is innocent, what is morally wrong and what is morally permissible. More broadly conceived, it could easily take in what is morally admirable and what is morally indifferent. We could even throw in what is shameful and what is dangerous.[13]

The important thing is the pattern of analysis, and it can apply in all these realms. An action is morally admirable, we can say, if on the part both of the agent and of others it makes sense to feel moral approbation toward the agent for having done it. An action is shameful if it makes sense for the agent to feel ashamed for having done it, and for others to disdain him for having done it. An act is dangerous if it makes sense for the agent to feel afraid on account of having done it. All these notions concern the ways it makes sense to feel about things people do, the feelings that are warranted.

All norms, we might say, are primarily norms of rationality. The various different kinds of norms governing a thing—moral norms, aesthetic norms, norms of propriety—are each norms for the rationality of some one kind of attitude one can have toward it. Just as moral norms are norms for the rationality of guilt and resentment, so aesthetic norms are norms for the rationality of kinds of aesthetic appreciation. Norms of propriety are norms for the rationality of shock, so that something is improper if it makes sense to be shocked by it.[14]

Return, though, to the opponent of guilt or anger. He might think, say, that guilt is always irrational because it is self-destructive, or that anger is rational whenever it makes us feel good. Those opinions, though, would not concern whether it is rational to feel guilty or angry, but whether it is rational to *want* ever to feel guilty or angry. When it makes sense to *want* to feel guilty is not, in my narrow sense, a moral question, whereas whether it makes sense to feel guilty is.

Suppose, though, he thinks that guilt itself is always irrational—say because it would only be rational if we had free will, which we don't. In that case, I am maintaining, he does deny that anything is ever morally reprehensible. Thus, in my narrow sense of the term, he denies that acts are ever morally wrong. He can still very well think that acts are bad in various other ways, and that some acts are much to be avoided. In some senses, then, he does think that acts can be morally wrong, and that many are. In my sense, though, he does not—and drawing the boundary where I do marks off a region in our moral thought that is worth exploring. Some of the moral questions that puzzle us may be questions of what norms to accept as governing guilt and resentment, and hence what acts to avoid as fit objects of guilt and resentment.[15]

Structural Problems

The analysis lets us reformulate questions about the structure of morality, and about what morality has to do with rationality. Is it always rational to be moral? On the broadest construal of morality, the problem is trivial: to be moral is simply to be, in the deepest sense, rational. On the narrow construal, in contrast, the question makes good sense. Does rationality ever require a person to do something morality forbids?[16] Diminished responsibility aside, this becomes, in my terms, two closely related questions. First, does it ever make sense to feel guilty over something it would not have made sense to omit? Second, does it ever make sense to resent something that it would not have made sense for the agent to omit?

The question, then, is how our norms for guilt and resentment are to tie in with our norms for action. Deciding whether rationality ever countermands morality is deciding whether to accept norms that can both permit an act and prescribe guilt and blame for it.

Turn next to moral dilemmas. Does the moral *ought* imply *can*, so that no matter how appalling the alternatives, at least one of them must be morally permissible? Or are there cases where anything one can do would be wrong?[17] Here again, the norm-expressivistic analysis provides an interpretation of the dispute. Diminished responsibility aside, the issue concerns the structure of well-founded guilt and anger. Are there situations in which, no matter what the agent does, it will make sense for him to feel guilty for having done it, and for others to be angry at him for having done it? Guilt here must be more than mere compunction, and part of the problem may be whether a distinction between compunction and full-fledged guilt can be drawn.

Is morality of value? It is sometimes held more of a burden than a blessing: we would all be better off, some claim, if morality were not part of our lives. Can we make enough sense of this claim to assess it? The question, I take it, is not whether it would be a good thing if there were more killing, cruelty, and other heinous deeds in the world, but whether, in light of its costs, morality is the best shield against such deeds. When people claim, then, that we would be better off without morality, how do they conceive "morality"? No doubt different people mean different things, but the norm-expressivistic analysis provides one possible interpretation—an interpretation on which the issue seems well worth pondering. It is a good thing, we may ask, for norms for guilt and resentment to play a big role in our lives? Or might other kinds of motivation—good will, wide sympathies, pride, a sense of shame, or some combination of these and others—bring many of the same benefits without the same costs?[18]

How much choice do we have? Are there cultures that get along without morality? Here again, much hinges on what is meant by the term. Some brand morality a peculiarly Western phenomenon, with its roots in the Judeo-Christian tradition; others think morality a cultural universal. I do not claim to know what in general is at issue in these claims, but the norm-expressivis-

tic analysis does direct us to a significant question: are norms for guilt and resentment universal? The question is not about norms in general, or about practices of criticism in general: it is not whether all cultures have norms or practices of criticism. The question is rather whether the emotions I have been calling "specifically moral" are culturally universal, and whether the existence of norms for these emotions is a cultural universal.

I have been reformulating old puzzles, not trying to solve them. The point is to see what Mill's proposal does. Once morality is delimited as he suggests, familiar problems can be put in new form, as questions about the structure of well-founded sentiments.

Notes

1. Quine (1960) gives an account much like this of what may properly be done, and calls such an analysis a "paraphrase". Stevenson (1944, 34–36) speaks of ordinary language as vague, and provides what he calls "working models". "They provide a meaning that can be *assigned* to the ethical terms, and which is well suited to certain contexts" (36).

2. "Moral realists" treat goodness and the like as properties, but as some recent moral realists conceive properties, telling which property a term picks out will not give its meaning. 'Hot' and 'of high mean kinetic energy' will pick out the same property, but no claim is made that the two have the same meaning. See Sturgeon (1985, 28–30), Railton (1986a, 1986b), and Boyd (1988). Such a theory of denotation will need a theory of meaning as well—a theory of what gives terms the references they have, and how we can reason about properties. Current moral realists, as I read them, are suspicious of the forms theories of meaning traditionally take, and are working to develop other forms.

3. Davidson (1980, 223) speaks of "the constitutive ideal of rationality" as control-

ling the evolution of a scheme of translation. Kripke (1982, 37) says, "The relation of meaning and intention to future action is *normative*, not *descriptive*." McDowell (1984, 336) quotes this approvingly, and talks of "the normativeness of meaning".

4. What I am calling "crude pragmatism" about belief is not the pragmatism of Peirce, James, or Dewey. James came closest: he thought that there are cases when we should believe whatever it is most beneficial to believe. The cases, though, are well circumscribed. The option to believe must be, in his terms, forced, living, and momentous, and one "that cannot be decided on intellectual grounds" (1897, 3–11).

5. A "category mistake", Ryle says (1949, 6–7), is the sort of mistake a child makes who, having come to the parade to see the division march by, sees the battalions, batteries, and squadrons, and asks when the division is coming.

6. Hume (1740, bk. 2, part 3, sec. 3) gives the classic defense of this position. See also Solomon (1976, 185), and Sabini and Silver (1982, 171). Others think an emotion involves an evaluation or appraisal, and that these can be assessed as rational or irrational. I discuss both beliefs and appraisals in Chapter 7 of *Wise Choices and Apt Feelings*.

7. Sidgwick (1907, esp. bk. 1, chap. 3, sec. 1). Kant (1785) is more difficult: he takes morality to be the realm of the "categorical imperative", which expresses the demands of pure practical reason. In addition, though, he recognizes non-moral "hypothetical imperatives", which express what is needed for one's own happiness. If we read him as taking hypothetical imperatives as demands of rationality, then we must not attribute the broad conception of morality to him.

8. Mill's theory was brought to recent philosophical attention by Lyons in a series of articles; see especially Lyons (1976).

9. This is roughly the analysis Ewing proposed for one sense of 'ought' (1939, 14).

'Ought' in another sense, he suggests, is simple and unanalyzable; this simple *ought* seems to correspond to my term 'rational'. Brandt (1946) develops this pattern of analysis for such terms as 'detestable' and 'meritorious'. He speaks of the emotions it is "fitting" to have toward an action, and a fitting emotion seems to be what I am calling a rational emotion. He is neutral on what fitting means, or whether it has any real meaning. Brentano (1889) offers a similar analysis for 'good': a thing is good if "love relating to it is correct" (*richtig*), if it is "worthy of love" (18). In some cases, he thinks, love is "experienced as being correct" (22), and that constitutes "insight—the clarity and evidence of certain judgments that is inseparable from their truth" (79). See the discussion by Carson (1984, 1–4 and elsewhere).

10. I argue this in Gibbard (1978, 95–96). It might be thought that we need objective rightness as an aim. Often, though, we should not do what we think most probably right in the objective sense; often to do so would be to run unconscionable risks. It may be thought that we need an objective sense to encourage people to get needed information. Information, though, is sometimes worth acquiring and sometimes not, and a subjective treatment can tell us when it is. For a decision-theoretic treatment of paying for information, see Raiffa (1968, 105–107 and chap. 7).

11. Brandt (1959, 458) makes this distinction, and argues that 'reprehensible' cannot be defined in terms of 'moral obligation'. He then offers a definition of 'reprehensible' that is quite close, in some respects, to the one I am offering.

12. Adam Smith (1790) holds something like this. Morality, he argues, concerns the propriety of moral sentiments. "The love of praise is the desire of obtaining the favorable sentiments of our brethren. The love of praise-worthiness is the desire of rendering ourselves the proper objects of those sentiments . . . The like affinity and resemblance take place between the dread of blame and that of blameworthiness"

(III.2.25; see all of III.2). Smith, though, unlike me, thinks that to call an emotion proper is to say that it is what a detached observer in fact would feel. See my discussion in Chapter 15.

13. Two recent works that mark off "morality" in a narrow sense are Brandt (1979, chaps. 9–10) and Williams (1985, esp. chap. 10). Brandt characterizes the "moral code" of a society as involving intrinsic motivation, guilt feelings and disapproval, believed importance, admiration or esteem, special terminology, and believed justification (164–176). Williams picks out morality as using a special notion of obligation and giving obligations a special significance (174). He does not try to define this special notion, but he does give some of its characteristics, and he contrasts obligations as they figure in the "morality system" with obligations "when they are rightly seen as merely one kind of consideration among others" (182). "Blame is the characteristic reaction of the morality system. The remorse or self-reproach or guilt I have already mentioned is the characteristic first-personal reaction within the system, and if an agent never felt such sentiments, he would not belong to the morality system or be a full moral agent in its terms" (177). Morality, he complains, turns everything into obligations; deliberation issues in oughts and mays (180, 175). In terms, then, of the narrow and broad conceptions of morality with which I started, we might read Williams's complaint as this: Morality takes narrowly moral notions, with their tie to blame, and invests them with the significance of moral notions in the broad sense. It treats them as figuring alone in the reasonable outcome of deliberation.

14. Brandt elaborates a proposal like this (1946). See also Adam Smith: "An amiable action, a respectable action, an horrid action, are all of them actions which naturally excite for the person who performs them, the love, the respect, or the horror of the spectator" (1790, III.4.10).

15. Scanlon proposes another characterization of morality. "An act is wrong if its performance . . . would be disallowed by any system of rules . . . which no one could reasonably reject as a basis for informed, unforced general agreement" (1982, 110). He proposes this as a substantive claim about morality, not as a theory of meaning (107). His proposal, then, is not a direct alternative to mine, but we can ask whether the two fit naturally together. Much in Scanlon's proposal remains to be worked out: we need to know about the term 'reasonable', about the conditions that will count as those of unforced agreement, and about the parties' motivations. Suppose all that is worked out though; would morality, on Scanlon's characterization, depend by its nature on sentiments of guilt and blame? If parties expected compliance by magic, they could reasonably decide what to accept or not without regard to these sentiments. Morality might help explain the sentiments, but not the reverse. Perhaps, though, the force the parties expect their agreement to have is moral: they will have some special motivation to keep the agreement. Must that motivation involve guilt and blame? This raises deep questions about whether guilt and blame have anything special to do with such things as agreements—questions I look to in Chapter 7 of *Wise Choices and Apt Feelings*.

16. Brandt formulates this question in terms of his own analyses of rationality and morality (1979, chap. 17).

17. This issue is discussed by van Fraassen (1973) and by Marcus (1980).

18. Nietzsche attacks *ressentiment* (1887, Essay I) and bad conscience (Essay II), and so he is attacking morality in the sense I am considering. "The bad conscience is an illness . . . but an illness as pregnancy is an illness" (II, sec. 19). It is needed in history "to breed an animal with the right to make promises" (II, sec. 1). His attack may be still broader, though, than the kind of attack I am contemplating: He seems willing to do without the protec-

tions I have assumed the antimoralist still wants; the self-torturing repression of natural inclinations that these protections exact will not be worth its cost when Zarathustra comes. "The attainment of this goal would require a *different* kind of spirit from that likely to appear in this present age: spirits strengthened by war and victory, for whom conquest, adventure, danger, and even pain have become needs; it would require habituation to the keen air of the heights, to winter journeys, to ice and mountains in every sense; it would require even a kind of sublime wickedness, an ultimate, supremely self-confident mischievousness in knowledge that goes with great health; it would require, in brief and alas, precisely this *great health*" (II. sec. 24). He does favor protection when it is mutual among those of roughly equal power. That is the origin of justice, he insists (1887, sec. 92).

References to the Notes

Boyd, Richard N. 1988. "How to Be a Moral Realist," pp. 181–228 in Geoffrey Sayre-McCord, ed., *Essays on Moral Realism*. Ithaca: Cornell University Press.

Brandt, Richard B. 1946. "Moral Valuation," *Ethics* 56:106–121.

———. 1959. *Ethical Theory*. Englewood Cliffs, N.J.: Prentice-Hall.

———. 1979. *A Theory of the Good and the Right*. Oxford: Clarendon Press.

Brentano, Franz. 1889. *Von Ursprung sitticher Erkenntnis*. Leipzig: Duncker & Humblot. Citations from *The Origin of Our Knowledge of Right and Wrong*, Oscar Kraus and Roderick Chisholm, eds., R. Chisholm and Elizabeth H. Schneewind, trans. London: Routledge and Kegan Paul, 1969.

Carson, Thomas. 1984. *The Status of Morality*. Dordrecht: Kluwer.

Davidson, Donald. 1980. *Essays on Actions and Events*. Oxford: Oxford University Press.

Ewing, A.C. 1939. "A Suggested Non-Naturalistic Analysis of Good," *Mind* 48:1–22.

Gibbard, Allan. 1978. "Act-Utilitarian Agreements," pp. 91–119 in Alvin Goldman and Jaegwon Kim,

eds., *Values and Morals*. Dordrecht, Holland: Reidel.

Hume, David. 1739. *Treatise of Human Nature*, vols. I and II. London: John Noon; vol. III, London: Thomas Longman, 1740.

James, William. 1897. *The Will to Believe and Other Essays in Popular Philosophy*. London: Longmans, Green. Cited edition, New York: Dover, 1956.

Kant, Immanuel. 1785. *Grundlegung der Metaphysic der Sitten*. Riga: Hartknoch. Trans. as *Foundations of the Metaphysics of Morals*, by Lewis White Beck. Indianapolis: Bobbs-Merrill, 1959. Standard page numbers from the Konigliche Preussische Akademie der Wissenschaft edition. Berlin, 1902–1938.

Kripke, Saul. 1982. *Wittgenstein on Rules and Private Language*. Cambridge: Harvard University Press.

Lyons, David. 1976. "Mill's Theory of Morality," *Nous* 10:101–120.

Marcus, Ruth Barcan. 1980. "Moral Dilemmas and Consistency, " *Journal of Philosophy* 77:121–136.

McDowell, John. 1984. "Wittgenstein on Following a Rule," *Synthese* 58:325–363.

Nietzsche, Friedrich. 1887. *Zur Geneologie der Moralen*. Trans. as *On the Geneology of Morals*, by Walter Kaufmann and R.J. Hollingdale. New York: Vintage Books, 1967.

Quine, W.V.O. 1960. *Word and Object*. Cambridge: MIT Press.

Raiffa, Howard. 1968. *Decision Analysis*. Reading, Mass.: Addison-Wesley.

Railton, Peter. 1986a. "Facts and Values," *Philosophical Topics* 14:5–31.

———. 1986b. "Moral Realism," *Philosophical Review* 95:163–207.

Ryle, Gilbert. 1949. *The Concept of Mind*. London: Hutchison.

Sabini, John, and Maury Silver. 1982. *Moralities of Everyday Life*. Oxford: Oxford University Press.

Scanlon, T.M. 1982. "Contractualism and Utilitarianism," pp. 103–128 in Amartya Sen and Bernard Williams, eds., *Utilitarianism and Beyond*. Cambridge: Cambridge University Press.

Sidgwick, Henry. 1907. *The Methods of Ethics*. 7th ed. London: Macmillan.

Smith, Adam. 1790. *The Theory of Moral Sentiments*. 6th ed. London: A. Strahan and T. Cadell.

Solomon, Robert C. 1976. *The Passions*. Garden City, N.Y.: Doubleday/Anchor.

Stevenson, Charles. 1944. *Ethics and Language*. New Haven: Yale University Press.

Sturgeon, Nicholas L. 1985. "Gibbard on Moral Judgment and Norms," *Ethics* 96:22–33.

Van Fraassen, Bas. 1973. "Values and the Heart's Command," *Journal of Philosophy* 70:5–19.

Williams, Bernard. 1985. *Ethics and the Limits of Philosophy*. Cambridge: Harvard University Press.

7 / R. M. HARE

DESCRIPTIVE MEANING AND MORAL PRINCIPLES

2.2. We must now notice the connexion between the fact that some judgements are descriptive and another feature which it has become the custom to call, when we are speaking of moral judgements, *universalizability*. It is important to emphasize that moral judgements *share* this feature with descriptive judgements, although the differences between them in other respects are, as we shall see, sufficient to make it misleading to say that moral judgements are descriptive. Nevertheless, in so far as moral judgements do have descriptive meaning, in addition to the other kind of meaning which they have, they share this characteristic, which is common to all judgements which carry descriptive meaning.

If a person says that a thing is red, he is committed to the view that anything which was like it in the relevant respects would likewise be red. The relevant respects are those which, he thought, entitled him to call the first thing red; in this particular case, they amount to one respect only: its red colour. This follows, according to the definitions given above, from the fact that 'This is red' is a descriptive judgement. 'This is red' entails 'Everything like this in the relevant respects is red' simply because to say that something is red while denying that some other thing which resembles it in the relevant respects is red is to misuse the word 'red'; and this is because 'red' is a descriptive term, and because therefore to say

Reprinted by permission of the publisher and copyright holder from R. M. Hare, *Freedom and Reason* (Oxford: Oxford University Press, 1963), pp. 10–25, 30–40.

that something is red is to say that it is of a certain kind, and so to imply that anything which is of that same kind is red.

The proposition 'Everything like this in the relevant respects is red' is not, indeed, formally and in the strictest sense a universal one; for it contains the singular term 'this'. But, as I have explained elsewhere,[1] when a singular term is governed by the word 'like' or its equivalent, it has the property of being turnable into a universal term by substituting for 'like this' a term which describes the respects in which the thing in question is being said to be like this. If no suitable word exists, it is always possible to invent one. And so if a person who says 'This is red' is committed also to the proposition 'Everything like this in the relevant respects is red', then he is, further, committed to the proposition that there is a property such that this has it and such that everything which has it is red. And the second part of this proposition contains no singular terms, and can therefore be called properly universal.

It may be observed that the proposition 'There is a property such that everything which has it is red' is a very trivial one, since the property in question is redness, and we know that there is such a property, once we know what sort of word 'red' is (i.e. a descriptive word). But note that there are in fact other properties such that everything that has them is red (e.g. the properties of being scarlet, or of being a ripe tomato of the commonest variety). We may admit, however, that, since this proposition, even if it were not non-trivially true, would still be trivially true, 'red' being the sort of word that it is, the thesis that descriptive judgements are universalizable is a quite trivial thesis. It is put forward here only because it will help us to shed light on the thesis, which is itself not so trivial, that moral judgements are, *in the same sense*, universalizable.

2.3. For the moment, however, let us merely observe that in an apparently trivial, but at any rate unobjectionable, sense, any singular descriptive judgement is universalizable: viz. in the sense that it commits the speaker to the further proposition that anything exactly like the subject of the first judgement, or like it in the relevant respects, possesses the property attributed to it in the first judgement. Let us now raise against this thesis some of the objections that are often raised against the corresponding thesis about value-judgements. First (it may be said) if, in the formulation of the thesis, we say 'exactly like', then the thesis becomes trivial and not worth stating. Nothing, it may be said, ever *is* exactly like anything else—whether this be regarded as analytic or not need not concern us. On the other hand (the objection goes on) if we say 'like in the relevant respects', we have on our hands the problem of how to determine and formulate what *are* the relevant respects. And if we cannot do this, it is alleged that the thesis is again valueless.

To this it may be replied, first, that it is wrong to take too narrowly utilitarian an attitude towards philosophical theses; let it suffice that they are true, and let it be left to the future to determine whether any useful results follow from them. Secondly, the thesis has indeed an important impact on the theory of meaning, just as the corresponding thesis about value-judgements has momentous consequences for ethics. The thesis enables us to illuminate the problem of what is meant by 'descriptive meaning'. This is not surprising; for we derived the thesis from a consideration of what it was for a term to be descriptive. One of the features of descriptive meaning, as opposed to other sorts of meaning, is that it relies upon the concept of *similarity*.

We might restate what we noticed above about descriptive meaning by saying that a descriptive meaning-rule is one which lays it down that we may apply an expression to objects which are similar to each other in certain respects. It is a direct consequence of this that we cannot without inconsistency apply a descriptive term to one thing, and refuse to apply it to another similar thing (either exactly similar or similar in the relevant respects). At any rate a person who admitted that two things were exactly similar, but applied some descriptive term to one while refusing to apply it to the other, though he claimed to be using the term unambiguously, would be showing that he either did not understand that the expression was a descriptive term, or did not understand what a descriptive term was.

It thus turns out that the universalizability of singular descriptive judgements is a consequence of the fact that the meaning-rules for the descriptive terms which they have to contain are universal rules, and universal rules of a certain type. The difficulty of formulating precisely the respect in which the two objects have to be similar is simply the difficulty of determining the precise meaning in which the speaker was using the term. For example, suppose that I say that X is red; I am committed to holding that anything which is like X in the relevant respect is also red. But suppose that I am asked what *is* the relevant respect. I shall be able to answer this question only by giving an indication, vague or precise, of what it was about X that made me call it red; i.e. by explaining what I meant by calling it red. This explanation, if I can give it, will determine in what respect another object has to resemble X before it becomes possible to, and impossible not to, apply to it the descriptive term 'red', in the sense in which I was using that term. In this particular case an ostensive explanation (possibly a very elaborate one) will be required.

I must emphasize again that I am not making language out to be more rigid than it is. It is, of course, true that the concept 'red' is one whose boundaries are ill-de-fined. One man might call an object red which another said was not red—and that, not because there was a difference in their colour-vision, but because they had learnt to use the word 'red' in slightly different ways. Colour-cards from different manu-facturers of paint often vary in this way; one card may, for example, classify as green a shade which is called on the other some sort of yellow. And a person might *change* his use of the word 'red' slightly; he might come to include in red, shades which previously he included in purple. The his-tory of the word 'purple' itself illustrates this sort of change; the dye from whose name the word 'purple' is derived would now be classified by almost everybody as a red. All I am saying is that on any one oc-casion of the use of the word 'red' the speaker must have *some* feature of an ob-ject in mind as that to which he is drawing attention in using the word. He may be very unclear about the precise boundaries of the concept he is employing (we can use 'red' without having decided what we would say about border-line cases); but there must be *something* about the object in question which, if it were repeated in an-other object, he would (provided that he went on using the word in the same sense) treat as entitling him to call that object red too. If this were not so, what he said would have no descriptive meaning at all. Thus (if I may be allowed to anticipate my future argument) the alleged difficulty of *formu-lating* the universal rule which is implied in any value-judgement is simply the same sort of difficulty which is encountered when we try to explain the meaning of a descriptive term as used on a particular oc-casion.

2.4. Let us now consider a further ob-jection, also on grounds of triviality. It might be said that the universal proposi-tion which is generated, in the way de-scribed above, by any singular descriptive judgement is merely a matter of the *mean-ing* of the descriptive term contained in the judgement; that it cannot be a matter of substance. If I say that X is red, I am com-mitted to holding that anything which is like X in a certain respect is red too. In us-ing the descriptive term 'red' I must be em-ploying *some* universal rule; but, it might be objected, this rule is only that which gives the meaning of 'red'; it is a purely verbal matter of how the word 'red' is used. Now this I do not wish to deny, in the case of purely descriptive terms; as we shall see, evaluative terms differ in this respect. The universal rules which are involved in the use of all descriptive expressions are mean-ing-rules; and since these are obviously in some sense universal (in what sense, I have tried to make clear), it seems hardly worth saying that singular descriptive proposi-tions commit the speaker to universal propositions. And perhaps in most philo-sophical contexts it would not be worth saying. But in the present context it is most important; for I am going on to speak about the universalizability of value-judgements (upon which a great deal hangs in ethics), and it is most necessary that it should be understood what I mean by this. The way which I have chosen of explaining what I mean is by saying that the feature of value-judgements which I call universalizability is simply that which they share with de-scriptive judgements; namely the fact that they both carry descriptive meaning. It thus becomes very important to elucidate accurately this feature of descriptive judge-ments.

If I call a thing red, I am committed to calling anything else like it red. And if I call a thing a good X, I am committed to call-ing any X like it good. But whereas the rea-son in the former case is that I must be us-ing the word 'red' in accordance with some *meaning*-rule, the reason in the latter case is much more complicated. For a naturalist, indeed, it would not be any more compli-cated; for naturalists hold that the rules which determine to what we can apply value-words are simply descriptive mean-ing-rules, and that these rules determine the meaning of these words completely, just as in the case of descriptive expres-sions. For him, a value-word is just one kind of descriptive expression. We may go further than this; for a naturalist is not the only sort of 'descriptivist'—if we may use this term for one who holds that value-words are simply one kind of descriptive word. It is true also of non-natural descriptivists such as Moore that for them value-words are descriptive terms whose meanings are completely determined by the sort of descriptive meaning-rules that I have been discussing. The difference between natural and non-natural descriptivists is important for our argument. The non-naturalist holds that the feature which has to be present in a thing before a value-word can be applied to it is something which can be described only by using that or some other value-word; it is *sui generis*. On the other hand, according to the naturalist such a feature is also describable, though perhaps at greater length, in non-evaluative (usually empirical) terms.

2.5. For the sake of a name, let me refer to the type of doctrine which I put forward in *The Language of Morals*, and still hold, as 'universal prescriptivism'—a combination, that is to say, of universalism (the view that moral judgements are universalizable) and prescriptivism (the view that they are, at any rate typically, prescriptive). It will be useful to make clear at this point that it is not easy with consistency to attack both sides of the doctrine at once. For, as we have seen, it follows from the definition of the expression 'descriptive term' that descriptive judgements are universalizable in just the same way as, according to my view, moral judgements are. It is impossible consistently to maintain that moral judgements are descriptive, and that they are not universalizable. To put the matter even more starkly: a philosopher who rejects universalizability is committed to the view that moral judgements have no descriptive meaning at all. Though there have been, no doubt, philosophers who are willing to go as far as this, they certainly do not include many of those who have declared themselves against universalizability.

The matter can perhaps be made clearer in the following way. Let us call the thesis that moral judgements are universalizable, *u*, and the thesis that they are prescriptive, *p*. Now there are two theses about the descriptive character of moral judgements which require to be carefully distinguished. The first and stronger of these (*d*') is that moral judgements are a kind of descriptive judgements, i.e. that their descriptive meaning exhausts their meaning. This is descriptivism. The second and weaker (*d*') is that moral judgements, though they may possess other elements in their meaning, do have descriptive meaning. I wish to affirm *p, u* and *d*'. These three theses are all mutually consistent. As we have seen, *d*' entails *u*. *p* is consistent with *d*', because to say that a judgement is prescriptive is not to say that prescriptive meaning is the only meaning that it carries, but merely that it does carry this element in its meaning among others. Now, as I hope to show, the combination of *p* and *u* (or *d*') is sufficient to establish the rationality of morals, or the possibility of cogent moral arguments—it is important that *p*, as I shall show, so far from being an obstacle to establishing this, is actually a necessary condition for it. But there are those who think that they require for this purpose not merely the weaker theses *u* or *d*' but the stronger thesis *d*. Now *d* is indeed inconsistent with *p*; and therefore these descriptivists think it necessary to deny *p*. But, because *p* has been affirmed by myself and others in conjunction with *u*, and because the connexion between *d*' and *u* has not been noticed, *u* has perhaps acquired, in the minds of some descriptivists, a kind of guilt by association: 'Some wicked prescriptivists have affirmed *u*,' they seem to be saying, 'therefore it must be attacked.' But since *d*, which the descriptivists affirm, entails the weaker thesis *d*', and this in turn entails *u*, it is impossible with consistency to affirm *d* and deny *u*. The major task of moral philosophy is to show how *p* and *u* are consistent. This task is not furthered by those who are so convinced that *d* is required as the basis of the rationality of morals that they reject out of hand *p*, because it is inconsistent with *d*; nor is it helped by those others who are so convinced of the truth of p that they reject u (which they wrongly think to be inconsistent with p). The subject will be understood when it is realized how p and u are both mutually consistent and jointly sufficient for establishing the rationality of morals; and that d is not only not necessary for this purpose, but actually prevents its realization, since it entails the abandonment of p, which, as we shall see, is an essential factor in moral arguments.

I shall argue shortly that a naturalist in particular cannot consistently deny the thesis of universalizability. But the non-natural descriptivist has, it must be allowed, a way of escape from this *argumentum ad hominem*. According to him, a word such as 'good', though descriptive, has meaning-rules which are logically independent of the meaning-rules of other, non-evaluative words. It is thus possible for him, if he wishes, to admit that moral judgements are, like other descriptive judgements, universalizable, but to admit this in such a trivial and innocuous way that he comes to no harm thereby, even if he wants at the same time to be, in substance, a particularist (if I may use that name for the opposite of a universalist). For suppose that we say to him: 'If you call X a good Y, you are committed to the judgement that anything which is like X in the relevant respects is also a good Y.' He can reply, 'Certainly; but the relevant respect is simply the possession of the *sui generis* non-natural property of goodness; an object might be like X in every other respect, and I could still refuse to call it a good Y if it had not got this property.'

Such a philosopher could indeed embrace, at any rate for all practical purposes, the extremest sort of particularism. He would be maintaining a thesis which is obviously false (for the reason given in LM 5.1ff.); but the argument which I have just put forward would not touch him. He could maintain a view similar in its effects to one attributed (wrongly, as we shall see) to the Existentialists by some of their British admirers: he could say that we have to examine every object in its uniqueness

for the property *goodness* and other moral properties; and that by attributing a moral property to one object we are not committed to attributing it to any other object, however similar in other respects. Of course, if we find another object possessing just this property, we shall have to say so; but since this property varies quite independently of the other, non-moral, properties, this commitment is the reverse of onerous. Everything that the particularist wishes to say can be said—in substance—in these old-fashioned terms without denying anything that I have established in this chapter, provided only that he sticks to non-naturalism.

There is, it is hardly necessary to point out, another kind of non-naturalist who thinks (quite correctly) that moral properties do *not* vary quite independently of non-moral properties, but are in some sense consequential or supervenient on them. *This* kind of non-naturalist will be, so far as the present argument goes, in the same position as the naturalists.

For the naturalist, the way of escape which I have just described is not open. For he is wedded to the view that when we apply a moral predicate to an object, we do so in virtue of a meaning-rule which lays it down that this predicate can be applied to objects of a certain kind; and that the question 'What kind?' is answered, not by pointing to a *sui generis* moral property, but by indicating *other*, non-moral, properties of the object (including perhaps negative properties—for the *absence* of properties may be as relevant as their presence). These are the properties which constitute *that* about the object which makes it a suitable subject for the application of this moral predicate. It follows that the kind of universalizability to which the naturalist is committed is not the relatively innocuous kind which, as we saw, the particularistically inclined non-naturalist can safely admit. For let us suppose that we are having the same argument as before, only with a particularist who wishes to be a naturalist. 'If you call X a good Y', we say to him, 'you are committed to the judgement that anything which is like X in the relevant respects is also a good Y'. He cannot, like the non-naturalist, while admitting this, claim that 'the relevant respects' are simply the possession of the *sui generis* non-natural property of goodness. They have to be, rather, some set of non-moral properties.

The effects, therefore, for the naturalist of his involvement in universalism are much more awkward for him, if he is inclined towards particularist views. For he is committed to the admission that, if he makes a moral judgement about one object, this must be in virtue of the possession by the object of certain non-moral features (*what* features is determined by the meaning-rule for the moral word in question); and that therefore any other object which possesses these features must also have the same moral judgement made about it. Thus it is quite impossible for a naturalist to be, consistently, any sort of particularist.

In the preceding paragraphs I have confined my attention, for the sake of simplicity, to the word 'good'. To avoid repetition, the reader who is in doubt as to whether the same remarks apply to other moral words is invited to go through the argument again, substituting other moral words for 'good', and confirming that it still carries conviction. For example, if 'right act' or 'wrong act' are substituted throughout for 'good object of a certain kind', all the same things can be said; and, in view of the very close connexion in meaning between 'ought' and 'right' and 'wrong', it will require only small modifications to carry through the same argument about 'ought'; this is clear from the fact that, for example, 'He ought not to do that' means the same as 'It would be wrong for him to do that'.

2.6. An illuminating way of approaching the thesis which I am maintaining (namely universal prescriptivism) is to look upon it as retaining what is sound in descriptivism (natural and non-natural), and adding to it an account of the other essential element in the meaning of moral judgements, the prescriptive. The truth in naturalism is that moral terms do indeed have descriptive meaning. It is not the only element in their meaning, and it is therefore misleading to refer to it, as do the naturalists, as *the* meaning of a moral term; but in virtue of possessing this descriptive meaning moral judgements are universalizable, and naturalism has the merit of implying this.

Another way of putting the point is this: both naturalism and my own view lay great stress on the fact that, when we make a moral judgement about something, we make it *because* of the possession by it of certain non-moral properties. Thus both views hold that moral judgements about particular things are made for reasons; and the notion of a reason, as always, brings with it the notion of a rule which lays down that something is a reason for something else. Both views, therefore, involve universalizability. The difference is that the naturalist thinks that the rule in question is a descriptive meaning-rule which exhausts the meaning of the moral term used; whereas in my own view the rule, though it is very analogous to a descriptive meaning-rule, and though, therefore, it is quite legitimate to speak of the 'descriptive meaning' of moral terms, does not exhaust their meaning. For a naturalist, therefore, the inference from a non-moral description of something to a moral conclusion about it is an inference whose validity is due solely to the meaning of the words in it. The rule permitting the inference would be simply the descriptive meaning-rule for the moral term used, and to accept such a rule would be simply to accept a meaning for the moral word. Conversely, if the meaning of the moral word be once understood, there can, for the naturalist, be no departing from the inference-rule; it is impossible to refuse the conclusion of the inference without altering the meaning of the word. But for me the position is different. Since the 'descriptive meaning' of moral terms does not exhaust their meaning, the other element in their meaning can make a difference to the logical behaviour of these terms in inferences. This is the point at issue in the controversy about whether an 'ought' can be derived from an 'is'.

2.7. It is now time, therefore, to ask what effect the introduction of the additional, prescriptive element in their meaning has upon the logical character of moral words.[2] I shall not try at this stage to define the word 'prescriptive'. Its meaning will not become clear until much later. But let us start by supposing that we have a word which carries the descriptive meaning of some value-word, but lacks its prescriptive meaning. Such a word would be, in its logical character, just like an ordinary descriptive word. To know how to use it, we should have to know to what kind of things it was properly applied, and no more. Now let us suppose that we try to *add* prescriptive meaning to such a word, thereby, according to my theory, recreating the original value-word. Let us, to take the same example as I used in *LM* 7.2, coin the word 'doog' to carry the descriptive meaning of the word 'good' as used in the sentence 'He is a good man', without its prescriptive meaning. Let us first notice, as before, that the statement '*X* is a doog man' will be universalizable. Anybody who makes it will be committed to the view that some man who was exactly like *X*, or like him in the relevant respects, would also be a doog man; and the relevant respects would be simply those which the descriptive meaning-rule for the word 'doog' specified.

Now what happens if we try to add prescriptive meaning to such a word? The inevitable consequence of such an addition is that the descriptive meaning-rule becomes more than a mere meaning-rule. Since our value-word 'good' is to be used with the same descriptive meaning as 'doog' the *content* of the rule will remain the same; but its logical character will change. The rule will still say that it is proper to apply the word 'good' to a certain kind of man; but in saying this (in enunciating the rule) we shall be doing more than specifying the meaning of the word. For in saying that it is proper to call a certain kind of man good (for example a man who feeds his children, does not beat his wife, &c.) we are not just explaining the meaning of a word; it is not mere verbal instruction that we are giving,

but something more: *moral* instruction. In learning that, of all kinds of man, *this* kind can be called good, our hearer will be learning something synthetic, a moral principle. It will be synthetic because of the added prescriptiveness of the word 'good'; in learning it, he will be learning, not merely to use a word in a certain way, but to commend, or prescribe for imitation, a certain kind of man. A man who wholeheartedly accepts such a rule is likely to *live*, not merely *talk*, differently from one who does not. Our descriptive meaning-rule has thus turned into a synthetic moral principle.

This change brings other consequences with it. To illustrate them, let us consider the context of the words' use in more detail. I have so far been assuming that the society which is using these expressions 'good man' and 'doog man' has very inflexible standards of human excellence, and that therefore no question arises of the descriptive meaning of either word changing. But in the real world standards of human excellence change (for example, on the wrongness of wife-beating);[3] and therefore, if the expression 'good man' is to be used (as it is) to express changing standards, its logical character has to be such as to allow for this. This is done by making the prescriptive meaning of the word primary, and its descriptive meaning secondary.

It is not *necessary* that a value-word should be treated in this way. There are other moral words whose prescriptive meaning is secondary to their descriptive: For example 'industrious' (*LM* 7.5), 'honest', and 'courageous'. Let us imagine a society which places a negative value upon industry; there seem to be such societies in the world, in which the industrious man is regarded as a mere nuisance. Such a society could never (if it spoke English) express its moral standards by using the word 'industrious', like us, for commending people, only with a totally different descriptive meaning—i.e. commending them for totally different qualities, for example that of doing as little work as possible. If they did that, we should say that they had changed *the meaning* of the English word 'industrious'. The descriptive meaning of 'industrious' is much too firmly attached to the word for this sort of thing to be allowed; these people would be much more likely to use the word in its normal descriptive meaning, but neutrally or pejoratively; i.e. to give it no, or an adverse, prescriptive meaning.

But it is not so mandatory, though it is possible, to treat the word 'good', like the word 'industrious', as one whose descriptive meaning is primary (*LM* 7.5). If we came to disapprove of industry, we should not stop calling the industrious man industrious; but, if we had previously called him a good man because, among other virtues, he was industrious, we should, if we came to disapprove of his industry very much, stop calling him good. This is because the commendation which is the prescriptive force of the word 'good' is more firmly attached to it than any part of its descriptive meaning; we should therefore be likely to keep the word 'good' as a prescriptive word (part of our vocabulary of commendation), and alter its descriptive meaning.

It is useful to have in our language both secondarily evaluative words like 'industrious' and primarily evaluative words like 'good'; and we should therefore be suspicious, if any philosopher seeks to persuade us that we ought in the interest of concreteness to neglect the study of words like 'good' and concentrate on words like 'industrious' and 'courageous'. The object of such a manœuvre might be to convince us that *all* moral words have their descriptive meaning irremovably attached to them; but, fortunately for the usefulness of moral language in expressing changing standards, this is not so. To take this line would be to give an account of moral language which is, so far as it goes, true, but not sufficiently general (in the sense in which Newtonian mechanics is not sufficiently general). The account would suffice for the moral language of an irrevocably closed society, in which a change in moral standards was unthinkable; but it does not do justice to the moral language of a society like our own, in which some people sometimes

think about ultimate moral questions, and in which, therefore, morality changes. Orwell's Newspeak in *1984* was a language so designed that in it dangerous thoughts could not be expressed. Much of Oldspeak is like this too—if we want, in the Southern States, to speak to a negro as an equal, we cannot do so by addressing him as a nigger; the word 'nigger' incapsulates the standards of the society, and, if we were confined to it, we could not break free of those standards. But fortunately we are not so confined; our language, as we have it, *can* be a vehicle for new ideas. . . .

3.1 I sought in the preceeding chapter to explain in what sense moral judgements are universalizable. The explanation may be summed up as follows: they are universalizable in just the same way as descriptive judgements are universalizable, namely the way which follows from the fact that both moral expressions and descriptive expressions have descriptive meaning; but in the case of moral judgements the universal rules which determine this descriptive meaning are not mere meaning-rules, but moral principles of substance. In this chapter, I am going to consider various other ways in which moral judgements might be said to be universal or universalizable—mainly in order to avoid future misinterpretation by indicating to which of these views I subscribe and to which I do not.

It is, first of all, most important to distinguish the logical thesis which I have been putting forward from various *moral* theses with which it is easy to confuse it. I said above that, because of universalizability, a person who makes a moral judgement commits himself, not merely to a meaning-rule, but to a substantial moral principle. The thesis of universalizability itself, however, is still a logical thesis. It is very important not to confuse the thesis of universalizability with the substantial moral principles to which, according to it, a person who makes a moral judgement commits himself.

By a 'logical' thesis I mean a thesis about the meanings of words, or dependent solely upon them. I have been maintaining that the meaning of the word 'ought' and other moral words is such that a person who uses them commits himself thereby to a universal rule. This is the thesis of universalizability. It is to be distinguished from *moral* views such as that everybody ought always to adhere to universal rules and govern all his conduct in accordance with them, or that one ought not to make exceptions in one's own favour. The logical thesis has, as we shall see, great potency in moral arguments; but for that very reason it is most important to make clear that it is no more than a logical thesis—for otherwise the objection will be made that a moral principle has been smuggled in disguised as a logical doctrine. In order to clarify this point I am going to take the two moral views just mentioned and show that they do not follow from the logical thesis, unless they themselves are interpreted in such a way as to be analytic (i.e. not to enjoin any one line of conduct rather than another). In the latter case, obviously, there would be no objection to deriving them from the logical thesis, because the accusation of smuggling in substantial moral principles could not then be raised.

3.2. Let us first consider the moral principle that everybody ought always to adhere to universal rules and govern all his conduct in accordance with them. The nature of this principle is best examined by asking what would constitute a breach of it. On one interpretation, it is impossible to break such a principle; for, given a description of a person's life, it is always, analytically, possible to find *some* universal rules according to which he has lived—if only the rule 'Live thus: . . .' followed by a minute description, in universal terms, of how he has lived.

To avoid this trivialization of the principle we are considering, let us stipulate that a man is not to be said to have *adhered* to a rule, nor to have *governed his conduct in accordance with* it, unless he has in some sense had the rule before his mind (at any rate from time to time) and unless his conduct has in some sense been motivated by the

desire to conform to it. Now on this interpretation, a man would be breaking the principle that everybody ought always to adhere to universal rules, and govern all his conduct in accordance with them, if he did something on some whim without considering any rule involved in the action. Does it follow from my logical thesis that such a person acts wrongly? Not in the least, it would seem; for the thesis does not say that a person who maintained that one ought always, in this man's circumstances, to act as he did, would be committing any logical fault, and still less does it say that the man himself is committing any *moral* fault. If, on a whim, I give a blind beggar a coin, this does not, according to the logical thesis of universalizability, stop my action being right; for it may be that one ought always to give alms to blind beggars—or even that one ought always to give alms to them without reflection. I do not wish to argue for or against such rules, but only to point out that they do not contravene my logical thesis. A person who acted thus without reflection could not, indeed, be thinking that this was the right thing to do; for that would involve consideration (in some sense) of a rule or principle; but he could do the right thing all the same. In the same way, one may use a word rightly without thinking whether it is the right word; but if one does think whether it is, one has thereby raised a question of principle: Is this the way the word is rightly used?

Offences against the thesis of universalizability are logical, not moral. If a person says 'I ought to act in a certain way, but nobody else ought to act in that way in relevantly similar circumstances', then, on my thesis, he is abusing the word 'ought'; he is implicitly contradicting himself. But the logical offence here lies in the *conjunction* of two moral judgements, not in either one of them by itself. The thesis of universalizability does not render self-contradictory any single, logically simple, moral judgement, or even moral principle, which is not already self-contradictory without the thesis; all it does is to force people to choose between judgements which cannot both be asserted without self-contradiction. And so no moral judgement or principle of substance follows from the thesis alone. Furthermore, a person may act, on a number of different occasions, in different ways, even if the occasions are qualitatively identical, without it following from the thesis that all, or that any particular one, of his actions must be wrong. The thesis does not even forbid us to say that *none* of the man's actions are wrong; for it is consistent with the thesis that the kinds of actions he did in the kind of situations described were morally indifferent. What the thesis does forbid us to do is to make different moral judgements about actions which we admit to be exactly or relevantly similar. The thesis tells us that this is to make two logically inconsistent judgements.

We might conceivably interpret the principle that one ought always to govern one's behaviour in accordance with universal rules as simply a denial, *en bloc*, of all such self-contradictory conjunctions of moral judgements. So interpreted, the principle becomes, like all denials of self-contradictions, analytic. It does not make much difference whether we say that it is a second-order statement about the logical properties of moral judgements, or that it is a first-order, but analytic, moral judgement. It could be put in either of these forms without substantially altering its character.

The same treatment can be given to the principle that one ought not to make exceptions in one's own favour. If this is interpreted merely as a denial that it can be the case that I ought to act in a certain way, but that others in relevantly similar circumstances ought not, then the principle is analytic (a repetition in other words of the logical thesis), and no moral judgement of substance follows from it. But if it is interpreted to mean that a man who acts in a certain way, while maintaining that others ought not so to act, is always *acting* wrongly, then not only is the principle synthetic, but most of us would dissent from

it; for the man may well be acting rightly, though the moral judgement that he makes about other people's actions is inconsistent with the judgement (if he makes it) that his own action is right. At any rate, the man's *action* cannot be a breach of the thesis of universalizability, although what he *says* may be; and this is what we should expect if, as I have been maintaining, it is a logical thesis and not a substantive moral principle.

I shall not go into detail concerning other possible moral principles which might be confused with the thesis of universalizability. Two famous ones may, however, be just mentioned. The first is the 'Golden Rule', if put in the form of a moral principle: One ought to treat others as one would wish them to treat oneself. If this were rewritten to read '. . . as others *ought* to treat oneself', then the same sort of account can be given of it as of the principles we have just discussed. By suitable interpretation, it can be made analytically true according to the universalist thesis; on other interpretations it becomes synthetic, but does not then follow from the thesis. If the word 'wish' is left in, the principle is obviously synthetic, and equally obviously does not follow from the thesis.

The second principle which may be mentioned is the Kantian one, which we may put in the form 'I ought never to act except in such a way that I can also will that my maxim should become a universal law'.[4] This, too, is capable of different interpretations; but it will be wisest, in a book of this character, while acknowledging a very great debt to Kant, to avoid becoming entangled in the spider's web of Kantian exegesis. If Kant is interpreted as meaning that a man who says that he ought to act in a certain way, but says 'Let others not act in this same way', is guilty of an implicit contradiction, then the Kantian principle is a way of stating a consequence of the logical thesis of universalizability. In this interpretation, *willing* (which is one of Kant's most elusive notions) is treated as roughly equivalent to *assenting to an imperative*, in the sense, not itself entirely clear, of *LM* 2.2. There is also a problem about the word 'can'; what I should wish to say about this will become apparent later). But it is a difficult enough task to make my own views clear to the reader, without trying to do the same for Kant's.

In general, I may anticipate my future argument by saying this: it looks at first sight as if we have a choice between two positions: (1) that the thesis of universalizability is itself a moral principle and therefore can have substantial moral consequences; and (2) that it is only a logical principle from which nothing of moral substance can follow, and that therefore it is useless for purposes of moral reasoning. It is the last clause ('it is useless . . .') which is here mistaken. Later, I shall try to show that, though the thesis is not a substantial moral principle but a logical one, and though, therefore, nothing moral follows from it by itself, it is capable of very powerful employment in moral argument when combined with other premisses. So the dilemma is a false one—though this has not prevented its being often used.

3.3. Having made it clear that universalism, as I am maintaining it, is a logical and not a moral thesis, I shall now try to remove certain sources of confusion as to its precise import. First of all, it may very well be asked whether this is a doctrine about *moral* uses of words only, or whether it is a doctrine about evaluative words in general.[5] The answer which I wish to give to this question is a somewhat complicated one, since we have to steer between at least two errors. It is a doctrine about evaluative words in general, but one which requires careful qualification. If we take as an example the word 'ought', it seems to me that, whatever the type of 'ought'-judgement that is being made (moral, aesthetic, technical, &c.) the judgement is universalizable.

This is one reason why the word 'ought' cannot be used in making legal judgements; if a person has a certain legal obligation, we cannot express this by saying that he *ought* to do such and such a thing, for the reason that 'ought'-judgements have

to be universalizable, which, in the strict sense, legal judgements are not. The reason why they are not is that a statement of law always contains an implicit reference to a particular jurisdiction; 'It is illegal to marry one's own sister' means, implicitly, 'It is illegal in (e.g.) England to marry one's own sister'. But 'England' is here a singular term, which prevents the whole proposition being universal; nor is it universalizable, in the sense of committing the speaker to the view that such a marriage would be illegal in any country that was otherwise like England. It is therefore impossible to use 'ought' in such a statement. The moral judgement that one *ought* not to marry one's sister is, however, universal; it implies no reference to a particular legal system.

It is even more necessary to distinguish 'ought'-judgements from ordinary *imperatives* in respect of universalizability. If, when the squad gets to the end of the parade-ground, the serjeant says 'Left wheel', this does not commit him (on pain of being accused of having changed his mind) to giving the same order, rather than 'Right wheel', on similar occasions in the future. But if, in a tactical exercise, the instructor says 'The situation being what it is, you ought to attack on the left', he will have changed his mind if, the next time this same exercise is gone through with a new group of cadets, he says 'The situation being what it is, you ought to attack on the right'. By 'changed his mind', I mean 'said something which is inconsistent with what he said before'.

Though, however, some philosophers have gone much too far in assimilating 'ought'-judgements (of all sorts) to simple imperatives, it may be that some people do sometimes use the word 'ought' when they should more properly have used a plain imperative, in order to give an instruction without any thought of reasons or grounds. Plain imperatives do not *have* to have reasons or grounds, though they normally do have; but 'ought'-judgements, strictly speaking, would be being misused if the demand for reasons or grounds were thought of as out of place—though the reasons need not be ulterior ones; some universal moral judgements already incorporate all the reasons they need or can have (*LM* 4.4).

Nevertheless, it may be that there is a debased use of 'ought' in which it is equivalent to a simple imperative (though I must confess that I have come across such a use only in the writings of philosophers). Just in case, however, there is such a use, it is convenient to put the matter in the following way: in by far the majority of judgements containing the word 'ought', it has the sense that requires them to be universalizable; there *may* be some peripheral cases where it does not have this sense; but at any rate in its *moral* uses (with which we are chiefly concerned) it always does. The word 'moral' plays here a far smaller role than I was at one time tempted to assign to it. It is the logic of the word 'ought' in its typical uses that requires universalizability, not that of the word 'moral'; the word 'moral' needs to be brought in only in order to identify one class of the typical uses, and that with which as moral philosophers we are most concerned. This means that the ambiguity of the word 'moral', which is notorious, need not worry us at this point. For in whichever of its current senses the word is being used, it suffices to exclude those peripheral uses of 'ought' (if they exist), in which it is not universalizable.

3.4. I now turn to the most serious of the misinterpretations to which universalism is subject. It is common to hear objection made to it on the ground that it implies that there are certain rather simple general moral principles which, in some unexplained sense, *exist* antecedently to the making of any moral judgement, and that all we have to do whenever we make such a judgement is to consult the relevant principle and, without more ado, the judgement is made. Such a doctrine would be that of a very hidebound moralist, whose moral principles were a set of copy-book headings.[6] This account of the matter differs from that which I wish to give in a number of respects. First of all, it is not

clear what is meant in this context by speaking of moral principles 'existing'; but even if they (in some sense) exist, I am sure that they do not always exist *antecedently*, so that all we have to do is to consult them. This is made sufficiently clear by considering almost any case of serious moral perplexity—for example Sartre's well-known case of the young man who was in doubt whether to join the Free French forces or to stay and look after his widowed mother.[7] Sartre uses the example in order to make the point that in such cases no antecedently 'existing' principle can be appealed to (*qui peut en decider a priori; aucune morale inscrite ne peut le dire*).[8] We have to consider the particular case and make up our minds what are its morally relevant features, and what, taking these features into account ought to be done in such a case. Nevertheless, when we do make up our minds, it is about a matter of principle which has a bearing outside the particular case. Sartre himself is as much of a universalist as I am, in the sense in which I am, to judge by the little book in which this example occurs.[9] He has also on occasion himself given his public support to universal moral principles.[10]

Secondly, the principles which are adhered to in making moral judgements are seldom very simple or general, at any rate when the judgements are made by intelligent people who have had any wide experience of life. It is most important here to distinguish between what may be called *universality* and *generality*, although these terms are often enough used interchangeably. The opposite of 'general' is 'specific'; the opposite of 'universal' is 'singular'—though the existence of the term 'particular', contrasted with both 'universal' and 'singular', introduces complications into which we do not need to enter. It will suffice for our purposes if we explain the terms informally in the following way. It will be remembered that we explained the notion of universalizability by reference to the term 'descriptive meaning'. Any judgement which has descriptive meaning must be universalizable, because the descriptive meaning-rules which determine this meaning are universal rules. But they are not necessarily general rules. A descriptive meaning-rule says that we can use a certain predicate of anything of a certain kind. And it is obvious that in the case of some descriptive predicates we shall have to go into a great deal of detail in order to specify what kind—if indeed this is formulable in words at all. Let the reader try specifying exactly what he means by a word like 'primitive', even in some particular context, and he will see what I mean. He will find that in order to distinguish it from other words such as 'archaic', 'unsophisticated', &c., he will have to enter into a great deal of detail, and may end up by having recourse to examples. Yet these are properly universal predicates. Other expressions create somewhat different difficulties owing to their complexity; in order to define the word 'barquentine' it is no use saying that it is a kind of vessel, nor even a kind of sailing-vessel; 'barquentine' is a very much less *general* term than 'vessel'; yet both are, equally, *universal* terms. Now universalism is not the doctrine that behind every moral judgement there has to lie a principle expressible in a few general terms; the principle, though universal, may be so complex that it defies formulation in words at all. But if it were formulated and specified, all the terms used in its formulation would be universal terms.

If I make a moral judgement about something, it must be because of some feature of the thing; but this feature may be one which requires much detail for its specification. It must be noticed that generality and specificity are, unlike universality and singularity, matters of degree. This enables us to put the difference between the two pairs of terms quite simply by means of examples. The moral principle 'One ought never to make false statements' is highly general; the moral principle 'One ought never to make false statements to one's wife' is much more specific. But both are universal; the second one forbids *anyone* who is married to make false statements to

his wife. It should be clear from these explanations that the thesis of universalizability does not require moral judgements to be made on the basis of highly general moral principles of the copy-book-heading type. As I explained in *LM* 3.6, ... our moral development, as we grow older, consists in the main in making our moral principles more and more specific, by writing into them exceptions and qualifications to cover kinds of case of which we have had experience. In the case of most people they soon become too complicated to admit of formulation, and yet give tolerably clear guidance in familiar situations. It is, indeed, always possible for a situation to arise which calls for a qualification of the principle; but, unless a person is plunged suddenly into an environment quite different to that in which he has grown up, this is likely to happen less and less as he grows older, because the situations which he encounters will more often resemble ones which he has encountered, and thought morally about, before.

Notes

1. *Aristotelian Society*, lv (1954/5), 307.
2. It must be emphasized that it is not part of my thesis that moral words are used prescriptively *in all contexts*; and it makes sense to call them 'moral' even when they are not so used. But on the prescriptive uses the other uses depend (LM 7.5, 9.3, 11.3). 'Prescriptive' is to be understood here in a wide sense to include permissions. Thus, the statement that an act is morally permissable is in this sense prescriptive. The logical relations between prescriptions and permissions are too complex to be dealt with here.
3. See G. M. Trevelyan, *English Social History*, p. 65: 'But the "lordship" was held [in the fifteenth century] to be vested in the husband, and when he asserted it by fist and stick, he was seldom blamed by public opinion.'

4. Kant, *Groundwork of the Metaphysic of Morals*, 2nd ed., p. 17 (tr. H. J. Paton, p. 70).

5. I must admit that what I said on this point in *Aristotelian Society*, lv (1954/5), 298, was worse than misleading.

6. See further *Aristotelian Society*, lv (1954/5), 309 f.

7. J.-P. Sartre, *L'Existentialisme est un Humanisme* (1946), pp. 39 ff. (tr. in W. Kaufmann, ed., *Existentialism*, pp. 295 f.).

8. Op. cit., p42 (Kaufmann, p. 296); cf. p. 47 (Kaufmann, p. 298), where the point is the same.

9. Cf. op. cit., pp. 31–32, 70–78 (Kaufmann, pp. 293, 304–6): 'I bear the responsibility of the choice which, in committing myself, also commits the whole of humanity'; 'In this sense we may say that there is a human universality, but it is not something given; it is being perpetually made'; '[The young man] was obliged to invent *the law* for himself' (my italics).

10. See *The Times*, 21 Sept. 1960, p. 10.

8 / PHILIPPA FOOT

Moral Beliefs

To many people it seems that the most notable advance in moral philosophy during the past 50 years or so has been the refutation of naturalism; and they are a little shocked that at this late date such an issue should be reopened. It is easy to understand their attitude: given certain apparently unquestionable assumptions, it would be about as sensible to try to reintroduce naturalism as to try to square the circle. Those who see it like this have satisfied themselves that they know in advance that any naturalistic theory must have a catch in it somewhere, and are put out at having to waste more time exposing an old fallacy. This paper is an attempt to persuade them to look critically at the premisses on which their arguments are based.

It would not be an exaggeration to say that the whole of moral philosophy, as it is now widely taught, rests on a contrast between statements of fact and evaluations, which runs something like this: "The truth or falsity of statements of fact is shewn by means of evidence; and what counts as evidence is laid down in the meaning of the expressions occurring in the statement of fact. (For instance, the meaning of 'round' and 'flat' made Magellan's voyages evidence for the roundness rather than the flatness of the Earth; someone who went on questioning whether the evidence was evidence could eventually be shewn to have made some linguistic mistake.) It follows that no two people can make the same

Reprinted by permission of the publisher and copyright holder from *Proceedings of the Aristotelian Society* 59 (1958–59): 83–104.

statement and count completely different things as evidence; in the end one at least of them could be convicted of linguistic ignorance. It also follows that if a man is given good evidence for a factual conclusion he cannot just refuse to accept the conclusion on the ground that in his scheme of things this evidence is not evidence at all. With evaluations, however, it is different. An evaluation is not connected logically with the factual statements on which it is based. One man may say that a thing is good because of some fact about it, and another may refuse to take that fact as any evidence at all, for nothing is laid down in the meaning of 'good' which connects it with one piece of 'evidence' rather than another. It follows that a moral eccentric could argue to moral conclusions from quite idiosyncratic premisses; he could say, for instance, that a man was a good man because he clasped and unclasped his hands, and never turned N.N.E. after turning S.S.W. He could also reject someone else's evaluation simply by denying that his evidence was evidence at all.

"The fact about 'good' which allows the eccentric still to use this term without falling into a morass of meaninglessness, is its 'action-guiding' or 'practical' function. This it retains; for like everyone else he considers himself bound to choose the things he calls 'good' rather than those he calls 'bad'. Like the rest of the world he uses 'good' in connexion only with a 'pro-attitude'; it is only that he has pro-attitudes to quite different things, and therefore calls them good."

There are here two assumptions about

'evaluations', which I will call assumption (1) and assumption (2).

Assumption (1) is that some individual may, without logical error, base his beliefs about matters of value entirely on premises which no one else would recognise as giving any evidence at all. Assumption (2) is that, given the kind of statement which other people regard as evidence for an evaluative conclusion, he may refuse to draw the conclusion because *this* does not count as evidence for *him*.

Let us consider assumption (1). We might say that this depends on the possibility of keeping the meaning of 'good' steady through all changes in the facts about anything which are to count in favour of its goodness. (I do not mean, of course, that a man can make changes as fast as he chooses; only that, whatever he has chosen, it will not be possible to rule him out of order.) But there is a better formulation, which cuts out trivial disputes about the meaning which 'good' happens to have in some section of the community. Let us say that the assumption is that the evaluative function of 'good' can remain constant through changes in the evaluative principle; on this ground it could be said that even if no one can call a man *good* because he clasps and unclasps his hands, he can commend him or express his *pro-attitude* towards him, and if necessary can invent a new moral vocabulary to express his unusual moral code.

Those who hold such a theory will naturally add several qualifications. In the first place, most people now agree with Hare, against Stevenson, that such words as 'good' only apply to individual cases through the application of general principles, so that even the extreme moral eccentric must accept principles of commendation. In the second place 'commending', 'having a pro-attitude', and so on, are supposed to be connected with doing and choosing, so that it would be impossible to say, *e.g.*, that a man was a good man only if he lived for a thousand years. The range of evaluation is supposed to be restricted to the range of possible action and choice.

I am not here concerned to question these supposed restrictions on the use of evaluative terms, but only to argue that they are not enough.

The crucial question is this. Is it possible to extract from the meaning of words such as 'good' some element called 'evaluative meaning' which we can think of as externally related to its objects? Such an element would be represented, for instance, in the rule that when any action was 'commended' the speaker must hold himself bound to accept an imperative 'let me do these things'. This is externally related to its object because, within the limitation which we noticed earlier, to possible actions, it would make sense to think of anything as the subject of such 'commendation'. On this hypothesis a moral eccentric could be described as commending the clasping of hands as the action of a good man, and we should not have to look for some background to give the supposition sense. That is to say, on this hypothesis the clasping of hands could be commended without any explanation; it could be what those who hold such theories call 'an ultimate moral principle'.

I wish to say that this hypothesis is untenable, and that there is no describing the evaluative meaning of 'good', evaluation, commending, or anything of the sort, without fixing the object to which they are supposed to be attached. Without first laying hands on the proper object of such things as evaluation, we shall catch in our net either something quite different such as accepting an order or making a resolution, or else nothing at all.

Before I consider this question, I shall first discuss some other mental attitudes and beliefs which have this internal relation to their object. By this I hope to clarify the concept of internal relation to an object, and incidentally, if my examples arouse resistance, but are eventually accepted, to show how easy it is to overlook an internal relation where it exists.

Consider, for instance, pride.

People are often surprised at the suggestion that there are limits to the things a man can be proud of, about which indeed he can feel pride. I do not know quite what account they want to give of pride; perhaps something to do with smiling and walking with a jaunty air, and holding an object up where other people can see it; or perhaps they think that pride is a kind of internal sensation, so that one might naturally beat one's breast and say 'pride is something I feel *here*'. The difficulties of the second view are well known; the logically private object cannot be what a name in the public language is the name of.[1] The first view is the more plausible, and it may seem reasonable to say that given certain behaviour a man can be described as showing that he is proud of something, whatever that something may be. In one sense this is true, and in another sense not. Given any description of an object, action, personal characteristic, etc., it is not possible to rule it out as an object of pride. Before we can do so we need to know what would be said about it by the man who is to be proud of it, or feels proud of it; but if he does not hold the right beliefs about it then whatever his attitude is it is not pride. Consider, for instance, the suggestion that someone might be proud of the sky or the sea: he looks at them and what he feels is *pride*, or he puffs out his chest and gestures with *pride* in their direction. This makes sense only if a special assumption is made about his beliefs, for instance, that he is under some crazy delusion and believes that he has saved the sky from falling, or the sea from drying up. The characteristic object of pride is something seen (*a*) as in some way a man's own, and (*b*) as some sort of achievement or advantage; without this object pride cannot be described. To see that the second condition is necessary, one should try supposing that a man happens to feel proud because he has laid one of his hands on the other, three times in an hour. Here again the supposition that it is pride that he feels will make perfectly good sense if a special background is filled in. Perhaps he is ill, and it is an achievement even to do this; perhaps this gesture has some religious or political significance, and he is a brave man who will so defy the gods or the rulers.

But with no special background there can be no pride, not because no one could psychologically speaking feel pride in such a case, but because whatever he did feel could not logically be pride. Of course, people can see strange things as achievements, though not just anything, and they can identify themselves with remote ancestors, and relations, and neighbours, and even on occasions with Mankind. I do not wish to deny there are many far-fetched and comic examples of pride.

We could have chosen many other examples of mental attitudes which are internally related to their object in a similar way. For instance, fear is not just trembling, and running, and turning pale; without the thought of some menacing evil no amount of this will add up to fear. Nor could anyone be said to feel dismay about something he did not see as bad; if his thoughts about it were that it was altogether a good thing, he could not say that (oddly enough) what he felt about it was dismay. "How odd, I feel dismayed when I ought to be pleased" is the prelude to a hunt for the adverse aspect of the thing, thought of as lurking behind the pleasant façade. But someone may object that pride and fear and dismay are feelings or emotions and therefore not a proper analogy for 'commendation', and there will be an advantage in considering a different kind of example. We could discuss, for instance, the belief that a certain thing is dangerous, and ask whether this could logically be held about anything whatsoever. Like 'this is good', 'this is dangerous' is an assertion, which we should naturally accept or reject by speaking of its truth or falsity; we seem to support such statements with evidence, and moreover there may seem to be a 'warning function' connected with the word 'dangerous' as there is supposed to be a 'commending function' connected with the word 'good'. For suppose that philosophers, puzzled about the property of dangerousness, decided that the word did not stand for a property at all, but was essentially a practical or action-guiding term, used for *warning*. Unless used in an 'inverted comma sense' the word 'dangerous' was used to warn, and this meant that anyone using it in such a sense committed himself to avoiding the things he called dangerous, to preventing other people from going near them, and perhaps to running in the opposite direction. If the conclusion were not obviously ridiculous, it would be easy to infer that a man whose application of the term was different from ours throughout might say that the oddest things were dangerous without fear of disproof; the idea would be that he could still be described as 'thinking them dangerous', or at least as 'warning', because by his attitude and actions he would have fulfilled the conditions for these things. This is nonsense because without its proper object *warning*, like *believing dangerous*, will not be there. It is logically impossible to warn about anything not thought of as threatening evil, and for danger we need a particular kind of serious evil such as injury or death.

There are, however, some differences between thinking a thing dangerous and feeling proud, frightened or dismayed. When a man says that something is dangerous he must support his statement with a special kind of evidence; but when he says that he feels proud or frightened or dismayed the description of the object of his pride or fright or dismay does not have quite this relation to his original statement. If he is shewn that the thing he was proud of was not his after all, or was not after all anything very grand, he may have to say that his pride was not justified, but he will not have to take back the statement that he was proud. On the other hand, someone who says that a thing is dangerous, and later sees that he made a mistake in thinking that an injury might result from it, has to go back on his original statement and admit that he was wrong. In neither case, however, is the speaker able to go on as before. A man who discovered that it was not his pumpkin but someone else's which had won the prize could only say that he still felt proud, if he could produce some other ground for pride. It is in this way that even feelings are logically vulnerable to facts.

It will probably be objected against these examples that for part of the way at least they beg the question. It will be said that indeed a man can only be proud of something he thinks a good action, or an achievement, or a sign of noble birth; as he can only feel dismay about something which he sees as bad, frightened at some threatened evil; similarly he can only warn if he is also prepared to speak, for instance, of injury. But this will only limit the range of possible objects of those attitudes and beliefs if the range of these terms is limited in its turn. To meet this objection I shall discuss the meaning of 'injury' because this is the simplest case. Anyone who feels inclined to say that anything could be counted as an achievement, or as the evil of which people were afraid, or about which they felt dismayed, should just try this out. I wish to consider the proposition that anything could be thought of as dangerous, because if it causes injury it is dangerous, and anything could be counted as an injury. I shall consider bodily injury because this is the injury connected with danger; it is not correct to put up a notice by the roadside reading 'Danger!' on account of bushes which might scratch a car. Nor can a substance be labelled 'dangerous' on the ground that it can injure delicate fabrics; although we can speak of the danger that it may do so, that is not the use of the word which I am considering here.

When a body is injured it is changed for the worse in a special way, and we want to know which changes count as injuries. First of all, it matters how an injury comes about; *e.g.*, it cannot be caused by natural decay. Then it seems clear that not just any kind of thing will do, for instance, any unusual mark on the body, however much trouble a man might take to have it removed. By far the most important class of injuries are injuries to a part of the body, counting as injuries because there is interference with the function of that part; injury to a leg, an eye, an ear, a hand, a muscle, the heart, the brain, the spinal cord. An injury to an eye is one that affects, or is likely to affect, its sight; an injury to a hand one which makes it less well able to reach out and grasp, and perform other operations of this kind. A leg can be injured because its movements and supporting power can be affected; a lung because it can become too weak to draw in the proper amount of air. We are most ready to speak of an injury where the function of a part of the body is to perform a characteristic operation, as in these examples. We might hesitate to say that a skull can be injured, and might prefer to speak of damage to it, since although there is indeed a function (a protective function) there is no operation. But thinking of the protective function of the skull we may want to speak of injury here. In so far as the concept of *injury* depends on that of *function* it is narrowly limited, since not even every use to which a part of the body is put will count as its function. Why is it that, even if it is the means by which they earn their living, we would never consider the removal of the dwarf's hump or the bearded lady's beard as a bodily injury? It will be tempting to say that these things are disfigurements, but this is not the point; if we suppose that a man who had some invisible extra muscle made his living as a court jester by waggling his ears, the ear would not have been injured if this were made to disappear. If it were natural to men to communicate by movements of the ear, then ears would have the function of signalling (we have no word for this kind of 'speaking') and an impairment of this function would be an injury; but things are not like this. This court jester would use his ears to make people laugh, but this is not the function of ears.

No doubt many people will feel impatient when such facts are mentioned, because they think that it is quite unimportant that this or that *happens* to be the case, and it seems to them arbitrary that the loss of the beard, the hump, or the ear muscle would not be called an injury. Isn't the loss of that by which one makes one's living a pretty catastrophic loss? Yet it seems quite natural that these are not counted as injuries if one thinks about the conditions of human life, and contrasts the loss of a spe-

cial ability to make people gape or laugh with the ability to see, hear, walk, or pick things up. The first is only needed for one very special way of living; the other in any foreseeable future for any man. This restriction seems all the more natural when we observe what other threats besides that of injury can constitute danger: of death, for instance, or mental derangement. A shock which could cause mental instability or impairment of memory would be called dangerous, because a man needs such things as intelligence, memory, and concentration as he needs sight or hearing or the use of hands. Here we do not speak of injury unless it is possible to connect the impairment with some physical change, but we speak of danger because there is the same loss of a capacity which any man needs.

There can be injury outside the range we have been considering; for a man may sometimes be said to have received injuries where no part of his body has had its function interfered with. In general, I think that any blow which disarranged the body in such a way that there was lasting pain would inflict an injury, even if no other ill resulted, but I do not know of any other important extension of the concept.

It seems therefore that since the range of things which can be called injuries is quite narrowly restricted, the word 'dangerous' is restricted in so far as it is connected with injury. We have the right to say that a man cannot decide to call just anything dangerous, however much he puts up fences and shakes his head.

So far I have been arguing that such things as pride, fear, dismay, and the thought that something is dangerous have an internal relation to their object, and hope that what I mean is becoming clear. Now we must consider whether those attitudes or beliefs which are the moral philosopher's study are similar, or whether such things as 'evaluation' and 'thinking something good' and 'commendation' could logically be found in combination with any object whatsoever. All I can do here is to give an example which may make this suggestion seem implausible, and to knock away a few of its supports. The example will come from the range of trivial and pointless actions such as we were considering in speaking of the man who clasped his hands three times an hour, and we can point to the oddity of the suggestion that this can be called a good action. We are bound by the terms of our question to refrain from adding any special background, and it should be stated once more that the question is about what can count in favor of the goodness or badness of a man or an action, and not what could be, or be thought, good or bad with a special background. I believe that the view I am attacking often seems plausible only because the special background is surreptitiously introduced.

Someone who said that clasping the hands three times in an hour was a good action would first have to answer the question 'How do you mean?' For the sentence 'this is a good action' is not one which has a clear meaning. Presumably, since our subject is moral philosophy, it does not here mean 'that was a good thing to do' as this might be said of a man who had done something sensible in the course of any enterprise whatever; we are to confine our attention to 'the moral use of "good"'. I am not clear that it makes sense to speak of 'a moral use of "good"', but we can pick out a number of cases which raise moral issues. It is because these are so diverse and because 'this is a good action' does not pick out any one of them, that we must ask 'How do you mean?' For instance, some things that are done fulfil a duty, such as the duty of parents to children or children to parents. I suppose that when philosophers speak of good actions they would include these. Some come under the heading of a virtue such as charity, and they will be included too. Others again are actions which require the virtues of courage or temperance, and here the moral aspect is due to the fact that they are done in spite of fear or the temptation of pleasure; they must indeed be done for the sake of some real or fancied good, but not necessarily what philosophers would want to call a moral good. Courage is not *particularly* concerned with saving other people's lives, or temperance with leaving them their share of the food and drink, and the goodness of *what is done* may here be all kinds of usefulness. It is because there are these very diverse cases included (I suppose) under the expression 'a good action' that we should refuse to consider applying it without asking what is meant, and we should now ask what is intended when someone is supposed to say that 'clasping the hands three times in an hour is a good action'. Is it supposed that this action fulfils a duty? Then in virtue of what does a man have this duty, and to whom does he owe it? We have promised not to slip in a special background, but he cannot possibly have a *duty* to clasp his hands unless such a background exists. Nor could it be an act of charity, for it is not thought to do anyone any good, nor again a gesture of humility unless a special assumption turns it into this. The action could be courageous, but only if it were done both in the face of fear and for the sake of a good, and we are not allowed to put in special circumstances which could make this the case.

I am sure that the following objection will now be raised. "Of course clasping one's hands three times in an hour cannot be brought under one of the virtues which we recognise, but that is only to say that it is not a good action by our current moral code. It is logically possible that in a quite different moral code quite different virtues should be recognised, for which we have not even got a name." I cannot answer this objection properly, for that would need a satisfactory account of the concept of a virtue. But anyone who thinks it would be easy to describe a new virtue connected with clasping the hands three times in an hour should just try. I think he will find that he has to cheat, and suppose that in the community concerned the clasping of hands has been given some special significance, or is thought to have some special effect. The difficulty is obviously connected with the fact that without a special background there is no possibility of answering the question 'What's the point?' It is no good saying that there would be a point in doing the action because the action was a morally good action: the question is how it can be given any such description if we cannot first speak about the point. And it is just as crazy to suppose that we can call *anything* the point of doing something without having to say what the point of *that* is. In clasping one's hands one may make a slight sucking noise, but what is the point of that? It is surely clear that moral virtues must be connected with human good and harm, and that it is quite impossible to call anything you like good or harm. Consider, for instance, the suggestion that a man might say he had been harmed because a bucket of water had been taken out of the sea. As usual it would be possible to think up circumstances in which this remark would make sense; for instance, when coupled with a belief in magical influences; but then the harm would consist in what was done by the evil spirits, not in the taking of the water from the sea. It would be just as odd if someone were supposed to say that harm had been done to him because the hairs of his head had been reduced to an even number.[2]

I conclude that assumption (1) is very dubious indeed, and that no one should be allowed to speak as if we can understand 'evaluation' 'commendation' or 'pro-attitude', whatever the actions concerned.

II.

I propose now to consider what was called Assumption (2), which said that a man might always refuse to accept the conclusion of an argument about values, because what counted as evidence for other people did not count for him. Assumption (2) could be true even if Assumption (1) were false, for it might be that once a particular question of values—say a moral question—had been accepted, any disputant was bound to accept particular pieces of evidence as relevant, the same pieces as every-

one else, but that he could always refuse to draw any moral conclusions whatsoever or to discuss any questions which introduced moral terms. Nor do we mean 'he might refuse to draw the conclusion' in the trivial sense in which anyone can perhaps refuse to draw *any* conclusion; the point is that any statement of value always seems to go beyond any statement of fact, so that he might have a reason for accepting the factual premises but refusing to accept the evaluative conclusion. That this is so seems to those who argue in this way to follow from the practical implications of evaluation. When a man uses a word such as 'good' in an 'evaluative' and not an 'inverted comma' sense, he is supposed to commit his will. From this it has seemed to follow inevitably that there is a logical gap between fact and value; for is it not one thing to say that a thing is so, and another to have a particular attitude towards its being so; one thing to see that certain effects will follow from a given action, and another to care? Whatever account was offered of the essential feature of evaluation—whether in terms of feelings, attitudes, the acceptance of imperatives or what not—the fact remained that with an evaluation there was a committal in a new dimension, and that this was not guaranteed by any acceptance of facts.

I shall argue that this view is mistaken; that the practical implication of the use of moral terms has been put in the wrong place, and that if it is described correctly the logical gap between factual premises and moral conclusion disappears.

In this argument it will be useful to have as a pattern the practical or 'action-guiding' force of the word 'injury', which is in some, though not all, ways similar to that of moral terms. It is clear I think that an injury is necessarily something bad and therefore something which as such anyone always has a reason to avoid, and philosophers will therefore be tempted to say that anyone who uses 'injury' in its full 'action-guiding' sense commits himself to avoiding the things he calls injuries. They will then be in the usual difficulties about the man who says he knows he ought to do something but does not intend to do it; perhaps also about weakness of the will. Suppose that instead we look again at the kinds of things which count as injuries, to see if the connexion with the will does not start here. As has been shown, a man is injured whenever some part of his body, in being damaged, has become less well able to fulfil its ordinary function. It follows that he suffers a disability, or is liable to do so; with an injured hand he will be less well able to pick things up, hold on to them, tie them together or chop them up, and so on. With defective eyes there will be a thousand other things he is unable to do, and in both cases we should naturally say that he will often be unable to get what he wants to get or avoid what he wants to avoid.

Philosophers will no doubt seize on the word 'want', and say that if we suppose that a man happens to want the things which an injury to his body prevents him from getting, we have slipped in a supposition about a 'pro-attitude' already; and that anyone who does not happen to have these wants can still refuse to use 'injury' in its prescriptive, or 'action-guiding' sense. And so it may seem that the only way to make a *necessary* connexion between 'injury' and the things that are to be avoided, is to say that it is only used in an 'action-guiding sense' when applied to something the speaker intends to avoid. But we should look carefully at the crucial move in that argument, and query the suggestion that someone might happen not to want anything for which he would need the use of hands or eyes. Hands and eyes, like ears and legs, play a part in so many operations that a man could only be said not to need them if he had no wants at all. That such people exist, in asylums, is not to the present purpose at all; the proper use of his limbs is something a man has reason to want if he wants anything.

I do not know just what someone who denies this proposition could have in mind. Perhaps he is thinking of changing the facts of human existence, so that merely wishing, or the sound of the voice, will bring the world to heel? More likely he is proposing to rig the circumstances of some individual's existence within the framework of the ordinary world, by supposing for instance that he is a prince whose servants will sow and reap and fetch and carry for him, and so use their hands and eyes in his service that he will not need the use of his. Let us suppose that such a story could be told about a man's life; it is wildly implausible, but let us pretend that it is not. It is clear that in spite of this we could say that any man had a reason to shun injury; for even if at the end of his life it could be said that by a strange set of circumstances he had never needed the use of his eyes, or his hands this could not possibly be foreseen. Only by once more changing the facts of human existence, and supposing every vicissitude foreseeable, could such a supposition be made.

This is not to say that an injury might not bring more incidental gain than necessary harm; one has only to think of times when the order has gone out that able-bodied men are to be put to the sword. Such a gain might even, in some peculiar circumstances, be reliably foreseen, so that a man would have even better reason for seeking than for avoiding injury. In this respect the word 'injury' differs from terms such as 'injustice'; the practical force of 'injury' means only that anyone has *a* reason to avoid injuries, not that he has an overriding reason to do so.

It will be noticed that this account of the 'action-guiding force of 'injury' links it with reasons for acting rather than with actually doing something. I do not think, however, that this makes it a less good pattern for the 'action-guiding' force of moral terms. Philosophers who have supposed that actual action was required if 'good' were to be used in a sincere evaluation have got into difficulties over weakness of will, and they should surely agree that enough has been done if we can show that any man has reason to aim at virtue and avoid vice. But is this impossibly difficult if we consider the kinds of things that count as virtue and vice? Consider, for instance, the cardinal virtues, prudence, temperance, courage and justice. Obviously any man needs prudence, but does he not also need to resist the temptation of pleasure when there is harm involved? And how could it be argued that he would never need to face what was fearful for the sake of some good? It is not obvious what someone would mean if he said that temperance or courage were not good qualities, and this not because of the 'praising' sense of these *words*, but because of the things that courage and temperance are.

I should like to use these examples to show the artificiality of the notions of 'commendation' and of 'pro-attitudes' as these are commonly employed. Philosophers who talk about these things will say that after the facts have been accepted—say that X is the kind of man who will climb a dangerous mountain, beard an irascible employer for a rise in pay, and in general face the fearful for the sake of something he thinks worth while—there remains the question of 'commendation' or 'evaluation'. If the word 'courage' is used they will ask whether or not the man who speaks of another as having courage is supposed to have commended him. If we say 'yes' they will insist that the judgement about courage *goes beyond the facts*, and might therefore be rejected by someone who refused to do so; if we say 'no' they will argue that 'courage' is being used in a purely descriptive or 'inverted comma sense', and that we have not got an example of the evaluative use of language which is the moral philosopher's special study. What sense can be made, however, of the question 'does he commend?' What is this extra element which is supposed to be present or absent after the facts have been settled? It is not a matter of liking the man who has courage, or of thinking him altogether good, but of 'commending him for his courage'. How are we supposed to do that? The answer that will be given is that we only commend someone else in speaking of him as courageous if we accept the imperative 'let me be courageous' for our-

selves. But this is quite unnecessary. I can speak of someone else as having the virtue of courage, and of course recognise it as a virtue in the proper sense, while knowing that I am a complete coward, and making no resolution to reform. I know that I should be better off if I were courageous, and so have a reason to cultivate courage, but I may also know that I will do nothing of the kind.

If someone were to say that courage was not a virtue he would have to say that it was not a quality by which a man came to act well. Perhaps he would be thinking that someone might be worse off for his courage, which is true, but only because an incidental harm might arise. For instance, the courageous man might have underestimated a risk, and run into some disaster which a cowardly man would have avoided because he was not prepared to take any risk at all. And his courage, like any other virtue, could be the cause of harm to him because possessing it he fell into some disastrous state of pride.[3] Similarly, those who question the virtue of temperance are probably thinking not of the virtue itself but of men whose temperance has consisted in resisting pleasure for the sake of some illusory good, or those who have made this virtue their pride.

But what, it will be asked, of justice? For while prudence, courage and temperance are qualities which benefit the man who has them, justice seems rather to benefit others, and to work to the disadvantage of the just man himself. Justice as it is treated here, as one of the cardinal virtues, covers all those things owed to other people: it is under injustice that murder, theft and lying come, as well as the withholding of what is owed for instance by parents to children and by children to parents, as well as the dealings which would be called unjust in everyday speech. So the man who avoids injustice will find himself in need of things he has returned to their owner, unable to obtain an advantage by cheating and lying; involved in all those difficulties painted by Thrasymachus in the first book of the Republic, in order to show that injustice is more profitable than justice to a man of strength and wit. We will be asked how, on our theory, justice can be a virtue and injustice a vice, since it will surely be difficult to show that any man whatsoever must need to be just as he needs the use of his hands and eyes, or needs prudence, courage and temperance?

Before answering this question I shall argue that if it cannot be answered, then justice can no longer be recommended as a virtue. The point of this is not to show that it must be answerable, since justice is a virtue, but rather to suggest that we should at least consider the possibility that justice is not a virtue. This suggestion was taken seriously by Socrates in the Republic, where it was assumed by everyone that if Thrasymachus could establish his premiss—that injustice was more profitable than justice—his conclusion would follow: that a man who had the strength to get away with injustice had reason to follow this as the best way of life. It is a striking fact about modern moral philosophy that no one sees any difficulty in accepting Thrasymachus' premiss and rejecting his conclusion and it is because Nietzsche's position is at this point much closer to that of Plato that he is remote from academic moralists of the present day.

In the Republic it is assumed that if justice is not a good to the just man, moralists who recommend it as a virtue are perpetrating a fraud. Agreeing with this, I shall be asked where exactly the fraud comes in; where the untruth that justice is profitable to the individual is supposed to be told? As a preliminary answer we might ask how many people are prepared to say frankly that injustice is more profitable than justice? Leaving aside, as elsewhere in this paper, religious beliefs which might complicate the matter, we will suppose that some tough atheistical character has asked 'Why should I be just?' (Those who believe that this question has something wrong with it can employ their favourite device for sieving out 'evaluating meaning', and suppose that the question is 'Why should I be "just"?') Are we prepared to reply 'As far

as you are concerned you will be better off if you are unjust, but it matters to the rest of us that you should be just, so we are trying to get you to be just'? He would be likely to enquire into our methods, and then take care not to be found out, and I do not think that many of those who think that it is not necessary to show that justice is profitable to the just man would easily accept that there was nothing more they could say.

The crucial question is: 'Can we give anyone, strong or weak, a reason why he should be just?'—and it is no help at all to say that since 'just' and 'unjust' are 'action-guiding words' no one can even ask 'Why should I be just?' Confronted with that argument the man who wants to do unjust things has only to be careful to avoid the *word*, and he has not been given a reason why he should not do the things which other people call 'unjust'. Probably it will be argued that he has been given a reason so far as anyone can ever be given a reason for doing or not doing anything, for the chain of reasons must always come to an end somewhere, and it may seem that one man may always reject the reason which another man accepts. But this is a mistake; some answers to the question 'why should I?' bring the series to a close and some do not. Hume showed how *one* answer closed the series in the following passage:

"Ask a man *why he uses exercise;* he will answer, *because he desires to keep his health.* If you then enquire, *why he desires health,* he will readily reply, *because sickness is painful.* If you push your enquiries farther, and desire a reason *why he hates pain,* it is impossible he can ever give any. This is an ultimate end, and is never referred to any other object." (*Enquiries,* Appendix I, V.) Hume might just as well have ended this series with boredom: sickness often brings boredom, and no one is required to give a reason why he does not want to be bored, any more than he has to give a reason why he does want to pursue what interests him. In general, anyone is given a reason for acting when he is shewn the way to something he wants; but for some wants the question

'Why do you want that?' will make sense, and for others it will not.[4] It seems clear that in this division justice falls on the opposite side from pleasure and interest and such things. 'Why shouldn't I do that?' is not answered by the words 'because it is unjust' as it is answered by showing that the action will bring boredom, loneliness, pain, discomfort or certain kinds of incapacity, and this is why (it is not true to say that 'it's unjust' gives a reason in so far as any reasons can ever be given. 'It's unjust' gives a reason only if the nature of justice can be shown to be such that it is necessarily connected with what a man wants.

This shows why a great deal hangs on the question of whether justice is or is not a good to the just man, and why those who accept Thrasymachus' premiss and reject his conclusion are in a dubious position.) They recommend justice to each man, as something he has a reason to follow, but when challenged to show why he should do so they will not always be able to reply. This last assertion does not depend on any 'selfish theory of human nature' in the philosophical sense. It is often possible to give a man a reason for acting by showing him that someone else will suffer if he does not; someone else's good may really be more to him than his own. But the affection which mothers feel for children, and lovers for each other, and friends for friends, will not take us far when we are asked for reasons why a man should be just; partly because it will not extend far enough, and partly because the actions dictated by benevolence and justice are not always the same. Suppose that I owe someone money; '... what if he be my enemy, and has given me just cause to hate him? What if he be a vicious man, and deserves the hatred of all mankind? What if he be a miser, and can make no use of what I would deprive him of? What if he be a profligate debauchee, and would rather receive harm than benefit from large possessions?'[5] Even if the general practice of justice could be brought under the motive of universal benevolence—the desire for the greatest happiness of the greatest number—many people certainly do not have any such desire. So that if justice is only to be recommended on these grounds a thousand tough characters will be able to say that they have been given no reason for practising justice, and many more would say the same if they were not too timid or too stupid to ask questions about the code of behaviour which they have been taught. Thus, given Thrasymachus' premiss Thrasymachus' point of view is reasonable; we have no particular reason to admire those who practise justice through timidity or stupidity.

It seems to me, therefore, that if Thrasymachus' thesis is accepted things cannot go on as before; we shall have to admit that the belief on which the status of justice as a virtue was founded is mistaken, and if we still want to get people to be just we must recommend justice to them in a new way. We shall have to admit that injustice is more profitable than justice, at least for the strong, and then do our best to see that hardly anyone can get away with being unjust. We have, of course, the alternative of keeping quiet, hoping that for the most part people will follow convention into a kind of justice, and not ask awkward questions, but this policy might be overtaken by a vague scepticism even on the part of those who do not know just what is lacking; we should also be at the mercy of anyone who was able and willing to expose our fraud.

Is it true, however, to say that justice is not something a man needs in his dealings with his fellows, supposing only that he be strong? Those who think that he can get on perfectly well without being just should be asked to say exactly how such a man is supposed to live. We know that he is to practise injustice whenever the unjust act would bring him advantage; but what is he to say? Does he admit that he does not recognise the rights of other people, or does he pretend? In the first case even those who combine with him will know that on a change of fortune, or a shift of affection, he may turn to plunder them, and he must be as wary of their treachery as they are of his. Presumably the happy unjust man is supposed, as in Book II of the Republic, to be a very cunning liar and actor, combining complete injustice with the appearance of justice: he is prepared to treat others ruthlessly, but pretends that nothing is further from his mind. Philosophers often speak as if a man could thus hide himself even from those around him, but the supposition is doubtful, and in any case the price in vigilance would be colossal. If he lets even a few people see his true attitude he must guard himself against them; if he lets no one into the secret he must always be careful in case the least spontaneity betray him. Such facts are important because the need a man has for justice in dealings with other men depends on the fact that they are men and not inanimate objects or animals. If a man only needed other men as he needs household objects, and if men could be manipulated like household objects, or beaten into a reliable submission like donkeys, the case would be different. As things are, the supposition that injustice is more profitable than justice is very dubious, although like cowardice and intemperance it might turn out incidentally to be profitable.

The reason why it seems to some people so impossibly difficult to show that justice is more profitable than injustice is that they consider in isolation particular just acts. It is perfectly true that if a man is just it follows that he will be prepared, in the event of very evil circumstances, even to face death rather than to act unjustly—for instance, in getting an innocent man convicted of a crime of which he has been accused. For him it turns out that his justice brings disaster on him, and yet like anyone else he had good reason to be a just and not an unjust man. He could not have it both ways and while possessing the virtue of justice hold himself ready to be unjust should any great advantage accrue. The man who has the virtue of justice is not ready to do certain things, and if he is too easily tempted we shall say that he was ready after all.

Notes

1. See Wittgenstein, *Philosophical Investigations*, especially §§243–315.

2. In face of this sort of example many philosophers take refuge in the thicket of aesthetics. It would be interesting to know if they are willing to let their whole case rest on the possibility that there might be aesthetic objections to what was done.

3. *Cp.* Aquinas, *Summa Theologica*, I–II, q. 55, Art. 4.

4. For an excellent discussion of reasons for action, see G. E. M. Anscombe, *Intention* §34–40.

5. Hume, *Treatise* Book III, Part II, Sect. 1.

KINDS OF GOODNESS

9 / CHRISTINE KORSGAARD

TWO DISTINCTIONS IN GOODNESS

In this paper I describe two distinctions in goodness which are often conflated, and try to show the importance of keeping them separate. The two distinctions in question are: the distinction between intrinsic and extrinsic goodness, and the distinction between ends or final goods, and means or instrumental goods.

It will help to begin by delineating the kind of value and the kind of judgment of value with which I am primarily concerned here. I take it that there are three primary categories of value with which the moral philosopher is concerned: namely, the rightness or justice of actions, policies, and institutions; the goodness of objects, purposes, lives, etc.: and the moral worth or moral goodness of characters, dispositions, or actions. My concern here is not with what constitutes moral worth or moral goodness but with the second category—with goodness as a feature of ordinary ends and purposes, states of affairs, objects, activities, and other things—that is, with the kind of goodness that marks a thing out as worthy of choice.

Within this category, we can distinguish, admittedly with some artificiality, three kinds of judgments of goodness that we make. We judge something to be good of its kind when we judge it to have the virtues appropriate to that kind. We may also judge something to be a good kind of thing, as when we say of friendship or

Reprinted by permission of the publisher and copyright holder from *The Philosophical Review* 92 (1983): 169–97.

books or health that they are good. And we also sometimes judge particular things to be good absolutely, meaning that here and now the world is a better place because of this thing. I am mostly concerned with this third sort of judgment in this paper, though part of what is in question is its relation to the other two.

II

It is rather standard fare in philosophy to distinguish two kinds of this value of goodness, often called "intrinsic" and "instrumental."[1] Objects, activities, or whatever, have an instrumental value if they are valued for the sake of something else—tools, money, and chores would be standard examples. A common explanation of the supposedly contrasting kind, intrinsic goodness, is to say that a thing is intrinsically good if it is valued for its own sake, that being the obvious alternative to a thing's being valued for the sake of something else. This is not, however, what the words "intrinsic value" mean. To say that something is intrinsically good is not by definition to say that it is valued for its own sake: it is to say that it has its goodness in itself. It refers, one might say, to the location or source of the goodness rather than the way we value the thing. The contrast between instrumental and intrinsic value is therefore misleading, a false contrast. The natural contrast to intrinsic goodness—the value a thing has "in itself"—is *extrinsic* goodness—the value a thing gets from some other source. The natural contrast to a thing that is valued instrumentally or as a means is a thing that is valued for its own sake or as an end. There are, therefore, two distinctions in goodness. One is the distinction between things valued for their own sakes and things valued for the sake of something else—between ends and means, or final and instrumental goods. The other is the distinction between things which have their value in themselves and things which derive their value from some other source: intrinsically good things versus extrinsically good things. Intrinsic and instrumental good should not be treated as correlatives, because they belong to two different distinctions.

If intrinsic is taken to be the opposite of instrumental, then it is under the influence of a theory: a theory according to which the two distinctions in goodness are the same, or amount to the same thing. According to such a theory, final goods or things valuable as ends will be the same as intrinsic goods, and instrumental goods or things valuable as means will be the same as extrinsic goods. It is worth considering what such a theory might be like.

The first part of the equivalence—that ends and intrinsic goods are the same—might be held in two very different ways: (1) The claim might be that anything we value for its own sake is thereby "intrinsically good"; that is, that this is all that can be meant by "intrinsically good." This amounts to a *reduction* of the intrinsic/extrinsic distinction to the end/means distinction; the significance of the former distinction drops out. This option, which in effect replaces the intrinsic/extrinsic distinction with the end/means distinction, is sometimes taken to render the conception of good "subjective," both in the sense of 'relative to the person' and of 'varying among individuals'. The thought goes this way: good things (on this account) are just those valued for their own sakes, but different people value different things for their own sakes. (2) The second way one might equate ends and intrinsically good things is by claiming that those things

which have intrinsic value are or ought to be treated as ends. In this case we have a significant, and rather metaphysical, claim about ethics and moral psychology: namely, that choice is or ought to be a response to an attribute that we perceive in things—the attribute of intrinsic goodness. Equating the two distinctions in goodness thus leads naturally to the idea that there are two alternative theories about final goods—either that "good" is subjective or that good things are the possessors of some particular attribute. Objectivity, in other words, is thought to amount to the possession of an attribute. I think that many people do have a tendency to think that these alternatives are exhaustive, and one thing I want to show is that if the two distinctions in goodness are kept separate, this need not be so.

The other side of the theory that equates the two distinctions is the equation of extrinsic with instrumental goods, or means. The consequences of this equation are serious. Since intrinsically good things (at least when "intrinsic" retains its significance) are thought to have their value *in* themselves, they are thought to have their goodness in any and all circumstances—to carry it with them, so to speak. If you find that a certain kind of thing is not good in any and all circumstances, that it is good in some cases and not others, its goodness is extrinsic—it is derived from or dependent upon the circumstances. If extrinsic value and instrumental value are equated, you are then forced to say of all such things that they are means or instruments. This way of thinking is part of what is behind the tendency to conclude that the final good must be pleasure or some sort of experience. The argument proceeds as follows: take an activity that we would naturally say is valuable for its own sake,—say, looking at a beautiful sunset. Now the question is raised: would you think this activity was a good one even if the person engaged in it found it tedious or painful? If you say "no" then you have admitted that the goodness of this activity is not intrinsic; that it depends, in some way, on the pleasantness of it. But if all extrinsic value is instrumental value, then the only option is that the activity is a *means* to pleasure. Now if the two distinctions are not equated, there is room for some other sorts of accounts of extrinsic value, and one may not be forced to this conclusion.

Because of these consequences this side of the equation has been more widely attacked than the other. It has been argued that instrumentality is not the only sort of extrinsic value, on the grounds that there are other sorts of contributions things can make to intrinsically good ends. So, for instance, it is common to identify a "part" of an intrinsically valuable "whole" as having "contributive" value. Another sort of value, suggested by C. I. Lewis, is called "inherent" value.[2] This is supposed to be the value that characterizes the object of an intrinsically good experience. A painting, for example, might have inherent value. The identification of these different kinds of extrinsic value serves as a reminder that things can bear other relations to good ends besides being their causes or tools for their production. Contributive value and inherent value, however, both share with instrumental value the fact of deriving their goodness from the contribution they make to the existence of a supposedly intrinsically good end.

Separating the two distinctions in goodness, however, opens up another possibility: that of something which is extrinsically good yet valued as an end. An example of this would be something that was good as an end because of the interest that someone took in it, or the desire that someone had for it, for its own sake. This is the case that I am going to be discussing in the rest of this paper. In particular, I am going to compare the very opposite treatments of this issue that appear in, on the one hand, the work of Moore and Ross at the beginning of our century and, on the other hand, Kant. These philosophers all separated the two distinctions, but they applied them to this case in opposite ways. Moore and Ross came to the conclusion that the goodness of ends is intrinsic and must be indepen-

dent of the interest that people take in them or the desires that people have for them. You might value something as an end because of its intrinsic goodness or in response to its intrinsic goodness, but a thing's possession of intrinsic goodness is quite independent of whether anyone cares about it or not. Kant's theory, on the other hand, both allows for and depends upon the idea of extrinsically valuable ends whose value comes from the interest that people take in them.

The fact that philosophers nowadays often oppose intrinsic to instrumental value and equate intrinsic value with the value of ends may just be taken to be sloppiness, of course. But it may also mean that these philosophers are working with some theory of the sort I have described—a theory of the equivalence of the two distinctions. As the Kantian option shows, such a theory is a substantive philosophical position and restricts the possibilities open to us in serious ways. It should not, in any case, be taken for granted.

III

In the early years of this century there was much discussion of the question whether or not a good thing has its value as a result of something like the interest taken in it or the desire someone has for it. Influential philosophers such as G. E. Moore, W. D. Ross, R. B. Perry, and others discussed this question at length. Probably the interest in the issue was aroused by a common utilitarian argument that pleasure is the only thing that is good in itself because it is the only thing that we can desire for its own sake. It quickly became, and still is, a commonplace in discussions of utilitarianism to argue that pleasure is not, after all, the only thing that we desire for its own sake. But that leaves open the further question whether the things we desire for their own sakes, whatever they might be, are therefore good in themselves, or intrinsically good. Moore, and following him. Ross, argued vigorously that this could not be so.

Goodness, they said, had nothing to do with mental attitudes taken towards things at all—even though it turned out that, as a matter of fact, goodness is a property of mental attitudes or a property of states of affairs that always include mental states or attitudes.

The idea of intrinsic value is central to Moore's theory. He believed that right actions are those that maximize intrinsic goods. Emphatically opposed to hedonism, he took the class of intrinsic goods to consist of such things as the appreciation of beauty, friendship, and love. In his attempt to account for the goodness of these things, he came back to the question of the nature of intrinsic value over and over again.[3]

In his paper "The Conception of Intrinsic Value," Moore argues that people who object to the idea that goodness is subjective are really worried about something quite different: the idea that goodness is nonintrinsic. This is shown, according to Moore, by the fact that there are theories which would render goodness objective to which the same people would still be opposed, and for the same reason. Moore gives as his example the theory that "better" means "better fitted to survive":[4] people who object to subjectivity, he says, would also object to this, although it renders "good" objective. So the problem with a subjectivist theory of the good is not merely the lack of objectivity, but something else. According to Moore, it is that it excludes the possibility that things are intrinsically valuable. Moore defines intrinsic value as follows:

> To say that a kind of value is "intrinsic" means merely that the question whether a thing possesses it, and in what degree it possesses it, depends solely on the intrinsic nature of the thing in question.[5]

Moore's definition of the intrinsic nature of a thing is rather complicated: he says that two things have a different intrinsic nature if they are not exactly alike; that the difference need not be a difference in qualities, since it may be in the degree of a quality or in the quality of a constituent; and that two numerically different things have the

same intrinsic nature if they are exactly alike.[6] In general, the intrinsic nature of a thing seems to consist of its nonrelational properties, for Moore insists that a thing would have the same intrinsic nature if transferred to another world or placed in a different set-up of causal laws.[7] This is what Moore supposes we want from the conception of intrinsic goodness, as his analysis of the trouble with the evolutionary account of goodness shows. He says that the difficulty is that the types better fitted to survive under our laws of nature would not be the same as the types better fitted to survive under other circumstances and with different laws of nature. "Good" therefore would not be dependent only on a thing's intrinsic nature but would be a property that is relative to the circumstances, even though in this case it would be objective. But the problem with subjectivism is the same: it makes "good" relative to the circumstances.

Intrinsic goodness is not an element in the thing's intrinsic nature, for to say that would be to commit the naturalistic fallacy. The elements in its intrinsic nature are natural properties and cannot be identified with the good. But it is dependent only on the thing's intrinsic nature and is just as constant: so long as the thing remains what it is, it has the same value: and the value is the same, of course, for everyone and so also objective. Since it is no part of a thing's intrinsic nature whether anybody likes it or not, intrinsic value is quite independent of people's desires and interests. To put it another way: the attribute of "being desired by somebody" is relational, and as such it obviously varies with the circumstances in which the thing is found.

In *Ethics*, Moore's definition is a little different. We judge a state of things to have intrinsic value when we judge that it would be a good thing for that state of things to exist, even if nothing else were to exist besides. Here again, the emphasis is on the thing's goodness being nonrelational in a certain way. This view of intrinsic goodness is behind Moore's method of determining which things have intrinsic goodness in *Principia Ethica:* the "method of isolation." In order to arrive at a correct decision on the question which things have intrinsic value, Moore says that we must consider whether a thing is such that, if it existed by itself, in absolute isolation, we should judge its existence to be good.[8] In *Ethics*, Moore says:

> We *can* consider with regard to any particular state of things whether it would be worth while that it should exist, even if there were absolutely nothing else in the Universe besides ... we *can* consider whether the existence of such a Universe would have been better than nothing, or whether it would have been just as good that nothing at all should ever have existed.[9]

These definitions, along with the method of isolation they suggest, seem to Moore to exclude easily any connection between intrinsic value and what people desire for its own sake, for, he tells us, it is obviously possible to desire something for its own sake, or believe that someone else does, and yet not regard the thing as the sort of thing that would be good if it existed in isolation. Indeed you might regard it as a bad thing, worse than nothing, for it to exist quite alone. Moore concludes:

> And if this is so, then it shows conclusively that to judge that a thing is intrinsically good is not the same thing as to judge that some man is pleased with it or desires it for its own sake.[10]

Moore, it should be noted, does not usually use the terminology of "relational" vs. "nonrelational" attributes in his discussions of intrinsic value, but these are the terms in which Ross and Perry, following Moore, take up the discussion. Ross, who is on Moore's side,[11] says that there are two kinds of theories of value. One kind treats value as an attribute, and the other treats it as a relation, usually to a state of mind such as interest or desire. If it is a relation, Ross complains, then nothing can be intrinsically good, since intrinsically good *means* "good even if nothing else exists."

But, he says,

> ... in that case value would seem always to be borrowed, and never owned; value would shine by a reflected glory having no original source.[12]

Ross, like Moore, finds it virtually self-evident that "intrinsically valuable" is not the same as "desired as an end." He insists that:

> It is surely clear that when we call something good we are thinking of it as possessing in itself a certain attribute and are not thinking of it as necessarily having an interest taken in it.[13]

The terms in which this discussion proceeded suggested that the question was whether final goods, whatever we ought to pursue, are intrinsically good and objective, the possessors of a property; or good because they are desired and therefore subjective, or at any rate "relational" and therefore unfixed. These are terms that those who followed Moore and Ross inherited.

IV

Kant, I am going to claim, was aware of and made use of the two distinctions in goodness, with results that were quite different from those arrived at by Moore and Ross.[14] In order to see this, we must begin by looking at Kant's own distinction between unconditioned and conditioned value. The *Foundations of the Metaphysics of Morals* opens with the famous claim:

> Nothing in the world—indeed nothing even beyond the world—can possibly be conceived which could be called good without qualification except a *good will* (G 9/392/393).[15]

As Kant presents the argument that follows, it becomes clear that what he means is that the good will is the only unconditionally good thing and "the supreme condition to which the private purposes of men must for the most part defer" (G 12/396). He says:

> This will must indeed not be the sole and complete good but the highest good and the condition of all others, even of the desire for happiness (G 12/396).

Happiness, by contrast to the good will, is referred to as a "conditional purpose" (G 12/396).

The fact that happiness is identified as a conditional purpose shows that the unconditioned/conditioned distinction is not the same as the end/means distinction, since happiness is certainly desired as an end. For Kant, the end/means distinction can be said to be a distinction in the *way* we value things. By contrast, the unconditioned/conditioned distinction is a distinction not in the way we value things but in the circumstances (conditions) in which they are objectively good. A thing is unconditionally good if it is good under any and all conditions, if it is good no matter what the context. In order to be unconditionally good, a thing must obviously carry its own value with it—have its goodness in itself (be an end in itself). Kant's notion of unconditional value therefore corresponds to the notion of intrinsic goodness as nonrelational that I have been discussing. The early passages of the *Foundations* emphasize the independence of the value of the good will from all surrounding circumstances as well as from its results. It is good in the world or even beyond it (G 9/393); it is not good because of what it effects or accomplishes; it sparkles like a jewel in its own right, as something that has its full worth in itself. Later in the *Foundations*, Kant uses the phrase "*inneren Wert,*" inner worth, to describe the special dignity of a morally good rational being as compared to the "*relativen Wert,*" relative worth, of anything else (G 53/435). But whereas Moore assigned intrinsic goodness to a range of things—to aesthetic appreciation, to friendship, and in general to the things that he thought we ought to pursue as ends—Kant assigns it only to the one thing, the good will.

If unconditional value is intrinsic value, conditional value is extrinsic value. Now a thing is conditionally valuable if it is good only when certain conditions are met: if it is good sometimes and not others. Thus, to elaborate on Kant's own examples, "the coolness of a villain makes him not only far more dangerous but also more directly abominable in our eyes than he would have seemed without it" (G 10/344), while coolness in a fireman or a surgeon is usually an excellent thing. Power, riches, and health are good or not depending upon what use is made of them. To say that a thing is conditionally valuable is to say that it is good when and only when the conditions of its goodness are met. We can say that a thing is good objectively (this is my terminology) either if it is unconditionally good or if it is a thing of conditional value and the conditions of its goodness are met. Here it is important to notice that "good objectively" is a judgment applying to real particulars: this woman's knowledge, this man's happiness, and so on. To say of a thing that it is good objectively is not to say that it is the type of thing that is usually good (a good kind of thing like knowledge or happiness) but that it contributes to the actual goodness of the world: here and now the world is a better place for *this*. We would not say that about the coolness of the villain or the happiness of the evil person: hence coolness and happiness are objectively good only when certain further conditions are met. Further, we might, under unusual conditions, attribute objective goodness to something that under more usual conditions is nearly always bad, as when a kind of occurrence normally unfortunate coincidentally contributes to someone's happiness.[16] When Kant says that the only thing good without qualification is a good will, he means that the good will is the one thing or kind of thing for which the world is always a better place, no matter "what it effects or accomplishes" (G 10/394).

The two distinctions interact in the following ways. When a thing is valued as a means or instrumentally (or is the sort of thing valued as a means) it will always be a conditionally or extrinsically valuable thing, and the goodness of the end to which it is a means will be a condition of its goodness. Instruments therefore can only be conditionally valuable. If the conditions of their goodness are met, however, they can be good objectively. The more important point is about things valued as ends. These are also conditionally or extrinsically good. In particular, happiness, under which Kant thinks all our other private purposes are subsumed, is only conditionally good, for:

> It need hardly be mentioned that the sight of a being adorned with no feature of a pure and good will, yet enjoying uninterrupted prosperity, can never give pleasure to a rational impartial observer. Thus the good will seems to constitute the indispensable condition even of worthiness to be happy (G 9/393).

But although happiness is conditionally valuable, it is, when the condition is met, objectively good.

In order to see this, it will help to keep in mind Kant's other uses of the unconditioned/conditioned distinction. If anything is conditioned in any way, reason seeks its condition, continually seeking the conditions of each condition until it reaches something unconditional. It is this characteristic activity of reason that generates the antinomies of theoretical speculative reason described in the *Critique of Pure Reason*. The usual example is causal explanation—if we explain a thing in terms of its cause, we then go on to explain the cause itself in terms of its cause, and this process continues. Reason does not want to rest until it reaches something that needs no explanation (although this turns out not to be available): say, something that is a first cause or its own cause. A causal explanation truly satisfying to reason would go all the way back to this evident first cause, thus *fully* explaining why the thing to be explained must be so. These are familiar sorts of moves in philosophy, so there is no need to belabor the point. To apply it here, it is only necessary to point out that just as to explain a thing fully we would have to find its unconditioned first cause, so to *justify* a

thing fully (where justify is "show that it is objectively good") we would have to show that all the conditions of its goodness were met, regressing on the conditions until we came to what is unconditioned. Since the good will is the only unconditionally good thing, this means that it must be the source and condition of all the goodness in the world; goodness, as it were, flows into the world from the good will, and there would be none without it. If a person has a good will, then that person's happiness (to the extent of his or her virtue) is good. This is why the highest good, the whole object of practical reason, is virtue and happiness in proportion to virtue: together these comprise all ends that are objectively good— the unconditional good and the private ends that are rendered good by its presence. (*Critique of Practical Reason*, 114–115/ 110). So also the Kingdom of Ends, defined as "a whole of rational beings as ends in themselves as well as of the particular ends which each may set for himself" (G 51/433), is a kingdom in which the objectively good is fully realized.

On the Kantian conception of goodness, then, an end is objectively good either if it is unconditionally (intrinsically) good *or* if it is conditionally good and the relevant conditions, whatever they are, are met. This conception of the good is used in his argument for one of the formulas of the categorical imperative, the Formula of Humanity as an End in Itself.[17] It is this argument that establishes the role of the good will in conferring value upon the ends of the person who has it.

The argument shows how Kant's idea of justification works. It can be read as a kind of regress upon the conditions, starting from an important assumption. The assumption is that when a rational being makes a choice or undertakes an action, he or she supposes the object to be good, and its pursuit to be justified. At least, if there is a categorical imperative there must be objectively good ends, for then there are necessary actions and so necessary ends (G 45–46/427–428 and *Doctrine of Virtue* 43–44/384–385). In order for there to be any objectively good ends, however, there must be something that is unconditionally good and so can serve as a sufficient condition of their goodness. Kant considers what this might be: it cannot be an object of inclination, for those have only a conditional worth, "for if the inclinations and the needs founded on them did not exist, their object would be without worth" (G 46/428). It cannot be the inclinations themselves because a rational being would rather be free from them. Nor can it be external things, which serve only as means. So, Kant asserts, the unconditionally valuable thing must be "humanity" or "rational nature," which he defines as "the power set to an end" (G 56/437 and DV 51/392). Kant explains that regarding your existence as a rational being as an end in itself is a "subjective principle of human action." By this I understand him to mean that we must regard ourselves as capable of conferring value upon the objects of our choice, the ends that we set, because we must regard our ends as good. But since "every other rational being thinks of his existence by the same rational ground which holds also for myself" (G 47/429), we must regard others as capable of conferring value by reason of their rational choices and so also as ends in themselves. Treating another as an end in itself thus involves making that person's ends as far as possible your own (G 49/430). The ends that are chosen by any rational being, possessed of the humanity or rational nature that is fully realized in a good will, take on the status of objective goods. They are not intrinsically valuable, but they are objectively valuable in the sense that every rational being has a reason to promote or realize them. For this reason it is our duty to promote the happiness of others—the ends that they choose—and, in general, to make the highest good our end.

It is worth emphasizing that the relation of intrinsic to extrinsic value in this case—the case of extrinsically valuable ends—is entirely different from that in the cases of extrinsic value mentioned earlier. Instrumental value, contributive value, and Lewis's inherent value were all forms of extrinsic value that derived from the pro-

duction of a supposedly intrinsically good end. The extrinsic value of an objectively good end—of something that forms part of the happiness of a good person—comes not from some further thing that that end promotes but from its status as the object of a rational and fully justified choice. Value in this case does not travel from an end to a means but from a fully rational choice to its object. Value is, as I have put it, "conferred" by choice. This formulation may seem paradoxical. A natural objection will be that the goodness of the chosen object is precisely what makes the choice rational, so that the choice cannot itself be what makes the object good. I will have more to say about this objection in the next section. The point I want to emphasize here is that the Kantian approach frees us from assessing the rationality of a choice by means of the apparently ontological task of assessing the thing chosen: we do not need to identify especially rational ends. Instead, it is the reasoning that goes into the choice itself—the procedures of full justification—that determines the rationality of the choice and so certifies the goodness of the object. Thus the goodness of rationally chosen ends is a matter of the demands of practical reason rather than a matter of ontology.[18] It is notable that on Kant's theory the goodness of means is handled the same way: it is not because of the ontological property of being productive of an intrinsically good end that means are good but rather because of the law of practical reason that "whoever wills the end, so far as reason has decisive influence on his action, wills also the indispensably necessary means to it that lie in his power" (G 34/417). Similarly, the argument for the objective goodness of the object of a rational choice is not an ontological one; rather, it is based on Kant's theory of rational action. If we regard our actions as rational, we must regard our ends as good; if so, we accord to ourselves a power of conferring goodness on the objects of our choice, and we must accord the same power—and so the same intrinsic worth—to others.

It will be helpful to pause for a moment to match up Kant's view and the Kantian terms to what has gone before. On Kant's view there is only one thing that has what he calls unconditional value and what Moore calls intrinsic value, and that is the power of rational choice (when the choices are made in a fully rational way, which is what characterizes the good will). The value of everything else whatever is extrinsic or conditional. Yet when a thing is conditionally valuable and the relevant conditions are met, the thing has objective value. Things that are valued for their own sakes or as ends have this status. Their value is conditional but can be objective, given the real circumstances of the case. Thus, although Kant, like Moore, firmly separates intrinsic value from a thing's being desired for its own sake, he has resources for saying that a thing is objectively good as an end *because* it is desired for its own sake. And most things that are good will in fact be good in this way: they will be good because they are part of the happiness of a deserving human being.

On Kant's theory, the goodness of most things is, in the way described by Ross, relational—relative to the desires and interests of people. But since it must also be appropriately related to one thing that has intrinsic value, it is not merely "subjective." Value does, in Ross's extravagant terms, "shine with a reflected glory," and it is "borrowed rather than owned" by most of the things that have it. But it does have an original source that brings it into the world—the value-conferring power of the good will.

V

In this section I want to focus on some advantages of the Kantian way of describing values. In the next section I will show how some of these advantages are shared by Moore. In the last section I will discuss what I take to be the most important advantage that Kant's theory of goodness has over Moore's.

Kant's treatment of the two distinctions and the relations between them allows us to describe certain kinds of everyday matters of value in a way that is more flexible and that I think is more natural than is available to us if the two distinctions are conflated or equated. This is especially so for certain cases of what we might call "mixed" values. I have in mind a variety of different mixtures. Take some examples: a luxurious instrument; a malicious pleasure; an unenjoyed exercise of one's higher faculties; or an undisplayed art object. Now the idea that a thing can have value under a condition, when combined with the reminder that instrumentality or usefulness is not the only possible condition (that is, some extrinsically good things are valued as ends), will help us to describe such cases.

Consider, for instance, a common symbol of aspiration—a mink coat. Is it valuable as a means or as an end? One hardly wants to say that it is valuable only as a means, to keep the cold out. The people who want mink coats are not willing to exchange them for plastic parkas, if those are better protection against the elements. A mink coat can be valued the way we value things for their own sakes: a person might put it on a list of the things he always wanted, or aspire to have some day, right alongside adventure, travel, or peace of mind. Yet it is also odd to say it is valued simply for its own sake. A coat is essentially instrumental: were it not for the ways in which human beings respond to cold, we would not care about them or ever think about them. To say that the coat is intrinsically or unconditionally valuable is absurd: its value is dependent upon an enormously complicated set of conditions, physiological, economic, and symbolic. Certainly, it does not pass Moore's isolation test, so far as I can see. A universe consisting of a mink coat or of someone's having one, without the associations that can only be provided by the particular relations and causal connections under which we live, is not really imaginable, much less valuable. What would a coat *be*? It seems hard even to apply the isolation test here, for one is tempted to say that its instrumentality *is* one of the elements in the "intrinsic nature" of a coat, even though it can hardly be said to be a property the coat would have under any set of laws of nature. If its instrumentality is not one of its intrinsic properties, then one is regarding the coat as something else—an animal skin sewed into a peculiar shape, perhaps. But then it seems as if one must strip away the practically relevant properties of the coat in order to ask about its intrinsic value—and that cannot be right. It is equally absurd to say of such a thing that it is a mere instrument, just because its value is conditioned. The Kantian distinctions allow us to say that the coat is valued in part for its own sake, although only under certain conditions. It even allows us to say of certain kinds of things, such as luxurious instruments, that they are valued for their own sakes under the condition of their usefulness. Mink coats and handsome china and gorgeously enameled frying pans are all things that human beings might choose partly for their own sakes under the condition of their instrumentality: that is, given the role such things play in our lives.

Another possible advantage is that the independent use of the two distinctions will provide us with a way of talking about the relation of pleasure, enjoyment, and appreciation to other kinds of value that does not turn these mental states into ends to which everything else is a means. Activities of various kinds might be thought to be good under the condition that we enjoy them and not good at all for those who, for one reason or another, cannot enjoy them, without forcing the conclusion that it is only for the sake of the enjoyment that they are valued. Certain difficulties concerning the "higher pleasures" described by Mill or those activities that Aristotle says are "pleasant in their own nature" although not necessarily "to a particular person" might be dealt with in this way. But this is a suggestion I cannot pursue here.

Consider also the example of an extraordinarily beautiful painting unsuspectedly locked up, perhaps permanently, in a closet. Now a beautiful painting, I am supposing, is valued for its own sake. If the

two distinctions are equated, we must say it has intrinsic value. Yet it is locked in a closet, utterly unseen, and no one is the better for its existence. Consider Moore's isolation test: is a universe with such a painting locked up somewhere intuitively better than one without it? Is a universe consisting of such a painting better than a universe consisting of something quite plain, with no viewers in either? These are curious puzzles: and Moore's isolation test seems to force us to ask the metaphysical-sounding question whether the painting has this property, intrinsic value, or not. Yet we *know* what the practically relevant property of the painting is: it is its beauty. Now on the Kantian type of account we can say that the painting is valuable for its own sake, yet so long as it remains locked up and unseen, it is no good at all. The condition of its goodness—the condition of the goodness of its beauty—is not met. That condition is that the painting be viewed. Yet although its value is not intrinsic, the painting may be objectively good for its own sake. If it were viewed, and the viewer were enraptured, or satisfied, or instructed by its loveliness, then the painting would be an objectively good thing: for the world would be, really, a better place for it: it would be a substantive contribution to the actual sum of goodness of the world. Notice, too, that this does not in the least mean that we have to say that the painting is only valued as a means to the experiences of appreciation. Those experiences are not an end to which the painting is a means, but the condition under which its value as an end is realized.

I am not suggesting that the Kantian treatment solves all the difficulties in our thinking about these things, but only that it does not drive us immediately to the conclusion that all of these things, valued only under conditions and only in a network of relations, must be mere instruments or contributors to some further thing—pleasure or some "mental" state, which supposedly has the real value. The conflation of the two distinctions does tend to have this effect. In particular, when conflation leads us to the conclusion that a thing can only be valued as an end when it is intrinsically valuable, or valuable independently of all conditions and relations, we find ourselves led inevitably to the curious conclusion to which modern moral philosophers are indeed frequently led—that everything good as an end must be something mental, some kind of experience. I have already mentioned one line of argument that leads to this conclusion: some sort of experience, such as pleasure, seems to be a condition of goodness of so many good things. Another line of thought that leads this way is this: no matter how much the philosopher wants to insist that the value of a good thing must be intrinsic and so nonrelational, the sense remains that the goodness of a good thing must have something to do with its goodness *for us*. It cannot merely be a property, metaphysical and simple, which we perceive in things and respond to in an extraordinary way. So the fact that goodness must lie in some relation to human beings, evidently at odds with the theory that goodness must be entirely nonrelational, is dealt with by making goodness a property of something belonging directly to the human being—our experiences or states of mind. By making goodness lie in the experiences themselves, the philosopher rids us of the worry: but what if no one is around to care about this good thing? What good is it then? Kant's way of looking at it, on the other hand, enables us to explain why ordinary good things are good only in virtue of the fact that people are around to care about them without tempting us to the conclusion that the only good things are mental states and experiences.

To some, it may seem paradoxical to claim that things are good because we desire or choose them, rather than to say that we desire or choose them because they are good. Ross, for example, finds it clear that when we call something good we are thinking of it as having some attribute, not as an object of interest; he thinks of our interest as inspired by the perception of the thing's goodness. We choose the thing because it is good. This picture is part of what gives

power to the theory that goodness is not relative to interest, and of course there is a way in which it is true. For instance, when we want a certain kind of thing, we usually want one with the virtues of that kind of thing. And it is also true that what makes a thing a good kind of thing is its virtues. In this sense our choice may be called forth by a thing's goodness, rather than the thing's being good because of our choice. But when we inquire into the basis for calling certain properties of a thing its "virtues," we always come back to something that is relative to certain conditions of human life. It is our interests and the bases of our interests that make certain qualities *virtues;* so these facts cannot make goodness a nonrelational attribute.

This shows up most clearly in the everyday kind of case of "mixed" value, in which the distinction between what we value for its own sake and what we value for the sake of something else is itself overstrained. Take this case: there are instrumental reasons, good ones, for eating. It keeps you alive. But most people could not really be said to eat in order to stay alive. Certainly, only someone who didn't enjoy eating, perhaps because of illness or some damage to the taste buds, would say that he ate "in order to stay alive." Are we then to say that eating is an activity that also has an *intrinsic* value? (Perhaps then we should be glad that we are so constituted that it is necessary for us?) Or shall we say that people eat for the sake of enjoyment—that pleasure is an end to which eating is a means? Of course, you cannot exchange another pleasure for it; hunger pains will prevent that. Perhaps then we should say we eat as a means, not to obtain life and health, but just to avoid pain. Now the philosopher wants to say: the real end is painlessness. But again, only someone in a particular situation would say that. Is this then a complicated case, to which the ends of life and health, enjoyment, and painlessness contribute in various ways? And if this is a complicated case, where are we going to find a simple one? It is easier to say that food is a good thing under the condition that you are hungry—or rather, under the set of physiological and psychological conditions that make it both necessary and pleasant for human beings to eat. Those conditions determine what the virtues of a good meal are, and not all of these virtues are instrumental properties. But this does not mean that you choose the meal in response to a perception of its intrinsic value, or of the intrinsic value of eating it. The conditions of our lives make various things valuable to us in various ways, and it is sometimes artificial to worry about whether we value those things as means or as ends. It is the conditions themselves that make the things good, that provide the various reasons for their goodness. The question is not whether the thing possesses a special attribute, but whether these reasons are sufficient to establish the goodness of the thing.

This point can be sharpened if we distinguish between the initial condition that makes an object a candidate for choice and the full complement of conditions that, when met, renders the thing good. In the cases under discussion in this paper, the initial condition is the thing's desirability as an end (or at least not merely as a means). I have tried to show that the sense in which we can be said to desire things because they are good—i.e., for their virtues—does not show that a desirable thing need have a nonrelational property of goodness. What we call virtues just are the features of the thing that, given our constitution and situation, we find appealing or interesting or satisfying to our needs. It remains just as true, as far as this goes, to say that the thing is good because we desire it as to say that we desire it because it is good. For its virtues are still relative to our desires, or, more accurately, to the conditions that give rise to those desires. The reason that one cannot, on a Kantian account, rest with the perhaps less paradoxical formulation that value is conferred by desire is that desire is not by itself a *sufficient* condition of the goodness of its object. This is shown initially by the sort of case in which one has a desire which one would

be better off without. Short of endorsing Kant's view that "the inclinations themselves, as sources of needs, however, are so lacking in absolute worth that the universal wish of every rational being must be to free himself completely from them" (G 46/428), we can agree that there are desires that conflict with one's health or happiness or that are self-destructive or pathological or simply burdensome out of all proportion to any gratification their fulfillment can provide. This already shows that the existence of a desire is not by itself a sufficient reason for the realization of its object; further conditions exist. The criterion that reasons be universalizable will also, on Kant's account, limit the capacity of desires to serve as reasons and so to confer value. But although desirability is not a sufficient condition of goodness, it is still the initial condition of the goodness of many good things, and so a main source of the goodness of those things.[19] On the Kantian view, not everything valued as an end need be intrinsically valuable or self-justifying for there to be a sufficient reason for it. A conditionally valuable thing can still be fully justified, if the unconditioned condition of its goodness is met. Things that are not self-justifying can be justified by something else. In particular, ends whose condition is their desirability can be justified by the rational choices of human beings.

VI

But I have not meant to suggest that Moore himself is prey to all of the difficulties that arise when the two distinctions are conflated. Moore has his own way of dealing with these issues of "mixed" value, a problem in which he was keenly interested. In order to handle cases of mixed value, Moore introduced a device which he regarded as one of his best discoveries: the theory of organic unities. The theory of organic unities involves two important points. First, it turns out that intrinsic value, on Moore's account, usually belongs to "organic" wholes or complexes of certain kinds, not to simple things. Second, it is true of such a complex whole that its value "bears no regular proportion to the sum of the values of its parts":

> It is certain that a good thing may exist in such a relation to another good thing that the value of the whole thus formed is immensely greater than the sum of the values of the two good things. It is certain that a whole formed of a good thing and an indifferent thing may have immensely greater value than that good thing itself possesses. It is certain that two bad things or a bad thing and an indifferent thing may form a whole much worse than the sum of badness of its parts. And, it seems as if indifferent things may also be the sole constituents of a whole which has great value, either positive or negative.[20]

In his last chapter, "The Ideal," Moore provides various examples. For instance: the mere existence of what is beautiful has *some* intrinsic value, but so little as to be negligible, compared to the consciousness of beauty. If the consciousness of beauty is taken to be the cognition of beauty, then it in turn is made much more valuable if accompanied by an appropriate emotional response, which Moore identifies with the appreciation. Yet appreciation of beauty is not an end to which the beautiful object is a mere means. If this were so it would not matter whether the appreciation were produced in us by something genuinely beautiful or not, and it does: appreciating something that is ugly may be bad. Instead of saying that the value of the appreciation is conditional upon its appropriateness, as one might expect, Moore says that the great intrinsic value of appreciating beauty does not belong either to the object or the appreciative state but only to the complex whole formed of both. But the goodness of the whole is not the sum of the value of the parts. For we have seen that the value of the beautiful object by itself is quite small, and the value of the appreciation, in another context, can be absolutely negative. Moore has similar things to say about his other cases: for instance love itself is a good thing, but if your beloved is a good person,

the whole is better by *more* than the addition of your beloved's goodness. These conclusions are arrived at by the method of isolation: we compare the value of various isolated wholes, with and without the relevant element. The important thing is to avoid the mistake of thinking that the element itself possesses all of the value of the difference its presence makes. It was because of this mistake that the Greeks attributed intrinsic value to knowledge. Moore explains that really, knowledge by itself has little or no value, but that it "is an absolutely essential constituent in the highest goods, and contributes immensely to their value."[21] Similarly, the great value that has been placed upon pleasure, and the delusion that pleasure is the sole good, is attributed to the fact that:

> Pleasure does seem to be a necessary constituent of most valuable wholes; and since the other constituents, into which we may analyse them, may easily seem not to have any value, it is natural to suppose that all the value belongs to pleasure.[22]

Indeed, getting the right account of the relation of pleasure to other sorts of value seems to have been one of Moore's major motives in introducing the idea of organic unities. Things like pleasure and knowledge have what the tradition has called "contributive value."

I hope it is evident from these examples that the principle of organic unities is meant to do the same job that the notion of a conditioned good in Kant's theory does: it allows us to say of certain things that they are valuable only under certain circumstances, or valuable only when certain other things are true or present, without forcing us to say that these kinds of things must be valuable merely as instruments. Contributive value takes on the role that conditional value plays in Kant's view. The remaining difference is that Moore makes no distinction between what would be in Kant's terms really unconditionally (or intrinsically) good and what would be objectively good as an end.

VII

The principle of organic unities is crucial to Moore, for it enables him to make some of the same distinctions and judgments that the Kantian divisions make possible. Like the Kantian distinctions, it gives us a more flexible way of talking about the value of everyday things; and like the Kantian distinctions, it makes it possible for us to explain the conditional character of a good thing without rendering that good thing a mere means. Moore, who separates pleasure from the consciousness of pleasure, even complains in one passage that if pleasure were the sole intrinsic good, consciousness would have to be regarded as a means to it.[23] But the principle of organic unities is also in a certain way perverse. The seeming difficulties that it solves in fact arise from the relational or conditional character of the value of most of the things that human beings regard as good. Yet it is precisely this relational character that Moore, with his insistence on intrinsic value, wants to deny.

Suppose someone said: on Kant's view happiness is a conditioned or extrinsic value and the good will its condition. But the happiness of a good person is, on Kant's view, always good, good under any and all circumstances, for its condition is met. So couldn't we say of this, as well as of the good will, that it is intrinsically valuable? What this would amount to would be constructing an organic unity out of happiness and the good will, and showing that on Moore's account it has intrinsic value. Then the Kantian notion of "objective value" and Moore's "intrinsic value" are not so different after all.[24]

And the answer to that is that there is still a difference. For Moore's view, and the intuitionistic method of isolation, veil or obscure the internal relations within the organic unity in virtue of which the organic unity has its value. Whereas the Kantian account, which focuses on rather than ignoring the internal relations of the valuable whole, allows us to see why happiness is valuable in just this case and not in another case. Moore can only say that the combi-nation of happiness and good will works (is a good recipe, so to speak) while happiness plus the bad will does not. Kant can say that happiness in the one case is good because the condition under which it is fully justified has been met (roughly, because its having been decently pursued makes it deserved). Those internal relations reveal the *reasons* for our views about what is valuable, while Moore's view tends to cover up these reasons. And this might be true in other cases as well: if we think that aesthetic response is only valuable when the object responded to is genuinely beautiful, or that friendship is only valuable when your friend is good, or even if we think that aesthetic response and friendship are just *more* valuable in these cases, then this has something to do with the reasons we think these kinds of things are valuable at all. On Moore's account the only relation in which the elements of an organic whole stand to each other is the relation of being elements in a single organic whole. They are all on a footing with one another. But if Kant is right there is an order within "valuable wholes," a conditioning of some elements by others, that is hidden by treating these elements as just so many *ingredients*. This order reflects the reason why the wholes are good.

Another way to put the point is this: Moore's theory drives a wedge between the reason why we care about something and the reason why it is good. Or rather, since on Moore's theory it is a mistake to talk about why something is good, we should say that it drives a wedge between our natural interest in something and our moral interest in it. On Moore's theory if you say that the reason something is good is because someone cares about it, that could only mean that the person's interest was an element in an organic whole which had intrinsic value. But according to Moore the question why such a whole has intrinsic value must not be raised: it just has the property of intrinsic value; there is no reason why it has that property.[25] Yet it is because it has intrinsic value that we ought to make it an end in our actions. A thing's goodness becomes a property that we intuit and respond to in a way that seems curiously divorced from our natural interests.

The interesting thing about that is that Moore took up the idea of intrinsic value because he saw that objectivity was not all that we wanted from a theory of value. He was certainly right to think that the same people who are discouraged by subjectivism are discouraged by an evolutionary theory or others of that kind. But to me it seems that this discouragement has to do with the way in which such theories undermine the nature of our concern for the good. For instance, if goodness is mere fitness to survive, then the only way goodness matters is the way the biological survival of the species matters—and that doesn't cover everything we feel about the importance of living a good life. But what is the nature of our concern for intrinsic values as Moore describes them? Moore seems to find it obvious that when we have determined what is intrinsically good we shall have an interest in bringing that into the world. His anti-naturalistic arguments prevent him from giving any account of why this nonnatural property should be so appealing to us. Of course, the isolation test by which intrinsic values are discerned guarantees that we will only attribute them to something that appeals to us. But that does not provide a justification of our interest in the intrinsically valuable or even a motivational explanation of it. On the Kantian account, by contrast, the good end is the object of a rational choice. The things that we want, need, care for, are good so long as certain conditions of rational choice are met. Thus, the reasons that things are good bear a definite relation to the reasons we have for caring about them.

The primary advantage of the Kantian theory of goodness is that it gives an account of the "objectivity" of goodness that does not involve assigning some sort of property to all good things. Good things are good in the way that Ross describes as relational, because of attitudes taken up towards them or because of other physical or psychological conditions that make them important to us. Only one thing—the good will itself—is assigned an intrinsic value or inner worth, and even the argument for that is not ontological. If we regard ourselves as having the power to justify our ends, the argument says, we must regard ourselves as having an inner worth—and we must treat others who can also place value on their ends in virtue of their humanity as having the same inner worth.

If human beings have an intrinsic value by virtue of the capacity for valuing things, then human beings bring goodness into the world. The distinction between a thing that is intrinsically good and a thing that is extrinsically good yet valuable as an end allows for the possibility that the things that are important to us have an objective value, yet have that value because they are important to us. Objective goodness is not a mysterious ontological attribute. The things that are important to us can be good: good because of our desires and interests and loves and because of the physiological, psychological, economic, historical, symbolic and other conditions under which human beings live.

Notes

1. Intrinsic is often directly opposed to instrumental; equally commonly, "extrinsic" is opposed to intrinsic but then "consequential" or "instrumental" is offered as a definition or explanation of that term. Or, in some of the literature, "intrinsic" is taken to be a particular theory about how ends are valued, and accepted or dismissed as such. All of these usages more or less imply the equivalence of the two distinctions; none leaves room for the Kantian theory described in this paper.

2. C. I. Lewis, *An Analysis of Knowledge and Valuation* (Open Court, 1946).

3. Moore's views on intrinsic value are mostly presupposed in *Principia Ethica* (Cambridge, 1903); but they are addressed explicitly in *Ethics* (Oxford, 1912); "The Conception of Intrinsic Value" written for

Philosophical Studies (Routledge and Kegan Paul, Ltd., 1922); and a symposium reply entitled "Is Goodness a Quality?" published in the Aristotelian Society Supplement in 1932 and reprinted in *Philosophical Papers* (1959). In the last, Moore tends to give way to a view that his earlier accounts avoid—namely, that only experiences can be intrinsically good. For that reason and because of its polemical nature I have not used it in this paper.

4. "The Conception of Intrinsic Value" p. 256.

5. *Ibid.*, p. 260.

6. *Ibid.*, pp. 260–65.

7. *Ibid.*, p. 256.

8. *Principia Ethica*, p. 187.

9. *Ethics*, p. 68.

10. *Ibid.*, p. 69.

11. In *The Right and The Good* (Oxford, 1930) Chapter IV, Ross argues explicitly in favor of Moore and against Ralph Barton Perry, who, in his *General Theory of Value* (Harvard, 1926), argues that value is relative to interest. The Kantian view defended in this paper is classified by Perry as one in which value is "the object of a qualified interest" and opposed by him in favor of the view that value is "the object of any interest."

12. *The Right and the Good*, p. 75.

13. *Ibid.*, p. 81.

14. I am not the first to set up Kant's view in opposition to Moore's. The same is done by H. J. Paton in "The Alleged Independence of Goodness" written for the Library of Living Philosophers Volume on Moore (Northwestern: Volume 4, 1942). Paton, however, is not concerned with the two distinctions, and he focuses on the goodness of actions, which he claims is relative to the circumstances in which they are performed. Moore's rather impatient response is to incorporate the choice into the action and consideration of the circumstances into the choice: thus under different circumstances you have different actions. Moore's reply may be fair in the case discussed, but it is an instance of a general strategy which I discuss in the paper: when someone brings forward an example of a good thing whose goodness seems relative to the circumstances, Moore and Ross incorporate the circumstances into the thing to maintain the nonrelational character of the goodness.

15. References to Kant's works are given in the text as shown. "G" stands for the *Foundations of the Metaphysics of Morals*; the first page number is that of the translation by Lewis White Beck (Library of Liberal Arts, 1959); the second is the Prussian Academy edition page number. Other titles are given in full. The translations used are: Lewis White Beck, *Critique of Practical Reason* (Library of Liberal Arts, 1956) and Mary J. Gregor, *The Doctrine of Virtue* (Harper Torchbooks, 1964).

16. I am indebted to the Editors of the *Philosophical Review* for this point.

17. A much fuller treatment of the ideas of this section is in my paper "Kant's Formula of Humanity," forthcoming in *Kant-Studien*.

18. Insofar as Moore's point in identifying the naturalistic fallacy is to deny the identity of goodness with any particular natural property and so to insist on the autonomy of ethical discourse, Kant could agree. But whereas Moore concludes that goodness must therefore be a nonnatural property, Kant understands it to be a practical, rather than a theoretical, characterization.

19. I would like to thank the Editors for prompting me to clarify the roles of desire and choice in conferring value.

20. *Principia Ethica*, pp. 27–28.

21. *Ibid.*, p. 199.

22. *Ibid.*, p. 93.

23. *Ibid.*, p. 89.

24. Ross does something very like this in his discussion of the relation of virtue and pleasure in *The Right and The Good*, pp. 135 ff.

25. See *Principia Ethica*, pp. 142–44.

PART II

WHAT THINGS ARE GOOD?

HEDONISM: DEFENSE AND CRITICISM

10 / HENRY SIDGWICK

ULTIMATE GOOD*

§ 1. At the outset of this treatise[1] I noticed that there are two forms in which the object of ethical inquiry is considered; it is sometimes regarded as a Rule or Rules of Conduct, 'the Right,' sometimes as an end or ends, 'the Good.' I pointed out that in the moral consciousness of modern Europe the two notions are *prima facie* distinct; since while it is commonly thought that the obligation to obey moral rules is absolute, it is not commonly held that the whole Good of man lies in such obedience; this view, we may say, is—vaguely and respectfully but unmistakably—repudiated as a Stoical paradox. The ultimate Good or Well-being of man is rather regarded as an ulterior result, the connexion of which with his Right Conduct is indeed commonly held to be certain, but is frequently conceived as supernatural, and so beyond the range of independent ethical speculation. But now, if the conclusions of the preceding chapters are to be trusted, it would seem that the practical determination of Right Conduct depends on the determination of Ultimate Good. For we have seen (a) that most of the commonly received maxims of Duty—even of those which at first sight appear absolute and independent—are found when closely examined to

*Editors' Note: For Sidgwick's definition of "pleasure," readers should consult the summary of this selection in the General Introduction.
Reprinted by permission of the publisher and copyright holder from Henry Sidgwick, *The Methods of Ethics*, 7th ed. (London: Macmillan, 1907), pp. 391–407.

contain an implicit subordination to the more general principles of Prudence and Benevolence: and (b) that no principles except these, and the formal principle of Justice or Equity can be admitted as at once intuitively clear and certain; while, again, these principles themselves, so far as they are self-evident, may be stated as precepts to seek (1) one's own good on the whole, repressing all seductive impulses prompting to undue preference of particular goods, and (2) others' good no less than one's own, repressing any undue preference for one individual over another. Thus we are brought round again to the old question with which ethical speculation in Europe began, 'What is the Ultimate Good for man?'—though not in the egoistic form in which the old question was raised. When, however, we examine the controversies to which this question originally led, we see that the investigation which has brought us round to it has tended definitely to exclude one of the answers which early moral reflection was disposed to give to it. For to say that 'General Good' consists solely in general Virtue,—if we mean by Virtue conformity to such prescriptions and prohibitions as make up the main part of the morality of Common Sense—would obviously involve us in a logical circle; since we have seen that the exact determination of these prescriptions and prohibitions must depend on the definition of this General Good.

Nor, I conceive, can this argument be evaded by adopting the view of what I

have called 'Aesthetic Intuitionism' and regarding Virtues as excellences of conduct
clearly discernible by trained insight, although their nature does not admit of being stated in definite formulae. For our notions of special virtues do not really
become more independent by becoming
more indefinite: they still contain, though
perhaps more latently, the same reference
to 'Good' or 'Wellbeing' as an ultimate
standard. This appears clearly when we
consider any virtue in relation to the cog-
nate vice—or at least *non-virtue*—into
which it tends to pass over when pushed
to an extreme, or exhibited under inappropriate conditions. For example, Common
Sense may seem to regard Liberality,
Frugality, Courage, Placability, as intrinsically desirable: but when we consider
their relation respectively to Profusion,
Meanness, Foolhardiness, Weakness, we
find that Common Sense draws the line in
each case not by immediate intuition, but
by reference either to some definite maxim
of duty, or to the general notion of 'Good'
or Wellbeing: and similarly when we ask
at what point Candour, Generosity,
Humility cease to be virtues by becoming
'excessive.' Other qualities commonly admired, such as Energy, Zeal, Self-control,
Thoughtfulness, are obviously regarded as
virtues only when they are directed to good
ends. In short, the only so-called Virtues
which can be thought to be essentially
and always such, and incapable of excess,
are such qualities as Wisdom, Universal
Benevolence, and (in a sense) Justice; of
which the notions manifestly involve this
notion of Good, supposed already determinate. Wisdom is insight into Good and
the means to Good; Benevolence is exhibited in the purposive actions called "doing
Good": Justice (when regarded as essentially and always a Virtue) lies in distributing Good (or evil) impartially according
to right rules. If then we are asked what is
this Good which it is excellent to know, to
bestow on others, to distribute impartially,
it would be obviously absurd to reply that
it is just this knowledge, these beneficent
purposes, this impartial distribution.

Nor, again, can I perceive that this difficulty is in any way met by regarding Virtue
as a quality of "character" rather than of
"conduct," and expressing the moral law
in the form, "Be this," instead of the form
"Do this."[2] From a practical point of view,
indeed, I fully recognise the importance of
urging that men should aim at an ideal of
character, and consider action in its effects
on character. But I cannot infer from this
that character and its elements—faculties,
habits, or dispositions of any kind—are the
constituents of Ultimate Good. It seems to
me that the opposite is implied in the very
conception of a faculty or disposition; it can
only be defined as a tendency to act or feel
in a certain way under certain conditions;
and such a tendency appears to me clearly
not valuable in itself but for the acts and
feelings in which it takes effect, or for the
ulterior consequences of these,—which
consequences, again, cannot be regarded as
Ultimate Good, so long as they are merely
conceived as modifications of faculties, dispositions, etc. When, therefore, I say that
effects on character are important, it is a
summary way of saying that by the laws of
our mental constitution the present act or
feeling is a cause tending to modify importantly our acts and feelings in the indefinite future: the comparatively permanent result supposed to be produced in the
mind or soul, being a tendency that will
show itself in an indefinite number of particular acts and feelings, may easily be
more important, in relation to the Ultimate
end, than a single act or the transient feeling of a single moment: but its comparative permanence appears to me no ground
for regarding it as itself a constituent of Ultimate Good.

§ 2. So far, however, I have been speaking only of particular virtues, as exhibited
in conduct judged to be objectively right:
and it may be argued that this is too external a view of the Virtue that claims to constitute Ultimate Good. It may be said that
the difficulty that I have been urging vanishes if we penetrate beyond the particular
virtues to the root and essence of virtue in
general,—the determination of the will to

do whatever is judged to be right and to aim at realising whatever is judged to be best—; since this subjective rightness or goodness of will, being independent of knowledge of what is objectively right or good, is independent of that presupposition of Good as already known and determined, which we have seen to be implied in the common conceptions of virtue as manifested in outward acts. I admit that if subjective rightness or goodness of Will is affirmed to be the Ultimate Good, the affirmation does not exactly involve the logical difficulty that I have been urging. None the less it is fundamentally opposed to Common Sense; since the very notion of subjective rightness or goodness of will implies an objective standard, which it directs us to seek, but does not profess to supply. It would be a palpable and violent paradox to set before the right-seeking mind no end except this right-seeking itself, and to affirm this to be the sole Ultimate Good, denying that any effects of right volition can be in themselves good, except the subjective rightness of future volitions, whether of self or of others. It is true that no rule can be recognised, by any reasonable individual, as more authoritative than the rule of doing what he judges to be right; for, in deliberating with a view to my own immediate action, I cannot distinguish between doing what is objectively right, and realising my own subjective conception of rightness. But we are continually forced to make the distinction as regards the actions of others and to judge that conduct may be objectively wrong though subjectively right: and we continually judge conduct to be objectively wrong because it tends to cause pain and loss of happiness to others,—apart from any effect on the subjective rightness of their volitions. It is as so judging that we commonly recognise the mischief and danger of fanaticism:—meaning by a fanatic a man who resolutely and unswervingly carries out his own conception of rightness, when it is a plainly mistaken conception.

The same result may be reached even without supposing so palpable a divorce between subjective and objective rightness of volition as is implied in the notion of fanaticism. As I have already pointed out,[3] though the 'dictates of Reason' are always to be obeyed, it does not follow that 'the dictation of Reason'—the predominance of consciously moral over nonmoral motives—is to be promoted without limits; and indeed Common Sense appears to hold that some things are likely to be better done, if they are done from other motives than conscious obedience to practical Reason or Conscience. It thus becomes a practical question how far the dictation of Reason, the predominance of moral choice and moral effort in human life, is a result to be aimed at: and the admission of this question implies that conscious rightness of volition is not the sole ultimate good. On the whole, then, we may conclude that neither (1) subjective rightness or goodness of volition, as distinct from objective, nor (2) virtuous character, except as manifested or realised in virtuous conduct, can be regarded as constituting Ultimate Good: while, again, we are precluded from identifying Ultimate Good with virtuous conduct, because our conceptions of virtuous conduct, under the different heads or aspects denoted by the names of the particular virtues, have been found to presuppose the prior determination of the notion of Good—that Good which virtuous conduct is conceived as producing or promoting or rightly distributing.

And what has been said of Virtue, seems to me still more manifestly true of the other talents, gifts, and graces which make up the common notion of human excellence or Perfection. However immediately the excellent quality of such gifts and skills may be recognised and admired, reflection shows that they are only valuable on account of the good or desirable conscious life in which they are or will be actualised, or which will be somehow promoted by their exercise.

§ 3. Shall we then say that Ultimate Good is Good or Desirable conscious or sentient Life—of which Virtuous action is one element, but not the sole constituent?

This seems in harmony with Common Sense; and the fact that particular virtues and talents and gifts are largely valued as means to ulterior good does not necessarily prevent us from regarding their exercise as also an element of Ultimate Good: just as the fact that physical action, nutrition, and repose, duly proportioned and combined, are means to the maintenance of our animal life, does not prevent us from regarding them as indispensable elements of such life. Still it seems difficult to conceive any kind of activity or process as both means and end, from precisely the same point of view and in respect of precisely the same quality: and in both the cases above mentioned it is, I think, easy to distinguish the aspect in which the activities or processes in question are to be regarded as means from that in which they are to be regarded as in themselves good or desirable. Let us examine this first in the case of the physical processes. It is in their purely physical aspect, as complex processes of corporeal change, that they are means to the maintenance of life: but so long as we confine our attention to their corporeal aspect,—regarding them merely as complex movements of certain particles of organised matter—it seems impossible to attribute to these movements, considered in themselves, either goodness or badness. I cannot conceive it to be an ultimate end of rational action to secure that these complex movements should be of one kind rather than another, or that they should be continued for a longer rather than a shorter period. In short, if a certain quality of human Life is that which is ultimately desirable, it must belong to human Life regarded on its physical side, or, briefly, Consciousness.

But again: it is not all life regarded on its psychical side which we can judge to be ultimately desirable: since psychical life as known to us includes pain as well as pleasure, and so far as it is painful it is not desirable. I cannot therefore accept a view of the wellbeing or welfare of human beings—as of other living things—which is suggested by current zoological conceptions and apparently maintained with more or less definiteness by influential writers; according to which, when we attribute goodness or badness to the manner of existence of any living organism, we should be understood to attribute to it a tendency either (1) to self-preservation, or (2) to the preservation of the community or race to which it belongs—so that what "Wellbeing" adds to mere "Being" is just promise of future being. It appears to me that this doctrine needs only to be distinctly contemplated in order to be rejected. If all life were as little desirable as some portions of it have been, in my own experience and in that (I believe) of all or most men, I should judge all tendency to the preservation of it to be unmitigatedly bad. Actually, no doubt, as we generally hold that human life, even as now lived, has on the average, a balance of happiness, we regard what is preservative of life as generally good, and what is destructive of life as bad: and I quite admit that a most fundamentally important part of the function of morality consists in maintaining such habits and sentiments as are necessary to the continued existence, in full numbers, of a society of human beings under their actual conditions of life. But this is not because the mere existence of human organisms, even if prolonged to eternity, appears to me in any way desirable; it is only assumed to be so because it is supposed to be accompanied by Consciousness on the whole desirable; it is therefore this Desirable Consciousness which we must regard as Ultimate Good.

In the same way, so far as we judge virtuous activity to be a part of Ultimate Good, it is, I conceive, because the consciousness attending it is judged to be in itself desirable for the virtuous agent; though at the same time this consideration does not adequately represent the importance of Virtue to human wellbeing, since we have to consider its value as a means as well as its value as an end. We may make the distinction clearer by considering whether Virtuous life would remain on the whole good for the virtuous agent, if we suppose it combined with extreme pain. The affirmative answer to this question was strongly supported in Greek philosophical discussion: but it is a paradox from which a modern thinker would recoil: he would hardly venture to assert that the portion of life spent by a martyr in tortures was in itself desirable,—though it might be his duty to suffer the pain with a view to the good of others, and even his interest to suffer it with a view to his own ultimate happiness.

§ 4. If then Ultimate Good can only be conceived as Desirable Consciousness—including the Consciousness of Virtue as a part but only as a part—are we to identify this notion with Happiness or Pleasure, and say with the Utilitarians that General Good is general happiness? Many would at this point of the discussion regard this conclusion as inevitable: to say that all other things called good are only means to the end of making conscious life better or more desirable, seems to them the same as saying that they are means to the end of happiness. But very important distinctions remain to be considered. According to the view taken in a previous chapter,[4] in affirming Ultimate Good to be Happiness or Pleasure, we imply (1) that nothing is desirable except desirable feelings, and (2) that the desirability of each feeling is only directly cognisable by the sentient individual at the time of feeling it, and that therefore this particular judgment of the sentient individual must be taken as final[5] on the question how far each element of feeling has the quality of Ultimate Good. Now no one, I conceive, would estimate in any other way the desirability of feeling considered merely as feeling: but it may be urged that our conscious experience includes besides Feelings, Cognitions and Volitions, and that the desirability of these must be taken into account, and is not to be estimated by the standard above stated. I think, however, that when we reflect on a cognition as a transient fact of an individual's psychical experience,—distinguishing it on the one hand from the feeling that normally accompanies it, and on the other hand from that relation of the knowing mind to the object known which

is implied in the term "true" or "valid cognition"[6]—it is seen to be an element of consciousness quite neutral in respect of desirability: and the same may be said of Volitions, when we abstract from their concomitant feelings, and their relation to an objective norm or ideal, as well as from all their consequences. It is no doubt true that in ordinary thought certain states of consciousness—such as Cognition of Truth, Contemplation of Beauty, Volition to realise Freedom or Virtue—are sometimes judged to be preferable on other grounds than their pleasantness: but the general explanation of this seems to be (as was suggested in Book ii. chap. ii. § 2) that what in such cases we really prefer is not the present consciousness itself, but either effects on future consciousness more or less distinctly foreseen, or else something in the objective relations of the conscious being, not strictly included in his present consciousness.

The second of these alternatives may perhaps be made clearer by some illustrations. A man may prefer the mental state of apprehending truth to the state of half-reliance on generally accredited fictions,[7] while recognising that the former state may be more painful than the latter, and independently of any effect which he expects either state to have upon his subsequent consciousness. Here, on my view, the real object of preference is not the consciousness of knowing truth, considered merely as consciousness,—the element of pleasure or satisfaction in this being more than outweighed by the concomitant pain,—but the relation between the mind and something else, which, as the very notion of 'truth' implies, is whatever it is independently of our cognition of it, and which I therefore call objective. This may become more clear if we imagine ourselves learning afterwards that what we took for truth is not really such: for in this case we should certainly feel that our preference had been mistaken; whereas if our choice had really been between two elements of transient consciousness, its reasonableness could not be affected by any subsequent discovery.

Similarly, a man may prefer freedom and penury to a life of luxurious servitude, not because the pleasant consciousness of being free outweighs in prospect all the comforts and securities that the other life would afford, but because he has a predominant aversion to that relation between his will and the will of another which we call slavery: or, again, a philosopher may choose what he conceives as 'inner freedom'—the consistent self-determination of the will—rather than the gratifications of appetite; though recognising that the latter are more desirable, considered merely as transient feelings. In either case, he will be led to regard his preference as mistaken, if he be afterwards persuaded that his conception of Freedom or self-determination was illusory; that we are all slaves of circumstances, destiny, etc.

So again, the preference of conformity to Virtue, or contemplation of Beauty, to a state of consciousness recognised as more pleasant seems to depend on a belief that one's conception of Virtue or Beauty corresponds to an ideal to some extent objective and valid for all minds. Apart from any consideration of future consequences, we should generally agree that a man who sacrificed happiness to an erroneous conception of Virtue or Beauty made a mistaken choice.

Still, it may be said that this is merely a question of definition: that we may take 'conscious life' in a wide sense, so as to include the objective relations of the conscious being implied in our notions of Virtue, Truth, Beauty, Freedom: and that from this point of view we may regard cognition of Truth, contemplation of Beauty, Free or Virtuous action, as in some measure preferable alternatives to Pleasure or Happiness—even though we admit that Happiness must be included as a part of Ultimate Good. In this case the principle of Rational Benevolence, which was stated in the last chapter as an indubitable intuition of the practical Reason, would not direct us to the pursuit of universal happiness alone, but of these "ideal goods" as well, as ends ultimately desirable for mankind generally.

§ 5. I think, however, that this view ought not to commend itself to the sober judgment of reflective persons. In order to show this, I must ask the reader to use the same twofold procedure that I before requested him to employ in considering the absolute and independent validity of common moral precepts. I appeal firstly to his intuitive judgment after due consideration of the question when fairly placed before it: and secondly to a comprehensive comparison of the ordinary judgments of mankind. As regards the first argument, to me at least it seems clear after reflection that these objective relations of the conscious subject, when distinguished from the consciousness accompanying and resulting from them, are not ultimately and intrinsically desirable; any more than material or other objects are, when considered apart from any relation to conscious existence. Admitting that we have actual experience of such preferences as have just been described of which the ultimate object is something that is not merely consciousness: it still seems to me that when (to use Butler's phrase) we "sit down in a cool hour," we can only justify to ourselves the importance that we attach to any of these objects by considering its conduciveness, in one way or another, to the happiness of sentient beings.

The second argument, that refers to the common sense of mankind, obviously cannot be made completely cogent; since, as above stated, several cultivated persons do habitually judge that knowledge, art, etc.— not to speak of Virtue—are ends independently of the pleasure derived from them. But we may urge not only that all these elements of "ideal good" are productive of pleasure in various ways; but also that they seem to obtain the commendation of Common Sense, roughly speaking, in proportion to the degree of this productiveness. This seems obviously true of Beauty; and will hardly be denied in respect of any kind of social ideal: it is paradoxical to maintain that any degree of Freedom, or any form of social order, would still be commonly regarded as desirable even if we were certain that it had no tendency to promote the general happiness. The case of knowledge is rather more complex; but certainly Common Sense is most impressed with the value of knowledge, when its 'fruitfulness' has been demonstrated. It is, however, aware that experience has frequently shown how knowledge, long fruitless, may become unexpectedly fruitful, and how light may be shed on one part of the field of knowledge from another apparently remote: and even if any particular branch of scientific pursuit could be shown to be devoid of even this indirect utility, it would still deserve some respect on utilitarian grounds; both as furnishing to the inquirer the refined and innocent pleasures of curiosity, and because the intellectual disposition which it exhibits and sustains is likely on the whole to produce fruitful knowledge. Still in cases approximating to this last, Common Sense is somewhat disposed to complain of the misdirection of valuable effort; so that the meed of honour commonly paid to Science seems to be graduated, though perhaps unconsciously, by a tolerably exact utilitarian scale. Certainly the moment the legitimacy of any branch of scientific inquiry is seriously disputed, as in the recent case of vivisection, the controversy on both sides is generally conducted on an avowedly utilitarian basis.

The case of Virtue requires special consideration: since the encouragement in each other of virtuous impulses and dispositions is a main aim of men's ordinary moral discourse; so that even to raise the question whether this encouragement can go too far has a paradoxical air. Still, our experience includes rare and exceptional cases in which the concentration of effort on the cultivation of virtue has seemed to have effects adverse to general happiness, through being intensified to the point of moral fanaticism, and so involving a neglect of other conditions of happiness. If, then, we admit as actual or possible such 'infelicific' effects of the cultivation of Virtue, I think we shall also generally admit that, in the case supposed, conducive-

ness to general happiness should be the criterion for deciding how far the cultivation of Virtue should be carried.

At the same time it must be allowed that we find in Common Sense an aversion to admit Happiness (when explained to mean a sum of pleasures) to be the sole ultimate end and standard of right conduct. But this, I think, can be fully accounted for by the following considerations.

I. The term Pleasure is not commonly used so as to include clearly *all* kinds of consciousness which we desire to retain or reproduce: in ordinary usage it suggests too prominently the coarser and commoner kinds of such feelings; and it is difficult even for those who are trying to use it scientifically to free their minds altogether from the associations of ordinary usage, and to mean by Pleasure only Desirable Consciousness or Feeling of whatever kind. Again, our knowledge of human life continually suggests to us instances of pleasures which will inevitably involve as concomitant or consequent either a greater amount of pain or a loss of more important pleasures: and we naturally shrink from including even hypothetically in our conception of ultimate good these—in Bentham's phrase—"impure" pleasures; especially since we have, in many cases, moral or aesthetic instincts warning us against such pleasures.

II. We have seen[8] that many important pleasures can only be felt on condition of our experiencing desires for other things than pleasure. Thus the very acceptance of Pleasure as the ultimate end of conduct involves the practical rule that it is not always to be made the conscious end. Hence, even if we are considering merely the good of one human being taken alone, excluding from our view all effects of his conduct on others, still the reluctance of Common Sense to regard pleasure as the sole thing ultimately desirable may be justified by the consideration that human beings tend to be less happy if they are exclusively occupied with the desire of personal happiness. *E.g.* (as was before shown) we shall miss the valuable pleasures which attend the exercise of the benevolent affections if we do not experience genuinely disinterested impulses to procure happiness for others (which are, in fact, implied in the notion of 'benevolent affections').

III. But again, I hold, as was expounded in the preceding chapter, that disinterested benevolence is not only thus generally in harmony with rational Self-love, but also in another sense and independently rational: that is, Reason shows me that if my happiness is desirable and a good, the equal happiness of any other person must be equally desirable. Now, when Happiness is spoken of as the sole Ultimate Good of man, the idea most commonly suggested is that each individual is to seek his own happiness at the expense (if necessary) or, at any rate, to the neglect of that of others: and this offends both our sympathetic and our rational regard for others' happiness. It is, in fact, rather the end of Egoistic than of Universal-istic Hedonism, to which Common Sense feels an aversion. And certainly one's individual happiness is, in many respects, an unsatisfactory mark for one's supreme aim, apart from any direct collision into which the exclusive pursuit of it may bring us with rational or sympathetic Benevolence. It does not possess the characteristics which, as Aristotle says, we "divine" to belong to Ultimate Good: being (so far, at least, as it can be empirically foreseen) so narrow and limited, of such necessarily brief duration, and so shifting and insecure while it lasts. But Universal Happiness, desirable consciousness or feeling for the innumerable multitude of sentient beings, present and to come, seems an End that satisfies our imagination by its vastness, and sustains our resolution by its comparative security.

It may, however, be said that if we require the individual to sacrifice his own happiness to the greater happiness of others on the ground that it is reasonable to do so, we really assign to the individual a different ultimate end from that which we lay down as the Ultimate Good of the universe of sentient beings: since we direct him to take, as ultimate, Happiness for the Universe, but Conformity to Reason for himself. I admit the substantial truth of this statement, though I should avoid the language as tending to obscure the distinction before explained between "obeying the dictates" and "prompting the dictation" of reason. But granting the alleged difference, I do not see that it constitutes an argument against the view here maintained, since the individual is essentially and fundamentally different from the larger whole—the universe of sentient beings—of which he is conscious of being a part; just because he has a known relation to similar parts of the same whole, while the whole itself has no such relation. I accordingly see no inconsistency in holding that while it *would* be reasonable for the aggregate of sentient beings, if it could act collectively, to aim at its own happiness only as an ultimate end— and would be reasonable for any individual to do the same, if he were the only sentient being in the universe—it may yet be *actually* reasonable for an individual to sacrifice his own Good or happiness for the greater happiness of others.[9]

At the same time I admit that, in the earlier age of ethical thought which Greek philosophy represents, men sometimes judged an act to be 'good' *for the agent*, even while recognising that its consequences would be on the whole painful to him,—as (*e.g.*) a heroic exchange of a life full of happiness for a painful death at the call of duty. I attribute this partly to a confusion of thought between what it is reasonable for an individual to desire, when he considers his own existence alone, and what he must recognise as reasonably to be desired, when he takes the point of view of a larger whole: partly, again, to a faith deeply rooted in the moral consciousness of mankind, that there cannot be really and ultimately any conflict between the two kinds of reasonableness.[10] But when 'Reasonable Self-love' has been clearly distinguished from Conscience, as it is by Butler and his followers, we find it is naturally understood to mean desire for one's own Happiness: so that in fact the interpretation of 'one's own good,' which was almost peculiar in ancient thought to the

Cyrenaic and Epicurean heresies, is adopted by some of the most orthodox of modern moralists. Indeed it often does not seem to have occurred to these latter that this notion can have any other interpretation.[11] If, then, when any one hypothetically concentrates his attention on himself, Good is naturally and almost inevitably conceived to be Pleasure, we may reasonably conclude that the Good of any number of similar beings, whatever their mutual relations may be, cannot be essentially different in quality.

IV. But lastly, from the universal point of view no less than from that of the individual, it seems true that Happiness is likely to be better attained if the extent to which we set ourselves consciously to aim at it be carefully restricted. And this not only because action is likely to be more effective if our effort is temporarily concentrated on the realisation of more limited ends—though this is no doubt an important reason:—but also because the fullest development of happy life for each individual seems to require that he should have other external objects of interest besides the happiness of other conscious beings. And thus we may conclude that the pursuit of the ideal objects before mentioned, Virtue, Truth, Freedom, Beauty, etc., *for their own sakes*, is indirectly and secondarily, though not primarily and absolutely, rational; on account not only of the happiness that will result from their attainment, but also of that which springs from their disinterested pursuit. While yet if we ask for a final criterion of the comparative value of the different objects of men's enthusiastic pursuit, and of the limits within which each may legitimately engross the attention of mankind, we shall none the less conceive it to depend upon the degree in which they respectively conduce to Happiness.

If, however, this view be rejected, it remains to consider whether we can frame any other coherent account of Ultimate Good. If we are not to systematise human activities by taking Universal Happiness as their common end, on what other principles are we to systematise them? It should

be observed that these principles must not only enable us to compare among themselves the values of the different nonhedonistic ends which we have been considering, but must also provide a common standard for comparing these values with that of Happiness; unless we are prepared to adopt the paradoxical position of rejecting happiness as absolutely valueless. For we have a practical need of determining not only whether we should pursue Truth rather than Beauty, or Freedom or some ideal constitution of society rather than either, or perhaps desert all of these for the life of worship and religious contemplation; but also how far we should follow any of these lines of endeavour, when we foresee among its consequences the pains of human or other sentient beings, or even the loss of pleasures that might otherwise have been enjoyed by them.[12]

I have failed to find—and am unable to construct—any systematic answer to this question that appears to me deserving of serious consideration: and hence I am finally led to the conclusion (which at the close of the last chapter seemed to be premature) that the Intuitional method rigorously applied yields as its final result the doctrine of pure Universalistic Hedonism,[13]—which it is convenient to denote by the single word, Utilitarianism.

Notes

1. See Book i. chap. i. § 2.

2. Cf. Stephen, *Science of Ethics*, chap. iv. § 16.

3. Chap. xi. § 3; see also chap. xii. § 3.

4. Book ii. chap. ii.

5. Final, that is, so far as the quality of the present feeling is concerned. I have pointed out that so far as any estimate of the desirability or pleasantness of a feeling involves comparison with feelings only represented in idea, it is liable to be erroneous through imperfections in the representation.

6. The term "cognition" without qualification more often implies what is signified by "true" or "valid": but for the present purpose it is necessary to eliminate this implication.

7. Cf. Leeky, *History of European Morals*, pp. 52 *seqq.*

8. Book i. chap. iv.; cf. Book ii. chap. iii.

9. I ought at the same time to say that I hold it no less reasonable for an individual to take his own happiness as his ultimate end. This "Dualism of the Practical Reason" will be further discussed in the concluding chapter of the treatise.

10. We may illustrate this double explanation by a reference to some of Plato's Dialogues, such as the *Gorgias*, where the ethical argument has a singularly mixed effect on the mind. Partly, it seems to us more or less dexterous sophistry, playing on a confusion of thought latent in the common notion of good: partly a noble and stirring expression of a profound moral faith.

11. Cf. Stewart, *Philosophy of the Active and Moral Powers*, Book ii. chap. i.

12. The controversy on vivisection, to which I referred just now, affords a good illustration of the need that I am pointing out. I do not observe that any one in this controversy has ventured on the paradox that the pain of sentient beings is not *per se* to be avoided.

13. I have before noticed (Book ii. chap. iii) the metaphysical objection taken by certain writers to the view that Happiness is Ultimate Good; on the ground that Happiness (=sum of pleasures) can only be realised in successive parts, whereas a "Chief Good" must be "something of which some being can be conceived in possession"—something, that is, which he can have all at once. On considering this objection it seemed to me that, in so far as it is even plausible, its plausibility depends on the exact form of the notion 'a Chief Good' (or 'Summum Bonum'), which is perhaps inappropriate as applied to Happiness. I have therefore in this chapter used the notion of 'Ultimate Happiness'. I have therefore in this chapter used the notion of 'Ultimate Good': as I can see no shadow of reason for affirming that that which is Good or Desirable *per se*, and not as a means to some further end, must *necessarily* be capable of being possessed all at once. I can understand that a man may aspire after a Good of this latter kind: but so long as Time is a necessary form of human existence, it can hardly be surprising that human good should be subject to the condition of being realised in successive parts.

11 / ROBERT NOZICK

VALUE AND PLEASURE

There are also substantial puzzles when we ask what matters other than how *people's* experiences feel "from the inside." Suppose there were an experience machine that would give you any experience you desired. Superduper neuropsychologists could stimulate your brain so that you would think and feel you were writing a great novel, or making a friend, or reading an interesting book. All the time you would be floating in a tank, with electrodes attached to your brain. Should you plug into this machine for life, preprogramming your life's experiences? If you are worried about missing out on desirable experiences, we can suppose that business enterprises have researched thoroughly the lives of many others. You can pick and choose from their large library or smorgasbord of such experiences, selecting your life's experiences for, say, the next two years. After two years have passed, you will have ten minutes or ten hours out of the tank, to select the experiences of your *next* two years. Of course, while in the tank you won't know that you're there; you'll think it's all actually happening. Others can also plug in to have the experiences they want, so there's no need to stay unplugged to serve them. (Ignore problems such as who will service the machines if everyone plugs in.) Would you plug in? *What else can matter to us, other than how our lives feel from the inside?* Nor should you refrain because of the few moments of distress between the mo-

ment you've decided and the moment you're plugged. What's a few moments of distress compared to a lifetime of bliss (if that's what you choose), and why feel any distress at all if your decision *is* the best one?

What does matter to us in addition to our experiences? First, we want to *do* certain things, and not just have the experience of doing them. In the case of certain experiences, it is only because first we want to do the actions that we want the experiences of doing them or thinking we've done them. (But *why* do we want to do the activities rather than merely to experience them?) A second reason for not plugging in is that we want to *be* a certain way, to be a certain sort of person. Someone floating in a tank is an indeterminate blob. There is no answer to the question of what a person is like who has long been in the tank. Is he courageous, kind, intelligent, witty, loving? It's not merely that it's difficult to tell; there's no way he is. Plugging into the machine is a kind of suicide. It will seem to some, trapped by a picture, that nothing about what we are like can matter except as it gets reflected in our experiences. But should it be surprising that what *we are* is important to us? Why should we be concerned only with how our time is filled, but not with what we are?

Thirdly, plugging into an experience machine limits us to a man-made reality, to a world no deeper or more important than that which people can construct.[1] There is no *actual* contact with any deeper reality, though the experience of it can be simulated. Many persons desire to leave them-

Reprinted by permission of the publisher and copyright holder from Robert Nozick, *Anarchy, State, and Utopia* (New York: Basic Books, 1974), pp. 43–45.

selves open to such contact and to a plumbing of deeper significance.[2] This clarifies the intensity of the conflict over psychoactive drugs, which some view as mere local experience machines, and others view as avenues to a deeper reality; what some view as equivalent to surrender to the experience machine, others view as following one of the reasons *not* to surrender!

We learn that something matters to us in addition to experience by imagining an experience machine and then realizing that we would not use it. We can continue to imagine a sequence of machines each designed to fill lacks suggested for the earlier machines. For example, since the experience machine doesn't meet our desire to *be* a certain way, imagine a transformation machine which transforms us into whatever sort of person we'd like to be (compatible with our staying us). Surely one would not use the transformation machine to become as one would wish, and thereupon plug into the experience machine![3] So something matters in addition to one's experiences *and* what one is like. Nor is the reason merely that one's experiences are unconnected with what one is like. For the experience machine might be limited to provide only experiences possible to the sort of person plugged in. Is it that we want to make a difference in the world? Consider then the result machine, which produces in the world any result you would produce and injects your vector input into any joint activity. We shall not pursue here the fascinating details of these or other machines. What is most disturbing about them is their living of our lives for us. Is it misguided to search for *particular* additional functions beyond the competence of machines to do for us? Perhaps what we desire is to live (an active verb) ourselves, in contact with reality. (And this, machines cannot do *for* us.) Without elaborating on the implications of this, which I believe connect surprisingly with issues about free will and causal accounts of knowledge, we need merely note the intricacy of the question of

what matters *for people* other then their experiences. Until one finds a satisfactory answer, and determines that this answer does not *also* apply to animals, one cannot reasonably claim that only the felt experiences of animals limit what we may do to them.

Notes

1. This point was suggested to me by Mr. Thom Krystofiak.

2. Traditional religious views differ on the *point* of contact with a transcendent reality. Some say that contact yields eternal bliss or Nirvana, but they have not distinguished this sufficiently from merely a *very* long run on the experience machine. Others think it is intrinsically desirable to do the will of a higher being which created us all, though presumably no one would think this if we discovered we had been created as an object of amusement by some superpowerful child from another galaxy or dimension. Still others imagine an eventual merging with a higher reality, leaving unclear its desirability, or where that merging leaves *us*.

3. Some wouldn't use the transformation machine at all; it seems like *cheating*. But the one-time use of the transformation machine would not remove all challenges; there would still be obstacles for the new us to overcome, a new plateau from which to strive even higher. And is this plateau any the less earned or deserved than that provided by genetic endowment and early childhood environment? But if the transformation machine could be used indefinitely often, so that we could accomplish anything by pushing a button to transform ourselves into someone who could do it easily, there would remain no limits we *need* to strain against or try to transcend. Would there by anything left *to do*? Do some theological views place God outside of time because an omniscient omnipotent being couldn't fill up his days?

THE DESIRE-SATISFACTION THEORY: DEFENSE AND CRITICISM

12 / G. H. VON WRIGHT

THE GOOD OF MAN

1. The notion of the good of man, which will be discussed in this chapter, is the central notion of our whole inquiry. The problems connected with it are of the utmost difficulty. Many things which I say about them may well be wrong. Perhaps the best I can hope for is that what I say will be interesting enough to be worth a refutation.

We have previously discussed the question, what kind of being has a good. We decided that it should make sense to talk of the good of everything, of the *life* of which it is meaningful to speak. On this ruling there can be no doubt that man *has* a good.

Granted that man has a good—what *is* it? The question can be understood in a multitude of senses. It can, for example, be understood as a question of a *name*, a verbal equivalent of that which we *also* call 'the good of man'.

We have already had occasion to point out that the German equivalent of the English substantive 'good', when this means the good of man or some other being, is *das Wohl*. There is no substantive 'well' with *this* meaning in English. But there are two related substantives, 'well-being' and 'welfare'.

Reprinted by permission of the publisher and copyright holder from G. H. von Wright, *The Varieties of Goodness*, chap. 5 (London: Routledge, 1963), pp. 86–113.

A being who, so to speak, 'has' or 'enjoys' its good, is also said to *be well* and, sometimes, to *do well*.

The notion of being well is related to the notion of health. Often 'to be well' means exactly the same as 'to be in good, bodily and mental, health'. A man is said to be well when he is all right, fit, in good shape generally. These various expressions may be said to refer to minimum requirements of enjoying one's good.

Of the being who does well, we also say that it flourishes, thrives, or prospers. And we call it happy. If health and well-being primarily connote something privative, absence of illness and suffering; happiness and well-doing again primarily refer to something positive, to an overflow or surplus of agreeable states and things.

From these observations on language three candidates for a name of the good of man may be said to emerge. These are 'happiness', 'well-being', and 'welfare'.

The suggestion might be made that 'welfare' is a comprehensive term which covers the whole of that which we also call 'the good of man' and of which happiness and well-being are 'aspects' or 'components' or 'parts'. It could further be suggested that there is a broad sense of 'happiness', and of 'well-being', to mean the same or roughly the same as 'welfare'. So that, on *one* way of understanding them, the three terms could be regarded as rough synonyms and alternative names of the good of man.

The suggestion that 'the good of man' and 'the welfare of man' are synonymous phrases I accept without discussion. That is: I shall use and treat them as synonyms.

It is hardly to be doubted that 'happiness' is sometimes used as a rough synonym of 'welfare'. More commonly, however, the two words are *not* used as synonyms. Happiness and welfare may, in fact, become distinguished as two concepts of different logical category or type. We shall here mention three features which may be used for differentiating the two concepts logically.

First of all, the two concepts have a primary connexion with two different forms of the good. One could say, though with caution, that happiness is a *hedonic*, welfare again a *utilitarian* notion. Happiness is allied to pleasure, and therewith to such notions as those of enjoyment, gladness, and liking. Happiness has no immediate logical connexion with the beneficial. Welfare again is primarily a matter of things beneficial and harmful, *i.e.* good and bad, for the being concerned. As happiness, through pleasure, is related to that which a man enjoys and likes, in a similar manner welfare, through the beneficial, is connected with that which a man wants and needs.

Further, happiness is more like a 'state' (state of affairs) than welfare is. A man can become happy, be happy, and cease to be happy. He can be happy and unhappy, more than once in his life. Happiness, like an end, can be achieved and attained. Welfare has not these same relationships to events, processes, and states *in time*.

Finally, a major logical difference between happiness and welfare is their relation to *causality*. Considerations of welfare are essentially considerations of how the doing and happening of various things will causally affect a being. One cannot pronounce on the question whether something is good or bad for a man, without considering the causal connexions in which this thing is or may become embedded. But one can pronounce on the question whether a man is happy or not, without necessarily considering what were the causal antecedents and what will be the consequences of his present situation.

The facts that happiness is primarily a hedonic and welfare primarily a utilitarian notion, and that they have logically different relationships to time and to causality, mark the two concepts as being of that which I have here called 'different logical category or type'. It does not follow, however, that the two concepts are logically entirely unconnected. They are, on the contrary, closely allied. What then is their mutual relation? This is a question, on which I have not been able to form a clear view. Welfare (the good of a being) is, somehow, the broader and more basic notion. It is also the notion which is of greater importance to ethics and to a general study of the varieties of goodness. Calling happiness an 'aspect' or 'component' or 'part' of the good of man is a non-committal mode of speech which is not meant to say more than this. Of happiness I could also say that it is the consummation or crown or flower of welfare. But these are metaphorical terms and do not illuminate the logical relationship between the two concepts.

2. By an end of action we shall understand anything, *for the sake of which* an action is undertaken. If something, which we want to do, is not wanted for the sake of anything else, the act or activity can be called an *end in itself*.

Ends can be intermediate or ultimate. Sometimes a man wants to attain an end for the sake of some further end. Then the first end is *intermediate*. An end, which is not pursued for the sake of any further end, is *ultimate*. We shall call a human act *end-directed*, if it is undertaken either as an end in itself or for the sake of some end.

What is an ultimate end of action is settled by the last answer, which the agent himself can give to the question, *why* he does or intends to do this or that. It is then understood that the question 'Why?' asks for a reason and not for a causal explanation of his behaviour.

In the terms which have here been introduced, we could redefine Psychological Hedonism as the doctrine that every end-directed human act is undertaken, ultimately, for the sake either of attaining some pleasure or avoiding something unpleasant. The doctrine again that every end-directed human act is undertaken, ultimately, for the sake of the acting agent's happiness we shall call Psychological Eudaimonism. A doctrine to the effect that every end-directed act is ultimately undertaken for the sake of the acting agent's welfare (good) has, to the best of my knowledge, never been defended. We need not here invent a name for it.

Aristotle sometimes talks[1] as though he had subscribed to the doctrine of psychological eudaimonism. If this was his view, he was certainly mistaken and, moreover, contradicting himself. It would be sheer nonsense to maintain that every chain of (noncausal) questions 'Why did you do this?' and answers to them must terminate in a reference to happiness. The view that man, in everything he does, is aiming at happiness (and the avoidance of misery) is even more absurd than the doctrine that he, in everything he does, is aiming at pleasure (and the avoidance of pain).

I said that, if Aristotle maintained psychological eudaimonism, he was contradicting himself. (And for this reason I doubt that Aristotle wanted to maintain it, though some of his formulations would indicate that he did.) For Aristotle also admits that there are ends, other than happiness, which we pursue for their own sake. He mentions pleasure and honour among them.[2] Even 'if nothing resulted from them, we should still choose each of them', he says.[3] On the other hand, those other final ends are sometimes desired, *not* for their own sake, but for the sake of something else. Whereas happiness, Aristotle thinks, is *never* desired for the sake of anything else.[4] Pleasure, *e.g.* pleasant amusement, can be desired for relaxation, and relaxation for the sake of continued activity.[5] *Then* pleasure is not a final end.

I would understand Aristotle's so-called eudaimonism in the following light: among possible ends of human action, *eudaimonia* holds a unique position. This unique position is *not* that *eudaimonia* is the final end of all action. It is that *eudaimonia* is the only end that is never anything except final. It is of the nature of *eudaimonia* that it cannot be desired for the sake of anything else. *This* is, so Aristotle seems to think, why *eudaimonia* is the highest good for man.[6]

It is plausible to think that a man can pursue, *i.e.* do things for the sake of promoting or safeguarding, his own happiness only as an ultimate end of his action. A man can also do things for the sake of promoting or safeguarding the happiness of some other being. It may be thought that he can do this only as an intermediate end of his action. The idea has an apparent plausibility, but is nevertheless a mistake. The truth seems to be that a man can pursue the happiness of others either as intermediate *or* as ultimate end.

The delight of a king can be the happiness of his subjects. He gives all his energies and work to the promotion of this end. Maybe he sacrifices his so-called 'personal happiness' for the good of those over whom he is set to rule. Yet, if this is what he likes to do, it is also that in which his happiness consists. To say this is not so distort facts logically. But to say that the king sacrifices himself for the sake of becoming happy and not for the sake of making others happy, would be a distortion. It would be a distortion similar to that of which psychological hedonism is guilty, when it maintains that everything is done for the sake of pleasure, on the ground that all satisfaction of desire may be thought intrinsically pleasant.

Can a man's *welfare* be an end of his own action? The question is equivalent to asking, whether a man can ever be truly said to do things for the sake of promoting or protecting his own good. It is not quite clear which is the correct answer.

On the view which is here taken of the good of a being, to do something for the sake of promoting one's own good, means to do something *because* one considers doing it *good for* oneself. And to do something for the sake of protecting one's own good means to do something *because* one considers neglecting it bad for oneself.

For all I can see, men sometimes do things for the reasons just mentioned. This would show that a man's welfare *can be* an end of his own action.

Yet the good of a being as an end of action is a very peculiar sort of 'end'. Normally, an end of action is a state of affairs, something which 'is there', when the end has been attained. But welfare is not a state of affairs. For this reason I shall say that welfare, the good of a being, can only in an *oblique* sense be called an end of action.

Obviously, the reason why a man does something, which he considers good for himself, is not always and necessarily *that* he considers doing it good for himself. Similarly, the reason why a man does something, which he considers bad for him to neglect, is not always and necessarily *that* he considers neglecting it bad for himself. This shows that a man's own welfare is not always an ultimate end of his action. It also shows that a man's own welfare is not always an end of his action at all. It does not show, however, that a man's own welfare is sometimes an intermediate end of his action. Whether it *can* be an intermediate end, I shall not attempt to decide. If the answer is negative, it would follow that, when a man's own welfare is an end of his action, it is necessarily an ultimate end.

Sometimes a man does something because he considers doing it good for another being, and neglects something because he considers doing it bad for another being. It is obvious that another man's good can be the *intermediate* end of a man's action. The reason why the master takes heed to promote and protect the welfare of his servants, can be that he expects them to serve him more efficiently if they thrive and are happy. Then his servants' welfare is an intermediate end of the master's. It may be suggested that, when the end of a man's action is another being's welfare, then it is necessarily an intermediate end. This suggestion, I think, is false. We shall

return to the topic later, when discussing egoism and altruism.

Beings can be handled or treated as means to somebody's ends. This is the case, *e.g.*, with domestic animals and slaves. Philosophers have sometimes entertained the idea that beings could also be treated as 'ends' or 'ends in themselves'. It is not clear what it means to say that a being, *e.g.* a man, is an 'end in itself'. But treating a man as an end in itself *could mean*, I suggest, that we do certain things because we consider them good for that man (and for no other ulterior reason) and abstain from doing certain things because we consider them bad for that man. In other words: whenever a being's good is an ultimate end of action, that being is treated as an end in itself. A man can treat other men thus, but also himself. That men *should be* thus treated is an interesting view of the nature of moral duty. We shall briefly talk of this in Chapter X.

In the next five sections of the present chapter we shall be dealing with various aspects of the concept of happiness and in the last five sections with questions relating to the concept of welfare.

3. Happiness, we said, is a hedonic notion. It is, of course, not *the same* as pleasure. Nor can it be defined, as has been suggested, as 'pleasure and the absence of pain'.

Moralists who have written about happiness have sometimes associated the notion more intimately with one, sometimes with another, of the three principal 'forms' of pleasure, which we have in this book distinguished. One could, accordingly, speak of three types of *ideals of happiness* or of the happy life.

The first I shall call *Epicurean ideals*. According to them, 'true happiness' derives above all from *having* things which please. 'Pleasure' need not here be understood in the 'grosser' sense of sensuous pleasure. It includes the enjoyment of agreeable recollections and thoughts, of good company, and of beautiful things. Moore's position in *Principia Ethica* can, I think, be called an Epicureanism in this broad sense.

Can a man find happiness entirely in passive pleasure? *i.e.* can following an Epicurean recipe of living make a man completely happy? I can see no *logical* impossibility in the idea. If a man's supreme desire happened to be to secure for himself a favourable balance of passive pleasure over passive 'unpleasure', *i.e.* of states he enjoys over states he dislikes, and if he were successful in this pursuit of his, then the Epicurean recipe of living would, by definition, make him happy. It may be argued—from considerations pertaining to the contingencies of life—that the chances are strongly against his succeeding. It may also be argued—this time from considerations pertaining to the psychology of human nature—that very few men are such pleasure-lovers that the supreme thing they want for themselves in life is a maximum of passive pleasure. But the facts—if they be facts—that Epicurean ideals are risky and not very commonly pursued throughout a whole life, must not induce us to deny that a man—if there be such a man—who successfully pursued such ideals was genuinely happy and flourishing. To deny this would be to misunderstand the notions of happiness and the good of man and would be symptomatic, I think, of some 'moralistic perversion'.

The second type of ideals of the happy life probably comes nearer than the Epicurean ideals to something which the classical writers of utilitarianism had in mind. It seems to me true to say that the utilitarians thought of happiness, not so much in terms of passive pleasure, as in terms of satisfaction of desire. Happiness, on such a view, is essentially contentedness—an equilibrium between needs and wants on the one hand and satisfaction on the other.

Yet one of the great utilitarians—protesting against unwanted consequences of a view which he was himself, though not whole-heartedly, defending—made the famous *dictum*, 'It is better to be a human being dissatisfied than a pig satisfied'. I am not a utilitarian myself. But I would like to protest, in a sense, against Mill's remark.

The ultimate reason why it is not good for man to live like a pig, is that the life of a pig *does not satisfy* man. The dissatisfied Socrates, to whom Mill refers, we may regard as a symbol of man in search of a better and therewith more satisfying form of life. If his cravings were all doomed to be nothing but 'vanity and the vexation of spirit', then to idealize the dissatisfied Socrates would be to cherish a perverted view of the good life.

If one adopts the view that happiness is essentially an equilibrium between desire and satisfaction, one may reach the further conclusion that the safest road to happiness is to have as few and modest wants as possible, thus minimizing the chances of frustration and maximizing those of satisfaction. This recipe of happiness I shall call *the ascetic ideal* of life.[7] When carried to the extreme, this ideal envisages complete happiness in the total abnegation of all desire whatsoever.

Ascetism, in this sense, can be termed a *crippled* view of happiness. In order to see in which respect it is crippled, it is helpful to consider the contrary of happiness, *i.e.* unhappiness or misery. It would seem that there is a more direct connexion between unhappiness and dissatisfaction of desire than there is between happiness and satisfaction. Frustration of desire is a main source of unhappiness. Never or seldom to get that for which one is craving, never or seldom to have a chance of doing that which one likes to do, *this* is above all what makes a man miserable.

To call extreme ascetism a crippled ideal is to accuse it of a logical mistake. This is the mistake of regarding happiness as the *contradictory*, and not as the *contrary*, of unhappiness. By escaping frustration a man escapes unhappiness—provided, of course, that it does not befall him in the form of such affliction, which accident or illness or the acts of evil neighbours may cause him. The man of *no* wants, if there existed such a creature, would not be unhappy. But it does not follow that he would be happy.

The third type of ideals of the happy life which I wanted to mention here, seeks happiness neither in passive pleasure nor in the satisfaction of desire, but in that which we have called active pleasure, *i.e.* the pleasure of doing that on which we are keen, which for its own sake we like *doing*. In the activities which we are keen on doing, we aim at technical goodness or perfection. The better we are in the art, the more do we enjoy practising it, the happier does it make us. Therefore, the more talented we are by nature for an art, the more can the development of our skill in it contribute to our happiness.

It may be argued—chiefly against Epicureanism I should think—that the pleasures of the active life are those which are best suited to secure the attainment of lasting happiness. It is more risky to be, for one's well-being, dependent upon things we *have* or *get* than upon things we *do* (or *are*). That is: it is more risky to seek happiness in passive than in active pleasure. There is probably a great deal of truth in the argument. But it would certainly be wrong to think that the road to happiness through an active life were completely risk-free.

4. The factors which determine whether a man will become happy, we shall call *conditions* of happiness. Of such conditions one may distinguish three main groups. Happiness, we shall say, is conditioned partly by *chance* or luck, partly by innate *disposition*, and partly by *action*. 'Action' here means action on the part of the individual concerned himself. That which is *done to* a man may, for present purposes, be counted as chance-factors conditioning his happiness.

Illness can befall a man or he can become bodily or mentally injured without any fault of his own. If such misfortune assumes a certain permanence, it may affect a man's happiness adversely. It may do so either as a cause of pain or as a cause of frustration of desire or because it prevents the victim from engaging in activity which, for its own sake, he enjoys. However, luck may also favour a man's good. The benefit a person draws from good friends or good teachers or financial benefactors has, partly if not wholly, the character of luck. It is

something which life has in store for some men but not for others to make them happier, independently of their own doings and precautions.

It is an aspect of that which we called the ascetic ideal of life, that man is well advised to *make* himself as independent as possible of chance and luck as conditions of his happiness. This he can try to do in various ways: by hardening himself to sustain pain, by withdrawing from political and social engagements, or by not aspiring too high even in those activities, which he enjoys for their own sake. The belief that a man could make himself altogether independent of external affectations of his good, is a conceit peculiar to certain 'ascetic' and 'stoic' attitudes to life. It overrates man's possibilities of conditioning his happiness and peace of mind by assuming a certain attitude to contingencies.

The innate dispositions of happiness have to do both with bodily health and with mental equipment and temper. A man of weak health is more exposed to certain risks of becoming unhappy than a man of good health. A man of many talents has more resources of happiness than a man of poor gifts. A man of good temper and cheerful outlook will not let adversities frustrate his efforts as easily as the impatient and gloomy man. To the extent that such temperamental dispositions can be developed or suppressed in a man, they fall under those conditions of happiness which a man controls through his action.

Human action, which is relevant to the happiness of the agent himself, is of two types. Action of the first type are things which the agent does, measures which he takes for the sake of promoting or protecting his happiness. Such action is *causally* relevant to his happiness. Action of the second type are things which the agent does or practises for their own sake, as ends in themselves, *i.e.* simply because he wants to do or likes to do them and for no other reason. Action in which a man delights one could call *constitutive* of his happiness, 'parts' of his happiness.

Now it may happen that action, which is

thus constitutive of a man's happiness, *also* affects his happiness causally. It may affect his happiness promotingly, but also affect it adversely. For example: a man is immensely fond of playing various games. He plays and enjoys playing them all day long. In so doing he neglects his education and his social duties and maybe his health too. Thus the very same thing, which is constitutive of his happiness, may, by virtue of its consequences, accumulate clouds of unhappiness over the agent's head, while he is rejoicing in this thing. This possibility is responsible for the major complications, which are connected with a man's own action as a conditioning factor of his happiness and welfare generally.

5. When is a man happy? It is obvious that a man can be truly praised happy, even though many painful and unpleasant things have happened to him in the course of his life. But not if he never had any pleasures. What must the preponderance of the pleasant over the unpleasant be, if he is still to be called happy?

Here it is helpful to consider the states which we call gladness and sadness. They occupy a kind of intermediate position between happiness and unhappiness on the one hand, and pleasure and its contrary on the other hand. It may be suggested that pleasant and unpleasant experiences and activities are constitutive of gladness and sadness in a manner similar to that in which states of joy and depression are constitutive of happiness and unhappiness. A man can be glad although he has toothache, and he can be a happy man even though he chances to be very sad for a time. But he could not be glad if he had no pleasures to compensate such pains as he may have at the time of his gladness; and he cannot be happy if he is not *on the whole* more glad than sad. But we cannot tell exactly what must be the balance.

Pleasure, joy, and happiness are things of increasing degrees of permanence and resistance to changes. Something can please a man without cheering him up, and cheer him up without making him happy. Something can be a terrible blow to a man and make him sad, but whether it makes him unhappy is another matter.

Consider, for example, a man whom we praise happy and who is hit by a sudden blow of bad luck, say, the loss of a child in an accident. He will experience painful agonies and extreme sadness. 'News of the disaster made him dreadfully unhappy,' we might say, thinking of these emotional effects on him. If, however, we were to say that the news made him *an unhappy man*, we should be thinking not only, or maybe even not at all, on those emotional effects, but on effects of a less immediate showing and of a longer lasting. If we can say of him some such things as, 'For years after he was as paralysed; none of the things, which used to delight him, gave him pleasure any longer,' or 'Life seemed to have lost meaning for him,—for a time he even contemplated suicide,' then the accident made him *unhappy* as distinct from merely *sad*. But whether things, bearing on the distinction, can be truly said of the man, is not to be seen in an inkling.

Analogous things can be said about changes in the reverse direction. A piece of news, say of an unexpected inheritance, can make a man jump with joy. But whether it makes him *happy* as distinct from merely *glad* can only be seen from effects of a longer lasting and less obvious showing on his subsequent life.

Should we say 'the *whole* of his subsequent life'? I think not. Happiness is neither a momentary state nor is it a sum total to be found out when we close our life's account. A man can *become* happy, *be* happy, and *change* from happy to unhappy. Thus, in the course of his life, a man can be both happy and unhappy. And he can be happy and unhappy more than once.

We could make a distinction between a happy *man* and a happy *life* and regard the second as a thing of wider scope. This would make it possible to say of somebody that he had a happy life although, for sometime, he was a most unhappy man.

6. A judgment to the effect that some being is happy or is not happy or is unhappy we shall call an *eudaimonic* judgment.

I think it is illuminating to compare the logic of the eudaimonic judgment to the logic of the statement 'This is pleasant'. Of the sentence 'This is pleasant' we said that it conceals a logical form. It suggests that pleasantness is a property which we attribute to some object or state, whereas in fact to judge something pleasant is to verbalize a relationship in which the judging subject stands to this thing. To judge something hedonically good is to manifest an *attitude*, one could also say, to certain things (activities, sensations, the causes of sensations). The logically most adequate form of the verbalization is therefore, it seems, the relational form 'I like this' or some similar relational form.

In an analogous sense the sentence 'He is happy' may be said, I think, to conceal a logical form. It suggests a view of happiness as a property which the happy individual exhibits—which shines forth from him. Whereas, in fact, to be happy is to be in a certain relationship. A relationship to what? it may be asked. A relationship to one's circumstances of life, I would answer. To say 'He is happy' is similar to saying 'He likes it', the 'it' not meaning this or that particular thing or activity but, so to speak, 'the whole thing'. One could also say, 'He likes his life as it is.'

On this view, if a man says of himself 'I am happy', he manifests in words an attitude which he takes, or a relationship, in which he stands, to his circumstances of life. Happiness *is* not in the circumstances—as it were awaiting the judgment—but springs into being with the relationship. (Just as hedonic goodness does not reside in the taste of an apple, but in somebody's liking the taste of an apple.) To judge oneself happy is to pass judgment on or value one's circumstances of life.

To say 'He is happy' can mean two different things. It can mean that the man, of whom we are talking, is in the relationship to his circumstances which, if *he* were to verbalize his attitude, he could express in the words 'I am happy'. Then 'He is happy' is not a value-judgment. It is a true or false statement to the effect that a certain subject values certain things, *i.e.* his circumstances of life, in a certain way. We could also call it a statement to the effect that a certain valuation *exists* (occurs, takes place).

Quite often, however, 'He is happy' is not a judgment about that which *he is* at all, but about that which *we should be*, if we happened to be in his circumstances. 'He is happy' then means roughly, 'He *must be* happy, *viz.* considering the circumstances he is in.' Such judgments are often an expression of envy. To say with conviction, 'Happy is he, who . . .' is usually to pronounce on that which we think would make ourselves happy.

We shall henceforth disregard the case, when the third person judgment 'He is happy' is only a disguise for our own valuations and thus really is a first person judgment.

7. On the view which I am defending here, judgments of happiness are thus very much like hedonic judgments. The third person judgments are true or false. In them is judged that so-and-so is or is not pleased with his circumstances of life. They are judgments *about* valuations—and therefore are no value-judgments. The first person judgments are not true or false. They *express* a subject's valuations of his own circumstances. They are genuine value-judgments, and yet in an important sense of 'judgment' they are no judgments.

Ultimately, a man is himself judge of his own happiness. By this I mean that any third person judgment which may be passed on his happiness, depends for its truth-value on how *he himself* values his circumstances of life. This is so independently of whether he verbalizes his attitude in a first person judgment or not.

In *a* sense, therefore, a man's own verdict 'I am happy' or 'I am unhappy', should he happen to pass it, will be final—whatever we may think *we* should say, if we were in his circumstances. We must never make the presence or absence of circumstances, which would determine our own first person judgments of happiness, the *criteria* of truth of third person judgments.

What may make it difficult to see clearly

this 'subjectivity' of the notion which we are discussing, is the fact that not every man is the best and most competent judge of his *prospects* of happiness. A man may strongly want to do something, think his life worthless if he is not allowed this thing. But another, more experienced man, may warn him that, if he follows his immediate impulses, he will in the end become a most miserable wretch. The more experienced man may be right. But the criterion, which proves him right, is *not* the mere fact that certain things—illness, destitution, and what not—befall this other man as a predicted consequence of his folly and wickedness. The criterion is that these consequences make that other man unhappy. If our fool accepts the consequences with a cheerful heart, the wise man cannot insist that he must be right. He cannot do so on the ground, say, that those same consequences would have made him, or most people, miserable. Nor can he pretend that the lightsome fellow is 'really' unhappy, though unaware of his own misery.

But cannot a man be mistaken in thinking that he *is* happy? In a sense he can *not*, but in another he *can*. 'He says he is happy, but in fact he is not' can express a true proposition. But does not the truth of this proposition entail that the person who professes to be happy is lying? And is this not uninteresting? The answer is that, beside uninteresting lies, there exist profoundly interesting lies in the matters, which we are now discussing. First person judgments of happiness can be insincere, and insincerity may be regarded as a species of lying.

The same, incidentally, holds good for first person hedonic judgments too. A youngster may profess to like the taste of tobacco, which in fact he detests, just for the sake of showing off. He may even make himself believe this, in some involved and twisted sense of 'believe'. A polite man may say he likes the taste of a wine merely to please his host. The insincerity of such first person judgments may be relatively easy to unmask.

In the case of first person judgments of happiness and misery, the problem of sincerity is most difficult—both psychologically and conceptually. I shall not here try to penetrate its logical aspects, which I find very bewildering. (I am not aware of any satisfactory discussion of the topic in the literature.) I shall make a shortcut through the difficulties and only say this much in conclusion:

However thoroughly a man may cheat himself with regard to his own happiness, the criterion of cheat or insincerity must be that *he* admits the fraud. A judgment is insincere when the subject 'in his innermost self' admits that it is not as he says it is. If his lips say 'I am happy' and he is not, then in his heart he must already be saying to himself 'I am not happy'. He, as it were, does not hear the voice of his heart. These are similes, and I am aware of the temptation to misuse them. (They are the same sort of similes that are used and misused in psychoanalysis—the similes of the subconscious, the super-ego, etc.) What I mean by them could perhaps be said most plainly as follows: The fact that first person judgments of happiness can be insincere must not be allowed to conflict logically with the fact that, whether a person is happy or not depends upon *his own* attitude to his circumstances of life. The supreme judge of the case *must be* the subject himself. To think that it could be otherwise is false objectivism.

8. Judgments of the beneficial and the harmful, *i.e.* of that which is good or bad for a man, involve two components. We have called them the *causal* and the *axiological* component. We must now say some words about each of them.

When something happens, *i.e.* the world changes in a certain respect, there will usually also be a number of subsequent changes, which are bound (by so-called 'natural necessity') to come about, once the first change took place. These subsequent changes we here call the *consequences* of the first change. If the first change is of that peculiar kind which we call a human act, then the subsequent changes are *consequences of action*. The change or changes upon which a certain further change is consequent (*i.e.*

the consequence of which this further change is) we shall call the *cause(s)* of this further change.

Most things which happen, perhaps all, would not have happened, *unless* certain antecedent changes had taken place in the world. These antecedent changes we shall call the *causal prerequisites* or *requirements* of the subsequent change. They are sometimes also called 'necessary causes.' The necessary causes may be, but need not be, 'causes' in the sense defined above.

These explanations are very summary. Not least of all considering the importance to ethics of the notion of consequences of action, it is an urgent *desideratum* that the logic of causal relationships be better elaborated than it is. We shall not, however, attempt this here. Only a few observations will be added to the above.

The notions both of consequences and of prerequisites and of causes of a change are relative to the further notion of a *state of the world*. Thus, *e.g.*, a change which is required in order to effect a certain change in the world as it is to-day, may not be required in order to effect this same change in the world as it is to-morrow.

It is sometimes said that every event (change) 'strictly speaking' has an infinite number of consequences throughout the whole of subsequent time, and that for this reason we can never know for certain what all the consequences of a given event are. These statements, if true at all, hold good for some different notion of consequence, but not for the notion with which we are here dealing. Exactly what could be meant by them is not clear. Yet we need not dismiss them as nonsense. When, for example, something which happens to-day is said to be a consequence of something which took place hundreds of years ago, what is meant is perhaps that, if we traced the 'causal history' of this event of to-day we should find among its 'causal ancestry' that event of hundreds of years ago. Here the notions of causal ancestry and causal history could be defined in terms of *our* notions of cause, consequence, and prerequisite and yet it need not follow that, if an

event belongs to the causal ancestry of another event, the first must be a cause or prerequisite of the second or the second a consequence of the first. For example: Let event *b* be a consequence (in our sense) of event *a* and a causal prerequisite (in our sense) of event *c*. It would then be reasonable to say that event *a* is a 'causal ancestor' of event *c*, or that tracing the 'causal history' of *c* takes us to *a*. In some loose sense of the words, *a* may be said to be a 'cause' of *c* and *c* a 'consequence' of *a*. But in the more precise sense, in which we are here employing the terms, *a* is not (necessarily) a cause of *c*, nor *c* (necessarily) a consequence of *a*.

The causes and consequences of things which happen, are often insufficiently known and therefore largely a matter of belief and conjecture. Sometimes, however, they *are* known to us. The statement, should it be made, that they *cannot* ('in principle') be known either is false or applies to some different notions of cause and consequence from ours.

By knowledge of the causes and consequences of things which happen, I here mean knowledge relating to *particulars*. An example would be knowledge that the death of N. N. was due to a dose of arsenic, which had been mixed into his food. Such knowledge of particulars is usually grounded on knowledge of general propositions—as for example that a dose of arsenic of a certain strength will (unless certain counteracting causes intervene) 'inevitably' kill a man. Whether all such knowledge of particulars is grounded on general knowledge, we shall not discuss.

When in the sequel we speak of *knowledge* of the causes and consequences of things, or of known causes and consequences, 'knowledge' is short for 'knowledge or belief' and 'known' for 'known or believed'. The consequences which are known (*i.e.* known or believed) at the time when the thing happens, we shall also call *foreseen* consequences.

So much for the causal component involved in judgments of the beneficial and the harmful. We now turn to the axiological component. A preliminary task will here be to clarify the notions of a *wanted* and an *unwanted* thing.

9. The notion of a wanted thing, which I shall now try to explain, is not the same as that of an end of action. I shall call it the notion of being *wanted in itself*. How things which are wanted in themselves, are related to things which are wanted as ends of action, will be discussed presently. Correlative with the notion of being . wanted in itself is the notion of being *unwanted in itself*. 'Between' the two falls a notion, which we shall call the notion of being *indifferent in itself*.

The notion of being wanted in itself is the nearest equivalent in my treatment here to the notion of *intrinsic value* in Moore and some other writers. Moore, when discussing the notion of intrinsic worth, often resorts to a logical fiction which, *mutatis mutandis*, may be resorted to also for explaining the meaning of a thing being wanted, unwanted, or indifferent 'in itself'.

This fiction is that of a preferential choice between two alternatives. A major difficulty is to formulate the terms of the choice correctly for the purpose of defining the axiological notions under discussion. (Moore's explanation of intrinsic value in terms of betterness of alternatives cannot be regarded as *logically* satisfactory—apart from questions of the meaningfulness of the very notion.[8]) Our proposal here of a solution to the problem is tentative only.

Assume you were offered a thing X which you did not already possess. Would you then rather take it than leave it, rather have it than (continue to) be without it? The offer must be considered apart from questions of causal requirements and of consequences. That is: considerations of things which you will have to do in order to get X, and of things which will happen to you as a consequence of your having got the thing X must not influence your choice. If then you would rather take X than leave it, X is *wanted in itself*. If you have the opposite preference, X is *unwanted in itself*. If you have no preference, X is *indifferent in itself*.

As readily noted, the ideas of the in it-self wanted and unwanted, which we have thus tried to explain in terms of a fictitious preferential choice, are necessarily relative to a *subject*. Nothing is wanted or unwanted 'in itself', if the words 'in itself' are supposed to mean 'apart from any rating or valuing subject'. The words 'in itself' mean 'causal prerequisites and consequences apart'. A thing, which for one subject is a wanted thing, may be regarded as unwanted by another subject. A thing, furthermore, which is wanted *now*, may be unwanted at another time—the subject being the same. The notion of being wanted or unwanted in itself is thus relative, not only to a subject, but also to a particular time in the life of this subject.

Moore did not think that intrinsic value was relative to subject and time. In this respect his 'objectivist' notion of the intrinsically good and bad differs from our 'subjectivist' notion of the in itself wanted and unwanted.

It is important to note that from our definition of the in itself wanted, unwanted, and indifferent it does not follow that, if X is wanted in itself, then not-X (the absence of X) is unwanted in itself. That not-X is wanted, unwanted, and indifferent in itself corresponds, on our definitions, to the following set of preferences:

Consider a thing X, which you have. Would you rather get rid of it than retain it, rather be without it than (continue to) possess it? The proposal must be considered apart from things which you will have to do in order to get rid of X and from things which will happen to you as a consequence of your having got rid of X. Then not-X is wanted in itself, if you prefer to get rid of X, unwanted in itself, if you prefer to retain X, and indifferent in itself, if you have no preference.

10. Anything which is an—intermediate or ultimate—end of action, can be called *a good* (for the subject in pursuit of the end). Anything which is an end of action, can also be said to be *a wanted thing*.

Also every thing, which is wanted in itself, can be called a good (for the subject to whom it is wanted). And every thing, which is unwanted in itself, can be called a bad (for the subject who shuns it).

Ends of action and things wanted in themselves thus both fall under the category 'goods'. Ends of action also fall under the category 'things wanted'.

The question may be raised, how ends of action and things wanted in themselves are mutually related. The question is complicated and I shall not discuss it in detail. It is reasonable to think that only things, which are attainable through action, *can be* ends of action. 'Craving for the moon' is not aiming at an end. But things other than those which are attainable through action, can be wanted in themselves—sunshine on a chilly day, for example. The only simple relationship between ends of action and things wanted in themselves, which I can suggest, is that ultimate ends of action are also things wanted in themselves.

Intermediate ends of action are either things wanted in themselves or things indifferent in themselves or, not infrequently, things unwanted in themselves. To get the in itself unwanted can never be an ultimate end of action, since the assumption that it is involves a contradiction. But to escape the in itself unwanted sometimes is an ultimate end of action. The unwanted is that which we shun, except when occasionally we pursue it as intermediate end for the sake of something else or suffer it as a necessary prerequisite of something coveted.

When a man gets something which is, to him, wanted in itself, without having pursued it as an end, we shall say that this wanted thing *befalls* him. Similarly, when a man gets something which is, to him, unwanted in itself and which he has not pursued as an intermediate end, we shall say that this thing befalls him.

The question may be raised whether a thing which befalls or happens to a man can appropriately be said to be 'wanted'. 'Wanted' in English has many meanings and must therefore be used with caution. Sometimes it means 'desired', sometimes 'needed', sometimes 'wished for'. When the wanted thing is an end of action, the nearest equivalent to 'wanted' is 'desired'.

Perhaps things which happen to a man and which satisfy our explanation of the in itself wanted, should better be called 'welcome'. They are things we 'gladly accept' or are 'happy to get'. Often we just call them 'good'. When I here call them 'wanted', it is by contrast to 'unwanted', which word is certainly correctly used for shunned things that befall or happen to a man.

11. Consider something, which an agent pursues as an ultimate end. Assume that he gets it. Attaining the end is usually connected with a number of things as its casual prerequisites and a number of other things as its consequences. Of the things which are thus causally connected with his end, some are perhaps known and others not known to the agent. Some, moreover, may be known to him already at the time when he pursues the end, others become known to him after he has attained it. That is: their causal relationship to the end is (becomes) known to him.

The thing which the agent pursues as an ultimate end, is to him a good and something he wants in itself. Of those things again which are causally connected—either as prerequisites or as consequences—with his attainment of the end, some are wanted in themselves (by him), others are unwanted in themselves (by him), others indifferent in themselves (to him). The sum total of those things, which are unwanted in themselves, we shall call the *price*, which the agent has to pay for the attainment of his ultimate end.

This notion of 'price', be it observed, includes consequences as well as causal prerequisites. On this definition of the notion, not only those things which the agent has to endure, in order to get his wanted thing, but also those which he has to suffer as a consequence of having got it, count as part of that which he has to *pay* for the good. One can define the notion of a price in different ways—for other purposes. This is how we define the notion for present purposes.

For anything which is wanted in itself, the question may be raised: Is this good worth its price? The question can be raised *prospectively*, with a view to things which have to be gone through as a consequence of starting to pursue this good as an end, or it can be raised *retrospectively*, with a view to things already suffered.

To answer the question whether a certain good is (was) worth its price, is to pass a value-judgment. It is to say of something, a good, that it is better or worse, more or less worth, than something else, its price. How shall this value-judgment be properly articulated?

I think we must resort here, for a second time, to the logical fiction of a preferential choice. We said that things which we do not have, are wanted in themselves when, ignoring their causes and consequences, we would rather get them than continue to be without them, and unwanted in themselves when we would rather continue to be without them than get them. This question of taking or leaving, having or being without, we can also raise for things, *considering their causes and consequences*. A correct way of presenting the choice which we should then be facing, is, I think, as follows:

Assume that X is something, which is not already in our world (life), *i.e.* is something which we do not already possess or which has not already happened or which we have not already done. Would we then want X to become introduced into our world (life), considering also the causal prerequisites of getting (doing) X and the consequences of having got (done) X? Or would we prefer to continue to be without X? In making up our mind we should also have to consider the causal prerequisites and the consequences of *not* having this change in our world (life). It may, for example, be necessary for us to take some in itself unwanted action to prevent X from coming into existence, if we wish to avoid having X, and it may be necessary for us to foresake some other in itself wanted thing Y as a consequence of *not* having had X.

We introduce the symbol 'X + C' for the complex whole, consisting of X and those other things, which are causally connected with it either as prerequisites or as consequences of its coming into being, *i.e.* of the change from not-X to X. The symbol 'not-X + C'' shall stand for the complex whole, consisting of the absence of X and the presence of those things which are causally connected, either as prerequisites or as consequences, with the continued absence of X.

The question which is presented for consideration in the fictitious preferential choice we are discussing, is whether we should prefer X + C to not-X + C' or whether we should have the reverse preference or whether we should be indifferent (have no preference).

Let the answer to the proposal be that we should rather have than continue to be without X, *i.e.* prefer X + C to not-X + C'. Then we shall say that X + C or the complex whole, consisting of X and the causal prerequisites and consequences of the coming into being of X, is a *positive constituent* of our good (welfare). Of the thing X itself we say that it is *good for us* or *beneficial*. This we say of X independently of whether X is wanted or unwanted or indifferent in itself.

Let the answer to the proposal be that we should rather continue to forego than have X, *i.e.* prefer not-X + C' to X + C. Then we shall say that X + C is a *negative constituent* of our good. Of the thing X itself we say that it is *bad for us* or *harmful*. This we say independently of whether X is wanted or unwanted or indifferent in itself.

The answer can, of course, also be that we should be indifferent to the alternatives. Then X + C is neither a positive nor a negative constituent of our good, and X is neither beneficial nor harmful.

Let us call X the *nucleus* of that complex whole, which consists of X and the causal prerequisites and consequences of the coming into existence of X. We could then say that the things which are beneficial or harmful, good or bad for a man, are nuclei of those complex causal wholes, which are positive or negative constituents of his good (welfare).

We can now state the conditions for answering the question whether a certain good is worth its 'price'. When a certain causal whole is a positive constituent of our good *and* its nucleus is a thing, which is wanted in itself, then we say that this thing or good *is* worth its price. When, however, the whole is a negative constituent of our good, *although* its nucleus is a thing, which is wanted in itself, then we say that this thing or good is *not* worth its price.

From our definitions of the beneficial and the harmful it does *not* follow that, if not-X is harmful, then X is beneficial, and *vice versa*. If, however, not-X is harmful, then X will be called *needed*. The needed is that, the lack or loss of which is a bad thing, an evil. The needed and the harmful are opposed as contradictories, *in the sense* that the contradictory of the needed is harmful, and *vice versa*. The beneficial and the harmful are opposed as contraries.

To provide a being with that which is beneficial for it is to *promote* its welfare. To provide it with that which it needs and to take care that it does not lose the needed is to *protect* its welfare. Things (acts, events) which are protective of a being's welfare are good for the being in the sense of 'good for' which can also be rendered by 'useful', but not in that sense of 'good for' which we call 'beneficial'.

12. The preferential choice, in the terms of which we have defined the notions of the beneficial and the harmful, we have called a 'logical fiction'. That it is a fiction implies two things. First, it implies that we are talking of how a man *would choose*, if he were presented with the choice, and not of what he actually chooses. Secondly, it implies that we assume the causal component involved in the value-judgment to be *completely known* to the subject at the time of the choice. This second assumption entails that there are no imperfections in the subject's knowledge which are such that, if they were detected and corrected, the subject would revise his preferences.

Thus, on our definitions, the answer to the question whether a certain thing is good or bad for a man, is independent of the following two factors: First, it is independent of whether he (or anybody else) *judges* or does not judge of the value of this thing for him. Secondly, it is independent

of what he (and everybody else) happens to *know* or not to know about the causal connexions of this thing. Yet, in spite of this independence of judgment and knowledge, the notions of the beneficial and the harmful are in an important sense *subjective*. Their subjectivity consists in their dependence upon the *preferences (wants)* of the subject concerned.

Considering what has just been said, it is clear that we must distinguish between that which *is* good or bad for a man and that which *appears*, *i.e.* is judged or considered or though (by himself or by others), to be good or bad for him.

Any judgment to the effect that something is good or bad for a man is based on such knowledge of the relevant causal connexions which the judging subject happens to possess. Since this knowledge may be imperfect, the judgment which he actually passes may be different from the judgment which he would pass, if he had perfect knowledge of the causal connexions. When there is this discrepancy between the actual and the potential judgment, we shall say that a man's *apparent* good is being mistaken for his *real* good.

Of certain things it is easier to judge correctly whether they are good or bad for us, than of certain other things. This means: the risks of mistaking our apparent good for our real good are sometimes greater, sometimes less. It is, on the whole, easier to judge correctly in matters relating to a person's health than in matters relating to his future career. For example: the judgment that it will do a man good to take regular exercise is, on the whole, safer than the judgment that it will be better for him to go into business than study medicine. Sometimes the difficulties to judge correctly are so great that it will be altogether idle and useless to try to form a judgment.

Sometimes we know for certain that a choice, which we are facing, is of great *importance* to us in the sense that it will make considerable *difference* to our future life, whether we choose the one or the other of two alternatives. An example could be a choice between getting married or remaining single or between accepting employment in a foreign country or continuing life at home. But certainty that the choice will make a great difference is fully compatible with uncertainty as to whether the difference will be for good or for bad. The feeling that our welfare *may* become radically affected by the choice, can make the choice very agonizing for us.

Also of many things in our past, which we did not deliberately choose, we may know for certain that they have been of great importance to us in the sense that our lives would have been very different, had these things not existed. This could be manifestly true, for example, of the influence which some powerful personality has had on our education or on the formation of our opinions. We may wonder whether it was not bad for us that we should have been so strongly under this influence. Yet, if we know only that our life would have been very different but cannot at all imagine *how* it would have been different, we may also be quite incompetent to form a judgment of the beneficial and harmful nature of this factor in our past history.

It is a deeply impressive fact about the condition of man that it should be difficult, or even humanly impossible, to judge confidently of many things which are known to affect our lives importantly, whether they are good or bad for us. I think that becoming *overwhelmed* by this fact is one of the things which can incline a man towards taking a religious view of life. 'Only God knows what is good or bad for us.' One could say thus—and yet accept that a man's welfare is a subjective notion in the sense that it is determined by what *he* wants and shuns.

13. Are judgments of the beneficial or harmful nature of things objectively true or false? When we try to answer this question, we must again observe the distinction between a first person judgment and a third person judgment.

When somebody judges of something that it is (was, will be) good or bad for somebody else, the judgment is a third person judgment. It depends for its truth-value on two things. The one is whether certain causal connexions are as the judging subject thinks that they are. The other is whether certain valuations (preferences, wants) of another subject are as the judging subject thinks that they are. Both to judge of causal connexions and to judge of the valuations of other subjects is to judge of empirical matters of fact. The judgment is 'objectively' true or false. It is, properly speaking, not a value-judgment, since the 'axiological' component involved in it is not a valuation but a judgment *about* (the existence or occurrence of) valuations.

The case of the first person judgment is more complicated. Its causal component is a judgment of matters of fact. In this respect the first person judgment is on a level with the third person judgment. Its axiological component, however, is a valuation and not a judgment about valuations. With regard to this component the judgment cannot be true or false. There is no 'room' for mistake concerning its truth-value. In this respect the first person judgment of the beneficial and the harmful is like the first person hedonic or eudaimonic judgment.

Although the first person judgment cannot be false in its axiological component, it can be *insincere*. The problem of sincerity of judgments concerning that which is good or bad for a man is most complicated. It is intimately connected with the problems relating to the notions of *regret* and of *weakness of will*. A few words will be said about them later.

A subject can also make a statement about his own valuations in the past or a conjecture about his valuations in the future. Such a statement or conjecture is, logically, a third person judgment. It is true or false both in its causal and in its axiological component.

Whether a judgment is, *logically*, a first person judgment, cannot be seen from the person and tense of its grammatical form alone. A man says 'This will do me good'. In saying this he could be anticipating certain consequences and *expressing* his valuation of them. But he could also be anticipating certain consequences and *antici-*

pating his valuation of them. In the first case, the judgment he makes is of the kind which I here call a first person judgment of the beneficial or harmful nature of things. In the second case, the judgment is (logically) a third person judgment. The subject is speaking *about* himself, *i.e.* about his future valuations.

Sometimes a judgment of the beneficial or the harmful is clearly anticipative both of consequences and of valuations. Sometimes it is clearly anticipative with regard to consequences and expressive with regard to valuations. But very often, it seems, the status of the judgment is not clear even to the judging subject himself. The judgment may contain *both* anticipations *and* expressions of valuations. Perhaps it is true to say that men's judgments of what is good or bad for themselves tend on the whole to be anticipative rather than expressive with regard to valuations.

The distinction between the *apparent* and the *real* good, it should be observed, can be upheld both for third person and for first person judgments of the beneficial and the harmful. In this respect judgments of the beneficial and the harmful differ from hedonic and eudaimonic judgments. (For the two last kinds of judgment the distinction vanishes in the first person case, *i.e.* in the genuine value-judgments.) Because of the presence of the causal component in the judgment, a subject can always be mistaken concerning the beneficial or the harmful nature of a thing—even when there is no 'room' for mistake with regard to valuation.

14. A man's answer to the question whether a certain good is worth its price or whether a thing is beneficial or harmful, may undergo alterations in the course of time. Such alterations in his judgments can be due either to changes in his knowledge of the relevant causal connexions or to changes in his valuations. For example: a man attains an end, which he considers worth while to have pursued, until years afterwards he comes to realize that he had

to pay for it with the ruin of his health. Then he revises his judgment and *regrets*.

There are two types of regret-situation relating to choices of ends and goods in general. Sometimes the choice can, in principle if not in practice, be repeated. To profess regret is then to say that one would not choose the same thing again next time, when there is an opportunity. But sometimes the choice is not repeatable. The reason for this could be that the consequences, of which one is aware and which are the ground for one's regret, continue to operate throughout one's whole life. There is no opportunity of making good one's folly in the past by acting more wisely in the future. Then to express regret is to pass judgment on one's *life*. It is like saying: If I were to live my life over again, I would, when arrived at the fatal station, act differently.

The value-judgments of regret and no-regret, like hedonic judgments and judgments of happiness, are neither true nor false. But they may be sincere or insincere. A person can say that he regrets, when in fact he does not, and he can stubbornly refuse to admit regret which he 'feels'. How is such insincerity unmasked? For example in this way: If a man, after having suffered the consequences, says he regrets his action, but on a new occasion repeats his previous choice, then we may doubt whether his remorse was not pretence only. He was perhaps annoyed at having had to pay so much for the coveted thing and therefore said it was not worth it, but at the bottom of his heart he was pleased at having got it. These are familiar phenomena.

Yet to think that a repetition of the professed folly were a sure sign of insincere regret, would be to ignore the complications of the practical problems relating to the good of man. A good, if strongly desired in itself and near at hand, may be a temptation to which a man succumbs, when the evil consequences are far ahead and the recollection of having suffered them in the past is perhaps already fading. There is no logical absurdity in the idea that a man sincerely regrets something as having been a mistake, a bad choice with a view to his welfare, *i.e.* with a view to what he 'really' wants for himself, and yet wilfully commits the same mistake over again, whenever there is an opportunity.

When a man succumbs to temptation and chooses a lesser immediate good, *i.e.* thing wanted in itself, rather than escapes a greater future bad, *i.e.* thing unwanted in itself, then he is acting wilfully against the interests of his own good. It is in such situations that those features of character which we call *virtues*, are needed to safeguard a man's welfare. We shall talk about them later.

That a man can do evil to himself through ignorance of the consequences of his acts or through negligence is obvious. That he can also harm himself through *akrasia* or weakness of will has a certain appearance of paradox. He then, as it were, both wants and does not want, welcomes and shuns, one and the same thing. When viewed in the short perspective, 'prerequisites and consequences apart', he wants it; when viewed in the prolonged perspective of the appropriate causal setting, he shuns it. One could say that, if he lets himself be carried away by the short perspective, then he was not capable of viewing *clearly* his situation in the long perspective. Or one could say that, if a man has an *articulated* *grasp* of what he wants, he can never harm himself through weakness of will. But saying this must not encourage an undue optimism about man's possibilities of acting in accordance with cool reasoning.

Notes

1. See, *e.g.*, *Ethica Nicomachea (EN)*, 1094a 18–21, 1095a 14–20, and 1176b 30–31.

2. *EN*, 1097b 1–2. See also 1172b 20–23.

3. *EN*, 1097b 2–3.

4. *EN*, 1097b 1 and again 1097b 5–6.

5. Cf. *EN*, 1176b 34–35.

6. There is no phrase in Aristotle's ethics which corresponds to our phrase 'the good of man'. *Eudaimonia* (happiness, well-being) Aristotle also calls the best or the highest good. The notion of a *summum bonum*, however, is not identical with the notion of the good of man as we use it here. But the two notions may be related.

7. Ascetism as an abnegation of worldly desire for the sake of the good of the soul must be distinguished from that which I here call ascetism as an ideal of life. To the first, ascetism is no 'end' or 'value' in itself, but an exercise and preparation for the good life.

8. See *Ethics*, pp. 42–44 and, in particular, Moore's reply to his critics in *The Philosophy of G. E. Moore*, pp. 554–557.

13 / RICHARD KRAUT

Desire and the Human Good

I

When we compare contemporary moral philosophy with the well-known moral systems of earlier centuries, we should be struck by the fact that a certain assumption about human well being that is now widely taken for granted was universally rejected in the past. The contemporary moral climate predisposes us to be pluralistic about the human good, whereas earlier systems of ethics embraced a conception of well being that we would now call narrow and restrictive. One way to convey the sort of contrast I have in mind is to note that according to Plato and Aristotle, there is one kind of life, that of the philosopher, that represents the summit of human flourishing, and all other lives are worth leading to the extent that they approximate this ideal. Certain other ethical theories of the past were in a way more narrow than this, for whereas Plato and Aristotle maintained that many things are in themselves worthwhile, others argued that there is only one intrinsic good—pleasure according to the Epicureans, virtue according to the Stoics. By contrast, it is now widely assumed that all such approaches are too exclusive, that not only are there many types of intrinsic goods but there is no one specific kind of life—whether it is that of a philosopher or a poet or anyone else—that is the single human ideal.[1] Even hedonism, a conception of the good that had a powerful influence

in the modern period, has few contemporary proponents. A consensus has arisen in our time that there is no single ultimate end that provides the measure by which the worth of all other goods must be assessed.[2]

But if we want not merely to take note of our departure from the past, but also to show why we are justified in being pluralists about the good, then we must have something to say about what human well being is. We should not simply assert that there are many goods and many kinds of good lives, but must offer some general account of what well being is that explains why it is so multiform. In response to this demand, many philosophers would, as a first approximation, equate the human good with the satisfaction of desire, and would explain the multiplicity of the good by pointing out that because of the enormous variety of our interests and tastes, our desires exhibit a similar heterogeneity. Roughly speaking, what makes a state of affairs good for someone is its satisfaction of one of that person's desires; accordingly, our lives go well to the extent that our desires, or the ones to which we give the greatest weight, are satisfied.[3]

A complication is created by the fact that sometimes we have desires—those created by addictions, for example—that we wish we were without. But this can easily be handled in familiar ways by giving special weight to second-order desires. The general idea is that so long as one wants something wholeheartedly and with open eyes, then it is good for one's desire to be satisfied, regardless of the content of the desire. The objects we now want or will want are

Reprinted by permission of the publisher and copyright holder from *Proceedings and Addresses of the American Philosophical Association* 68 (1994): 39–54.

made good for us by our wanting them; they are not already good for us, apart from our having a present or future desire for them. There are no facts about what is ultimately good for me that are independent of my aims, facts that I need to discover in order to know what to aim at. No wonder, then, that well being is multiform. Our good is invented and constructed rather than discovered; and because of the great variation in our personalities and abilities, we invent different plans of life and our desires are directed at many different kinds of objects.

Although the "desire theory," as it might be called, is widely accepted, in part because it gives some backing to the assumption that the good is multiform, I will argue that it nonetheless has weaknesses serious enough to justify its rejection.[4] At bottom, its main deficiency is that it is too accepting of desires as they stand, and cannot account for some of the ways in which they are subject to evaluation. What we need is a theory that is more objective and in this respect closer to the eudaimonistic theories of ancient and medieval philosophy. I would like to show how we can abandon the desire theory and still hold onto our sense that many different kinds of life are worth living—more than earlier systems realized, but not so many as the desire theory endorses.

II

I begin with a point that, despite its familiarity, cannot easily be accommodated by the desire theory. It is conceptually and psychologically possible for people to decide, voluntarily and with due deliberation, to renounce their good in favor of an alternative goal. They can clearheadedly design a long-range plan and fulfill it, thereby satisfying their deepest desires, in spite of the fact that they realize all the while that what they are doing is bad for them. In fact, they can carry out certain plans precisely *because* they think that it is bad for them to do so. For example, sup-

pose a man has committed a serious crime at an earlier point in his life, and although he now regrets having done so, he realizes that no one will believe him if he confesses. So he decides to inflict a punishment upon himself for a period of several years. He abandons his current line of work, which he loves, and takes a job that he considers boring, arduous, and insignificant. He does not regard this as a way of serving others, because he realizes that what he will be doing is useless. His aim is simply to balance the evil he has done to others with a comparable evil for himself. Taking a pill to relieve his pangs of guilt would be of no use, since his aim is to do himself harm, not to make himself feel good. He punishes himself because he regards this as a moral necessity, and when he carries out his punishment, he does so from a sense of duty rather than a joyful love of justice and certainly with no relish for the particular job he is doing. In an ordinary sense of "want," he doesn't want to punish himself, but the desire theory cannot take refuge in this point, since it uses a much broader notion of desire, according to which what we voluntarily seek is what we desire. And in this sense, our self-punisher does want above all to punish himself.

Spending one's days performing a task that one rightly regards as boring, arduous and useless is not something we would ordinarily consider advantageous, and so we can plausibly assume that when the self-punisher carries out his plan, he is not only trying to act against his good, but he succeeds in harming himself, despite the fact that he gets precisely what he wants. It would be dogmatic and counter-intuitive to insist that he must benefit from his punishment simply because he desires it. The more reasonable response is to concede that sometimes carrying out one's plans and getting what one above all wants conflicts with one's good.

Furthermore, I see no plausible way for the desire theory to make adjustments that convincingly accommodate this sort of counter-example. Bringing in the notions of rationality and full information will not help. The self-punisher is not violating any obvious principle of rationality and he has all the empirical information he needs.[5] The moral that is most naturally drawn from this case is that there are circumstances in which people voluntarily renounce their good. When they do so, they are still getting what they want, and so we cannot equate well being with the satisfaction of desires, even when these desires are rational and exposed to full information. Other sorts of cases in which this happens, which are more common than self-punishment, are those in which we willingly make sacrifices in our wellbeing in order to promote the good of others. But rather than pursue this idea, I will turn to another type of objection to the desire theory. The weakness of the theory is best appreciated when we see the variety of difficulties it encounters.

III

Imagine a boy who, while walking through the park, sees a duck, and at the same time spots a rock on the ground. Impulsively, he picks up the rock and throws it at the duck. Is it good for him, to some extent, if his desire to hit the duck is satisfied? I find that implausible. Surely he would be no worse off if he had never felt an impulse to hit the duck; and once this impulse does arise, he would be no worse off if it evaporated before he acted on it.[6] We might even say, with some plausibility, that it is *bad* for him to satisfy this desire, that for his own good he should be free of such destructive impulses. Someone who wants to defend the desire theory may suggest that we should salvage it by making a slight modification. The boy's desire to hit the duck is a mere passing whim, and so what we should say is that satisfying desires is good for us only when they are more enduring than fleeting urges.[7] The desires that are good to satisfy are those that organize our lives and lead to projects that absorb considerable time and energy. The problem with this idea is that we can easily imagine desires that are

unobjectionable as whims but become perverse when given more significance than that. Consider for example the impulse one might feel on a winter walk to reach out and knock an icicle to the ground. And imagine someone who has more than a fleeting urge to do this. Rather, he has the project of knocking down as many icicles as he can before they melt. He hires a crew of workers and a fleet of trucks, so that he can reach icicles hanging from tall buildings; and this is how he spends his winters. It is implausible to suppose that now that this desire is no mere whim but a grand project, its satisfaction has become good.[8] Rather, our reaction to the example is that the subject has become the victim of a senseless passion. The amount of time and effort he devotes to his plan does not make us confident that this is where his good lies; on the contrary, this feature of the example is precisely what inclines us to think that he is wasting his time.[9]

Some philosophers will react to this case by saying that if the icicle fanatic really has carefully considered all of the alternatives available to him, and decides after due deliberation that this is the plan he wishes to pursue, then, peculiar as it may seem, the satisfaction of this desire *is* where his good lies.[10] Who are we, it might be asked rhetorically, to stand in judgment of his conception of the good? To this it can be replied that we cannot responsibly avoid considering the specific content of people's projects when we make decisions about whether we should assist them. If the icicle fanatic appealed to us for financial support, we would not and should not set aside doubts about whether he is doing himself any good, and these doubts arise precisely because we focus on the object of his desire and fail to see why it is worth his while to undertake this project.

IV

There is one other aspect of the desire theory that should be considered, before I propose an alternative approach. The theory holds that it is the satisfaction of *my* desires that constitutes my good. We can gain a better perspective on the theory if we construe it as one among a family of closely related views. For example, what we might call the parental desire theory would hold that what makes something good for a person is the fact that it is something *his parents* want for him. The sibling desire theory and the grandparent desire theory would have the same structure: each would identify the good of X with the satisfaction of the desires some Y has regarding X, alternative versions of the theory picking out a different Y. The desire theory is the special case in which Y is identical to X. This leads us to ask why we should take the desire theory to be more plausible than the parental desire theory or any other member of this family of theories. We cannot reply: because each person knows where his best interest lies. For we recognize that as a hazardous generalization. If the parental desire theory must be rejected because there are times when parents fail to have the necessary love and knowledge to guide the lives of their children, then we will be faced with the question why these failures cannot also occur in the relation one has to oneself.

Perhaps the parental desire theory (and all other variations in which X is not identical to Y) should be rejected because its general acceptance would lead to passivity and submissiveness. Children would continually make their most important decisions by looking to the blueprint for their lives drawn up by others, and they would fail to develop such qualities as self-reliance, creativity, autonomy and the like. But why should we think that these are qualities that children should develop? An appealing answer is that it is part of a person's good to be a designer of one's life and a molder of one's desires. But that is not a suggestion the desire theorist can accept because, according to that theory, if my good consists partly in exercising initiative and expressing autonomy, then that is true only on condition that these are qualities I want to have. If I don't want them because

I haven't been educated to value them, then, according to the desire theory, my lacking them is in itself no loss.

Although no one thinks that the parental desire theory is correct, there is nonetheless a modest and obvious truth that lies in its vicinity, namely that in the first stages of human life, it is best for children to be looked after by adults who take responsibility for their present and future good. And one reason why this is so is because there are many things that are or will be good for children that they are in no position to know about and cannot be said to want. A baby wants food, warmth, stimulation, and contact; but we cannot attribute to it a desire to develop its capacities or to be nurtured in the customs of its society. Education about these matters is beneficial for children, but the desire-theory cannot easily explain why, because children are for a time too young to have any desire for such learning. The desire-theory says that one's well-being is constituted by the satisfaction of one's desires, but the example of small children forces us to recognize a gap in the theory: it cannot be one's present desires alone that constitute one's well-being.

The gap could be filled if we say that the satisfaction of one's future desires is also a component of well-being. Even though a child may not now want an education she will want this at some future time, and so it is in her interests if we prepare her for the satisfaction of this future desire. But this way of expanding the desire theory does not fully capture our reasons for educating children: the child isn't going to have a desire to be educated independently of the way we bring her up; rather we train her so that she develops this desire and can satisfy it, and we do so because we think that having and satisfying this desire will be good for her. We encourage the interest children show in music, or their curiosity about the natural world, because we think it is and will be good for them to have a love of music or of nature. But there is nothing inevitable about their developing these desires. When we promote the future good of young children, we do not merely aim at desire satisfaction in general, but we try to instill certain desires rather than others on the grounds that some things are worth developing a desire for, and others are not.[11]

V

I conclude from what I have said so far that wanting something does not by itself confer desirability on what we want or getting it. It is intelligible and at times appropriate to act on the thought, "I want to do this, even though I don't think that it's good for me or will make my life better." That expresses the attitude many of us normally have towards our whims and impulses. Although we act on them, and need not be subject to criticism for doing so, we don't puff up the importance of these desires by supposing that it will be good even to the slightest degree if they are satisfied.[12]

But if wanting something does not make it good for the want to be satisfied, then we have to ask what does. My response is that what makes a desire good to satisfy is its being a desire for something that has features that make it worth wanting. Notice the difference between this approach and the one that lies behind the desire theory. It says that we confer goodness on objects by wanting them; by contrast, my idea is that the objects we desire must prove themselves worthy of being wanted by having certain characteristics. If they lack features that make them worth wanting, then the fact that we want them does not make up for that deficiency.

The sort of view I have in mind can also be expressed if I switch for the moment from talking about what people want to talking about what they love. It is widely accepted that someone who is living a good life should love something or someone. If one has no interests or attachments at all, how can one's life be going well? Or if one is only slightly interested in things, if one has no strong emotional attachments, then that too is a deficiency, because there are

objects to which a more enthusiastic response is appropriate. But, according to the conception of the good that I am presenting, some things are worthy of our interest and love, whereas others are not. So what makes one's life a good one is one's caring about something worth caring about. But of course that cannot be the whole story, because we can care a great deal about what is worthy of love and yet be cut off from it in some way. Imagine someone who loves painting but is imprisoned and unable to carry out her work; or someone who loves his children but is prevented from having any relationship with them. These people may love what is worth loving, but they don't have a satisfactory relationship with what they love, and as a result their lives are not going well.[13] So, there are at least three conditions that make a life a good one: one must love something, what one loves must be worth loving, and one must be related in the right way to what one loves.[14] Perhaps other conditions must be specified, but I will not explore that possibility here.

It might be objected that the thesis I am proposing is empty unless it is backed by a systematic theory that enables us to decide which among alternative ways of life is most worth living and which objects are most worth loving. It would of course be nice to have such a theory, but it is possible to do without one and still make defensible judgments about what is worth wanting and what is not. Recall the examples used earlier: we can judge, without having a systematic conception of the good, that the self-punisher is harming himself by doing boring, arduous, and insignificant work; or that the icicle fanatic is wasting his time. To take other cases: We believe that in normal circumstances only a certain amount of attention deserves to be paid to such things as neatness, appearance, or health, and we consider an interest that goes beyond this to be obsessive, because it undermines a person's good. We think that certain intellectual or artistic projects would be a waste of time because they would produce uninteresting results or none at all. To take another sort of case: if someone devotes considerable time to friendships with people who are contemptible and undeserving of affection, then we think that his life is to some degree misspent.

What these examples suggest is that when we choose the objects of our interests successfully we can justify our choice of a way of life by pointing to the qualities of those objects. We have more to say in these cases than "this is what I want to do;" we can explain why we want to do these things by describing the admirable qualities of the objects we love. And by educating others to recognize and care about those qualities, we can rationally persuade them that it was worth their while for them to develop an interest in objects to which they were initially indifferent.

If this approach is correct, then certain widespread and powerful human desires may be such that their satisfaction does us no good. Consider, for example, the desire to have positions of power over other people, simply for its own sake. Those who love power in this way are not making any obvious error of fact or reasoning. Yet, if one asks what it is about power that makes it worth loving, it is hard to know how to answer or even to see that the question admits of an answer. Someone who develops a desire for power does not do so by being trained to focus on its properties; we don't become sensitized or educated so that we can respond to or articulate the admirable qualities that power has. So it's no wonder that we draw a blank when we ask what it is about power that makes it desirable.

Notice how different the situation is when it comes to certain other things we care about. If we are experienced and articulate, we can say a great deal about why we love our favorite novel or piece of music or friend.[15] This is because we become attached to these objects through a process of training that makes us adept at recognizing and articulating certain properties that we respond to. Power, by contrast, is typically sought for no reason at all. And if we reject the desire theory, then we have

no reason to think that satisfying the desire for power is in itself good for people.[16] The same holds true of other deep-seated worldly motives, such as the desires for fame, recognition, and wealth.

It is here that we find one of the greatest contrasts between certain traditional conceptions of the good and the desire theory. The older conceptions took the desires for power, reputation, wealth, and the like to be, at best, of limited value; in fact, despite many disagreements among Platonists, Aristotelians, Stoics, Epicureans, and Christians about what the good is, there was until recent times a striking consensus among philosophers in these traditions that strong desires for power, status, material goods, and the like are contrary to self-interest properly understood. By contrast, the desire theory must hold that, so long as we pursue these goals without psychological division and with open eyes, making no mistake of fact or logic, then they are no less worth pursuing as ends than any other possible goals. That is why I said earlier that the chief weakness of the desire theory is that it is too accepting of desires as they stand and that it underestimates the ways in which we can subject desires to criticism. The desire theory does not demand that the objects in which we take an interest have in themselves desirable features, since its basic idea is that we invest those objects with desirability by being attracted to them. Traditional conceptions are more able to criticize desires as they stand because they insist that the objects we love prove themselves worthy of our interest by their possession of desirable characteristics.

VI

The controversial nature of the proposal I am making can be brought out still further if we notice what it says about pain. It is often taken to be obvious that physical pain is in itself bad;[17] but my doubts about the intrinsic goodness of power lead me also to question the intrinsic badness of pain.

When I said that power is not good in itself, my reason was that I saw no feature of it that makes it worth wanting. Similarly, even though we all want to avoid pain, I see no feature of it that makes it worthy of avoidance. We don't notice any characteristic of pain that grounds our aversion to it; we just hate the way it feels. But according to my proposal that is not enough to show that it really is bad in itself.[18] Just as our going for something does not show it to be good, so our avoiding it does not show it to be bad. And the fact that we *all* avoid it, and instinctively so, does not show it to be bad either. Our instincts are subject to evaluation, and so something more must be said about our aversion to pain besides its instinctual character, if we are to conclude that it is bad in itself.

To avoid misunderstanding, let me add that of course I think that pain is almost always bad to some extent. But my reason for thinking this has to do with the things that physical pain normally accompanies, namely some injury or the interruption of healthy processes. Almost every pain distracts us from devoting full attention to the things we care about, and over time pain depresses the level of energy we have. Pain is an animal's generally reliable mechanism for keeping it out of harm's way, and this applies no less to human animals than others. When we take into account the other events that accompany pain, we can see why it is generally bad for us to some degree. What I am questioning is whether, when we leave aside these other features of pain and just concentrate on the way it feels, we have any reason to think it is bad, and not merely something we dislike.[19]

Perhaps I can create some doubt about whether pain is intrinsically bad by calling attention to a number of other sensations that are disliked even though they are not physically painful: for example, foul odors and grating noises. Should we say that these are in themselves bad to experience, apart from the harm they typically bring about by distracting or annoying us? Suppose I am the only person who is repelled by a certain sound, and everyone else is indifferent to it: if we say that it is intrinsically bad for me but not for others to hear the sound, then we are presupposing that it is a person's likes and dislikes that create what is good and bad for him.[20] And we will then have to say that satisfying our whims and urges is good, and in particular that it is good for the boy in our earlier example to hit the duck. On the other hand, if we say that a grating sound is bad for me to hear only if everyone else has the same response then we have to explain why the reaction of others should be so important to my good. The most plausible way of disposing of this whole problem is to say that we should not infer from our aversion to something that it is contrary to our good, just as we should not infer from the presence of an urge that it does some good to satisfy it. If we accept this proposal, then we should become doubtful about the intrinsic badness of pain.

VII

There is one further matter that should be addressed before we return to the theme of pluralism with which we began. I have been focusing exclusively on the *human* good and have said nothing about the good of other sorts of animals. But it might be objected that this is the wrong way to go about things, because we need to locate the human good within a framework that has broader application. And it should be obvious that much of what I have said about the human good does not apply to other animals. I claim that for a human life to go well one must love something worth loving. But it would be absurd to hold that the life of a non-human animal goes well only on this condition. What in the life of a salmon or a snake or a mole is worth loving? Can these animals be said to love anything at all?

The inapplicability of these conditions of human well being to non-human life might suggest that we have been on the wrong track all along. Perhaps we should have begun by looking for an account of well being that covers all cases, not just the human condition. Such a thought may partially account for the attraction of hedonism to earlier thinkers. Pleasure and pain guide the behavior of all animals; and hedonists, ancient and modern, have always appealed to the universality of these forces to support their doctrine. Hedonism has an apparent advantage in that it determines the good of all animals with one fell swoop. But we should not be impressed, for the implausibility of hedonism as applied to human life still stands. What we must do therefore is find some substitute for it. We need a general account of the well being of all animals, and then we must ask how the more specific conception of human well being is related to this broader framework.

The general formula that we should apply across the board is one that we find in Aristotle and the Stoics, namely that the good for each animal consists in leading the kind of life that is appropriate to its nature. And since each animal species has a different nature, we must consider the peculiar physical characteristics of each species to determine more specifically where its good lies. The nature of non-human animals is fixed by their bodies and physical capacities, and so for them living well consists in the maintenance of physical health and the full use of the capacities of their bodies. That is why the confinement of a bird to a small space would be contrary to its good, even if it were attached during its confinement to a machine that constantly stimulated the pleasure center of its brain.

But what should we say about the peculiar nature of human beings? Because of our possession of the kind of brain we have, the lives we can lead are far less restricted than are those of other animals. Our intellectual capacity allows far greater plasticity in our development, and it makes the kind of life we lead far more a matter of choice than it is for other animals. The good of a non-human animal is, as it were, built into its body, whereas for human beings the good is an object of rational choice and its achievement requires the training of desires and emotions so that they take

appropriate objects as determined by reason. This is not to deny that we have a nature. Rather, it is to say that it is our nature to be choosers, to be capable of using reason to make choices and to mold our desires and emotions. And so the nature of human beings is reflected in our theory of the good when we say that in order for our lives to go well our desires and emotions must be directed at objects whose features make them appropriate choices for us. It is implicit in the notion of choiceworthiness that the objects of our desires are open to evaluation by means of reflection. By insisting that desire satisfaction is not in itself good, that the object of the desire must be worth wanting, we bring in the need for evaluation and reflection, and we thus ground our good in our capacity for rational choice. We explain the human good not as hedonism does, by means of a single comprehensive theory applicable to all animals, but by a two-stage process in which a broad account that applies universally is then made more specific by being tied to the peculiarities of the human situation.

Since I have accepted the traditional view that our nature as human beings consists in the exercise of our capacity for rational choice, it might be asked why I do not go further and accept a more determinate conception of the good, one that holds that human lives are worthwhile to the extent that they are devoted to reasoning. My reply is that the extent to which it is intrinsically worthwhile to engage in reasoning, or good reasoning, is itself a matter that is subject to rational evaluation; there is no self-contradiction in the idea that one might *reason* to the conclusion that there are activities that are better than *reasoning*, or that one's life goes best if reason plays a secondary or minor role. So the fact that reasoning is distinctive of human beings does not itself determine the proper place of reasoning in a human life. The best way of establishing the importance of reason in a good life is to take note of the various kinds of worthwhile activities there are, and recognize how many of them we would be incapable of undertaking, if our capacity for reasoning were seriously impaired.

VIII

We can now return to the ideas with which we started: that the good for human beings is highly varied, that there is no single master good that measures the worth of all others; that there is no specific kind of life that is best for everyone. Pluralism, so construed, is a newcomer to the philosophical scene, and it is worth asking whether any arguments can be found for it. One of the apparent attractions of the desire theory is that it offers an explanation for this variety, but in light of that theory's deficiencies we have reason to seek an alternative account of why pluralism about the good might be true.

A better way to defend pluralistic intuitions, I suggest, is to accept the general thesis that some objects of human pursuit have qualities that make them objectively worth wanting and that others are without merit, but to reject any of the more specific theses that have been proposed in the past about how to achieve a more determinate ranking of human lives. The modern philosopher's sense that many different kinds of lives are worth living, but that we cannot arrange them in a hierarchy ranging from best to worst, is best supported by concrete illustration rather than a highly general argument: the favored strategy should be to take note of all of the different objects that are worth pursuing and the diversity of worthwhile lives devoted to these pursuits, and then to show that none of the objective conceptions of the good with which we are familiar from the history of philosophy does justice to this rich variety. But this pluralistic project cannot succeed simply by pointing to the great variety of lives people in fact lead; what must be shown is considerably more difficult, namely that these different kinds of lives are worth living, and none more so than any others.

If this is correct, then the hierarchical conceptions of the good that are now out

of favor cannot be undermined with a single blow; if there is no supremely desirable object or life, in comparison with which all other objects or lives must be evaluated, then this must be established on a case-by-case basis by showing why each proposed candidate fails to provide a plausible standard. The defender of the multiplicity of the human good must support this thesis by persuading us that many different types of thing are worth wanting and by showing why we should reject attempts to assign each of them a discrete place on a single hierarchical scale. Although I am sympathetic to such a project, I have not undertaken it here. My main point has been that the multiplicity of the good cannot be directly inferred from the variability of human desire. So my conclusion is a conditional one: if we wish to be pluralists, then we should accept the point, once widely taken for granted, that in deciding which sorts of lives it is good to live, we cannot bypass the task of evaluating our desires by asking whether their objects possess the qualities that make them worth wanting.[21]

Notes

1. Pluralism about the human good is given special emphasis in Isaiah Berlin, "Two Concepts of Liberty," in *Four Essays on Liberty*, London, Oxford University Press, 1969, p. 171; Robert Nozick, *Anarchy, State, and Utopia*, New York, Basic Books, 1974, pp. 309–312; and Stuart Hampshire, *Innocence and Experience*, Cambridge, Mass., Harvard University Press, p. 31. But this frame of mind is evident in practically every substantive work of contemporary moral philosophy.

2. I admit that it is difficult to characterize the contrast between pluralism and more restrictive theories in a precise way. For example, consider the complex thesis that (a) the intellectual life is best; (b) there are many types of intellectual lives (one may study botany, mathematics, literature . . .); (c) and all such lives are equally

worthwhile. This will strike the contemporary pluralist as insufficiently pluralistic, even though there is nothing "formally" incorrect about the thesis, since it holds that there is no one best kind of life. The modern intuition, I think, is best characterized in historical rather than formal terms; it holds, in other words, that theories of the past went wrong in being unduly restrictive.

3. Here the word "satisfaction" must be construed not as a reference to a feeling but merely to the obtaining of a desired state of affairs. What makes something good for us is our wanting and getting it, not any felt response.

4. Highly sophisticated versions of the "desire theory" are elaborated with great subtlety by John Rawls, *A Theory of Justice*, Cambridge, Mass., Belknap Press, 1971, pp. 395–424; Richard B. Brandt, *A Theory of the Good and the Right*, Oxford, Clarendon Press, 1979, Part I; James Griffin, *Well-Being*, Oxford, Clarendon Press, 1986, pp. 7–39. There are also many significant differences between them, of course. Parts of my discussion of the desire theory will consider a version of it less complex than the varieties they propose; this is because I think it is helpful to consider weaknesses in the simpler version before we ask whether more complex versions succeed in remedying those weaknesses. For criticism of some of the more sophisticated versions of the theory, see J. David Velleman, "Brandt's Definition of 'Good'," *The Philosophical Review* 97 (1988): 353–71; Connie S. Rosati, "Naturalism, Normativity, and the Open Question Argument," unpublished.

5. Perhaps it will be suggested that we need to distinguish two senses of a person's "good;" in some sense, the self-punisher is promoting his good, since he is carrying out his plan, but in some other sense he is making himself worse off. But this approach runs the risk of inventing a purely technical sense of well-being, one whose only justification is that it salvages the desire theory. Another alternative

would be to restrict the desire theory so that the only desires whose satisfaction are good are the ones that have no moral content. That would enable the desire theory to avoid the conclusion that the self-punisher is promoting his good, but the theory so modified would rule out far too much. Desires to be a good friend, a good father, or a good citizen all have moral content; and it is hard to see why we should rule out the possibility that satisfying these desires can be good. Still another move would be to say that our good consists in satisfying desires that are formed under favorable conditions; since the desire to punish oneself is a response to an *un*favorable condition, namely an earlier crime, it might not be counted as the sort of desire whose satisfaction is good. But this modification would also rule out too much. Many lives are governed by a desire to find remedies for such unfavorable circumstances as disease, injustice, and ignorance; but lives devoted to the alleviation of these conditions can certainly be good, in spite of the fact that they are responsive to unfavorable conditions.

6. One could resist this step by saying that satisfying the desire to hit the duck is only slightly good for the boy. But why so? What if his desire to hit the duck is extremely strong? And what if the stone is rather small, so that the injury to the duck will be slight? We can say that the boy should suppress his desire to hit the duck because the duck has a right not to be injured. But rights can be justifiably infringed when doing so does enough good; so, if the boy's desire is strong enough, will hitting the duck do him enough good to justify his infringing the duck's right? I should add that I think nothing in this example would be changed if the person throwing the stone is an adult in full charge of his faculties rather than a boy.

7. Amartya Sen also questions conceptions of the human good that allow the satisfaction of whims to be in one's interests. See *Inequality Reexamined*, Harvard Uni-

versity Press, Cambridge, Mass., 1992, p. 56 n. 1; and his "Well-being, Agency and Freedom: The Dewey Lectures 1984," *The Journal of Philosophy* 82. Sen also develops the point that individuals living in conditions of severe deprivation might satisfy their desires simply by limiting them to what is attainable. See *Inequality Reexamined*, pp. 7, 55. This corresponds to the point made by Rawls that a "plan of life" must be "drawn up under (more or less) favorable conditions" if its execution is to constitute a person's happiness. See *A Theory of Justice*, p. 409.

8. It might be objected that the icicle fanatic is doing himself some good because his project is giving him pleasure. But it should be recalled once again that the desire theory does not make the value of satisfying desires depend on the pleasure that in many cases comes when desires are satisfied. And in any case even when we take into account the pleasure the icicle fanatic gets, we have to ask why getting pleasure is always to some extent good for a person. Is it because we desire pleasure? In that case, it cannot be the pleasure achieved by the icicle fanatic that makes his activity good for him, but the fact that his desire for the pleasure of knocking down icicles is satisfied. But we can still demand an explanation for why the satisfaction of this desire is good for him.

9. ". . . here we meet ideas which are curiously elusive, such as the thought that some pursuits are more worthwhile than others, and some matters trivial and some important in human life. Since it makes good sense to say that most men waste a lot of their lives in ardent pursuit of what is trivial and unimportant it is not possible to explain the important and the trivial in terms of the amount of attention given to different subjects by the average man. But I have never seen, or been able to think out, a true account of this matter . . ." Phillipa Foot, *Virtues and Vices*, Berkeley: University of California Press, 1978, p. 6.

10. We can ask philosophers who take this position why we should think that a person who has reflected about what he wishes and has made no logical or factual errors is guaranteed not to be in error about the worthwhileness of what he proposes to do. It is only in rare and contrived situations that going through an intellectual process guarantees a correct result. Pure and perfect procedural justice are examples of this, but in these cases we can see why a certain process must give rise to the right outcome. In general, however, if someone has thought long and hard about some question, including a normative question, and has avoided obvious and elementary errors, this does not insure that he has answered the questions correctly.

11. This example also reveals a weakness in a different way of expanding the desire theory: we might say that a person's well being is constituted by the satisfaction of the desires he *would* have if he were rational and well-informed. On this basis, we might say that what makes it good for a child to be educated is the fact that she would want to be educated were she rational and well-informed. But once again this does not capture the way we think about the education of a child. We do not give a child a musical education, for example, because we ask what she would do if she were completely rational and fully informed, and then somehow come to the conclusion that she would want to develop a love of music. Rather, we already have the conviction, based on our own experience and that of others, that it is good for people to develop a love of music.

12. Some philosophers—Aquinas is a prominent example—have held that whatever is wanted is wanted on the grounds that it is good. That is precisely what I am questioning. Furthermore, Aquinas, following Aristotle, held that whatever is desired by *everyone* must *be* and not merely seem good, to some extent. But if everyone had a desire to knock icicles to

the ground, that would not show that doing so is a part, even a small part, of the human good. That one person feels an internal push does not show that it is good for the push to have its way; even if everyone feels the same kind of push and gives way to it, we need not infer that it is good for us to satisfy that desire.

13. What it is to be properly related to objects one loves varies according to the kind of object it is. The idea is that if one is in some way cut off from what one loves, then one is not faring well; but what being cut off amounts to depends on the kind of object it is. (My use of the term "object" should not be taken to mean that persons are excluded from being objects.) Being properly related to an object one loves presumably involves the satisfaction of desires, so I am not suggesting that such satisfaction is irrelevant to well-being. For this reason I would not want to describe this conception of the good as an "objective list" theory, in Derek Parfit's sense. But neither does it fit his two other alternatives: hedonistic and desire-fulfillment theories. See *Reasons and Persons*, Oxford, Clarendon Press, 1984, p. 493. I also assume that being properly related to an object one loves involves some degree of enjoyment of the object. It should be noticed that the idea I am proposing has something important in common with the desire theory: a person's good, I think, consists partly in his being in a certain psychological state. This should be contrasted with a view according to which one's life is going well if one perfects certain capacities, regardless of how one feels about doing so.

14. Notice that this gives us an easy and natural way to account for the phenomenon of self-renunciation that was discussed earlier. Although it would be extraordinary to have no desire to do and take delight in what one loves doing, one might nonetheless decide that this desire ought to give way to something else one considers more important. That is the situation we described earlier when we discussed the person who punishes himself by leaving a job he loves and condemning himself to several years of useless drudgery. For a period of time there is nothing in his life that he loves, and so one of the conditions of living well is not fulfilled. Similarly, one might decide not to promote one's good not as a punishment but as a sacrifice for the good of others. One might think for example that one will be of greatest use to others if one chooses to do something that, as it happens, one unfortunately does not love doing. A life of drudgery can in certain cases be of great value to humanity, and if one voluntarily accepts such a life for moral reasons that should not be taken to mean that one is aiming at or doing what is best for oneself.

15. I am not saying that such sophistication is a necessary condition of leading a good life. What is necessary is that the objects of one's desire have features that make them worth wanting—not that one be articulate about what those features are.

16. This of course does not mean that power is intrinsically bad or instrumentally worthless. If the pursuit of power has a proper role in human life, as it presumably does, then this must be shown indirectly, by establishing a connection between the desire for power and some further purpose already determined to be worthwhile.

17. For a powerful presentation of this position, see Thomas Nagel, *The View from Nowhere*, New York, Oxford University Press, 1986, pp. 156–8.

18. To this it may be objected that since all justification comes to an end, we should not be impressed by the point that we cannot say what it is about a painful sensation that makes it worth avoiding. Painfulness simply is a quality of a sensation that makes it undesirable; why should there have to be some further feature of pain that makes it worthy of our aversion? In reply: Justification in ethics involves systematization, but the thesis that pain is inherently undesirable is one

that does no real work in the process of systematization. If we give up the belief that pain is bad in itself and hold instead that we don't like pain, we have lost nothing we need for theoretical or practical purposes. Nothing is gained, for the moral life or for moral philosophy, by upholding the thesis that pain is not only disliked but worthy of being disliked. By contrast, we would be justifiably disturbed to be told about certain other things we love or hate that there is nothing lovable or hateful about them. There is a big difference, for example, between saying that I dislike another person and saying that he merits my aversion. It is true that after I have said everything I have to say about why he is awful (and this will involve saying why certain personal qualities are objectionable), my justification comes to an end. But by pointing to certain personal features, I am entitled to say that I have given a justification for my attitude. In the case of pain, however, this sort of justification is unavailable; and appealing to my aversion to pain does not constitute a justification of that attitude. Opponents of my thesis might nonetheless insist that we simply "see" that pain is bad in itself, and that we do not have to support this intuition by linking it to any other judgments we make. But this conception of justification in ethics has serious difficulties.

19. A critic of my proposal might nonetheless persist by focusing on hypothetical situations in which we must make a choice between undergoing two medical procedures: they are equally effective in producing a good result, but in one of them we feel some pain whereas in the other we do not. We can suppose, for the sake of argument, that there is no advantage in taking the painful alternative and no drawback in undergoing the operation painlessly. In such a situation, everyone would of course opt for the painless procedure. But what does this thought experiment tell us? It shows that pain is in itself bad for us only if we also accept the thesis that what everyone would want in a certain situation must be good. But that thesis is precisely what is at issue. Another objection to my proposal is that unless pain is by itself bad we have no reason not to cause others to feel it. If we can be sure that causing someone pain will lead to no other harm, and if it is not in itself bad, then why is it wrong? We can reply that how we treat others cannot be determined simply by asking what is good or bad for them. We show our concern and respect for them by paying attention to their desires and aversions, and not merely their good and bad. If someone else is repelled by a certain kind of sound, then that by itself is reason for me not to make it; and similarly, the fact that others dislike pain is all the reason one needs for not inflicting it on them. We need not affirm the badness of pain to provide a basis for refraining from cruelty.

20. Nagel, op. cit. p. 158, holds that "we have reason to seek/avoid sensations we immediately and strongly like/dislike," and applies this to "experiences to which not everyone reacts in the same way, like the sound of squeaking chalk." But he does not accept the broader principle, "Seek what you want and avoid what you don't want." Why then is it good for one to avoid *noises* one does not like, but not, more generally, *whatever* one does not like? He replies: because noises are sensations or experiences, and one's dislike of them is "immediately and unreflective." This strikes me as artificial. Why should the immediacy and unreflectiveness of a sensation make a difference to its intrinsic goodness or badness?

21. I benefitted greatly from the criticism and encouragement of Samantha Brennan, Tom Christiano, David Copp, John Deigh, Walter Edelberg, Bill Hart, Dan Hausman, Terry Irwin, Shelly Kagan, Douglas MacLean, Connie Rosati, Susan Wolf; and audiences at Cornell University, the University of Arizona, and the University of Illinois at Chicago.

OBJECTIVIST THEORIES

14 / G. E. MOORE

THE IDEAL

110. The title of this chapter is ambiguous. When we call a state of things 'ideal' we may mean three distinct things, which have only this in common: that we always do mean to assert, of the state of things in question, not only that it is good in itself, but that it is good in itself in a much higher degree than many other things. The first of these meanings of 'ideal' is (1) that to which the phrase *'The* Ideal' is most properly confined. By this is meant the *best* state of things *conceivable*, the Summum Bonum or Absolute Good. It is in this sense that a right conception of Heaven would be a right conception of the Ideal: we mean by the Ideal a state of things which would be absolutely perfect. But this conception may be quite clearly distinguished from a second, namely, (2) that of the best *possible* state of things in this world. This second conception may be identified with that which has frequently figured in philosophy as the 'Human Good,' or the *ultimate* end towards which our action should be directed. It is in this sense that Utopias are said to be Ideals. The constructor of an Utopia may suppose many things to be possible, which are in fact impossible; but he always assumes that some things, at least, are rendered impossible by natural laws, and hence his construction differs essentially from one which may disregard *all*

Reprinted by permission of the publisher and copyright holder from G. E. Moore, *Principia Ethica*, chap. 6 (Cambridge: Cambridge University Press, 1903), pp. 183–222.

natural laws, however certainly established. At all events the question 'What is the best state of things which we could *possibly* bring about?' is quite distinct from the question 'What would be the best state of things conceivable?' But, thirdly, we may mean by calling a state of things 'ideal' merely (3) that it is good in itself in a high degree. And it is obvious that the question what things are 'ideal' in this sense is one which must be answered before we can pretend to settle what is the Absolute or the Human Good. It is with the Ideal, in this third sense, that this chapter will be principally concerned. Its main object is to arrive at some positive answer to the fundamental question of Ethics—the question: 'What things are good or ends in themselves?' To this question we have hitherto obtained only a negative answer: the answer that pleasure is certainly not the *sole* good.

111. I have just said that it is upon a correct answer to this question that correct answers to the two other questions, What is the Absolute Good? and What is the Human Good? must depend; and, before proceeding to discuss it, it may be well to point out the relation which it has to these two questions.

(1) It is just possible that the Absolute Good may be entirely composed of qualities which we cannot even imagine. This is possible, because, though we certainly do know a great many things that are good-in-themselves, and good in a high degree, yet what is best does not necessarily con-

tain all the good things there are. That this is so follows from the principle explained in Chap. I. (§§ 18–22), to which it was there proposed that the name 'principle of organic unities' should be confined. This principle is that the intrinsic value of a whole is neither identical with nor proportional to the sum of the values of its parts. It follows from this that, though in order to obtain the greatest possible sum of values in its parts, the Ideal would necessarily contain all the things which have intrinsic value in any degree, yet the whole which contained all these parts might not be so valuable as some other whole, from which certain positive goods were omitted. But if a whole, which does not contain all positive goods, may yet be better than a whole which does, it follows that the best whole *may* be one, which contains *none* of the positive goods with which we are acquainted.

It is, therefore, *possible* that we cannot discover what the Ideal is. But it is plain that, though this possibility cannot be denied, no one can have any right to assert that it is realised—that the Ideal *is* something unimaginable. We cannot judge of the comparative values of things, unless the things we judge are before our minds. We cannot, therefore, be entitled to assert that anything, which we cannot imagine, would be better than some of the things which we can; although we are also not entitled to deny the possibility that this may be the case. Consequently our search for the Ideal must be limited to a search for that one, among all the wholes composed of elements known to us, which seems to be better than all the rest. We shall never be entitled to assert that this whole is Perfection, but we shall be entitled to assert that it is *better* than any other which may be presented as a rival.

But, since anything which we can have any *reason* to think ideal must be composed of things that are known to us, it is plain that a comparative valuation of these must be our chief instrument for deciding what is ideal. The best ideal we can construct will be that state of things which contains the greatest number of things having positive

value, and which contains nothing evil or indifferent—*provided* that the presence of none of these goods, or the absence of things evil or indifferent, seems to diminish the value of the whole. And, in fact, the chief defect of such attempts as have been made by philosophers to construct an Ideal—to describe the Kingdom of Heaven—seems to consist in the fact that they omit many things of very great positive value, although it is plain that this omission does *not* enhance the value of the whole. Where this is the case, it may be confidently asserted that the ideal proposed is not ideal. And the review of positive goods, which I am about to undertake, will, I hope, shew that no ideals yet proposed are satisfactory. Great positive goods, it will appear, are so numerous, that any whole, which shall contain them all, must be of vast complexity. And though this fact renders it difficult, or, humanly speaking, impossible, to decide what is The Ideal, what is the absolutely best state of things imaginable, it is sufficient to condemn those Ideals, which are formed by omission, without any visible gain in consequence of such omission. Philosophers seem usually to have sought only for the *best* of single things; neglecting the fact that a whole composed of two great goods, even though one of these be obviously inferior to the other, may yet be often seen to be decidedly superior to either by itself.

(2) On the other hand, Utopias—attempted descriptions of a Heaven upon Earth—commonly suffer not only from this, but also from the opposite defect. They are commonly constructed on the principle of merely omitting the great positive evils, which exist at present, with utterly inadequate regard to the goodness of what they retain: the so-called goods, to which they have regard, are, for the most part, things which are, at best, mere means to good—things, such as freedom, *without* which, possibly, nothing very good can exist in this world, but which are of no value in themselves and are by no means certain even to produce anything of value. It is, of course, necessary to the purpose of their

authors, whose object is merely to construct the best that may be possible in this world, that they should include, in the state of things which they describe, many things, which are themselves indifferent, but which, according to natural laws, seem to be absolutely necessary for the existence of anything which is good. But, in fact, they are apt to include many things, of which the necessity is by no means apparent, under the mistaken idea that these things are goods-in-themselves, and not merely, here and now, a means to good: while, on the other hand, they also omit from their description great positive goods, of which the attainment seems to be quite as possible as many of the changes which they recommend. That is to say, conceptions of the Human Good commonly err, not only, like those of the Absolute Good, in omitting some great goods, but also by including things indifferent; and they both omit and include in cases where the limitations of natural necessity, by the consideration of which they are legitimately differentiated from conceptions of the Absolute Good, will not justify the omission and inclusion. It is, in fact, obvious that in order to decide correctly at what state of things we ought to aim, we must not only consider what results it is possible for us to obtain, but also which, among equally possible results, will have the greatest value. And upon this second enquiry the comparative valuation of known goods has a no less important bearing than upon the investigation of the Absolute Good.

112. The method which must be employed in order to decide the question 'What things have intrinsic value, and in what degrees?' has already been explained in Chap. III. (§§ 55, 57). In order to arrive at a correct decision on the first part of this question, it is necessary to consider what things are such that, if they existed *by themselves,* in absolute isolation, we should yet judge their existence to be good; and, in order to decide upon the relative *degrees* of value of different things, we must similarly consider what comparative value seems to attach to the isolated existence of each. By employing this method, we shall guard against two errors, which seem to have been the chief causes which have vitiated previous conclusions on the subject. The first of these (1) that which consists in supposing that what seems absolutely necessary here and now, for the existence of anything good—what we cannot do without—is therefore good in itself. If we isolate such things, which are mere means to good, and suppose a world in which they alone, and nothing but they, existed, their intrinsic worthlessness becomes apparent. And, secondly, there is the more subtle error (2) which consists in neglecting the principle of organic unities. This error is committed, when it is supposed, that, if one part of a whole has no intrinsic value, the value of the whole must reside entirely in the other parts. It has, in this way, been commonly supposed, that, if all valuable wholes could be seen to have one and only one common properly, the wholes must be valuable solely *because* they possess this property; and the illusion is greatly strengthened, if the common property in question seems, considered by itself, to have more value than the other parts of such wholes, considered by themselves. But, if we consider the property in question, *in isolation,* and then compare it with the whole, of which it forms a part, it may become easily apparent that, existing by itself, the property in question has not nearly so much value, as has the whole to which it belongs. Thus, if we compare the value of a certain amount of pleasure, *existing absolutely by itself,* with the value of certain 'enjoyments,' containing an equal amount of pleasure, it may become apparent that the 'enjoyment' is much better than the pleasure, and also, in some cases, much worse. In such a case it is plain that the 'enjoyment' does *not* owe its value *solely* to the pleasure it contains, although it might easily have appeared to do so, when we only considered the other constituents of the enjoyment, and seemed to see that, without the pleasure, they would have had no value. It is now apparent, on the contrary, that the whole 'enjoyment' owes its value quite equally to the presence of the other constituents, *even though* it may

be true that the pleasure is the only constituent having any value by itself. And similarly, if we are told that all things owe their value solely to the fact that they are 'realisations of the true self,' we may easily refute this statement, by asking whether the predicate that is meant by 'realising the true self,' supposing that it could exist alone, would have any value whatsoever. Either the *thing*, which does 'realise the true self,' has intrinsic value or it has not; and if it has, then it certainly does not owe its value solely to the fact that it realises the true self.

113. If, now, we use this method of absolute isolation, and guard against these errors it appears that the question we have to answer is far less difficult than the controversies of Ethics might have led us to expect. Indeed, once the meaning of the question is clearly understood, the answer to it, in its main outlines, appears to be so obvious, that it runs the risk of seeming to be a platitude. By far the most valuable things, which we know or can imagine, are certain states of consciousness, which may be roughly described as the pleasures of human intercourse and the enjoyment of beautiful objects. No one, probably, who has asked himself the question, has ever doubted that personal affection and the appreciation of what is beautiful in Art or Nature, are good in themselves; nor, if we consider strictly what things are worth having *purely for their own sakes*, does it appear probable that any one will think that anything else has *nearly* so great a value as the things which are included under these two heads. I have myself urged in Chap. III. (§ 50) that the mere existence of what is beautiful does appear to have *some* intrinsic value; but I regard it as indubitable that Prof. Sidgwick was so far right, in the view there discussed, that such mere existence of what is beautiful has value, so small as to be negligible, in comparison with that which attaches to the *consciousness* of beauty. This simple truth may, indeed, be said to be universally recognised. What has *not* been recognised is that it is the ultimate and fundamental truth of Moral Philos-

ophy. That it is only for the sake of these things—in order that as much of them as possible may at some time exist—that any one can be justified in performing any public or private duty; that they are the *raison d'être* of virtue; that it is they—these complex wholes *themselves*, and not any constituent or characteristic of them—that form the rational ultimate end of human action and the sole criterion of social progress: these appear to be truths which have been generally overlooked.

That they are truths—that personal affections and aesthetic enjoyments include *all* the greatest, and *by far* the greatest, goods we can imagine, will, I hope, appear more plainly in the course of that analysis of them, to which I shall now proceed. All the things, which I have meant to include under the above descriptions, are highly complex *organic unities*; and in discussing the consequences, which follow from this fact, and the elements of which they are composed, I may hope at the same time both to confirm and to define my position.

114. I. I propose to begin by examining what I have called aesthetic enjoyments, since the case of personal affections presents some additional complications. It is, I think, universally admitted that the proper appreciation of a beautiful object is a good thing in itself; and my question is: What are the main elements included in such an appreciation?

(1) It is plain that in those instances of aesthetic appreciation, which we think most valuable, there is included, not merely a bare cognition of what is beautiful in the object, but also some kind of feeling or emotion. It is not sufficient that a man should merely see the beautiful qualities in a picture and know that they are beautiful, in order that we may give his state of mind the highest praise. We require that he should also *appreciate* the beauty of that which he sees and which he knows to be beautiful—that he should feel and see *its beauty*. And by these expressions we certainly mean that he should have an appropriate emotion towards the beautiful qualities which he cognises. It is perhaps the

case that all aesthetic emotions have some common quality; but it is certain that differences in the emotion seem to be appropriate to differences in the kind of beauty perceived: and by saying that different emotions are *appropriate* to different kinds of beauty, we mean that the whole which is formed by the consciousness of that kind of beauty *together with* the emotion appropriate to it, is better than if any other emotion had been felt in contemplating that particular beautiful object. Accordingly we have a large variety of different emotions, each of which is a necessary constituent in some state of consciousness which we judge to be good. All of these emotions are essential elements in great positive goods; they are *parts* of organic wholes, which have great intrinsic value. But it is important to observe that these wholes are organic, and that, hence, it does not follow that the emotion, *by itself*, would have any value whatsoever, nor yet that, if it were directed to a different object, the whole thus formed might not be positively bad. And, in fact, it seems to be the case that if we distinguish the emotional element, in any aesthetic appreciation, from the cognitive element, which accompanies it and is, in fact, commonly thought of as a part of the emotion; and if we consider what value this emotional element would have, *existing by itself*, we can hardly think that it has any great value, even if it has any at all. Whereas, if the same emotion be directed to a different object, if, for instance, it is felt towards an object that is positively ugly, the whole state of consciousness is certainly often positively bad in a high degree.

115. (2) In the last paragraph I have pointed out the two facts, that the presence of some emotion is necessary to give any very high value to a state of aesthetic appreciation, and that, on the other hand, this same emotion, in itself, may have little or no value: it follows that these emotions give to the wholes of which they form a part a value far greater than that which they themselves possess. The same is obviously true of the cognitive element which must be combined with these emotions in order to form these highly valuable wholes; and the present paragraph will attempt to define what is meant by this cognitive element, so far as to guard against a possible misunderstanding. When we talk of seeing a beautiful object, or, more generally, of the cognition or consciousness of a beautiful object, we may mean by these expressions something which forms no part of any valuable whole. There is an ambiguity in the use of the term 'object,' which has probably been responsible for as many enormous errors in philosophy and psychology as any other single cause. This ambiguity may easily be detected by considering the proposition, which, though a contradiction in terms, is obviously true: That when a man sees a beautiful picture, he may see nothing beautiful whatever. The ambiguity consists in the fact that, by the 'object' of vision (or cognition), may be meant *either* the qualities actually seen *or* all the qualities possessed by the thing seen. Thus in our case: when it is said that the picture is beautiful, it is meant that it contains qualities which are beautiful; when it is said that the man sees the picture, it is meant that he sees a great number of the qualities contained in the picture; and when it is said that, nevertheless, he sees nothing beautiful, it is meant that he does *not* see those qualities of the picture which are beautiful. When, therefore, I speak of the cognition of a beautiful object, as an essential element in a valuable aesthetic appreciation, I must be understood to mean only the cognition of *the beautiful qualities* possessed by that object, and *not* the cognition of other qualities of the object possessing them. And this distinction must itself be carefully distinguished from the other distinction expressed above by the distinct terms 'seeing the beauty of a thing' and 'seeing its beautiful qualities.' By 'seeing the beauty of a thing' we commonly mean the having an emotion towards its beautiful qualities; whereas in the 'seeing of its beautiful qualities' we do not include any emotion. By the cognitive element, which is equally necessary with emotion to the existence of a valuable appreciation, I mean merely the

actual cognition or consciousness of any or all of an object's *beautiful qualities*—that is to say any or all of those elements in the object which possess any positive beauty. That such a cognitive element is essential to a valuable whole may be easily seen, by asking: What value should we attribute to the proper emotion excited by hearing Beethoven's Fifth Symphony, if that emotion were entirely unaccompanied by any consciousness, either of the notes, or of the melodic and harmonic relations between them? And that the mere *hearing* of the Symphony, even accompanied by the appropriate emotion, is not sufficient, may be easily seen, if we consider what would be the state of a man, who should hear all the notes, but should *not* be aware of any of those melodic and harmonic relations, which are necessary to constitute the smallest beautiful elements in the Symphony.

116. (3) Connected with the distinction just made between 'object' in the sense of the qualities actually before the mind, and 'object' in the sense of the whole thing which possesses the qualities actually before the mind, is another distinction of the utmost importance for a correct analysis of the constituents necessary to a valuable whole. It is commonly and rightly thought that to see beauty in a thing which has no beauty is in some way inferior to seeing beauty in that which really has it. But under this single description of 'seeing beauty in that which has no beauty,' two very different facts, and facts of very different value, may be included. We may mean *either* the attribution to an object of really beautiful qualities which it does not possess *or* the feeling towards qualities, which the object does possess but which are in reality not beautiful, an emotion which is appropriate only to qualities really beautiful. Both these facts are of very frequent occurrence; and in most instances of emotion both no doubt occur together: but they are obviously quite distinct, and the distinction is of the utmost importance for a correct estimate of values. The former may be called an error of judgment, and the latter an error of taste; but it is important to observe

that the 'error of taste' commonly involves a false judgment *of value;* whereas the 'error of judgment' is merely a false judgment *of fact.*

Now the case which I have called an error of taste, namely, where the actual qualities we admire (whether possessed by the 'object' or not) are ugly, can in any case have no value, except such as may belong to the emotion *by itself;* and in most, if not in all, cases it is a considerable positive evil. In this sense, then, it is undoubtedly right to think that seeing beauty in a thing which has no beauty is inferior in value to seeing beauty where beauty really is. But the other case is much more difficult. In this case there is present all that I have hitherto mentioned as necessary to constitute a great positive good: there is a cognition of qualities really beautiful, together with an appropriate emotion towards these qualities. There can, therefore, be no doubt that we have here a great positive good. But there is present also something else; namely, a belief that these beautiful qualities exist, and that they exist in a certain relation to other things—namely, to some properties of the object to which we attribute these qualities: and further the object of this belief is false. And we may ask, with regard to the whole thus constituted, whether the presence of the belief, and the fact that what is believed is false, make any difference to its value? We thus get three different cases of which it is very important to determine the relative values. Where both the cognition of beautiful qualities and the appropriate emotion are present we may *also* have either, (1) a belief in the existence of these qualities, of which the object, *i.e.* that they exist, is true: or (2) a mere cognition, without belief, when it is (*a*) true, (*b*) false, that the object of the cognition, *i.e.* the beautiful qualities, exists: or (3) a belief in the existence of the beautiful qualities, when they do not exist. The importance of these cases arises from the fact that the second defines the pleasures of imagination, including a great part of the appreciation of those works of art which are *representative;* whereas the first contrasts with these the appreciation of what is beautiful in Nature, and the human affections. The third, on the other hand, is contrasted with both, in that it is chiefly exemplified in what is called misdirected affection; and it is possible also that the love of God, in the case of a believer, should fall under this head.

117. Now all these three cases, as I have said, have something in common, namely, that, in them all, we have a cognition of really beautiful qualities together with an appropriate emotion towards those qualities. I think, therefore, it cannot be doubted (nor is it commonly doubted) that all three include great positive goods; they are all things of which we feel convinced that they are worth having for their own sakes. And I think that the value of the second, in either of its two subdivisions, is precisely the same as the value of the element common to all three. In other words, in the case of purely imaginative appreciations we have merely the cognition of really beautiful qualities together with the appropriate emotion; and the question, whether the object cognised exists or not, seems here, where there is no belief either in its existence or in its non-existence, to make absolutely no difference to the value of the total state. But it seems to me that the two other cases do differ in intrinsic value both from this one and from one another, even though the object cognised and the appropriate emotion should be identical in all three cases. I think that the additional presence of a belief in the reality of the object makes the total state much better, if the belief is true; and worse, if the belief is false. In short, where there is belief, in the sense in which we *do* believe in the existence of Nature and horses, and do *not* believe in the existence of an ideal landscape and unicorns, the *truth* of what is believed does make a great difference to the value of the organic whole. If this be the case, we shall have vindicated the belief that *knowledge*, in the ordinary sense, as distinguished on the one hand from belief in what is false and on the other from the mere awareness of what is true, does contribute towards in-trinsic value—that, at least in some cases, its presence as a part makes a whole more valuable than it could have been without.

Now I think there can be no doubt that we do judge that there is a difference of value, such as I have indicated, between the three cases in question. We do think that the emotional contemplation of a natural scene, supposing its qualities equally beautiful, is in some way a better state of things than that of a painted landscape: we think that the world would be improved if we could substitute for the best works of representative art *real* objects equally beautiful. And similarly we regard a misdirected affection or admiration, even where the error involved is a mere error of judgment and not an error of taste, as in some way unfortunate. And further, those, at least, who have a strong respect for truth, are inclined to think that a merely poetical contemplation of the Kingdom of Heaven *would* be superior to that of the religious believer, *if* it were the case that the Kingdom of Heaven does not and will not really exist. Most persons, on a sober, reflective judgment, would feel some hesitation even in preferring the felicity of a madman, convinced that the world was ideal, to the condition either of a poet imagining an **ideal** world, or of themselves enjoying and **appreciating** the lesser goods which do and will exist. But, in order to assure ourselves that these judgments are really judgments of intrinsic value upon the question before us, and to satisfy ourselves that they are correct, it is necessary clearly to distinguish our question from two others which have a very important bearing upon our total judgment of the cases in question.

118. In the first place (*a*) it is plain that, where we believe, the question whether what we believe is true or false, will generally have a most important bearing upon the value of our belief *as a means.* Where we believe, we are apt to act upon our belief, in a way in which we do not act upon our cognition of the events in a novel. The truth of what we believe is, therefore, very important as preventing the pains of disappointment and still more serious conse-

quences. And it might be thought that a misdirected attachment was unfortunate solely for this reason: that it leads us to count upon results, which the real nature of its object is not of a kind to ensure. So too the Love of God, where, as usual, it includes the belief that he will annex to certain actions consequences, either in this life or the next, which the course of nature gives no reason to expect, may lead the believer to perform actions of which the actual consequences, supposing no such God to exist, may be much worse than he might otherwise have effected: and it might be thought that this was the sole reason (as it is a sufficient one) why we should hesitate to encourage the Love of God, in the absence of any proof that he exists. And similarly it may be thought that the only reason why beauty in Nature should be held superior to an equally beautiful landscape or imagination, is that its existence would ensure greater permanence and frequency in our emotional contemplation of that beauty. It is, indeed, certain that the chief importance of most *knowledge*—of the truth of most of the things which we believe— does, in this world, consist in its extrinsic advantages: it is immensely valuable *as a means*.

And secondly, (b) it may be the case that the existence of that which we contemplate is itself a great positive good, so that, for this reason alone, the state of things described by saying, that the object of our emotion really exists, would be intrinsically superior to that in which it did not. This reason for superiority is undoubtedly of great importance in the case of human affections, where the object of our admiration is the mental qualities of an admirable person; for that *two* such admirable persons should exist is greatly better than that there should be only one: and it would also discriminate the admiration of inanimate nature from that of its representations in art, in so far as we may allow a small intrinsic value to the existence of a beautiful object, apart from any contemplation of it. But it is to be noticed that this reason would not account for any difference in value between

the cases where the truth was believed and that in which it was merely cognised, without either belief or disbelief. In other words, so far as this reason goes, the difference between the two subdivisions of our second class (that of imaginative contemplation) would be as great as between our first class and the second subdivision of our second. The superiority of the mere *cognition* of a beautiful object, when that object also happened to exist, over the same cognition when the object did not exist, would, on this count, be as great as that of the *knowledge* of a beautiful object over the mere imagination of it.

119. These two reasons for discriminating between the value of the three cases we are considering, must, I say, be carefully distinguished from that, of which I am now questioning the validity, if we are to obtain a correct answer concerning this latter. The question I am putting is this: Whether the *whole* constituted by the fact that there is an emotional contemplation of a beautiful object, which both is believed to be and is *real*, does not derive some of its value from the fact that the object *is* real? I am asking whether the value of this whole, *as a whole*, is not greater than that of those which differ from it, *either* by the absence of belief, with or without truth, *or*, belief being present, by the mere absence of truth? I am not asking *either* whether it is not superior to them as a means (which it certainly is), *nor* whether it may not contain a more valuable *part*, namely, the existence of the object in question. My question is solely whether the existence of its object does not constitute an addition to the value of the whole, quite distinct from the addition constituted by the fact that this whole does contain a valuable part.

If, now, we put this question, I cannot avoid thinking that it should receive an affirmative answer. We can put it clearly by the method of isolation; and the sole decision must rest with our reflective judgment upon it, as thus clearly put. We can guard against the bias produced by a consideration of value *as a means* by supposing the case of an illusion as complete and permanent as illusions in this world never can be. We can imagine the case of a single person, enjoying throughout eternity the contemplation of scenery as beautiful, and intercourse with persons as admirable, as can be imagined; while yet the whole of the objects of his cognition are absolutely unreal. I think we should definitely pronounce the existence of a universe, which consisted solely of such a person, to be *greatly* inferior in value to one in which the objects, in the existence of which he believes, did really exist just as he believes them to do; and that it would be thus inferior *not only* because it would lack the goods which consist in the existence of the objects in question, but *also* merely because his belief would be false. That it would be inferior *for this reason alone* follows if we admit, what also appears to me certain, that the case of a person, merely imagining, without believing, the beautiful objects in question, would, *although these objects really existed*, be yet inferior to that of the person who also believed in their existence. For here all the additional good, which consists in the existence of the objects, is present, and yet there still seems to be a great difference in value between this case and that in which their existence is believed. But I think that my conclusion may perhaps be exhibited in a more convincing light by the following considerations. (1) It does not seem to me that the small degree of value which we may allow to the existence of beautiful inanimate objects is nearly equal in amount to the difference which I feel that there is between the appreciation (accompanied by belief) of such objects, when they really exist, and the purely imaginative appreciation of them when they do not exist. This inequality is more difficult to verify where the object is an admirable person, since a *great* value must be allowed to his existence. But yet I think it is not paradoxical to maintain that the superiority of reciprocal affection, where both objects are worthy and both exist, over an unreciprocated affection, where both are worthy but one does not exist, does not lie solely in the fact that, in the former case, we have two good things instead of one, but also in the fact that each is such as the other believes him to be. (2) It seems to me that the important contribution to value made by true belief may be very plainly seen in the following case. Suppose that a worthy object of affection does really exist and is believed to do so, but that there enters into the case this error of fact, that the qualities loved, though exactly like, are yet not the *same* which really do exist. This state of things is easily imagined, and I think we cannot avoid pronouncing that, *although* both persons here exist, it is yet not so satisfactory as where the very person loved and believed to exist is also the one which actually does exist.

120. If all this be so, we have, in this third section, added to our two former results the third result that a true belief in the reality of an object greatly increases the value of many valuable wholes. Just as in sections (1) and (2) it was maintained that aesthetic and affectionate emotions had little or no value apart from the cognition of appropriate objects, and that the cognition of these objects had little or no value apart from the appropriate emotion, so that the whole, in which both were combined, had a value greatly in excess of the sum of the values of its parts; so, according to this section, if there be added to these wholes a true belief in the reality of the object, the new whole thus formed has a value greatly in excess of the sum obtained by adding the value of the true belief, considered in itself, to that of our original wholes. This new case only differs from the former in this, that, whereas the true belief, by itself, has quite as little value as either of the two other constituents taken singly, yet they, taken together, seem to form a whole of very great value, whereas this is not the case with the two wholes which might be formed by adding the true belief to either of the others.

The importance of the result of this section seems to lie mainly in two of its consequences. (1) That it affords some justification for the immense intrinsic value, which seems to be commonly attributed to the mere *knowledge* of some truths, and which was expressly attributed to some kinds of knowledge by Plato and Aristotle. Perfect knowledge has indeed competed with perfect love for the position of Ideal. If the results of this section are correct, it appears that knowledge, though having little or no value by itself, is an absolutely essential constituent in the highest goods, and contributes immensely to their value. And it appears that this function may be performed not only by that case of knowledge, which we have chiefly considered, namely, knowledge of the reality of the beautiful object cognised, but also by knowledge of the numerical identity of this object with that which really exists, and by the knowledge that the existence of that object is truly good. Indeed all knowledge, which is directly concerned with the nature of the constituents of a beautiful object, would seem capable of adding greatly to the value of the contemplation of that object, although, by itself, such knowledge would have no value at all.—And (2) The second important consequence, which follows from this section, is that the presence of true belief may, in spite of a great inferiority in the value of the emotion and the beauty of its object, constitute with them a whole equal or superior in value to wholes, in which the emotion and beauty are superior, but in which a true belief is wanting or a false belief present. In this way we may justify the attribution of equal or superior value to an appreciation of an inferior real object, as compared with the appreciation of a greatly superior object which is a mere creature of the imagination. Thus a just appreciation of nature and of real persons may maintain its equality with an equally just appreciation of the products of artistic imagination, in spite of much greater beauty in the latter. And similarly though God may be admitted to be a more perfect object than any actual human being, the love of God may yet be inferior to human love, *if* God does not exist.

121. (4) In order to complete the discussion of this first class of goods—goods which have an essential reference to *beau-*tiful objects—it would be necessary to attempt a classification and comparative valuation of all the different forms of beauty, a task which properly belongs to the study called Aesthetics. I do not, however, propose to attempt any part of this task. It must only be understood that I intend to include among the essential constituents of the goods I have been discussing, every form and variety of beautiful object, if only it be truly beautiful; and, *if* this be understood, I think it may be seen that the consensus of opinion with regard to what is positively beautiful and what is positively ugly, and even with regard to great differences in degree of beauty, is quite sufficient to allow us a hope that we need not greatly err in our judgments of good and evil. In anything which is thought beautiful by any considerable number of persons, there is probably *some* beautiful quality; and differences of opinion seem to be far more often due to exclusive attention, on the part of different persons, to different qualities in the same object, than to the positive error of supposing a quality that is ugly to be really beautiful. When an object, which some think beautiful, is denied to be so by others, the truth is *usually* that it lacks some beautiful quality or is deformed by some ugly one, which engage the exclusive attention of the critics.

I may, however, state two general principles, closely connected with the results of this chapter, the recognition of which would seem to be of great importance for the investigation of what things are truly beautiful. The first of these is (1) a definition of beauty, of what is meant by saying that a thing is truly beautiful. The naturalistic fallacy has been quite as commonly committed with regard to beauty as with regard to good: its use has introduced as many errors into Aesthetics as into Ethics. It has been even more commonly supposed that the beautiful may be *defined* as that which produces certain effects upon our feelings; and the conclusion which follows from this—namely, that judgments of taste are merely *subjective*—that precisely the same thing may, according to circumstances, be *both* beautiful *and* not beautiful—has very frequently been drawn. The conclusions of this chapter suggest a definition of beauty, which may partially explain and entirely remove the difficulties which have led to this error. It appears probable that the beautiful should be *defined* as that of which the admiring contemplation is good in itself. That is to say: To assert that a thing is beautiful is to assert that the cognition of it is an essential element in one of the intrinsically valuable wholes we have been discussing; so that the question, whether it is *truly* beautiful or not, depends upon the *objective* question whether the whole in question is or is not truly good, and does not depend upon the question whether it would or would not excite particular feelings in particular persons. This definition has the double recommendation that it accounts both for the apparent connection between goodness and beauty and for the no less apparent difference between these two conceptions. It appears, at first sight, to be a strange coincidence, that there should be two *different* objective predicates of value, 'good' and 'beautiful,' which are nevertheless so related to one another that whatever is beautiful is also good. But, if our definition be correct, the strangeness disappears; since it leaves only one *unanalysable* predicate of value, namely 'good,' while 'beautiful,' though not identical with, is to be defined by reference to this, being thus, at the same time, different from and necessarily connected with it. In short, on this view, to say that a thing is beautiful is to say, not indeed that it is *itself* good, but that it is a necessary element in something which is: to prove that a thing is truly beautiful is to prove that a whole, to which it bears a particular relation as a part, is truly good. And in this way we should explain the immense predominance, among objects commonly considered beautiful, of *material* objects—objects of the external senses; since these objects, though themselves having, as has been said, little or no intrinsic value, are yet essential constituents in the largest group of wholes which have intrinsic value. These wholes themselves may be, and are, also

beautiful; but the comparative rarity, with which we regard them as themselves *objects* of contemplation, seems sufficient to explain the association of beauty with external objects.

And secondly (2) it is to be observed that beautiful objects are themselves, for the most part, organic unities, in this sense, that they are wholes of great complexity, such that the contemplation of any part, by itself, may have no value, and yet that, unless the contemplation of the whole includes the contemplation of that part, it will lose in value. From this it follows that there can be no single criterion of beauty. It will never be true to say: This object owes its beauty *solely* to the presence of this characteristic; nor yet that: Wherever this characteristic is present, the object must be beautiful. All that can be true is that certain objects are beautiful, *because* they have certain characteristics, in the sense that they would not be beautiful *unless* they had them. And it may be possible to find that certain characteristics are more or less universally present in all beautiful objects, and are, in this sense, more or less important conditions of beauty. But it is important to observe that the very qualities, which differentiate one beautiful object from all others, are, if the object be truly beautiful, as *essential* to its beauty, as those which it has in common with ever so many others. The object would no more have the beauty it has, without its specific qualities, than without those that are generic; and the generic qualities, *by themselves*, would fail, as completely, to give beauty, as those which are specific.

122. II. It will be remembered that I began this survey of great unmixed goods, by dividing all the greatest goods we know into the two classes of aesthetic enjoyments, on the one hand, and the pleasures of human intercourse or of personal affection, on the other. I postponed the consideration of the latter on the ground that they presented additional complications. In what this additional complication consists, will now be evident; and I have already been obliged to take account of it, in

discussing the contribution to value made by true belief. It consists in the fact that in the case of personal affection, the object itself is not *merely* beautiful, while possessed of little or no intrinsic value, but is itself, in part at least, of great intrinsic value. All the constituents which we have found to be necessary to the most valuable aesthetic enjoyments, namely, appropriate emotion, cognition of truly beautiful qualities, and true belief, are equally necessary here; but here we have the additional fact that the object must be not only truly beautiful, but also truly good in a high degree.

It is evident that this additional complication only occurs in so far as there is included in the object of personal affection some of the *mental* qualities of the person towards whom the affection is felt. And I think it may be admitted that, wherever the affection is most valuable, the appreciation of mental qualities must form a large part of it, and that the presence of this part makes the whole far more valuable than it could have been without it. But it seems very doubtful whether this appreciation, by itself, can possess as much value as the whole in which it is combined with an appreciation of the appropriate *corporeal* expression of the mental qualities in question. It is certain that in all actual cases of valuable affection, the bodily expressions of character, whether by looks, by words, or by actions, do form a part of the object towards which the affection is felt, and that the fact of their inclusion appears to heighten the value of the whole state. It is, indeed, very difficult to imagine what the cognition of mental qualities *alone*, unaccompanied by *any* corporeal expression, would be like; and, in so far as we succeed in making this abstraction, the whole considered certainly appears to have less value. I therefore conclude that the importance of an admiration of admirable mental qualities lies chiefly in the immense superiority of a whole, in which it forms a part, to one in which it is absent, and not in any high degree of intrinsic value which it possesses by itself. It even appears to be doubtful, whether, in itself, it possesses so

much value as the appreciation of mere corporeal beauty undoubtedly does possess; that is to say, whether the appreciation of what has great intrinsic value is so valuable as the appreciation of what is merely beautiful.

But further if we consider the nature of admirable mental qualities, by themselves, it appears that a proper appreciation of them involves a reference to purely material beauty in yet another way. Admirable mental qualities do, if our previous conclusions are correct, consist very largely in an emotional contemplation of beautiful objects; and hence the appreciation of them will consist essentially in the contemplation of such contemplation. It is true that the most valuable appreciation of persons appears to be that which consists in the appreciation of their appreciation of other persons: but even here a reference to material beauty appears to be involved, *both* in respect of the fact that what is appreciated in the last instance may be the contemplation of what is merely beautiful, *and* in respect of the fact that the most valuable appreciation of a person appears to *include* an appreciation of his corporeal expression. Though, therefore, we may admit that the appreciation of a person's attitude towards other persons, or, to take one instance, the love of love, is far the most valuable good we know, and far more valuable than the mere love of beauty, yet we can only admit this if the first be understood to *include* the latter, in various degrees of directness.

With regard to the question what *are* the mental qualities of which the cognition is essential to the value of human intercourse, it is plain that they include, in the first place, all those varieties of aesthetic appreciation, which formed our first class of goods. They include, therefore, a great variety of different emotions, each of which is appropriate to some different kind of beauty. But we must now add to these the whole range of emotions, which are appropriate to persons, and which are different from those which are appropriate to mere corporeal beauty. It must also be remembered that just as these emotions have little value in themselves, and as the state of mind in which they exist may have its value greatly heightened, or may entirely lose it and become positively evil in a great degree, according as the cognitions accompanying the emotions are appropriate or inappropriate; so too the appreciation of these emotions, though it may have some value in itself, may yet form part of a whole which has far greater value or no value at all, according as it is or is not accompanied by a perception of the appropriateness of the emotions to their objects. It is obvious, therefore, that the study of what is valuable in human intercourse is a study of immense complexity; and that there may be much human intercourse which has little or no value, or is positively bad. Yet here too, as with the question what is beautiful, there seems no reason to doubt that a reflective judgment will in the main decide correctly both as to what are positive goods and even as to any *great* differences in value between these goods. In particular, it may be remarked that the emotions, of which the contemplation is essential to the greatest values, and which are also themselves appropriately excited by such contemplation, appear to be those which are commonly most highly prized under the name of affection.

123. I have now completed my examination into the nature of those great positive goods, which do not appear to include among their constituents anything positively evil or ugly, though they include much which is in itself indifferent. And I wish to point out certain conclusions which appear to follow, with regard to the nature of the Summum Bonum, or that state of things which would be the most perfect we can conceive. Those idealistic philosophers, whose views agree most closely with those here advocated, in that they deny pleasure to be the sole good and regard what is completely good as having some complexity, have usually represented a purely spiritual state of existence as the Ideal. Regarding matter as essentially imperfect, if not positively evil, they have concluded that the total absence of all material properties is necessary to a state of perfection. Now, according to what has been said, this view would be correct so far as it asserts that any great good must be *mental*, and so far as it asserts that a purely material existence, *by itself*, can have little or no value. The superiority of the spiritual over the material has, in a sense, been amply vindicated. But it does not follow, from this superiority, that a perfect state of things must be one, from which all material properties are rigidly excluded: on the contrary, if our conclusions are correct, it would seem to be the case that a state of things, in which they are included, must be vastly better than any conceivable state in which they were absent. In order to see that this is so, the chief thing necessary to be considered is *exactly what it is* which we declare to be good when we declare that the appreciation of beauty in Art and Nature is so. That this appreciation *is* good, the philosophers in question do not for the most part deny. But, if we admit it, then we should remember Butler's maxim that: Everything is what it is, and not another thing. I have tried to shew, and I think it is too evident to be disputed, that such appreciation is an organic unity, a complex whole; and that, in its most undoubted instances, part of what is included in this whole is *a cognition of material qualities*, and particularly of a vast variety of what are called *secondary* qualities. If, then, it is *this* whole, which we know to be good, and not another thing, then we know that material qualities, even though they be perfectly worthless in themselves, are yet essential constituents of what is far from worthless. What we know to be valuable is the apprehension of just these qualities, and not of any others; and, if we propose to subtract them from it, then what we have left is *not* that which we know to have value, but something else. And it must be noticed that this conclusion holds, even if my contention, that a true belief in the existence of these qualities adds to the value of the whole in which it is included, be disputed. We should then, indeed, be entitled to assert that the *existence* of a material world

was wholly immaterial to perfection; but the fact that what we knew to be good was a cognition of *material qualities* (though purely imaginary), would still remain. It must, then, be admitted on pain of self-contradiction—on pain of holding that things are not what they are, but something else—that a world, from which material qualities were wholly banished, would be a world which lacked many, if not all, of those things, which we know most certainly to be great goods. That it *might* nevertheless be a far better world than one which retained these goods, I have already admitted (§ 111 (1)). But in order to shew that any such world *would* be thus better, it would be necessary to shew that the retention of these things, though good in themselves, impaired, in a more than equal degree, the value of some whole, to which they might belong; and the task of shewing this has certainly never been attempted. Until it be performed, we are entitled to assert that material qualities are a necessary constituent of the Ideal; that, though something utterly unknown *might* be better than any world containing either them or any other good we know, yet we have no reason to suppose that anything whatever would be better than a state of things in which they were included. To deny and exclude matter, is to deny and exclude the best we know. That a thing may retain its value, while losing some of its qualities, is utterly untrue. All that is true is that the changed thing may have more value than, or as much value as, that of which the qualities have been lost. What I contend is that nothing, which we *know* to be good and which contains no material qualities, has such great value that we can declare it, *by itself*, to be superior to the whole which would be formed by the addition to it of an appreciation of material qualities. That a *purely* spiritual good may be the *best* of single things, I am not much concerned to dispute, although, in what has been said with regard to the nature of personal affection, I have given reasons for doubting it. But that by adding to it some appreciation of material qualities, which, though perhaps

inferior by itself, is certainly a great positive good, we should obtain a greater sum of value, which no corresponding decrease in the value of the whole, as a whole, could counterbalance—this, I maintain, we have certainly no reason to doubt.

124. In order to complete this discussion of the main principles involved in the determination of intrinsic values, the chief remaining topics, necessary to be treated, appear to be two. The first of these is the nature of great intrinsic *evils*, including what I may call *mixed* evils; that is to say, those evil wholes, which nevertheless contain, as essential elements, something positively good or beautiful. And the second is the nature of what I may similarly call *mixed* goods; that is to say, those wholes, which, though intrinsically good *as wholes*, nevertheless contain, as essential elements, something positively evil or ugly. It will greatly facilitate this discussion, if I may be understood throughout to use the terms 'beautiful' and 'ugly,' not necessarily with reference to things of the kind which most naturally occur to us as instances of what is beautiful and ugly, but in accordance with my own proposed definition of beauty. Thus I shall use the word 'beautiful' to denote that of which the admiring contemplation is good in itself; and 'ugly' to denote that of which the admiring contemplation is evil in itself.

I. With regard, then, to great positive evils, I think it is evident that, if we take all due precautions to discover *precisely what* those things are, of which, *if they existed absolutely by themselves*, we should judge the existence to be a great evil, we shall find most of them to be organic unities of exactly the same nature as those which are the greatest positive goods. That is to say, they are cognitions of some object, accompanied by some emotion. Just as neither a cognition nor an emotion, *by itself*, appeared capable of being greatly good, so (with one exception), neither a cognition nor an emotion, *by itself*, appears capable of being greatly evil. And just as a whole formed of both, even without the addition of any other element, appeared undoubtedly capable of being a great good, so such a whole, *by itself*, appears capable of being a great evil. With regard to the *third* element, which was discussed as capable of adding greatly to the value of a good, namely, *true belief*, it will appear that it has different relations towards different kinds of evils. In some cases the addition of true belief to a positive evil seems to constitute a far worse evil; but in other cases it is not apparent that it makes any difference.

The greatest positive evils may be divided into the following three classes.

125. (1) The first class consists of those evils, which seem always to include an enjoyment or admiring contemplation of things which are themselves either evil or ugly. That is to say these evils are characterised by the fact that they include precisely the same emotion, which is also essential to the greatest unmixed goods, from which they are differentiated by the fact that this emotion is directed towards an inappropriate object. In so far as this emotion is either a slight good in itself or a slightly beautiful object, these evils would therefore be cases of what I have called 'mixed' evils; but, as I have already said, it seems very doubtful whether an emotion, completely isolated from its object, has either value or beauty: it certainly has not much of either. It is, however, important to observe that the very same emotions, which are often loosely talked of as the greatest or the only goods, may be essential constituents of the very worst wholes: that, according to the nature of the cognition which accompanies them, they may be conditions either of the greatest good, or of the greatest evil.

In order to illustrate the nature of evils of this class, I may take two instances—cruelty and lasciviousness. That these are great intrinsic evils, we may, I think, easily assure ourselves, by imagining the state of a man, whose mind is solely occupied by either of these passions, in their worst form. If we then consider what judgment we should pass upon a universe which consisted *solely* of minds thus occupied, without the smallest hope that there would ever

exist in it the smallest consciousness of any object other than those proper to these passions, or any feeling directed to any such object, I think we cannot avoid the conclusion that the existence of such a universe would be a far worse evil than the existence of none at all. But, if this be so, it follows that these two vicious states are not only, as is commonly admitted, bad as means, but also bad in themselves.—And that they involve in their nature that complication of elements, which I have called a love of what is evil or ugly, is, I think, no less plain. With regard to the pleasures of lust, the nature of the cognition, by the presence of which they are to be defined, is somewhat difficult to analyse. But it appears to include both cognitions of organic sensations and perceptions of states of the body, of which the enjoyment is certainly an evil in itself. So far as these are concerned, lasciviousness would, then, include in its essence an admiring contemplation of what is ugly. But certainly one of its commonest ingredients, in its worst forms, is an enjoyment of the same state of mind in other people: and in this case it would therefore also include a love of what is evil. With regard to cruelty, it is easy to see that an enjoyment of pain in other people is essential to it; and, as we shall see, when we come to consider pain, this is certainly a love of evil: while, in so far as it also includes a delight in the bodily signs of agony, it would also comprehend a love of what is ugly. In both cases, it should be observed, the evil of the state is heightened not only by an increase in the evil or ugliness of the object, but also by an increase in the enjoyment.

It might be objected, in the case of cruelty, that our disapproval of it, even in the isolated case supposed, where no considerations of its badness as a means could influence us, may yet be really directed to the pain of the persons, which it takes delight in contemplating. This objection may be met in the first place, by the remark that it entirely fails to explain the judgment, which yet, I think, no one, on reflection, will be able to avoid making, that even though the amount of pain contemplated be the same, yet the greater the delight in its contemplation, the worse the state of things. But it may also, I think, be met by notice of a fact, which we were unable to urge in considering the similar possibility with regard to goods—namely the possibility that the reason why we attribute greater value to a worthy affection for a *real* person, is that we take into account the additional good consisting in the existence of that person. We may I think urge, in the case of cruelty, that its intrinsic odiousness is equally great, whether the pain contemplated really exists or is purely imaginary. I, at least, am unable to distinguish that, in this case, the presence of *true belief* makes any difference to the intrinsic value of the whole considered, although it undoubtedly may make a great difference to its value *as a means*. And so also with regard to other evils of this class: I am unable to see that a true belief in the *existence* of their objects makes any difference in the degree of their positive demerits. On the other hand, the presence of another class of beliefs seems to make a considerable difference. When we enjoy what is evil or ugly, in spite of our knowledge that it is so, the state of things seems considerably worse than if we made no judgment at all as to the object's value. And the same seems also, strangely enough, to be the case when we make a false judgment of value. When we admire what is ugly or evil, believing that it is beautiful and good, this belief seems also to enhance the intrinsic vileness of our condition. It must, of course, be understood that, in both these cases, the judgment in question is merely what I have called a judgment of taste; that is to say, it is concerned with the worth of the qualities actually cognised and not with the worth of the object, to which those qualities may be rightly or wrongly attributed.

Finally it should be mentioned that evils of this class, *beside* that emotional element (namely enjoyment and admiration) which they share with great unmixed goods, appear always also to include some specific emotion, which does not enter in the same way into the constitution of any good. The presence of this specific emotion seems certainly to enhance the badness of the whole, though it is not plain that, by itself, it would be either evil or ugly.

126. (2) The second class of great evils are undoubtedly mixed evils; but I treat them next, because, in a certain respect, they appear to be the *converse* of the class last considered. Just as it is essential to this last class that they should include an emotion, appropriate to the cognition of what is good or beautiful, but directed to an inappropriate object; so to this second class it is essential that they should include a cognition of what is good or beautiful, but accompanied by an inappropriate emotion. In short, just as the last class may be described as cases of the love of what is evil or ugly, so this class may be described as cases of the hatred of what is good or beautiful.

With regard to these evils it should be remarked: First, that the vices of hatred, envy and contempt, where these vices are evil in themselves, appear to be instances of them; and that they are frequently accompanied by evils of the first class, for example, where a delight is felt in the pain of a good person. Where they are thus accompanied, the whole thus formed is undoubtedly worse than if either existed singly.

And secondly: That in their case a true belief in the existence of the good or beautiful object, which is hated, does appear to enhance the badness of the whole, in which it is present. Undoubtedly also, as in our first class, the presence of a true belief as to the *value* of the objects contemplated, increases the evil. But, contrary to what was the case in our first class, a *false* judgment of value appears to lessen it.

127. (3) The third class of great positive evils appears to be the class of *pains*.

With regard to these it should first be remarked that, as in the case of pleasure, it is not pain itself, but only the consciousness of pain, towards which our judgments of value are directed. Just as in Chap. III., it was said that pleasure, however intense, which no one felt, would be no good at all;

so it appears that pain, however intense, of which there was no consciousness, would be no evil at all.

It is, therefore, only the consciousness of intense pain, which can be maintained to be a great evil. But that this, *by itself*, may be a great evil, I cannot avoid thinking. The case of pain thus seems to differ from that of pleasure: for the mere consciousness of pleasure, however intense, does not, *by itself*, appear to be a *great* good, even if it has some slight intrinsic value. In short, pain (if we understand by this expression, the consciousness of pain) appears to be a far worse evil than pleasure is a good. But, if this be so, then *pain* must be admitted to be an exception from the rule which seems to hold both of all *other* great evils and of *all* great goods: namely that they are all organic unities to which *both* a cognition of an object *and* an emotion directed towards that object are essential. In the case of pain and of pain alone, it seems to be true that a mere cognition, by itself, may be a great evil. It is, indeed, *an* organic unity, since it involves both the cognition and the object, neither of which, by themselves, has either merit or demerit. But it is a less complex organic unity than any other great evil and than any great good, *both* in respect of the fact that it does not involve, *beside* the cognition, an emotion directed towards its object, *and also* in respect of the fact that the *object* may here be absolutely simple, whereas in most, if not all, other cases, the object itself is highly complex.

This want of analogy between the relation of pain to intrinsic evil and of pleasure to intrinsic good, seems also to be exhibited in a second respect. Not only is it the case that consciousness of intense pain is, by itself, a great evil, whereas consciousness of intense pleasure is, by itself, no great good; but also the *converse* difference appears to hold of the contribution which they make to the value of the whole, when they are combined respectively with another great evil or with a great good. That is to say, the presence of pleasure (though not in proportion to its intensity) does appear to enhance the value of a whole, in

which it is combined with any of the great unmixed goods which we have considered: it might even be maintained that it is *only* wholes, in which *some* pleasure is included, that possess any great value: it is certain, at all events, that the presence of pleasure makes a contribution to the value of good wholes greatly in excess of its own intrinsic value. On the contrary, if a feeling of pain be combined with any of the evil states of mind which we have been considering, the difference which its presence makes to the value of the whole, *as a whole*, seems to be rather for the better than the worse: in any case, the only additional evil which it introduces, is that which it, by itself, intrinsically constitutes. Thus, whereas pain is *in itself* a great evil, but makes no addition to the badness of a whole, in which it is combined with some other bad thing, except that which consists in its own intrinsic badness; pleasure, conversely, is not *in itself* a great good, but does make a great addition to the goodness of a whole in which it is combined with a good thing, quite apart from its own intrinsic value.

128. But finally, it must be insisted that pleasure and pain are completely analogous in this: that we cannot assume either that the presence of pleasure always makes a state of things better *on the whole*, or that the presence of pain always makes it worse. This is the truth which is most liable to be overlooked with regard to them; and it is because this is true, that the common theory, that pleasure is the only good and pain the only evil, has its grossest consequences in misjudgments of value. Not only is the pleasantness of a state *not* in proportion to its intrinsic worth; it may even add positively to its vileness. We do not think the successful hatred of a villian the less vile and odious, because he takes the keenest delight in it; nor is there the least need, in logic, why we should think so, apart from an unintelligent prejudice in favour of pleasure. In fact it seems to be the case that wherever pleasure is added to an evil state of either of our first two classes, the whole thus formed is *always* worse than if no pleasure had been there. And similarly with re-

gard to pain. If pain be added to an evil state of either of our first two classes, the whole thus formed is *always* better, *as a whole*, than if no pain had been there; though here, if the pain be too intense, since that is a great evil, the state may not be better *on the whole*. It is in this way that the theory of vindictive punishment may be vindicated. The infliction of pain on a person whose state of mind is bad may, if the pain be not too intense, create a state of things that is better *on the whole* than if the evil state of mind had existed unpunished. Whether such a state of things can ever constitute a *positive* good, is another question.

129. II. The consideration of this other question belongs properly to the second topic, which was reserved above for discussion—namely the topic of 'mixed' goods. 'Mixed' goods were defined above as things, which, though positively good *as wholes*, nevertheless contain, as essential elements, something intrinsically evil or ugly. And there certainly seem to be such goods. But for the proper consideration of them, it is necessary to take into account a new distinction—the distinction just expressed as being between the value which a thing possesses 'as a whole,' and that which it possesses 'on the whole.'

When 'mixed' goods were defined as things positively good *as wholes*, the expression was ambiguous. It was meant that they were positively good *on the whole*; but it must now be observed that the value which a thing possesses *on the whole* may be said to be equivalent to the sum of the value which it possesses *as a whole, together with* the intrinsic values which may belong to any of its parts. In fact, by the 'value which a thing possesses as a whole,' there may be meant two quite distinct things. There may be meant either (1) That value which arises solely *from the combination* of two or more things; or else (2) The total value formed by the addition to (1) of any intrinsic values which may belong to the things combined. The meaning of the distinction may perhaps be most easily seen by considering the supposed case of vindictive punishment. If it is true that the combined existence of two evils may yet constitute a less evil than would be constituted by the existence of either singly, it is plain that this can only be because there arises from the combination a positive good which is greater than the *difference* between the sum of the two evils and the demerit of either singly: this positive good would then be the value of the whole, *as a whole*, in sense (1). Yet if this value be not so great a good as the sum of the two evils is an evil, it is plain that the value of the whole state of things will be a positive evil; and this value is the value of the whole, *as a whole*, in sense (2). Whatever view may be taken with regard to the particular case of vindictive punishment, it is plain that we have here *two distinct things*, with regard to *either* of which a separate question may be asked in the case of every organic unity. The first of these two things may be expressed as *the difference* between the value *of the whole thing* and the sum of the value of its parts. And it is plain that where the parts have little or no intrinsic value (as in our first class of goods, §§ 114, 115), this difference will be nearly or absolutely identical with the value of the whole thing. The distinction, therefore, only becomes important in the case of wholes, of which one or more parts have a great intrinsic value, positive or negative. The first of these cases, that of a whole, in which one part has a great *positive* value, is exemplified in our 2nd and 3rd classes of great unmixed goods (§§ 120, 122); and similarly the Summum Bonum is a whole of which *many* parts have a great *positive* value. Such cases, it may be observed, are also very frequent and very important objects of Aesthetic judgment; since the essential distinction between the 'classical' and the 'romantic' styles consists in the fact that the former aims at obtaining the greatest possible value for the whole, *as a whole*, in sense (1), whereas the latter sacrifices this in order to obtain the greatest possible value for some *part*, which is itself an organic unity. It follows that we cannot declare either style to be necessarily superior, since an equally good result *on the whole*, or 'as a whole' in sense (2), may be obtained by either method; but the distinctively *aesthetic* temperament seems to be characterised by a tendency to prefer a good result obtained by the classical, to an equally good result obtained by the romantic method.

130. But what we have now to consider are cases of wholes, in which one or more parts have a great *negative* value—are great positive evils. And first of all, we may take the *strongest* cases, like that of retributive punishment, in which we have a whole, exclusively composed of two great positive evils—wickedness and pain. Can such a whole ever be positively good *on the whole?*

(1) I can see no reason to think that such wholes ever are positively good *on the whole.* But from the fact that they may, nevertheless, be less evils, than either of their parts taken singly, it follows that they have a characteristic which is most important for the correct decision of practical questions. It follows that, quite apart from *consequences* or any value which an evil may have as a mere means, it may, *supposing* one evil already exists, be worth while to create another, since, by the mere creation of this second, there may be constituted a whole less bad than if the original evil had been left to exist by itself. And similarly, with regard to all the wholes which I am about to consider, it must be remembered, that, even if they are not goods *on the whole,* yet, where an evil already exists, as in this world evils do exist, the existence of the other part of these wholes will constitute a thing desirable *for its own sake*—that is to say, not merely a means to future goods, but one of the *ends* which must be taken into account in estimating what that best possible state of things is, to which every right action must be a means.

131. (2) But, as a matter of fact, I cannot avoid thinking that there are wholes, containing something positively evil and ugly, which are, nevertheless, great positive goods on the whole. Indeed, it appears to be to this class that those instances of virtue, which contain anything intrinsically good, chiefly belong. It need not, of course, be denied that there is sometimes included in a virtuous disposition more or less of those unmixed goods which were first discussed—that is to say, a real love of what is good or beautiful. But the typical and characteristic virtuous dispositions, so far as they are not mere means, seem rather to be examples of mixed goods. We may take as instances (a) Courage and Compassion, which seem to belong to the second of the three classes of virtues distinguished in our last chapter (§ 107); and (b) the specifically 'moral' sentiment, by reference to which the third of those three classes was defined (§ 108).

Courage and compassion, in so far as they contain an intrinsically desirable state of mind, seem to involve essentially a cognition of something evil or ugly. In the case of courage the object of the cognition may be an evil of any of our three classes; in the case of compassion, the proper object is pain. Both these virtues, accordingly, must contain precisely the same cognitive element, which is also essential to evils of class (1); and they are differentiated from these by the fact that the emotion directed to these objects is, in their case, an emotion of the same kind which was essential to evils of class (2). In short, just as evils of class (2) seemed to consist in a hatred of what was good or beautiful, and evils of class (1) in a love of what was evil or ugly; so these virtues involve a *hatred* of what is evil or ugly. Both these virtues do, no doubt, also contain other elements, and, among these, each contains its specific emotion; but that their value does not depend solely upon these other elements, we may easily assure ourselves, by considering what we should think of an attitude of endurance or of defiant contempt toward an object intrinsically good or beautiful, or of the state of a man whose mind was filled with pity for the happiness of a worthy admiration. Yet pity for the undeserved sufferings of others, endurance of pain to ourselves, and a defiant hatred of evil dispositions in ourselves or in others, seem to be undoubtedly admirable in themselves; and if so, there are admirable things, which must be lost, if there were no cognition of evil.

Similarly the specifically 'moral' senti-ment, in all cases where it has any consid-erable intrinsic value, appears to include a hatred of evils of the first and second classes. It is true that the emotion is here excited by the idea that an action is right or wrong; and hence the object of the idea which excites it is generally not an intrin-sic evil. But, as far as I can discover, the emotion with which a conscientious man views a real or imaginary right action, con-tains, as an essential element, the same emotion with which he views a wrong one: it seems, indeed, that this element is nec-essary to make his emotion specifically *moral*. And the specifically moral emotion excited by the idea of a wrong action, seems to me to contain essentially a more or less vague cognition of the kind of intrinsic evils, which are usually caused by wrong actions, whether they would or would not be caused by the particular action in ques-tion. I am, in fact, unable to distinguish, in its main features, the moral sentiment ex-cited by the idea of rightness and wrong-ness, wherever it is intense, from the total state constituted by a cognition of some-thing intrinsically evil together with the emotion of hatred directed towards it. Nor need we be surprised that this mental state should be the one chiefly associated with the idea of rightness, if we reflect on the nature of those actions which are most commonly recognised as duties. For by far the greater part of the actions, of which we commonly think as duties, are *negative:* what we feel to be our duty is to *abstain* from some action to which a strong natural impulse tempts us. And these wrong ac-tions, in the avoidance of which duty con-sists, are usually such as produce, very im-mediately, some bad consequence in pain to others; while, in many prominent in-stances, the inclination, which prompts us to them, is itself an intrinsic evil, contain-ing, as where the impulse is lust or cruelty, an anticipatory enjoyment of something evil or ugly. That right action does thus so frequently entail the suppression of some evil impulse, is necessary to explain the plausibility of the view that virtue *consists*

in the control of passion by reason. Ac-cordingly, the truth seems to be that, when-ever a strong moral emotion is excited by the idea of rightness, this emotion is ac-companied by a vague cognition of the kind of evils usually suppressed or avoided by the actions which most frequently occur to us as instances of duty; and that the emo-tion is directed towards this evil quality. We may, then, conclude that the specific moral emotion owes almost all its intrinsic value to the fact that it includes a cognition of evils accompanied by a hatred of them: mere rightness, whether truly or untruly attributed to an action, seems incapable of forming the object of an emotional con-templation, which shall be any great good.

132. If this be so, then we have, in many prominent instances of virtue, cases of a whole, greatly good in itself, which yet con-tains the cognition of something, whereof the existence would be a great evil: a great good is absolutely dependent for its value, upon its inclusion of something evil or ugly, although it does not owe its value *solely* to this element in it. And, in the case of virtues, this evil object does, in general, actually exist. But there seems no reason to think that, when it does exist, the whole state of things thus constituted is therefore the better *on the whole*. What seems indu-bitable, is only that the feeling contempla-tion of an object, whose existence *would* be a great evil, or which is ugly, may be es-sential to a valuable whole. We have an-other undoubted instance of this in the ap-preciation of tragedy. But, in tragedy, the sufferings of Lear, and the vice of Iago may be purely imaginary. And it seems certain that, if they really existed, the evil thus ex-isting, while it must detract from the good consisting in a proper feeling towards them, will add no positive value to that good great enough to counterbalance such a loss. It does, indeed, seem that the exis-tence of a true belief in the object of these mixed goods does add *some* value to the whole in which it is combined with them: a conscious compassion for real suffering seems to be better, *as a whole*, than a com-passion for sufferings merely imaginary;

and this may well be the case, even though the evil involved in the actual suffering makes the total state of things bad *on the whole*. And it certainly seems to be true that a *false* belief in the actual existence of its object makes a worse mixed good than if our state of mind were that with which we normally regard pure fiction. Accordingly we may conclude that the only mixed goods, which are positively good *on the whole*, are those in which the object is something which *would* be a great evil, if it existed, or which *is* ugly.

133. With regard, then, to those mixed goods, which consist in an appropriate attitude of the mind towards things evil or ugly, and which include among their number the greater part of such virtues as have any intrinsic value whatever, the following three conclusions seem to be those chiefly requiring to be emphasized:—

(1) There seems no reason to think that where the object is a thing evil in itself, which *actually exists*, the total state of things is ever positively *good on the whole*. The appropriate mental attitude towards a really existing evil contains, of course, an element which is absolutely identical with the same attitude towards the same evil, where it is purely imaginary. And this element, which is common to the two cases, may be a great positive good, on the whole. But there seems no reason to doubt that, where the evil is *real*, the amount of this real evil is always sufficient to reduce the total sum of value to a negative quantity. Accordingly we have no reason to maintain the paradox that an ideal world would be one in which vice and suffering must exist in order that it may contain the goods consisting in the appropriate emotion towards them. It is not a positive good that suffering should exist, in order that we may compassionate it; or wickedness, that we may hate it. There is no reason to think that any actual evil whatsoever would be contained in the Ideal. It follows that we cannot admit the actual validity of any of the arguments commonly used in Theodicies; no such argument succeeds in justifying the fact that there does exist even the smallest of the many evils which this world contains. The most that can be said for such arguments is that, when they make appeal to the principle of organic unity, their appeal is valid *in principle*. It *might* be the case that the existence of evil was necessary, not merely as a means, but analytically, to the existence of the greatest good. But we have no reason to think that this *is* the case in any instance whatsoever.

But (2) there *is* reason to think that the cognition of things evil or ugly, which are purely imaginary, is essential to the Ideal. In this case the burden of proof lies the other way. It cannot be doubted that the appreciation of tragedy is a great positive good; and it seems almost equally certain that the virtues of compassion, courage, and self-control contain such goods. And to all these the cognition of things which would be evil, if they existed, is analytically necessary. Here then we have things of which the existence must add value to any whole in which they are contained; nor is it possible to assure ourselves that any whole, from which they were omitted, would thereby gain more in its value *as a whole*, than it would lose by their omission. We have no reason to think that any whole, which did not contain them, would be so good *on the whole* as some whole in which they were obtained. The case for their inclusion in the Ideal is as strong as that for the inclusion of material qualities (§ 123, above). *Against* the inclusion of these goods nothing can be urged except a bare possibility.

Finally (3) it is important to insist that, as was said above, these mixed virtues have a great practical value, in addition to that which they possess either in themselves or as mere means. Where evils do exist, as in this world they do, the fact that they are known and properly appreciated, constitutes a state of things having greater value *as a whole* even than the same appreciation of purely imaginary evils. This state of things, it has been said, is never positively good *on the whole*; but where the evil, which reduces its total value to a negative quantity, already unavoidably exists, to obtain the intrinsic value which belongs to it *as a whole* will obviously produce a better state of things than if the evil had existed by itself, quite apart from the good element in it which is identical with the appreciation of imaginary evils, and from any ulterior consequences which its existence may bring about. The case is here the same as with retributive punishment. Where an evil already exists, it is well that it should be pitied or hated or endured, according to its nature; just as it may be well that some evils should be punished. Of course, as in all practical cases, it often happens that the attainment of this good is incompatible with the attainment of another and a greater one. But it is important to insist that we have here a real intrinsic value, which must be taken into account in calculating that greatest possible balance of intrinsic value, which it is always our duty to produce.

15 / W. D. ROSS

What Things Are Good?

Our next step is to inquire what kinds of things are intrinsically good. (1) The first thing for which I would claim that it is intrinsically good is virtuous disposition and action, i.e. action, or disposition to act, from any one of certain motives, of which at all events the most notable are the desire to do one's duty, the desire to bring into being something that is good, and the desire to give pleasure or save pain to others. It seems clear that we regard all such actions and dispositions as having value in themselves apart from any consequence. And if any one is inclined to doubt this and to think that, say, pleasure alone is intrinsically good, it seems to me enough to ask the question whether, of two states of the universe holding equal amounts of pleasure, we should really think no better of one in which the actions and dispositions of all the persons in it were thoroughly virtuous than of one in which they were highly vicious. To this there can be only one answer. Most hedonists would shrink from giving the plainly false answer which their theory requires, and would take refuge in saying that the question rests on a false abstraction. Since virtue, as they conceive it, is a disposition to do just the acts which will produce most pleasure, a universe full of virtuous persons would be bound, they might say, to contain more pleasure than a universe full of vicious persons. To this two answers may be made.

Reprinted by permission of the publisher and copyright holder from W. D. Ross, *The Right and the Good* (Oxford: Oxford University Press, 1930), pp. 131–141, 149–153, 155–165, 168–173.

(a) Much pleasure, and much pain, do not spring from virtuous or vicious actions at all but from the operation of natural laws. Thus even if a universe filled with virtuous persons were bound to contain more of the pleasure and less of the pain that springs from human action than a universe filled with vicious persons would, that inequality of pleasantness might easily be supposed to be precisely counteracted by, for instance, a much greater incidence of disease. The two states of affairs would then, on balance, be equally pleasant; would they be equally good? And (b) even if we could not imagine any circumstances in which two states of the universe equal in pleasantness but unequal in virtue could exist, the supposition is a legitimate one, since it is only intended to bring before us in a vivid way what is really self-evident, that virtue is good apart from its consequences.

(2) It seems at first sight equally clear that pleasure is good in itself. Some will perhaps be helped to realize this if they make the corresponding supposition to that we have just made; if they suppose two states of the universe including equal amounts of virtue but the one including also widespread and intense pleasure and the other widespread and intense pain. Here too it might be objected that the supposition is an impossible one, since virtue always tends to promote general pleasure, and vice to promote general misery. But this objection may be answered just as we have answered the corresponding objection above.

Apart from this, however, there are two ways in which even the most austere moralists and the most anti-hedonistic philosophers are apt to betray the conviction that pleasure is good in itself. (*a*) One is the attitude which they, like all other normal human beings, take towards kindness and towards cruelty. If the desire to give pleasure to others is approved, and the desire to inflict pain on others condemned, this seems to imply the conviction that pleasure is good and pain bad. Some may think, no doubt, that the mere thought that a certain state of affairs would be *painful* for another person is enough to account for our conviction that the desire to produce it is bad. But I am inclined to think that there is involved the further thought that a state of affairs in virtue of being painful is *prima facie* (i.e. where other considerations do not enter into the case) one that a rational spectator would not approve, i.e. is *bad;* and that similarly our attitude towards kindness involves the thought that pleasure is good. (*b*) The other is the insistence, which we find in the most austere moralists as in other people, on the conception of merit. If virtue deserves to be rewarded by happiness (whether or not vice also deserves to be rewarded by unhappiness), this seems at first sight to imply that happiness and unhappiness are not in themselves things indifferent, but are good and bad respectively.

Kant's view on this question is not as clear as might be wished. He points out that the Latin *bonum* covers two notions, distinguished in German as *das Gute* (the good) and *das Wohl* (well-being, i.e. pleasure or happiness); and he speaks of 'good' as being properly applied only to actions,[1] i.e. he treats 'good' as equivalent to 'morally good', and by implication denies that pleasure (even deserved pleasure) is good. It might seem then that when he speaks of the union of virtue with the happiness it deserves as the *bonum consummatum* he is not thinking of deserved happiness as good but only as *das Wohl*, a source of satisfaction to the person who has it. But if this exhausted his meaning, he would have no right to speak of virtue, as he repeatedly does, as *das oberste Gut;* he should

call it simply *das Gute*, and happiness *das Wohl*. Further, he describes the union of virtue with happiness not merely as 'the object of the desires of rational finite beings', but adds that it approves itself 'even in the judgement of an impartial reason' as 'the whole and perfect good', rather than virtue alone. And he adds that 'happiness, while it is pleasant to the possessor of it, is not of itself absolutely and in all respects good, but always presupposes morally right behaviour as its condition'; which implies that *when* that condition is fulfilled, happiness *is* good.[2] All this seems to point to the conclusion that in the end he had to recognize that while virtue alone is morally good, deserved happiness also is not merely a source of satisfaction to its possessor, but objectively good.

But reflection on the conception of merit does not support the view that pleasure is always good in itself and pain always bad in itself. For while this conception implies the conviction that pleasure when deserved is good, and pain when undeserved bad, it also suggests strongly that pleasure when undeserved is bad and pain when deserved good.

There is also another set of facts which casts doubt on the view that pleasure is always good and pain always bad. We have a decided conviction that there are bad pleasures and (though this is less obvious) that there are good pains. We think that the pleasure taken either by the agent or by a spectator in, for instance, a lustful or cruel action is bad; and we think it a good thing that people should be pained rather than pleased by contemplating vice or misery.

Thus the view that pleasure is always good and pain always bad, while it seems to be strongly supported by some of our convictions, seems to be equally strongly opposed by others. The difficulty can, I think, be removed by ceasing to speak simply of pleasure and pain as good or bad, and by asking more carefully what it is that we mean. Consideration of the question is aided if we adopt the view (tentatively adopted already)[3] that what is good or bad is always something properly expressed by a that-clause, i.e. an objective, or as I should prefer to call it, a *fact*. If we look at the matter thus, I think we can agree that the fact that a sentient being is in a state of pleasure is always in itself good, and the fact that a sentient being is in a state of pain always in itself bad, when this fact is not an element in a more complex fact having some other characteristic relevant to goodness or badness. And where considerations of desert or of moral good or evil do not enter, i.e. in the case of animals, the fact that a sentient being is feeling pleasure or pain is the whole fact (or the fact sufficiently described to enable us to judge of its goodness or badness), and we need not hesitate to say that the pleasure of animals is always good, and the pain of animals always bad, in itself and apart from its consequences. But when a moral being is feeling a pleasure or pain that is deserved or undeserved, or a pleasure or pain that implies a good or a bad disposition, the total fact is quite inadequately described if we say 'a sentient being is feeling pleasure, or pain'. The total fact may be that 'a sentient and moral being is feeling a pleasure that is undeserved, or that is the realization of a vicious disposition', and though the fact included in this, that 'a sentient being is feeling pleasure' would be good if it stood alone, that creates only a presumption that the total fact is good, and a presumption that is outweighed by the other element in the total fact.

Pleasure seems, indeed, to have a property analogous to that which we have previously recognized under the name of conditional or *prima facie* rightness. An act of promise-keeping has the property, not necessarily of being right but of being something that is right if the act has no other morally significant characteristic (such as that of causing much pain to another person). And similarly a state of pleasure has the property, not necessarily of being good, but of being something that is good if the state has no other characteristic that prevents it from being good. The two characteristics that may interfere with its being good are (*a*) that of being contrary to desert,

and (*b*) that of being a state which is the realization of a bad disposition. Thus the pleasures of which we can say without doubt that they are good are (i) the pleasures of non-moral beings (animals), (ii) the pleasures of moral beings that are deserved and are either realizations of good moral dispositions or realizations of neutral capacities (such as the pleasures of the senses).

In so far as the goodness or badness of a particular pleasure depends on its being the realization of a virtuous or vicious disposition, this has been allowed for by our recognition of virtue as a thing good in itself. But the mere recognition of virtue as a thing good in itself, and of pleasure as a thing *prima facie* good in itself, does not do justice to the conception of merit. If we compare two imaginary states of the universe, alike in the total amounts of virtue and vice and of pleasure and pain present in the two, but in one of which the virtuous were all happy and the vicious miserable, while in the other the virtuous were miserable and the vicious happy, very few people would hesitate to say that the first was a much better state of the universe than the second. It would seem then that, besides virtue and pleasure, we must recognize (3), as a third independent good, the apportionment of pleasure and pain to the virtuous and the vicious respectively. And it is on the recognition of this as a separate good that the recognition of the duty of justice, in distinction from fidelity to promises on the one hand and from beneficence on the other, rests.

(4) It seems clear that knowledge, and in a less degree what we may for the present call 'right opinion', are states of mind good in themselves. Here too we may, if we please, help ourselves to realize the fact by supposing two states of the universe equal in respect of virtue and of pleasure and of the allocation of pleasure to the virtuous, but such that the persons in the one had a far greater understanding of the nature and laws of the universe than those in the other. Can any one doubt that the first would be a better state of the universe?

From one point of view it seems doubtful whether knowledge and right opinion, no matter what it is of or about, should be considered good. Knowledge of mere matters of fact (say of the number of stories in a building), without knowledge of their relation to other facts, might seem to be worthless; it certainly seems to be worth much less than the knowledge of general principles, or of facts as depending on general principles—what we might call insight or understanding as opposed to mere knowledge. But on reflection it seems clear that even about matters of fact right opinion is in itself a better state of mind to be in than wrong, and knowledge than right opinion.

There is another objection which may naturally be made to the view that knowledge is as such good. There are many pieces of knowledge which we in fact think it well for people *not* to have; e.g. we may think it a bad thing for a sick man to know how ill he is, or for a vicious man to know how he may most conveniently indulge his vicious tendencies. But it seems that in such cases it is not the knowledge but the consequences in the way of pain or of vicious action that we think bad.

It might perhaps be objected that knowledge is not a better state than right opinion, but merely a source of greater satisfaction to its possessor. It no doubt is a source of greater satisfaction. Curiosity is the desire to *know*, and is never really satisfied by mere opinion. Yet there are two facts which seem to show that this is not the whole truth. (*a*) While opinion recognized to be such is never thoroughly satisfactory to its possessor, there is another state of mind which is not knowledge—which may even be mistaken—yet which through lack of reflection is not distinguished from knowledge by its possessor, the state of mind which Professor Cook Wilson has called 'that of being under the impression that so-and-so is the case'.[4] Such a state of mind may be as great a source of satisfaction to its possessor as knowledge, yet we should all think it to be an inferior state of mind to knowledge.

This surely points to a recognition by us that knowledge has a worth other than that of being a source of satisfaction to its possessor. (*b*) Wrong opinion, so long as its wrongness is not discovered, may be as great a source of satisfaction as right. Yet we should agree that it is an inferior state of mind, because it is to a less extent founded on knowledge and is itself a less close approximation to knowledge; which again seems to point to our recognizing knowledge as something good in itself.

Four things, then, seem to be intrinsically good—virtue, pleasure, the allocation of pleasure to the virtuous, and knowledge (and in a less degree right opinion). And I am unable to discover anything that is intrinsically good, which is not either one of these or a combination of two or more of them. And while this list of goods has been arrived at on its own merits, by reflection on what we really think to be good, it perhaps derives some support from the fact that it harmonizes with a widely accepted classification of the elements in the life of the soul. It is usual to enumerate these as cognition, feeling, and conation. Now knowledge is the ideal state of the mind, and right opinion an approximation to the ideal, on the cognitive or intellectual side; pleasure is its ideal state on the side of feeling; and virtue is its ideal state on the side of conation; while the allocation of happiness to virtue is a good which we recognize when we reflect on the ideal relation between the conative side and the side of feeling. It might of course be objected that there are or may be intrinsic goods that are not states of mind or relations between states of mind at all, but in this suggestion I can find no plausibility. Contemplate any imaginary universe from which you suppose mind entirely absent, and you will fail to find anything in it that you can call good in itself. That is not to say, of course, that the existence of a material universe may not be a necessary condition for the existence of many things that are good in themselves. Our knowledge and our true opinions are to a large extent about the material world, and to that extent could not exist unless it existed. Our pleasures are to a large extent derived from material objects. Virtue owes many of its opportunities to the existence of material conditions of good and material hindrances to good. But the value of material things appears to be purely instrumental, not intrinsic.

Of the three elements virtue, knowledge, and pleasure are compounded all the complex states of mind that we think good in themselves. Aesthetic enjoyment, for example, seems to be a blend of pleasure with insight into the nature of the object that inspires it. Mutual love seems to be a blend of virtuous disposition of two minds towards each other, with the knowledge which each has of the character and disposition of the other, and with the pleasure which arises from such disposition and knowledge. And a similar analysis may probably be applied to all other complex goods. . . .

The 'greatest wave' now awaits us—the question whether virtue, knowledge, and pleasure can be compared with one another in value, and whether they can be measured against one another. I do not pretend that the views I shall express are certainly true, still less that I can prove them to be so. I will only say that they are the result of a good deal of reflection about the comparative value of these things, and that they agree, so far as I can judge, with the views of many others who have reflected on it. I think, then, that pleasure is definitely inferior in value to virtue and knowledge. There are certain facts which support this view. (1) Most people are convinced that human life is in itself something more valuable than animal life, though it seems highly probable that the lives of many animals contain a greater balance of pleasure over pain than the lives of many human beings. Most people would accept Mill's dictum that 'it is better to be a human being dissatisfied than a pig satisfied',[5] though they may think such a view inconsistent with Mill's own principles. The very fact that he felt bound to make an admission so fatal to his cherished hedonism is some testimony to the truth of the admission. (2)

Many people whose opinion deserves the greatest respect have undoubtedly thought that the promotion of the general happiness was the highest possible ideal. But the happy state of the human race which they aimed at producing was such a state as the progress of civilization naturally leads us to look forward to, a state much of whose pleasantness would spring from such things as the practice of virtue, the knowledge of truth, and the appreciation of beauty. The ideal has owed its attractiveness in a large degree not to its being a state of maximum happiness, but to its being a state whose happiness would spring from such sources; and if they thought that the state of maximum happiness would be one whose happiness sprang from such things as the indulgence of cruelty, the lighthearted adoption of ill-grounded opinions, and enjoyment of the ugly, they would immediately reject such an ideal. They would no doubt argue that such a state as I have just described could not in fact be one of maximum happiness. But that, if true, is simply a consequence of the laws of the world we live in, and does not absolve them from facing the problem, what if the laws of nature *were* such as to make such a life the most pleasant possible? Would they then prefer it to a state less pleasant but more virtuous and intelligent? They have, in fact, in pronouncing pleasure to be the sole good, not had in mind mere pleasant consciousness, such as we suppose animals to enjoy, but to a very large extent what I have called[6] good (i. e. morally good) pleasures, those which are themselves actualizations of morally good dispositions (such as love for other men and love of truth and beauty) and which owe their goodness much more to this than to their pleasantness.

This argument, if it is sound, only proves that a certain amount of virtue and knowledge would more than outweigh a certain amount of pleasure, and it might still be held that a certain larger amount of pleasure would more than outweigh the given amount of virtue and intelligence. But if we take this view we are faced by the question, *what* amount of pleasure is precisely equal in value to a given amount of virtue or of knowledge? And to this question, so long as we think that *some* amount is equal, I see no possibility of an answer or of an approach to one. With regard to pleasure and virtue, it seems to me much more likely to be the truth that *no* amount of pleasure is equal to any amount of virtue, that in fact virtue belongs to a higher order of value, beginning at a point higher on the scale of value than that which pleasure ever reaches; in other words, that while pleasure is comparable in value with virtue (i. e. can be said to be less valuable than virtue) it is not commensurable with it, as a finite duration is not commensurable with infinite duration. Pleasure will then be an object worthy of production, but only when this does not interfere with the production of virtue.

(3) The question seems to become clearer when one turns from considering virtue and pleasure in the abstract to consider which of them seems the most worth while to get for ourselves. It seems clear that, viewed in this way, pleasure reveals itself as a cheap and ignoble object in comparison with virtue. This manifests itself clearly in the fact that the acquisition of pleasure for oneself rarely, if ever, presents itself as a duty, and usually only as something permissible when it does not interfere with duty, while the attainment of moral goodness habitually presents itself as a duty. This surely points to an infinite superiority of virtue over pleasure, a superiority such that no gain in pleasure can make up for a loss in virtue.

But if virtue is better worth aiming at for ourselves than pleasure, it is better worth trying to promote for man in general. For that which is good owes its goodness not to being possessed by one person or by another, but to its nature.

(4) A further argument in favour of this view seems to arise from the consideration of pleasures which are realizations of a bad disposition, such as the pleasure of cruelty. It seems clear that when we consider such a pleasure we are able to say at once that it is bad, that it would have been better that it should not have existed. If the goodness of pleasure were commensurable with the goodness or badness of moral disposition, it would be possible that such a pleasure if sufficiently intense should be good on the whole. But in fact its intensity is a measure of its badness, because it is a measure of the viciousness of the disposition realized.

(5) It is, on the face of it, much less obvious that knowledge completely transcends pleasure in value than that virtue does so. In fact it would be paradoxical to say that the slightest possible increase in knowledge would outweigh the greatest possible loss of pleasure; I do not think that this can reasonably be maintained about knowledge considered simply as a condition of the intellect. But in fact most (if not all) states of knowledge are themselves to some extent the actualization of a desire for knowledge. And the desire or disposition expressed and manifested in them has *moral* worth, is of the nature of virtue, and has thus a value completely transcending that of pleasure (i. e. pleasure that is the actualization not of a good disposition but of a neutral capacity, as sensuous pleasure is). It is to be noted, however, that this desire is expressed just as much in the search for knowledge as in the attainment of it. While in its own nature knowledge seems to be a better state than inquiry, the moral virtue of desire for knowledge may be much more fully present in many an unsuccessful search for difficult knowledge than in the successful attainment of knowledge that is easy to get.

The view that virtue and knowledge are much better things than pleasure does not in practice work out in so ascetic a way as might appear, and that for two reasons. (1) It is quite certain that by promoting virtue and knowledge in ourselves and in others we shall inevitably produce much pleasant consciousness. These are, by general agreement, among the surest sources of happiness for their possessors. And still more are they among the surest sources of general happiness, for a variety of reasons which will readily suggest themselves.

And (2) it is pretty clear that our pursuit of the greater goods is made all the more effective by intervals in which we give ourselves up to enjoying ourselves and helping others to enjoy themselves. The desire for pleasure is so strong in every one that any one who tries to ignore or suppress it entirely will find himself defeated by the laws of human nature; *naturam expellas furca, tamen usque recurret.* There is a place for asceticism in the best life, but it cannot safely be made the general rule of the best life.

When we turn to consider the relative value of moral goodness and knowledge as ends, here again I am inclined to think that moral goodness is infinitely better than knowledge. Here too the question seems to become clearer when one considers these two goods not in the abstract but as objects to be striven after for ourselves as individuals. When I ask myself whether any increase of knowledge, however great, is worth having at the cost of a wilful failure to do my duty or of a deterioration of character, I can only answer in the negative. The infinite superiority of moral goodness to anything else is clearest in the case of the highest form of moral goodness, the desire to do one's duty. But even of the lesser virtues the same appears to be true. And if virtue is always the thing best worth aiming at for oneself, it is the thing best worth trying to promote in others. . . .

Goodness is always a consequential attribute; that which is good is good by virtue of something else in its nature, by being of a certain kind. I think that I can best explain what I understand by *'morally good'* by saying that it means 'good either by being a certain sort of character or by being related in one of certain definite ways to a certain sort of character'. It seems necessary to put the matter in this alternative way, because a variety of kinds of thing can be said to be morally good. We may say that such and such a *man* is morally good or that a certain *action* or a certain sort of *feeling* (e.g. sympathy with misfortune) is morally good. But it seems clear that a man is morally good by virtue of having a char-

acter of a certain kind, and that an action or a feeling is morally good by virtue of proceeding from a character of a certain kind. This account of the meaning of 'morally good' seems to be confirmed by studying the usage of the phrase. Suppose it were said, for instance, that while conscientious action, knowledge, and pleasure are all good, conscientious action is the only one of the three that is morally good, what we should mean is that while conscientious action is good in virtue of proceeding from a certain sort of character, knowledge and pleasure are good not in virtue of this but in virtue of being, respectively, knowledge and pleasure.

If this account of what we mean by 'morally good' is correct, the general answer to our next question, what kinds of thing are morally good, is clear. Only what is a certain sort of character or is related to a certain sort of character in one of certain ways, can be good in virtue of being a certain sort of character or of being so related to it. Of the things that are morally good, I will take for consideration morally good actions, and ask what can be said about the nature of these. If we could agree about this, we are not likely to disagree about what sort of men or what sort of feelings are morally good; they will be the men that have, and the feelings that spring from, the same sort of character that morally good actions spring from. Now when we ask what is the general nature of morally good actions, it seems quite clear that it is in virtue of the motives that they proceed from that actions are morally good. Moral goodness is quite distinct from and independent of rightness, which (as we have seen)[7] belongs to acts *not* in virtue of the motives they proceed from, but in virtue of the nature of what is done. Thus a morally good action need not be the doing of a right act, and the doing of a right act need not be a morally good action. The ethical theories that stress the thing done and those that stress the motive from which it is done both have some justification, for both 'the right act' and 'the morally good action' are notions of the first importance in ethics; but the two types of theory have been at cross-purposes, because they have failed to notice that they are talking about different things. Thus Kant has tried to deduce from his conception of the nature of a morally good action rules as to what types of act are right; and others have held a view which amounts to saying that so long as our motive is good it does not matter what we do. And, on the other side, the tendency of acts to produce good or bad results has sometimes been treated as if it made them morally good or bad. The drawing of a rigid distinction between the right and the morally good frees us from such confusion.

We can perhaps now substitute something more definite for our preliminary statement that moral goodness is that goodness which is connected with a certain type or types of character. If we ask in particular what the moral goodness of morally good actions arises from, the answer seems (as we have seen) to be 'from a certain kind of motivation'. When we ask what the moral goodness of morally good *feelings* arises from, we cannot answer 'from motivation', for the term 'motive' is inappropriate here, being appropriate only when action is in question. But cannot we say that the moral goodness both of actions and of feelings arises from their proceeding from a certain kind of desire? We think that sorrow at the misfortune of others is morally good because we think that it springs from an interest in their happiness, or, to put the matter more plainly, from a desire that they shall be happy. As regards actions, the only objection that might be made to saying their goodness is due to their proceeding from a certain sort of desire would be the objection that conscientious action does not spring from desire, but from something quite different.

Kant, whose greatest service to ethics is the vindication of the distinct character and the supreme worth of conscientious action, against the open or covert egoism of most of the eighteenth-century theories, insists that what is operative in it is something distinct from desire of any kind. It is for him something so mysterious that he is driven

to assign it not to man's phenomenal nature, which he believes to be moved solely by desire, but to his real or noumenal nature, and to hold (as his theory of freedom implies) that it is not operative in time at all. Against this it must be maintained that while a general sense of duty (i.e. an apprehension that there are things we ought to do) is present, active or latent, in us throughout our adult lives, it is no more true to say that than to say that a desire for food, for instance, is present in us, active or latent, throughout our lives; and that the thought of a particular act as being our duty, which is what operates when we act from the sense of duty, arises in us at a particular time just as does the particular desire to eat, which is what operates when we, in fact, proceed to eat. The familiar conflict between the sense of duty and other motives could not take place unless both were operating in the same field, and that the field of ordinary 'phenomenal' consciousness.

Regarding the sense of duty as an operation of reason distinct from any form of desire, and accepting the *general* truth of Aristotle's dictum that thought alone sets nothing going,[8] Kant found one of his greatest puzzles to lie in the fact that pure reason can become practical, that the mere thought of an act as one's duty can by itself induce us to do the act. In comparison with this, actions from desire seemed to him easily intelligible. But it may be maintained that there is no more mystery in the fact that the thought of an act as one's duty should arouse an impulse to do it, than in the fact that the thought of an act as pleasant, or as leading to pleasure, should arouse an impulse to do it. Human nature being what it is, the latter thought arouses an impulse to action much more constantly than the former; but it is only if we have already assumed (on quite insufficient grounds) that pleasure is the only object of desire, that we shall find it difficult to suppose that the thought of an act as right can arouse a desire to do it. Kant himself, of course, allows that the thought of duty arouses *emotion*—the emotion which he calls *Achtung*, respect or reverence; and this seems to be part of the truth. But to hold this is not incompatible with holding that the thought of duty also arouses desire. Now people often describe themselves as 'wanting' to do their duty. It seems to be often a perfectly straightforward description of their state of mind, and when we examine ourselves we find something of which this appears to be a correct description. All that Kant has said of the uniqueness and the moral supremacy of action arising from the awareness of duty is justified; but it owes its uniqueness and supremacy not to not proceeding from desire, but to proceeding from a desire which is specifically distinct because it is a desire for a specifically distinct object, not for the attainment of pleasure nor even for the conferring of it on others, but just for the doing of our duty. It is in virtue of the specific quality of the attribute 'obligatory', and not of arousing something other than desire, that the thought of duty has the humbling and at the same time uplifting effect that Kant ascribes to it.

When it is denied that we desire to do our duty, that in us which leads us to do our duty tends to be thought of as being in necessary conflict with desire. The sense of duty tends to be described as the sense that one should do certain acts, though on other grounds (e.g. on the ground of their painfulness) one wants not to do them. But 'the sense of duty' really means the sense that we ought to do certain acts, *whether or not* on other grounds we desire to do them, and no matter with what intensity we may desire, on other grounds, not to do them. One of the effects of the forming of a habit of dutiful action is that any natural repugnance one may have to dutiful acts on other grounds tends to diminish. If we form a habit of early rising, for example, it becomes easier, and less unpleasant, to rise early. But when the doing of a dutiful action is thought of as necessarily involving a resistance to desire, the paradoxical consequence follows that the forming of a good habit, since it leads to less and less resistance to desire being necessary, has to be

held to involve that we act less and less from a sense of duty as the habit grows stronger, so that (if, as Kant holds, sense of duty is the only good motive, or even if it is the best motive) to form a good habit is to become a person who acts less well, and therefore a less good person.

If habitual action could become so automatic that it ceased to be done from the thought that it is right, there would certainly be less moral worth in the doing of it. But so long as the act is still done because it is right, it will have no less moral worth because it has become easy. The agent's devotion to duty has not been impaired, but its whole intensity is not needed, as it was at the beginning, to enable him to do the right act. Some of it has now become surplus. The view that there may be a reserve or surplus of good motive, more than is needed to produce the right act,[9] enables us to avoid the paradoxical consequence that to form good habits is to become less good. Goodness is measured not by the intensity of the conflict but by the strength of the devotion to duty. The stronger the motives that oppose the doing of the right act, the more *sure* we can be that when the right act has been done the sense of duty must have been strong; but it may well *be* equally strong when resisting motives are feeble or nonexistent.

Tending, as he does, to think of obligation as thwarting desire, and holding that a perfect character must have no desires adverse to the doing of what is right, Kant finds himself obliged to say that a perfect character or 'holy will' would act not under a sense of obligation but only under a sense of the goodness or rightness of certain acts. But, as we have seen, an act, as distinct from the doing of it from a certain motive, is never *good*; and to think of an act as *right* is to think of it either as being obligatory or as being one of certain alternatives, the doing of one or other of which is obligatory;[10] so that the distinction which Kant draws between the right and the obligatory does not answer to the real difference. When we realize that obligation is not necessarily in conflict with desire, but merely independent of desire, we need not hesitate to say that a holy will would act under a sense of obligation; only it would be an obligation that would not necessarily be irksome, because there need not be actually present any desire adverse to it. In fact, the better a man is, the more intensely will he feel himself bound to act in certain ways and not in others, though it will also be true that he will have less desire to act in these other ways. It would, however, be a mistake to say that *all* internal conflict is incompatible with a perfect character. A perfect character would, *ex hypothesi*, have no bad desires; it would not, for instance, desire the pleasure of contemplating another's pain. But its perfection would not exclude the desire for innocent sensuous pleasures, such as those of food or rest, and these desires might incidentally be in conflict with the desire to do what was right. The possibility of such conflict as this seems inseparable from human nature, and at the same time quite compatible with a perfect character.

It would seem, then, that conscientious action springs from a certain desire (the desire to do one's duty), and owes its goodness to the specific nature of this desire. And if this be granted, we have removed the only objection that seems likely to be made to the contention that all morally good actions (and feelings) owe their goodness to the kind of desire they spring from.

If 'morally good' means what I have taken it to mean, it seems that besides (1) conscientious action two other kinds of action are morally good; and these too owe their goodness to the nature of the desire they spring from. These are (2) action springing from the desire to bring into being something good, and (3) action springing from the desire to produce some pleasure, or prevent some pain, for another being.

Under (2) I would include actions in which we are aiming at improving our own character or that of another, without thinking of this as a duty. And believing as I do that a certain state of our intellectual nature also is good, I would include actions

in which we are aiming at improving our own intellectual condition or that of others. Some writers would maintain that such action, and that in which we aim at producing pleasure for others, is not morally good, but virtuous. But if I am right in the account I have given of what we mean by moral goodness, viz. that it is goodness due to the character, or (more definitely) to the desire, involved, it seems clear that such actions are morally good. And it would seem contrary to the natural usage of the word 'virtuous' to deny that conscientious action is virtuous. In fact 'morally good' and 'virtuous' appear to mean the same thing, and to be applicable to actions from any one of these three desires.

It may seem at first sight doubtful whether the second and third of these desires are really different. Some might be inclined to hold, and I have sometimes myself believed, that to think of something as being a pleasant state of consciousness for another being necessarily involves thinking of it as good, or *is* thinking of it as good in a particular way, just as thinking of an action as virtuous is thinking of it as good in another particular way. There is no doubt that the two thoughts are often closely associated. Many people undoubtedly do think that pleasure is good, and in aiming at the production of pleasure for another are aiming at the production of something thought of as good. Nevertheless it appears to me that the thought of something as pleasant for another being is both different and separable from the thought of it as good.[11] For (*a*) there are many states of consciousness of other people that we think to be pleasant and also bad (e.g. states of enjoying the contemplation of some one else's pain). It can only be by overlooking such cases that any one can come to hold that to think of something as pleasant for another being either is or necessarily involves thinking of it as good. And (*b*) quite apart from such vicious pleasures, it seems clear that (i) the thought of a state of consciousness as pleasant for another cannot be the thought of it as good in a particular way; for if it were, the thought of a state of consciousness as pleasant for oneself would equally be the thought of it as good in a particular way (since being pleasant is, on this view, just being good in a particular way); and then the desire to get such an experience for oneself would be the desire to bring into being something thought of as good, and would itself have to be deemed morally good; whereas we are convinced that the desire of an innocent sensuous pleasure (such as that of rest after work) is morally indifferent. And (ii) it seems clear that the thought of a state of mind as pleasant either for oneself or for another does not necessarily *involve* the thought of it as good, since we should then on reflection always be able to detect the distinct presence of the second thought whenever the first is present; which we certainly are not.

It seems, therefore, that we must distinguish the desire to bring something pleasant for another person into being, from the desire to bring something good into being (of which an instance would be the desire to help a friend to improve his character).[12] And both are evidently different from the desire to do what is right. Yet there is this amount of connexion between the thought of an act as right on the one hand and the thought of a good, or pleasure for another, to be brought into being, on the other hand, that when we think of an act as right we think that either something good or some pleasure for another will be brought into being. When we consider ourselves bound, for instance, to fulfil a promise, we think of the fulfilment of the promise as the bringing into existence of some source of pleasure or satisfaction for the person to whom we have made the promise. And when we consider the other main types of duty—the duties of reparation, of gratitude, of justice, of beneficence, of self-improvement—we find that in the thought of any of these there is involved the thought that what the dutiful act is the origination of is either an objective good of a pleasure (or source of pleasure) for some one else. The conscientious attitude is one which *involves* the thought either of good or of pleasure for some one else, but it is a more reflective attitude than that in which we aim directly at the production of some good or some

pleasure for another, since in it the mere thought of some particular good, or of a particular pleasure for another, does not immediately incite us to action, but we stop to think whether in all the circumstances the bringing of that good or pleasure into existence is what is really incumbent upon us; the difference is well illustrated by that between discriminate and indiscriminate charity.

If there be these three types of virtuous action, it seems that in principle there might be three corresponding types of vicious action, (1) the desire to do what is wrong, (2) the desire to bring into being some particular evil, (3) the desire to inflict some pain on another. It seems clear that all of these, if they exist, are vicious, and that they are different from one another as are the three corresponding forms of good action. But it is not quite obvious that any one of them ever really occurs. (1) Men seem to be attracted to the doing of wrong acts by the thought of the pleasantness of the particular acts or of their consequences, or it may be by the thought of the pleasure of flouting authority and convention; it seems very doubtful whether they are ever attracted by the mere thought of the wrongness of an act. 'Evil, be thou my good', which is (I suppose) meant to indicate this attitude, is the maxim not of a man but of a devil. (2) Again, when some one sets himself to bring something evil into existence, e.g. to corrupt some one's character, it may be doubted whether it is the badness of what he is bringing into being that attracts him, or the pleasant sense of power or some other pleasure that will attend the action. The corrupting of the character of another, for the sake of corrupting it, is again the traditional role of the devil; but I am inclined to think it not impossible for a man. (3) The existence of disinterested malevolence seems at first sight doubtful; it may be argued that what incites any one to do a malevolent act is not the thought of the pain of his victim, but the thought of the pleasure he will himself derive from watching or thinking of the other's pain. But the true view seems to be that the very thought that that experience will be pleasant to oneself presupposes the existence of an independent desire for the pain of the victim. And a vindictive death-bed will is pretty good evidence of disinterested malevolence, as one of the opposite kind is of disinterested benevolence.

Between the three types of good desire (and of consequent good action), and similarly between the three conceivable types of bad desire and action, it seems possible to establish a scale of goodness, or of badness. For, firstly, it seems clear that the desire to do one's duty is the morally best motive. Many will question this, and think that acts springing from love, from an interest in the well-being of a particular person or persons, are better than those dictated by the 'cold', 'hard', and 'rigid' sense of duty. But let us reflect. Suppose that some one is drawn towards doing act *A* by a sense of duty, and towards doing another, incompatible, act *B* by love for a particular person. *Ex hypothesi*, he thinks he will not be doing his duty in doing *B*. Can we possibly say that he will be acting better if he does what he thinks not his duty than if he does what he thinks *is* his duty? Evidently not. What those who hold this view mean by 'acting from the sense of duty' is obeying a traditional, conventional code rather than following the warm impulses of the heart. But what is properly meant by the sense of duty is the thought that one *ought* to act in a certain way, not the thought that one has been brought up to or is expected to act in a certain way. And it seems clear that when a genuine sense of duty is in conflict with any other motive we must recognize its precedence. If you seriously think you ought to do *A*, you are bound to think you will be acting morally worse in doing anything else instead.

Suppose, now, that love and sense of duty incline us to the *same* act. Will our action be morally better if we act from the first motive or from the second? It seems clear that since the sense of duty is recognized as the better motive when the two are in conflict, it is still the better when they are in agreement. We may like better the man who acts more instinctively, from

love, but we are bound to think the man who acts from sense of duty the better man. And this is not merely because instinctive affection is a more wayward, capricious motive than sense of duty, more apt to lead to wrong acts. It is because the sense of duty is different in kind from, and superior in kind to, any other motive.

We have considered (*a*) the case in which sense of duty and another motive, present in the same person, point to different acts, (*b*) that in which they point to the same act. But there is a third comparison to be considered. Many people would say that a man who helps his neighbour from sympathy, without thinking whether this or any other action is his duty, does a better action than another man who helps his neighbour from a sense of duty; though thay might admit that *when* the sense of duty arises in a man, it is better that he should act from it than from any other motive; and this is at first sight an attractive view. Nevertheless, it appears that action from the sense of duty, which we have seen to be better than action from any motive which conflicts or conspires with it, is also better than action not preceded by the thought of duty. The attractiveness of the opposite view seems to arise from the following fact: The sense of duty is more obviously present when it has to fight against opposing inclinations; i. e. is more obviously present in an imperfect character than in one all of whose inclinations urge it in the direction which duty also indicates.[13] We are therefore apt to associate it with an imperfect character, and to prefer the characters of those whose inclinations are good and who act on them without thought of duty. But in truth the thought that an act is my duty is not the thought that an act is my duty though I want to do something else, but the thought that an act is my duty whether or not I want to do something else; though *if* I do not want to do things incompatible with duty the act done from sense of duty is done immediately, without the necessity of a moral conflict and without the thought of duty having to be held for any length of time before the mind. The man who acts from a sense of duty without fuss or conflict appears to be a better character than the man who acts from inclination without any thought of duty; though, as I suggest later, the man who acts from both sense of duty and virtuous inclination is in a still better state.

So far I have spoken as if each action sprang from one and only one motive; we have next to consider actions (if there are any) done from mixed motives. Is it possible to do an act partly from sense of duty, partly from love, and, if so, is such an action morally better or worse than one done from pure sense of duty? Again, is it possible to do an act partly from a good, partly from an indifferent or bad motive, and, if so, what are we to say of the moral value of such an action? . . .

It is clear that a mother, for instance, may want her child to be happy or good, and may also think it her duty to produce for it the conditions of happiness or of goodness. But can she really act from both motives together; must not one be operative and the other ineffective? The metaphor of 'mixture of motives' seems a questionable one, but we must at least recognize the co-operation of motives, or perhaps we should rather say 'the co-operation of elements to form a single motive'. We are familiar, I think, with cases in which conscience alone or self-interest alone would not have induced some one to do some difficult act, but the two together have induced him to do it. The activities of most statesmen are probably correctly attributed to the co-operation of ambition, party feeling, and patriotism, in varying proportions; and it does not seem as if we can always say, 'This act was due to ambition and that to party feeling and that to patriotism'; in many of their acts it seems that two, or perhaps all three, of these motives are at work. Again, if we want to induce a man to undertake a certain task, we probably put various arguments before him representing the points in its favour, and we do so not merely in the faith that if one point does not appeal to him another will, but in the belief that the various points, or some of them, may have a cumulative influence on him; and this seems, in fact, often to be the case.

Can we go further, and say that all motives that are present at all in a man's mind at a particular moment are *bound* to cooperate in producing his action, the mind being subject to a law of composition of forces of its own? This is clearly not the case. If motive A inclines us towards a certain act and motive B towards a different act, our doing of the first act is not necessarily altered (though the state of feeling with which we do it is) by our desire to do the second, nor do we necessarily do an act intermediate in character between the two. The doing of such an act (e.g. when there are two safe ways across a street, and we take an unsafe way between them) is a mark of distraction and loss of self-control. When we act with self-control we do the one act resolutely, irrespective of a lingering wish to do the other. We must, however, consider separately the case in which two motives point to the *same* act. We *may* act from both motives together; *must* we do so? We have seen that a motive adverse to the doing of a particular act may be so disregarded that the act is done just as it would have been done had the motive been absent; it seems reasonable to suppose that a motive favourable to the doing of the act may equally be disregarded; e. g. that when both sense of duty and ambition would incline a man to do an act, he may, though he is sensible of both motives, do the act wholly from the one or wholly from the other; and attention to one's own experience seems to support this view.

Where, however, a higher and a lower motive do co-operate in inducing us to act, what degree of moral worth has the action—more, or less, than if it had been done from the higher motive only? Kant assumes that its worth will be less, since it will no longer be 'pure'. The question can be looked at in either of two entirely different ways. It will suffice if we take account of two morally good motives, one higher than the other, of one morally indifferent motive, and of one bad motive; and must suppose that each of these motives has a definite amount of effectiveness in inducing the agent to act. We are far from being in a position to assign correctly definite numerical amounts either to the value or to the strength of motives; but it will help us to attack the problem if we assign (admittedly arbitrarily) such amounts. Let us suppose, then, that in the scale of values sense of duty is represented by 10, love by 8, desire of an innocent sensuous pleasure by 0, malice by −8: and let us suppose an act in which two of these motives cooperate with equal strength in producing an act. To assign other values to the motives, or unequal strengths to them, would not affect the argument. Kant, in insisting that the worth of an action is degraded by the presence in it of any motive lower than the sense of duty, is really assuming that its value must then be the value half-way between that which it would have had if done wholly from sense of duty, and that which it would have had if done wholly from the lower motive; e.g. an act done from sense of duty + desire of an innocent sensuous pleasure will have the value 10 + 0/2. An action done from sense of duty + malice[14] will have the value $10-8/2$. And since Kant assigns no value, positive or negative, to 'pathological' love, an action done from sense of duty + love will have the value 10 + 0/2. If we amend his view, as we have seen reason to do,[15] by assigning a positive value (say 8) to love, an action done from sense of duty + love will have the value 10 + 8/2.

It is, however, possible to take quite a different view; to hold that, for instance, sense of duty may be present with undiminished strength when another motive co-operates with it, and that when it is, the addition of a morally indifferent motive does not lessen the value of the action, and the addition of a good, though less good, motive increases it. The action done from sense of duty + desire of an innocent sensuous pleasure may be estimated at 10 + 0; that done from sense of duty + malice at $10-8$; that done from sense of duty + love at 10 + 8. If we call sense of duty A, love B, desire of innocent sensuous pleasure C, malice D, the value of the actions we have been considering will be estimated thus:

Action	Kant	Kant Modified	Alternative View
from A	10	10	10
from $A + B$	5	9	18
from $A + C$	5	5	10
from $A + D$	1	1	2

It is now, perhaps, easier to see the principles on which the two modes of estimation are based. In insisting (as in principle he does) that when two motives are equally effective, their total (or net) value must be divided by two in order to assess the value of the action, Kant is really assuming that all similar actions have an equal total intensity of motivation, so that by the extent to which any other motive is effective, the sense of duty must be less effective than it would have been if acting alone. We, on the other hand, are suggesting that the sense of duty may be present with equal intensity and effectiveness whether another motive is or is not effective. Or, to put it otherwise, he is assuming that the motivation is always exactly enough to produce the doing of the given act, while we are suggesting that there may be some to spare, so that in a man who does an act, e. g., from sense of duty + love, the sense of duty may yet be strong enough to have secured the doing of the act from it alone; i.e., while we agree with Kant that there are cases in which, say, sense of duty + a morally indifferent motive are just strong enough to produce a certain act, and that then the value of the act, if both motives are equally effective, is only half what it would have been if done from pure sense of duty, we suggest that there are other actions in which, while a morally indifferent motive is present, the sense of duty is strong enough to have secured by itself the doing of the act, and that in that case the action is as good as if it had been done from sense of duty alone. And while we hold that there are actions in which sense of duty + an inferior good motive are just enough to secure the doing of the act, and that in that case the value of the action is reduced, we suggest that there are other cases in which, though an inferior good motive is present, the sense of duty is strong enough to have secured by itself the doing of the act, and that in such a case the value of the action is greater than if it had been done from duty alone. On the question whether such a reserve or surplus of motivation exists, there seems to be no appeal except to introspection, and it seems clear on introspection that there are many cases in which, while a variety of motives inclines us to do an act, one of them or some of them would have been enough to induce us to do it. Thus we can, while agreeing with Kant that the sense of duty is the best motive, justify the generally entertained preference for actions in which some more instinctive generous impulse is present as well. And experience suggests that the presence and effectiveness of instinctive generous emotions are by no means adverse to the operation of the sense of duty. It is *not* the case that men in whom the sense of duty is strong are usually less affected by the generous emotions than those in whom it is weak. And it is possible, as we have tried to show, to value highly the presence and operation of warm personal feeling, without disparaging, as it has so often been thought necessary to do, the supreme moral value of the sense of duty.

Notes

1. *Kritik der pr. Vernunft*, 59–60 (Akad. Ausgabe, vol. v), 150–1 (Abbott's Trans., ed. 6).

2. Ib. 110–11 (Akad. Ausgabe), 206–7 (Abbott).

3. Ross, *The Right and the Good*, pp. 111–113.

4. *Statement and Inference*, i. 113.

5. *Util.*, 14 (copyright editions).

6. Cf. Ross. *The Right and the Good*, p. 166.

7. Ross, *The Right and the Good*, pp. 4–6.

8. *Nic. Eth.* 1139a 35.

9. Cf. Ross, *The Right and the Good*, p. 172.

10. Cf. Ross, *The Right and the Good*, pp. 3–4.

11. On this question, as on some others, I wish to retract the view put forward by me in *Proceedings of the Aristotelian Society*, 1928–9, 251–74.

12. This may be held whether or not we consider that all pleasures, or that some pleasures, are in fact good. The desire to bring them into being *qua* pleasant for another will in either case be different from the desire to bring them into being *qua* good.

13. Cf. Kant, *Grundlegung* (Akad. Ausg. iv. 397–9. Abbott's *Kant's Theory of Ethics*, 13–15). One fact which makes the presence of the sense of duty more obvious in the former case is that in this case there is present not only the thought that I ought to do so-and-so, but also the consequential thought that I ought to resist the inclination which would prevent me from doing so-and-so.

14. This combination may sound paradoxical; but a little reflection will show that it is not impossible, nor, indeed, at all uncommon.

15. Cf. Ross, *The Right and the Good*, pp. 160–1.

16 / THOMAS HURKA

PERFECTIONISM

1.1

Some moral theories have been carefully studied in recent moral philosophy, but one, as important as any, has been largely neglected.

This moral theory starts from an account of the good human life, or the intrinsically desirable life. And it characterizes this life in a distinctive way. Certain properties, it says, constitute human nature or are definitive of humanity—they make humans humans. The good life, it then says, develops these properties to a high degree or realizes what is central to human nature. Different versions of the theory may disagree about what the relevant properties are and so disagree about the content of the good life. But they share the foundational idea that what is good, ultimately, is the development of human nature.

This theory appears in the work of many great moralists. Aristotle and Aquinas think it is human nature to be rational, and that a good human exercises rationality to a high degree. Marx views humans as both productive, because we transform nature through our labour, and social, because we do so co-operatively. The best life, he concludes, develops both capacities maximally, as will happen under communism. For Idealists such as Hegel and Bradley, humans are but one manifestation of Absolute Spirit, and their best activities most fully realize identity with Spirit, as social life does

Reprinted by permission of the publisher and copyright holder from Thomas Hurka, *Perfectionism* (Oxford: Oxford University Press, 1993), pp. 3, 10–22, 31–44.

in one realm, and art, religion, and philosophy do in another. Even Nietzsche reasons this way, saying that humans essentially exercise a will to power and are most admirable when their wills are most powerful.

These are just some adherents of the theory; others are Plato, Spinoza, Leibniz, Kant, Green, and Bosanquet. Despite differing in their more specific moral claims, they all offer variants on a single theory, one centred on an ideal of the good life defined in terms of human nature. . . .

2.1 Distinctiveness and Essence

What, then, is human nature? Different views are defended in the perfectionist tradition.

2.1.1

One view equates human nature with the properties *distinctive of* humans, or *possessed only by* humans. These properties are important, the view says, because they separate us from other species; no other animal has them. And our good comes in their full development.

Plato suggests this view in *Republic* I, where a thing's good is said to be whatever "it alone can perform, or perform better than anything else."[1] And there are echoes in other writers. Aristotle says human excellence cannot include nutrition or perception because these functions are shared by plants and animals;[2] Kant defines "perfection" as the development of powers "characteristic of humanity (as distinguished from animality)."[3] Even Marx wants to know how humans "distinguish themselves from animals"[4] and tries in several places to show how human labour differs from any activity of animals.[5] So a first view identifies human nature with the properties found only in humans.

Although it appears simple, this view can be difficult to apply. Consider the properties associated with the human digestive system. At the most general level they are shared by other organisms, which leads Aristotle to deny value to their development. Described more specifically, however, they are unique. No other species processes food in exactly the same way as humans or has a digestive system with precisely the same structure. Is there not a distinctive property here? To say no, the distinctiveness view must have some way of excluding specifically described properties, and what this could be is not clear.

Even when it can be applied, the distinctiveness view faces a decisive objection. Humans have some attractive distinctive properties, but they have many others that are morally trivial. Humans may be uniquely rational, but they are also the only animals who make fires, despoil the environment, and kill things for fun.[6] A distinctiveness perfectionism implies that developing these properties is intrinsically good—an absurd implication.

We will see this pattern again: a concept of nature falling to the wrong-properties objection. But in this case the objection's success has deeper roots. If the distinctiveness view fails the second test about consequences it is because it fails the first test, that is, it fails to respect our original understanding of "nature."

Whatever it is, human nature must be something located in humans and dependent only on facts about humans. For this reason it cannot consist in distinctive properties. To say that a property is distinctive of humans is not just to say something about humans. It is to say that the property is possessed by humans *and not by other species*. It is to say as much about non-humans as about humans, and how can facts about non-humans affect *our* nature and

our good? The point has been well made by Robert Nozick.[7] At present, humans are the only beings with full rationality. But what if dolphins develop rationality? Will this development make its exercise no longer good in humans? What if we discover beings on another planet that have always been rational? Will our rationality never have been good? The distinctiveness view makes the human good depend implausibly on facts about other species, and it does so because its central concept refers to more than humans. It does not capture our intuitive sense of "nature" and, not surprisingly, has absurd implications.

2.1.2

A more promising view uses the concept of essence. It equates human nature with the properties *essential to* humans, or that constitute *the human essence*. "Essence" is used here in the manner of Saul Kripke.[8] For Kripke, an essential property of a kind is one the kind possesses necessarily, or possesses in every possible world where it exists. If a property is essential to a kind, nothing can be a member of the kind and lack it; in every world where the kind exists, its members all possess it. These claims concern necessity, but necessity *de re*, not *de dicto*: that is, they depend, not on conventions of language, but on a kind's own nature. The properties essential to humans are those any being must have to count as human, and the second view says that these properties define the human good.

This view is much closer to the perfectionist idea than was the earlier one about distinctiveness. That a property is essential to humans is a fact only about humans; it involves no other species. Moreover, it seems a fact of just the right kind. A kind's essential properties fix its boundaries or extension; they determine what is and is not a member. Surely this role makes essential properties suitable for a perfectionist concept of nature. If our original ideal was to become fully human or to develop human nature, surely the properties that make us human must figure in its best formulation.

The view also clarifies the appeal of perfectionism. In formulating its ideal, the theory assumes that being human is not just another of our properties, like being a lawyer or a hockey fan. It is fundamental to us. In developing human nature we do not realize something tangential to our identity, but realize what at bottom we are.

The concept of essence clarifies this assumption, for each of us is essentially a human. In every possible world in which we exist, we belong to the human species; in none are we frogs or fish. The essence view therefore makes double use of the concept of essence: to define human nature, and to tie that nature to individual humans. The properties fundamental to the human species are in the same way fundamental to its individual members.

The essence view is well represented in the perfectionist tradition. Hegel calls "universality" the "essence" of human consciousness, and says that only in the society he recommends are humans "in possession of their own essence or their own inner universality."[9] Marx says that capitalism alienates workers from their "human essence," whereas communism will involve "the real reappropriation of the human essence."[10] Similar language appears in Nietzsche. He speaks of "a world whose essence is will to power" and of the will to power itself as "the innermost essence of being."[11] Other writers use equivalent expressions. Aristotle and Aquinas say that goodness consists in actuality or in realizing form, both of which they equate with realizing essence. Still other perfectionists make identity-claims. Plato says in the *Phaedo* that a human is identical to her soul and distinct from her body, from which she is separated before and after earthly life. This statement seems equivalent to a claim about essence. To say that a human is identical to her soul seems to imply that some properties of her soul, such as intellect, are essential to her, whereas those of her body are not.[12]

In its simple form, however, the essence view is too inclusive and falls to the wrong-properties objection. Whatever their other essential properties, all humans are necessarily self-identical, necessarily red if red, and necessarily occupiers of space. None of these properties seems intrinsically worth developing. However well it does on the first test, the essence view fails the second test by including in our nature some intuitively trivial properties.

It may be replied that these trivial properties do not admit of degrees, so including them in human nature cannot affect the important perfectionist judgements distinguishing different modes of living. There may be something to this reply, but I doubt that there is enough. Can we be certain that no trivial essential properties admit of degrees? If humans necessarily occupy space, may some not do so more by occupying more space? More importantly, a concept of nature that includes morally idle properties is, to put it mildly, inelegant. If narrow perfection is a serious moral ideal, it should be specifiable without such useless clutter.

The objections should not make us abandon the concept of essence; it does too well by the first test. We should instead try to narrow the concept of nature so it includes some essential properties and not others: ones that avoid the wrong-properties objection but not ones that are trivial.

2.1.3

The most obvious move is to combine our first two views and equate human nature with the properties *essential to and distinctive of* humans. These are properties possessed by humans in all the possible worlds where they exist and by them alone in the actual world. They are both necessary to and unique to the species.

This essence-and-distinctiveness view has several attractive features. For one, it seems likely to do well against the wrong-properties objection. Because it imposes two conditions for belonging to human nature, it seems likely to select only a few properties and to exclude those most common in wrong-properties objections. Making fires and despoiling the environment are ruled out because, although distinctive, they are not essential; occupying space is out because it is not distinctive. We do not yet know what properties the view positively selects; work would be needed to identify them. But the view seems likely to exclude most trivial properties.

The view also gives probably the truest reflection of the perfectionist tradition. Many perfectionists, among them Aristotle, Aquinas, and Marx, speak both of essence and of distinctiveness, and for consistency must be ascribed a compound view. So, on a different ground, must many others. Writers who claim to value distinctive properties surely cannot mean *all* distinctive properties; the implications are too absurd. They must mean what are distinctive among humans' important properties, that is, among something like their essential properties.

Unfortunately, however, the view inherits defects from the distinctiveness view. It shares the difficulty about what is and is not distinctive, say, about the human digestive system. It also makes our good depend on facts about other animals. Just as a property can cease to be distinctive because of changes in other species, it can also cease to be essential-and-distinctive. Finally, the view pushes perfectionism in a direction I find unattractive. When it works as it is meant to, the distinctiveness test excludes from our good the development of any bodily properties. It supports ideals that are purely mental or even intellectual, such as those of Plato and Aristotle. But these ideals are surely too narrow. That we are embodied animals is a deep fact about us—some would say as deep a fact as any—and one an acceptable perfectionism should reflect. If its aim for us is to develop our nature, surely the bodily parts of that nature must be included. Our physical properties may not be our morally most significant properties or their development our greatest good, but a final objection to the compound view is that it gives our physical properties no value at all.

To avoid these defects, we could try amending the view to include only prop-

erties that are *essential and necessarily distinctive*, that is, those properties had by humans alone in this world and by humans alone in any world. This amendment helps with the first and especially the second defect. If only necessarily distinctive properties count, we cannot imagine another species's acquiring a property (formerly) in our nature. But it magnifies the third defect, by excluding from our nature properties that many want included. Many perfectionists think rationality is essential to humans, and in its sophisticated forms it is actually distinctive. But it is not necessarily distinctive, for we can imagine other beings with the same rational powers. In fact, we can wonder whether any human essential property, considered on its own, could not in principle be had by another species. If so, the amended view is so restrictive that it lets no properties whatever into our nature.

It seems that no tinkering with distinctiveness will yield an acceptable concept of nature:[13] we need some other device for defining a subset of essential properties. To find this subset, let us look more closely at the different essential properties each human has.

2.2. Essence and Life

Each individual human has six classes of essential properties, distinguished by the range of objects they are shared by. First are the essential properties shared by all objects, such as self-identity and being red if red and, following that, a narrower class found only in physical objects. These properties include being made of (or being) elementary particles and occupying space. Let us identify these two classes as, first, the properties essential to a human qua object and, second, those essential to her qua physical object. Third come essential properties found only in living things and, fourth, those found only in animals. Both these classes contain structural properties. Inanimate matter is made of the same elementary particles as living flesh, obeying the same physical laws. What distinguishes the latter must thus be the particles' organization. To count as animate, matter must be organized for functions such as nutrition, growth, and movement, and what is essential to a human qua living thing or qua animal is that her body is structured for these organic functions. The fifth class contains the essential properties that distinguish humans from other animals, perhaps including rationality. Finally, there are the essential properties that distinguish one human from others. These last properties are essential to her, not qua member of a species, but qua individual, and at the deepest level they are unique to her. Based ultimately on her material origin, they include the particular sperm and egg from which she developed and any further properties deriving from that.

Of these six classes, only the last could not figure in an ideal of narrow perfection. Because this ideal involves a nature common to all humans, it cannot depend on essential differences among them. Nonetheless, individually essential properties may be thought morally significant and deserve some discussion.

2.2.1

Alongside narrow perfectionism there runs, as a secondary theme in our tradition, the idea that humans have individual natures and are better the more fully they develop them. Rousseau says:[14]

Aside from the nature common to the species each individual brings with him at birth a distinctive temperament, which determines his spirit and character. There is no question of changing or putting a restraint on this temperament, only of training it and bringing it to perfection.

Like the concept of human nature, that of individual nature needs specification and may find it in individual essence. If *individual perfection* develops individually essential properties, is it a value to supplement or even replace that of developing human nature?

Although perhaps initially appealing, the idea does not withstand scrutiny. Consider, first, the fundamental individually essential property, that of being descended from a particular sperm and egg. This property cannot be developed to varying degrees—one either has it or not—and in any case seems morally trivial. Why should facts about a person's material origin affect what is good in her now? Nor do we do better if we consider what her origin brings, namely a continuing genetic endowment. This endowment does not normally give a human the ability to do things others cannot, for example, the ability to do F when no one else can do F. Instead, it gives her a possibly (but not necessarily) unique profile of abilities to do G-to-as-much-as-degree-m, H-to-as-much-as-degree-n, and so on. In itself, this profile cannot be developed to varying degrees; one either has it or not. But it can be used to shape a life. A human can assign time to pursuits in accordance with their place in her profile so that her distribution of activity fits her (possibly unique) configuration of talents. This idea of individual perfection is at least coherent, but it does not have plausible consequences.

If a person's profile contains abilities for fire-lighting and killing, the idea faces a familiar objection. It values intrinsically activities that do not seem of worth. Even if we consider only attractive abilities, there are still implausible consequences. Any broad perfectionism, including human-nature perfectionism, agrees that we should normally be more active where we have more talent. To test the individual-essence view, therefore, we must imagine a case where this will not have the best consequences on other theories of value. Imagine that a person with more talent for music than for writing finds that, because of factors such as the availability of teachers, she can achieve more in writing than in music. Should she still be guided by her profile and give more time to music than to writing? The individual-essence view says yes, but most of us surely say no. For us a profile of talents matters instrumentally, as showing where a person can achieve most, but it does not have intrinsic significance.

An individualist ideal might be plausible if each human's genes gave him a unique style of acting, which could be manifested in all he did and could be developed to higher degrees. Rousseau's talk of a "distinctive temperament" present from birth seems to suggest this idea. But humans do not have genetically based unique styles of acting. Some may develop unique styles, but this is a cultural matter, and contingent. When we consider individual natures as they actually are, there seems little promise in individual-essence perfectionism.

2.2.2

Let us return to our main argument and the five classes of essential property relevant to human-nature perfectionism. Using only the second test, about consequences, which of these classes do we want in our concept of nature? It is easy to eliminate the first class, properties essential to humans qua objects. Shared by numbers and other abstract entities, they are, intuitively, of no moral significance. The same holds for the second class, properties essential to humans qua physical objects. But the remaining three classes—those essential to humans qua living things, qua animals, and (only) qua humans—do seem worth retaining. Considering only consequences, the most promising perfectionism identifies human nature with the essential properties in these three classes. Its ideal is the development of whatever properties are *essential to humans and conditioned on their being living things*. These are essential properties that humans could not have if they were not living; they presuppose life, or are necessarily distinctive of living things.

This essence-and-life view retains several virtues from the essence-and-distinctiveness view. It retains part of the answer to the wrong-properties objection because it excludes the trivial essential properties we share with inanimate matter, such as self-identity and occupying space. We do not yet know what properties the view pos-

itively selects, and work will be needed to identify these, but the view does exclude many trivial properties. It is also reasonably close to the perfectionist tradition. Unlike the earlier view, however, it does not require difficult decisions about distinctiveness or make our good depend on other species. If some previously inanimate matter acquires a property in our nature, our nature has not changed. Instead, the matter has come alive. Finally, the view recognizes that we are embodied. When fully elaborated, it may not give the development of our physical nature great moral weight—this is a subject for later—but it does make it one intrinsic good.

The view avoids certain objections, but does it have a positive rationale? Does our initial perfectionist idea point to just this concept of nature? If not, this is no disaster. The perfectionist idea has taken us a long way, to the equation of human nature with some essential properties. If consequences are then needed to decide exactly which essential properties, this is legitimate fine-tuning of an already substantive ideal. But I believe we can do better. By looking more closely at traditional formulations of the ideal, we can justify this particular specification.

In characterizing perfection, perfectionists speak often of the "good human life." They describe, not a momentary state or achievement, but a whole mode of living. Aristotle, for example, says that perfection can be achieved only "in a complete life"[15] and in weighing the leading accounts of it, compares, not politics and contemplation as such, but whole political and contemplative lives.[16] This emphasis on the life is multiply important. It reflects assumptions about how perfectionist values are aggregated and combined, and it also bears on our present concern. The centrality of the "good life" in perfectionism suggests that, whatever properties define it, they must presuppose that we are living. They must contribute to a way of living by themselves being forms of life. Properties shared by inanimate matter are not only intuitively trivial but also irrelevant to an outlook that asks above all how we should live. This outlook can justify its account of nature as follows: We start with the plausible idea that nature is essence and then narrow essence to living essence. This approach keeps our nature within ourselves—there is no dependence on other species—and also fits our original ideal. If that ideal was of a certain human life, we ensure that its elaboration will have an appropriate content.

The justification is deepened in a generalized perfectionism. If we apply perfectionist concepts to non-humans, we do so only to living things. It is only to animate kinds that we attribute perfection or a nature worth developing. (We do not speak of the good or flourishing of a rock or chemical.) The essence-and-life view reflects this division between kinds in its demarcation of human essential properties. It counts as relevant to our perfection what could be relevant to some species's perfection, and excludes what could not.

The best perfectionism, then, equates human nature with the properties essential to humans and conditioned on their being living things. We cannot yet endorse this perfectionism. We do not yet know what properties *are* essential to humans as living, as we must if we are to decide finally how perfectionism fares against the wrong-properties objection and, more generally, how attractive it is. But, given its account of nature, this perfectionism offers the best hope for a defensible morality. I will underscore this claim shortly by using the account to answer some common objections against perfectionism. But first a clarification is needed.

2.2.3

The perfectionist ideal is a *moral* ideal in the following sense: It is an ideal people ought to pursue regardless of whether they now want it or would want it in hypothetical circumstances, and apart from any pleasures it may bring. In Kant's terminology, the ideal supports categorical, not hypothetical, imperatives, ones that are not contingent on impulses or desires.

The ideal need not be moral in a nar-

rower sense that is sometimes used. In this sense, moral evaluations concern only the choices people make or the traits and dispositions behind their choices. On all theories of human nature, a person's perfection depends partly on her choices, but on many it also depends on factors outside her choices, such as her natural abilities, supply of material resources, and treatment by others. Given such a theory, the perfectionist ideal is moral in the broader sense of supporting categorical imperatives, but not in the narrower sense concerned only with choice and character.

Once it is understood as moral, the ideal can be expressed in several ways. A common formulation is in terms of the "good human life," one in which living essential properties are developed to a high degree. One can also speak of the "good human" (who develops these properties to a high degree) or simply of what is "good" (that the properties are developed). As well, one can speak of what is "good for" a human, if this is defined in terms of the preceding expressions. If something is "good for" a person whenever it is, for example, (simply) good and a state of the person, then developing human nature is "good for" us all. (If I use "good for," and the related expressions "benefit" and "harm," my use will always be in this derivative sense.) But the ideal is not about what is "good for" humans in a more common sense.

In this more common sense, "good for" is tied to the concepts of well-being or welfare and interests: Something is "good for" a person if it increases his well-being or furthers his interests. Well-being itself is often characterized subjectively, in terms of actual or hypothetical desires. Given this subjective characterization, perfectionism cannot concern well-being. Its ideal cannot define the "good for" a human because the ideal is one he ought to pursue regardless of his desires. In my view, perfectionism should never be expressed in terms of well-being.[17] It gives an account of the good human life, or of what is good in a human, but not of what is "good for" a human in the sense tied to well-being.

2.3 Nature: Objections

The wrong-properties objection is the most important against perfectionism, but there are others. When the concept of nature is undefined, the theory has difficulty answering these objections, but with nature as essence (from now on the restriction to living essence will be assumed) it can respond.

2.3.1

Philosophers used to dismiss perfectionism by saying the concept of human nature is incoherent or obscure. This attitude is less common since Kripke, but a related objection remains: that the concept of nature, although coherent, is partly evaluative.

To include a property in "human nature," the objection says, is not to make a factual claim about it. It is to say the property is somehow important or desirable, and so to use prior evaluative standards. To be a free-standing morality, perfectionism needs a descriptive concept of nature, but this is not available. Its heart, or the heart of any particular version of it, is not an ideal of developing human nature, but whatever criteria guide this prior selection of important properties.

A full answer to this objection requires a positive account of how natures are known. But even here we can see how, with nature as essence, the objection's main claims misfire.

These claims, first, are dubious if they concern the *meaning* of sentences attributing essential properties. The standard analyses of these sentences—and several have been proposed—use the same semantic tools, principally the concept of truth, as analyses of clearly factual language. They contain no explicitly evaluative elements and give no hint of normative content. If the best-known semantics are correct, the concept of essence is descriptive; if nature is essence, so is the concept of human nature.

Second, not just any evaluative content would undermine perfectionism. Only *morally* evaluative content would have this effect, and it is very unlikely.

It is well known that objects can be evaluated from different points of view or by different standards of goodness. Thus, a person can be evaluated first as a musician and then as a potential soldier. Because the criteria relevant to these evaluations are different, the evaluations are logically independent. A good musician may or may not be a good soldier, but his being the one does not entail his being the other. For the same reason, a principle characterizing one good in terms of another—for example, "Good musicians make the best soldiers"—is not damagingly circular. It borrows standards from another evaluative point of view but, relative to its own purposes, these standards are descriptive. It can serve, well or ill, as a ground-level principle for evaluating soldiers.

The same point applies to the evaluation of properties. A principle that uses values to identify the morally important properties of humans will be under only if the values it uses are moral. This is unlikely when the properties are picked out as essential.

If we believe, with Kripke, that its atomic structure is essential to an element such as gold, this is not because of a *moral* preference for atomic properties. If anything, it may be because of an explanatory preference. A common epistemological view holds that essential properties are identified by their central role in good scientific explanations. We know that its atomic structure is essential to gold, the view holds, because this structure is central to the best explanations of gold's weight, colour, and other properties. Even if this view contained the whole truth about essentialism—even if attributions of essence just were claims about good explanation—this would not undermine perfectionism. To say that humans ought morally to develop the properties central to good scientific explanations is to characterize their good by using standards that are not moral. It is to borrow standards from science, and for moral purposes these standards are descriptive. Their descriptive character can, moreover, always be made explicit. If our standards for good explanations demand truth, simplicity, and predictive power, then, on the view we are considering, the perfectionist ideal is equivalent to the following: "The good human life develops to a high degree the properties central to the truest, simplest, and most predictively powerful explanations of humans' other properties." Whether or not this ideal is attractive, it can ground a free-standing morality.

So the concept of nature is not evaluative if nature is essence, and even if it were, this would damage perfectionism only if the concept were morally evaluative. We do not use moral standards to identify the essences of non-human kinds, and there is no reason to think we must use them with humans.

2.3.2

Although perfectionism in general can answer this objection, the same is not true of all versions of perfectionism. In fact, it is not true of many versions. Many perfectionists allow their views about human nature to be shaped by moral considerations and, as a result, make claims about that nature that are false.

This is especially true of perfectionists whose theories are *moralistic*. A moralistic perfectionism takes one human essential property to be something like practical rationality and characterizes this property in such a way that realizing it to a high degree requires developing the dispositions commonly considered virtuous, such as temperance, justice, and honesty, or abiding by the rules—"Do not kill," "Do not lie"—commonly counted as moral. Moralism makes goodness by perfectionist standards in part the same as goodness by the lights of commonsense morality. It makes the degree to which humans develop their natures depend on the degree to which they fulfil popular notions of morality.

Moralism is present in the perfectionisms of Aristotle, Aquinas, and Green, and it dominates that of Kant. In my view it is a fundamental error. Humans are by

no means necessarily virtuous, and if moralism implies that they are, it embodies a clear falsehood. Even if it does not imply this strong claim, it embodies a falsehood. Moralism makes claims about the degree to which humans develop their nature that are incompatible with any plausible account of what that nature is. In any sense of "rational" in which it is plausible that humans are essentially rational, it is not plausible that conventionally moral humans are always more rational than immoral ones. Here rationality connotes deliberation and the effective pursuit of ends, which can be found no less in a successful burglar than in a philanthropist. And if there is a sense in which conventionally moral humans are more rational than immoral ones (which I doubt), the rationality it defines is not essential to humans. It is not true that humans could not exist without this morally loaded rationality.

It is one thing to use moral judgements to fine-tune a concept of nature; doing so is acceptable and even necessary. It is quite another to let moral considerations affect one's claims about what falls under a concept of nature once that is defined. Moralistic perfectionists, too eager to square themselves with commonsense morality, do the latter and make claims about human nature that, on any acceptable definition of nature, are false.

Nor is this the only defect in moralism. We are interested in perfectionism as a distinctive morality, with distinctive implications. But moralism threatens this distinctiveness. If a moralistic perfectionism says that to develop our nature we must follow such-and-such rules, its consequences will coincide with those of a morality that contains only these rules. The theory's use of perfectionist concepts will still have some importance. It will imply that in following the moral rules, we not only do what is right but also make our own lives best. But this claim will not affect the theory's specific content, that is, its specific claims about what we ought to do. Given this, moralistic perfectionism can seem, not an alternative to other moralities, but at best a variant formulation of them.

This is Sidgwick's reaction in *The Methods of Ethics*. He initially lists perfectionism as one of the main moralities he will discuss, but it quickly loses this status. Having defined "perfection" as "Excellence of Human Nature," Sidgwick says that the principal element in perfection is "commonly conceived" to be virtue, in the conventionally moral sense of virtue.[18] This definition is not surprising, given that Sidgwick's models for perfectionism are Kant and Green, but it has unfortunate results. Because achieving virtue involves following rules similar to those of an intuitionist morality, Sidgwick calls perfectionism a special case of intuitionism and then drops it from his discussion. This is an understandable response to perfectionism as Sidgwick conceives it. Not only does this perfectionism make unsupportable claims about human nature, but it effectively reduces itself to some other morality.

Because moralism is such an error, the best perfectionism must be free of it. It must never characterize the good by reference to conventional moral rules, but always non-morally; and in defending its claims about essence, it must likewise appeal only to non-moral considerations. Its acceptability will still depend on whether it fits our moral convictions, including some in commonsense morality. But this fit cannot be built into its content by moralistic claims about essence. It must instead exploit features of the theory's structure.

2.3.3

A second objection claims that, even if the concept of nature is descriptive, the concept of its full development is not. Having identified the properties in human nature, perfectionism must explain what develops them to a high degree, and it cannot do so without appealing to moral considerations outside its main idea.

Even with nature as essence, this objection's first claim is partly true. For some essential properties what their full development involves may be uncontroversial, and for all there are conceptual limits on what degrees of them can mean. But these limits

do not always determine a unique measure. Consider, for example, theoretical rationality. How far people develop this property depends presumably on some features of their beliefs, but which features? The concept of rationality itself excludes the idea that the best beliefs are those acquired on a Tuesday or while walking north. But are the best beliefs then true, justified, explanatorily powerful, or some combination of these? To characterize theoretical perfection fully, we do need some decisions, which cannot be justified on narrow perfectionist grounds, about what degrees of it involve.

But this defect in perfectionism is not serious. By the time it specifies degrees, the theory has done considerable work. Its basic idea has selected the properties whose development matters for excellence, and these properties impose substantial limits on what degrees of them can mean. That some room for play is left where further decisions are needed should not make us doubt the importance of perfectionism. It means only that different versions of perfectionism can agree in their central ideal and agree about human nature, but disagree slightly about how that nature is developed. This point will be important later, for in describing the Aristotelian perfections we will often face choices between different principles of measurement. But these principles will never be so diverse, nor the play room they exploit so large, that they threaten the theory's distinctiveness.

2.3.4

Finally, there is a weakened version of the wrong-properties objection. It claims, not that perfectionism does have implausible consequences, but only that it could have such consequences if things were different.

Let us concede, the objection begins, that, given the true theory of human nature, perfectionism has attractive implications. Even so, human nature could have turned out to be different. It could have been our essence to be cruel and aggressive, as a caricature of Nietzsche maintains. On this hypothesis, perfectionism has implausible consequences, and this possibility undermines its claim to acceptance in actual conditions.

We could respond to this objection by simply denying, as some philosophers do, that merely hypothetical consequences can count against a moral theory, but this response would not be persuasive. Even if possible consequences count less than actual ones, it is too much to say they count for nothing, especially when the possibilities are realistic and the claims about them dramatic.

A better answer begins by noting that, if nature is essence, there are no real possibilities to consider. The human essence contains the properties humans possess in every possible world where they exist and, on standard assumptions, possess essentially in every such world. If humans are necessarily rational, then, given the most accepted modal logic, they are necessarily necessarily rational.[19] Therefore, when we speculate about what the human essence might have "turned out to be," we cannot be considering a real possibility. We can only be considering what Kripke calls an "epistemic possibility,"[20] that is, the (barely logical) possibility that, given the knowledge we once had, we could have gone on to acquire evidence that the human essence is other than what it is. But this possibility cannot undermine perfectionism. Although it shows that it was once possible for us to acquire the justified belief that perfectionism has repellent consequences, it does nothing to alter the falsity (in all possible worlds) of that belief. If our essence is attractive in the actual world, it is attractive in all worlds, and perfectionism is attractive in all worlds too.

Of course, we can consider the real possibility of there existing beings who are essentially cruel and aggressive, as long as we do not call them humans, but this changes the objection. It does not touch an ideal defined only for humans and not generalized to other species. Nor does it really damage a more inclusive perfectionism. Given the intimate connection between a kind's essence and its other properties, essentially cruel beings would have to differ from us in countless other ways. Because their explanatory properties were different, their explained properties would have to be different as well. This makes the earlier skepticism about hypothetical consequences relevant. How can we have reliable moral views about beings so far removed from our experience? How can specific judgements about them outweigh the intrinsic appeal of a morality based on natures? The present objection seems powerful because it seems to show that perfectionism could have implausible consequences for us, living the lives we are now, or for beings very like us. This, however, the logic of essentialism prevents it from showing.

It is not that there is no difficulty here. A generalized perfectionism does imply that, if essentially cruel beings existed, the development of cruelty in them would be intrinsically good. The question is what this implication shows. Given the beings' nature, their perfection would be highly competitive, in that one's achieving it would prevent others from doing the same. What was intrinsically good might therefore be instrumentally bad because of its effects on the victims. In fact, the situation for these beings' perfection would be bleak: It would be impossible for any one of them to achieve it without directly blocking some others. The generalized perfectionism abstracts from these facts. It allows that a being's exercising cruelty might be instrumentally bad, and even bad all things considered. It claims only that the cruelty, insofar as it realized the being's nature, would be intrinsically good. This is not a claim that, given the beings' remoteness from our experience, our specific judgements give us good reason to reject. And an attractive general ideal gives us reason to accept it. . . .

3.3 Defending Perfectionism

3.3.1

A substantive defence of perfectionism must follow the same lines as a defence of any morality. It must show that the theory coheres with our intuitive moral judgements at all levels of generality, or, in Rawls's phrase, is in "reflective equilibrium"[21] with all these judgements. Because perfectionism is complex, a full defence of it must be complex. It must show, first, that the general perfectionist ideal, that of developing human nature, is attractive when considered by itself and as a potential foundation for morality. The theory's basic idea must have intrinsic appeal. Second, the defence must show that the ideal has attractive consequences, both at the middle level, where it identifies the properties whose development is intrinsically good, and at lower levels, where it makes particular claims about which activities are best and right. Finally, perfectionism must work as a systematic whole, with its general ideas explaining its particular claims. Then the theory not only matches our intuitions but also gives them a satisfying rationale.

This kind of defence is most persuasive when there is some logical distance between a morality's parts, so that judgements about one are not infected by knowledge of the others. There often is this logical distance within perfectionism. Because it takes argument to identify the properties essential to humans, we can evaluate the theory's general ideal without knowing what specific values it supports and, conversely, have views about the value of developing, say, rationality without knowing whether rationality is part of human nature. Similar logical gaps appear elsewhere in the theory. A general ideal of rationality does not reveal immediately what specific activities realize it best, and there will be further confirmation for the theory if these activities turn out to be attractive. Because perfectionism's parts can be considered in relative isolation from each other, its passing reflective equilibrium tests is especially impressive. If the most plausible concept of nature turns out to contain only independently attractive properties, with independently attractive realizations, the theory is independently confirmed at all its levels.

The defence is made easier by the fact that, at each more general level, perfectionism can make adjustments to avoid unwanted consequences at lower levels. It can refine its concept of nature to exclude morally trivial properties and, in specifying degrees of perfection, can prefer measures with more attractive implications. But the room for adjustment is limited. Not just anything can count as a concept of nature, and not just anything can define degrees of rationality. Throughout perfectionism, the more general levels impose constraints on what can be affirmed at levels below. If despite these constraints the theory's particular claims are still attractive, this supports its general ideal.

The second and third parts of the defence turn on perfectionism's consequences. In the remainder of this book, I will argue that, in its best version, perfectionism has many attractive consequences and does not have unacceptable ones, as it would do if it assigned value to what are clearly trivial properties. Ideally, the theory would yield every attractive consequence or capture every intuitively appealing moral claim. This may not happen; there may be intuitively appealing properties that cannot be connected to an ideal of human nature. (Perhaps the capacity for pleasure is one.) If so, this failing is less damaging to perfectionism than if the theory valued intuitively trivial properties. At most, it shows that the perfectionist ideal must be combined with other moral ideas in a pluralist theory. And whether it shows this depends partly on the first part of the defence: whether the perfectionist ideal is attractive when considered by itself.

If the ideal was not attractive by itself, its plausibility would depend entirely on its ability to yield and explain attractive consequences. That there were desirable consequences it could not capture would suggest strongly that it needs to be supplemented in a pluralist theory. If the ideal is attractive by itself, however, the situation is different. Then we may hold it against an initially appealing moral claim that it cannot be connected to human nature. We may even reject the claim, deciding that it is mistaken if it cannot be connected to human nature. This issue is one we can discuss here: the intrinsic appeal of the perfectionist ideal.

3.3.2

I believe the ideal does have intrinsic appeal: The goal of developing human nature, or exercising essential human powers, is deeply attractive. This is reflected in its widespread acceptance. The ideal is implicit in non-philosophical talk of living a "fully human" or "truly human" life and is endorsed by diverse philosophers. Writers such as Aquinas, Nietzsche, Green, and Marx have very different particular visions of the good life. Some value contemplation; others value action. Some value a communal life; others value a life of solitude. If, despite these differences, these philosophers all ground their particular values in a single ideal of human nature, that ideal must have intrinsic appeal.

Some of this appeal can be explained, if nature is essence. Because each of us is essentially a human, to develop human nature is not to develop some temporary or tangential property, such as being a lawyer or a hockey fan. It is to develop what makes us what we are.

The ideal is also attractive as a potential foundation for morality. It may not exclude a justification in terms of more basic principles; perhaps no moral ideas does. But it does not require such a justification. It is of sufficient depth and generality to be in itself the basis of all moral claims; in human nature we have something that can be ethical bedrock. In fact, the perfectionist ideal makes a peremptory claim: As a potential foundation for morality, it dismisses any moral judgements that cannot be derived from it. However appealing they seem in themselves, it counts against them that they cannot be connected to human nature.

It may be objected that these claims for the ideal are less plausible if we have rejected the accretions discussed earlier in this chapter. If developing human nature was each human's purpose, given her by God, it would make sense that doing so was good. Stripped of these claims, the ideal has less appeal.

There may indeed be some cost to abandoning these accretions. If each human had a metaphysical purpose, the claim that it was good to fulfil that purpose might have intrinsic appeal. If so, a perfectionism that talked of purposes would have two attractive basic ideas, one about human nature and one about purposes, and in rejecting the accretion we lose the support of the second idea. But the loss here is not great: The perfectionist ideal, considered apart from any accretions, is attractive enough to ground a moral theory. And there may be no loss at all. Do teleological perfectionists believe first that it is good to fulfil the human purpose, and only then, because perfection is our purpose, that perfection is good? Or do they believe first that perfection is good, and then, because our purpose must be good, that our purpose is perfection? I suspect their reasoning often follows the second course. If it does, teleological claims add nothing to the appeal of perfectionism.

The same is true of accretions about a divine creator. That an all-powerful being wishes us to pursue some goal is no reason to do so unless we know, independently, that what the being wishes is good. Unless perfection is intrinsically desirable, someone's desire that we pursue it has no moral weight. This point is reflected in the perfectionist tradition. Theological perfectionists such as Aquinas do not derive the perfectionist ideal from claims about God; they apply it to him. If God is supremely good, they hold, it is because he fully realizes his unlimited nature. In addition, there are important non-theological perfectionists. Marx and Nietzsche are resolutely irreligious and have a purely mechanistic view of nature. Nevertheless, both endorse an ideal based on human nature.

It may also be said that perfectionism loses by rejecting the natural tendency doctrines. If a strong desire or pleasure doctrine were true, perfectionism could explain why some moralists equate the good with satisfaction: They mistake something strictly correlated with the good for the good itself. Again, there may be some loss here. But if a moderate view like Green's is true (3.1.4), perfectionism can give some explanation of these moralists' error: Satisfaction, although not strictly correlated with perfection, does often go with it. And even if Green's view is false, it is hardly a decisive objection to a moral theory that it must sometimes say that other theories are simply false.

The intrinsic appeal of the perfectionist ideal is not seriously diminished by the rejection of various accretions. We have good reason to examine the substantive moral theory it generates.

3.4 How Are Essences Known?

To elaborate this perfectionism, we must first determine what properties do belong to human nature or actually are essential to humans and conditioned on their being living things. This inquiry in turn requires a method for identifying these properties. Deciding which essential properties are conditioned on humans' being living seems straightforward; the difficult question is how we discover which properties are essential. How in general are essences known?

3.4.1

Epistemological questions have received less attention than one might have expected in the recent literature on essentialism, but philosophers who defend particular claims about essences use one of two methods.

The first method, associated with Kripke,[22] is *intuitive*. It says that we discover essential properties by making intuitive judgements in thought experiments involving candidate members of a kind. To learn whether its atomic structure is essential to

gold, for example, we imagine a series of possible substances with gold's atomic structure but a different outward appearance. If we judge all these substances to be gold, our judgement shows that its inner constitution is essential to gold and its phenomenal properties contingent. We learn what could and could not be gold by asking how we could and could not imagine gold's existing.

The second method examines *scientific explanations*. Associated with Hilary Putnam,[23] it says that we identify essential properties by their central role in the explanations given by good scientific theories. That gold has a certain atomic structure explains its colour, weight, and other phenomenal properties, but is not in turn explained by them. Gold's atomic structure is thus explanatorily prior to these properties, and this shows, on the second view, that it is essential. For the explanatory view, properties central to scientific explanations are essential, and in gold these cluster around its inner constitution.

These two methods agree in their conclusions about many particular essential properties, for example, those of gold. But they are very different, and the choice between them is important for epistemology. The choice is also difficult. Each method faces difficulties, and in each case they threaten to reduce it to its rival.

The intuitive method faces the standard objection to any appeal to "intuitive" knowledge. Do we really have direct intuitions about *de re* necessity? Are our judgements about possible objects really self-standing? In this particular case the objection is especially pressing, for no one can make these judgements without having some collateral knowledge. No one can know that a kind has a property essentially without knowing first that it (simply) has that property. Thus, no one can know that gold has its atomic structure essentially without knowing first that it (simply) has that structure. Moreover, one may need further knowledge. Of the intuitive method we must ask: If people knew all the properties of gold but did not know their explanatory relations—whether its structure explains its appearance or vice versa—could they make confident judgements about possible instances of gold? Could they decide which were and were not gold? If not, this would undermine the intuitive approach. Our supposedly free-standing verdicts in thought experiments would reflect prior explanatory knowledge, and the intuitive view would collapse into the explanatory.

The difficulty facing the explanatory method appears when we try to analyze "explanation." The best-known account of explanation is Carl Hempel's "deductive-nomological" account,[24] but it will not do for identifying essences. It notoriously fails to capture certain "asymmetries of explanation," of which one is that essential properties explain accidental properties but are not explained by them. If there is a deduction of gold's phenomenal properties from its atomic properties plus some bridge principles—which is all the account requires—there is also a deduction of its atomic properties from its phenomenal properties plus some (reversed) bridge principles. Explanations are supposed, on the second view, to distinguish essential from accidental properties; as analyzed by Hempel, they cannot.

To capture the asymmetries of explanation, we must supplement Hempel's account with further material conditions. Some philosophers have proposed the following: A deduction counts as explanatory only if it derives accidental properties from essential properties and not vice versa.[25] But this proposal undermines the explanatory approach. If we need to know which properties are essential before we can know which deductions are explanatory, we cannot use explanations to identify essential properties. On the contrary, we must have some prior, perhaps intuitive, knowledge of essential properties. This most obvious supplement to the deductive-nomological account undermines the explanatory method, and it is not clear whether any other supplement gives the right results about explanation.

Given these difficulties, I cannot take either method and show that it provides the one canonical means for discovering essences. Nonetheless, it seems that *at least one* of the methods must be canonical. And, since whichever is not canonical seems likely to collapse into the other, it may not matter practically which is which. If we are interested in a practical question such as "What is human nature?" we can proceed as follows. We can use both methods simultaneously, testing our claims about the human essence both intuitively and against explanatory theories. We can count as essential to humans whatever properties are picked out by both methods together. With gold these properties seem to coincide, and, if the previous arguments are correct, they should coincide generally. Epistemologists may differ about which method is doing the real work in our arguments and which is dependent, but if the same conclusions follow from both methods, then adherents of both should find them well grounded.

3.4.2

Against this double approach, an objection may be raised. How can we use the second, explanatory method if we have rejected all strong tendency doctrines? If there was some property that all humans wanted to develop, or that history was tending to develop, the method would be easy to apply. A teleological human science would give this property a central role, and explanatory considerations would then show that the property was essential. Without tendencies, however, no teleological science is possible, and in the absence of such a science, how can the second method be used?

A teleological science would, if true, bear on questions about our nature, and many perfectionists do use such a science to ground their essentialist claims. Aristotle's belief that formal and final causes coincide implies that we discover a kind's nature by seeing what it naturally grows towards. Hegel and Marx make essential to humans the very properties whose development is the end state in their theories of history, and Nietzsche says:[26]

> Suppose, finally, we succeeded in explaining our entire instinctive life as the development and ramification of *one* basic form of the will—namely of the will to power, as *my* proposition has it; suppose all organic functions could be traced back to this will to power and one could also find in it the solution of the problem of procreation and nourishment—it is *one* problem—then one would have gained the right to determine *all* efficient force univocally as—*will to power*. The world viewed from inside, the world defined and determined according to its "intelligible character"—it would be "will to power" and nothing else.

This epistemic use of teleology is, in fact, central to the teleological formulation of perfectionism. This formulation claims that, if humans naturally desire some property, its development must be part of their good. It can claim on the same ground that the property must be part of human nature. The fact about desire gives the property a central role in explaining human behaviour and thereby shows it is essential.

Although the explanatory method can use a teleological science, it need not. Think again of gold. No scientific theory says that gold tends to develop its atomic structure to higher degrees; such a theory is impossible. What our best science does, rather, is to use gold's atomic structure to explain the many different changes it can undergo. If gold is heated to a certain point, it melts; if it is immersed in aqua regia, it dissolves; and in each case the explanation starts from the same facts about its atomic structure. Something similar is possible for humans. Even if their behaviour does not always aim at one goal, there can be a single theory that explains how they pursue their different goals, and a single property that is central to all the explanations this theory supports. Even if human action is diverse, its explanation can always start from the same property. If so, explanatory considerations will make this property essential even though it is not the goal in any teleological science. . . .

4.1 The Aristotelian Theory: Physical Essence

4.1.1

A first deliverance of the intuitive method is that humans necessarily have bodies. We can imagine purely spiritual beings and, perhaps, understand their psychology. But if they have no physical form they are not, intuitively, of our species. Beyond this, intuition tells us that humans necessarily have bodies with a fairly determinate structure. No human can remain alive without a functioning respiratory, muscular, digestive, circulatory, and nervous system, and, analogously, no possible being without these systems passes the intuitive test for humanity. Unless its body permits it somehow to breathe, move, process nutrients, and exercise central control, it is not a human.

These claims are confirmed by the explanatory method. One explanation of human behaviour is physical explanation, and it makes central the very systems picked out by intuition. To explain why a runner is panting, we say her circulatory system needs to carry more oxygen to her muscles, which causes her respiratory system to process air at a greater rate than usual. If she pushes off with her legs, we say her nervous system is sending messages to her thigh muscles, causing them to contract. These explanations supervene on and may reduce to the explanations of some more basic science such as chemistry or physics. But this reduction is irrelevant in our version of perfectionism. We have defined human nature to exclude any properties shared by inanimate matter, which means that the explanations we look to must likewise be restricted to living things. Chemical and physical explanations apply to rocks and gases as well as to humans, and we must therefore consider only explanations that presuppose some organic structure. In humans this structure is expressed in certain major physiological systems—in respiratory, muscular, digestive, circulatory, and nervous systems—

and the relevant explanations cite their operation.

Both methods have difficulty making these initial claims more precise. If humans essentially have some respiratory system, must they have the specific arrangement of organs they have? If we imagine beings like us in all respects except that they have three lungs, are we imagining humans? What of beings whose respiratory systems operate on different chemical principles? These questions are difficult, and I cannot answer them decisively, but they may not be important in a moral study of perfectionism. In our world, no human can grow a third lung or alter chemical laws; we are stuck with the physiological systems we have. Given this, our physical perfection can depend only on how our actual systems function, that is, on events in our actual bodies. If a general description of our physical essence—one saying only that we need some respiratory system—defines clear degrees of our physical perfection, it may not matter whether more specific descriptions do or do not remain essential.

4.1.2

What, then, defines degrees of physical perfection? This is more a question for physiology than for philosophy, but a rough answer is as follows. Each system in our body has a characteristic activity. The respiratory system extracts oxygen from air, the circulatory system distributes nutrients, and so on. For a human to remain alive, each system must perform its activity to some minimal degree; for her to achieve reasonable physical perfection, it must do so to a reasonable degree. But a system does this when it is free from outside interference and operating healthily. So the basic level of physical perfection is good bodily health, when all our bodily systems function in an efficient, unrestricted way. Then essential physical processes occur to a reasonable degree, and we have reasonable physical perfection.

This first implication is attractive. Even apart from their effects on other values, illness and poor organic functioning are intrinsically regrettable. The loss of a limb or of full activity in an important organ detracts from the completeness of a human life, and robustness adds to it. It makes the life more fully human. Physical health may not be a major perfectionist good, and it may receive less moral weight than the development of rationality. But a perfectionism that gives it some value acknowledges that some of our nature is bodily and that, like others, this part can be more or less developed.

This connection with health is no accident, but has evolutionary origins. Like other aspects of our nature, our bodily systems were selected as those most likely to make for our survival and reproduction. Their unimpeded operation is healthy because otherwise beings possessed of them would be adaptively disadvantaged. In their present form the systems are essential to humans, who cannot exist without them. But, like humankind itself, they emerged from natural selection and were favoured over alternatives precisely because of their connection with healthy, self-maintaining activity.

Higher physical perfection comes in vigorous bodily activity. Here our major physical systems perform to higher degrees, processing more air, carrying more nutrients, and moving greater weights longer distances. This activity occurs most notably in athletics, and Aristotelian perfectionism finds the highest physical good in great athletic feats. These feats often embody perfections other than physical perfection. They require skill and dexterity and can follow months of careful planning. In both these ways they realize practical rationality, and this can account for much of their value. But there is also a physical dimension. When a human runs 100 meters in 9.86 seconds or long-jumps 29 feet, something physically splendid occurs. His bodily powers are realized to the full in a way that is intrinsically admirable and of intrinsic perfectionist worth.

Most of us are not outstanding athletes and cannot achieve the highest physical perfection. Still, we can preserve our basic health and pursue whatever mild athletics are compatible with our main projects. We have instrumental reasons to do both these things. Physical activity keeps us alert and can be the medium for some exercise of rationality. If Aristotelian perfectionism is correct, however, this activity is also a modest intrinsic good, as the development of our physical nature.

4.2 The Aristotelian Theory: Rationality

4.2.1

The most important Aristotelian claim is that humans are essentially rational. Its elaboration requires an account of degrees of theoretical and practical rationality, which will be given later. But its core is this: Humans are rational because they can form and act on beliefs and intentions. More specifically, they are rational because they can form and act on sophisticated beliefs and intentions, ones whose contents stretch across persons and times and that are arranged in complex hierarchies. These last features distinguish human rationality from that of lower animals. Animals have isolated perceptual beliefs, but only humans can achieve explanatory understanding. They can grasp generalizations that apply across objects and times and can use them to explain diverse phenomena. A similar point holds for practical rationality. Animals have just local aims, but humans can envisage patterns of action that stretch through time or include other agents and can perform particular acts as means to them. By constructing hierarchies of ends, they can engage in intelligent tool use and have complex interactions with others. Distinctive properties do not matter as such in our perfectionism, but the Aristotelian theory makes essential a kind of rationality that at present is found only in humans.

That humans are essentially rational is supported, first, by the intuitive method. We do not think there were humans in the world until primates developed with suffi-cient intelligence, and the same view colours our judgements about possibilities. If we imagine a species with no capacity for a mental life, or with none more sophisticated than other animals', we do not take ourselves to be imagining humans. Whatever their physical form, they are not of our species. The degree to which humans exercise rationality varies from time to time in their lives, being lower, for example, when they are asleep. But beings who never envisage or plan for a future are not, intuitively, humans.

Again, this claim is confirmed by the explanatory method. Alongside the physical explanation of human behaviour is psychological explanation, which explains at least intentional human action by citing beliefs and aims that make it rational. This explanation presupposes theoretical and practical rationality and ascribes their current exercise in all its particular accounts. It deserves closer examination.

4.2.2

A psychological explanation of person A's act of ϕ-ing has the following form:

> A intended to make it the case that p.
>
> A believed that ϕ-ing was the most effective means to p.
>
> A was acting as a rational agent.
>
> A was physically able to ϕ.
>
> Therefore, A ϕ-ed intentionally.

Two features of this schema deserve comment. One is that it begins with an intention that p, rather than going back to a desire or wish that p. This point highlights the central role of intentions in practical reasoning. We have many desires that we never act on, because their objects are unattainable or because we think satisfying them is on balance unwise. These desires never affect our behaviour. Only when a desire generates an intention do we think seriously about its satisfaction or set ourselves properly to pursue it. The second feature is the claim that A was acting as a rational agent. This claim is required for the success of any psychological explanation but, within that explanation, is always contingent. Even if humans are essentially rational, they do not exercise full rationality at every moment. On the contrary, they sometimes succumb to weakness of will, self-deception, and other lapses from full rational control. To be subjects of psychological explanation, they must be generally rational, and generally do what their beliefs and aims make appropriate. But full rationality need not always be present, and, when it is not, full rational explanation is not possible.

In this general form, psychological explanation applies to some other animals who also act on beliefs and aims.[27] This is not so, however, when the ascribed mental states are sophisticated, with extended contents and hierarchical relations. Then the premises of the explanation—beliefs about scientific laws or intentions for the distant future—are beyond other animals, and the conclusion may be as well. It may involve intelligent tool use or willed co-operation with others. The scope of the explanation also alters given sophisticated mental states. Instead of taking A's intention that p as given, sophisticated psychology can say that she intends p as a means to q, which she in turn wills as a means to r. It can explain a particular end as a means to others that appear above it in a rational hierarchy. It can also explain many beliefs. If A believes that ϕ-ing is the most effective means to p, sophisticated psychology may say:

A has evidence that ϕ-ing is the most effective means to p.

A is forming beliefs as a rational agent.

Therefore, A believes that ϕ-ing is the most effective means to p.

The rationality ascribed here is no longer the practical rationality that derives acts from intentions and beliefs, but the theoretical rationality that grounds beliefs in evidence. It is the rationality exercised when sophisticated beings use general principles to move from initial evidential beliefs to other, more speculative beliefs. The explanation does not claim that A is perfectly rational or always forms beliefs on the basis of evidence. She may sometimes suffer from slips of reasoning, wishful thinking, or self-deception. For her beliefs to be generally explicable, however, she must generally derive them from evidence, and for this particular explanation to succeed she must be doing so now.

The content of sophisticated psychology, then, gives it a sophisticated form. Instead of treating items of behaviour one by one, it ascribes a system of connected beliefs and aims to explain, not just a person's acts, but many of the mental states behind them. It explains aims in terms of beliefs and other aims, and beliefs in terms of other beliefs. The central role in this psychology is clearly played by the properties of theoretical and practical rationality. These properties are, first, presupposed in every premise of a psychological explanation. No one can have a belief or intention about p, especially if p is sophisticated, without the mental capacity to grasp its content. In saying that she believes or intends p, we assume that she has that degree of rationality. Nor can she have a belief or aim about p unless she generally acts on her beliefs and aims as reason requires. Unless she generally does what she believes will promote her goals, no goals can be ascribed to her. Unless she generally derives beliefs from evidence, she cannot have beliefs. Finally, a premise ascribing the present exercise of rationality is a crucial part of every psychological explanation. Unless A is now acting or forming beliefs rationally, the premises of the explanation will not entail its conclusion. Unless her rational powers are now being exercised, her having certain mental states will not explain a thing.

That the two forms of rationality are central does not, however, imply any natural tendency doctrine. Sophisticated psychology does not say that humans have an overriding desire to develop rationality or a supreme tendency in that direction. On the contrary, it places no restriction on the content of their goals. What it does, rather, is use the one property of rationality to explain how humans' different goals all issue in action. Its structure is therefore like that of explanations of gold. It starts from one ascription of rationality and shows how, given this rationality, people with different initial aims, experiences, and evidence will end up believing, intending, and acting differently. It uses reason to explain goal-directed behaviour without making reason itself a goal.

Psychology also makes rationality essential without supporting moralism, the view that developing one's own nature requires the other-regarding virtues. Because the rationality it ascribes is formal, defined only by the scope and inter-relations of a person's beliefs and aims, it can be realized as much in conventional immorality as in morality. If the immorality is wrong, it cannot be because it reduces the agent's own perfection.

4.2.3

This first explanatory argument gives us good reason to conclude that humans are essentially rational, but it is not the only such argument available.

As described to this point, sophisticated psychology uses pairs of beliefs and aims to explain human acts. How does it decide which pairs to use? How does it know which specific mental states to ascribe? In the case where A ϕ's intentionally, we may say that she intended p and believed that ϕ-ing was a means to p. But it would also explain her act if she intended some different end q or r and believed that ϕ-ing was a means to that, or intended not-p and believed mistakenly that ϕ-ing would prevent p. To give a determinate explanation of her ϕ-ing, psychology must be able to select one of these intention-belief pairs above the others. How does it do so?

The only answer I know makes rationality even more central to sophisticated psychology. Several writers, among them Donald Davidson, argue that this psychology is governed by a "principle of charity" requiring us to make an agent's overall behaviour as rational as possible.[28] In explaining a particular act, we must ascribe those beliefs and aims that make the most sense of her conduct as a whole. Different intention-belief pairs may do equally well in rationalizing her present act, but they will differ in their capacity to fit into a larger scheme explaining her total conduct through time. One allows us to find rational origins for most of her other beliefs and acts; another forces us to leave many ungrounded in reasons. The principle of charity exploits this difference and, by requiring us to prefer the first ascription, permits a determinate explanation of what she has done.

Without something like a principle of charity, it is hard to see how psychology could give determinate explanations. But again, some clarifications are needed.

The principle of charity does not imply that everyone's behaviour is highly rational. It tells us to interpret for maximum rationality, but it cannot say what result this effort will have. One person's conduct may be such that its most charitable interpretation makes him very rational, whereas another's leaves him, even on the kindest construal, much further down a scale of coherence. An ideal of charity guides psychological explanation, but it cannot determine its final content. That depends on empirical facts about a person's behaviour.

Second, a plausible principle of charity has two parts, one theoretical and one practical. It tells us to maximize both theoretical and practical rationality, or rationality in belief and rationality in action. These different maximands can sometimes conflict, as in cases that suggest self-deception. To say that someone has deceived himself is to explain an act of belief formation as a rational means to some goal, for example, avoiding distress, but it is also to ascribe an unjustified belief. In deciding whether to interpret someone as self-deceived, we decide whether to maximize his theoretical or practical rationality, where we cannot do both.

A final point concerns the substance of the ideal of charity. When sophisticated psychology tells us to maximize theoretical and practical rationality, what exactly does it intend? What is the precise content of its interpretive goal? According to a simple view, rationality involves just acting on some intentions and believing on some evidence, so a charitable interpretation maximizes just the number of a person's acts and beliefs with some rational origin. But this view is not the only one possible. Davidson, for example, says that interpretations should make a person so far as possible "consistent, a believer of truths, and a lover of the good."[29] This proposal goes beyond the simple view because a belief based in evidence may still be false and an act aimed at an end far from laudable. In fact, Davidson's account of charity is just one of many possible. On the theoretical side, we can imagine a weak principle telling us to maximize just the number of a person's beliefs that are consistent; two stronger principles telling us to maximize either the number that are justified or the number that are true; and a still stronger one telling us to maximize the number that are both justified and true, or that constitute knowledge.

There are further possibilities. Charity can tell us to prefer ascribing beliefs that are more sophisticated. It can, and in my view should, say that, other things equal, we should prefer ascribing beliefs with more extended contents and more elaborate inter-relations. We make agents more rational, and explain them better, if we assign states with greater reach and explanatory coherence. Unfortunately, views like this last one are hard to defend. However plausible it is that psychology requires *some* concept of charity, it is difficult to argue that this concept must take one rather than another specific form. Can we show that one account of charity is truer than all others to our everyday explanatory practice? Or that it gives what by independent criteria are clearly better explanations? I do not see a decisive argument here, and it may be that there is none. It may be that, despite the general importance to psychology of using some principle of charity, there is no one content that principle must have.

If this is right, there may be some indeterminacy in the concept of charity, but the indeterminacy does not undermine the general conclusion we can draw from Davidson. Even without a specific principle of charity, we can know what range an acceptable principle must fall within, and we can also know its importance. If sophisticated psychology tells us to maximize the rationality (in some sense) of all agents, then rationality (in that sense) is even more central than before. Rationality is presupposed in the premises of every psychological explanation, and its current exercise must also be explicitly ascribed. Now we see, beyond this, that it is a regulative ideal governing psychology and determining which of the many rationalizations consistent with its general structure are indeed explanations. If psychology uses charity constraints, rationality is doubly central to it, and we have doubly good reason to include rationality in the human essence.

Alongside physical perfection, then, Aristotelian perfectionism recognizes two further goods, which we can call *theoretical* and *practical perfection*. Although their full description will come later, they already look promising, and a perfectionism containing them seems likely to have attractive consequences. This is impressive, because in deriving the goods from the human essence we did not use moralism or any moral arguments. The claim that humans are essentially rational first emerged from thought experiments and then was confirmed by psychological explanations. When this is added to the intrinsic appeal of the perfectionist idea, the prospects for Aristotelian perfectionism look good.

Notes

1. Plato, *Republic*, 353a.

2. Aristotle, *Nicomachean Ethics*, 10797b33–1098a2.

3. Kant, *The Doctrine of Virtue*, University of Pennsylvania Press, 1964, p. 51.

4. Marx and Engels, *The German Ideology*, in *Karl Marx*, ed.D. McLellan, Oxford University Press, 1977, p. 160.

5. Marx, *Economic and Philosophical Manu-*

scripts, p. 82; and *Capital*, vol. 1, pp. 283–84.

6. Williams, *Morality: An Introduction to Ethics*, p. 64; see also Nielsen, "Alienation and Self-Realization," *Philosophy* 48 (1973) pp. 23–24. Williams intends some of his properties, especially the last ones, to be not just morally trivial but repugnant. The issue is tricky, however. If killing things for fun is repugnant, it is primarily because of its effect on the things killed. That the killing is intrinsically evil, or makes the killer's life worse, is a more contentious claim that, in my view, perfectionism need not affirm. In any case, it is sufficient for Williams's objection if his properties are valueless, that is, lack positive worth.

7. Nozick, *Philosophical Explanations*, pp. 515–17.

8. Kripke, *Naming and Necessity*.

9. Hegel, *The Phenomenology of Spirit*, Oxford University Press, 1977, p. 297; and *The Philosophy of Right*, sec. 153.

10. Marx, *Economic and Philosophical Manuscripts*, in *Karl Marx*, pp. 83, 89.

11. Nietzsche, *Beyond Good and Evil*, sec. 1986; and *The Will to Power*, sec. 693.

12. Other claims that seem equivalent to ones about essence are: that perfection consists in the conformity of human existence with its "idea" or "concept" (Hegel, Marx, Bradley), that something is the "species-being" or "species-activity" of humans (Marx), that something constitutes "life" or humans' "life-activity" (Marx, Nietzsche), and that certain capacities belong to a human's "real" or "true self," as opposed to his "apparent self" (Kant, Bradley).

13. Another possibility is to apply the distinctiveness test to conjunctions of essential properties. Essential property A may not be distinctive of humans, nor essential property B, but no other species may have A and B together. If so, then a further compound view says the conjunction $A \& B$ belongs to human nature. As initially stated, this view collapses into the simple essence view. If the conjunction $A \& B$ is unique to humans, it will remain so if essential property C is added; species that do not have the smaller conjunction will not have the larger one. So the conjunction of all human essential properties is, as a conjunction, always distinctive. We might try equating human nature with the smallest set of essential properties that is distinctive, but in many cases this collapses into the original essence-and-distinctiveness view. If there is one property that is, individually, both essential and distinctive, the smallest set contains only it.

14. Jean-Jacques Rousseau, *La Nouvelle Héloise*, cinquième partie, lettre 3, quoted in Passmore, *The Perfectability of Man*, p. 178. See also Nietzsche, *Schopenhauer as Educator*, pp. 1–6; Norton, *Personal Destinies: A Philosophy of Ethical Individualism*; and, for a theory that combines species and individual essences, Unger, *Knowledge and Politics*, pp. 239–40.

15. Aristotle, *Nicomachean Ethics*, 1098a18–20.

16. Aristotle, *Nicomachean Ethics*, 1095b14–1096a10, 1177a11–1179a33; *Eudemian Ethics*, 1215a26–b14; and *Politics*, 1324a24–b1. See also Aquinas, *Summa Theologica*, 2a2ae, q. 182.

17. Could there not be an objective or perfectionist account of well-being, which characterizes well-being not in terms of desires, but in terms of developing human nature? I do not believe there is conceptual room for such an account, for I do not believe "well-being" has any meaning independent *both* of particular accounts of well-being *and* of the moral predicate "good." I do not see that "developing human nature constitutes well-being and is therefore good" says anything over and above "developing human nature is good," and prefer to confine perfectionism to the second, simpler claim.

18. Sidgwick, *The Methods of Ethics*, p. 11.

19. I here assume the modal axiom "If necessarily *p*, then necessarily necessarily *p*." This axiom characterizes the modal system S4 (and stronger systems) and is widely thought to state an intuitively plausible principle about necessity.

20. Kripke, *Naming and Necessity*, pp. 103–5.

21. Rawls, *A Theory of Justice*, p. 20.

22. Kripke, *Naming and Necessity*, pp. 123–25.

23. Putnam, "Is Semantics Possible?" and "The Meaning of 'Meaning," both in Putnam, *Mind, Language, and Reality*, Cambridge University Press, 1975.

24. Hempel, *Aspects of Scientific Explanation*, pp. 381–412.

25. See, for example, Brody, *Identity and Essence*, pp. 144–51.

26. Nietzsche, *Beyond Good and Evil*, sec. 36. Note that "intelligible character" is an Idealist synonym for "essence."

27. Some may deny that lower animals have intentions, as opposed to mere desires. If so, distinctively human psychology begins earlier than I claim.

28. Davidson, *Essays on Actions and Events*.

29. Davidson, "Mental Events," in *Essays on Actions and Events*, p. 222.

17 / DEREK PARFIT

What Makes Someone's Life Go Best?

What would be best for someone, or would be most in this person's interests, or would make this person's life go, for him, as well as possible? Answers to this question I call *theories about self-interest*. There are three kinds of theory. On *Hedonistic Theories*, what would be best for someone is what would make his life happiest. On *Desire-Fulfilment Theories*, what would be best for someone is what, throughout his life, would best fulfil his desires. On *Objective List Theories*, certain things are good or bad for us, whether or not we want to have the good things, or to avoid the bad things.

Narrow Hedonists assume, falsely, that pleasure and pain are two distinctive kinds of experience. Compare the pleasures of satisfying an intense thirst or lust, listening to music, solving an intellectual problem, reading a tragedy, and knowing that one's child is happy. These various experiences do not contain any distinctive common quality.

What pains and pleasures have in common are their relations to our desires. On the use of 'pain' which has rational and moral significance, all pains are when experienced unwanted, and a pain is worse or greater the more it is unwanted. Similarly, all pleasures are when experienced wanted, and they are better or greater the more they are wanted. These are the claims of *Preference-Hedonism*. On

Reprinted by permission of the publisher and copyright holder from Derek Parfit, *Reasons and Persons* (Oxford: Oxford University Press, 1984), pp. 493–502.

this view, one of two experiences is more pleasant if it is preferred.

This theory need not follow the ordinary uses of the words 'pain' and 'pleasure'. Suppose that I could go to a party to enjoy the various pleasures of eating, drinking, laughing, dancing, and talking to my friends. I could instead stay at home and read *King Lear*. Knowing what both alternatives would be like, I prefer to read *King Lear*. It extends the ordinary use to say that this would give me more pleasure. But on Preference-Hedonism, if we add some further assumptions given below, reading *King Lear* would give me a better evening. Griffin cites a more extreme case. Near the end of his life Freud refused pain-killing drugs, preferring to think in torment than to be confusedly euphoric. Of these two mental states, euphoria is more pleasant. But on Preference-Hedonism thinking in torment was, for Freud, a better mental state. It is clearer here not to stretch the meaning of the word 'pleasant'. A Preference-Hedonist should merely claim that, since Freud preferred to think clearly though in torment, his life went better if it went as he preferred.[1]

Consider next Desire-Fulfilment Theories. The simplest is the *Unrestricted* Theory. This claims that what is best for someone is what would best fulfil *all* of his desires, throughout his life. Suppose that I meet a stranger who has what is believed to be a fatal disease. My sympathy is aroused, and I strongly want this stranger to be cured. Much later, when I have forgotten our meeting, the stranger is cured. On the Unrestricted Desire-Fulfilment Theory, this event is good for me, and makes my life go better. This is not plausible. We should reject this theory.

Another theory appeals only to someone's desires about his own life. I call this the *Success Theory*. This theory differs from Preference-Hedonism in only one way. The Success Theory appeals to all of our preferences about our own lives. A Preference-Hedonist appeals only to preferences about those present features of our lives that are introspectively discernible. Suppose that I strongly want not to be deceived by other people. On Preference-Hedonism it would be better for me if I believe that I am not being deceived. It would be irrelevant if my belief is false, since this makes no difference to my state of mind. On the Success Theory, it would be worse for me if my belief is false. I have a strong desire about my own life—that I should not be deceived in this way. It is bad for me if this desire is not fulfilled, even if I falsely believe that it is.

When this theory appeals only to desires that are about our own lives, it may be unclear what this excludes. Suppose that I want my life to be such that all my desires, whatever their objects, are fulfilled. This may seem to make the Success Theory, when applied to me, coincide with the Unrestricted Desire-Fulfilment Theory. But a Success Theorist should claim that this desire is not really about my own life. This is like the distinction between a real change in some object, and a so-called *Cambridge-change*. An object undergoes a Cambridge-change if there is any change in the true statements that can be made about this object. Suppose that I cut my cheek while shaving. This causes a real change in me. It also causes a change in Confucius. It becomes true, of Confucius, that he lived on a planet in which later one more cheek was cut. This is merely a Cambridge-change.

Suppose that I am an exile, and cannot communicate with my children. I want their lives to go well. I might claim that I want to live the life of someone whose children's lives go well. A Success Theorist should again claim that this is not really a desire about my own life. If unknown to me one of my children is killed by an avalanche, this is not bad for me, and does not make my life go worse.

A Success Theorist *would* count some similar desires. Suppose that I try to give my children a good start in life. I try to give them the right education, good habits, and psychological strength. Once again, I am now an exile, and will never be able to learn what happens to my children. Suppose that, unknown to me, my children's lives go badly. One finds that the education that I gave him makes him unemployable, another has a mental breakdown, another becomes a petty thief. If my children's lives fail in these ways, and these failures are in part the result of mistakes I made as their parent, these failures in my children's lives would be judged to be bad for me on the Success Theory. One of my strongest desires was to be a successful parent. What is now happening to my children, though it is unknown to me, shows that this desire is not fulfilled. My life failed in one of the ways in which I most wanted it to succeed. Though I do not know this fact, it is bad for me, and makes it true that I have had a worse life. This is like the case where I strongly want not to be deceived. Even if I never know, it is bad for me both if I am deceived and if I turn out to be an unsuccessful parent. These are not introspectively discernible differences in my conscious life. On Preference-Hedonism, these events are not bad for me. On the Success Theory, they are.

Because they are thought by some to need special treatment. I mention next the desires that people have about what happens after they are dead. For a Preference-Hedonist, once I am dead, nothing bad can happen to me. A Success Theorist should deny this. Return to the case where all my children have wretched lives, because of the mistakes I made as their parent. Suppose that my children's lives all go badly only after I am dead. My life turns out to have been a failure, in the one of the ways I cared about most. A Success Theorist should claim that, here too, this makes it true that I had a worse life.

Some Success Theorists would reject this claim. Their theory ignores the desires of the dead. I believe this theory to be indefensible. Suppose that I was asked. 'Do you want it to be true that you were a successful parent even after you are dead?' I would answer 'Yes'. It is irrelevant to my desire whether it is fulfilled before or after I am dead. These Success Theorists count it as bad for me if my desire is not fulfilled, even if, because I am an exile, I never know this. How then can it matter whether, when my desire is not fulfilled. I am dead? All that my death does is to *ensure* that I will never know this. If we think it irrelevant that I never know about the non-fulfilment of my desire, we cannot defensibly claim that my death makes a difference.

I turn now to questions and objections which arise for both Preference-Hedonism and the Success Theory.

Should we appeal only to the desires and preferences that someone actually has? Return to my choice between going to a party or staying at home to read *King Lear*. Suppose that, knowing what both alternatives would be like, I choose to stay at home. And suppose that I never later regret this choice. On one theory, this shows that staying at home to read *King Lear* gave me a better evening. This is a mistake. It might be true that, if I had chosen to go to the party, I would never have regretted that choice. According to this theory, this would have shown that going to the party gave me a better evening. This theory thus implies that each alternative would have been better than the other. Since this theory implies such contradictions, it must be revised. The obvious revision is to appeal not only to my actual preferences, in the alternative I choose, but also to the preferences that I would have had if I had chosen otherwise.[2]

In this example, whichever alternative I choose, I would never regret this choice. If this is true, can we still claim that one of the alternatives would give me a better evening? On some theories, when in two alternatives I would have such contrary preferences, neither alternative is better or worse for me. This is not plausible when one of my contrary preferences would have been much stronger. Suppose that, if I choose to go to the party, I shall be only mildly glad that I made this choice, but that, if I choose to stay and read *King Lear*, I shall be extremely glad. If this is true, reading *King Lear* gives me a better evening.

Whether we appeal to Preference-Hedonism or the Success Theory, we should not appeal only to the desires or preferences that I actually have. We should also appeal to the desires and preferences that I would have had, in the various alternatives that were, at different times, open to me. One of these alternatives would be best for me if it is the one in which I would have the strongest desires and preferences fulfilled. This allows us to claim that some alternative life would have been better for me, even if throughout my actual life I am glad that I chose this life rather than this alternative.

There is another distinction which applies both to Preference-Hedonism and to the Success Theory. These theories are *Summative* if they appeal to all of someone's desires, actual and hypothetical, about his own life. In deciding which alternative would produce the greatest total net sum of desire-fulfilment, we assign some positive number to each desire that is fulfilled, and some negative number to each desire that is not fulfilled. How great these numbers are depends on the intensity of the desires in question. (In the case of the Success Theory, which appeals to past desires, it may also depend on how long these desires were had. As I suggest in Chapter 8, this may be a weakness in this theory. The issue does not arise for Preference-Hedonism, which appeals only to desires about one's present state of mind.) The total net sum of desire-fulfilment is the sum of the positive numbers minus the negative numbers. Provided that we can compare the relative strength of different desires, this calculation could in theory be performed. The choice of a unit for the numbers makes no difference to the result.

Another version of both theories does not appeal, in this way, to all of a person's desires and preferences about his own life. It appeals only to *global* rather than *local* desires and preferences. A preference is global if it is about some part of one's life considered as a whole, or is about one's whole life. The *Global* versions of these theories I believe to be more plausible.

Consider this example. Knowing that you accept a Summative theory, I tell you that I am about to make your life go better. I shall inject you with an addictive drug. From now on, you will wake each morning with an extremely strong desire to have another injection of this drug. Having this desire will be in itself neither pleasant nor painful, but if the desire is not fulfilled within an hour it would then become extremely painful. This is no cause for concern, since I shall give you ample supplies of this drug. Every morning, you will be able at once to fulfil this desire. The injection, and its after-effects, would also be neither pleasant nor painful. You will spend the rest of your days as you do now.

What would the Summative theories imply about this case? We can plausibly suppose that you would not welcome my proposal. You would prefer not to become addicted to this drug, even though I assure you that you will never lack supplies. We can also plausibly suppose that, if I go ahead, you will always regret that you became addicted to this drug. But it is likely that your initial desire not to become addicted, and your later regrets that you did, would not be as strong as the desires you have each morning for another injection. Given the facts as I described them, your reason to prefer not to become addicted would not be very strong. You might dislike the thought of being addicted to anything. And you would regret the minor inconvenience that would be involved in remembering always to carry with you, like a diabetic, sufficient supplies. But these desires might be far weaker than the desires you would have each morning for a fresh injection.

On the Summative Theories, if I make

you an addict, I would be increasing the sum-total of your desire-fulfilment. I would be causing one of your desires not to be fulfilled: your desire not to become an addict, which, after my act, becomes a desire to be cured. But I would also be giving you an indefinite series of extremely strong desires, one each morning, all of which you can fulfil. The fulfilment of all these desires would outweigh the non-fulfilment of your desires not to become an addict, and to be cured. On the Summative Theories, by making you an addict, I would be benefiting you—making your life go better.

This conclusion is not plausible. Having these desires, and having them fulfilled, are neither pleasant nor painful. We need not be Hedonists to believe, more plausibly, that it is in no way better for you to have and to fulfil this series of strong desires.

Could the Summative Theories be revised, so as to meet this objection? Is there some feature of the addictive desires which would justify the claim that we should ignore them when we calculate the sum total of your desire-fulfilment? We might claim that they can be ignored because they are desires that you would prefer not to have. But this is not an acceptable revision. Suppose that you are in great pain. You now have a very strong desire not to be in the state that you are in. On our revised theory, a desire does not count if you would prefer not to have this desire. This must apply to your intense desire not to be in the state you are in. You would prefer not to have this desire. If you did not dislike the state you are in, it would not be painful. Since our revised theory does not count desires that you would prefer not to have, it implies, absurdly, that it cannot be bad for you to be in great pain.

There may be other revisions which could meet these objections. But it is simpler to appeal to the Global versions of both Preference-Hedonism and the Success Theory. These appeal only to someone's desires about some part of his life, considered as a whole, or about his whole life. The Global Theories give us the right answer in the case where I make you an addict. You would prefer not to become addicted, and you would later prefer to cease to be addicted. These are the only preferences to which the Global Theories appeal. They ignore your particular desires each morning for a fresh injection. This is because you have yourself taken these desires into account in forming your global preference.

This imagined case of addiction is in its essentials similar to countless other cases. There are countless cases in which it is true both (1) that, if someone's life goes in one of two ways, this would increase the sum total of his local desire-fulfilment, but (2) that the other alternative is what he would globally prefer, *whichever* way his actual life goes.

Rather than describing another of the countless actual cases, I shall mention an imaginary case. This is the analogue, within one life, of the *Repugnant Conclusion* that I discuss in Part Four. Suppose that I could either have fifty of years of life of an extremely high quality, or an indefinite number of years that are barely worth living. In the first alternative, my fifty years would, on any theory, go extremely well. I would be very happy, would achieve great things, do much good, and love and be loved by many people. In the second alternative my life would always be, though not by much, worth living. There would be nothing bad about this life, and it would each day contain a few small pleasures.

On the Summative Theories, if the second life was long enough, it would be better for me. In each day within this life I have some desires about my life that are fulfilled. In the fifty years of the first alternative, there would be a very great sum of local desire-fulfilment. But this would be a finite sum, and in the end it would be outweighed by the sum of desire-fulfilment in my indefinitely long second alternative. A simpler way to put this point is this. The first alternative would be good. In the second alternative, since my life is worth living, living each extra day is good for me. If we merely add together whatever is good for me, some number of these extra days would produce the greatest total sum.

I do not believe that the second alternative would give me a better life. I therefore reject the Summative Theories. It is likely that, in both alternatives, I would globally prefer the first. Since the Global Theories would then imply that the first alternative gives me a better life, these theories seem to me more plausible.[3]

Turn now to the third kind of Theory that I mentioned: the Objective List Theory. According to this theory, certain things are good or bad for people, whether or not these people would want to have the good things, or to avoid the bad things. The good things might include moral goodness, rational activity, the development of one's abilities, having children and being a good parent, knowledge, and the awareness of true beauty. The bad things might include being betrayed, manipulated, slandered, deceived, being deprived of liberty or dignity, and enjoying either sadistic pleasure, or aesthetic pleasure in what is in fact ugly.[4]

An Objective List Theorist might claim that his theory coincides with the Global version of the Success Theory. On this theory, what would make my life go best depends on what I would prefer, now and in the various alternatives, if I knew all of the relevant facts about these alternatives. An Objective List Theorist might say that the most relevant facts are what his theory claims—what would in fact be good or bad for me. And he might claim that anyone who knew these facts would want what is truly good for him, and want to avoid what would be bad for him.

If this was true, though the Objective List Theory would coincide with the Success Theory, the two theories would remain distinct. A Success Theorist would reject this description of the coincidence. On his theory, nothing is good or bad for people, whatever their preferences are. Something is bad for someone only if, knowing the facts, he wants to avoid it. And the relevant facts do not include the alleged facts cited by the Objective List Theorist. On the Success Theory it is, for instance, bad for someone to be deceived if and because this is not what he wants. The Objective List Theorist makes the reverse claim. People want not to be deceived because this is bad for them.

As these remarks imply, there is one important difference between on the one hand Preference-Hedonism and the Success Theory, and on the other hand the Objective List Theory. The first two kinds of theory give an account of self-interest which is entirely factual, or which does not appeal to facts about value. The account appeals to what a person does and would prefer, given full knowledge of the purely non-evaluative facts about the alternatives. In contrast, the Objective List Theory appeals directly to facts about value.

In choosing between these theories, we must decide how much weight to give to imagined cases in which someone's fully informed preferences would be bizarre. If we can appeal to these cases, they cast doubt on both Preference-Hedonism and the Success Theory. Consider the man that Rawls imagined who wants to spend his life counting the numbers of blades of grass in different lawns. Suppose that this man knows that he could achieve great progress if instead he worked in some especially useful part of Applied Mathematics. Though he could achieve such significant results, he prefers to go on counting blades of grass. On the Success Theory, if we allow this theory to cover all imaginable cases, it could be better for this person if he counts his blades of grass rather than achieves great and beneficial results in Mathematics.

The counter-example might be more offensive. Suppose that what someone would most prefer, knowing the alternatives, is a life in which, without being detected, he causes as much pain as he can to other people. On the Success Theory, such a life would be what is best for this person.

We may be unable to accept these conclusions. Ought we therefore to abandon this theory? This is what Sidgwick did, though those who quote him seldom notice this. He suggests that 'a man's future good on the whole is what he would now desire and seek on the whole if all the consequences of all the different lines of conduct open to him were accurately foreseen and adequately realised in imagination at the present point of time'.[5] As he comments: 'The notion of "Good" thus attained has an ideal element: it is something that *is* not always actually desired and aimed at by human beings: but the ideal element is entirely interpretable in terms of *fact*, actual or hypothetical, and does not introduce any judgement of value'. Sidgwick then rejects this account, claiming that what is ultimately good for someone is what this person *would* desire if his desires were in harmony with reason. This last phrase is needed, Sidgwick thought, to exclude the cases where the someone's desires are irrational. He assumes that there are some things that we have good reason to desire, and others that we have good reason not to desire. These might be the things which are held to be good or bad for us by Objective List Theories.

Suppose we agree that, in some imagined cases, what someone would most want both now and later, fully knowing about the alternatives, would *not* be what would be best for him. If we accept this conclusion, it may seem that we must reject both Preference-Hedonism and the Success Theory. Perhaps, like Sidgwick, we must put constraints on what can be rationally desired.

It might be claimed instead that we can dismiss the appeal to such imagined cases. It might be claimed that what people would in fact prefer, if they knew the relevant facts, would always be something that we could accept as what is really good for them. Is this a good reply? If we agree that in the imagined cases what someone would prefer might be something that is bad for him, in these cases we have abandoned our theory. If this is so, can we defend our theory by saying that, in the actual cases, it would not go astray? I believe that this is not an adequate defence. But I shall not pursue this question here.

This objection may apply with less force

to Preference-Hedonism. On this theory, what can be good or bad for someone can only be discernible features of his conscious life. These are the features that, at the time, he either wants or does not want. I asked above whether it is bad for people to be deceived because they prefer not to be, or whether they prefer not to be deceived because this is bad for them. Consider the comparable question with respect to pain. Some have claimed that pain is intrinsically bad, and that this is why we dislike it. As I have suggested, I doubt this claim. After taking certain kinds of drug, people claim that the quality of their sensations has not altered, but they no longer dislike these sensations. We would regard such drugs as effective analgesics. This suggests that the badness of a pain consists in its being disliked, and that it is not disliked because it is bad. The disagreement between these views would need much more discussion. But, if the second view is better, it is more plausible to claim that whatever someone wants or does not want to experience—however bizarre we find his desires—should be counted as being for this person truly pleasant or painful, and as being for that reason good or bad for him. There may still be cases where it is plausible to claim that it would be bad for someone if he enjoys certain kinds of pleasure. This might be claimed, for instance, about sadistic pleasure. But there may be few such cases.

If instead we appeal to the Success Theory, we are not concerned only with the experienced quality of our conscious life. We are concerned with such things as whether we are achieving what we are trying to achieve, whether we are being deceived, and the like. When considering this theory, we can more often plausibly claim that, even if someone knew the facts, his preferences might go astray, and fail to correspond to what would be good or bad for him.

Which of these different theories should we accept? I shall not attempt an answer here. But I shall end by mentioning another theory, which might be claimed to combine what is most plausible in these conflicting theories. It is a striking fact that those who have addressed this question have disagreed so fundamentally. Many philosophers have been convinced Hedonists; many others have been as much convinced that Hedonism is a gross mistake.

Some Hedonists have reached their view as follows. They consider an opposing view, such as that which claims that what is good for someone is to have knowledge, to engage in rational activity, and to be aware of true beauty. These Hedonists ask, 'Would these states of mind be good, if they brought no enjoyment, and if the person in these states of mind had not the slightest desire that they continue?' Since they answer No, they conclude that the value of these states of mind must lie in their being liked, and in their arousing a desire that they continue.

This reasoning assumes that the value of a whole is just the sum of the value of its parts. If we remove the part to which the Hedonist appeals, what is left seems to have no value, hence Hedonism is the truth.

Suppose instead that we claim that the value of a whole may not be a mere sum of the value of its parts. We might then claim that what is best for people is a composite. It is not just their being in the conscious states that they want to be in. Nor is it just their having knowledge, engaging in rational activity, being aware of true beauty, and the like. What is good for someone is neither just what Hedonists claim, nor just what is claimed by Objective List Theorists. We might believe that if we had *either* of these, *without the other*, what we had would have little or no value. We might claim, for example, that what is good or bad for someone is to have knowledge, to be engaged in rational activity, to experience mutual love, and to be aware of beauty, while strongly wanting just these things. On this view, each side in this disagreement saw only half of the truth. Each put forward as sufficient something that was only necessary. Pleasure with many other kinds of object has no value. And, if they are entirely devoid of pleasure, there is no value in knowledge, rational activity, love, or the awareness of beauty. What is of value, or is good for someone, is to have both; to be engaged in these activities, and to be strongly wanting to be so engaged.

Notes

1. Griffin, J. P., 'Are There Incommensurable Values?', *Philosophy and Public Affairs 7*, No. 1, Fall 1977.

2. See "Prudence' by P. Bricker, *Journal of Philosophy*, July 1980.

3. See, for example, Moore, G. E., *Principia Ethica*, Cambridge University Press, 1903, and Ross, W. D., *The Foundations of Ethics*, Oxford: The Clarendon Press, 1939.

4. Sidgwick, H., *The Methods of Ethics*, London: MacMillan, 1907, pp. 111–12.

5. See Edwards, R. B., *Pleasures and Pains*, Ithaca, N.Y.: Cornell University Press, 1979, throughout. A similar suggestion is made by Plato in *The Philebus*. For a deeper discussion of the different theories about self-interest, see J. Griffin, *Well-Being*, Oxford: Oxford University Press, 1986.

Part III

VIRTUES AND ETHICS

18 / G. E. M. ANSCOMBE

MODERN MORAL PHILOSOPHY

I will begin by stating three theses which I present in this paper. The first is that it is not profitable for us at present to do moral philosophy; that should be laid aside at any rate until we have an adequate philosophy of psychology, in which we are conspicuously lacking. The second is that the concepts of obligation, and duty—*moral* obligation and *moral* duty, that is to say—and of what is *morally* right and wrong, and of the *moral* sense of "ought," ought to be jettisoned if this is psychologically possible; because they are survivals, or derivatives from survivals, from an earlier conception of ethics which no longer generally survives, and are only harmful without it. My third thesis is that the differences between the well-known English writers on moral philosophy from Sidgwick to the present day are of little importance.[1]

Anyone who has read Aristotle's *Ethics* and has also read modern moral philosophy must have been struck by the great contrasts between them. The concepts which are prominent among the moderns seem to be lacking, or at any rate buried or far in the background, in Aristotle. Most noticeably, the term "moral" itself, which we have by direct inheritance from Aristotle, just doesn't seem to fit, in its modern sense, into an account of Aristotelian ethics. Aristotle distinguishes virtues as moral and intellectual. Have some of what he calls "intellectual" virtues what *we* should call a "moral" aspect? It would seem so; the criterion is

presumably that a failure in an "intellectual" virtue—like that of having good judgment in calculating how to bring about something useful, say in municipal government—may be *blameworthy*. But—it may reasonably be asked—cannot *any* failure be made a matter of blame or reproach? Any derogatory criticism, say of the workmanship of a product or the design of a machine, can be called blame or reproach. So we want to put in the word "morally" again: sometimes such a failure may be *morally* blameworthy, sometimes not. Now has Aristotle got this idea of *moral* blame, as opposed to any other? If he has, why isn't it more central? There are some mistakes, he says, which are causes, not of involuntariness in actions, but of scoundrelism, and for which a man is blamed. Does this mean that there is a *moral* obligation not to make certain intellectual mistakes? Why doesn't he discuss obligation in general, and this obligation in particular? If someone professes to be expounding Aristotle and talks in a modern fashion about "moral" such-and-such, he must be very imperceptive if he does not constantly feel like someone whose jaws have somehow got out of alignment: the teeth don't come together in a proper bite.

We cannot, then, look to Aristotle for any elucidation of the modern way of talking about "moral" goodness, obligation, etc. And all the best-known writers on ethics in modern times, from Butler to Mill, appear to me to have faults as thinkers on the subject which make it impossible to hope for any direct light on it from them. I will state these objections with the brevity which their character makes possible.

Reprinted by permission of the publisher and copyright holder from *Philosophy* 33 (1958): 1–19.

Butler exalts conscience, but appears ignorant that a man's conscience may tell him to do the vilest things.

Hume defines "truth" in such a way as to exclude ethical judgments from it, and professes that he has proved that they are so excluded. He also implicitly defines "passion" in such a way that aiming at anything is having a passion. His objection to passing from "is" to "ought" would apply equally to passing from "is" to "owes" or from "is" to "needs." (However, because of the historical situation, he has a point here, which I shall return to.)

Kant introduces the idea of "legislating for oneself," which is as absurd as if in these days, when majority votes command great respect, one were to call each reflective decision a man made a *vote* resulting in a majority, which as a matter of proportion is overwhelming, for it is always 1–0. The concept of legislation requires superior power in the legislator. His own rigoristic convictions on the subject of lying were so intense that it never occurred to him that a lie could be relevantly described as anything but just a lie (e.g. as "a lie in such-and-such circumstances"). His rule about universalizable maxims is useless without stipulations as to what shall count as a relevant description of an action with a view to constructing a maxim about it.

Bentham and Mill do not notice the difficulty of the concept "pleasure." They are often said to have gone wrong through committing the "naturalistic fallacy"; but this charge does not impress me, because I do not find accounts of it coherent. But the other point—about pleasure—seems to me a fatal objection from the very outset. The ancients found this concept pretty baffling. It reduced Aristotle to sheer babble about "the bloom on the cheek of youth" because, for good reasons, he wanted to make it out both identical with and different from the pleasurable activity. Generations of modern philosophers found this concept quite unperplexing, and it reappeared in the literature as a problematic one only a year or two ago when Ryle wrote about it. The reason is simple: since Locke, pleasure was taken to be some sort of internal impression. But it was superficial, if that was the right account of it, to make it the point of actions. One might adapt something Wittgenstein said about "meaning" and say "Pleasure cannot be an internal impression, for no internal impression could have the consequences of pleasure."

Mill also, like Kant, fails to realize the necessity for stipulation as to relevant descriptions, if his theory is to have content. It did not occur to him that acts of murder and theft could be otherwise described. He holds that where a proposed action is of such a kind as to fall under some one principle established on grounds of utility, one must go by that; where it falls under none or several, the several suggesting contrary views of the action, the thing to do is to calculate particular consequences. But pretty well any action can be so described as to make it fall under a variety of principles of utility (as I shall say for short) if it falls under any.

I will now return to Hume. The features of Hume's philosophy which I have mentioned, like many other features of it, would incline me to think that Hume was a mere—brilliant—sophist; and his procedures are certainly sophistical. But I am forced, not to reverse, but to add to, this judgment by a peculiarity of Hume's philosophizing: namely that although he reaches his conclusions—with which he is in love—by sophistical methods, his considerations constantly open up very deep and important problems. It is often the case that in the act of exhibiting the sophistry one finds oneself noticing matters which deserve a lot of exploring: the obvious stands in need of investigation as a result of the points that Hume pretends to have made. In this, he is unlike, say, Butler. It was already well known that conscience could dictate vile actions; for Butler to have written disregarding this does not open up any new topics for us. But with Hume it is otherwise: hence he is a very profound and great philosopher, in spite of his sophistry. For example:

Suppose that I say to my grocer "Truth consists in *either* relations of ideas, as that

20s. = £1, *or* matters of fact, as that I ordered potatoes, you supplied them, and you sent me a bill. So it doesn't apply to such a proposition as that I *owe* you such-and-such a sum."

Now if one makes this comparison, it comes to light that the relation of the facts mentioned to the description "X owes Y so much money" is an interesting one, which I will call that of being "brute relative to" that description. Further, the "brute" facts mentioned here themselves have descriptions relative to which *other* facts are "brute"—as, e.g., *he had potatoes carted to my house* and *they were left there* are brute facts relative to "he supplied me with potatoes." And the fact X *owes Y money* is in turn "brute" relative to other descriptions—e.g. "X is solvent." Now the relation of "relative bruteness" is a complicated one. To mention a few points: if xyz is a set of facts brute relative to a description A, then xyz is a set out of a range some set among which holds if A holds; but the holding of some set among these does not necessarily entail A, because exceptional circumstances can always make a difference; and what are exceptional circumstances relatively to A can generally only be explained by giving a few diverse examples, and *no* theoretically adequate provision can be made for exceptional circumstances, since a further special context can theoretically always be imagined that would reinterpret any special context. Further, though in normal circumstances, xyz would be a justification for A, that is not to say that A just comes to the same as "xyz"; and also there is apt to be an institutional context which gives its point to the description A, of which institution A is of course not itself a description. (E.g. the statement that I give someone a shilling is not a description of the institution of money or of the currency of this country.) Thus, though it would be ludicrous to pretend that there can be no such thing as a transition from, e.g., "is" to "owes," the character of the transition is in fact rather interesting and comes to light as a result of reflecting on Hume's arguments.[2]

That I owe the grocer such-and-such a sum would be one of a set of facts which would be "brute" in relation to the description "I am a bilker." "Bilking" is of course a species of "dishonesty" or "injustice." (Naturally the consideration will not have any effect on my actions unless I want to commit or avoid acts of injustice.)

So far, in spite of their strong associations, I conceive "bilking," "injustice" and "dishonesty" in a merely "factual" way. That I can do this for "bilking" is obvious enough; "justice" I have no idea how to define, except that its sphere is that of actions which relate to someone else, but "injustice," its defect, can for the moment be offered as a generic name covering various species. E.g.: "bilking," "theft" (which is relative to whatever property institutions exist), "slander," "adultery," "punishment of the innocent."

In present-day philosophy an explanation is required how an unjust man is a bad man, or an unjust action a bad one; to give such an explanation belongs to ethics; but it cannot even be begun until we are equipped with a sound philosophy of psychology. For the proof that an unjust man is a bad man would require a positive account of justice as a "virtue." This part of the subject-matter of ethics is, however, completely closed to us until we have an account of what *type of characteristic* a virtue is—a problem, not of ethics, but of conceptual analysis—and how it relates to the actions in which it is instanced: a matter which I think Aristotle did not succeed in really making clear. For this we certainly need an account at least of what a human action is at all, and how its description as "doing such-and-such" is affected by its motive and by the intention or intentions in it; and for this an account of such concepts is required.

The terms "should" or "ought" or "needs" relate to good and bad: e.g. machinery needs oil, or should or ought to be oiled, in that running without oil is bad for it, or it runs badly without oil. According to this conception, of course, "should" and "ought" are not used in a special "moral" sense when one says that a man should not bilk. (In Aristotle's sense of the term "moral" (ἠθικός), they are being used in connection with a *moral* subject-matter: namely that of human passions and (non-technical) actions.) But they have now acquired a special so-called "moral" sense—i.e. a sense in which they imply some absolute verdict (like one of guilty/not guilty on a man) on what is described in the "ought" sentences used in certain types of context: not merely the contexts that *Aristotle* would call "moral"—passions and actions—but also some of the contexts that he would call "intellectual."

The ordinary (and quite indispensable) terms "should," "needs," "ought," "must"—acquired this special sense by being equated in the relevant contexts with "is obliged," or "is bound," or "is required to," in the sense in which one can be obliged or bound by law, or something can be required by law.

How did this come about? The answer is in history: between Aristotle and us came Christianity, with its *law* conception of ethics. For Christianity derived its ethical notions from the Torah. (One might be inclined to think that a law conception of ethics could arise only among people who accepted an allegedly divine positive law; that this is not so is shown by the example of the Stoics, who also thought that whatever was involved in conformity to human virtues was required by divine law.)

In consequence of the dominance of Christianity for many centuries, the concepts of being bound, permitted, or excused became deeply embedded in our language and thought. The Greek word "ἁμαρτάνειν," the aptest to be turned to that use, acquired the sense "sin," from having meant "mistake," "missing the mark," "going wrong." The Latin *peccatum* which roughly corresponded to ἁμαρτάνει was even apter for the sense "sin," because it was already associated with "culpa"—"guilt"—a juridical notion. The blanket term "illicit," "unlawful," meaning much the same as our blanket term "wrong," explains itself. It is interesting that Aristotle did not have such a blanket term. He has blanket terms for wickedness—"villain," "scoundrel"; but of course a man is not a villain or a scoundrel by the performance of one bad action, or a few bad actions. And he has terms like "disgraceful," "impious"; and specific terms signifying defect of the relevant virtue, like "unjust"; but no term corresponding to "illicit." The extension of this term (i.e. the range of its application) could be indicated in his terminology only by a quite lengthy sentence: that is "illicit" which, whether it is a thought or a consented-to passion or an action or an omission in thought or action, is something contrary to one of the virtues the lack of which shows a man to be bad *qua* man. That formulation would yield a concept co-extensive with the concept "illicit."

To have a *law* conception of ethics is to hold that what is needed for conformity with the virtues failure in which is the mark of being bad *qua* man (and not merely, say, *qua* craftsman or logician)—that what is needed for *this*, is required by divine law. Naturally it is not possible to have such a conception unless you believe in God as a law-giver; like Jews, Stoics, and Christians. But if such a conception is dominant for many centuries, and then is given up, it is a natural result that the concepts of "obligation," of being bound or required as by a law, should remain though they had lost their root; and if the word "ought" has become invested in certain contexts with the sense of "obligation," it too will remain to be spoken with a special emphasis and a special feeling in these contexts.

It is as if the notion "criminal" were to remain when criminal law and criminal courts had been abolished and forgotten. A Hume discovering this situation might conclude that there was a special sentiment, expressed by "criminal," which alone gave the word its sense. So Hume discovered the situation in which the notion "obligation" survived, and the notion "ought" was invested with that peculiar force having which it is said to be used in a "moral" sense, but in which the belief in divine law had long since been abandoned: for it was substantially given up among

Protestants at the time of the Reformation.[3] The situation, if I am right, was the interesting one of the survival of a concept outside the framework of thought that made it a really intelligible one.

When Hume produced his famous remarks about the transition from "is" to "ought," he was, then, bringing together several quite different points. One I have tried to bring out by my remarks on the transition from "is" to "owes" and on the relative "bruteness" of facts. It would be possible to bring out a different point by enquiring about the transition from "is" to "needs"; from the characteristics of an organism to the environment that it needs, for example. To say that it needs that environment is not to say, e.g., that you want it to have that environment, but that it won't flourish unless it has it. Certainly, it all depends whether you *want* it to flourish! as Hume would say. But what "all depends" on whether you want it to flourish is whether the fact that it needs that environment, or won't flourish without it, has the slightest influence on your actions, Now *that* such-and-such "ought" to be or "is needed" is supposed to have an influence on your actions: from which it seemed natural to infer that to judge that it "ought to be" was in fact to grant what you judged "ought to be" influence on your actions. And no amount of truth as to what *is* the case could possibly have a logical claim to have influence on your actions. (It is not judgment as such that sets us in motion; but our judgment on how to get or do something we *want*.) Hence it *must* be impossible to infer "needs" or "ought to be" from "is." But in the case of a plant, let us say, the inference from "is" to "needs" is certainly not in the least dubious. It is interesting and worth examining; but not at all fishy. Its interest is similar to the interest of the relation between brute and less brute facts: these relations have been very little considered. And while you can contrast "what it needs" with "what it's got"— like contrasting *de facto* and *de iure*—that does not make its needing this environment less of a "truth."

Certainly in the case of what the plant needs, the thought of a need will only affect action if you want the plant to flourish. Here, then, there is no necessary connection between what you can judge the plant "needs" and what you want. But there is some sort of necessary connection between what you think *you* need, and what you want. The connection is a complicated one; it is possible *not* to want something that you judge you need. But, e.g., it is not possible never to want *anything* that you judge you need. This, however, is not a fact about the meaning of the word "to need," but about the phenomenon of *wanting*. Hume's reasoning, we might say, in effect, leads one to think it must be about the word "to need," or "to be good for."

Thus we find two problems already wrapped up in the remark about a transition from "is" to "ought"; now supposing that we had clarified the "relative bruteness" of facts on the one hand, and the notions involved in "needing," and "flourishing" on the other—there would *still* remain a third point. For, following Hume, someone might say: Perhaps you have made out your point about a transition from "is" to "owes" and from "is" to "needs": but only at the cost of showing "owes" and "needs" sentences to express a *kind* of truths, a *kind* of facts. And it remains impossible to infer *"morally ought"* from "is" sentences.

This comment, it seems to me, would be correct. This word "ought," having become a word of mere mesmeric force, could not, in the character of having that force, be inferred from anything whatever. It may be objected that it could be inferred from other "morally ought" sentences: but that cannot be true. The appearance that this is so is produced by the fact that we say "All men are φ " and "Socrates is a man" implies "Socrates is φ." But here "φ" is a dummy predicate. We mean that if you substitute a real predicate for "φ" the implication is valid. A real predicate is required; not just a word containing no intelligible thought: a word retaining the suggestion of force, and apt to have a strong psychological effect, but which no longer signifies a real concept at all.

For its suggestion is one of a *verdict* on my action, according as it agrees or disagrees with the description in the "ought" sentence. And where one does not think there is a judge or a law, the notion of a verdict may retain its psychological effect, but not its meaning. Now imagine that just this word "verdict" *were* so used—with a characteristically solemn emphasis—as to retain its atmosphere but not its meaning, and someone were to say: "For a *verdict*, after all, you need a law and a judge." The reply might be made: "Not at all, for if there were a law and a judge who gave a verdict, the question for us would be whether accepting that verdict is something that there is a *verdict* on." This is an analogue of an argument which is so frequently referred to as decisive: If someone does have a divine law conception of ethics, all the same, he has to agree that he has to have a judgment that he *ought* (morally ought) to obey the divine law; so his ethic is in exactly the same position as any other: he merely has a "practical major premise"[4]: "Divine law ought to be obeyed" where someone else has, e.g., "The greatest happiness principle ought to be employed in all decisions."

I should judge that Hume and our present-day ethicists had done a considerable service by showing that no content could be found in the notion "morally ought"; if it were not that the latter philosophers try to find an alternative (very fishy) content and to retain the psychological force of the term. It would be most reasonable to drop it. It has no reasonable sense outside a law conception of ethics; they are not going to maintain such a conception; and you can do ethics without it, as is shown by the example of Aristotle. It would be a great improvement if, instead of "morally wrong," one always named a genus such as "untruthful," "unchaste," "unjust." We should no longer ask whether doing something was "wrong," passing directly from some description of an action to this notion; we should ask whether, e.g., it was unjust; and

the answer would sometimes be clear at once.

I now come to the epoch in modern English moral philosophy marked by Sidgwick. There is a startling change that seems to have taken place between Mill and Moore. Mill assumes, as we saw, that there is no question of calculating the particular consequences of an action such as murder or theft; and we saw too that his position was stupid, because it is not at all clear how an action *can* fall under just one principle of utility. In Moore and in subsequent academic moralists of England we find it taken to be pretty obvious that "the right action" is the action which produces the best possible consequences (reckoning among consequences the intrinsic values ascribed to certain kinds of act by some "Objectivists"[5]). Now it follows from this that a man does well, subjectively speaking, if he acts for the best in the particular circumstances according to his judgment of the total consequences of this particular action. I say that this follows, not that any philosopher has said precisely that. For discussion of these questions can of course get extremely complicated: e.g. it can be doubted whether "such-and-such is the right action" is a satisfactory formulation, on the grounds that things have to exist to have predicates—so perhaps the best formulation is "I am obliged"; or again, a philosopher may deny that "right" is a "descriptive" term, and then take a roundabout route through linguistic analysis to reach a view which comes to the same thing as "the right action is the one productive of the best consequences" (e.g. the view that you frame your "principles" to effect the end you choose to pursue, the connexion between "choice" and "best" being supposedly such that choosing reflectively means that you choose how to act so as to produce the best consequences); further, the roles of what are called "moral principles" and of the "motive of duty" have to be described; the differences between "good" and "morally good" and "right" need to be explored, the special characteristics of "ought" sentences investigated. Such discussions generate an appearance of significant diversity of views where what is really significant is an overall similarity. The overall similarity is made clear if you consider that every one of the best known English academic moral philosophers has put out a philosophy according to which, e.g., it is not possible to hold that it cannot be right to kill the innocent as a means to any end whatsoever and that someone who thinks otherwise is in error. (I have to mention both points; because Mr. Hare, for example, while teaching a philosophy which would encourage a person to judge that killing the innocent would be what he "ought" to choose for over-riding purposes, would also teach, I think, that if a man chooses to make avoiding killing the innocent for any purpose his "supreme practical principle," he cannot be impugned for error: that just is his "principle." But with that qualification, I think it can be seen that the point I have mentioned holds good of every single English academic moral philosopher since Sidgwick.) Now this is a significant thing: for it means that all these philosophies are quite incompatible with the Hebrew-Christian ethic. For it has been characteristic of that ethic to teach that there are certain things forbidden whatever *consequences* threaten, such as: choosing to kill the innocent for any purpose, however good; vicarious punishment; treachery (by which I mean obtaining a man's confidence in a grave matter by promises of trustworthy friendship and then betraying him to his enemies); idolatry; sodomy; adultery; making a false profession of faith. The prohibition of certain things simply in virtue of their description as such-and-such identifiable kinds of action, regardless of any further consequences, is certainly not the whole of the Hebrew-Christian ethic; but it is a noteworthy feature of it; and if every academic philosopher since Sidgwick has written in such a way as to exclude this ethic, it would argue a certain provinciality of mind not to see this incompatibility as the most important fact about these philoso-

phers, and the differences between them as somewhat trifling by comparison.

It is noticeable that none of these philosophers displays any consciousness that there is such an ethic, which he is contradicting: it is pretty well taken for obvious among them all that a prohibition such as that on murder does not operate in face of some consequences. But of course the strictness of the prohibition has as its point *that you are not to be tempted by fear or hope of consequences.*

If you notice the transition from Mill to Moore, you will suspect that it was made somewhere by someone; Sidgwick will come to mind as a likely name; and you will in fact find it going on, almost casually, in him. He is rather a dull author; and the important things in him occur in asides and footnotes and small bits of argument which are not concerned with his grand classification of the "methods of ethics." A divine law theory of ethics is reduced to an insignificant variety by a footnote telling us that "the best theologians" (God knows whom he meant) tell us that God is to be obeyed in his capacity of a *moral* being. ἡ φορτικός ὁ ἔπαινος; one seems to hear Aristotle saying: "Isn't the praise vulgar?"[6]—But Sidgwick *is* vulgar in that kind of way: he thinks, for example, that humility consists in underestimating your own merits—i.e. in a species of untruthfulness; and that the ground for having laws against blasphemy was that it was offensive to believers; and that to go accurately into the virtue of purity is to offend against its canons, a thing he reproves "medieval theologians" for not realizing.

From the point of view of the present enquiry, the most important thing about Sidgwick was his definition of intention. He defines intention in such a way that one must be said to intend any foreseen consequences of one's voluntary action. This definition is obviously incorrect, and I dare say that no one would be found to defend it now. He uses it to put forward an ethical thesis which would now be accepted by many people: the thesis that it does not make any difference to a man's responsibility for something that he foresaw, that he felt no desire for it, either as an end or as a means to an end. Using the language of intention more correctly, and avoiding Sidgwick's faulty conception, we may state the thesis thus: it does not make any difference to a man's responsibility for an effect of his action which he can foresee, that he does not intend it. Now this sounds rather edifying; it is I think quite characteristic of very bad degenerations of thought on such questions that they sound edifying. We can see what it amounts to by considering an example. Let us suppose that a man has a responsibility for the maintenance of some child. Therefore deliberately to withdraw support from it is a bad sort of thing for him to do. It would be bad for him to withdraw its maintenance because he didn't want to maintain it any longer; *and* also bad for him to withdraw it because by doing so he would, let us say, compel someone else to do something. (We may suppose for the sake of argument that compelling that person to do that thing is in itself quite admirable.) But now he has to choose between doing something disgraceful and going to prison; if he goes to prison, it will follow that he withdraws support from the child. By Sidgwick's doctrine, there is no difference in his responsibility for ceasing to maintain the child, between the case where he does it for its own sake or as a means to some other purpose, and when it happens as a foreseen and unavoidable consequence of his going to prison rather than do something disgraceful. It follows that he must weigh up the relative badness of withdrawing support from the child and of doing the disgraceful thing; and it may easily be that the disgraceful thing is in fact a less vicious action than intentionally withdrawing support from the child would be; if then the fact that withdrawing support from the child is a side effect of his going to prison does not make any difference to his responsibility, this consideration will incline him to do the disgraceful thing; which can still be pretty bad. And of course, once he has started to look at the matter in this light, the only rea-

sonable thing for him to consider will be the consequences and not the intrinsic badness of this or that action. So that, given that he judges reasonably that no *great* harm will come of it, he can do a much more disgraceful thing than deliberately withdrawing support from the child. And if his calculations turn out in fact wrong, it will appear that he was not responsible for the consequences, because he did not foresee them. For in fact Sidgwick's thesis leads to its being quite impossible to estimate the badness of an action except in the light of *expected* consequences. But if so, then *you* must estimate the badness in the light of the consequences *you* expect; and so it will follow that you can exculpate yourself from the *actual* consequences of the most disgraceful actions, so long as you can make out a case for not having foreseen them. Whereas I should contend that a man is responsible for the bad consequences of his bad actions, but gets no credit for the good ones; and contrariwise is not responsible for the bad consequences of good actions.

The denial of *any* distinction between foreseen and intended consequences, as far as responsibility is concerned, was not made by Sidgwick in developing any one "method of ethics"; he made this important move on behalf of everybody and just on its own account; and I think it plausible to suggest that *this* move on the part of Sidgwick explains the difference between old-fashioned Utilitarianism and that *consequentialism*, as I name it, which marks him and every English academic moral philosopher since him. By it, the kind of consideration which would formerly have been regarded as a temptation, the kind of consideration urged upon men by wives and flattering friends, was given a status by moral philosophers in their theories.

It is a necessary feature of consequentialism that it is a shallow philosophy. For there are always borderline cases in ethics. Now if you are either an Aristotelian, or a believer in divine law, you will deal with a borderline case by considering whether doing such-and-such in such-and-such circumstances is, say, murder, or is an act of injustice; and according as you decide it is or it isn't, you judge it to be a thing to do or not. This would be the method of casuistry; and while it may lead you to stretch a point on the circumference, it will not permit you to destroy the centre. But if you are a consequentialist, the question "What is it right to do in such-and-such circumstances?" is a stupid one to raise. The casuist raises such a question only to ask "Would it be *permissible* to do so-and-so?" or "Would it be permissible *not* to do so-and-so?" Only if it would *not* be permissible *not* to do so-and-so could he say *"This would be the thing to do."*[7] Otherwise, though he may speak *against* some action, he cannot prescribe any—for in an *actual* case, the circumstances (beyond the ones imagined) might suggest all sorts of possibilities, and you can't know in advance what the possibilities are going to be. Now the consequentialist has no footing on which to say "This would be permissible, this not"; because by his own hypothesis, it is the consequences that are to decide, and he has no business to pretend that he can lay it down what possible twists a man could give doing this or that; the most he can say is: a man must not *bring about* this or that; he has no right to say he will, in an actual case, bring about such-and-such unless he does so-and-so. Further, the consequentialist, in order to be imagining borderline cases at all, has of course to assume some sort of law or standard according to which this is a borderline case, Where then does he get the standard from? In practice the answer invariably is: from the standards current in his society or his circle. And it has in fact been the mark of all these philosophers that they have been extremely conventional; they have nothing in them by which to revolt against the conventional standards of their sort of people; it is impossible that they should be profound. But the chance that a whole range of conventional standards will be decent is small.—Finally, the point of considering hypothetical situations, perhaps very improbable ones, *seems* to be to elicit from yourself or someone else a hypothetical decision to do something of a bad kind. I don't doubt this has the effect of predisposing people—who will never get into the situations for which they have made hypothetical choices—to consent to similar bad actions, or to praise and flatter those who do them, so long as their crowd does so too, when the desperate circumstances imagined don't hold at all.

Those who recognize the origins of the notions of "obligation" and of the emphatic, "moral," *ought*, in the divine law conception of ethics, but who reject the notion of a divine legislator, sometimes look about for the possibility of retaining a law conception without a divine legislator. This search, I think, has some interest in it. Perhaps the first thing that suggests itself is the "norms" of a society. But just as one cannot be impressed by Butler when one reflects what conscience can tell people to do, so, I think, one cannot be impressed by this idea if one reflects what the "norms" of a society can be like. That legislation can be "for oneself" I reject as absurd; whatever you do "for yourself" may be admirable; but is not legislating. Once one sees this, one may say: I have to frame my own rules, and these are the best I can frame, and I shall go by them until I know something better: as a man might say "I shall go by the customs of my ancestors." Whether this leads to good or evil will depend on the *content* of the rules or of the customs of one's ancestors. If one is lucky it will lead to good. Such an attitude would be hopeful in this at any rate: it seems to have in it some Socratic doubt where, from having to fall back on such expedients, it should be clear that Socratic doubt is good; in fact rather generally it must be good for anyone to think "Perhaps in some way I can't see, I may be on a bad path, perhaps I am hopelessly wrong in some essential way".—The search for "norms" might lead someone to look for laws of nature, as if the universe were a legislator; but in the present day this is not likely to lead to good results: it might lead one to eat the weaker according to the laws of nature, but would hardly lead anyone nowadays to notions of justice; the pre-Socratic feeling about justice as comparable to the balance or harmony which kept things going is very remote to us.

There is another possibility here: "obligation" may be contractual. Just as we look at the law to find out what a man subject to it is required by it to do, so we look at a contract to find out what the man who has made it is required by it to do. Thinkers, admittedly remote from us, might have the idea of a *foedus rerum*, of the universe not as a legislator but as the embodiment of a contract. Then if you could find out what the contract was, you would learn your obligations under it. Now, you cannot be under a law unless it has been promulgated to you; and the thinkers who believed in "natural divine law" held that it was promulgated to every grown man in his knowledge of good and evil. Similarly you cannot be in a contract without having contracted, i.e. given signs of entering upon the contract. Just possibly, it might be argued that the use of language which one makes in the ordinary conduct of life amounts in some sense to giving the signs of entering into various contracts. If anyone had this theory, we should want to see it worked out. I suspect that it would be largely formal; it might be possible to construct a system embodying the law (whose status might be compared to that of "laws" of logic): "what's sauce for the goose is sauce for the gander," but hardly one descending to such particularities as the prohibition on murder or sodomy. Also, while it is clear that you can be subject to a law that you do not acknowledge and have not thought of as law, it does not seem reasonable to say that you can enter upon a contract without knowing that you are doing so; such ignorance is usually held to be destructive of the nature of a contract.

It might remain to look for "norms" in human virtues: just as *man* has so many teeth, which is certainly not the average number of teeth men have, but is the number of teeth for the species, so perhaps the species *man*, regarded not just biologically, but from the point of view of the activity of thought and choice in regard to the various departments of life—powers and faculties and use of things needed—"has" such-and-such virtues: and this "man" with the complete set of virtues is the "norm," as "man" with, e.g., a complete set of teeth is a norm. But in *this* sense "norm" has ceased to be roughly equivalent to "law." In *this* sense the notion of a "norm" brings us nearer to an Aristotelian than a law conception of ethics. There is, I think, no harm in that; but if someone looked in this direction to give "norm" a sense, then he ought to recognize what has happened to the notion "norm," which he wanted to mean "law—without bringing God in"—it has ceased to mean "law" at all; and *so* the notions of "moral obligation," "the moral ought," and "duty" are best put on the Index, if he can manage it.

But meanwhile—is it not clear that there are several concepts that need investigating simply as part of the philosophy of psychology and,—as I should recommend—*banishing ethics totally* from our minds? Namely—to begin with: "action," "intention," "pleasure," "wanting." More will probably turn up if we start with these. Eventually it might be possible to advance to considering the concept "virtue"; with which, I suppose, we should be beginning some sort of a study of ethics.

I will end by describing the advantages of using the word "ought" in a non-emphatic fashion, and not in a special "moral" sense; of discarding the term "wrong" in a "moral" sense, and using such notions as "unjust."

It is possible, if one is allowed to proceed just by giving examples, to distinguish between the intrinsically unjust, and what is unjust given the circumstances. To arrange to get a man judicially punished for something which it can be clearly seen he has not done is intrinsically unjust. This might be done, of course, and often has been done, in all sorts of ways; by suborning false witnesses, by a rule of law by which something is "deemed" to be the case which is admittedly not the case as a matter of fact, and by open insolence on the part of the judges and powerful people when they more or less openly say: "A fig for the fact that you did not do it; we mean to sentence you for it all the same." What is unjust given, e.g., normal circumstances is to deprive people of their ostensible property without legal procedure, not to pay debts, not to keep contracts, and a host of other things of the kind. Now, the circumstances can clearly make a great deal of difference in estimating the justice or injustice of such procedures as these; and these circumstances may *sometimes* include expected consequences; for example, a man's claim to a bit of property can become a nullity when its seizure and use can avert some obvious disaster: as, e.g., if you could use a machine of his to produce an explosion in which it would be destroyed, but by means of which you could divert a flood or make a gap which a fire could not jump. Now this certainly does not mean that what would ordinarily be an act of injustice, but is not intrinsically unjust, can always be rendered just by a reasonable calculation of better consequences; far from it; but the problems that would be raised in an attempt to draw a boundary line (or boundary area) here are obviously complicated. And while there are certainly some general remarks which ought to be made here, and some boundaries that can be drawn, the decision on particular cases would for the most part be determined κατὰ τὸν ὀρθὸν λόγον "according to what's reasonable."— E.g. that *such-and-such* a delay of payment of a *such-and-such* debt to a person *so* circumstanced, on the part of a person *so* circumstanced, would or would not be unjust, is really only to be decided "according to what's reasonable"; and for this there can *in principle* be no canon other than giving a few examples. That is to say, while it is because of a big gap in philosophy that we can give no general account of the concept of virtue and of the concept of justice, but have to proceed, using the concepts, only by giving examples; still there is an area where it is not because of any gap, but is in principle the case, that there is no ac-

count except by way of examples: and that is where the canon is "what's reasonable": which of course is *not* a canon.

That is all I wish to say about what is just in some circumstances, unjust in others; and about the way in which expected consequences can play a part in determining what is just. Returning to my example of the intrinsically unjust: if a procedure *is* one of judicially punishing a man for what he is clearly understood not to have done, there can be absolutely no argument about the description of this as unjust. No circumstances, and no expected consequences, which do *not* modify the description of the procedure as one of judicially punishing a man for what he is known not to have done can modify the description of it as unjust. Someone who attempted to dispute this would only be pretending not to know what "unjust" means: for this is a paradigm case of injustice.

And here we see the superiority or the term "unjust" over the terms "morally right" and "morally wrong." For in the context of English moral philosophy since Sidgwick it appears legitimate to discuss whether it *might* be "morally right" in some circumstances to adopt that procedure; but it cannot be argued that the procedure would in any circumstance be just.

Now I am not able to do the philosophy involved—and I think that no one in the present situation of English philosophy *can* do the philosophy involved—but it is clear that a good man is a just man; and a just man is a man who habitually refuses to commit or participate in any unjust actions for fear of any consequences, or to obtain any advantage, for himself or anyone else. Perhaps no one will disagree. But, it will be said, what *is* unjust is sometimes determined by expected consequences; and certainly that is true. But there are cases where it is not: now if someone says, "I agree, but all this wants a lot of explaining," then he is right, and, what is more, the situation at present is that we can't do the explaining; we lack the philosophic equipment. But if someone really thinks, *in advance*,[8] that it is open to question whether such an action as procuring the judicial execution of the innocent should be quite excluded from consideration—I do not want to argue with him; he shows a corrupt mind.

In such cases our moral philosophers seek to impose a dilemma upon us. "If we have a case where the term 'unjust' applies purely in virtue of a factual description, can't one raise the question whether one sometimes conceivably ought to do injustice? If 'what is unjust' is determined by consideration of whether it is right to do so-and-so in such-and-such circumstances, then the question whether it is 'right' to commit injustice can't arise, just because 'wrong' has been built into the definition of injustice. But if we have a case where the description 'unjust' applies purely in virtue of the facts, without bringing 'wrong' in, then the question can arise whether one 'ought' perhaps to commit an injustice, whether it might not be 'right' to? And of course 'ought' and 'right' are being used in their *moral* senses here. Now either you must decide what is 'morally right' in the light of certain *other* 'principles,' or you make a 'principle' about *this* and decide that an injustice is never 'right'; but even if you do the latter you are going beyond the facts; you are making a decision that you will not, or that it is wrong to, commit injustice. But in either case, *if* the term 'unjust' is determined simply by the facts, it is not the term 'unjust' that determines that the term 'wrong' applies, but a decision that injustice is *wrong*, together with the diagnosis of the 'factual' description as entailing injustice. But the man who makes an absolute decision that injustice is 'wrong' has no footing on which to criticize someone who does *not* make that decision as judging falsely."

In this argument "wrong" of course is explained as meaning "morally wrong," and all the atmosphere of the term is retained while its substance is guaranteed quite null. Now let us remember that "morally wrong" is the term which is the heir of the notion "illicit," or "what there is an obligation *not* to do"; which belongs in a divine law theory or ethics. Here it re-

ally does add something to the description "unjust" to say there is an obligation not to do it; for what obliges is the divine law— as rules oblige in a game. So if the divine law obliges not to commit injustice by forbidding injustice, it really does add something to the description "unjust" to say there is an obligation not to do it, And it is because "morally wrong" is the heir of this concept, but an heir that is cut off from the family of concepts from which it sprang, that "morally wrong" *both* goes beyond the mere factual description "unjust" *and* seems to have no discernible content except a certain compelling force, which I should call purely psychological. And such is the force of the term that philosophers actually suppose that the divine law notion can be dismissed as making no essential difference even if it is held—*because* they think that a "practical principle" running "I *ought* (i.e. am morally obliged) to obey divine laws" is required for the man who believes in divine laws. But actually this notion of obligation is a notion which only operates in the context of law. And I should be inclined to congratulate the present-day moral philosophers on depriving "morally ought" of its now delusive appearance of content, if only they did not manifest a detestable desire to retain the atmosphere of the term.

It may be possible, if we are resolute, to discard the notion "morally ought," and simply return to the ordinary "ought", which, we ought to notice, is such an extremely frequent term of human language that it is difficult to imagine getting on without it. Now if we do return to it, can't it reasonably be asked whether one might ever need to commit injustice, or whether it won't be the best thing to do? Of course it can. And the answers will be various. One man—a philosopher—may say that since justice is a virtue, and injustice a vice, and virtues and vices are built up by the performances of the action in which they are instanced, an act of injustice will tend to make a man bad; and essentially the flourishing of a man *qua* man consists in his being good (e.g. in virtues); but for any X to which such terms apply, X needs what makes it flourish, so a man needs, or ought to perform, only virtuous actions; and even if, as it must be admitted may happen, he flourishes less, or not at all, in inessentials, by avoiding injustice, his life is spoiled in essentials by not avoiding injustice—so he still needs to perform only just actions. That is roughly how Plato and Aristotle talk; but it can be seen that philosophically there is a huge gap, at present unfillable as far as we are concerned, which needs to be filled by an account of human nature, human action, the type of characteristic a virtue is, and above all of human "flourishing." And it is the last concept that appears the most doubtful. For it is a bit much to swallow that a man in pain and hunger and poor and friendless is "flourishing," as Aristotle himself admitted. Further, someone might say that one at least needed to stay alive to "flourish." Another man unimpressed by all that will say in a hard case "What we need is such-and-such, which we won't get without doing this (which is unjust)—so this is what we ought to do." Another man, who does not follow the rather elaborate reasoning of the philosophers, simply says "I know it is in any case a disgraceful thing to say that one had better commit this unjust action." The man who believes in divine laws will say perhaps "It is forbidden, and however it looks, it cannot be to anyone's profit to commit injustice"; he like the Greek philosophers can think in terms of "flourishing." If he is a Stoic, he is apt to have a decidedly strained notion of what "flourishing consists" in; if he is a Jew or Christian, he need not have any very distinct notion: the way it will profit him to abstain from injustice is something that he leaves it to God to determine, himself only saying "It can't do me any good to go against his law." (But he also hopes for a great reward in a new life later on, e.g. at the coming of Messiah; but in this he is relying on special promises.)

It is left to modern moral philosophy—the moral philosophy of all the well-known English ethicists since Sidgwick—to construct systems according to which the man who says "We need such-and-such, and will only get it this way" *may* be a virtuous character: that is to say, it is left open to debate whether such a procedure as the judicial punishment of the innocent may not in some circumstances be the "right" one to adopt; and though the present Oxford moral philosophers would accord a man *permission* to "make it his principle" not to do such a thing, they teach a philosophy according to which the particular consequences of such an action *could* "morally" be taken into account by a man who was debating what to do; and if they were such as to conflict with his "ends," it might be a step in his moral education to frame a moral principle under which he "managed" (to use Mr. Nowell-Smith's phrase[9]) to bring the action; or it might be a new "decision of principle," making which was an advance in the formation of his moral thinking (to adopt Mr. Hare's conception), to decide: in such-and-such circumstances one ought to procure the judicial condemnation of the innocent. And that is my complaint.

Notes

1. This paper was originally read to the Voltaire Society in Oxford.

2. The above two paragraphs are an abstract of a paper "On Brute Facts" forthcoming in *Analysis*.

3. They did not deny the existence of divine law; but their most characteristic doctrine was that it was given, not to be obeyed, but to show man's incapacity to obey it, even by grace; and this applied not merely to the ramified prescriptions of the Torah, but to the requirements of "natural divine law." Cf. in this connection the decree of Trent against the teaching that Christ was only to be trusted in as mediator, not obeyed as legislator.

4. As it is absurdly called. Since major premise = premise containing the term

which is predicate in the conclusion, it is a solecism to speak of it in the connection with practical reasoning.

5. Oxford Objectivists of course distinguish between "consequences" and "intrinsic values" and so produce a misleading appearance of not being "consequentialists." But they do not hold—and Ross explicitly denies—that the gravity of, e.g., procuring the condemnation of the innocent is such that it cannot be outweighed by, e.g., national interest. Hence their distinction is of no importance.

6. E.N. 1178b16.

7. Necessarily a rare case: for the positive precepts, e.g. "Honour your parents," hardly ever prescribe, and seldom even necessitate, any particular action.

8. If he thinks it in the concrete situation, he is of course merely a normally tempted human being. In discussion when this paper was read, as was perhaps to be expected, this case was produced: a government is required to have an innocent man tried, sentenced and executed under threat of a "hydrogen bomb war." It would seem strange to me to have much hope of so averting a war threatened by such men as made this demand. But the most important thing about the way in which cases like this are invented in discussions, is the assumption that only two courses are open: here, compliance and open defiance. No one can say in advance of such a situation what the possibilities are going to be—e.g. that there is none of stalling by a feigned willingness to comply, accompanied by a skillfully arranged "escape" of the victim.

9. *Ethics*, p. 308.

19 / PHILIPPA FOOT

Virtues and Vices

For many years the subject of the virtues and vices was strangely neglected by moralists working within the school of analytic philosophy. The tacitly accepted opinion was that a study of the topic would form no part of the fundamental work of ethics; and since this opinion was apparently shared by philosophers such as Hume, Kant, Mill, G. E. Moore, W. D. Ross, and H. A. Prichard, from whom contemporary moral philosophy has mostly been derived, perhaps the neglect was not so surprising after all. However that may be, things have recently been changing. During the past ten or fifteen years several philosophers have turned their attention to the subject; notably G. H. von Wright and Peter Geach. Von Wright devoted a not at all perfunctory chapter to the virtues in his book *The Varieties of Goodness*[1] published in 1963, and Peter Geach's book called *The Virtues*[2] appeared in 1977. Meanwhile a number of interesting articles on the topic have come out in the journals.

In spite of this recent work, it is best when considering the virtues and vices to go back to Aristotle and Aquinas. I myself have found Plato less helpful, because the individual virtues and vices are not so clearly or consistently distinguished in his work. It is certain, in any case, that the most systematic account is found in Aristotle, and in the blending of Aristotelian and Christian philosophy found in St. Thomas. By and large Aquinas followed Aristotle—

Reprinted by permission of the author from *Virtues and Vices* (Berkeley: University of California Press, 1978), pp. 1–18.

sometimes even heroically—where Aristotle gave an opinion, and where St. Thomas is on his own, as in developing the doctrine of the theological virtues of faith, hope and charity, and in his theocentric doctrine of happiness, he still uses an Aristotelian framework where he can: as for instance in speaking of happiness as man's last end. However, there are different emphases and new elements in Aquinas's ethics: often he works things out in far more detail than Aristotle did, and it is possible to learn a great deal from Aquinas that one could not have got from Aristotle. It is my opinion that the *Summa Theologica* is one of the best sources we have for moral philosophy, and moreover that St. Thomas's ethical writings are as useful to the atheist as to the Catholic or other Christian believer.

There is, however, one minor obstacle to be overcome when one goes back to Aristotle and Aquinas for help in constructing a theory of virtues, namely a lack of coincidence between their terminology and our own. For when we talk about the virtues we are not taking as our subject everything to which Aristotle gave the name *aretē* or Aquinas *virtus*, and consequently not everything called a virtue in translations of these authors. 'The virtues' to us are the moral virtues whereas *aretē* and *virtus* refer also to arts, and even to excellences of the speculative intellect whose domain is theory rather than practice. And to make things more confusing we find some dispositions called moral virtues in translations from the Greek and Latin, although the class of virtues that Aristotle calls *aretai ēthikai* and Aquinas *virtutes morales* does not exactly correspond with our class of moral virtues. For us there are four cardinal moral virtues: courage, temperance, wisdom and justice. But Aristotle and Aquinas call only three of these virtues moral virtues; practical wisdom (Aristotle's *phronēsis* and Aquinas's *prudentia*) they class with the intellectual virtues, though they point out the close connexions between practical wisdom and what they call moral virtues; and sometimes they even use *aretē* and *virtus* very much as we use 'virtue'.

I will come back to Aristotle and Aquinas, and shall indeed refer to them frequently in this paper. But I want to start by making some remarks, admittedly fragmentary, about the concept of a moral virtue as we understand the idea.

First of all it seems clear that virtues are, in some general way, beneficial. Human beings do not get on well without them. Nobody can get on well if he lacks courage, and does not have some measure of temperance and wisdom, while communities where justice and charity are lacking are apt to be wretched places to live, as Russia was under the Stalinist terror, or Sicily under the Mafia. But now we must ask to whom the benefit goes, whether to the man who has the virtue or rather to those who have to do with him? In the case of some of the virtues the answer seems clear. Courage, temperance and wisdom benefit both the man who has these dispositions and other people as well; and moral failings such as pride, vanity, worldliness, and avarice harm both their possessor and others, though chiefly perhaps the former. But what about the virtues of charity and justice? These are directly concerned with the welfare of others, and with what is owed to them; and since each may require sacrifice of interest on the part of the virtuous man both may seem to be deleterious to their possessor and beneficial to others. Whether in fact it is so has, of course, been a matter of controversy since Plato's time or earlier. It is a reasonable opinion that on the whole a man is better off for being char-

itable and just, but this is not to say that circumstances may not arise in which he will have to sacrifice everything for charity or justice.

Nor is this the only problem about the relation between virtue and human good. For one very difficult question concerns the relation between justice and the common good. Justice, in the wide sense in which it is understood in discussions of the cardinal virtues, and in this paper, has to do with that to which someone has a right— that which he is owed in respect of non-interference and positive service—and rights may stand in the way of the pursuit of the common good. Or so at least it seems to those who reject utilitarian doctrines. This dispute cannot be settled here, but I shall treat justice as a virtue independent of charity, and standing as a possible limit on the scope of that virtue.

Let us say then, leaving unsolved problems behind us, that virtues are in general beneficial characteristics, and indeed ones that a human being needs to have, for his own sake and that of his fellows. This will not, however, take us far towards a definition of a virtue, since there are many other qualities of a man that may be similarly beneficial, as for instance bodily characteristics such as health and physical strength, and mental powers such as those of memory and concentration. What is it, we must ask, that differentiates virtues from such things?

As a first approximation to an answer we might say that while health and strength are excellences of the body, and memory and concentration of the mind, it is the will that is good in a man of virtue. But this suggestion is worth only as much as the explanation that follows it. What might we mean by saying that virtue belongs to the will?

In the first place we observe that it is primarily by his intentions that a man's moral dispositions are judged. If he does something unintentionally this is usually irrelevant to our estimate of his virtue. But of course this thesis must be qualified, because failures in performance rather than intention may show a lack of virtue. This will be so when, for instance, one man brings harm to another without realising he is doing it, but where his ignorance is itself culpable. Sometimes in such cases there will be a previous act or omission to which we can point as the source of the ignorance. Charity requires that we take care to find out how to render assistance where we are likely to be called on to do so, and thus, for example, it is contrary to charity to fail to find out about elementary first aid. But in an interesting class of cases in which it seems again to be performance rather than intention that counts in judging a man's virtue there is no possibility of shifting the judgement to previous intentions. For sometimes one man succeeds where another fails not because there is some specific difference in their previous conduct but rather because his heart lies in a different place; and the disposition of the heart is part of virtue.

Thus it seems right to attribute a kind of moral failing to some deeply discouraging and debilitating people who say, without lying, that they mean to be helpful; and on the other side to see virtue *par excellence* in one who is prompt and resourceful in doing good. In his novel *A Single Pebble* John Hersey describes such a man, speaking of a rescue in a swift flowing river:

It was the head tracker's marvellous swift response that captured my admiration at first, his split second solicitousness when he heard a cry of pain, his finding in mid-air, as it were, the only way to save the injured boy. But there was more to it than that. His action, which could not have been mulled over in his mind, showed a deep, instinctive love of life, a compassion, an optimism, which made me feel very good. . . .

What this suggests is that a man's virtue may be judged by his innermost desires as well as by his intentions; and this fits with our idea that a virtue such as generosity lies as much in someone's attitudes as in his actions. Pleasure in the good fortune of others is, one thinks, the sign of a generous spirit; and small reactions of pleasure and displeasure often the surest signs of a man's moral disposition.

None of this shows that it is wrong to think of virtues as belonging to the will; what it does show is that 'will' must here be understood in its widest sense, to cover what is wished for as well as what is sought.

A different set of considerations will, however, force us to give up any simple statement about the relation between virtue and will, and these considerations have to do with the virtue of wisdom. Practical wisdom, we said, was counted by Aristotle among the intellectual virtues, and while our *wisdom* is not quite the same as *phronēsis* or *prudentia* it too might seem to belong to the intellect rather than the will. Is not wisdom a matter of knowledge, and how can knowledge be a matter of intention or desire? The answer is that it isn't, so that there is good reason for thinking of wisdom as an intellectual virtue. But on the other hand wisdom has special connexions with the will, meeting it at more than one point.

In order to get this rather complex picture in focus we must pause for a little and ask what it is that we ourselves understand by wisdom: what the wise man knows and what he does. Wisdom, as I see it, has two parts. In the first place the wise man knows the means to certain good ends; and secondly he knows how much particular ends are worth. Wisdom in its first part is relatively easy to understand. It seems that there are some ends belonging to human life in general rather than to particular skills such as medicine or boatbuilding, ends having to do with such matters as friendship, marriage, the bringing up of children, or the choice of ways of life; and it seems that knowledge of how to act well in these matters belongs to some people but not to others. We call those who have this knowledge wise, while those who do not have it are seen as lacking wisdom. So, as both Aristotle and Aquinas insisted, wisdom is to be contrasted with cleverness because cleverness is the ability to take the right steps to any end, whereas wisdom is related only to good ends, and to human life in general rather than to the ends of particular arts.

Moreover, we should add, there belongs to wisdom only that part of knowledge which is within the reach of any ordinary adult human being: knowledge that can be acquired only by someone who is clever or who has access to special training is not counted as part of wisdom, and would not be so counted even if it could serve the ends that wisdom serves. It is therefore quite wrong to suggest that wisdom cannot be a moral virtue because virtue must be within the reach of anyone who really wants it and some people are too stupid to be anything but ignorant even about the most fundamental matters of human life. Some people are wise without being at all clever or well informed: they make good decisions and they know, as we say, 'what's what'.

In short wisdom, in what we called its first part, is connected with the will in the following ways. To begin with it presupposes good ends: the man who is wise does not merely know *how* to do good things such as looking after his children well, or strengthening someone in trouble, but must also want to do them. And then wisdom, in so far as it consists of knowledge which anyone can gain in the course of an ordinary life, is available to anyone who really wants it. As Aquinas put it, it belongs 'to a power under the direction of the will'.[3]

The second part of wisdom, which has to do with values, is much harder to describe, because here we meet ideas which are curiously elusive, such as the thought that some pursuits are more worthwhile than others, and some matters trivial and some important in human life. Since it makes good sense to say that most men waste a lot of their lives in ardent pursuit of what is trivial and unimportant it is not possible to explain the important and the trivial in terms of the amount of attention given to different subjects by the average man. But I have never seen, or been able to think out, a true account of this matter, and

I believe that a complete account of wisdom, and of certain other virtues and vices must wait until this gap can be filled. What we can see is that one of the things a wise man knows and a foolish man does not is that such things as social position, and wealth, and the good opinion of the world, are too dearly bought at the cost of health or friendship or family ties. So we may say that a man who lacks wisdom 'has false values', and that vices such as vanity and worldliness and avarice are contrary to wisdom in a special way. There is always an element of false judgement about these vices, since the man who is vain for instance sees admiration as more important than it is, while the worldly man is apt to see the good life as one of wealth and power. Adapting Aristotle's distinction between the weak-willed man (the akratēs) who follows pleasure though he knows, in some sense, that he should not, and the licentious man (the akolastos) who sees the life of pleasure as the good life,[4] we may say that moral failings such as these are never purely 'akratic'. It is true that a man may criticise himself for his worldliness or vanity or love of money, but then it is his values that are the subject of his criticism.

Wisdom in this second part is, therefore, partly to be described in terms of apprehension, and even judgement, but since it has to do with a man's attachments it also characterises his will.

The idea that virtues belong to the will, and that this helps to distinguish them from such things as bodily strength or intellectual ability has, then, survived the consideration of the virtue of wisdom, albeit in a fairly complex and slightly attenuated form. And we shall find this idea useful again if we turn to another important distinction that must be made, namely that between virtues and other practical excellences such as arts and skills.

Aristotle has sometimes been accused, for instance by von Wright, of failing to see how different virtues are from arts or skills;[5] but in fact one finds, among the many things that Aristotle and Aquinas say about this difference, the observation that seems to go the heart of the matter. In the matter of arts and skills, they say, voluntary error is preferable to involuntary error, while in the matter of virtues (what we call virtues) it is the reverse.[6] The last part of the thesis is actually rather hard to interpret, because it is not clear what is meant by the idea of involuntary viciousness. But we can leave this aside and still have all we need in order to distinguish arts or skills from virtues. If we think, for instance, of someone who deliberately makes a spelling mistake (perhaps when writing on the blackboard in order to explain this particular point) we see that this does not in any way count against his skill as a speller: 'I did it deliberately' rebuts an accusation of this kind. And what we can say without running into any difficulties is that there is no comparable rebuttal in the case of an accusation relating to lack of virtue. If a man acts unjustly or uncharitably, or in a cowardly or intemperate manner, 'I did it deliberately' cannot on any interpretation lead to exculpation. So, we may say, a virtue is not, like a skill or an art, a mere capacity: it must actually engage the will.

II

I shall now turn to another thesis about the virtues, which I might express by saying that they are *corrective*, each one standing at a point at which there is some temptation to be resisted or deficiency of motivation to be made good. As Aristotle put it, virtues are about what is difficult for men, and I want to see in what sense this is true, and then to consider a problem in Kant's moral philosophy in the light of what has been said.

Let us first think about courage and temperance. Aristotle and Aquinas contrasted these virtues with justice in the following respect. Justice was concerned with operations and courage and temperance with passions.[7] What they meant by this seems to have been, primarily, that the man of courage does not fear immoderately nor the man of temperance have immoderate desires for pleasure, and that there was no corresponding moderation of a passion implied in the idea of justice. This particular account of courage and temperance might be disputed on the ground that a man's courage is measured by his action and not by anything as uncontrollable as fear; and similarly that the temperate man who must on occasion refuse pleasures need not *desire* them any less than the intemperate man. Be that as it may (and something will be said about it later) it is obviously true that courage and temperance have to do with particular springs of action as justice does not. Almost any desire can lead a man to act unjustly, not even excluding the desire to help a friend or to save a life, whereas a cowardly act must be motivated by fear or a desire for safety, and an act of intemperance by a desire for pleasure, perhaps even for a particular range of pleasures such as those of eating or drinking or sex. And now, going back to the idea of virtues as correctives one may say that it is only because fear and the desire for pleasure often operate as temptations that courage and temperance exist as virtues at all. As things are we often want to run away not only where that is the right thing to do but also where we should stand firm; and we want pleasure not only where we should seek pleasure but also where we should not. If human nature had been different there would have been no need of a corrective disposition in either place, as fear and pleasure would have been good guides to conduct throughout life. So Aquinas says, about the passions:

> They may incite us to something against reason, and so we need a curb, which we name *temperance*. Or they may make us shirk a course of action dictated by reason, through fear of dangers or hardships. Then a person needs to be steadfast and not run away from what is right; and for this *courage* is named.[8]

As with courage and temperance so with many other virtues: there is, for instance, a virtue of industriousness only because idleness is a temptation; and of humility only because men tend to think too well of themselves. Hope is a virtue because despair too is a temptation; it might have been that no one cried that all was lost except where he could really see it to be so, and in this case there would have been no virtue of hope.

With virtues such as justice and charity it is a little different, because they correspond not to any particular desire or tendency that has to be kept in check but rather to a deficiency of motivation; and it is this that they must make good. If people were as much attached to the good of others as they are to their own good there would no more be a general virtue of benevolence than there is a general virtue of self-love. And if people cared about the rights of others as they care about their own rights no virtue of justice would be needed to look after the matter, and rules about such things as contracts and promises would only need to be made public, like the rules of a game that everyone was eager to play.

On this view of the virtues and vices everything is seen to depend on what human nature is like, and the traditional catalogue of the two kinds of dispositions is not hard to understand. Nevertheless it may be defective, and anyone who accepts the thesis that I am putting forward will feel free to ask himself where the temptations and deficiencies that need correcting are really to be found. It is possible, for example, that the theory of human nature lying behind the traditional list of the virtues and vices puts too much emphasis on hedonistic and sensual impulses, and does not sufficiently take account of less straightforward inclinations such as the desire to be put upon and dissatisfied, or the unwillingness to accept good things as they come along.

It should now be clear why I said that virtues should be seen as correctives; and part of what is meant by saying that virtue is about things that are difficult for men should also have appeared. The further application of this idea is, however, controversial, and the following difficulty presents itself: that we both are and are not inclined to think that the harder a man finds it to act virtuously the more virtue he shows if he does act well. For on the one hand great virtue is needed where it is particularly hard to act virtuously; yet on the other it could be argued that difficulty in acting virtuously shows that the agent is imperfect in virtue: according to Aristotle, to take pleasure in virtuous action is the mark of true virtue, with the self-mastery of the one who finds virtue difficult only a second best. How then is this conflict to be decided? Who shows most courage, the one who wants to run away but does not, or the one who does not even want to run away? Who shows most charity, the one who finds it easy to make the good of others his object, or the one who finds it hard?

What is certain is that the thought that virtues are corrective does not constrain us to relate virtue to difficulty in each individual man. Since men in general find it hard to face great dangers or evils, and even small ones, we may count as courageous those few who without blindness or indifference are nevertheless fearless even in terrible circumstances. And when someone has a natural charity or generosity it is, at least part of the virtue that he has; if natural virtue cannot be the whole of virtue this is because a kindly or fearless disposition could be disastrous without justice and wisdom, and these virtues have to be learned, not because natural virtue is too easily acquired. I have argued that the virtues can be seen as correctives in relation to human nature in general but not that each virtue must present a difficulty to each and every man.

Nevertheless many people feel strongly inclined to say that it is for moral effort that moral praise is to be bestowed, and that in proportion as a man finds it easy to be virtuous so much the less is he to be morally admired for his good actions. The dilemma can be resolved only when we stop talking about difficulties standing in the way of virtuous action as if they were of only one kind. The fact is that some kinds of difficulties do indeed provide an occasion for much virtue, but that others rather show that virtue is incomplete.

To illustrate this point I shall first consider an example of honest action. We may suppose for instance that a man has an opportunity to steal, in circumstances where stealing is not morally permissible, but that he refrains. And now let us ask our old question. For one man it is hard to refrain from stealing and for another man it is not: which shows the greater virtue in acting as he should? It is not difficult to see in this case that it makes all the difference whether the difficulty comes from circumstances, as that a man is poor, or that his theft is unlikely to be detected, or whether it comes from something that belongs to his own character. The fact that a man is *tempted* to steal is something about him that shows a certain lack of honesty: of the thoroughly honest man we say that it 'never entered his head', meaning that it was never a real possibility for him. But the fact that he is poor is something that makes the occasion more *tempting*, and difficulties of this kind make honest action all the more virtuous.

A similar distinction can be made between different obstacles standing in the way of charitable action. Some circumstances, as that great sacrifice is needed, or that the one to be helped is a rival, give an occasion on which a man's charity is severely tested. Yet in given circumstances of this kind it is the man who acts easily rather than the one who finds it hard who shows the most charity. Charity is a virtue of attachment, and that sympathy for others which makes it easier to help them is part of the virtue itself.

These are fairly simple cases, but I am not supposing that it is always easy to say where the relevant distinction is to be drawn. What, for instance, should we say about the emotion of fear as an obstacle to action? Is a man more courageous if he fears much and nevertheless acts, or if he is relatively fearless? Several things must be said about this. In the first place it seems that the emotion of fear is not a necessary condition for the display of courage; in face of a great evil such as death or injury a man

may show courage even if he does not tremble. On the other hand even irrational fears may give an occasion for courage: if someone suffers from claustrophobia or a dread of heights he may require courage to do that which would not be a courageous action for others. But not all fears belong from this point of view to the circumstances rather than to a man's character. For while we do not think of claustrophobia or a dread of heights as features of character, a general timorousness may be. Thus, although pathological fears are not the result of a man's choices and values some fears may be. The fears that count against a man's courage are those that we think he could overcome, and among them, in a special class, those that reflect the fact that he values safety too much.

In spite of problems such as these, which have certainly not all been solved, both the distinction between different kinds of obstacles to virtuous action, and the general idea that virtues are correctives, will be useful in resolving a difficulty in Kant's moral philosophy closely related to the issues discussed in the preceding paragraphs. In a passage in the first section of the *Groundwork of the Metaphysics of Morals* Kant notoriously tied himself into a knot in trying to give an account of those actions which have as he put it 'positive moral worth'. Arguing that only actions done out of a sense of duty have this worth he contrasts a philanthropist who 'takes pleasure in spreading happiness around him' with one who acts out of respect for duty, saying that the actions of the latter but not the former have moral worth. Much scorn has been poured on Kant for this curious doctrine, and indeed it does seem that something has gone wrong, but perhaps we are not in a position to scoff unless we can give our own account of the idea on which Kant is working. After all it does seem that he is right in saying that some actions are in accordance with duty, and even required by duty, without being the subjects of moral praise, like those of the honest trader who deals honestly in a situation in which it is in his interest to do so.

It was this kind of example that drove Kant to his strange conclusion. He added another example, however, in discussing acts of self-preservation; these he said, while they normally have no positive moral worth, may have it when a man preserves his life not from inclination but without inclination and from a sense of duty. Is he not right in saying that acts of self-preservation normally have no moral significance but that they may have it, and how do we ourselves explain this fact?

To anyone who approaches this topic from a consideration of the virtues the solution readily suggests itself. Some actions are in accordance with virtue without requiring virtue for their performance, whereas others are both in accordance with virtue and such as to show possession of a virtue. So Kant's trader was dealing honestly in a situation in which the virtue of honesty is not required for honest dealing, and it is for this reason that his action did not have 'positive moral worth'. Similarly, the care that one ordinarily takes for one's life, as for instance on some ordinary morning in eating one's breakfast and keeping out of the way of a car on the road, is something for which no virtue is required. As we said earlier there is no general virtue of self-love as there is a virtue of benevolence or charity, because men are generally attached sufficiently to their own good. Nevertheless in special circumstances virtues such as temperance, courage, fortitude, and hope may be needed if someone is to preserve his life. Are these circumstances in which the preservation of one's own life is a duty? Sometimes it is so, for sometimes it is what is owed to others that should keep a man from destroying himself, and then he may act out of a sense of duty. But not all cases in which acts of self-preservation show virtue are like this. For a man may display each of the virtues just listed even where he does not do any harm to others if he kills himself or fails to preserve his life. And it is this that explains why there may be a moral aspect to suicide which does not depend on possible injury to other people. It is not that suicide is 'always wrong', whatever that would mean, but that suicide is *sometimes* contrary to virtues such as courage and hope.

Let us now return to Kant's philanthropists, with the thought that it is action that is in accordance with virtue and also displays a virtue that has moral worth. We see at once that Kant's difficulties are avoided, and the happy philanthropist reinstated in the position which belongs to him. For charity is, as we said, a virtue of attachment as well as action, and the sympathy that makes it easier to act with charity is part of the virtue. The man who acts charitably out of a sense of duty is not to be undervalued, but it is the other who most shows virtue and therefore to the other that most moral worth is attributed. Only a detail of Kant's presentation of the case of the dutiful philanthropist tells on the other side. For what he actually said was that this man felt no sympathy and took no pleasure in the good of others because 'his mind was clouded by some sorrow of his own', and this is the kind of circumstance that increases the virtue that is needed if a man is to act well.

III

It was suggested above that an action with 'positive moral worth', or as we might say a positively good action, was to be seen as one which was in accordance with virtue, by which I mean contrary to no virtue, and moreover one for which a virtue was required. Nothing has so far been said about another case, excluded by the formula, in which it might seem that an act displaying one virtue was nevertheless contrary to another. In giving this last description I am thinking not of two virtues with competing claims, as if what were required by justice could nevertheless be demanded by charity, or something of that kind, but rather of the possibility that a virtue such as courage or temperance or industry which overcomes a special temptation, might be displayed in an act of folly or villainy. Is this something that we must allow for, or is it only good or innocent actions which can be acts of these virtues? Aquinas, in his definition of virtue, said that virtues can produce only good actions, and that they are dispositions 'of which no one can make bad use',[9] except when they are treated as objects, as in being the subject of hatred or pride. The common opinion nowadays is, however, quite different. With the notable exception of Peter Geach hardly anyone sees any difficulty in the thought that virtues may sometimes be displayed in bad actions. Von Wright, for instance, speaks of the courage of the villain as if this were a quite unproblematic idea, and most people take it for granted that the virtues of courage and temperance may aid a bad man in his evil work. It is also supposed that charity may lead a man to act badly, as when someone does what he has no right to do, but does it for the sake of a friend.

There are, however, reasons for thinking that the matter is not as simple as this. If a man who is willing to do an act of injustice to help a friend, or for the common good, is supposed to act out of charity, and he so acts where a just man will not, it should be said that the unjust man has more charity than the just man. But do we not think that someone not ready to act unjustly may yet be perfect in charity, the virtue having done its whole work in prompting a man to do the acts that are permissible? And is there not more difficulty than might appear in the idea of an act of injustice which is nevertheless an act of courage? Suppose for instance that a sordid murder were in question, say a murder done for gain or to get an inconvenient person out of the way, but that this murder had to be done in alarming circumstances or in the face of real danger; should we be happy to say that such an action was an act of courage or a courageous act? Did the murderer, who certainly acted boldly, or with intrepidity, if he did the murder, also act courageously? Some people insist that they are ready to say this, but I have noticed that they like to move over to a murder for the sake of conscience, or to some other act done in the course of

a villainous enterprise but whose immediate end is innocent or positively good. On their hypothesis, which is that bad acts can easily be seen as courageous acts or acts of courage, my original example should be just as good.

What are we to say about this difficult matter? There is no doubt that the murderer who murdered for gain was *not a coward*: he did not have a second moral defect which another villain might have had. There is no difficulty about this because it is clear that one defect may neutralise another. As Aquinas remarked, it is better for a blind horse if it is slow.[10] It does not follow, however, that an act of villainy can be courageous; we are inclined to say that it 'took courage', and yet it seems wrong to think of courage as equally connected with good actions and bad.

One way out of this difficulty might be to say that the man who is ready to pursue bad ends does indeed have courage, and shows courage in his action, but that in him courage is not a virtue. Later I shall consider some cases in which this might be the right thing to say, but in this instance it does not seem to be. For unless the murderer consistently pursues bad ends his courage will often result in good; it may enable him to do many innocent or positively good things for himself or for his family and friends. On the strength of an individual bad action we can hardly say that in him courage is not a virtue. Nevertheless there is something to be said even about the individual action to distinguish it from one that would readily be called an act of courage or a courageous act. Perhaps the following analogy may help us to see what it is. We might think of words such as 'courage' as naming characteristics of human beings in respect of a certain power, as words such as 'poison' and 'solvent' and 'corrosive' so name the properties of physical things. The power to which virtue-words are so related is the power of producing good action, and good desires. But just as poisons, solvents and corrosives do not always operate characteristically, so it could be with virtues. If P (say arsenic) is a poison it does not follow that P acts as a poison wherever it is found. It is quite natural to say on occasion 'P does not act as a poison here' though P is a poison and it is P that is acting here. Similarly courage is not operating as a virtue when the murderer turns his courage, which is a virtue to bad ends. Not surprisingly the resistance that some of us registered was not to the expression 'the courage of the murderer' or to the assertion that what he did 'took courage' but rather to the description of that action as an act of courage or a courageous act. It is not that the action *could* not be so described, but that the fact that courage does not here have its characteristic operation is a reason for finding the description strange.

In this example we were considering an action in which courage was not operating as a virtue, without suggesting that in that agent it generally failed to do so. But the latter is also a possibility. If someone is both wicked and foolhardy this may be the case with courage, and it is even easier to find examples of a general connection with evil rather than good in the case of some other virtues. Suppose, for instance, that we think of someone who is over-industrious, or too ready to refuse pleasure, and this is characteristic of him rather than something we find on one particular occasion. In this case the virtue of industry, or the virtue of temperance, has a systematic connexion with defective action rather than good action; and it might be said in either case that the virtue did not operate as a virtue in this man. Just as we might say in a certain setting 'P is not a poison here' though P is a poison and P is here, so we might say that industriousness, or temperance, is not a virtue in some. Similarly in a man habitually given to wishful thinking, who clings to false hopes, hope does not operate as a virtue and we may say that it is not a virtue in him.

The thought developed in the last paragraph, to the effect that not every man who has a virtue has something that is a virtue in him, may help to explain a certain dis-

comfort that one may feel when discussing the virtues. It is not easy to put one's finger on what is wrong, but it has something to do with a disparity between the moral ideals that may seem to be implied in our talk about the virtues, and the moral judgements that we actually make. Someone reading the foregoing pages might, for instance, think that the author of this paper always admired most those people who had all the virtues, being wise and temperate as well as courageous, charitable, and just. And indeed it is sometimes so. There are some people who do possess all these virtues and who are loved and admired by all the world, as Pope John XXIII was loved and admired. Yet the fact is that many of us look up to some people whose chaotic lives contain rather little of wisdom or temperance, rather than to some others who possess these virtues. And while it may be that this is just romantic nonsense I suspect that it is not. For while wisdom always operates as a virtue, its close relation prudence does not, and it is prudence rather than wisdom that inspires many a careful life. Prudence is not a virtue in everyone, any more than industriousness is, for in some it is rather an over-anxious concern for safety and propriety, and a determination to keep away from people or situations which are apt to bring trouble with them; and by such defensiveness much good is lost. It is the same with temperance. Intemperance can be an appalling thing, as it was with Henry VIII of whom Wolsey remarked that

rather than he will either miss or want any part of his will or appetite, he will put the loss of one half of his realm in danger.

Nevertheless in some people temperance is not a virtue, but is rather connected with timidity or with a grudging attitude to the acceptance of good things. Of course what is best is to live boldly yet without imprudence or intemperance, but the fact is that rather few can manage that.

Notes

I am indebted to friends in many universities for their help in forming my views on this subject; and particularly to John Giuliano of UCLA, whose unpublished work on the unity of the virtues I have consulted with profit, and to Rosalind Hursthouse who commented on a draft of the middle period.

1. G. H. von Wright, *The Varieties of Goodness* (London, 1963).

2. Peter Geach, *The Virtues* (Cambridge, 1977).

3. Aquinas, *Summa Theologica*, 1a2ae Q.56 a.3.

4. Aristotle, *Nicomachean Ethics*, especially bk. VII.

5. von Wright op. cit. chapter VIII.

6. Aristotle op. cit. 1140 b 22–25. Aquinas op. cit. 1a2ae Q.57 a.4.

7. Aristotle op. cit. 1106 b 15 and 1129 a.4 have this implication; but Aquinas is more explicit in op. cit. 1a2ae Q.60 a.2.

8. Aquinas op. cit. 1a2ae Q.61 a.3.

9. Aquinas op. cit. 1a2ae Q.56 a.5.

10. Aquinas op. cit. 1a2ae Q.58 a.4.

20 / ALASDAIR MACINTYRE

The Nature of the Virtues

One response to the history which I have narrated so far might well be to suggest that even within the relatively coherent tradition of thought which I have sketched there are just too many different and incompatible conceptions of a virtue for there to be any real unity to the concept or indeed to the history. Homer, Sophocles, Aristotle, the New Testament and medieval thinkers differ from each other in too many ways. They offer us different and incompatible lists of the virtues; they give a different rank order of importance to different virtues; and they have different and incompatible theories of the virtues. If we were to consider later Western writers on the virtues, the list of differences and incompatibilities would be enlarged still further; and if we extended our enquiry to Japanese, say, or American Indian cultures, the differences would become greater still. It would be all too easy to conclude that there are a number of rival and alternative conceptions of the virtues, but, even within the tradition which I have been delineating, no single core conception.

The case for such a conclusion could not be better constructed than by beginning from a consideration of the very different lists of items which different authors in different times and places have included in their catalogues of virtues. Some of these catalogues—Homer's, Aristotle's and the New Testament's—I have already noticed at greater or lesser length. Let me at the risk of some repetition recall some of their key features and then introduce for further comparison the catalogues of two later Western writers, Benjamin Franklin and Jane Austen.

The first example is that of Homer. At least some of the items in a Homeric list of the *aretai* would clearly not be counted by most of us nowadays as virtues at all, physical strength being the most obvious example. To this it might be replied that perhaps we ought not to translate the word *aretê* in Homer by our word 'virtue', but instead by our word 'excellence'; and perhaps, if we were so to translate it, the apparently surprising difference between Homer and ourselves would at first sight have been removed. For we could allow without any kind of oddity that the possession of physical strength is the possession of an excellence. But in fact we would not have removed, but instead would merely have relocated, the difference between Homer and ourselves. For we would now seem to be saying that Homer's concept of an *aretê*, an excellence, is one thing and that our concept of a virtue is quite another since a particular quality can be an excellence in Homer's eyes, but not a virtue in ours and *vice versa*.

But of course it is not that Homer's list of virtues differs only from our own; it also notably differs from Aristotle's. And Aristotle's of course also differs from our own. For one thing, as I noticed earlier, some Greek virtue-words are not easily translatable into English or rather out of Greek. Moreover consider the importance of friendship as a virtue in Aristotle's list—how different from us! Or the place of *phronêsis*—how different from Homer and from us! The mind receives from Aristotle the kind of tribute which the body receives from Homer. But it is not just the case that the difference between Aristotle and Homer lies in the inclusion of some items and the omission of others in their respective catalogues. It turns out also in the way in which those catalogues are ordered, in which items are ranked as relatively central to human excellence and which marginal.

Moreover the relationship of virtues to the social order has changed. For Homer the paradigm of human excellence is the warrior; for Aristotle it is the Athenian gentleman. Indeed according to Aristotle certain virtues are only available to those of great riches and of high social status; there are virtues which are unavailable to the poor man, even if he is a free man. And those virtues are on Aristotle's view ones central to human life; magnanimity—and once again, any translation of *megalopsuchia* is unsatisfactory—and munificence are not just virtues, but important virtues within the Aristotelian scheme.

At once it is impossible to delay the remark that the most striking contrast with Aristotle's catalogue is to be found neither in Homer's nor in our own, but in the New Testament's. For the New Testament not only praises virtues of which Aristotle knows nothing—faith, hope and love—and says nothing about virtues such as *phronêsis* which are crucial for Aristotle, but it praises at least one quality as a virtue which Aristotle seems to count as one of the vices relative to magnanimity, namely humility. Moreover since the New Testament quite clearly sees the rich as destined for the pains of Hell, it is clear that the key virtues cannot be available to them; yet they *are* available to slaves. And the New Testament of course differs from both Homer and Aristotle not only in the items included in its catalogue, but once again in its rank ordering of the virtues.

Turn now to compare all three lists of virtues considered so far—the Homeric, the Aristotelian, and the New Testament's—with two much later lists, one which can be compiled from Jane Austen's novels and the other which Benjamin Franklin constructed for himself. Two features stand out in Jane Austen's list. The first is the importance that she allots to the virtue which she calls 'constancy', a virtue about which I shall say more in a later chapter. In some ways constancy plays a role in Jane Austen analogous to that of *phronêsis* in Aristotle; it is a virtue the possession of which is a prerequisite for the possession of other virtues. The second is the fact that what Aristotle treats as the virtue of agreeableness (a virtue for which he says there is no name) she treats as only the simulacrum of a genuine virtue—the genuine virtue in question is the one she calls amiability. For the man who practices agreeableness does so from considerations of honour and expediency, according to Aristotle; whereas Jane Austen thought it possible and necessary for the possessor of that virtue to have a certain real affection for people as such. (It matters here that Jane Austen is a Christian.) Remember that Aristotle himself had treated military courage as a simulacrum of true courage. Thus we find here yet another type of disagreement over the virtues; namely, one as to which human qualities are genuine virtues and which mere simulacra.

In Benjamin Franklin's list we find almost all the types of difference from at least one of the other catalogues we have considered and one more. Franklin includes virtues which are new to our consideration such as cleanliness, silence and industry; he clearly considers the drive to acquire itself a part of virtue, whereas for most ancient Greeks this is the vice of *pleonexia*; he treats some virtues which earlier ages had considered minor as major; but he also redefines some familiar virtues. In the list of thirteen virtues which Franklin compiled as part of his system of private moral accounting, he elucidates each virtue by citing a maxim obedience to which *is* the virtue in question. In the case of chastity the maxim is 'Rarely use venery but for health or offspring—never to dullness, weakness or the injury of your own or another's peace or reputation'. This is clearly not what earlier writers had meant by 'chastity'.

We have therefore accumulated a startling number of differences and incompatibilities in the five stated and implied accounts of the virtues. So the question which I raised at the outset becomes more urgent. If different writers in different times and places, but all within the history of Western culture, include such different sets and types of items in their lists, what grounds have we for supposing that they do indeed aspire to list items of one and the same kind, that there is any shared concept at all? A second kind of consideration reinforces the presumption of a negative answer to this question. It is not just that each of these five writers lists different and differing kinds of items; it is also that each of these lists embodies, is the expression of a different theory about what a virtue is.

In the Homeric poems a virtue is a quality the manifestation of which enables someone to do exactly what their well-defined social role requires. The primary role is that of the warrior king and that Homer lists those virtues which he does becomes intelligible at once when we recognise that the key virtues therefore must be those which enable a man to excel in combat and in the games. It follows that we cannot identify the Homeric virtues until we have first identified the key social roles in Homeric society and the requirements of each of them. The concept of *what anyone filling such-and-such a role ought to do* is prior to the concept of a virtue; the latter concept has application only via the former.

On Aristotle's account matters are very different. Even though some virtues are available only to certain types of people, none the less virtues attach not to men as inhabiting social roles, but to man as such. It is the *telos* of man as a species which determines what human qualities are virtues. We need to remember however that although Aristotle treats the acquisition and exercise of the virtues as means to an end, the relationship of means to end is internal and not external. I call a means internal to a given end when the end cannot be adequately characterised independently of a characterisation of the means. So it is with the virtues and the *telos* which is the good life for man on Aristotle's account. The exercise of the virtues is itself a crucial component of the good life for man. This distinction between internal and external means to an end is not drawn by Aristotle himself in the *Nicomachean Ethics*, as I noticed earlier, but it is an essential distinction to be drawn if we are to understand what Aristotle intended. The distinction *is* drawn explicitly by Aquinas in the course of his defence of St Augustine's definition of a virtue, and it is clear that Aquinas understood that in drawing it he was maintaining an Aristotelian point of view.

The New Testament's account of the virtues, even if it differs as much as it does in content from Aristotle's—Aristotle would certainly not have admired Jesus Christ and he would have been horrified by St Paul—does have the same logical and conceptual structure as Aristotle's account. A virtue is, as with Aristotle, a quality the exercise of which leads to the achievement of the human telos. *The* good for man is of course a supernatural and not only a natural good, but supernature redeems and completes nature. Moreover the relationship of virtues as means to the end which is human incorporation in the divine kingdom of the age to come is internal and not external, just as it is in Aristotle. It is of course this parallelism which allows Aquinas to synthesise Aristotle and the New Testament. A key feature of this parallelism is the way in which the concept of *the good life for man* is prior to the concept of a virtue in just the way in which on the Homeric account the concept of a social role was prior. Once again it is the way in which the former concept is applied which determines how the latter is to be applied. In both cases the concept of a virtue is a secondary concept.

The intent of Jane Austen's theory of the

virtues is of another kind. C.S. Lewis has rightly emphasised how profoundly Christian her moral vision is and Gilbert Ryle has equally rightly emphasised her inheritance from Shaftesbury and from Aristotle. In fact her views combine elements from Homer as well, since she is concerned with social roles in a way that neither the New Testament nor Aristotle are. She is therefore important for the way in which she finds it possible to combine what are at first sight disparate theoretical accounts of the virtues. But for the moment any attempt to assess the significance of Jane Austen's synthesis must be delayed. Instead we must notice the quite different style of theory articulated in Benjamin Franklin's account of the virtues.

Franklin's account, like Aristotle's, is teleological; but unlike Aristotle's, it is utilitarian. According to Franklin in his *Autobiography* the virtues are means to an end, but he envisages the means-ends relationship as external rather than internal. The end to which the cultivation of the virtues ministers is happiness, but happiness understood as success, prosperity in Philadelphia and ultimately in heaven. The virtues are to be useful and Franklin's account continuously stresses utility as a criterion in individual cases: 'Make no expence but to do good to others or yourself; i.e. waste nothing', 'Speak not but what may benefit others or yourself. Avoid trifling conversation' and, as we have already seen, 'Rarely use venery but for health or offspring . . .' When Franklin was in Paris he was horrified by Parisian architecture: 'Marble, porcelain and gilt are squandered without utility.'

We thus have at least three very different conceptions of a virtue to confront: a virtue is a quality which enables an individual to discharge his or her social role (Homer); a virtue is a quality which enables an individual to move towards the achievement of the specifically human *telos*, whether natural or supernatural (Aristotle, the New Testament and Aquinas); a virtue is a quality which has utility in achieving earthly and heavenly success (Franklin).

Are we to take these as three rival accounts of the same thing? Or are they instead accounts of three different things? Perhaps the moral structures in archaic Greece, in fourth-century Greece, and in eighteenth-century Pennsylvania were so different from each other that we should treat them as embodying quite different concepts, whose difference is initially disguised from us by the historical accident of an inherited vocabulary which misleads us by linguistic resemblance long after conceptual identity and similarity have failed. Our initial question has come back to us with redoubled force.

Yet although I have dwelt upon the *prima facie* case for holding that the differences and incompatibilities between different accounts at least suggest that there is no single, central, core conception of the virtues which might make a claim for universal allegiance. I ought also to point out that each of the five moral accounts which I have sketched so summarily does embody just such a claim. It is indeed just this feature of those accounts that makes them of more than sociological or antiquarian interest. Every one of these accounts claims not only theoretical, but also an institutional hegemony. For Odysseus the Cyclopes stand condemned because they lack agriculture, on *agora* and *themis*. For Aristotle the barbarians stand condemned because they lack the *polis* and are therefore incapable of politics. For New Testament Christians there is no salvation outside the apostolic church. And we know that Benjamin Franklin found the virtues more at home in Philadelphia than in Paris and that for Jane Austen the touchstone of the virtues is a certain kind of marriage and indeed a certain kind of naval officer (that is, a certain kind of *English* naval officer).

The question can therefore now be posed directly: are we or are we not able to disentangle from these rival and various claims a unitary core concept of the virtues of which we can give a more compelling account than any of the other accounts so far? I am going to argue that we can in fact discover such a core concept and that it turns out to provide the tradition of which I have written the history with its conceptual unity. It will indeed enable us to distinguish in a clear way those beliefs about the virtues which genuinely belong to the tradition from those which do not. Unsurprisingly perhaps it is a complex concept, different parts of which derive from different stages in the development of the tradition. Thus the concept itself in some sense embodies the history of which it is the outcome.

One of the features of the concept of a virtue which has emerged with some clarity from the argument so far is that it always requires for its application the acceptance of some prior account of certain features of social and moral life in terms of which it has to be defined and explained. So in the Homeric account the concept of a virtue is secondary to that of *a social role*, in Aristotle's account it is secondary to that of *the good life for man* conceived as the *telos* of human action and in Franklin's much later account it is secondary to that of utility. What is it in the account which I am about to give which provides in a similar way the necessary background against which the concept of a virtue has to be made intelligible? It is in answering this question that the complex, historical, multilayered character of the core concept of virtue becomes clear. For there are no less than three stages in the logical development of the concept which have to be identified in order, if the core conception of a virtue is to be understood, and each of these stages has its own conceptual background. The first stage requires a background account of what I shall call a practice, the second an account of what I have already characterised as the narrative order of a single human life and the third an account a good deal fuller than I have given up to now of what constitutes a moral tradition. Each later stage presupposes the earlier, but not *vice versa*. Each earlier stage is both modified by and reinterpreted in the light of, but also provides an essential constituent of each later stage. The progress in the development of the concept is closely related to, although it

does not recapitulate in any straightforward way, the history of the tradition of which it forms the core.

In the Homeric account of the virtues— and in heroic societies more generally—the exercise of a virtue exhibits qualities which are required for sustaining a social role and for exhibiting excellence in some well-marked area of social practice: to excel is to excel at war or in the games, as Achilles does, in sustaining a household, as Penelope does, in giving counsel in the assembly, as Nestor does, in the telling of a tale, as Homer himself does. When Aristotle speaks of excellence in human activity, he sometimes, though not always, refers to some well-defined type of human practice: flute-playing, or war, or geometry. I am going to suggest that this notion of a particular type of practice as providing the arena in which the virtues are exhibited and in terms of which they are to receive their primary, if incomplete, definition is crucial to the whole enterprise of identifying a core concept of the virtues. I hasten to add two *caveats* however.

The first is to point out that my argument will not in any way imply that virtues are *only* exercised in the course of what I am calling practices. The second is to warn that I shall be using the word 'practice' in a specially defined way which does not completely agree with current ordinary usage, including my own previous use of that word. What am I going to mean by it?

By a 'practice' I am going to mean any coherent and complex form of socially established cooperative human activity through which goods internal to that form of activity are realised in the course of trying to achieve those standards of excellence which are appropriate to, and partially definitive of, that form of activity, with the result that human powers to achieve excellence, and human conceptions of the ends and goods involved, are systematically extended. Tic-tac-toe is not an example of a practice in this sense, nor is throwing a football with skill; but the game of football is, and so is chess. Bricklaying is not a practice; architecture is. Planting turnips is not a practice; farming is. So are the enquiries of physics, chemistry and biology, and so is the work of the historian, and so are painting and music. In the ancient and medieval worlds the creation and sustaining of human communities—of households, cities, nations—is generally taken to be a practice in the sense in which I have defined it. Thus the range of practices is wide: arts, sciences, games, politics in the Aristotelian sense, the making and sustaining of family life, all fall under the concept. But the question of the precise range of practices is not at this stage of the first importance. Instead let me explain some of the key terms involved in my definition, beginning with the notion of goods internal to a practice.

Consider the example of a highly intelligent seven-year-old child whom I wish to teach to play chess, although the child has no particular desire to learn the game. The child does however have a very strong desire for candy and little chance of obtaining it. I therefore tell the child that if the child will play chess with me once a week I will give the child 50¢ worth of candy; moreover I tell the child that I will always play in such a way that it will be difficult, but not impossible, for the child to win and that, if the child wins, the child will receive an extra 50¢ worth of candy. Thus motivated the child plays and plays to win. Notice however that, so long as it is the candy alone which provides the child with a good reason for playing chess, the child has no reason not to cheat and every reason to cheat, provided he or she can do so successfully. But, so we may hope, there will come a time when the child will find in those goods specific to chess, in the achievement of a certain highly particular kind of analytical skill, strategic imagination and competitive intensity, a new set of reasons, reasons now not just for winning on a particular occasion, but for trying to excel in whatever way the game of chess demands. Now if the child cheats, he or she will be defeating not me, but himself or herself.

There are thus two kinds of good possibly to be gained by playing chess. On the one hand there are those goods externally and contingently attached to chess-playing and to other practices by the accidents of social circumstance—in the case of the imaginary child candy, in the case of real adults such goods as prestige, status and money. There are always alternative ways for achieving such goods, and their achievement is never to be had *only* by engaging in some particular kind of practice. On the other hand there are the goods internal to the practice of chess which cannot be had in any way but by playing chess or some other game of that specific kind. We call them internal for two reasons: first, as I have already suggested, because we can only specify them in terms of chess or some other game of that specific kind and by means of examples from such games (otherwise the meagerness of our vocabulary for speaking of such goods forces us into such devices as my own resort to writing of 'a certain highly particular kind of'); and secondly because they can only be identified and recognised by the experience of participating in the practice in question. Those who lack the relevant experience are incompetent thereby as judges of internal goods.

This is clearly the case with all the major examples of practices: consider for example—even if briefly and inadequately—the practice of portrait painting as it developed in Western Europe from the late middle ages to the eighteenth century. The successful portrait painter is able to achieve many goods which are in the sense just defined external to the practice of portrait painting—fame, wealth, social status, even a measure of power and influence at courts upon occasion. But those external goods are not to be confused with the goods which are internal to the practice. The internal goods are those which result from an extended attempt to show how Wittgenstein's dictum 'The human body is the best picture of the human soul' (*Investigations*) might be made to become true by teaching us 'to regard ... the picture on our wall as the object itself (the men, landscape and so on) depicted there' in a quite new way. What is misleading about Wittgenstein's dictum as it stands is its neglect of the truth in George Orwell's thesis 'At 50 everyone has the face he deserves'. What painters from Giotto to Rembrandt learnt to show was how the face at any age may be revealed as the face that the subject of a portrait deserves.

Originally in medieval paintings of the saints the face was an icon; the question of a resemblance between the depicted face of Christ or St Peter and the face that Jesus or Peter actually possessed at some particular age did not even arise. The antithesis to this iconography was the relative naturalism of certain fifteenth-century Flemish and German painting. The heavy eyelids, the coifed hair, the lines around the mouth undeniably represent some particular woman, either actual or envisaged. Resemblance has usurped the iconic relationship. But with Rembrandt there is, so to speak, synthesis: the naturalistic portrait is now rendered as an icon, but an icon of a new and hitherto inconceivable kind. Similarly in a very different kind of sequence mythological faces in a certain kind of seventeenth-century French painting become aristocratic faces in the eighteenth century. Within each of these sequences at least two different kinds of good internal to the painting of human faces and bodies are achieved.

There is first of all the excellence of the products, both the excellence in performance by the painters and that of each portrait itself. This excellence—the very verb 'excel' suggests it—has to be understood historically. The sequences of development find their point and purpose in a progress towards and beyond a variety of types and modes of excellence. There are of course sequences of decline as well as of progress, and progress is rarely to be understood as straightforwardly linear. But it is in participation in the attempts to sustain progress and to respond creatively to moments that the second kind of good internal to the practices of portrait painting is to be found. For what the artist discovers within the pursuit of excellence in portrait painting—

and what is true of portrait painting is true of the practice of the fine arts in general— is the good of a certain kind of life. That life may not constitute the whole of life for someone who is a painter by a very long way or it may at least for a period, Gauguin-like, absorb him or her at the expense of almost everything else. But it is the painter's living out of a greater or lesser part of his or her life *as a painter* that is the second kind of good internal to painting. And judgment upon these goods requires at the very least the kind of competence that is only to be acquired either as a painter or as someone willing to learn systematically what the portrait painter has to teach.

A practice involves standards of excellence and obedience to rules as well as the achievement of goods. To enter into a practice is to accept the authority of those standards and the inadequacy of my own performance as judged by them. It is to subject my own attitudes, choices, preferences and tastes to the standards which currently and partially define the practice. Practices of course, as I have just noticed, have a history: games, sciences and arts all have histories. Thus the standards are not themselves immune from criticism, but none the less we cannot be initiated into a practice without accepting the authority of the best standards realised so far. If, on starting to listen to music, I do not accept my own incapacity to judge correctly, I will never learn to hear, let alone to appreciate, Bartok's last quartets. If, on starting to play baseball, I do not accept that others know better than I when to throw a fast ball and when not, I will never learn to appreciate good pitching let alone to pitch. In the realm of practices the authority of both goods and standards operates in such a way as to rule out all subjectivist and emotivist analyses of judgment. De gustibus est disputandum.

We are now in a position to notice an important difference between what I have called internal and what I have called external goods. It is characteristic of what I have called external goods that when achieved they are always some individual's property and possession. Moreover characteristically they are such that the more someone has of them, the less there is for other people. This is sometimes necessarily the case, as with power and fame, and sometimes the case by reason of contingent circumstance as with money. External goods are therefore characteristically objects of competition in which there must be losers as well as winners. Internal goods are indeed the outcome of competition to excel, but it is characteristic of them that their achievement is a good for the whole community who participate in the practice. So when Turner transformed the seascape in painting or W.G. Grace advanced the art of batting in cricket in a quite new way their achievement enriched the whole relevant community.

But what does all or any of this have to do with the concept of the virtues? It turns out that we are now in a position to formulate a first, even if partial and tentative definition of a virtue: *A virtue is an acquired human quality the possession and exercise of which tends to enable us to achieve those goods which are internal to practices and the lack of which effectively prevents us from achieving any such goods.* Later this definition will need amplification and amendment. But as a first approximation to an adequate definition it already illuminates the place of the virtues in human life. For it is not difficult to show for a whole range of key virtues that without them the goods internal to practices are barred to us, but not just barred to us generally, barred in a very particular way.

It belongs to the concept of a practice as I have outlined it—and as we are all familiar with it already in our actual lives, whether we are painters or physicists or quarterbacks or indeed just lovers of good painting or first-rate experiments or a well-thrown pass—that its goods can only be achieved by subordinating ourselves to the best standard so far achieved, and that entails subordinating ourselves within the practice in our relationship to other practitioners. We have to learn to recognise what

is due to whom; we have to be prepared to take whatever self-endangering risks are demanded along the way; and we have to listen carefully to what we are told about our own inadequacies and to reply with the same carefulness for the facts. In other words we have to accept as necessary components of any practice with internal goods and standards of excellence the virtues of justice, courage and honesty. For not to accept these, to be willing to cheat as our imagined child was willing to cheat in his or her early days at chess, so far bars us from achieving the standards of excellence or the goods internal to the practice that it renders the practice pointless except as a device for achieving external goods.

We can put the same point in another way. Every practice requires a certain kind of relationship between those who participate in it. Now the virtues are those goods by reference to which, whether we like it or not, we define our relationships to those other people with whom we share the kind of purposes and standards which inform practices. Consider an example of how reference to the virtues has to be made in certain kinds of human relationship.

A, B, C, and D are friends in that sense of friendship which Aristotle takes to be primary: they share in the pursuit of certain goods. In my terms they share in a practice. D dies in obscure circumstances, A discovers how D died and tells the truth about it to B while lying to C. C discovers the lie. What A cannot then intelligibly claim is that he stands in the same relationship of friendship to both B and C. By telling the truth to one and lying to the other he has partially defined a difference in the relationship. Of course it is open to A to explain this difference in a number of ways; perhaps he was trying to spare C pain or perhaps he is simply cheating C. But some difference in the relationship now exists as a result of the lie. For their allegiance to each other in the pursuit of common goods has been put in question.

Just as, so long as we share the standards and purposes characteristic of practices, we define our relationships to each other, whether we acknowledge it or not, by reference to standards of truthfulness and trust, so we define them too by reference to standards of justice and of courage. If A, a professor, gives B and C the grades that their papers deserve, but grades D because he is attracted by D's blue eyes or is repelled by D's dandruff, he has defined his relationship to D differently from his relationship to the other members of the class, whether he wishes it or not. Justice requires that we treat others in respect of merit or desert according to uniform and impersonal standards; to depart from the standards of justice in some particular instance defines our relationship with the relevant person as in some way special or distinctive.

The case with courage is a little different. We hold courage to be a virtue because the care and concern for individuals, communities and causes which is so crucial to so much in practices requires the existence of such a virtue. If someone says that he cares for some individual, community or cause, but is unwilling to risk harm or danger on his, her or its own behalf, he puts in question the genuineness of his care and concern. Courage, the capacity to risk harm or danger to oneself, has its role in human life because of this connection with care and concern. This is not to say that a man cannot genuinely care and also be a coward. It is in part to say that a man who genuinely cares and has not the capacity for risking harm or danger has to define himself, both to himself and to others, as a coward.

I take it then that from the standpoint of those types of relationship without which practices cannot be sustained truthfulness, justice and courage—and perhaps some others—are genuine excellences, are virtues in the light of which we have to characterise ourselves and others, whatever our private moral standpoint or our society's particular codes may be. For this recognition that we cannot escape the definition of our relationships in terms of such goods is perfectly compatible with the acknowledgment that different societies have

and have had different codes of truthfulness, justice and courage. Lutheran pietists brought up their children to believe that one ought to tell the truth to everybody at all times, whatever the circumstances or consequences, and Kant was one of their children. Traditional Bantu parents brought up their children not to tell the truth to unknown strangers, since they believed that this could render the family vulnerable to witchcraft. In our culture many of us have been brought up not to tell the truth to elderly great-aunts who invite us to admire their new hats. But each of these codes embodies an acknowledgment of the virtue of truthfulness. So it is also with varying codes of justice and of courage.

Practices then might flourish in societies with very different codes; what they could not do is flourish in societies in which the virtues were not valued, although institutions and technical skills serving unified purposes might well continue to flourish. (I shall have more to say about the contrast between institutions and technical skills mobilised for a unified end, on the one hand, and practices on the other, in a moment.) For the kind of cooperation, the kind of recognition of authority and of achievement, the kind of respect for standards and the kind of risk-taking which are characteristically involved in practices demand for example fairness in judging oneself and others—the kind of fairness absent in my example of the professor, a ruthless truthfulness without which fairness cannot find application—the kind of truthfulness absent in my example of A, B, C and D—and willingness to trust the judgments of those whose achievement in the practice give them an authority to judge which presupposes fairness and truthfulness in those judgments, and from time to time the taking of self-endangering, reputation-endangering and even achievement-endangering risks. It is no part of my thesis that great violinists cannot be vicious or great chess-players mean-spirited. Where the virtues are required, the vices also may flourish. It is just that the vicious and mean-spirited necessarily rely on the virtues of others for the practices in which they engage to flourish and also deny themselves the experience of achieving those internal goods which may reward even not very good chess-players and violinists.

To situate the virtues any further within practices it is necessary now to clarify a little further the nature of a practice by drawing two important contrasts. The discussion so far I hope makes it clear that a practice, in the sense intended, is never just a set of technical skills, even when directed towards some unified purpose and even if the exercise of those skills can on occasion be valued or enjoyed for their own sake. What is distinctive of a practice is in part the way in which conceptions of the relevant goods and ends which the technical skills serve—and every practice does require the exercise of technical skills—are transformed and enriched by these extensions of human powers and by that regard for its own internal goods which are partially definitive of each particular practice or type of practice. Practices never have a goal or goals fixed for all time—painting has no such goal nor has physics—but the goals themselves are transmuted by the history of the activity. It therefore turns out not to be accidental that every practice has its own history and a history which is more and other than that of the improvement of the relevant technical skills. This historical dimension is crucial in relation to the virtues.

To enter into a practice is to enter into a relationship not only with its contemporary practitioners, but also with those who have preceded us in the practice, particularly those whose achievements extended the reach of the practice to its present point. It is thus the achievement, and *a fortiori* the authority, of a tradition which I then confront and from which I have to learn. And for this learning and the relationship to the past which it embodies the virtues of justice, courage and truthfulness are prerequuisite in precisely the same way and for precisely the same reasons as they are in sustaining present relationships within practices.

It is not only of course with sets of technical skills that practices ought to be contrasted. Practices must not be confused with institutions. Chess, physics and medicine are practices; chess clubs, laboratories, universities and hospitals are institutions. Institutions are characteristically and necessarily concerned with what I have called external goods. They are involved in acquiring money and other material goods; they are structured in terms of power and status, and they distribute money, power and status as rewards. Nor could they do otherwise if they are to sustain not only themselves, but also the practices of which they are the bearers. For no practices can survive for any length of time unsustained by institutions. Indeed so intimate is the relationship of practices to institutions—and consequently of the goods external to the goods internal to the practices in question—that institutions and practices characteristically form a single causal order in which the ideals and the creativity of the practice are always vulnerable to the acquisitiveness of the institution, in which the cooperative care for common goods of the practice is always vulnerable to the competitiveness of the institution. In this context the essential function of the virtues is clear. Without them, without justice, courage and truthfulness, practices could not resist the corrupting power of institutions.

Yet if institutions do have corrupting power, the making and sustaining of forms of human community—and therefore of institutions—itself has all the characteristics of a practice, and moreover of a practice which stands in a peculiarly close relationship to the exercise of the virtues in two important ways. The exercise of the virtues is itself apt to require a highly determinate attitude to social and political issues; and it is always within some particular community with its own specific institutional forms that we learn or fail to learn to exercise the virtues. There is of course a crucial difference between the way in which the relationship between moral character and political community is envisaged from the standpoint of liberal individualist modernity and the way in which that relationship was envisaged from the standpoint of the type of ancient and medieval tradition of the virtues which I have sketched. For liberal individualism a community is simply an arena in which individuals each pursue their own self-chosen conception of the good life, and political institutions exist to provide that degree of order which makes such self-determined activity possible. Government and law are, or ought to be, neutral between rival conceptions of the good life for man, and hence, although it is the task of government to promote law-abidingness, it is on the liberal view no part of the legitimate function of government to inculcate any one moral outlook.

By contrast, on the particular ancient and medieval view which I have sketched political community not only requires the exercise of the virtues for its own sustenance, but it is one of the tasks of government to make its citizens virtuous, just as it is one of the tasks of parental authority to make children grow up so as to be virtuous adults. The classical statement of this analogy is by Socrates in the *Crito*. It does not of course follow from an acceptance of the Socratic view of political community and political authority that we ought to assign to the modern state the moral function which Socrates assigned to the city and its laws. Indeed the power of the liberal individualist standpoint partly derives from the evident fact that the modern state is indeed totally unfitted to act as moral educator of any community. But the history of how the modern state emerged is of course itself a moral history. If my account of the complex relationship of virtues to practices and to institutions is correct, it follows that we shall be unable to write a true history of practices and institutions unless that history is also one of the virtues and vices. For the ability of a practice to retain its integrity will depend on the way in which the virtues can be and are exercised in sustaining the institutional forms which are the social bearers of the practice. The integrity of a practice causally requires the

exercise of the virtues by at least some of the individuals who embody it in their activities; and conversely the corruption of institutions is always in part at least an effect of the vices.

The virtues are of course themselves in turn fostered by certain types of social institution and endangered by others. Thomas Jefferson thought that only in a society of small farmers could the virtues flourish; and Adam Ferguson with a good deal more sophistication saw the institutions of modern commercial society as endangering at least some traditional virtues. It is Ferguson's type of sociology which is the empirical counterpart of the conceptual account of the virtues which I have given, a sociology which aspires to lay bare the empirical, causal connection between virtues, practices and institutions. For this kind of conceptual account has strong empirical implications; it provides an explanatory scheme which can be tested in particular cases. Moreover my thesis has empirical content in another way; it does entail that without the virtues there could be a recognition only of what I have called external goods and not at all of internal goods in the context of practices. And in any society which recognised only external goods competitiveness would be the dominant and even exclusive feature. We have a brilliant portrait of such a society in Hobbes's account of the state of nature; and Professor Turnbull's report of the fate of the Ik suggests that social reality does in the most horrifying way confirm both my thesis and Hobbes's.

Virtues then stand in a different relationship to external and to internal goods. The possession of the virtues—and not only of their semblance and simulacra—is necessary to achieve the latter; yet the possession of the virtues may perfectly well hinder us in achieving external goods. I need to emphasise at this point that external goods genuinely are goods. Not only are they characteristic objects of human desire, whose allocation is what gives point to the virtues of justice and of generosity, but no one can despise them altogether without a certain hypocrisy. Yet notoriously the cultivation of truthfulness, justice and courage will often, the world being what it contingently is, bar us from being rich or famous or powerful. Thus although we may hope that we can not only achieve the standards of excellence and the internal goods of certain practices by possessing the virtues *and* become rich, famous and powerful, the virtues are always a potential stumbling block to this comfortable ambition. We should therefore expect that, if in a particular society the pursuit of external goods were to become dominant, the concept of the virtues might suffer first attrition and then perhaps something near total effacement, although simulacra might abound.

The time has come to ask the question of how far this partial account of a core conception of the virtues—and I need to emphasise that all that I have offered so far is the first stage of such an account—is faithful to the tradition which I delineated. How far, for example, and in what ways is it Aristotelian? It is—happily—not Aristotelian in two ways in which a good deal of the rest of the tradition also dissents from Aristotle. First, although this account of the virtues is teleological, it does not require the identification of any teleology in nature, and hence it does not require any allegiance to Aristotle's metaphysical biology. And secondly, just because of the multiplicity of human practices and the consequent multiplicity of goods in the pursuit of which the virtues may be exercised—goods which will often be contingently incompatible and which will therefore make rival claims upon our allegiance—conflict will not spring solely from flaws in individual character. But it was just on these two matters that Aristotle's account of the virtues seemed most vulnerable; hence if it turns out to be the case that this socially teleological account can support Aristotle's general account of the virtues as well as does his own biologically teleological account, these differences from Aristotle himself may well be regarded as strengthening rather than weakening the case for a generally Aristotelian standpoint.

There are at least three ways in which the account that I have given *is* clearly Aristotelian. First it requires for its completion a cogent elaboration of just those distinctions and concepts which Aristotle's account requires: voluntariness, the distinction between the intellectual virtues and the virtues of character, the relationship of both to natural abilities and to the passions and the structure of practical reasoning. On every one of these topics something very like Aristotle's view has to be defended, if my own account is to be plausible.

Secondly my account can accommodate an Aristotelian view of pleasure and enjoyment, whereas it is interestingly irreconcilable with any utilitarian view and more particularly with Franklin's account of the virtues. We can approach these questions by considering how to reply to someone who, having considered my account of the differences between goods internal to and goods external to a practice required into which class, if either, does pleasure or enjoyment fall? The answer is, 'Some types of pleasure into one, some into the other.'

Someone who achieves excellence in a practice, who plays chess or football well or who carries through an enquiry in physics or an experimental mode in painting with success, characteristically enjoys his achievement and his activity in achieving. So does someone who, although not breaking the limit of achievement, plays or thinks or acts in a way that leads towards such a breaking of limit. As Aristotle says, the enjoyment of the activity and the enjoyment of achievement are not the ends at which the agent aims, but the enjoyment supervenes upon the successful activity in such a way that the activity achieved and the activity enjoyed are one and the same state. Hence to aim at the one is to aim at the other; and hence also it is easy to confuse the pursuit of excellence with the pursuit of enjoyment *in this specific sense*. This particular confusion is harmless enough; what is not harmless is the confusion of enjoyment *in this specific sense* with other forms of pleasure.

For certain kinds of pleasure are of course external goods along with prestige, status, power and money. Not all pleasure is the enjoyment supervening upon achieved activity; some is the pleasure of psychological or physical states independent of all activity. Such states—for example that produced on a normal palate by the closely successive and thereby blended sensations of Colchester oyster, cayenne pepper and Veuve Cliquot—may be sought as external goods, as external rewards which may be purchased by money or received in virtue of prestige. Hence the pleasures are categorised neatly and appropriately by the classification into internal and external goods.

It is just this classification which can find no place within Franklin's account of the virtues which is formed entirely in terms of external relationships and external goods. Thus although by this stage of the argument it is possible to claim that my account does capture a conception of the virtues which is at the core of the particular ancient and medieval tradition which I have delineated, it is equally clear that there is more than one possible conception of the virtues and that Franklin's standpoint and indeed any utilitarian standpoint is such that to accept it will entail rejecting the tradition and *vice versa*.

One crucial point of incompatibility was noted long ago by D.H. Lawrence. When Franklin asserts, 'Rarely use venery but for health or offspring . . .', Lawrence replies, 'Never *use* venery.' It is of the character of a virtue that in order that it be effective in producing the internal goods which are the rewards of the virtues it should be exercised without regard to consequences. For it turns out to be the case that—and this is in part at least one more empirical factual claim—although the virtues are just those qualities which tend to lead to the achievement of a certain class of goods, none the less unless we practice them irrespective of whether in any particular set of contingent circumstances they will produce those goods or not, we cannot possess them at all. We cannot be genuinely courageous or

truthful and be so only on occasion. Moreover, as we have seen, cultivation of the virtues always may and often does hinder the achievement of those external goods which are the mark of worldly success. The road to success in Philadelphia and the road to heaven may not coincide after all.

Furthermore we are now able to specify one crucial difficulty for *any* version of utilitarianism—in addition to those which I noticed earlier. Utilitarianism cannot accommodate the distinction between goods internal to and goods external to a practice. Not only is that distinction marked by none of the classical utilitarians—it cannot be found in Bentham's writings nor in those of either of the Mills or of Sidgwick—but internal goods and external goods are not commensurable with each other. Hence the notion of summing goods—and a fortiori in the light of what I have said about kinds of pleasure and enjoyment the notion of summing happiness—in terms of one single formula or conception of utility, whether it is Franklin's or Bentham's or Mill's, makes no sense. None the less we ought to note that although *this* distinction is alien to J.S. Mill's thought, it is plausible and in no way patronising to suppose that something like this is the distinction which he was trying to make in *Utilitarianism* when he distinguished between 'higher' and 'lower' pleasures. At the most we can say 'something like this'; for J.S. Mill's upbringing had given him a limited view of human life and powers, had unfitted him, for example, for appreciating games just because of the way it had fitted him for appreciating philosophy. None the less the notion that the pursuit of excellence in a way that extends human powers is at the heart of human life is instantly recognisable as at home in not only J.S. Mill's political and social thought, but also in his and Mrs Taylor's life. Were I to choose human exemplars of certain of the virtues as I understand them, there would of course be many names to name, those of St Benedict and St Francis of Assisi and St Theresa *and* those of Frederick Engels and Eleanor Marx and Leon Trotsky among them. But that of John Stuart Mill would have to be there as certainly as any other.

Thirdly my account is Aristotelian in that it links evaluation and explanation in a characteristically Aristotelian way. From an Aristotelian standpoint to identify certain actions as manifesting or failing to manifest a virtue or virtues is never only to evaluate; it is also to take the first step towards explaining why those actions rather than some others were performed. Hence for an Aristotelian quite as much as for a Platonist the fate of a city or an individual can be explained by citing the injustice of a tyrant or the courage of its defenders. Indeed without allusion to the place that justice and injustice, courage and cowardice play in human life very little will be genuinely explicable. It follows that many of the explanatory projects of the modern social sciences, a methodological canon of which is the separation of 'the facts'—this conception of 'the facts' is the one which I delineated in Chapter 7—from all evaluation, are bound to fail. For the fact that someone was or failed to be courageous or just cannot be recognised as 'a fact' by those who accept that methodological canon. The account of the virtues which I have given is completely at one with Aristotle's on this point. But now the question may be raised: your account may be in many respects Aristotelian, but is it not in some respects false? Consider the following important objection.

I have defined the virtues partly in terms of their place in practices. But surely, it may be suggested, some practices—that is, some coherent human activities which answer to the description of what I have called a practice—are evil. So in discussions by some moral philosophers of this type of account of the virtues it has been suggested that torture and sado-masochistic sexual activities might be examples of practices. But how can a disposition be a virtue if it is the kind of disposition which sustains practices and some practices issue in evil? My answer to this objection falls into two parts.

First I want to allow that there *may* be

practices—in the sense in which I understand the concept—which simply *are* evil. I am far from convinced that there are, and I do not in fact believe that either torture or sado-masochistic sexuality answer to the description of a practice which my account of the virtues employs. But I do not want to rest my case on this lack of conviction, especially since it is plain that as a matter of contingent fact many types of practice may on particular occasions be productive of evil. For the range of practices includes the arts, the sciences and certain types of intellectual and athletic game. And it is at once obvious that any of these may under certain conditions be a source of evil: the desire to excel and to win can corrupt, a man may be so engrossed by his painting that he neglects his family, what was initially an honourable resort to war can issue in savage cruelty. But what follows from this?

It certainly is not the case that my account entails *either* that we ought to excuse or condone such evils *or* that whatever flows from a virtue is right. I do have to allow that courage sometimes sustains injustice, that loyalty has been known to strengthen a murderous aggressor and that generosity has sometimes weakened the capacity to do good. But to deny this would be to fly in the face of just those empirical facts which I invoked in criticising Aquinas' account of the unity of the virtues. That the virtues need initially to be defined and explained with reference to the notion of a practice thus in no way entails approval of all practices in all circumstances. That the virtues—as the objection itself presupposed—*are* defined not in terms of good and right practices, but of practices, does not entail or imply that practices as actually carried through at particular times and places do not stand in need of moral criticism. And the resources for such criticism are not lacking. There is in the first place no inconsistency in appealing to the requirements of a virtue to criticise a practice. Justice may be initially defined as a disposition which in its particular way is necessary to sustain practices; it does not follow that in pursuing the requirements of a practice violations of justice are not to be condemned. Moreover I already pointed out in Chapter 12 that a morality of virtues requires as its counterpart a conception of moral law. Its requirements too have to be met by practices. But, it may be asked, does not all this imply that more needs to be said about the place of practices in some larger moral context? Does not this at least suggest that there is more to the core concept of a virtue than can be spelled out in terms of practices? I have after all emphasised that the scope of any virtue in human life extends beyond the practices in terms of which it is initially defined. What then is the place of the virtues in the larger arenas of human life?

I stressed earlier that any account of the virtues in terms of practices could only be a partial and first account. What is required to complement it? The most notable difference so far between my account and any account that could be called Aristotelian is that although I have in no way restricted the exercise of the virtues to the context of practices, it is in terms of practices that I have located their point and function. Whereas Aristotle locates that point and function in terms of the notion of a type of whole human life which can be called good. And it does seem that the question 'What would a human being lack who lacked the virtues?' must be given a kind of answer which goes beyond anything which I have said so far. For such an individual would not merely fail *in a variety of particular ways* in respect of the kind of excellence which can be achieved through participation in practices and in respect of the kind of human relationship required to sustain such excellence. His own life *viewed as a whole* would perhaps be defective; it would not be the kind of life which someone would describe in trying to answer the question 'What is the best kind of life for this kind of man or woman to live?' And that question cannot be answered without at least raising Aristotle's own question. 'What is the good life for man?' Consider

three ways in which a human life informed only by the conception of the virtues sketched so far would be defective.

It would be pervaded, first of all, by *too many* conflicts and *too much* arbitrariness. I argued earlier that it is a merit of an account of the virtues in terms of a multiplicy of goods that it allows for the possibility of tragic conflict in a way in which Aristotle's does not. But it may also produce even in the life of someone who is virtuous and disciplined too many occasions when one allegiance points in one direction, another in another. The claims of one practice may be incompatible with another in such a way that one may find oneself oscillating in an arbitrary way, rather than making rational choices. So it seems to have been with T.E. Lawrence. Commitment to sustaining the kind of community in which the virtues can flourish may be incompatible with the devotion which a particular practice—of the arts, for example—requires. So there may be tensions between the claims of family life and those of the arts—the problem that Gauguin solved or failed to solve by fleeing to Polynesia, or between the claims of politics and those of the arts—the problem that Lenin solved or failed to solve by refusing to listen to Beethoven.

If the life of the virtues is continuously fractured by choices in which one allegiance entails the apparently arbitrary renunciation of another, it may seem that the goods internal to practices do after all derive their authority from our individual choices; for when different goods summon in different and in incompatible directions, 'I' have to choose between their rival claims. The modern self with its criterionless choices apparently reappears in the alien context of what was claimed to be an Aristotelian world. This accusation might be rebutted in part by returning to the question of why both goods and virtues do have authority in our lives and repeating what was said earlier in this chapter. But this reply would only be partly successful; the distinctively modern notion of choice would indeed have reappeared, even if with a more limited scope for its exercise than it has usually claimed.

Secondly without an overriding conception of the *telos* of a whole human life, conceived as a unity, our conception of certain individual virtues has to remain partial and incomplete. Consider two examples. Justice, on an Aristotelian view, is defined in terms of giving each person his or her due or desert. To deserve well is to have contributed in some substantial way to the achievement of those goods, the sharing of which and the common pursuit of which provide foundations for human community. But the goods internal to practices, including the goods internal to the practice of making and sustaining forms of community, need to be ordered and evaluated in some way if we are to assess relative desert. Thus only substantive application of an Aristotelian concept of justice requires an understanding of goods and of the good that goes beyond the multiplicity of goods which inform practices. As with justice, so also with patience. Patience is the virtue of waiting attentively without complaint, but not of waiting thus for anything at all. To treat patience as a virtue presupposes some adequate answer to the question: waiting for what? Within the context of practices a partial, although for many purposes adequate, answer can be given: the patience of a craftsman with refractory material, of a teacher with a slow pupil, of a politician in negotiations, are all species of patience. But what if the material is just too refractory, the pupil too slow, the negotiations too frustrating? Ought we always at a certain point just to give up in the interests of the practice itself? The medieval exponents of the virtue of patience claimed that there are certain types of situation in which the virtue of patience requires that I do not ever give up on some person or task, situations in which, as they would have put it, I am required to embody in my attitude to that person or task something of the patient attitude of God towards his creation. But this could only be so if patience served some overriding good, some *telos* which warranted putting other goods in a subordinate place. Thus it turns out that the content of the virtue of patience depends upon how we order various goods in a hierarchy and a *fortiori* on whether we are able rationally so to order these particular goods.

I have suggested so far that unless there is a *telos* which transcends the limited goods of practices by constituting the good of a whole human life, the good of a human life conceived as a unity, it will *both* be the case that a certain subversive arbitrariness will invade the moral life *and* that we shall be unable to specify the context of certain virtues adequately. These two considerations are reinforced by a third: that there is at least one virtue recognised by the tradition which cannot be specified at all except with reference to the wholeness of a human life—the virtue of integrity or constancy. 'Purity of heart,' said Kierkegaard, 'is to will one thing.' This notion of singleness of purpose in a whole life can have no application unless that of a whole life does.

It is clear therefore that my preliminary account of the virtues in terms of practices captures much, but very far from all, of what the Aristotelian tradition taught about the virtues. It is also clear that to give an account that is at once more fully adequate to the tradition and rationally defensible, it is necessary to raise a question to which the Aristotelian tradition presupposed an answer, an answer so widely shared in the pre-modern world that it never had to be formulated explicitly in any detailed way. This question is: is it rationally justifiable to conceive of each human life as a unity, so that we may try to specify each such life as having its good and so that we may understand the virtues as having their function in enabling an individual to make of his or her life one kind of unity rather than another?

Part IV

REALISM VS.
ANTI-REALISM

21 / J. L. MACKIE

The Subjectivity of Values

1. Moral Scepticism

There are no objective values. This is a bald statement of the thesis of this chapter, but before arguing for it I shall try to clarify and restrict it in ways that may meet some objections and prevent some misunderstanding.

The statement of this thesis is liable to provoke one of three very different reactions. Some will think it not merely false but pernicious; they will see it as a threat to morality and to everything else that is worthwhile, and they will find the presenting of such a thesis in what purports to be a book on ethics paradoxical or even outrageous. Others will regard it as a trivial truth, almost too obvious to be worth mentioning, and certainly too plain to be worth much argument. Others again will say that it is meaningless or empty, that no real issue is raised by the question whether values are or are not part of the fabric of the world. But, precisely because there can be these three different reactions, much more needs to be said.

The claim that values are not objective, are not part of the fabric of the world, is meant to include not only moral goodness, which might be most naturally equated with moral value, but also other things that could be more loosely called moral values or disvalues—rightness and wrongness, duty, obligation, an action's being rotten and contemptible, and so on. It also in-

Reprinted by permission of the publisher and copyright holder from J. L. Mackie, *Ethics* (New York: Penguin, 1977), pp. 15–49.

cludes non-moral values, notably aesthetic ones, beauty and various kinds of artistic merit. I shall not discuss these explicitly, but clearly much the same considerations apply to aesthetic and to moral values, and there would be at least some initial implausibility in a view that gave the one a different status from the other.

Since it is with moral values that I am primarily concerned, the view I am adopting may be called moral scepticism. But this name is likely to be misunderstood: 'moral scepticism' might also be used as a name for either of two first order views, or perhaps for an incoherent mixture of the two. A moral sceptic might be the sort of person who says 'All this talk of morality is tripe,' who rejects morality and will take no notice of it. Such a person may be literally rejecting all moral judgements; he is more likely to be making moral judgements of his own, expressing a positive moral condemnation of all that conventionally passes for morality; or he may be confusing these two logically incompatible views, and saying that he rejects all morality, while he is in fact rejecting only a particular morality that is current in the society in which he has grown up. But I am not at present concerned with the merits or faults of such a position. These are first order moral views, positive or negative: the person who adopts either of them is taking a certain practical, normative, stand. By contrast, what I am discussing is a second order view, a view about the status of moral values and the nature of moral valuing, about where and how they fit into the world. These first and second order views are not merely distinct but completely independent: one could be a second order moral sceptic without being a first order one, or again the other way round. A man could hold strong moral views, and indeed ones whose content was thoroughly conventional, while believing that they were simply attitudes and policies with regard to conduct that he and other people held. Conversely, a man could reject all established morality while believing it to be an objective truth that it was evil or corrupt.

With another sort of misunderstanding moral scepticism would seem not so much pernicious as absurd. How could anyone deny that there is a difference between a kind action and a cruel one, or that a coward and a brave man behave differently in the face of danger? Of course, this is undeniable; but it is not to the point. The kinds of behaviour to which moral values and disvalues are ascribed are indeed part of the furniture of the world, and so are the natural, descriptive, differences between them; but not, perhaps, their differences in value. It is a hard fact that cruel actions differ from kind ones, and hence that we can learn, as in fact we all do, to distinguish them fairly well in practice, and to use the words 'cruel' and 'kind' with fairly clear descriptive meanings; but is it an equally hard fact that actions which are cruel in such a descriptive sense are to be condemned? The present issue is with regard to the objectivity specifically of value, not with regard to the objectivity of those natural, factual, differences on the basis of which differing values are assigned.

2. Subjectivism

Another name often used, as an alternative to 'moral scepticism', for the view I am discussing is 'subjectivism'. But this too has more than one meaning. Moral subjectivism too could be a first order, normative, view, namely that everyone really ought to do whatever he thinks he should. This plainly is a (systematic) first order view; on examination it soon ceases to be plausible, but that is beside the point, for it is quite independent of the second order thesis at present under consideration. What is more confusing is that different second order views compete for the name 'subjectivism'. Several of these are doctrines about the meaning of moral terms and moral statements. What is often called moral subjectivism is the doctrine that, for example, 'This action is right' *means* 'I approve of this action', or more generally that moral judgements are equivalent to reports of the speaker's own feelings or attitudes. But the view I am now discussing is to be distinguished in two vital respects from any such doctrine as this. First, what I have called moral scepticism is a negative doctrine, not a positive one: it says what there isn't, not what there is. It says that there do not exist entities or relations of a certain kind, objective values or requirements, which many people have believed to exist. Of course, the moral sceptic cannot leave it at that. If his position is to be at all plausible, he must give some account of how other people have fallen into what he regards as an error, and this account will have to include some positive suggestions about how values fail to be objective, about what has been mistaken for, or has led to false beliefs about, objective values. But this will be a development of his theory, not its core: its core is the negation. Secondly, what I have called moral scepticism is an ontological thesis, not a linguistic or conceptual one. It is not, like the other doctrine often called moral subjectivism, a view about the meanings of moral statements. Again, no doubt, if it is to be at all plausible, it will have to give some account of their meanings, and I shall say something about this in Section 7 of this chapter and again in Chapters 2, 3, and 4. But this too will be a development of the theory, not its core.

It is true that those who have accepted the moral subjectivism which is the doctrine that moral judgements are equivalent to reports of the speaker's own feelings or attitudes have usually presupposed what I am calling moral scepticism. It is because they have assumed that there are no objective values that they have looked elsewhere for an analysis of what moral statements might mean, and have settled upon subjective reports. Indeed, if all our moral statements were such subjective reports, it would follow that, at least so far as we are aware, there are no objective moral values. If we were aware of them, we would say something about them. In this sense this sort of subjectivism entails moral scepticism. But the converse entailment does not hold. The denial that there are objective values does not commit one to any particular view about what moral statements mean, and certainly not to the view that they are equivalent to subjective reports. No doubt if moral values are not objective they are in some very broad sense subjective, and for this reason I would accept 'moral subjectivism' as an alternative name to 'moral scepticism'. But subjectivism in this broad sense must be distinguished from the specific doctrine about meaning referred to above. Neither name is altogether satisfactory: we simply have to guard against the (different) misinterpretations which each may suggest.

3. The Multiplicity of Second Order Questions

The distinctions drawn in the last two sections rest not only on the well-known and generally recognized difference between first and second order questions, but also on the more controversial claim that there are several kinds of second order moral question. Those most often mentioned are questions about the meaning and use of ethical terms, or the analysis of ethical concepts. With these go questions about the logic of moral statements: there may be special patterns of moral argument, licensed, perhaps, by aspects of the meanings of moral terms—for example, it may be part of the meaning of moral statements that they are universalizable. But there are also ontological, as contrasted with linguistic or conceptual, questions about the nature and status of goodness or rightness or whatever it is that first order moral statements are distinctively about. These are questions of factual rather than conceptual analysis: the problem of what goodness is cannot be settled conclusively or exhaustively by finding out what the word 'good' means, or what it is conventionally used to say or to do.

Recent philosophy, biased as it has been towards various kinds of linguistic inquiry, has tended to doubt this, but the distinction between conceptual and factual analysis in ethics can be supported by analogies with other areas. The question of what perception is, what goes on when someone perceives something, is not adequately answered by finding out what words like 'see' and 'hear' mean, or what someone is doing in saying 'I perceive . . .', by analysing, however fully and accurately, any established concept of perception. There is a still closer analogy with colours. Robert Boyle and John Locke called colours 'secondary qualities', meaning that colours as they occur in material things consist simply in patterns of arrangement and movement of minute particles on the surfaces of objects, which make them, as we would now say, reflect light of some frequencies better than others, and so enable these objects to produce colour sensations in us, but that colours as we see them do not literally belong to the surfaces of material things. Whether Boyle and Locke were right about this cannot be settled by finding out how we use colour words and what we mean in using them. Naïve realism about colours might be a correct analysis not only of our pre-scientific colour concepts but also of the conventional meanings of colour words, and even of the meanings with which scientifically sophisticated people use them when they are off their guard, and yet it might not be a correct account of the status of colours.

Error could well result, then, from a failure to distinguish factual from conceptual analysis with regard to colours, from taking an account of the meanings of statements as a full account of what there is. There is a similar and in practice even greater risk of error in moral philosophy. There is another reason, too, why it would be a mistake to concentrate second order ethical discussions on questions of meaning. The more work philosophers have done on meaning, both in ethics and elsewhere, the more complications have come to light. It is by now pretty plain that no simple account of the meanings of first order moral statements will be correct, will cover adequately even the standard, conventional, senses of the main moral terms; I think, none the less, that there is a relatively clear-cut issue about the objectivity of moral values which is in danger of being lost among the complications of meaning.

4. Is Objectivity a Real Issue?

It has, however, been doubted whether there is a real issue here. I must concede that it is a rather old-fashioned one. I do not mean merely that it was raised by Hume, who argued that 'The vice entirely escapes you . . . till you turn your reflexion into your own breast,' and before him by Hobbes, and long before that by some of the Greek sophists. I mean rather that it was discussed vigorously in the nineteen thirties and forties, but since then has received much less attention. This is not because it has been solved or because agreement has been reached: instead it seems to have been politely shelved.

But was there ever a genuine problem? R.M. Hare has said that he does not understand what is meant by 'the objectivity of values', and that he has not met anyone who does. We all know how to recognize the activity called 'saying, thinking it to be so, that some act is wrong', and he thinks that it is to this activity that the subjectivist and the objectivist are both alluding, though one calls it 'an attitude of disapproval' and the other 'a moral intuition': these are only different names for the same thing. It is true that if one person says that a certain act is wrong and another that it is not wrong the objectivist will say that they are contradicting one another; but this

yields no significant discrimination between objectivism and subjectivism, because the subjectivist too will concede that the second person is negating what the first has said, and Hare sees no difference between contradicting and negating. Again, the objectivist will say that one of the two must be wrong; but Hare argues that to say that the judgement that a certain act is wrong is itself wrong is merely to negate that judgement, and the subjectivist too must negate one or other of the two judgements, so that still no clear difference between objectivism and subjectivism has emerged. He sums up his case thus: 'Think of one world into whose fabric values are objectively built; and think of another in which those values have been annihilated. And remember that in both worlds the people in them go on being concerned about the same things—there is no difference in the "subjective" concern which people have for things, only in their "objective" value. Now I ask, "What is the difference between the states of affairs in these two worlds?" Can any answer be given except "None whatever"?'

Now it is quite true that it is logically possible that the subjective concern, the activity of valuing or of thinking things wrong, should go on in just the same way whether there are objective values or not. But to say this is only to reiterate that there is a logical distinction between first and second order ethics: first order judgements are not necessarily affected by the truth or falsity of a second order view. But it does not follow, and it is not true, that there is no difference whatever between these two worlds. In the one there is something that backs up and validates some of the subjective concern which people have for things, in the other there is not. Hare's argument is similar to the positivist claim that there is no difference between a phenomenalist or Berkeleian world in which there are only minds and their ideas and the common-sense realist one in which there are also material things, because it is logically possible that people should have the same experiences in both. If we reject the positivism that would make the dispute between realists and phenomenalists a pseudo-question, we can reject Hare's similarly supported dismissal of the issue of the objectivity of values.

In any case, Hare has minimized the difference between his two worlds by considering only the situation where people already have just such subjective concern; further differences come to light if we consider how subjective concern is acquired or changed. If there were something in the fabric of the world that validated certain kinds of concern, then it would be possible to acquire these merely by finding something out, by letting one's thinking be controlled by how things were. But in the world in which objective values have been annihilated the acquiring of some new subjective concern means the development of something new on the emotive side by the person who acquires it, something that eighteenth-century writers would put under the head of passion or sentiment.

The issue of the objectivity of values needs, however, to be distinguished from others with which it might be confused. To say that there are objective values would not be to say merely that there are some things which are valued by everyone, nor does it entail this. There could be agreement in valuing even if valuing is just something that people do, even if this activity is not further validated. Subjective agreement would give intersubjective values, but intersubjectivity is not objectivity. Nor is objectivity simply universalizability: someone might well be prepared to universalize his prescriptive judgements or approvals—that is, to prescribe and approve in just the same ways in all relevantly similar cases, even ones in which he was involved differently or not at all—and yet he could recognize that such prescribing and approving were his activities, nothing more. Of course if there were objective values they would presumably belong to *kinds* of things or actions or states of affairs, so that the judgements that reported them would be universalizable; but the converse does not hold.

A more subtle distinction needs to be made between objectivism and descriptivism. Descriptivism is again a doctrine about the meanings of ethical terms and statements, namely that their meanings are purely descriptive rather than even partly prescriptive or emotive or evaluative, or that it is not an essential feature of the conventional meaning of moral statements that they have some special illocutionary force, say of commending rather than asserting. It contrasts with the view that commendation is in principle distinguishable from description (however difficult they may be to separate in practice) and that moral statements have it as at least part of their meaning that they are commendatory and hence in some uses intrinsically action-guiding. But descriptive meaning neither entails nor is entailed by objectivity. Berkeley's subjective idealism about material objects would be quite compatible with the admission that material object statements have purely descriptive meaning. Conversely, the main tradition of European moral philosophy from Plato onwards has combined the view that moral values are objective with the recognition that moral judgements are partly prescriptive or directive or action-guiding. Values themselves have been seen as at once prescriptive and objective. In Plato's theory the Forms, and in particular the Form of the Good, are eternal, extra-mental, realities. They are a very central structural element in the fabric of the world. But it is held also that just knowing them or 'seeing' them will not merely tell men what to do but will ensure that they do it, overruling any contrary inclinations. The philosopher-kings in the *Republic* can, Plato thinks, be trusted with unchecked power because their education will have given them knowledge of the Forms. Being acquainted with the Forms of the Good and Justice and Beauty and the rest they will, by this knowledge alone, without any further motivation, be impelled to pursue and promote these ideals. Similarly, Kant believes that pure reason can by itself be practical, though he does not pretend to be able to explain how it can be so. Again, Sidgwick argues that if there is to be a science of ethics—and he assumes that there can be, indeed he defines ethics as 'the science of conduct'—what ought to be 'must in another sense have objective existence: it must be an object of knowledge and as such the same for all minds'; but he says that the affirmations of this science 'are also precepts', and he speaks of happiness as 'an end *absolutely* prescribed by reason'. Since many philosophers have thus held that values are objectively prescriptive, it is clear that the ontological doctrine of objectivism must be distinguished from descriptivism, a theory about meaning.

But perhaps when Hare says that he does not understand what is meant by 'the objectivity of values' he means that he cannot understand how values could be objective, he cannot frame for himself any clear, detailed, picture of what it would be like for values to be part of the fabric of the world. This would be a much more plausible claim; as we have seen, even Kant hints at a similar difficulty. Indeed, even Plato warns us that it is only through difficult studies spread over many years that one can approach the knowledge of the Forms. The difficulty of seeing how values could be objective is a fairly strong reason for thinking that they are not so; this point will be taken up in Section 9 but it is not a good reason for saying that this is not a real issue.

I believe that as well as being a real issue it is an important one. It clearly matters for general philosophy. It would make a radical difference to our *metaphysics* if we had to find room for objective values—perhaps something like Plato's Forms—somewhere in our picture of the world. It would similarly make a difference to our epistemology if it had to explain how such objective values are or can be known, and to our philosophical psychology if we had to allow such knowledge, or Kant's pure practical reason, to direct choices and actions. Less obviously, how this issue is settled will affect the possibility of certain kinds of moral argument. For example, Sidgwick

considers a discussion between an egoist and a utilitarian, and points out that if the egoist claims that his happiness or pleasure is objectively desirable or good, the utilitarian can argue that the egoist's happiness 'cannot be more objectively desirable or more a good than the similar happiness of any other person: the mere fact . . . that *he is he* can have nothing to do with its objective desirability of goodness'. In other words, if ethics is built on the concept of objective goodness, then egoism as a first order system or method of ethics can be refuted, whereas if it is assumed that goodness is only subjective it cannot. But Sidgwick correctly stresses what a number of other philosophers have missed, that this argument against egoism would require the objectivity specifically of goodness: the objectivity of what ought to be or of what it is rational to do would not be enough. If the egoist claimed that it was objectively rational, or obligatory upon him, to seek his own happiness, a similar argument about the irrelevance of the fact that he is he would lead only to the conclusion that it was objectively rational or obligatory for each other person to seek *his* own happiness, that is, to a universalized form of egoism, not to the refutation of egoism. And of course insisting on the universalizability of moral judgements, as opposed to the objectivity of goodness, would yield only the same result.

5. Standards of Evaluation

One way of stating the thesis that there are no objective values is to say that value statements cannot be either true or false. But this formulation, too, lends itself to misinterpretation. For there are certain kinds of value statements which undoubtedly can be true or false, even if, in the sense I intend, there are no objective values. Evaluations of many sorts are commonly made in relation to agreed and assumed standards. The classing of wool, the grading of apples, the awarding of prizes at sheepdog trials, flower shows, skating and diving championships, and even the marking of examination papers are carried out in relation to standards of quality or merit which are peculiar to each particular subject-matter or type of contest, which may be explicitly laid down but which, even if they are nowhere explicitly stated, are fairly well understood and agreed by those who are recognized as judges or experts in each particular field. Given any sufficiently determinate standards, it will be an objective issue, a matter of truth and falsehood, how well any particular specimen measures up to those standards. Comparative judgements in particular will be capable of truth and falsehood: it will be a factual question whether this sheepdog has performed better than that one.

The subjectivist about values, then, is not denying that there can be objective evaluations relative to standards, and these are as possible in the aesthetic and moral fields as in any of those just mentioned. More than this, there is an objective distinction which applies in many such fields, and yet would itself be regarded as a peculiarly moral one: the distinction between justice and injustice. In one important sense of the word it is a paradigm case of injustice if a court declares someone to be guilty of an offence of which it knows him to be innocent. More generally, a finding is unjust if it is at variance with what the relevant law and the facts together require, and particularly if it is known by the court to be so. More generally still, any award of marks, prizes, or the like is unjust if it is at variance with the agreed standards for the contest in question: if one diver's performance in fact measures up better to the accepted standards for diving than another's, it will be unjust if the latter is awarded higher marks or the prize. In this way the justice or injustice of decisions relative to standards can be a thoroughly objective matter, though there may still be a subjective element in the interpretation or application of standards. But the statement that a certain decision is thus just or unjust will not be objectively prescriptive: in so far as it can be simply true it leaves open the question whether there is any objective requirement to do what is just and to refrain from what is unjust, and equally leaves open the practical decision to act in either way.

Recognizing the objectivity of justice in relation to standards, and of evaluative judgements relative to standards, then, merely shifts the question of the objectivity of values back to the standards themselves. The subjectivist may try to make his point by insisting that there is no objective validity about the choice of standards. Yet he would clearly be wrong if he said that the choice of even the most basic standards in any field was completely arbitrary. The standards used in sheepdog trials clearly bear some relation to the work that sheepdogs are kept to do, the standards for grading apples bear some relation to what people generally want in or like about apples, and so on. On the other hand, standards are not as a rule strictly validated by such purposes. The appropriateness of standards is neither fully determinate nor totally indeterminate in relation to independently specifiable aims or desires. But however determinate it is, the objective appropriateness of standards in relation to aims or desires is no more of a threat to the denial of objective values than is the objectivity of evaluation relative to standards. In fact it is logically no different from the objectivity of goodness relative to desires. Something may be called good simply in so far as it satisfies or is such as to satisfy a certain desire; but the objectivity of such relations of satisfaction does not constitute in our sense an objective value.

6. Hypothetical and Categorical Imperatives

We may make this issue clearer by referring to Kant's distinction between hypothetical and categorical imperatives, though what he called imperatives are more naturally expressed as 'ought'-statements than in the imperative mood. 'If you want X, do Y' (or 'You ought to do Y')' will be a hypothetical imperative if it is based on the supposed fact that Y is, in the circumstances, the only (or the best) available means to X, that is, on a causal relation between Y and X. The reason for doing Y lies in its causal connection with the desired end, X; the oughtness is contingent upon the desire. But 'You ought to do Y' will be a categorical imperative if you ought to do Y irrespective of any such desire for any end to which Y would contribute, if the oughtness is not thus contingent upon any desire. But this distinction needs to be handled with some care. An 'ought'-statement is not in this sense hypothetical merely because it incorporates a conditional clause. 'If you promised to do Y, you ought to do Y' is not a hypothetical imperative merely on account of the stated if-clause; what is meant may be either a hypothetical or a categorical imperative, depending upon the implied reason for keeping the supposed promise. If this rests upon some such further unstated conditional as 'If you want to be trusted another time', then it is a hypothetical imperative; if not, it is categorical. Even a desire of the agent's can figure in the antecedent of what, though conditional in grammatical form, is still in Kant's sense of a categorical imperative. 'If you are strongly attracted sexually to young children you ought not to go in for school teaching' is not, in virtue of what it explicitly says, a hypothetical imperative: the avoidance of school teaching is not being offered as a means to the satisfaction of the desires in question. Of course, it could still be a hypothetical imperative, if the implied reason were a prudential one; but it could also be a categorical imperative, a moral requirement where the reason for the recommended action (strictly, avoidance) does not rest upon that action's being a means to the satisfaction of any desire that the agent is supposed to have. Not every conditional ought-statement or command, then, is a hypothetical imperative; equally, not every non-conditional one is a categorical imperative. An appropriate if-clause may be left unstated. Indeed, a simple command in the imperative mood, say a parade-ground order, which might seem most lit-

erally to qualify for the title of a categorical imperative, will hardly ever be one in the sense we need here. The implied reason for complying with such an order will almost always be some desire of the person addressed, perhaps simply the desire to keep out of trouble. If so, such an apparently categorical order will be in our sense a hypothetical imperative. Again, an imperative remains hypothetical even if we change the 'if' to 'since': the fact that the desire for X is actually present does not alter the fact that the reason for doing Y is contingent upon the desire for X by way of Y's being a means to X. In Kant's own treatment, while imperatives of skill relate to desires which an agent may or may not have, imperatives of prudence relate to the desire for happiness which, Kant assumes, everyone has. So construed, imperatives of prudence are no less hypothetical than imperatives of skill, no less contingent upon desires that the agent has at the time the imperatives are addressed to him. But if we think rather of a counsel of prudence as being related to the agent's future welfare, to the satisfaction of desires that he does not yet have—not even to a present desire that his future desires should be satisfied—then a counsel of prudence is a categorical imperative, different indeed from a moral one, but analogous to it.

A categorical imperative, then, would express a reason for acting which was unconditional in the sense of not being contingent upon any present desire of the agent to whose satisfaction the recommended action would contribute as a means—or more directly: 'You ought to dance', if the implied reason is just that you want to dance or like dancing, is still a hypothetical imperative. Now Kant himself held that moral judgements are categorical imperatives, or perhaps are all applications of one categorical imperative, and it can plausibly be maintained at least that many moral judgements contain a categorically imperative element. So far as ethics is concerned, my thesis that there are no objective values is specifically the denial that any such categorically imperative element is objectively valid. The objective values which I am denying would be action-directing absolutely, not contingently (in the way indicated) upon the agent's desires and inclinations.

Another way of trying to clarify this issue is to refer to moral reasoning or moral arguments. In practice, of course, such reasoning is seldom fully explicit: but let us suppose that we could make explicit the reasoning that supports some evaluative conclusion, where this conclusion has some action-guiding force that is not contingent upon desires or purposes or chosen ends. Then what I am saying is that somewhere in the input to this argument—perhaps in one or more of the premisses, perhaps in some part of the form of the argument—there will be something which cannot be objectively validated—some premiss which is not capable of being simply true, or some form of argument which is not valid as a matter of general logic, whose authority or cogency is not objective, but is constituted by our choosing or deciding to think in a certain way.

7. The Claim to Objectivity

If I have succeeded in specifying precisely enough the moral values whose objectivity I am denying, my thesis may now seem to be trivially true. Of course, some will say, valuing, preferring, choosing, recommending, rejecting, condemning, and so on, are human activities, and there is no need to look for values that are prior to and logically independent of all such activities. There may be widespread agreement in valuing, and particular value-judgements are not in general arbitrary or isolated: they typically cohere with others, or can be criticized if they do not, reasons can be given for them, and so on: but if all that the subjectivist is maintaining is that desires, ends, purposes, and the like figure somewhere in the system of reasons, and that no ends or purposes are objective as opposed to being merely intersubjective, then this may be conceded without much fuss.

But I do not think that this should be conceded so easily. As I have said, the main tradition of European moral philosophy includes the contrary claim, that there are objective values of just the sort I have denied. I have referred already to Plato, Kant, and Sidgwick. Kant in particular holds that the categorical imperative is not only categorical and imperative but objectively so: though a rational being gives the moral law to himself, the law that he thus makes is determinate and necessary. Aristotle begins the *Nicomachean Ethics* by saying that the good is that at which all things aim, and that ethics is part of a science which he calls 'politics', whose goal is not knowledge but practice; yet he does not doubt that there can be *knowledge* of what is the good for man, nor, once he has identified this as well-being or happiness, *eudaimonia*, that it can be known, rationally determined, in what happiness consists; and it is plain that he thinks that this happiness is intrinsically desirable, not good simply because it is desired. The rationalist Sámuel Clarke holds that:

> these eternal and necessary differences of things make it *fit and reasonable* for creatures so to act . . . even separate from the consideration of these rules being the *positive will* or *command of God*; and also antecedent to any respect or regard, expectation or apprehension, of any *particular private and personal advantage or disadvantage, reward or punishment*, either present or future. . . .

Even the sentimentalist Hutcheson defines moral goodness as 'some quality apprehended in actions, which procures approbation . . .', while saying that the moral sense by which we perceive virtue and vice has been given to us (by the Author of nature) to direct our actions. Hume indeed was on the other side, but he is still a witness to the dominance of the objectivist tradition, since he claims that when we 'see that the distinction of vice and virtue is not founded merely on the relations of objects, nor is perceiv'd by reason', this 'wou'd subvert all the vulgar systems of morality'.

And Richard Price insists that right and wrong are 'real characters of actions', not 'qualities of our minds', and are perceived by the understanding; he criticizes the notion of moral sense on the ground that it would make virtue an affair of taste, and moral right and wrong 'nothing in the objects themselves'; he rejects Hutcheson's view because (perhaps mistakenly) he sees it as collapsing into Hume's.

But this objectivism about values is not only a feature of the philosophical tradition. It has also a firm basis in ordinary thought, and even in the meanings of moral terms. No doubt it was an extravagance for Moore to say that 'good' is the name of a non-natural quality, but it would not be so far wrong to say that in moral contexts it is used as if it were the name of a supposed non-natural quality, where the description 'non-natural' leaves room for the peculiar evaluative, prescriptive, intrinsically action-guiding aspects of this supposed quality. This point can be illustrated by reflection on the conflicts and swings of opinion in recent years between non-cognitivist and naturalist views about the central, basic, meanings of ethical terms. If we reject the view that it is the function of such terms to introduce objective values into discourse about conduct and choices of action, there seem to be two main alternative types of account. One (which has importantly different subdivisions) is that they conventionally express either attitudes which the speaker purports to adopt towards whatever it is that he characterizes morally, or prescriptions or recommendations, subject perhaps to the logical constraint of universalizability. Different views of this type share the central thesis that ethical terms have, at least partly and primarily, some sort of non-cognitive, non-descriptive, meaning. Views of the other type hold that they are descriptive in meaning, but descriptive of natural features, partly of such features as everyone, even the non-cognitivist, would recognize as distinguishing kind actions from cruel ones, courage from cowardice, politeness from rudeness, and so on, and partly (though these two over-

lap) of relations between the actions and some human wants, satisfactions, and the like. I believe that views of both these types capture part of the truth. Each approach can account for the fact that moral judgements are action-guiding or practical. Yet each gains much of its plausibility from the felt inadequacy of the other. It is a very natural reaction to any non-cognitive analysis of ethical terms to protest that there is more to ethics than this, something more external to the maker of moral judgements, more authoritative over both him and those of or to whom he speaks, and this reaction is likely to persist even when full allowance has been made for the logical, formal, constraints of full-blooded prescriptivity and universalizability. Ethics, we are inclined to believe, is more a matter of knowledge and less a matter of decision than any non-cognitive analysis allows. And of course naturalism satisfies this demand. It will not be a matter of choice or decision whether an action is cruel or unjust or imprudent or whether it is likely to produce more distress than pleasure. But in satisfying this demand, it introduces a converse deficiency. On a naturalist analysis, moral judgements can be practical, but their practicality is wholly relative to desires or possible satisfactions of the person or persons whose actions are to be guided; but moral judgements seem to say more than this. This view leaves out the categorical quality of moral requirements. In fact both naturalist and non-cognitive analyses leave out the apparent authority of ethics, the one by excluding the categorically imperative aspect, the other the claim to objective validity or truth. The ordinary user of moral language means to say something about whatever it is that he characterizes morally, for example a possible action, as it is in itself, or would be if it were realized, and not about, or even simply expressive of, his, or anyone else's, attitude or relation to it. But the something he wants to say is not purely descriptive, certainly not inert, but something that involves a call for action or for the refraining from action, and one that is absolute, not contingent upon any desire or preference or policy or choice, his own or anyone else's. Someone in a state of moral perplexity, wondering whether it would be wrong for him to engage, say, in research related to bacteriological warfare, wants to arrive at some judgement about this concrete case, his doing this work at this time in these actual circumstances; his relevant characteristics will be part of the subject of the judgement, but no relation between him and the proposed action will be part of the predicate. The question is not, for example, whether he really wants to do this work, whether it will satisfy or dissatisfy him, whether he will in the long run have a proattitude towards it, or even whether this is an action of a sort that he can happily and sincerely recommend in all relevantly similar cases. Nor is he even wondering just whether to recommend such action in all relevantly similar cases. He wants to know whether this course of action would be wrong in itself. Something like this is the everyday objectivist concept of which talk about non-natural qualities is a philosopher's reconstruction.

The prevalence of this tendency to objectify values—and not only moral ones—is confirmed by a pattern of thinking that we find in existentialists and those influenced by them. The denial of objective values can carry with it an extreme emotional reaction, a feeling that nothing matters at all, that life has lost its purpose. Of course this does not follow; the lack of objective values is not a good reason for abandoning subjective concern or for ceasing to want anything. But the abandonment of a belief in objective values can cause, at least temporarily, a decay of subjective concern and sense of purpose. That it does so is evidence that the people in whom this reaction occurs have been tending to objectify their concerns and purposes, have been giving them a fictitious external authority. A claim to objectivity has been so strongly associated with their subjective concerns and purposes that the collapse of the former seems to undermine the latter as well.

This view, that conceptual analysis would reveal a claim to objectivity, is some-

times dramatically confirmed by philosophers who are officially on the other side. Bertrand Russell, for example, says that 'ethical propositions should be expressed in the optative mood, not in the indicative'; he defends himself effectively against the charge of inconsistency in both holding ultimate ethical valuations to be subjective and expressing emphatic opinions on ethical questions. Yet at the end he admits:

> Certainly there *seems* to be something more. Suppose, for example, that some one were to advocate the introduction of bull-fighting in this country. In opposing the proposal, I should *feel*, not only that I was expressing my desires, but that my desires in the matter are *right*, whatever that may mean. As a matter of argument, I can, I think, show that I am not guilty of any logical inconsistency in holding to the above interpretation of ethics and at the same time expressing strong ethical preferences. But in feeling I am not satisfied.

But he concludes, reasonably enough, with the remark: 'I can only say that, while my own opinions as to ethics do not satisfy me, other people's satisfy me still less.'

I conclude, then, that ordinary moral judgements include a claim to objectivity, an assumption that there are objective values in just the sense in which I am concerned to deny this. And I do not think it is going too far to say that this assumption has been incorporated in the basic, conventional, meanings of moral terms. Any analysis of the meanings of moral terms which omits this claim to objective, intrinsic, prescriptivity is to that extent incomplete; and this is true of any non-cognitive analysis, any naturalist one, and any combination of the two.

If second order ethics were confined, then, to linguistic and conceptual analysis, it ought to conclude that moral values at least are objective: that they are so is part of what our ordinary moral statements mean: the traditional moral concepts of the ordinary man as well as of the main line of western philosophers are concepts of objective value. But it is precisely for this reason that linguistic and conceptual analysis is not enough. The claim to objectivity, however ingrained in our language and thought, is not self-validating. It can and should be questioned. But the denial of objective values will have to be put forward not as the result of an analytic approach, but as an 'error theory', a theory that although most people in making moral judgements implicitly claim, among other things, to be pointing to something objectively prescriptive, these claims are all false. It is this that makes the name 'moral scepticism' appropriate.

But since this is an error theory, since it goes against assumptions ingrained in our thought and built into some of the ways in which language is used, since it conflicts with what is sometimes called common sense, it needs very solid support. It is not something we can accept lightly or casually and then quietly pass on. If we are to adopt this view, we must argue explicitly for it. Traditionally it has been supported by arguments of two main kinds, which I shall call the argument from relativity and the argument from queerness, but these can, as I shall show, be supplemented in several ways.

8. The Argument from Relativity

The argument from relativity has as its premiss the well-known variation in moral codes from one society to another and from one period to another, and also the differences in moral beliefs between different groups and classes within a complex community. Such variation is in itself merely a truth of descriptive morality, a fact of anthropology which entails neither first order nor second order ethical views. Yet it may indirectly support second order subjectivism: radical differences between first order moral judgements make it difficult to treat those judgements as apprehensions of objective truths. But it is not the mere occurrence of disagreements that tells against the objectivity of values. Disagreement on questions in history or biology or cosmol-

ogy does not show that there are no objective issues in these fields for investigators to disagree about. But such scientific disagreement results from speculative inferences or explanatory hypotheses based on inadequate evidence, and it is hardly plausible to interpret moral disagreement in the same way. Disagreement about moral codes seems to reflect people's adherence to and participation in different ways of life. The causal connection seems to be mainly that way round: it is that people approve of monogamy because they participate in a monogamous way of life rather than that they participate in a monogamous way of life because they approve of monogamy. Of course, the standards may be an idealization of the way of life from which they arise: the monogamy in which people participate may be less complete, less rigid, than that of which it leads them to approve. This is not to say that moral judgements are purely conventional. Of course there have been and are moral heretics and moral reformers, people who have turned against the established rules and practices of their own communities for moral reasons, and often for moral reasons that we would endorse. But this can usually be understood as the extension, in ways which, though new and unconventional, seemed to them to be required for consistency, of rules to which they already adhered as arising out of an existing way of life. In short, the argument from relativity has some force simply because the actual variations in the moral codes are more readily explained by the hypothesis that they reflect ways of life than by the hypothesis that they express perceptions, most of them seriously inadequate and badly distorted, of objective values.

But there is a well-known counter to this argument from relativity, namely to say that the items for which objective validity is in the first place to be claimed are not specific moral rules or codes but very general basic principles which are recognized at least implicitly to some extent in all society—such principles as provide the foundations of what Sidgwick has called different methods of ethics: the principle of universalizability, perhaps, or the rule that one ought to conform to the specific rules of any way of life in which one takes part, from which one profits, and on which one relies, or some utilitarian principle of doing what tends, or seems likely, to promote the general happiness. It is easy to show that such general principles, married with differing concrete circumstances, different existing social patterns or different preferences, will beget different specific moral rules; and there is some plausibility in the claim that the specific rules thus generated will vary from community to community or from group to group in close agreement with the actual variations in accepted codes.

The argument from relativity can be only partly countered in this way. To take this line the moral objectivist has to say that it is only in these principles that the objective moral character attaches immediately to its descriptively specified ground or subject: other moral judgements are objectively valid or true, but only derivatively and contingently—if things had been otherwise, quite different sorts of actions would have been right. And despite the prominence in recent philosophical ethics of universalization, utilitarian principles, and the like, these are very far from constituting the whole of what is actually affirmed as basic in ordinary moral thought. Much of this is concerned rather with what Hare calls 'ideals' or, less kindly, 'fanaticism'. That is, people judge that some things are good or right, and others are bad or wrong, not because—or at any rate not only because—they exemplify some general principle for which widespread implicit acceptance could be claimed, but because something about those things arouses certain responses immediately in them, though they would arouse radically and irresolvably different responses in others. 'Moral sense' or 'intuition' is an initially more plausible description of what supplies many of our basic moral judgements than 'reason'. With regard to all these starting points of moral thinking the argument from relativity remains in full force.

9. The Argument from Queerness

Even more important, however, and certainly more generally applicable, is the argument from queerness. This has two parts, one metaphysical, the other epistemological. If there were objective values, then they would be entities or qualities or relations of a very strange sort, utterly different from anything else in the universe. Correspondingly, if we were aware of them, it would have to be by some special faculty of moral perception or intuition, utterly different from our ordinary ways of knowing everything else. These points were recognized by Moore when he spoke of non-natural qualities, and by the intuitionists in their talk about a 'faculty of moral intuition'. Intuitionism has long been out of favour, and it is indeed easy to point out its implausibilities. What is not so often stressed, but is more important, is that the central thesis of intuitionism is one to which any objectivist view of values is in the end committed: intuitionism merely makes unpalatably plain what other forms of objectivism wrap up. Of course the suggestion that moral judgements are made or moral problems solved by just sitting down and having an ethical intuition is a travesty of actual moral thinking. But, however complex the real process, it will require (if it is to yield authoritatively prescriptive conclusions) some input of this distinctive sort, either premises or forms of argument or both. When we ask the awkward question, how we can be aware of this authoritative prescriptivity, of the truth of these distinctively ethical premises or of the cogency of this distinctively ethical pattern of reasoning, none of our ordinary accounts of sensory perception or introspection or the framing and confirming of explanatory hypotheses or inference or logical construction or conceptual analysis, or any combination of these, will provide a satisfactory answer; 'a special sort of intuition' is a lame answer, but it is the one to which the clear-headed objectivist is compelled to resort.

Indeed, the best move for the moral objectivist is not to evade this issue, but to look for companions in guilt. For example, Richard Price argues that it is not moral knowledge alone that such an empiricism as those of Locke and Hume is unable to account for, but also our knowledge and even our ideas of essence, number, identity, diversity, solidity, inertia, substance, the necessary existence and infinite extension of time and space, necessity and possibility in general, power; and causation. If the understanding, which Price defines as the faculty within us that discerns truth, is also a source of new simple ideas of so many other sorts, may it not also be a power of immediately perceiving right and wrong, which yet are real characters of actions?

This is an important counter to the argument from queerness. The only adequate reply to it would be to show how, on empiricist foundations, we can construct an account of the ideas and beliefs and knowledge that we have of all these matters. I cannot even begin to do that here, though I have undertaken some parts of the task elsewhere. I can only state my belief that satisfactory accounts of most of these can be given in empirical terms. If some supposed metaphysical necessities or essences resist such treatment, then they too should be included, along with objective values, among the targets of the argument from queerness.

This queerness does not consist simply in the fact that ethical statements are 'unverifiable'. Although logical positivism with its verifiability theory of descriptive meaning gave an impetus to non-cognitive accounts of ethics, it is not only logical positivists but also empiricists of a much more liberal sort who should find objective values hard to accommodate. Indeed, I would not only reject the verifiability principle but also deny the conclusion commonly drawn from it, that moral judgements lack descriptive meaning. The assertion that there are objective values or intrinsically prescriptive entities or features of some kind, which ordinary moral judgements presuppose, is, I hold, not meaningless but false.

Plato's Forms give a dramatic picture of what objective values would have to be. The Form of the Good is such that knowledge of it provides the knower with both a direction and an overriding motive; something's being good both tells the person who knows this to pursue it and makes him pursue it. An objective good would be sought by anyone who was acquainted with it, not because of any contingent fact that this person, or every person, is so constituted that he desires this end, but just because the end has to-be-pursuedness somehow built into it. Similarly, if there were objective principles of right and wrong, any wrong (possible) course of action would have not-to-be-doneness somehow built into it. Or we should have something like Clarke's necessary relations of fitness between situations and actions, so that a situation would have a demand for such-and-such an action somehow built into it.

The need for an argument of this sort can be brought out by reflection on Hume's argument that 'reason'—in which at this stage he includes all sorts of knowing as well as reasoning—can never be an 'influencing motive of the will'. Someone might object that Hume has argued unfairly from the lack of influencing power (not contingent upon desires) in ordinary objects of knowledge and ordinary reasoning, and might maintain that values differ from natural objects precisely in their power, when known, automatically to influence the will. To this Hume could, and would need to, reply that this objection involves the postulating of value-entities or value-features of quite a different order from anything else with which we are acquainted, and of a corresponding faculty with which to detect them. That is, he would have to supplement his explicit argument with what I have called the argument from queerness.

Another way of bringing out this queerness is to ask, about anything that is supposed to have some objective moral quality, how this is linked with its natural features. What is the connection between the natural fact that an action is a piece of deliberate cruelty—say, causing pain just for fun—and the moral fact that it is wrong? It cannot be an entailment, a logical or semantic necessity. Yet it is not merely that the two features occur together. The wrongness must somehow be 'consequential' or 'supervenient'; it is wrong because it is a piece of deliberate cruelty. But just what *in the world* is signified by this 'because'? And how do we know the relation that it signifies, if this is something more than such actions being socially condemned, and condemned by us too, perhaps through our having absorbed attitudes from our social environment? It is not even sufficient to postulate a faculty which 'sees' the wrongness: something must be postulated which can see at once the natural features that constitute the cruelty, and the wrongness, and the mysterious consequential link between the two. Alternatively, the intuition required might be the perception that wrongness is a higher order property belonging to certain natural properties; but what is this belonging of properties to other properties, and how can we discern it? How much simpler and more comprehensible the situation would be if we could replace the moral quality with some sort of subjective response which could be causally related to the detection of the natural features on which the supposed quality is said to be consequential.

It may be thought that the argument from queerness is given an unfair start if we thus relate it to what are admittedly among the wilder products of philosophical fancy—Platonic Forms, non-natural qualities, self-evident relations of fitness, faculties of intuition, and the like. Is it equally forceful if applied to the terms in which everyday moral judgements are more likely to be expressed—though still, as has been argued in Section 7, with a claim to objectivity—'you must do this', 'you can't do that', 'obligation', 'unjust', 'rotten', 'disgraceful', 'mean', or talk about good reasons for or against possible actions? Admittedly not; but that is because the objective prescriptivity, the element a claim for whose authoritativeness is embedded in ordinary moral thought and language, is not yet isolated in these forms of speech, but is presented along with relations to desires and feelings, reasoning about the means to desired ends, interpersonal demands, the injustice which consists in the violation of what are in the context the accepted standards of merit, the psychological constituents of meanness, and so on. There is nothing queer about any of these, and under cover of them the claim for moral authority may pass unnoticed. But if I am right in arguing that it is ordinarily there, and is therefore very likely to be incorporated almost automatically in philosophical accounts of ethics which systematize our ordinary thought even in such apparently innocent terms as these, it needs to be examined, and for this purpose it needs to be isolated and exposed as it is by the less cautious philosophical reconstructions.

10. Patterns of Objectification

Considerations of these kinds suggest that it is in the end less paradoxical to reject than to retain the common-sense belief in the objectivity of moral values, provided that we can explain how this belief, if it is false, has become established and is so resistant to criticisms. This proviso is not difficult to satisfy.

On a subjectivist view, the supposedly objective values will be based in fact upon attitudes which the person has who takes himself to be recognizing and responding to those values. If we admit what Hume calls the mind's 'propensity to spread itself on external objects', we can understand the supposed objectivity of moral qualities as arising from what we can call the projection or objectification of moral attitudes. This would be analogous to what is called the 'pathetic fallacy', the tendency to read our feelings into their objects. If a fungus, say, fills us with disgust, we may be inclined to ascribe to the fungus itself a non-natural quality of foulness. But in moral contexts there is more than this propensity at work. Moral attitudes themselves are at

least partly social in origin: socially established—and socially necessary—patterns
of behaviour put pressure on individuals,
and each individual tends to internalize
these pressures and to join in requiring
these patterns of behaviour of himself and
of others. The attitudes that are objectified
into moral values have indeed an external
source, though not the one assigned to
them by the belief in their absolute authority. Moreover, there are motives that
would support objectification. We need
morality to regulate interpersonal relations, to control some of the ways in which
people behave towards one another, often
in opposition to contrary inclinations. We
therefore want our moral judgements to be
authoritative for other agents as well as for
ourselves: objective validity would give
them the authority required. Aesthetic values are logically in the same position as
moral ones; much the same metaphysical
and epistemological considerations apply
to them. But aesthetic values are less
strongly objectified than moral ones; their
subjective status, and an 'error theory' with
regard to such claims to objectivity as are
incorporated in aesthetic judgements, will
be more readily accepted, just because the
motives for their objectification are less
compelling.

But it would be misleading to think of
the objectification of moral values as primarily the projection of feelings, as in the
pathetic fallacy. More important are wants
and demands. As Hobbes says, 'whatsoever is the object of any man's Appetite or
Desire, that is it, which he for his part cal-
leth *Good*'; and certainly both the adjective
'good' and the noun 'goods' are used in
non-moral contexts of things because they
are such as to satisfy desires. We get the
notion of something's being objectively
good, or having intrinsic value, by revers-
ing the direction of dependence here, by
making the desire depend upon the goodness, instead of the goodness on the desire.
And this is aided by the fact that the desired thing will indeed have features that
make it desired, that enable it to arouse a
desire or that make it such as to satisfy

some desire that is already there. It is fairly
easy to confuse the way in which a thing's
desirability is indeed objective with its having in our sense objective value. The fact
that the word 'good' serves as one of our
main moral terms is a trace of this pattern
of objectification.

Similarly related uses of words are cov-
ered by the distinction between hypothetical and categorical imperatives. The statement that someone 'ought to' or, more
strongly, 'must' do such-and-such may be
backed up explicitly or implicitly by reference to what he wants or to what his purposes and objects are. Again, there may be
a reference to the purposes of someone else,
perhaps the speaker: 'You must do this'—
'Why?'—'Because I want such-and-such'.
The moral categorical imperative which
could be expressed in the same words can
be seen as resulting from the suppression
of the conditional clause in a hypothetical
imperative without its being replaced by
any such reference to the speaker's wants.
The action in question is still required in
something like the way in which it would
be if it were appropriately related to a
want, but it is no longer admitted that there
is any contingent want upon which its being required depends. Again this move can
be understood when we remember that at
least our central and basic moral judgements represent social demands, where the
source of the demand is indeterminate and
diffuse. Whose demands or wants are in
question, the agent's, or the speaker's, or
those of an indefinite multitude of other
people? All of these in a way, but there are
advantages in not specifying them precisely. The speaker is expressing demands
which he makes as a member of a community, which he has developed in and by
participation in a joint way of life; also,
what is required of this particular agent
would be required of any other in a relevantly similar situation; but the agent too
is expected to have internalized the relevant demands, to act as if the ends for
which the action is required were his own.
By suppressing any explicit reference to demands and making the imperatives cate-

gorical we facilitate conceptual moves from one such demand relation to another. The moral uses of such words as 'must' and 'ought' and 'should', all of which are used also to express hypothetical imperatives, are traces of this pattern of objectification.

It may be objected that this explanation links normative ethics too closely with descriptive morality, with the mores or socially enforced patterns of behaviour that anthropologists record. But it can hardly be denied that moral thinking starts from the enforcement of social codes. Of course it is not confined to that. But even when moral judgements are detached from the mores of any actual society they are liable to be framed with reference to an ideal community of moral agents, such as Kant's kingdom of ends, which but for the need to give God a special place in it would have been better called a commonwealth of ends.

Another way of explaining the objectification of moral values is to say that ethics is a system of law from which the legislator has been removed. This might have been derived either from the positive law of a state or from a supposed system of divine law. There can be no doubt that some features of modern European moral concepts are traceable to the theological ethics of Christianity. The stress on quasi-imperative notions, on what ought to be done or on what is wrong in a sense that is close to that of 'forbidden', are surely relics of divine commands. Admittedly, the central ethical concepts for Plato and Aristotle also are in a broad sense prescriptive or intrinsically action-guiding, but in concentrating rather on 'good' than on 'ought' they show that their moral thought is an objectification of the desired and the satisfying rather than of the commanded. Elizabeth Anscombe has argued that modern, non-Aristotelian, concepts of *moral* obligation, *moral* duty, of what is *morally* right and wrong, and of the *moral* sense of 'ought' are survivals outside the framework of thought that made them really intelligible, namely the belief in divine law. She infers that 'ought' has 'become a word of mere mesmeric force', with only a 'delusive ap-

pearance of content', and that we would do better to discard such terms and concepts altogether, and go back to Aristotelian ones.

There is much to be said for this view. But while we can explain some distinctive features of modern moral philosophy in this way, it would be a mistake to see the whole problem of the claim to objective prescriptivity as merely local and unnecessary, as a post-operative complication of a society from which a dominant system of theistic belief has recently been rather hastily excised. As Cudworth and Clarke and Price, for example, show, even those who still admit divine commands, or the positive law of God, may believe moral values to have an independent objective but still action-guiding authority. Responding to Plato's *Euthyphro* dilemma, they believe that God commands what he commands because it is in itself good or right, not that it is good or right merely because and in that he commands it. Otherwise God himself could not be called good. Price asks, 'What can be more preposterous, than to make the Deity nothing but will; and to exalt this on the ruins of all his attributes?' The apparent objectivity of moral value is a widespread phenomenon which has more than one source: the persistence of a belief in something like divine law when the belief in the divine legislator has faded out is only one factor among others. There are several different patterns of objectification, all of which have left characteristic traces in our actual moral concepts and moral language.

11. The General Goal of Human Life

The argument of the preceding sections is meant to apply quite generally to moral thought, but the terms in which it has been stated are largely those of the Kantian and post-Kantian tradition of English moral philosophy. To those who are more familiar with another tradition, which runs through Aristotle and Aquinas, it may seem wide of the mark. For them, the fundamental notion is that of the good for man, or the general end or goal of human life, or perhaps of a set of basic goods or primary human purposes. Moral reasoning consists partly in achieving a more adequate understanding of this basic goal (or set of goals), partly in working out the best way of pursuing and realizing it. But this approach is open to two radically different interpretations. According to one, to say that something is the good for man or the general goal of human life is just to say that this is what men in fact pursue or will find ultimately satisfying, or perhaps that it is something which, if postulated as an implicit goal, enables us to make sense of actual human strivings and to detect a coherent pattern in what would otherwise seem to be a chaotic jumble of conflicting purposes. According to the other interpretation, to say that something is the good for man or the general goal of human life is to say that this is man's proper end, that this is what he ought to be striving after, whether he in fact is or not. On the first interpretation we have a descriptive statement, on the second a normative or evaluative or prescriptive one. But this approach tends to combine the two interpretations, or to slide from one to the other, and to borrow support for what are in effect claims of the second sort from the plausibility of statements of the first sort.

I have no quarrel with this notion interpreted in the first way. I would only insert a warning that there may well be more diversity even of fundamental purposes, more variation in what different human beings will find ultimately satisfying, than the terminology of 'the good for man' would suggest. Nor indeed, have I any quarrel with the second, prescriptive, interpretation, provided that it is recognized as subjectively prescriptive, that the speaker is here putting forward his own demands or proposals, or those of some movement that he represents, though no doubt linking these demands or proposals with what he takes to be already in the first, descriptive, sense fundamental human

goals. In fact, I shall myself make use of the notion of the good for man, interpreted in both these ways, when I try in Chapter 8 to sketch a positive moral system. But if it is claimed that something is objectively the right or proper goal of human life, then this is tantamount to the assertion of something that is objectively categorically imperative, and comes fairly within the scope of our previous arguments. Indeed, the running together of what I have here called the two interpretations is yet another pattern of objectification: a claim to objective prescriptivity is constructed by combining the normative element in the second interpretation with the objectivity allowed by the first, by the statement that such and such are fundamentally pursed or ultimately satisfying human goals. The argument from relativity still applies: the radical diversity of the goals that men actually pursue and find satisfying makes it implausible to construe such pursuits as resulting from an imperfect grasp of a unitary true good. So too does the argument from queerness; we can still ask what this objectively prescriptive rightness of the true goal can be, and how this is linked on the one hand with the descriptive features of this goal and on the other with the fact that it is *to some extent* an actual goal of human striving.

To meet these difficulties, the objectivist may have recourse to the purpose of God: the true purpose of human life is fixed by what God intended (or, intends) men to do and to be. Actual human strivings and satisfactions have some relation to this true end because God made men for this end and made them such as to pursue it—but only *some* relation, because of the inevitable imperfection of created beings.

I concede that if the requisite theological doctrine could be defended, a kind of objective ethical prescriptivity could be thus introduced. Since I think that theism cannot be defended, I do not regard this as any threat to my argument. But I shall take up the question of relations between morality and religion again in Chapter 10. Those who wish to keep theism as a live option can read the arguments of the intervening chapters hypothetically, as a discussion of what we can make of morality without recourse to God, and hence of what we can say about morality if, in the end, we dispense with religious belief.

12. Conclusion

I have maintained that there is a real issue about the status of values, including moral values. Moral scepticism, the denial of objective moral values, is not to be confused with any one of several first order normative views, or with any linguistic or conceptual analysis. Indeed, ordinary moral judgements involve a claim to objectivity which both non-cognitive and naturalist analyses fail to capture. Moral scepticism must, therefore, take the form of an error theory, admitting that a belief in objective values is built into ordinary moral thought and language, but holding that this ingrained belief is false. As such, it needs arguments to support it against 'common sense'. But solid arguments can be found. The considerations that favour moral scepticism are: first, the relatively or variability of some important starting points of moral thinking and their apparent dependence on actual ways of life; secondly, the metaphysical peculiarity of the supposed objective values, in that they would have to be intrinsically action-guiding and motivating; thirdly, the problem of how such values could be consequential or supervenient upon natural features; fourthly, the corresponding epistemological difficulty of accounting for our knowledge of value entities or features and of their links with the features on which they would be consequential; fifthly, the possibility of explaining, in terms of several different patterns of objectification, traces of which remain in moral language and moral concepts, how even if there were no such objective values people not only might have come to suppose that there are but also might persist firmly in that belief. These five points sum up the case for moral scepticism; but of al-

most equal importance are the preliminary removal of misunderstandings that often prevent this thesis from being considered fairly and explicitly, and the isolation of those items about which the moral sceptic is sceptical from many associated qualities and relations whose objective status is not in dispute.

But what if we can establish this negative conclusion, that there are no objective values? How does it help us to say anything positively about ethics? Does it not at one stroke rule out all normative ethics, laying it down that all affirmative first order judgements are false, since they include, by virtue of the very meanings of their terms, unwarranted claims to objectivity? I shall take up these questions in Chapter 5; but first I want to amplify and reinforce the conclusion of this chapter by some investigations of the meanings and logical connections of moral terms.

Notes

My views on the subject of this chapter were first put forward in 'A Refutation of Morals', published in the *Australasian Journal of Psychology and Philosophy* 24 (1946), but substantially written in 1941. Discussions current at about that time which helped to determine the main outlines of my position are recorded in, for example, Charles L. Steven-son's *Ethics and Language* (New Haven, 1941) and A.J. Ayer's *Language, Truth, and Logic* (London, 1936). An unjustly neglected work which anticipates my stress on objectification is E. Westermarck's *Ethical Relativity* (London, 1932). But the best illustration and support for the arguments of this chapter, and for much else in the book, are provided by the works of such earlier writers as Hobbes, Locke, Samuel Clarke, Hutcheson, Butler, Balguy, Hume, and Richard Price, of which substantial selections are edited by D.D. Raphael in *British Moralists 1650–1800* (Oxford, 1969): for example, Balguy brings out very clearly what I call the 'claim to objectivity'.

There is a full survey of recent controversy

between critics and defenders of naturalism in 'Recent Work on Ethical Naturalism' by R.L. Franklin in *Studies in Ethics, American Philosophical Quarterly Monograph No. 7* (1973). Concentration on questions of meaning is criticized by P. Singer in 'The Triviality of the Debate over "Is-ought" and the Defini-tion of "Moral" ' in the *American Philosophical Quarterly* 10 (1973).

The quotations from R.M. Hare are from 'Nothing Matters', in his *Applications of Moral Philosophy* (London, 1972). This article was written in 1957. Hare's present view is given in 'Some Confusions about Subjectivity' in *Freedom and Morality*, edited by J. Bricke (University of Kansas Lindley Lectures—forthcoming). References to Sidgwick throughout this book are to *Methods of Ethics* (London, 1874), and those to Kant are to *Groundwork of the Metaphysic of Morals*, translated (for example) by H.J. Paton in The Moral Law (London, 1948). The quotation from Russell is from his 'Reply to Criticisms' in *The Philosophy of Bertrand Russell*, edited by P.A. Schlipp (Evanston, 1944). G.E.M. Anscombe's view is quoted from 'Modern Moral Philosophy', in *Philosophy* 33 (1958), reprinted in *The Definition of Morality*, edited by G. Wallace and A.D.M. Walker (London, 1970). The argument of Section 11 owes much to private discussion with J.M. Finnis.

22 / JOHN MCDOWELL

Values and Secondary Qualities

1 J. L. Mackie insists that ordinary evaluative thought presents itself as a matter of sensitivity to aspects of the world.[1] And this phenomenological thesis seems correct. When one or another variety of philosophical non-cognitivism claims to capture the truth about what the experience of value is like, or (in a familiar surrogate for phenomenology[2]) about what we mean by our evaluative language, the claim is never based on careful attention to the lived character of evaluative thought or discourse. The idea is, rather, that the very concept of the cognitive or factual rules out the possibility of an undiluted representation of how things are, enjoying, nevertheless, the internal relation to 'attitudes' or the will that would be needed for it to count as evaluative.[3] On this view the phenomenology of value would involve a mere incoherence, if it were as Mackie says—a possibility that then tends (naturally enough) not to be so much as entertained. But, as Mackie sees, there is no satisfactory justification for supposing that the factual is, by definition, attitudinatively and motivationally neutral. This clears away the only obstacle to accepting his phenomenological claim; and the upshot is that non-cognitivism must offer to correct the phenomenology of value, rather than to give an account of it.[4]

In Mackie's view the correction is called for. In this paper I want to suggest that he attributes an unmerited plausibility to this thesis, by giving a false picture of what one is committed to if one resists it.

2 Given that Mackie is right about the phenomenology of value, an attempt to accept the appearances makes it virtually irresistible to appeal to a perceptual model. Now Mackie holds that the model must be perceptual awareness of *primary* qualities. And this makes it comparatively easy to argue that the appearances are misleading. For it seems impossible—at least on reflection—to take seriously the idea of something that is like a primary quality in being simply *there*, independently of human sensibility, but is nevertheless intrinsically (not conditionally on contingencies about human sensibility) such as to elicit some 'attitude' or state of will from someone who becomes aware of it. Moreover, the primary-quality model turns the epistemology of value into mere mystification. The perceptual model is no more than a model: perception, strictly so called, does not mirror the role of reason in evaluative thinking, which seems to require us to regard the apprehension of value as an intellectual rather than a merely sensory matter. But if we are to take account of this, while preserving the model's picture of values as brutely and absolutely *there*, it seems that we need to postulate a faculty—'intuition'—about which all that can be said is that it makes us aware of objective rational connections: the model itself ensures that there is nothing helpful to say about how such a faculty might work, or why its deliverances might deserve to count as knowledge.

But why is it supposed that the model

Reprinted by permission of the publisher and copyright holder from *Morality and Objectivity*, ed. Ted Honderich (London: Routledge, 1985), pp. 110–129.

must be awareness of primary qualities rather than secondary qualities? The answer is that Mackie, following Locke, takes secondary-quality perception, as conceived by a pre-philosophical consciousness, to involve a projective error: one analogous to the error he finds in ordinary evaluative thought. He holds that we are prone to conceive secondary-quality experience in a way that would be appropriate for experience of primary qualities. So a pre-philosophical secondary-quality model for awareness of value would in effect be, after all, a primary-quality model. And to accept a philosophically corrected secondary-quality model for the awareness of value would be simply to give up trying to go along with the appearances.

I believe, however, that this conception of secondary-quality experience is seriously mistaken.

3 A secondary quality is a property the ascription of which to an object is not adequately understood except as true, if it is true, in virtue of the object's disposition to present a certain sort of perceptual appearance: specifically, an appearance characterizable by using a word for the property itself to say how the object perceptually appears. Thus an object's being red is understood as obtaining in virtue of the object's being such as (in certain circumstances) to look, precisely, red.

This account of secondary qualities is faithful to one key Lockean doctrine, namely the identification of secondary qualities with 'powers to produce various sensations in us'.[5] (The phrase 'perceptual appearance', with its gloss, goes beyond Locke's unspecific 'sensations', but harmlessly; it serves simply to restrict our attention, as Locke's word may not, to properties that are in a certain obvious sense perceptible.[6])

I have written of what property-ascriptions are understood to be true in virtue of, rather than of what they are true in virtue of. No doubt it is true that a given thing is red in virtue of some microscopic textural property of its surface; but a predication understood only in such terms—not in

terms of how the object would look—would not be an ascription of the secondary quality of redness.[7]

Secondary-quality experience presents itself as perceptual awareness of properties genuinely possessed by the objects that confront one. And there is no general obstacle to taking that appearance at face value.[8] An object's being such as to look red is independent of its actually looking red to anyone on any particular occasion; so, notwithstanding the conceptual connection between being red and being experienced as red, an experience of something as red can count as a case of being presented with a property that is there anyway—there independently of the experience itself.[9] And there is no evident ground for accusing the appearance of being misleading. What would one expect it to be like to experience something's being such as to look red, if not to experience the thing in question (in the right circumstances) as looking, precisely, red?

On Mackie's account, by contrast, to take experiencing something as red at face value, as a non-misleading awareness of a property that really confronts one, is to attribute to the object a property which is 'thoroughly objective', in the sense that it does not need to be understood in terms of experiences that the object is disposed to give rise to; but which nevertheless resembles redness as it figures in our experience—this to ensure that the phenomenal character of the experience need not stand accused of misleadingness, as it would if the 'thoroughly objective' property of which it constituted an awareness were conceived as a microscopic textural basis for the object's disposition to look red. This use of the notion of resemblance corresponds to one key element in Locke's exposition of the concept of a primary quality.[10] In these Lockean terms Mackie's view amounts to accusing a naive perceptual consciousness of taking secondary qualities for primary qualities.

According to Mackie, this conception of primary qualities that resemble colours as we see them is coherent; that nothing is characterized by such qualities is established by merely empirical argument. But is the idea coherent? This would require two things: first, that colours figure in perceptual experience neutrally, so to speak, rather than as essentially phenomenal qualities of objects, qualities that could not be adequately conceived except in terms of how their possessors would look; and, second, that we command a concept of resemblance that would enable us to construct notions of possible primary qualities out of the idea of resemblance to such neutral elements of experience. The first of these requirements is quite dubious. (I shall return to this.) But even if we try to let it pass, the second requirement seems impossible. Starting with, say, redness as it (putatively neutrally) figures in our experience, we are asked to form the notion of a feature of objects which resembles that, but which is adequately conceivable otherwise than in terms of how its possessors would look (since if it were adequately conceivable only in those terms it would simply be secondary). But the second part of these instructions leaves it wholly mysterious what to make of the first: it precludes the required resemblance being in phenomenal respects, but it is quite unclear what other sense we could make of the notion of resemblance to redness as it figures in our experience. (If we find no other, we have failed to let the first requirement pass; redness as it figures in our experience proves stubbornly phenomenal.)[11] I have indicated how we can make error-free sense of the thought that colours are authentic objects of perceptual awareness; in face of that, it seems a gratuitous slur on perceptual 'common sense' to accuse it of this wildly problematic understanding of itself.

Why is Mackie resolved, nevertheless, to convict 'common sense' of error? Secondary qualities are qualities not adequately conceivable except in terms of certain subjective states, and thus subjective themselves in a sense that that characterization defines. In the natural contrast, a primary quality would be objective in the sense that what it is for something to have it can be adequately understood otherwise than in terms of dispositions to give rise to subjective states. Now this contrast between objective and subjective is not a contrast between veridical and illusory experience. But it is easily confused with a different contrast, in which to call a putative object of awareness 'objective' is to say that it is there to be experienced, as opposed to being a mere figment of the subjective state that purports to be an experience of it. If secondary qualities were subjective in the sense that naturally contrasts with this, naive consciousness would indeed be wrong about them, and we would need something like Mackie's Lockean picture of the error it commits. What is acceptable, though, is only that secondary qualities are subjective in the first sense, and it would be simply wrong to suppose that this gives any support to the idea that they are subjective in the second.[12]

More specifically, Mackie seems insufficiently whole-hearted in an insight of his about perceptual experiences. In the case of 'realistic' depiction, it makes sense to think of veridicality as a matter of resemblance between aspects of a picture and aspects of what it depicts.[13] Mackie's insight is that the best hope of a philosophically hygienic interpretation for Locke's talk of 'ideas', in a perceptual context, is in terms of 'intentional objects': that is, aspects of representational content—aspects of how things seem to one in the enjoyment of a perceptual experience. Now it is an illusion to suppose, as Mackie does, that this warrants thinking of the relation between a quality and an 'idea' of it on the model of the relation between a property of a picture's subject and an aspect of the picture. Explaining 'ideas' as 'intentional objects' should direct our attention to the relation between how things are and how an experience represents them as being—in fact identity, not resemblance, if the representation is veridical.[14] Mackie's Lockean appeal to resemblance fits something quite different: a relation borne to aspects of how things are by intrinsic aspects of a bearer of representational content—not how things are represented to be, but features of an item that does the representing, with particular aspects of its content carried by particular aspects of what it is intrinsically (non-representationally) like.[15] Perceptual experiences have representational content; but nothing in Mackie's defence of the 'intentional objects' gloss on 'ideas' would force us to suppose that they have it in that sort of way.[16]

The temptation to which Mackie succumbs, to suppose that intrinsic features of experience function as vehicles for particular aspects of representational content, is indifferent to any distinction between primary and secondary qualities in the representational significance that these features supposedly carry. What it is for a colour to figure in experience and what it is for a shape to figure in experience would be alike, on this view, in so far as both are a matter of an experience's having a certain intrinsic feature. If one wants, within this framework, to preserve Locke's intuition that primary-quality experience is distinctive in potentially disclosing the objective properties of things, one will be naturally led to Locke's use of the notion of resemblance. But no notion of resemblance could get us from an essentially experiential state of affairs to the concept of a feature of objects intelligible otherwise than in terms of how its possessors would strike us. (A version of this point told against Mackie's idea of possible primary qualities answering to 'colours as we see them'; it tells equally against the Lockean conception of shapes.)

If one gives up the Lockean use of resemblance, but retains the idea that primary and secondary qualities are experientially on a par, one will be led to suppose that the properties attributed to objects in the 'manifest image' are all equally phenomenal—intelligible, that is, only in terms of how their possessors are disposed to appear. Properties that are objective, in the contrasting sense, can then figure only in the 'scientific image'.[17] On these lines one altogether loses hold of Locke's intuition

that primary qualities are distinctive in being both objective and perceptible.[18]

If we want to preserve the intuition, as I believe we should, then we need to exorcize the idea that what it is for a quality to figure in experience is for an experience to have a certain intrinsic feature: in fact I believe that we need to reject these supposed vehicles of content altogether. Then we can say that colours and shapes figure in experience, not as the representational significance carried by features that are—being intrinsic features of experience—indifferently subjective (which makes it hard to see how a difference in respect of objectivity could show up in their representational significance); but simply as properties that objects are represented as having, distinctively phenomenal in the one case and not so in the other. (Without the supposed intrinsic features, we should be immune to the illusion that experiences cannot represent objects as having properties that are not phenomenal—properties that are adequately conceivable otherwise than in terms of dispositions to produce suitable experiences.[19]) What Locke unfelicitously tried to yoke together, with his picture of real resemblances of our 'ideas', can now divide into two notions that we must insist on keeping separate: first, the possible veridicality of experience (the objectivity of its object, in the second of the two senses I distinguished), in respect of which primary and secondary qualities are on all fours; and, second, the not essentially phenomenal character of some properties that experience represents objects as having (their objectivity in the first sense), which marks off the primary perceptible qualities from the secondary ones.

In order to deny that a quality's figuring in experience consists in an experience's having a certain intrinsic feature, we do not need to reject the intrinsic features altogether; it would suffice to insist that a quality's figuring in experience consists in an experience's having a certain intrinsic feature *together with* the quality's being the representational significance carried by that feature. But I do not believe that this yields a position in which acceptance of the supposed vehicles of content coheres with a satisfactory account of perception. This position would have it that the fact that an experience represents things as being one way rather than another is strictly additional to the experience's intrinsic nature, and so extrinsic to the experience itself (it seems natural to say 'read into it'). There is a phenomenological falsification here. (This brings out a third role for Locke's resemblance, namely to obviate the threat of such a falsification by constituting a sort of intrinsic representationality: Locke's 'ideas' carry the representational significance they do by virtue of what they are like, and this can be glossed both as 'how they are intrinsically' and as 'what they resemble'.) In any case, given that we cannot project ourselves from features of experience to nonphenomenal properties of objects by means of an appeal to resemblance, it is doubtful that the metaphor of representational significance being 'read into' intrinsic features can be spelled out in such a way as to avoid the second horn of our dilemma. How could representational significance be 'read into' intrinsic features of experience in such a way that what was signified did not need to be understood in terms of them? How could a not intrinsically representational feature of experience become imbued with objective significance in such a way that an experience could count, by virtue of having that feature, as a direct awareness of a not essentially phenomenal property of objects?[20]

How things strike someone as being is, in a clear sense, a subjective matter: there is no conceiving it in abstraction from the subject of the experience. Now a motive for insisting on the supposed vehicles of aspects of content might lie in an aspiration, familiar in philosophy, to bring subjectivity within the compass of a fundamentally objective conception of reality.[21] If aspects of content are not carried by elements in an intrinsic structure, their subjectivity is irreducible. By contrast, one might hope to objectivize any 'essential subjectivity' that needs to be attributed to not intrinsically

representational features of experience, by exploiting a picture involving special access on a subject's part to something conceived in a broadly objective way—its presence in the world not conceived as constituted by the subject's special access to it.[22] Given this move, it becomes natural to suppose that the phenomenal character of the 'manifest image' can be explained in terms of a certain familiar picture: one in which a confronted 'external' reality, conceived as having only an objective nature, is processed through a structured 'subjectivity', conceived in this objectivistic manner. This picture seems to capture the essence of Mackie's approach to the secondary qualities.[23] What I have tried to suggest is that the picture is suspect in threatening to cut us off from the *primary* (not essentially phenomenal) qualities of the objects that we perceive: either (with the appeal to resemblance) making it impossible, after all, to keep an essentially phenomenal character out of our conception of the qualities in question, or else making them merely hypothetical, not accessible to perception. If we are to achieve a satisfactory understanding of experience's openness to objective reality, we must put a more radical construction on experience's essential subjectivity. And this removes an insidious obstacle—one whose foundation is summarily captured in Mackie's idea that it is not simply wrong to count 'colours as we see them' as items in our minds—that stands in the way of understanding how secondary-quality experience can be awareness, with nothing misleading about its phenomenal character, of properties genuinely possessed by elements in a not exclusively phenomenal reality.

4 The empirical ground that Mackie thinks we have for not postulating 'thoroughly objective features which resemble our ideas of secondary qualities' is that attributing such features to objects is surplus to the requirements of explaining our experience of secondary qualities. If it would be incoherent to attribute such features to objects, as I believe, this empirical argu-

ment falls away as unnecessary. But it is worth considering how an argument from explanatory superfluity might fare against the less extravagant construal I have suggested for the thought that secondary qualities genuinely characterize objects: not because the question is difficult or contentious, but because of the light it casts on how an explanatory test for reality—which is commonly thought to undermine the claims of values—should be applied.

A 'virtus dormitiva' objection would tell against the idea that one might mount a satisfying explanation of an object's looking red on its being such as to look red. The weight of the explanation would fall through the disposition to its structural ground.[24] Still, however optimistic we are about the prospects for explaining colour experience on the basis of surface textures,[25] it would be obviously wrong to suppose that someone who gave such an explanation could in consistency deny that the object was such as to look red. The right explanatory test is not whether something pulls its own weight in the favoured explanation (it may fail to do so without thereby being explained away), but whether the explainer can consistently deny its reality.[26]

Given Mackie's view about secondary qualities, the thought that values fail an explanatory test for reality is implicit in a parallel that he commonly draws between them. It is nearer the surface in his 'argument from queerness' and explicit in his citing 'patterns of objectification' to explain the distinctive phenomenology of value experience.[27] Now it is, if anything, even more obvious with values than with essentially phenomenal qualities that they cannot be credited with causal efficacy: values would not pull their weight in any explanation of value experience even remotely analogous to the standard explanations of primary-quality experience. But reflection on the case of secondary qualities has already opened a gap between that admission and any concession that values are not genuine aspects of reality. And the point is reinforced by a crucial disanalogy

between values and secondary qualities. To press the analogy is to stress that evaluative 'attitudes', or states of will, are like (say) colour experience in being unintelligible except as modifications of a sensibility like ours. The idea of value experience involves taking admiration, say, to represent its object as having a property which (although there in the object) is essentially subjective in much the same way as the property that an object is represented as having by an experience of redness—that is, understood adequately only in terms of the appropriate modification of human (or similar) sensibility. The disanalogy, now, is that a virtue (say) is conceived to be not merely such as to elicit the appropriate 'attitude' (as a colour is merely such as to cause the appropriate experiences), but rather such as to *merit* it. And this makes it doubtful whether merely causal explanations of value experience are relevant to the explanatory test, even to the extent that the question to ask is whether someone could consistently give such explanations while denying that the values involved are real. It looks as if we should be raising that question about explanations of a different kind.

For simplicity's sake, I shall elaborate this point in connection with something that is not a value, though it shares the crucial feature: namely danger or the fearful. On the face of it, this might seem a promising subject for a projectivist treatment (a treatment that appeals to what Hume called the mind's 'propensity to spread itself on external objects').[28] At any rate the response that, according to such a treatment, is projected into the world can be characterized, without phenomenological falsification, otherwise than in terms of seeming to find the supposed product of projection already there.[29] And it would be obviously grotesque to fancy that a case of fear might be explained as the upshot of a mechanical (or perhaps para-mechanical) process initiated by an instance of 'objective fearfulness'. But if what we are engaged in is an 'attempt to understand ourselves',[30] then merely causal explanations of responses like fear will not be satisfying anyway.[31] What we want here is a style of explanation that makes sense of what is explained (in so far as sense can be made of it). This means that a technique for giving satisfying explanations of cases of fear—which would perhaps amount to a satisfactory explanatory theory of danger, though the label is possibly too grand—must allow for the possibility of criticism; we make sense of fear by seeing it as a response to objects that *merit* such a response, or as the intelligibly defective product of a propensity towards responses that would be intelligible in that way.[32] For an object to merit fear just is for it to be fearful. So explanations of fear that manifest our capacity to understand ourselves in this region of our lives will simply not cohere with the claim that reality contains nothing in the way of fearfulness.[33]

The shared crucial feature suggests that this disarming of a supposed explanatory argument for unreality should carry over to the case of values. There is, of course, a striking disanalogy in the contentiousness that is typical of values; but I think it would be a mistake to suppose that this spoils the point. In so far as we succeed in achieving the sort of understanding of our responses that is in question, we do so on the basis of preparedness to attribute, to at least some possible objects of the responses, properties that would validate the responses. What the disanalogy makes especially clear is that the explanations that preclude our denying the reality of the special properties that are putatively discernible from some (broadly) evaluative point of view are themselves constructed from that point of view. (We already had this in the case of the fearful, but the point is brought home when the validation of the responses is controversial.) However, the critical dimension of the explanations that we want means that there is no question of just any actual response pulling itself up by its own bootstraps into counting as an undistorted perception of the relevant special aspect of reality.[34] Indeed, awareness that values are contentious tells against an unreflective contentment with the current state of one's

critical outlook, and in favour of a readiness to suppose that there may be something to be learned from people with whom one's first inclination is to disagree. The aspiration to understand oneself is an aspiration to change one's responses, if that is necessary for them to become intelligible otherwise than as defective. But although a sensible person will never be confident that his evaluative outlook is incapable of improvement, that need not stop him supposing, of some of his evaluative responses, that their objects really do merit them. He will be able to back up this supposition with explanations that show how the responses are well-placed; the explanations will share the contentiousness of the values whose reality they certify, but that should not stop him accepting the explanations any more than (what nobody thinks) it should stop him endorsing the values.[35] There is perhaps an air of bootstrapping about this. But if we restrict ourselves to explanations from a more external standpoint, at which values are not in our field of view, we deprive ourselves of a kind of intelligibility that we aspire to; and projectivists have given no reason whatever to suppose that there would be anything better about whatever different kind of self-understanding the restriction would permit.

5 It will be obvious how these considerations undermine the damaging effect of the primary-quality model. Shifting to a secondary-quality analogy renders irrelevant any worry about how something that is brutely *there* could nevertheless stand in an internal relation to some exercise of human sensibility. Values are not brutely there—not there independently of our sensibility—any more than colours are: though, as with colours, this does not stop us supposing that they are there independently of any particular apparent experience of them. As for the epistemology of value, the epistemology of danger is a good model. (Fearfulness is not a secondary quality, although the model is available only after the primary-quality model has been dislodged. A secondary-quality anal-

ogy for value experience gives out at certain points, no less than the primary-quality analogy that Mackie attacks.) To drop the primary-quality model in this case is to give up the idea that fearfulness itself, were it real, would need to be intelligible from a standpoint independent of the propensity to fear; the same must go for the relations of rational consequentiality in which fearfulness stands to more straight-forward properties of things.[36] Explanations of fear of the sort I envisaged would not only establish, from a different standpoint, that some of its objects are really fearful, but also make plain, case by case, what it is about them that makes them so; this should leave it quite unmysterious how a fear response rationally grounded in awareness (unproblematic, at least for present purposes) of these 'fearful-making characteristics' can be counted as being, or yielding, knowledge that one is confronted by an instance of real fearfulness.[37]

Simon Blackburn has written, on behalf of a projectivist sentimentalism in ethics, that 'we profit ... by realizing that a training of the feelings rather than a cultivation of a mysterious ability to spot the immutable fitnesses of things is the foundation of how to live.'[38] This picture of what an opponent of projectivism must hold is of a piece with Mackie's primary-quality model; it simply fails to fit the position I have described.[39] Perhaps with Aristotle's notion of practical wisdom in mind, one might ask why a training of the feelings (as long as the notion of feeling is comprehensive enough) cannot be the cultivation of an ability—utterly unmysterious just because of its connections with feelings—to spot (if you like) the fitnesses of things; even 'immutable' may be all right, so long as it is not understood (as I take it Blackburn intends) to suggest a 'platonistic' conception of the fitnesses of things, which would reimport the characteristic ideas of the primary-quality model.[40]

Mackie's response to this suggestion used to be, in effect, that it simply conceded his point.[41] Can a projectivist claim that the position I have outlined is at best a nota-

tional variant, perhaps an inferior notational variant, of his own position?

It would be inferior if, in eschewing the projectivist metaphysical framework, it obscured some important truth. But what truth would this be? It will not do at this point to answer 'The truth of projectivism'. I have disarmed the explanatory argument for the projectivist's thin conception of genuine reality. What remains is rhetoric expressing what amounts to a now unargued primary-quality model for genuine reality.[42] The picture that this suggests for value experience—objective (value-free) reality processed through a moulded subjectivity—is no less questionable than the picture of secondary-quality experience on which, in Mackie at any rate, it is explicitly modelled. In fact I should be inclined to argue that it is projectivism that is inferior. Deprived of the specious explanatory argument, projectivism has nothing to sustain its thin conception of reality (that on to which the projections are effected) but a contentiously substantial version of the correspondence theory of truth, with the associated picture of genuinely true judgment as something to which the judger makes no contribution at all.[43]

I do not want to argue this now. The point I want to make is that even if projectivism were not actually worse, metaphysically speaking, than the alternative I have described, it would be wrong to regard the issue between them as nothing but a question of metaphysical preference.[44] In the projectivist picture, having one's ethical or aesthetic responses rationally suited to their objects would be a matter of having the relevant processing mechanism functioning acceptably. Now projectivism can of course perfectly well accommodate the idea of assessing one's processing mechanism. But it pictures the mechanism as something that one can contemplate as an object in itself. It would be appropriate to say 'something one can step back from', were it not for the fact that one needs to use the mechanism itself in assessing it; at any rate one is supposed to be able to step back from any naively realistic acceptance of the values that the first-level employ-ment of the mechanism has one attribute to items in the world. How, then, are we to understand this pictured availability of the processing mechanism as an object for contemplation, separated off from the world of value? Is there any alternative to thinking of it as capable of being captured, at least in theory, by a set of principles for superimposing values on to a value-free reality? The upshot is that the search for an evaluative outlook that one can endorse as rational becomes, virtually irresistibly, a search for such a set of principles: a search for a *theory* of beauty or goodness. One comes to count 'intuitions' respectable only in so far as they can be validated by an approximation to that ideal.[45] (This is the shape that the attempt to objectivize subjectivity takes here.) I have a hunch that such efforts are misguided; not that we should rest content with an 'anything goes' irrationalism, but that we need a concep-tion of rationality in evaluation that will cohere with the possibility that particular cases may stubbornly resist capture in any general net. Such a conception is straight-forwardly available within the alternative to projectivism that I have described. I al-lowed that being able to explain cases of fear in the right way might amount to hav-ing a theory of danger, but there is no need to generalize that feature of the case; the explanatory capacity that certifies the spe-cial objects of an evaluative outlook as real, and certifies its responses to them as ra-tional, would need to be exactly as creative and case-specific as the capacity to discern those objects itself. (It would be the same capacity: the picture of 'stepping back' does not fit here.)[46] I take it that my hunch poses a question of moral and aesthetic taste, which—like other questions of taste—should be capable of being argued about. The trouble with projectivism is that it threatens to bypass that argument, on the basis of a metaphysical picture whose purported justification falls well short of making it compulsory. We should not let the question seem to be settled by what stands revealed, in the absence of com-pelling argument, as a prejudice claiming the honour due to metaphysical good taste.

Acknowledgment

This paper grew out of my contributions to a seminar on J. L. Mackie's *Ethics: Inventing Right and Wrong* (Penguin, Harmonds-worth, 1977: I refer to this as E) which I had the privilege of sharing with Mackie and R. M. Hare in 1978. I do not believe that John Mackie would have found it strange that I should pay trib-ute to a sadly missed colleague by continuing a strenuous disagreement with him.

Notes

1. See E, pp. 31–5. I shall also abbreviate ref-erences to the following other books by Mackie: *Problems from Locke* (Clarendon Press, Oxford, 1976; hereafter *PFL*); and *Hume's Moral Theory* (Routledge & Kegan Paul, London, 1980; hereafter *HMT*).

2. An inferior surrogate: it leads us to exag-gerate the extent to which expressions of our sensitivity to values are signalled by the use of a special vocabulary. See my 'Aesthetic value, objectivity, and the fab-ric of the world', in Eva Schaper, ed., *Pleasure, Preference, and Value* (Cambridge University Press, Cambridge, 1983), pp. 1–16, at pp. 1–2.

3. I am trying here to soften a sharpness of focus that Mackie introduces by stressing the notion of prescriptivity. Mackie's sin-

gleness of vision here has the perhaps unfortunate effect of discouraging a distinction such as David Wiggins has drawn between 'valuations' and 'directives or deliberative (or practical) judgements' (see 'Truth, invention, and the meaning of life', *Proceedings of the British Academy* LXII (1976), pp. 331–78, at pp. 338–9). My topic here is really the former of these. (It may be that the distinction does not matter in the way that Wiggins suggests: see n. 35 below.)

4. I do not believe that the 'quasi-realism' that Simon Blackburn has elaborated is a real alternative to this. (See p. 358 of his 'Truth, realism, and the regulation of theory', in Peter A. French, Theodore E. Uehling, Jr., and Howard Wettstein, eds, *Midwest Studies in Philosophy V: Studies in Epistemology* (University of Minnesota Press, Minneapolis, 1980), pp. 353–71.) In so far as the quasi-realist holds that the values, in his thought and speech about which he imitates the practices supposedly characteristic of realism, are *really* products of projecting 'attitudes' into the world, he must have a conception of genuine reality—that which the values lack and the things on to which they are projected have. And the phenomenological claim ought to be that *that* is what the appearances entice us to attribute to values.

5. *An Essay concerning Human Understanding*, II.viii.10.

6. Being stung by a nettle is an actualization of a power in the nettle that conforms to Locke's description, but it seems wrong to regard it as a perception of that power; the experience lacks an intrinsically representational character which that would require. (It is implausible that looking red is intelligible independently of being red; combined with the account of secondary qualities that I am giving, this sets up a circle. But it is quite unclear that we ought to have the sort of analytic or definitional aspirations that would make the circle problematic. See Colin McGinn, *The Subjective View* (Clarendon Press, Oxford, 1983), pp. 6–8.)

7. See McGinn, op. cit. pp. 12–14.

8. Of course there is room for the concept of illusion, not only because the senses can malfunction but also becuse of the need for a modifier like my '(in certain circumstances)', in an account of what it is for something to have a secondary quality. (The latter has no counterpart with primary qualities.)

9. See the discussion of (one interpretation of the notion of) objectivity at pp. 77–8 of Gareth Evans, 'Things without the mind', in Zak van Straaten, ed., *Philosophical Subjects: Essays presented to P. F. Strawson* (Clarendon Press, Oxford, 1980), pp. 76–116. Throughout the present section I am heavily indebted to this most important paper.

10. See *Essay*, II.viii.1.5.

11. Cf. pp. 56–7 of P. F. Strawson, 'Perception and its objects', in G. F. Macdonald, ed., *Perception and Identity: Essays presented to A. J. Ayer* (Macmillan, London, 1979), pp. 41–60.

12. This is a different way of formulating a point made by McGinn, op. cit., p. 121. Mackie's phrase 'the fabric of the world' belongs with the second sense of 'objective', but I think his arguments really address only the first. *Pace* p. 103 of A. W. Price, 'Varieties of objectivity and values', *Proceedings of the Aristotelian Society* LXXXII (1982–3), 103–19, I do not think the phrase can be passed over as unhelpful, in favour of what the arguments do succeed in establishing, without missing something that Mackie wanted to say. (A gloss on 'objective' as 'there to be experienced' does not figure in Price's inventory, p. 104. It seems to be the obvious response to his challenge at pp. 118–19.)

13. I do not say it is correct: scepticism about this is very much in point. (See Nelson Goodman, *Languages of Art* (Oxford University Press, London, 1969), chapter I.)

14. When resemblance is in play, it functions as a palliative to lack of veridicality, not as what veridicality consists in.

15. Intrinsic features of experience, functioning as vehicles for aspects of content,

seem to be taken for granted in Mackie's discussion of Molyneux's problem (*PFL*, pp. 28–32). The slide from talk of content to talk that fits only bearers of content seems to happen also in Mackie's discussion of truth, in *Truth, Probability, and Paradox* (Clarendon Press, Oxford, 1973), with the idea that a formulation like 'A true statement is one such that the way things are is the way it represents things as being' makes truth consist in a relation of correspondence (rather than identity) between how things are and how things are represented as being; pp. 56–7 come too late to undo the damage done by the earlier talk of 'comparison', e.g. at pp. 50, 51. (A subject matter for the talk that fits bearers is unproblematically available in this case; but Mackie does not mean to be discussing truth as a property of sentences or utterances.)

16. Indeed, this goes against the spirit of a passage about the word 'content' at *PFL*, p. 48. Mackie's failure to profit by his insight emerges particularly strikingly in his remarkable claim (*PFL*, p. 50) that the 'intentional object' conception of the content of experience yields an account of perception that is within the target area of 'the stock objections against an argument from an effect to a supposed cause of a type which is never directly observed'. (Part of the trouble here is a misconception of direct realism as a surely forlorn attempt to make perceptual knowledge unproblematic: *PFL*, p. 43.)

17. The phrases 'manifest image' and 'scientific image' are due to Wilfrid Sellars; see 'Philosophy and the scientific image of man', in *Science, Perception and Reality* (Routledge & Kegan Paul, London, 1963).

18. This is the position of Strawson, op. cit. (and see also his 'Reply to Evans' in van Straaten, ed., op. cit., pp. 273–82). I am suggesting a diagnosis, to back up McGinn's complaint, op. cit., p. 124n.

19. Notice Strawson's sleight of hand with phrases like 'shapes-as-seen', at p. 280 of 'Reply to Evans'. Strawson's understanding of what Evans is trying to say fails altogether to accommodate Evans's remark ('Things without the mind', p. 96) that 'to deny that . . . primary properties are *sensory* is not at all to deny that they are *sensible* or *observable*'. Shapes as seen are shapes—that is, non-sensory properties; it is one thing to deny, as Evans does, that experience can furnish us with the concepts of such properties, but quite another to deny that experience can disclose instantiations of them to us.

20. Features of physiologically specified states are not to the point here. Such features are not apparent in experience; whereas the supposed features that I am concerned with would have to be aspects of what experience is like for us, in order to function intelligibly as carriers for aspects of the content that experience presents to us. There may be an inclination to ask why it should be any harder for a feature of experience to acquire an objective significance than it is for a word to do so. But the case of language affords no counterpart to the fact that the objective significance in the case we are concerned with is a matter of how things (e.g.) *look* to be; the special problem is how to stop that 'look' having the effect that a supposed intrinsic feature of experience gets taken up into its own representational significance, thus ensuring that the significance is phenomenal and not primary.

21. See Thomas Nagel, 'Subjective and objective', in *Mortal Questions* (Cambridge University Press, Cambridge, 1979), pp. 196–213.

22. Cf. Bernard Williams, *Descartes: The Project of Pure Enquiry* (Penguin, Harmondsworth, 1978), p. 295.

23. Although McGinn, op. cit., is not taken in by the idea that 'external' reality has only objective characteristics, I am not sure that he sufficiently avoids the picture that underlies that idea: see pp. 106–9. (This connects with a suspicion that at pp. 9–10 he partly succumbs to a temptation to objectivize the subjective properties of objects that he countenances: it is not as clear as he seems to suppose that, say, redness can be, so to speak, abstracted from the way things strike *us* by an ap-

peal to relativity. His worry at pp. 132–6, that secondary-quality experience may after all be phenomenologically misleading, seems to betray the influence of the idea of content-bearing intrinsic features of experience.)

24. See McGinn, op. cit., p. 14.

25. There are difficulties over how complete such explanations could aspire to be: see Price, op. cit., pp. 114–15, and my 'Aesthetic value, objectivity, and the fabric of the world', op. cit., pp. 10–12.

26. Cf. pp. 206–8, especially p. 208, of David Wiggins, 'What would be a substantial theory of truth?', in van Straaten, ed., op. cit., pp. 189–221. The test of whether the explanations in question are consistent with rejecting the item in contention is something that Wiggins once mooted, in the course of a continuing attempt to improve that formulation: I am indebted to discussion with him.

27. See also Simon Blackburn, 'Rule-following and moral realism', in Steven Holtzman and Christopher Leich, eds, *Wittgenstein: To Follow a Rule* (Routledge & Kegan Paul, London, 1981), pp. 163–87; and the first chapter of Gilbert Harman, *The Nature of Morality* (Oxford University Press, New York, 1977).

28. *A Treatise of Human Nature*, I.iii.14. 'Projectivist' is Blackburn's useful label: see 'Rule-following and moral realism', op. cit., and 'Opinions and chances', in D. H. Mellor, ed., *Prospects for Pragmatism* (Cambridge University Press, Cambridge, 1980), pp. 175–96.

29. At pp. 180–1 of 'Opinions and chances', Blackburn suggests that a projectivist need not mind whether or not this is so; but I think he trades on a slide between 'can . . . only be understood in terms of' and 'our best vocabulary for identifying' (which allows that there may be an admittedly inferior alternative).

30. The phrase is from p. 165 of Blackburn, 'Rule-following and moral realism'.

31. I do not mean that satisfying explanations will not be causal. But they will not be *merely* causal.

32. I am assuming that we are not in the presence of a theory according to which no responses of the kind in question *could* be well-placed. That would have a quite unintended effect. (See E, p. 16.) Notice that it will not meet my point to suggest that calling a response 'well-placed' is to be understood only quasi-realistically. Explanatory indispensability is supposed to be the test for the *genuine* reality supposedly lacked by what warrants only quasi-realistic treatment.

33. Cf. Blackburn, 'Rule-following and moral realism', op. cit., p. 164.

34. This will be so even in a case in which there are no materials for constructing standards of criticism except actual responses: something that is not so with fearfulness, although given a not implausible holism it will be so with values.

35. I can see no reason why we should not regard the contentiousness as ineliminable. The effect of this would be to detach the explanatory test of reality from a requirement of convergence (cf. the passage by Wiggins cited in n. 26 above). As far as I can see, this separation would be a good thing. It would enable resistance to projectivism to free itself, with a good conscience, of some unnecessary worries about relativism. It might also discourage a misconception of the appeal to Wittgenstein that comes naturally to such a position. (Blackburn, 'Rule-following and moral realism', pp. 170–4, reads into my 'Non-cognitivism and rule-following', in Holtzman and Leich, eds, op. cit., pp. 141–62, an interpretation of Wittgenstein as, in effect, making truth a matter of consensus, and has no difficulty in arguing that this will not make room for hard cases; but the interpretation is not mind.) With the requirement of convergence dropped, or at least radically relativized to a point of view, the question of the claim to truth of directives may come closer to the question of the truth status of evaluations than Wiggins suggests, at least in 'Truth, invention, and the meaning of life', op. cit.

36. Mackie's question (*E*, p. 41) 'Just what *in*

the world is signified by this "because"?' involves a tendentious notion of 'the world'.

37. See Price, op. cit., pp. 106–7, 115.

38. 'Rule-following and moral realism', p. 186.

39. Blackburn's realist evades the explanatory burdens that sentimentalism discharges, by making the world rich (cf. p. 181) and then picturing it as simply setting its print on us. Cf. *E*, p. 22: 'If there were something in the fabric of the world that validated certain kinds of concern, then it would be possible to acquire these merely by finding something out, by letting one's thinking be controlled by how things were'. This saddles an opponent of projectivism with a picture of awareness of value as an exercise of pure receptivity, preventing him from deriving any profit from an analogy with secondary-quality perception.

40. On 'platonism', see my 'Non-cognitivism and rule-following', op. cit., at pp. 156–7. On Aristotle, see M. F. Burnyeat, 'Aristotle on learning to be good', in Amelie O. Rorty, ed., *Essays on Aristotle's Ethics* (University of California Press, Berkeley, Los Angeles, London, 1980), pp. 69–92.

41. Price, op. cit. p. 107, cites Mackie's response to one of my contributions to the 1978 seminar (see Acknowledgment above).

42. We must not let the confusion between the two notions of objectivity distinguished in §3 above seem to support this conception of reality.

43. Blackburn uses the correspondence theorist's pictures for rhetorical effect, but he is properly sceptical about whether this sort of realism makes sense (see 'Truth, realism, and the regulation of theory', op. cit.). His idea is that the explanatory argument makes a counterpart to its metaphysical favouritism safely available to a projectivist about values in particular. Deprived of the explanatory argument, this projectivism should simply wither away. (See 'Rule-following and moral realism', p. 165. Of course I am not saying that the thin conception of reality that

Blackburn's projectivism needs is unattainable, in the sense of being unformulable. What we lack is reasons of a respectable kind to recognize it as a complete conception of *reality*.)

44. Something like this seems to be suggested by Price, op. cit., pp. 107–8.

45. It is hard to see how a rational *invention* of values could take a more piecemeal form.

46. Why do I suggest that a particularistic conception of evaluative rationality is unavailable to a projectivist? (See Blackburn, 'Rule-following and moral realism', pp. 167–70.) In the terms of that discussion, the point is that (with no good explanatory argument for his metaphysical favouritism) a projectivist has no alternative to being 'a *real* realist' about the world on which he thinks values are superimposed. He cannot stop this from generating a quite un-Wittgensteinian picture of what *really* going in in the same way would be; which means that *he* cannot appeal to Wittgenstein in order to avert, as Blackburn puts it, 'the threat which shaplessness poses to a respectable notion of consistency' (p. 169). So, at any rate, I meant to argue in my 'Non-cognitivism and rule-following', to which Blackburn's paper is a reply. Blackburn thinks his projectivism is untouched by the argument, because he thinks he can sustain its metaphysical favouritism without appealing to 'real realism', on the basis of the explanatory argument. But I have argued that this is an illusion. (At p. 181, Blackburn writes: 'Of course, it is true that our reactions are "simply felt" and, in a sense, not rationally explicable.' He thinks he can comfortably say this because our conception of reason will go along with the quasi-realist truth that his projectivism confers on some evaluations. But how can one restrain the metaphysical favouritism that a projectivist must show from generating some such thought as 'This is not *real* reason'? If that is allowed to happen, a remark like the one I have quoted will merely threaten—like an ordinary nihilism—to dislodge us from our ethical and aesthetic convictions.)

23 / SIMON BLACKBURN

Errors and the Phenomenology of Value

Oh Is there not one maiden breast
That does not feel the moral beauty
Of Making worldly interest
Subordinate to sense of duty?
    W.S. Gilbert
    The Pirates of Penzance

I

John Mackie described himself as a moral sceptic, and he described his theory of ethics as an error theory. The ordinary user of moral language wants to claim something which, according to Mackie, cannot be claimed without error: he wants to claim 'something that involves a call for action or for the refraining from action, and one that is absolute, not contingent upon any desire or preference or policy or choice, his own or anyone else's'.[1] Again, someone in moral perplexity may want to know whether a course of action is wrong 'in itself', and 'something like this in the everyday objectivist concept' which is erroneous. For, according to Mackie, ordinary judgments and perplexities include an assumption that there are objective values, in a sense in which he denies that there are. This assumption is ingrained enough to count as part of the meaning of ordinary moral terms, but it is false.

Reprinted by permission of the publisher and copyright holder from *Morality and Objectivity*, ed. Ted Honderich (London: Routledge, 1985), pp. 1–22.

Mackie did not draw quite the consequences one might have expected from this position. If a vocabulary embodies an error, then it would be better if it were replaced by one which avoids the error. Slightly more accurately, if a vocabulary embodies an error *in some use* it would be better if either it, or a replacement vocabulary, were used differently. We could better describe this by saying that our old, infected moral concepts or ways of thought should be replaced by ones which serve our legitimate needs, but avoid the mistake. Yet Mackie does not say what such a way of thought would look like, and how it would differ in order to show its innocence of the old error. On the contrary, in the second part of the book, he is quite happy to go on to express a large number of straightforward moral views, about the good life, about whether it is permissible to commit suicide or abortion, and so on. All these are expressed in the old, supposedly infected vocabulary. Mackie does, of course, notice the problem. He explicitly asks whether his error theory rules out all first-order ethics, and when he returns to the question there is a real threat that ideally there would be no such activity as first-order moralizing. The threat is only averted, supposedly, by introducing the general Humean theme about the social function of morality: 'Morality is not to be discovered but to be made: we have to decide what moral views to adopt, what moral stands to take.' Yet from the standpoint of an error theory it is quite extraordinary that we should have to do any such thing. Why should we have to choose to fall into error? Surely it would be better if we avoided *moral* (erroneous) views altogether, and contended ourselves with some lesser, purged commitments which can be held without making metaphysical mistakes? Let us call these shmoral views, and a vocabulary which expresses them a shmoral vocabulary. Then the puzzle is why, in the light of the error theory, Mackie did not at least indicate how a shmoral vocabulary would look, and did not himself go on only to shmoralize, not to moralize. And in my view this is enough of a puzzle to cast doubt back on to the original diagnosis of error. In other words, it would obviously have been a silly thing to do, to try to substitute some allegedly hygienic set of concepts for moral ones; but that in itself suggests that no error can be incorporated in mere use of those concepts.

In reply to this it may be said that appearances notwithstanding, Mackie did actually only go on to shmoralize. He rids himself of the error, but uses the Humean reconstruction of practical needs and practical reasoning to advocate various shmoral views. These are only accidentally expressed in a vocabulary looking so like that of ordinary moralists: the identity of shape of words does not signify identity of concept, although there is sufficient overlap in function between moralizing and shmoralizing to justify retention of the same words. This is certainly possible. But it leaves an acute problem of identifying just where shmoralizing differs from moralizing: what shows us whether Mackie is moralizing or shmoralizing? Does it determine the issue that he will say things like 'there is no objective prescriptivity built into the fabric of the world'? Troubles multiply. Firstly it is

clear that not all moralists will deny this (many moralists will not even understand it). Secondly it seems gratuitous to infer that there are two different activities from the fact that there are two or more different theories about the nature of the activity. It would be much more natural to say that Hume and Mackie moralize, just as ordinary people do, but with a developed and different theory about what it is that they are doing. The error theory then shrinks to the claim that most ordinary moralists have a bad theory, or at least no very good theory, about what it is to moralize, and in particular that they falsely imagine a kind of objectivity for values, obligations, and so on. This may be true, but it does not follow that the error infects the practice of moralizing, nor the concepts used in ways defined by that practice.

Here, however, a fairly blanket holism can be introduced to rescue Mackie, or at least to urge that it is profitless to oppose him. Our theories infect our meanings; so a different theory about the nature of the activity of moralizing will yield a different meaning for the terms with which we do it; hence Mackie is right that the ordinary meanings do embody error. It becomes profitless to split things in two, so that on the one hand there is the error-free practice, and on the other hand a multiplicity of possibly erroneous theories about its nature. Indeed, the split appeals no more than the despised analytic-synthetic distinction, and if the opponents of an error theory need that, they will gain few supporters.

It is important, and not just to this philosophical issue, to see that this defence fails. To answer it, distinguish between the activity or practice of moralizing and the 'full meaning' of moral terms, where this is determined as the holist wishes, by both the practice and whatever theory the subjects hold about the nature of their practice. Then the holist may have the thesis about 'full meaning', with the consequence that Hume and Mackie may give a different full meaning to their terms, simply through having a different theory of their point and purpose. But it will not follow that their *practice* will differ from that of other people. Hence, it will not follow that other people's practice embodies error. For it is in principle possible that we should observe the practice of some subjects as closely as we wish, and know as much as there is to know about their ways of thinking, commending, approving, deliberating, worrying, and so on, yet be unable to tell from all that which theory they hold. The practice could be clipped on to either metaphysic. The holist will have it that this alters meanings throughout. But we can give him that, yet still maintain that no difference is discernible in the practice, and therefore that no error is embodied in the practice of those who hold the wrong theory. To use a close analogy, there are different theories about the nature of arithmetical concepts. Hence a holist may claim that a subject will give a different total meaning to numerals depending on which theory he accepts, and this difference will apply just as much when the subject is counting as when he is doing matamathematics. All that may be true, yet it would not follow that any practice of counting embodies error. That would be so only if one could tell just by observing it which of the competing metamathematical theories the subject accepts. In the arithmetical case this would not be true. Similarly, I maintain, in the moral case one ought not to be able to tell from the way in which someone conducts the activity of moralizing, whether he has committed the 'objectivist' mistake or not; hence any such mistake is better thought of as accidental to the practice.

Obviously there is *an* answer to this. It is that the objectivist error does so permeate the practice that you can tell, from the way people moralize, that they are in its grip. It is as if a strict finitist theory, say, of arithmetic led someone to deny that you could count certain sets which others can happily enumerate. But which features of the practice show this? They are to be features which lie beyond the scope of what I have called 'quasi-realism': the enterprise of showing how much of the apparently 're-

alist' appearance of ordinary moral thought is explicable and justifiable on an anti-realist picture.[2] According to me quasi-realism is almost entirely successful, and I do not think John Mackie provided reasons for thinking otherwise. In other words, proper shmoralizing is proper moralizing.

II

So far, I have tried to show that there is something fishy about holding an error theory, yet continuing to moralize, and I have argued that the 'holistic' or Quinean defence of such a position would fail. The argument can now move in different directions. Let us call the Humean picture of the nature of morality, and of the metaphysics of the issue, projectivism. On this view we have sentiments and other reactions, caused by natural features of things, and we 'gild or stain' the world by describing it as if it contained features answering to these sentiments, in the way that the niceness of an ice-cream answers to the pleasure it gives us. Then we could say that Mackie is right about the metaphysical issue, and ought to have been more thoroughgoing in replacing moral terms and concepts by different ones—in other words, that the projectivist in ethics should conduct his practical reasoning in a different way: his shmoralizing would not be moralizing. Let us call this a *revisionist* projectivism. By contrast, there is the quasi-realist identification of shmoralizing with moralizing. In effect the skirmishes in part I of this paper urge that quasi-realism needs to be taken seriously, because even projectivists are going to find themselves indulging in a practice which is apparently identical with moralizing. Of course, in opposition to each of these views, there is the realist charge that projectivism is false in any case; finally there is the 'quietist' view, urged for instance by Professor Hare, that no real issue can be built around the objectivity or otherwise of moral values.

If we are to say that the practices characteristic of moralizing are or are not available to a projectivist, we should be careful to identify the practices at issue. In previous papers I have tried to show how the realist-seeming *grammar* of moral discourse can be explained on that metaphysic. This involved, for instance, addressing the Geach-Frege problem of accounting for unasserted occurrence of sentences using moral terms, explaining the propositional form which we give to moral utterances, explaining why we may legitimately worry whether one of our moral views is correct, and hence explaining the role of a concept of truth in ethics, and so on. If this work is successful there is no way of arguing that the grammar of moral discourse either refutes projectivism, or forces it to take a revisionist course. This means, of course, that Mackie cannot properly use these aspects of our practice in support of the error theory. And sometimes he does just this. For instance, he cites Russell's feeling that on a particular moral issue (opposition to the introduction of bull-fighting into England) one does not just express a desire that the thing should not happen, but does so while feeling that one's desires on such a matter are *right*.[3] Mackie thinks that this is a claim to objectivity, and as such erroneous. The quasi-realist will see it instead as a proper, necessary expression of an attitude to our own attitudes. It is not something that should be wrenched out of our moral psychology; it is something we need to cultivate to the right degree and in the right places, to avoid the (moral) defect of indifference to things that merit passion. This actually illustrates a central quasi-realist tactic: what seems like a thought which embodies a particular second-order metaphysic of morals is seen instead as a kind of thought which expresses a first-order attitude or need. Perhaps the nicest example comes from counter-factuals which seem to assert an anti-projectivist, mind-independence of moral facts: 'even if we had approved of it or enjoyed it or desired to do it, bear-baiting would still have been wrong' can sound like a second-order, realist commitment directly in opposition to

projectivism. But in fact, on the construal of indirect contexts which I offer, it comes out as a perfectly sensible first-order commitment to the effect that it is not our enjoyments or approvals which you should look to in discovering whether bear-baiting is wrong (it is at least mainly the effect on the bear).

For the rest of this paper I shall suppose that this aspect of quasi-realism is successful. So projectivism can accommodate the propositional grammar of ethics. It need not seek to revise that. On the contrary, properly protected by quasi-realism it supports and indeed explains this much of our ordinary moral thought. But in my experience this explanation is apt to leave a residual unease. People feel uncomfortable with the idea that this is the true explanation of our propensity to find and to respect values, obligations, duties and rights. They feel an unease perhaps rather like that of nineteenth-century thinkers who found it so difficult to do ethics without God. This unease is located in a tension between the subjective source which projectivism gives to morality, and the objective 'feel' that a properly working morality has. It is this objective feel or phenomenology which people find threatened by projectivism, and they may go on to fear the threat as one which strikes at the core of morality. We may scoff at those who thought that if God is dead everything is permitted. But it is harder to really shake off the feeling that if duties, rights, etc. come down to that—to the projectivist earth—then they do not have quite the power or force, the title to respect, which we were brought up to believe.

It is, I think, particularly the side of morality associated with *obligation* which is felt to be subject to this threat. Obligation needs to be 'peremptory and absolute', as George Eliot famously said; it often needs to be perceived as something sufficiently external to us to act as a *constraint* or bound on our other sentiments and desires. The chains and shackles of obligation must come from outside us. Can anything both be felt to have this power, and yet be ex-

plained as a projection of our own sentiments? The charge will then be that projectivism falsifies this aspect of morality; it
will be unable to endorse this kind of perception of obligation, but must explain it
away as a phenomenological distortion. It
will be the result of an error, and realist opponents of projectivism will join with revisionists to urge that it marks a point at
which quasi-realism fails.[4] The realists will
trust the phenomenology, and revisionists
will regret it. We can notice in this connection that when Mackie identifies the error
of ordinary thought, it is the 'intrinsic' or
'absolute' to-be-done-ness which certain
actions are felt to possess which he often
points to.[5] It is not just the 'intrinsic' value
of happiness or pleasure, because it is less
surprising that these values should receive
a projective explanation. It is as if the objectivists' error is to think of certain things
as obligatory in a way which has nothing
to do with us, and about which we can do
nothing: a way which could in principle
stand opposed to the whole world of human desire and need. Now admittedly
from this it might seem that the error is to
adopt a deontological rather than a teleological first-order morality. But surely this
is wrong, for Mackie did not want the error to be purely one of adopting a defective or non-consequentialist first-order
morality. Doing that may be a natural consequence of a metaphysical mistake but it
is not in itself an 'error' intrinsic to the very
nature of morality. I think instead that
Mackie chose the word, and chose to concentrate upon obligation, because of the absolute and external 'feel' which he wanted
to indicate, and which he felt was not explicable or defensible on a projective metaphysic. And if he were right, then by threatening this part of the feeling of obligation,
projectivism would indeed threaten one of
the most important and characteristic parts
of morality. But is there any reason to believe that he is right?

The issue will look rather different depending on whether the difficulty is supposed to concern the explanation of moral
psychology, or its justification. Consider a

very pure case of someone in the grip of a
duty. Mabel and Fred want to marry each
other. The opportunity is there, the desires
are aflame, the consequences are pre-
dictably acceptable or even desirable.
There is only one thought to oppose it: they
have a duty to do otherwise, so it would
be wrong. And this feeling that it would be
wrong can wrestle with and sometimes
even overcome all the rest. Isn't this mysterious? Called conscience, it used to be
mysterious enough to suggest an internal
voice of God standing outside the natural
world of sentiments and desires. On the
present line of thought, it is mysterious
enough to suggest perception of an external or objective moral fact, also standing
outside the natural world of sentiments
and desires. Unfortunately, neither of these
explanations is more than a gesture. It is
trivial to point out the gaps they leave. But
there is a better explanation: Fred has been
brought up in a certain way and a consequence of this upbringing is that he looks
on certain courses of action with horror. He
will only keep his self-respect, only be able
to live with himself if he conducts his life
in a particular way, and this is a range of
feeling sufficiently strong to oppose immediate desire, and which gains expression
when he describes the conduct as wrong.
Whether it was a good thing that Fred was
brought up like that is a matter of judgment, but it can hardly be doubted that it
is a good thing that people should sometimes feel like that, for otherwise they are
more likely to do the most awful things. It
is of course a brute fact about human beings that our sources of self-respect are
malleable in this way, but that is a matter
of common observation. Equally, it is a
matter of common observation that there
are cultural ways of reinforcing such feelings in elements of the population which
may be in particular need of them: traditionally soldiers and girls get strong injec-
tions of honour and duty.

At the level of explanation, then, it is
hard to see why there is any problem for
the projectivist. Indeed, it is hard to see
how there *could* be. For many of the ingre-

dients of his account will be needed by any other account. For instance, his observations on the plasticity of our sensibilities, and on the various devices which lead people to respect different sets of obligations and to value different aspects of things, will be simply copied by a realist, who will need to say that our perceptions of moral facts are similarly trained and adapted. As usual, however, the extra ingredients the realist adds (the values or obligations which, in addition to normal features of things, are cognized and the respect we then feel for these cognized qualities) are pulling no explanatory weight: they just sit on top of the story which tells how our sentiments relate to natural features of things. If Fred poses a problem, then, it cannot be one of the explanation of moral psychology, but must be one of justification.

If Fred is rational, can his virtue survive his own awareness of its origin and nature? If Mabel throws into her wooing a whole projective plus quasi-realist explanation of what Fred is doing when he maintains that it's wrong, and if Fred is rational, will this not destroy his resolve? Shouldn't he think something like this: that although he has been brought up to use moral categories and to think that there are moral obligations etc., *there are none really*—they are a fiction, or useful, regulative myth: hence—forget them? Once again we are reminded of those thinkers who felt that if there were no God or no afterlife, then it would be rational to ignore the claims of morality whenever self-interest suggested it. Their anxiety was grounded on a mistake about rationality, for the altruistic or principled man is no more nor less rational than the self-interested—he is just different in ways which affect his happiness and the happiness of communities composed of people like him. Rationality in itself does not force one sensibility or another on us *just* because we have some belief about the origin of that sensibility. This is obvious if we take a parallel: Mabel may be tempted to laugh at Fred's moustache; Fred may seek to dissuade her by telling a projectivist story about the judgment that something is

funny, but there is no reason for him to succeed. Finding things very funny is perfectly compatible with believing that it is a tendency to laugh which we project on the world when we do so. It is not uniquely rational to try to smother our sense of humour because of this belief about its nature. So Mabel is not irrational if she accepts Fred's theory of laughter and continues to laugh at his moustache, and by analogy he may be perfectly rational to accept the projectivist account of morality, and to maintain his resolve just as forcefully as before.

I say that he may be rational to do this. But it is possible that he is not, for an explanation of the origin of a sentiment can diminish its force. For example, psychologists sometimes connect humour with sublimated or concealed aggression. Believing this explanation, and being ashamed of aggressive instincts, it would be rational for me to find fewer and fewer things funny. The explanation *coupled with* other values undermines the sentiment. Similarly a morality might contain values whose effect, coupled with a projective explanation, is to diminish a subject's respect for some obligations. For example, a child may be brought up to believe that things really matter only in so far as God cares about them; learning not to think of conscience as the voice of God would couple with this attitude to diminish the force with which he feels obligations. Or, someone might suppose that only commitments which describe the constitution of the real world have any importance and that all others are better ignored: a projective explanation of morality may then diminish the attention he is prepared to pay to it.[6] This latter attitude is actually quite common. For example, when people feel uncomfortable about trying to impose a morality on other people it is the idea that moral commitments lack real, objective truth values certified by an independent reality that troubles them. The hope of rehabilitating morality by making it an object of perception or reason, and thereby having a better claim on our attention, bears witness to the same idea. In each case however it is not the explanation of the practice *per se* which has the sceptical consequence. It is only the effect of the explanation on sensibilities which have been brought up to respect only particular kinds of thing. So when people fear that projectivism carries with it a loss of status to morality, their fear ought to be groundless, and will only appear if a defective sensibility leads them to respect the wrong things.

So far I have considered this problem only as it affects obligations. But similar remarks can be apposite in connection with values. It is not initially so surprising that we can go on valuing the good things of life whilst knowing that the valuing is an expression of our own subjective sentiments. This need be no more odd than that we should go on finding things funny or painful, or worth while or beautiful, although God is dead, or although we accept subjective responses as the source of these reactions. However, David Wiggins has found a problem even here for the position which he called non-cognitivism, which shares with projectivism the Humean theme that 'ends are supplied by feeling or will, which are not conceived either as percipient or as determinants in any interesting way of perception'.[7] The core of the charge is, I think, that projectivism cannot co-exist with the way in which we perceive values as residing in things outside ourselves. It is not entirely clear, because Wiggins associates with projectivism the repugnant (first-order) doctrine that the only things which possess any intrinsic value are human states of consciousness. But a projectivist's sensibility need not, and in my view should not, take this shape. He can admire features of things regardless of their effects on us: his first-order morality need no more be anthropocentric than it need be egocentric. Remember here that a projectivist who avails himself of quasi-realism can assert those tantalizing expressions of apparent mind-independence: it is not my sentiments that make bear-baiting wrong; it is not because we disapprove of it that mindless violence is abominable; it is preferable that the world should be a

beautiful place even after all consciousness of it ceases. The explanation of what we are doing when we say such things in no way impugns our right to hold them, nor the passion with which we should do so. But if we dissociate ourselves from this target then at this point Wiggins seems to threaten projectivism no more than the attack deflected in the last paragraph. It might be that there are people who cannot 'put up with' the idea that values have a subjective source; who cannot put up with the idea that the meaning of their life and their activities is ultimately something they confer, and that even critical reflection on how best to confer them conducts itself in the light of other sentiments which must be taken simply as given. But this will be because such people have a defect elsewhere in their sensibilities—one which has taught them that things do not matter unless they matter to God, or throughout infinity, or to a world conceived apart from any particular set of concerns or desires, or whatever. One should not adjust one's metaphysics to pander to such defects.

There is still that nagging feel that on this metaphysic 'there are no obligations etc. *really*' (otherwise, why call the position anti-realist?). But urging this as a problem confuses two different contexts in which such a remark might occur. Protected by quasi-realism, my projectivist says the things that sound so realist to begin with—that there are real obligations and values, and that many of them are independent of us, for example. It is *not* the position that he says these for public consumption but denies them in his heart, so to speak. He affirms *all that could ever properly be meant* by saying that there are real obligations.[8] When the context of discussion is that of first-order commitment, he is as solid as the most virtuous moralist. It is just that the explanation of why there are obligations and the rest is not quite that of untutored commonsense. It deserves to be called anti-realist because it avoids the view that when we moralize we respond to, and describe, an independent aspect of reality. Again, a useful model for understanding this is provided by mathematics. There are anti-realist views of what we are doing when we practise arithmetic. But they need not and should not lead to anyone wondering whether 7 + 5 is 'really' 12, for that would be an expression of first-order doubt which would not be a consequence of the second-order theory. Arithmetical practice would remain as solid and certain as could be, but explained without reference to an independent mathematical reality.

III

Thus far I have been using quasi-realism to protect the appearance of morality: to urge that there is no error in our ordinary ways of thought and our ordinary commitments and passions. This enterprise will interest a projectivist most, because it defends him against the most forceful attack he faces, which is that he cannot accommodate the rich phenomena of the moral life. But realist opponents of projectivism need to notice quasi-realism as well, since otherwise they do not know how to launch an attack on projectivism. They would not have correctly located its strengths or weaknesses. Nevertheless, they could concede that its defence is successful on these fronts, yet still maintain their hostility. They can urge that the metaphor of projection fails, or is better replaced by a comparison between our knowledge of ethics and our knowledge of other things, such as mathematics, or colours. It is this latter comparison which I now wish to explore. It is not, in my view, right to suppose that there is immediately an issue between two rival theories of morality. This is partly because some of the writers I shall mention, who might seem to be offering a perceptual account of morality, are at least half-inclined to deny that they wish to offer a theory at all, although that does leave the status of some of their remarks regrettably unclear. At any rate, as I see it there are in the beginning two invitations, but they are not so much rivals as complementary to each other. The one is to explore the idea of a projection upon the world of a sentiment which we feel. The other is to explore the idea of a perception of a real property, but one which is intimately related to our own sensibilities. These mark different directions of exploration, and it should not be obvious at first sight which will prove the more profitable. I believe that at the end the first provides illumination where the second runs into obstacles, disanalogies, and an ultimate inability to say anything. I also believe that the first can explain and soothe away the fears which lead people to the second—the fear I addressed in part II, that without obligations of a reality which he cannot aspire to, everything is permitted, for example. I shall try to make good these claims by presenting the 'perceptual' direction in the light of the writings of David Wiggins, Thomas Nagel and John McDowell, and more recently Hilary Putnam,[9] but as I mentioned, I am conscious that it is not easy to extract one theory, or just one theory, from those writings. However, at least they suggest a direction of thought, and it is this direction which I want to block.

The opposition understands that projectivism is an explanatory theory, which maintains that moral values are projections of sentiment because we have a better explanation of moral practices if we see ourselves as responsive only to a value-free world. But according to the opposition, a number of considerations make this an insufficient basis for projectivism. Disquiet can perhaps be focused under three headings.

(1) Consider secondary properties. Colours (etc.) are real properties of objects, and this is true even if the best causal explanation of how we detect them proceeds by mentioning primary properties. Colours really exist, although the reality which contains them is not independent of the fact that there also exist human modes of perception.

(2) The thesis just put forward will only appear surprising (i) because of a prejudice that only primary properties, or the properties of some 'ultimate' scientific theory of things, are real, or (ii) because we forget the

truth that the world cannot be 'prised away from' our manner of conceiving it, nor from our interests and concerns when we do so. Since neither of these motives is legitimate, there is no obstacle to (1), and to using the parallel with colours to allow a reality to values etc.

(3) It is true that a training of a particular kind is needed to enable people properly to perceive values etc., but this is harmless: people need training to detect, e.g., features of tunes or shades.

I do not suppose that each of the writers I have mentioned would assent to each of these. For example, although the work of Nagel is prominent in opening up the idea of a reality which is yet subject-dependent, his own work on moral motivation is much more concerned with rationality than with any analogy to the perception of secondary qualities. And Wiggins thinks that the question of the truth of moral commitments looks very different if we consider values and if we consider obligations. But I shall put questions of attribution to one side, simply taking these three themes to form the core of a *perceptual* model of moralizing which at least appears to be a rival to projectivism. Is it a rival, and if it is, then how are we to tell which is better?

Wiggins writes that he has 'long marvelled' at the fact that philosophers have dwelt frequently upon the difference between 'good' and 'red' or 'yellow'. I do not think he should have, unless indeed it is marvellous that philosophers should emphasize things that are banal, and basic. At any rate, it is very easy to rattle off significant differences between secondary properties and those involved in value and obligation. Here are half a dozen.

(a) Moral properties supervene upon others in quite a different way from any in which secondary properties do so. It is a scientific fact that secondary properties supervene upon primary properties. It may even be a metaphysical fact, at least inasmuch as it would offend deep metaphysical commitments to imagine secondary properties changing whilst primary properties do not. But it is not a criterion of in-

competence in the ascription of secondary properties to fail to realize that they must supervene upon others. On the other hand, that moral properties supervene upon natural ones is not a scientific fact, and it *is* criterial of incompetence in moralizing to fail to realize that they must do so.

(b) The receptive mechanisms whereby we are acquainted with secondary properties are well-known objects of scientific study. For example, the kinds of damage to the retina or the ear or taste buds which result in defective perception of secondary qualities can be studied. These studies are not at all similar to studies of defects of character which lead to moral blindness: these latter studies have no receptive or causal mechanisms as their topic. This is just as well, for we need to put things in a particular moral light after we are told about their *other* properties; we do not *also* have to wheel a particular sensory mechanism up against them. Connected with this, and with (a), is the thought that if our secondary-property-detecting mechanisms fail we know that immediately: it presents as a loss of immediately felt phenomenal quality, just as it does when the light fails or we stick cotton wool in our ears. There is no such loss when we become, say, corrupt. We cannot become corrupt overnight, and usually we cannot tell when we have done so. Indeed, it would be a hallmark of many kinds of moral blindness that this is so. The really coarse man thinks that he is perfectly in order, but that other people are too fastidious (recognizing that you have become really coarse is in this way self-refuting: the realization itself shows some residual delicacy).

(c) It is not altogether simple to characterize the 'mind-dependence' of secondary qualities. But it is plausible to say that these are relative to our perceptions of them in this way: if we were to change so that everything in the world which had appeared blue came to appear red to us, this is what it is for the world to cease to contain blue things, and come to contain only red things. The analogue with moral qualities fails dramatically: if everyone comes to think of it as permissible to maltreat animals, this does nothing at all to make it permissible: it just means that everybody has deteriorated.[10]

(d) The way in which moral practices vary with the forms of life of a society is not at all similar to the way, if any, in which perceptions of secondary qualities can vary with those forms of life. Roughly, we expect such perceptions to vary in acuity depending on whether the property perceived is important to a culture. But once a predicate is located as expressing such a property, there is no prospect of finding that it has a radically different extension. Whereas many things are evaluated quite differently in different groups or at different times. Similarly, apart from rare borderline cases, there is nothing in secondary quality ascription parallel to the 'essentially contested' character of many moral verdicts.

(e) It is up to a subject whether he cares about any particular secondary property in any way. If morality consisted in the perception of qualities, there would be a theoretical space for a culture which perceived the properties perfectly, but paid no attention to them. But however it is precisely fixed, the practical nature of morality is clearly intrinsic to it, and there is not this theoretical space.

(f) Evaluative predicates are typically attributive: a thing may be good *qua* action of a commander-in-chief, but bad *qua* action of a father, just as a man may be a good burglar but a bad batsman. Secondary properties just sit there: a red tomato is a red fruit and a red object just bought at the grocer's. (Wiggins notices this asymmetry after the passage quoted.)

Of course, the extent to which these constitute disanalogies can be debated. But perhaps by way of illustrating their strength in the moral case, we can notice that sometimes they will not present such a clear picture. For example it is very doubtful whether they apply with equal force to the perception of physical *beauty*. For at least (a), (c), (e) and (f) can be queried in this case. And this in turn connects with the sense we can have that sometimes the beauty of a thing needs perception, and cannot be told. Whereas when it cannot be told how good something was, this is always because some other fact about it resists communication—how happy we were, or how brave we needed to be. So unlike John Mackie I incline to find the projective nature of morality much better motivated than the projective theory applied to aesthetic evaluation. But applied to ethics the cumulative effect of these considerations seems to me to be great enough for it to appear a severe error of philosophical taste to expect a theory of moralizing to look very much like a theory of secondary quality perception. Nevertheless we cannot depend entirely upon this cumulative effect. For it will be retorted that mention of secondary qualities just provided an illustration of a combination, a shape of theory, which can also apply to ethics, however different the subject matter is in other respects. This is the combination or shape of theory illustrated by (1)–(3). So the disqualification of secondary properties wins one battle, but it does not by itself win the war against a 'perceptual' direction.

I will not try to show that once they are properly distanced from other perceptual analogues, (1)–(3) provide no theory of ethics at all, let alone one capable of standing up against projectivism. The first thing to realize is that there is nothing to prevent a projectivist *talking of* the perception of moral properties, of the world containing obligations, and so on. We talk of the perception of every single category of thing and fact which we ever communicate. We talk of perception of numerical truths, truths about the future, truths about the past, possibilities, other minds, theoretical entities of all kinds. We talk of perception whenever we think of ourselves as properly indicating the truth: in other words, whenever we feel able to say that 'if it hadn't been the case that *p* I would not be committed to *p*'. But this is not the end of epistemology, but its beginning, for the theorist's job is to reflect upon our right to hold such conditionals. Merely reporting that we hold them is not doing this. Now in the ethical case, the projectivist, protected again by quasi-realism, has a story to tell about this: he can explain why people who are satisfied that their moral sensibilities are functioning well express themselves in this way. But genuine cases of perception standardly demand stories with different ingredients. 'If it hadn't been the case that the shape was square, I would not have believed that it was' can be said because we are causally affected by shapes and can use those effects to deliver verdicts on them. 'If it hadn't been red, I would not have believed that it was' can be said because I know enough of my normality in relation to other people to know that only when a thing disposes most people, in good light conditions, to say that it is red, do I say that it is red. And of course I can be wrong about that on an occasion of bad light or bad brain state or whatever.

The important point is that talking of moral perception by itself provides no theory whatsoever of such conditionals. It provides only a misleading sense of security that somewhere there is such a theory. The theory is not causal, as in the case of shape, nor can it be a matter of conformity with a community, for that just misplaces moral reality, which is not created by community consensus, as (c) reminds us. So what is it? It just doesn't exist. But this means that the invitation to explore the perceptual direction has simply petered out. It is as if someone thought that they could seriously provide a theory of mathematical truth which based itself on the idea that we perceive that 7 + 5 = 12, and then simply turned its back on the disanalogies between such knowledge and ordinary sense perception. It is obvious that until the question of the status of these conditionals, and our right to believe them, is prosecuted nothing has been said, or at any rate nothing that cannot be tacked on to the end of any genuinely successful account of arithmetic. Similarly with ethics.

The nub of the matter, then, is that the projectivist provides explanation, making

moralizing an intelligible human activity with its own explanation and its own propriety, and the opposition provides none, but gestures at an evidently lame analogy. In his paper in this volume John McDowell counters both by claiming that the explanatory pretensions of projectivism are 'spurious', and by mounting an opposition case for being able to do something better. I take this last claim first. In effect it uses the 'interest-relative' nature of explanation to cite contexts in which proper explanations of various verdicts can be given by citing supposedly projected states of affairs. 'Why did I find that frightening/funny/appalling?' It can satisfy the interest behind such questions to answer 'Because it *merited* fright/mirth/horror'. 'Why do we find human happiness good?' 'Because it *is* good'. Citing the supposedly projected state of affairs here plays a part in an explanation, and one which in certain contexts can meet the need behind the question.

This is true, but by itself it is quite inert. Compare: 'why do we say that the cube root of 1728 is 12?' 'Because it *is* 12'. At least if the motive behind the question is fear that this is an anomalous, surprising thing for us to say, then the answer can allay it: we are, as it were, only running true to form in such a verdict. We are not in the grip of strange or local arithmetical error. This provides an explanation relative to an interest in whether the thing that we say shows us making a mistake: the reply says that it does not. Similarly in the first cases: a suspicion that there is something odd about, say, finding the dark frightening, can be allayed by saying that it is what you would expect, that darkness merits fear. But of course allowing all this goes no way to disallowing another, wider, explanatory interest which these answers quite fail to engage. This questioner may be asking why we find something frightening because he finds any such reaction puzzling: why do human beings ever feel fear, or get as far as supposing that anything merits fear? No doubt there is an answer to hand: one which talks of the behavioral consequences of the emotion, and their evolutionary advantages to creatures which have it. In a similar vein we try to place the activity of moralizing, or the reaction of finding things funny, or the practice of arithmetic. In particular we try to fit our commitments in these areas into a metaphysical understanding of the kinds of fact the world contains: a metaphysical view which can be properly hostile to an unanalysed and *sui generis* area of moral or humorous or mathematical facts. And relative to this interest, answers which merely cite the truth of various such verdicts are quite beside the point. This, again, is because there is no theory connecting these truths to devices whereby we know about them—in other words, no way of protecting our right to the conditionals I identified.

Could it be held that this explanatory interest is somehow unjustified: that explanations of a certain type cannot be had, or that the desire for them is the desire for an illusory, 'external' viewpoint outside of all human standpoints and perspectives? This is the justification for not having or wanting to have an explanatory theory along my lines at all. There are two reasons to resist this 'quietist' idea (again, I hesitate to attribute it directly, because the opponents to projectivism that I have mentioned tend to ride both the perceptual, explanatory line, and the suggestion that we need no line at all, in uncomfortable tandem). The first reason for rejecting it is that we know that it is a common human option to moralize about more or fewer things in greater or lesser strengths. The scope of morality can wax and wane, and this makes it urgent to find an explanation of the practice which goes some way to defining its *proper* scope. Secondly, there can never be an *a priori* right to claim that our activity in making judgments X permits of no explanation (except the gesture which says that we perceive X-type states of affairs). You just have to try the various explanations out. And of course it is particularly perverse to say that any explanatory attempt in a direction must fail when many appear to have succeeded well (I myself think that there is precious little surprising left about morality: its meta-theory seems to me to be pretty well exhaustively understood. The difficulty is enabling people to appreciate it). Could it be said that although these wider explanatory interests are legitimate, they mark a boundary between the philosopher and the natural scientist? The evolutionary explanation of the emotion of fear is not only empirical, but marks a recognizable divide between any enterprise of understanding fear as we all feel it and know it, and understanding it discursively, in terms of its origins or function. Can the philosopher rest with the phenomenology, and dismiss the rest as sociology, psychology, or someone else's science? The trouble then is that the philosopher gets to say nothing: Hobbes and Hume and Mackie become classified as natural scientists, and the only philosophical activity left is playing variations on the theme of everything being what it is and not another thing. The philosophical spade becomes by definition the one that is turned on the first shove.

IV

There is one final question I would like to raise, but not to settle. So far I have discussed metaphysics as if it were exclusively a second-order issue, with no necessary consequences for first-order moral theory. But we saw in part II that when Mackie characterizes the mistake which according to my kind of projectivism need not be made, he found it natural to describe it by using a deontological moral vocabulary. And it is, I think, not a mistake to expect that a projective theory will consort with consequentialist first-order views. Since those views are generally downgraded today it will be important to get that connection a little bit further into focus, lest projectivism gets damned by association.

It should be said at the outset that there is no essential connection between projectivism and a consequentialist view in ethics. It could be that all human beings found it natural to feel certain sentiments, which gain expression as approval, when faced with some features of action, although those features have no consequences which explain the approval. This would be parallel to the way in which certain gestures or timings of actions are hugely funny, although for no apparent reason. If we had this kind of propensity, then it would not alter the metaphysics— it would not in itself make a realistic theory easier to define properly, or more likely to be true. But we would say that those features are good (or right, or whatever) and perhaps we would be unable to envisage admirable moralities which did not do so: we would have a deontological ethics. As a metaphysical view, projectivism explains what we are doing when we moralize. It does not follow that it can explain, or be asked to explain, all the features of the particular way we moralize. First-order quirks would be as mysterious to a Humean as they are to anyone else. Nevertheless, it is natural to associate projectivism with consequentialist moralities, in the following way. A projectivist is unlikely to take the moral sentiments as simply given. He will fill out the story by attempting an explanation of the practice of moralizing. This turns to its function, and particularly to its social function. In Mackie's terms, morality is an invention which is successful because it enables things to go well amongst people with a natural inheritance of needs and desires which they must together fulfil. Moral thought becomes a practice with a purpose. Saying this goes beyond the metaphysical view, as I have tried to explain, but it is a natural addendum to it. And if it is right, there must at least be a limit to the extent to which moral thought can oppose consequentialist, teleological reasoning. It will be unclear how wholeheartedly a moralist who understands this second-order theory can endorse deontological views which stand in the way of all human purpose or fulfilment. Perhaps this is part of the trouble with Fred and Mabel. Perhaps Fred has a psychology which motivates him one way, when his and Mabel's happiness would be found another way. So

should he not regard this as an encumbrance: isn't he the victim of an upbringing, and should he not see his particular psychology as a defect, whether or not he can effectively work to change it?

This is another version of the problem of part II, except that this time it is the peculiarly deontological cast of mind which is threatened. But Fred need not regard himself as a victim, so long as he can endorse the general policy of producing human beings whose motivational states are like his. What we really have is a 'motive consequentialism'—a grown-up brother of rule-utilitarianism.[11] The motivations people obey are good in proportion as the consequences of people being like that (and knowing that other people are like that) are good.[12] Actions are then judged either in the light of the motivations that prompted them, or in the different dimension of their actual effects in the world, depending on the purposes for which we are judging them. But the position does not collapse into ordinary act-consequentialism, because for well-known reasons one would expect a society of people motivated solely by consequentialist considerations to do pretty badly. Nor need any such position share the other prominent feature of utilitarianism which causes dislike: the idea that all values are ultimately commensurable. The features of human life which we value, and which would be drawn into any remotely plausible sketch of human flourishing, very probably represent a bundle of ultimately incommensurable goods, amongst which there is no systematic way of making choices. In any case, there is ample room for a projectivist to respect the reasons which make this seem plausible. His explanatory project can start from the heterogeneity of ways in which life can flourish, or fail. On the whole, then, I regard the alliance with consequentialism as a strength rather than anything else—to put it another way, it is only an alliance with the best features of that direction in ethical thought. Of course, there may be features of some people's moralities which even this diluted motive-consequentialism cannot well explain, and these it will regret.

But I hope I have said enough to show that none of them could possibly count as integral to moral thought itself.

Notes

1. Unless otherwise stated page references are to *Ethics: Inventing Right and Wrong* (Penguin, 1977).
2. 'Truth realism and the regulation of theory', in *Midwest Studies in Philosophy, vol. V (Epistemology)*, ed. French, Uehling and Wettstein; 'Rule following and moral realism', in *Wittgenstein: to Follow a Rule*, ed. Holtzman and Leich (Routledge & Kegan Paul, 1981); and chapter 6 of *Spreading The Word* (Oxford University Press, 1984).
3. p. 34.
4. See for instance the first paragraph of John McDowell's careful continuation of the realist-projectivist issue, in this volume.
5. *The Miracle of Theism* (Oxford University Press, 1982) p. 104, 115 ff.
6. Mackie mentions this kind of psychology on p. 24.
7. 'Truth, invention and the meaning of life', British Academy Lecture (Oxford University Press, 1976).
8. Compare Evans on the unintelligibility of one way of thinking of colours as real ('Things without the mind' in *Philosophical Subjects*, ed. Z. van Straaten (Oxford University Press, 1980)). I want to maintain that any genuinely anti-projective attempt to think of obligations or values as 'real' is either similarly unintelligible, or marks a mistake about explanation. This is why I would deny that there is an aspect of moral *phenomenology* which gives morality an objective appearance which quasi-realism must regard as illusory (as McDowell claims in note 4 to his paper in this volume). For there is nothing in the appearance of morality to force us to make the mistake about explanation. Obligations and so

forth appear in exactly the way I would predict.
9. Wiggins, 'Truth, invention and the meaning of life', op. cit.; T. Nagel, 'Subjective and objective', in *Moral Questions* (Cambridge University Press, 1979); J. McDowell, 'Are moral requirements hypothetical imperatives?' (*Proceedings of the Aristotelian Society Supplementary Volume* 1978) and in this volume; H. Putnam, *Reason, Truth and History* (Cambridge University Press, 1981).
10. I stressed this in 'Rule following and moral realism'. McGinn concentrates upon the point in *The Subjective View* (Oxford University Press, 1983), p. 150.
11. And, fairly clearly, the one that Hume endorsed. Talking of motives is better than talking of rules (rule-utilitarianism can be charged with 'rule worship' when it tries to give the verdict to a rule rather than to utility in a hard case. But what charge is there of motive worship?), and as explained in the text, consequentialism is not subject to at least some of the main objections to utilitarianism.
12. Rule-utilitarianism is falsely supposed to collapse into act-utilitarianism partly through neglecting this qualification, (e.g. B. Williams, *Utilitarianism For and Against* (Cambridge University Press, 1973), p. 118 ff). I am contesting what Williams calls the 'act-adequacy premise'. The consequences of a rule being embedded in a society go well beyond the consequences of definite commissions or omissions for which the rule is responsible. There is also the consequence of mutual knowledge that the rule is likely to order action. To illustrate the effect of this consider a rule that promises that dead people should be respected. The main part of the good such a rule does lies not in any surplus utility of acts performed in accordance with it, but in the dignity with which one can approach old age or death in a society where it is known that people have such respect. This value resides not in acts, but in states of mind for which respect for the rule is responsible.

24 / NICHOLAS STURGEON

MORAL EXPLANATIONS

There is one argument for moral skepticism that I respect even though I remain unconvinced. It has sometimes been called the argument from moral diversity or relativity, but that is somewhat misleading, for the problem arises not from the diversity of moral views, but from the apparent difficulty of *settling* moral disagreements, or even of knowing what would be required to settle them, a difficulty thought to be noticeably greater than any found in settling disagreements that arise in, for example, the sciences. This provides an argument for moral skepticism because one obviously possible explanation for our difficulty in settling moral disagreements is that they are really unsettleable, that there is no way of justifying one rather than another competing view on these issues; and a possible further explanation for the unsettleability of moral disagreements, in turn, is moral nihilism, the view that on these issues there just is no fact of the matter, that the impossibility of discovering and establishing moral truths is due to there not being any.

I am, as I say, unconvinced: partly because I think this argument exaggerates the difficulty we actually find in settling moral disagreements, partly because there are alternative explanations to be considered for the difficulty we do find. Under the latter heading, for example, it certainly matters to what extent moral disagreements depend on disagreements about other questions which, however disputed they may be, are nevertheless regarded as having objective answers: questions such as which, if any, religion is true, which account of human psychology, which theory of human society. And it also matters to what extent consideration of moral questions is in practice skewed by distorting factors such as personal interest and social ideology. These are large issues. Although it is possible to say some useful things to put them in perspective,[1] it appears impossible to settle them quickly or in any a priori way. Consideration of them is likely to have to be piecemeal, and, in the short run at least, frustratingly indecisive.

These large issues are not my topic here. But I mention them, and the difficulty of settling them, to show why it is natural that moral skeptics have hoped to find some quicker way of establishing their thesis. I doubt that any exist, but some have of course been proposed. Verificationist attacks on ethics should no doubt be seen in this light, and J. L. Mackie's "argument from queerness" is a clear instance (Mackie, *Ethics: Inventing Right and Wrong* [Harmondsworth, England, 1977], pp. 38–42). The quicker argument on which I shall concentrate, however, is neither of these, but instead an argument by Gilbert Harman designed to bring out the "basic problem" about morality, which in his view is "its apparent immunity from observational testing" and "the seeming irrelevance of observational evidence" (Harman, *The Nature of Morality: An Introduction to Ethics* [New York, 1977], pp. vii, viii. Parenthetical page

Reprinted by permission of the publisher and copyright holder from Nicholas Sturgeon, *Morality, Reason, and Truth*, ed. David Copp and David Zimmerman (Totowa, N.J.: Rowman and Littlefield, 1985), pp. 49–78.

338

Harman Qute

references are to this work). The argument is that reference to moral facts appears unnecessary for the *explanation* of our moral observations and beliefs.

Harman's view, I should say at once, is not in the end a skeptical one, and he does not view the argument I shall discuss as a decisive defense of moral skepticism or moral nihilism. Someone else might easily so regard it, however. For Harman himself regards it as creating a strong *prima facie* case for skepticism and nihilism, strong enough to justify calling it "the problem with ethics."[2] And he believes it shows that the only recourse for someone who wishes to avoid moral skepticism is to find defensible reductive definitions for ethical terms; so skepticism would be the obvious conclusion for anyone to draw who doubted the possibility of such definitions. I believe, however, that Harman is mistaken on both counts. I shall show that his argument for skepticism either rests on claims that most people would find quite implausible (and so cannot be what constitutes, for *them*, the problem with ethics); or else it becomes just the application to ethics of a familiar *general* skeptical strategy, one which, if it works for ethics, will work equally well for unobservable theoretical entities, or for other minds, or for an external world (and so, again, can hardly be what constitutes the distinctive problem with *ethics*). In the course of my argument, moreover, I shall suggest that one can in any case be a moral realist, and indeed an ethical naturalist, without believing that we are now or ever will be in possession of reductive naturalistic definitions for ethical terms.

I. The Problem with Ethics

Moral theories are often tested in thought experiments, against imagined examples; and, as Harman notes, trained researchers often test scientific theories in the same way. The problem, though, is that scientific theories can also be tested against the world, by observations or real experiments; and, Harman asks, "can moral principles be tested in the same way, out in the world?" (p. 4).

This would not be a very interesting or impressive challenge, of course, if it were merely a resurrection of standard verificationist worries about whether moral assertions and theories have any testable empirical implications, implications statable in some relatively austere "observational" vocabulary. One problem with that form of the challenge, as Harman points out, is that there are no "pure" observations, and in consequence no purely observational vocabulary either. But there is also a deeper problem that Harman does not mention, one that remains even if we shelve worries about "pure" observations and, at least for the sake of argument, grant the verificationist his observational language, pretty much as it was usually conceived: that is, as lacking at the very least any obviously theoretical terminology from any recognized science, and of course as lacking any moral terminology. For then the difficulty is that moral principles fare just as well (or just as badly) against the verificationist challenge as do typical scientific principles. For it is by now a familiar point about scientific principles—principles such as Newton's law of universal gravitation or Darwin's theory of evolution—that they are entirely devoid of empirical implications when considered in isolation.[3] We do of course base observational predictions on such theories and so test them against experience, but that is because we do not consider them in isolation. For we can derive these predictions only by relying at the same time on a large background of additional assumptions, many of which are equally theoretical and equally incapable of being tested in isolation. A less familiar point, because less often spelled out, is that the relation of moral principles to observation is similar in *both* these respects. Candidate moral principles—for example, that an action is wrong just in case there is something else the agent could have done that would have produced a greater net balance of pleasure over pain—lack empirical implications when considered in isolation. But it is easy to derive empirical consequences from them, and thus to test them against experience, if we allow ourselves, as we do in the scientific case, to rely on a background of other assumptions of comparable status. Thus, if we conjoin the act-utilitarian principle I just cited with the further view, also untestable in isolation, that it is always wrong deliberately to kill a human being, we can deduce from these two premises together the consequence that deliberately killing a human being always produces a lesser balance of pleasure over pain than some available alternative act; and this claim is one any positivist would have conceded we know, in principle at least, how to test. If we found it to be false, moreover, then we would be forced by this empirical test to abandon at least one of the moral claims from which we derived it.

It might be thought a worrisome feature of this example, however, and a further opening for skepticism, that there could be controversy about which moral premise to abandon, and that we have not explained how our empirical test can provide an answer to *this* question. And this may be a problem. It should be a familiar problem, however, because the Duhemian commentary includes a precisely corresponding point about the scientific case: that if we are at all cautious in characterizing what we observe, then the requirement that our theories merely be *consistent* with observation is an astoundingly weak one. There are always many, perhaps indefinitely many, different mutually inconsistent ways to adjust our views to meet this constraint. Of course, in practice we are often confident of how to do it: If you are a freshman chemistry student, you do not conclude from your failure to obtain the predicted value in an experiment that it is all over for the atomic theory of gases. And the decision can be equally easy, one should note, in a moral case. Consider two examples. From the surprising moral thesis that Adolf Hitler was a morally admirable person, together with a modest piece of moral theory to the effect that no morally admirable per-

son would, for example, instigate and oversee the degradation and death of millions of persons, one can derive the testable consequence that Hitler did not do this. But he did, so we must give up one of our premises; and the choice of which to abandon is neither difficult nor controversial.

Or, to take a less monumental example, contrived around one of Harman's own, suppose you have been thinking yourself lucky enough to live in a neighborhood in which no one would do anything wrong, at least not in public; and that the modest piece of theory you accept, this time, is that malicious cruelty, just for the hell of it, is wrong. Then, as in Harman's example, "you round a corner and see a group of young hoodlums pour gasoline on a cat and ignite it." At this point, either your confidence in the neighborhood or your principle about cruelty has got to give way. But the choice is easy, if dispiriting, so easy as hardly to require thought. As Harman says, "You do not need to *conclude* that what they are doing is wrong; you do not need to figure anything out; you can *see* that it is wrong" (p. 4). But a skeptic can still wonder whether this practical confidence, or this "seeing," rests in either sort of case on anything more than deeply ingrained conventions of thought—respect for scientific experts, say, and for certain moral traditions—as opposed to anything answerable to the facts of the matter, any reliable strategy for getting it right about the world.

Now, Harman's challenge is interesting partly because it does not rest on these verificationist doubts about whether moral beliefs have observational implications, but even more because what it does rest on is a partial answer to the kind of general skepticism to which, as we have seen, reflection on the verificationist picture can lead. Many of our beliefs are justified, in Harman's view, by their providing or helping to provide a reasonable *explanation* of our observing what we do. It would be consistent with your failure, as a beginning student, to obtain the experimental result predicted by the gas laws, that the laws are mistaken. That would even be one explanation of your failure. But a better explanation, in light of your inexperience and the general success experts have had in confirming and applying these laws, is that you made some mistake in running the experiment. So our scientific beliefs can be justified by their explanatory role; and so too, in Harman's view, can mathematical beliefs and many commonsense beliefs about the world.

Not so, however moral beliefs: They appear to have no such explanatory role. That is "the problem with ethics." Harman spells out his version of this contrast:

> You need to make assumptions about certain physical facts to explain the occurrence of the observations that support a scientific theory, but you do not seem to need to make assumptions about any moral facts to explain the occurrence of the so-called moral observations I have been talking about. In the moral case, it would seem that you need only make assumptions about the psychology or moral sensibility of the person making the moral observation. (p. 6)

More precisely, and applied to his own example, it might be reasonable, in order to explain your judging that the hoodlums are wrong to set the cat on fire, to assume "that the children really are pouring gasoline on a cat and you are seeing them do it." But there is no

> obvious reason to assume anything about "moral facts," such as that it is really wrong to set the cat on fire. . . . Indeed, an assumption about moral facts would seem to be totally irrelevant to the explanation of your making the judgment you make. It would seem that all we need assume is that you have certain more or less well articulated moral principles that are reflected in the judgments you make, based on your moral sensibility. (p. 7)

And Harman thinks that if we accept this conclusion, suitably generalized, then, subject to a possible qualification I shall come to shortly, we must conclude that moral theories cannot be tested against the world

as scientific theories can, and that we have no reason to believe that moral facts are part of the order of nature or that there is any moral knowledge (pp. 23, 35).

My own view is that Harman is quite wrong, not in thinking that the explanatory role of our beliefs is important to their justification, but in thinking that moral beliefs play no such role.[4] I shall have to say something about the initial plausibility of Harman's thesis as applied to his own example, but part of my reason for dissenting should be apparent from the other example I just gave. We find it easy (and so does Harman [p. 108]) to conclude from the evidence not just that Hitler was not morally admirable, but that he was morally depraved. But isn't it plausible that Hitler's moral depravity—the fact of his really having been morally depraved—forms part of a reasonable explanation of why we believe he was depraved? I think so, and I shall argue concerning this and other examples that moral beliefs commonly play the explanatory role Harman denies them. Before I can press my case, however, I need to clear up several preliminary points about just what Harman is claiming and just how his argument is intended to work.

II. Observation, Explanation, and Reduction

(1) For there are several ways in which Harman's argument invites misunderstanding. One results from his focusing at the start on the question of whether there can be moral *observations*.[5] But this question turns out to be a side issue, in no way central to his argument that moral principles cannot be tested against the world. There are a couple of reasons for this, of which the more important[6] by far is that Harman does not really require of moral facts, if belief in them is to be justified, that they figure in the explanation of moral observations. It would be enough, on the one hand, if they were needed for the explanation of moral beliefs that are not in any interesting sense observations. For example,

Harman thinks belief in moral facts would be vindicated if they were needed to explain our drawing the moral conclusions we do when we reflect on hypothetical cases, but I think there is no illumination in calling these conclusions observations.[7] It would also be enough, on the other hand, if moral facts were needed for the explanation of what were clearly observations, but not moral observations. Harman thinks mathematical beliefs are justified, but he does not suggest that there are mathematical observations; it is rather that appeal to mathematical truths helps to explain why we make the physical observations we do (p. 10). Moral beliefs would surely be justified, too, if they played such a role, whether or not there are any moral observations.

So the claim is that moral facts are not needed to explain our having any of the moral beliefs we do, whether or not those beliefs are observations, and are equally unneeded to explain any of the observations we make, whether or not those observations are moral. In fact, Harman's view appears to be that moral facts aren't needed to explain anything at all: although it would perhaps be question-begging for him to begin with this strong a claim, since he grants that if there were any moral facts, then appeal to other moral facts, more general ones, for example, might be needed to explain *them* (p. 8). But he is certainly claiming, at the very least, that moral facts aren't needed to explain any nonmoral facts we have any reason to believe in.

This claim has seemed plausible even to some philosophers who wish to defend the existence of moral facts and the possibility of moral knowledge. Thus, Thomas Nagel has recently retreated to the reply that

> it begs the question to assume that *explanatory* necessity is the test of reality in this area. . . . To assume that only what has to be included in the best explanatory picture of the world is real, is to assume that there are no irreducibly normative truths.[8]

But this retreat will certainly make it more difficult to fit moral knowledge into any-

thing like a causal theory of knowledge, which seems plausible for many other cases, or to follow Hilary Putnam's suggestion that we "apply a generally causal account of reference . . . to moral terms" (Putnam, "Language and Reality," in *Mind, Language, and Reality. Philosophical Papers*, vol. 2 [Cambridge, 1975], p. 290). In addition, the concession is premature in any case, for I shall argue that moral facts do fit into our explanatory view of the world, and in particular into explanations of many moral observations and beliefs.

(2) Other possible misunderstandings concern what is meant in asking whether reference to moral facts is *needed* to explain moral beliefs. One warning about this question I save for my comments on reduction below; but another, about what Harman is clearly *not* asking, and about what sort of answer I can attempt to defend to the question he is asking, can be spelled out first. For, to begin with, Harman's question is clearly not just whether there is *an* explanation of our moral beliefs that does not mention moral facts. Almost surely there is. Equally surely, however, there is *an* explanation of our commonsense nonmoral beliefs that does not mention an external world: one which cites only our sensory experience, for example, together with whatever needs to be said about our psychology to explain why with that history of experience we would form just the beliefs we do. Harman means to be asking a question that will lead to skepticism about moral facts, but not to skepticism about the existence of material bodies or about well-established scientific theories of the world.

Harman illustrates the kind of question he is asking, and the kind of answer he is seeking, with an example from physics which it will be useful to keep in mind. A physicist sees a vapor trail in a cloud chamber and thinks, "There goes a proton." What explains his thinking this? Partly, of course, his psychological set, which largely depends on his beliefs about the apparatus and all the theory he has learned; but partly also, perhaps, the hypothesis that "there really was a proton going through the cloud chamber, causing the vapor trail, which he saw as a proton." We will *not* need this latter assumption, however, "if his having made that observation could have been equally well explained by his psychological set alone, without the need for any assumption about a <u>proton</u>" (p. 6).[9] So for reference to moral facts to be *needed* in the explanation of our beliefs and observations, is for this reference to be required for an explanation that is somehow *better* than competing explanations. Correspondingly, reference to moral facts will be unnecessary to an explanation, in Harman's view, not just because we can find some explanation that does not appeal to them, but because *no* explanation that appeals to them is any better than some competing explanation that does not.

Now, fine discriminations among <u>competing explanations</u> of almost anything are likely to be difficult, controversial, and provisional. Fortunately, however, my discussion of Harman's argument will not require any fine discriminations. This is because Harman's thesis, as we have seen, is *not* that moral explanations lose out by a small margin; nor is it that moral explanations, although sometimes initially promising, always turn out on further examination to be inferior to nonmoral ones. It is, rather, that reference to moral facts always looks, right from the start, to be "completely irrelevant" to the explanation of any of our observations and beliefs. And my argument will be that this is mistaken: that many moral explanations appear to be good explanations, or components in good explanations, that are not obviously undermined by anything else that we know. <u>My suspicion, in fact, is that moral facts are needed in the sense explained, that they will turn out to belong in our best overall explanatory picture of the world, even in the long run,</u> but I shall not attempt to establish that here. Indeed, it should be clear why I could not pretend to do so. For I have explicitly put to one side the issue (which I regard as incapable in any case of quick resolution) of whether and to what extent actual moral disagreements can be settled satisfactorily.

But I assume it would count as a defect in any sort of explanation to rely on claims about which rational agreement proved unattainable. So I concede that it *could* turn out, for anything I say here, that moral explanations are all defective and should be discarded. What I shall try to show is merely that many moral explanations look reasonable enough to be in the running; and, more specifically, that nothing Harman says provides any reason for thinking they are not. This claim is surely strong enough (and controversial enough) to be worth defending.

(3) It is implicit in this statement of my project, but worth noting separately, that I take Harman to be proposing an *independent* <u>skeptical argument</u>—independent not merely of the argument from the difficulty of settling disputed moral questions, but also of other standard arguments for moral skepticism. Otherwise his argument is not worth independent discussion. For <u>any</u> of these more familiar skeptical arguments will of course imply that moral explanations are defective, on the reasonable assumption that it would be a defect in any explanation to rely on claims as doubtful as these arguments attempt to show all moral claims to be. But if *that* is why there is a problem with moral explanations, one should surely just cite the relevant skeptical argument, rather than this derivative difficulty about moral explanations, as the basic "problem with ethics," and it is that argument we should discuss. So I take Harman's interesting suggestion to be that there is a *different* difficulty that remains even if we put other arguments for moral skepticism aside and *assume*, for the sake of argument, that there are moral facts (for example, that what the children in his example are doing is really wrong): namely, that these assumed facts *still* seem to play no explanatory role.

This understanding of Harman's thesis crucially affects my argumentative strategy in a way to which I should alert the reader in advance. For it should be clear that assessment of this thesis not merely permits, but *requires*, that we provisionally assume the existence of moral facts. I can see no way of evaluating the claim that *even if* we assumed the existence of moral facts they would still appear explanatorily irrelevant, without assuming the existence of some, to see how they would look. So I do freely assume this in each of the examples I discuss in the next section. (I have tried to choose plausible examples, moreover, moral facts most of us would be inclined to believe in if we did believe in moral facts, since those are the easiest to think about; but the precise examples don't matter, and anyone who would prefer others should feel free to substitute his own.) I grant, furthermore, that if Harman were right about the outcome of this thought experiment—that even after we assumed these facts they still looked irrelevant to the explanation of our moral beliefs and of other nonmoral facts—then we might conclude with him that there were, after all, no such facts. But I claim he is wrong: Once we have provisionally assumed the existence of moral facts, they *do* appear relevant, by perfectly ordinary standards, to the explanation of moral beliefs and of a good deal else besides. Does this prove that there *are* such facts? Well of course it helps support that view, but here I carefully make no claim to have shown so much. What I *show* is that any remaining reservations about the existence of moral facts must be based on those *other* skeptical arguments, of which Harman's argument is independent. In short, there may still be a "problem with ethics," but it has *nothing* special to do with moral explanations.

(4) A final preliminary point concerns a qualification Harman adds himself. As I have explained his argument so far, it assumes that we could have reason to believe in moral facts only if this helped us "explain why we observe what we observe" (p. 13); but, he says, this assumption is too strong, for we can have evidence for the truth of some beliefs that play no such explanatory role. We might, for example, come to be able to explain color perception without saying that objects have colors, by citing certain physical and psychological facts. But this would not show that there

are no colors; it would show only that facts about color are "somehow reducible" to these physical and psychological facts. And this leaves the possibility that moral facts, too, even if they ultimately play no explanatory role themselves, might be "reducible to certain other facts that can help explain our observations" (p. 14). So a crucial question is: What would justify a belief in reducibility? What makes us think color facts might be reducible to physical (or physical and psychological) facts, and what would justify us in thinking moral facts reducible to explanatory natural facts of some kind?

Harman's answer is that it is still the *apparent* explanatory role of color facts, or of moral facts, that matters; and hence that this qualification to his argument is not so great as it might seem. We know of no precise reduction for facts of either sort. We believe even so that reduction is possible for color facts because even when we are able to explain color perception without saying that objects are colored.

> we will still *sometimes* refer to the actual colors of objects in explaining color perception, if only for the sake of simplicity. . . . We will continue to believe that objects have colors because we will continue to refer to the actual colors of objects in the explanations that we will in practice give.

But Harman thinks that no comparable point holds for moral facts. "There does not ever seem to be, even in practice, any point to explaining someone's moral observations by appeal to what is actually right or wrong, just or unjust, good or bad" (p. 22).

Now I shall argue shortly that this is just wrong: that sober people frequently offer such explanations of moral observations and beliefs, and that many of these explanations look plausible enough on the evidence to be worth taking seriously. So a quick reply to Harman, strictly adequate for my purpose, would be simply to accept his concession that this by itself should lead us to regard moral facts as (at worst) reducible to explanatory facts.[10] Concern about the need for, and the role of, reductive definitions has been so central to meta-ethical discussion in this century, however, and has also proved enough of a sticking point in discussions I have had of the topic of this essay, that I should say a bit more.

As a philosophical naturalist, I take natural facts to be the only facts there are.[11] If I am prepared to recognize moral facts, therefore, I must take them, too, to be natural facts: But which natural facts? It is widely thought that an ethical naturalist must answer this question by providing reductive naturalistic definitions[12] for moral terms and, indeed, that until one has supplied such definitions one's credentials as a *naturalist* about any supposed moral facts must be in doubt. Once such definitions are in hand, however, it seems that moral explanations should be dispensable, since any such explanations can then be paraphrased in nonmoral terms; so it is hard to see why an ethical naturalist should attach any importance to them. Now, there are several problems with this reasoning, but the main one is that the widely held view on which it is based is mistaken: mistaken about where a scheme of reductive naturalistic definitions would be found, if there were to be one, but also about whether, on a naturalistic view of ethics, one should expect there to be such a thing at all. I shall take up these points in reverse order, arguing first (a) that it is a mistake to require of ethical naturalism that it even promise reductive definitions for moral terms, and then (b) that even if such definitions are to be forthcoming it is, at the very least, no special problem for ethical naturalism that we are not *now* in confident possession of them.

(a) Naturalism is in one clear sense a "reductionist" doctrine of course, for it holds that moral facts are nothing but natural facts. What I deny, however, is that from this metaphysical doctrine about what sort of facts moral facts are, anything follows about the possibility of reduction in another sense (to which I shall henceforth confine the term) more familiar from the philosophical literature: that is, about whether moral expressions can be given re-ductive definitions in some distinctive nonmoral vocabulary, in which any plausible moral explanations could then be recast. The difficulty with supposing naturalism to require this can be seen by pressing the question of just what this distinctive vocabulary is supposed to be. It is common to say merely that this reducing terminology must be "factual" or "descriptive" or must designate natural properties; but unless ethical naturalism has already been ruled out, this is no help, for what naturalists of course contend is that moral discourse is *itself* factual and descriptive (although it may be other things as well), and that moral terms themselves stand for natural properties. The idea, clearly, is supposed to be that the *test* of whether these naturalistic claims about moral discourse are correct is whether this discourse is reducible to some other; but what other? I consider two possibilities.

(i) Many would agree that it is too restrictive to understand ethical naturalism as requiring that moral terms be definable in the terminology of fundamental physics. One reason it is too restrictive is that philosophical naturalism might be true even if physicalism, the view that everything is physical, is not. Some form of emergent dualism might be correct, for example. A different reason, which I find more interesting (because I think physicalism *is* true), is that physicalism entails nothing in any case about whether even biology or psychology, let alone ethics, is reducible to physics. There are a number of reasons for this, but a cardinality problem noted by Richard Boyd is sufficient to secure the point ("Materialism without Reductionism: Non-Humean Causation and the Evidence for Physicalism," in *The Physical Basis of Mind* [Cambridge, Mass., forthcoming]). If there are (as there appear to be) any continuous physical parameters, then there are continuum many physical states of the world, but there are at most countably many predicates in any language, including that of even ideal physics; so there are more physical properties than there are physical expressions to represent them. Thus, although physicalism certainly entails that biological and psychological properties (and ethical properties, too, if there are any) are physical, nothing follows about whether we have any but biological or psychological or ethical terminology for representing these particular physical properties.

(ii) Of course, not many discussions of ethical naturalism have focused on the possibility of reducing ethics to physics; social theory, psychology, and occasionally biology have appeared more promising possibilities. But that facts might be *physical* whether or not all the disciplines that deal with them are reducible to *physics*, helps give point to my question of why we should think that if all ethical facts are *natural* (or, for that matter, *social* or *psychological* or *biological*), it follows that they can equally well be expressed in some other, nonmoral idiom; and it also returns us to the question of just what this alternative idiom is supposed to be. The answer to this latter question simply assumed in most discussions of ethical naturalism, I think, is that there are a number of disciplines that we pretty well know to deal with a single natural world, for example, physics, biology, psychology, and social theory; that it is a matter of no great concern whether any of *these* disciplines is reducible to some one of the others or to anything else; but that the test of whether ethical naturalism is true *is* whether ethics is reducible to some (nonmoral) combination of *them*.[13]

But what rationale is there for holding ethics alone to this reductive test? Perhaps there would be one if ethics appeared in some salient respect strikingly dissimilar to these other disciplines: if, for example, Harman were right what whereas physics, biology, and the rest offer plausible explanations of many obviously natural facts, including facts about our beliefs and observations, ethics never does. Perhaps ethics could then plausibly be required to earn its place by some alternative route. But I shall of course argue that Harman is wrong about this alleged dissimilarity, and I take

my argument to provide part of the defense required for a naturalistic but nonreductive view of ethics.

(b) A naturalist, however, will certainly want (and a critic of naturalism will likely demand) a fuller account than this of just where moral facts are supposed to fit in the natural world. For all I have shown, moreover, this account might even provide a scheme of reduction for moral discourse: My argument has been not that ethical naturalism could not take this form, but only that it need not. So where should one look for such a fuller account or (if it is to be had) such a reduction? The answer is that the account will have to be derived from our best moral theory, together with our best theory of the rest of the natural world—exactly as, for example, any reductive account of colors will have to be based on all we know about colors, including our best optical theory together with other parts of physics and perhaps psychology. If hedonistic act-utilitarianism (and enough of its associated psychology) turns out to be true, for example, then we can define the good as pleasure and the absence of pain, and a right action as one that produces at least as much good as any other, and that will be where the moral facts fit. If, more plausibly, some other moral theory turns out to be correct, we will get a different account and (if the theory takes the right form) different reductive definitions. It would of course be a serious objection to ethical *naturalism* if we discovered that the *only* plausible moral theories had to invoke supernatural facts of some kind, by making right and wrong depend on the will of a deity, for example, or by implying that only persons with immortal souls could have moral obligations. We would then have to choose between a naturalistic world view and a belief in moral facts. But an ethical naturalist can point out that there are familiar moral theories that lack implications of this sort and that appear defensible in the light of all we know about the natural world; and any of them, if correct, could provide a naturalistic account of moral facts and even (if one is to be had) a naturalistic reduction of moral discourse.

Many philosophers will balk at this confident talk of our discovering some moral theory to be correct. But their objection is just the familiar one whose importance I acknowledged at the outset, before putting it to one side: For I grant that the difficulty we experience in settling moral issues, including issues in moral theory, is a problem (although perhaps not an insuperable one) for any version of moral realism. All I contend here is that there is not, in addition to this acknowledged difficulty, any special further (or prior) problem of finding reductive definitions for moral terms or of figuring out where moral facts fit in the natural world. Our moral theory, if once we get it, will provide whatever reduction is to be had and will tell us where the moral facts fit. The suspicion that there must be more than this to the search for reductive definitions almost always rests, I believe, on the view that these definitions must be suited to a special epistemic role: for example, that they will have to be analytic or conceptual truths and so provide a privileged basis for the rest of our theory. But I am confident that moral reasoning, like reasoning in the sciences, is inevitably dialectical and lacks a priori foundations of this sort. I am also sure that no ethical naturalist need think otherwise.[14]

The relevance of these points is this: It is true that if we once obtained correct reductive definitions for moral terms, moral explanations would be in principle dispensable; so if ethical naturalism had to promise such definitions, it would also have to promise the eliminability in principle of explanations couched in moral terms. But note three points. First, it should be no surprise, and should be regarded as no special difficulty for naturalism even on a reductionist conception of it, that we are not now in possession of such definitions, and so not *now* in a position to dispense with any moral explanations that seem plausible. To be confident of such definitions we would need to know just which moral theory is correct; but ethics is an area of great controversy, and I am sure we do not yet know this. Second,

if some moral explanations do seem plausible, as I shall argue, then one important step toward improving this situation in ethics will be to see what sort of theory emerges if we attempt to refine these explanations in the light both of empirical evidence and theoretical criticism. So it is easy to see, again even on a reductionist understanding of naturalism that promises the eliminability of moral explanations in the long run, why any naturalist will think that for the foreseeable short run such explanations should be taken seriously on their own terms.

The third and most important point, finally, is that the eliminability of moral explanations for *this* reason, if actually demonstrated, would of course not represent a triumph of ethical skepticism but would rather derive from its defeat. So we must add one further caution, as I promised, concerning Harman's thesis that no reference to moral facts is *needed* in the explanation of moral beliefs. For there are, as we can now see, two very different reasons one might have for thinking this. One—Harman's reason, and my target in the remainder of this essay—is that no moral explanations even seem plausible, that reference to moral facts always strikes us as "completely irrelevant" to the explanation of moral beliefs. This claim, if true, would tend to support moral skepticism. The other reason—which I have just been considering, and with which I also disagree—is that any moral explanations that *do* seem plausible can be paraphrased without explanatory loss in entirely nonmoral terms. I have argued that it is a mistake to understand ethical naturalism as promising this kind of reduction even in principle; and I think it in any case absurd overconfidence to suppose that anyone can spell out an adequate reduction now. But any reader unconvinced by my arguments should note also that this *second* reason is no version of moral skepticism: For what anyone convinced by it must think, is that we either are or will be able to say, in entirely nonmoral terms, exactly which natural properties moral terms refer to.[15] So

Harman is right to present reductionism as an alternative to skepticism; part of what I have tried to show is just that it is neither the only nor the most plausible such alternative, and that no ethical naturalist need be committed to it.

III. Moral Explanations

With these preliminary points aside, I turn to my arguments against Harman's thesis. I shall first add to my example of Hitler's moral character several more in which it seems plausible to cite moral facts as part of an explanation of nonmoral facts, and in particular of people's forming the moral opinions they do. I shall then argue that Harman gives us no plausible reason to reject or ignore these explanations; I shall claim, in fact, that the same is true for his own example of the children igniting the cat. I shall conclude, finally, by attempting to diagnose the source of the disagreement between Harman and me on these issues.

My Hitler example suggests a whole range of extremely common cases that appear not to have occurred to Harman, cases in which we cite someone's moral character as part of an explanation of his or her deeds, and in which that whole story is then available as a plausible further explanation of someone's arriving at a correct assessment of that moral character. Take just one other example. Bernard DeVoto, in *The Year of Decision: 1846*, describes the efforts of American emigrants already in California to rescue another party of emigrants, the Donner Party, trapped by snows in the High Sierras, once their plight became known. At a meeting in Yerba Buena (now San Francisco), the relief efforts were put under the direction of a recent arrival, Passed Midshipman Selim Woodworth, described by a previous acquaintance as "a great busybody and ambitious of taking a command among the emigrants."[16] But Woodworth not only failed to lead rescue parties into the mountains himself, where other rescuers were counting on him (leaving children to be picked up by him, for example), but had to be "shamed, threatened, and bullied" even into organizing the efforts of others willing to take the risk; he spent time arranging comforts for himself in camp, preening himself on the importance of his position; and as a predictable result of his cowardice and his exercises in vainglory, many died who might have been saved, including four known still to be alive when he turned back for the last time in mid-March. DeVoto concludes: "Passed Midshipman Woodworth was just no damned good" (1942, p. 442). I cite this case partly because it has so clearly the structure of an inference to a reasonable explanation. One can think of competing explanations, but the evidence points against them. It isn't, for example, that Woodworth was a basically decent person who simply proved too weak when thrust into a situation that placed heroic demands on him. He volunteered, he put no serious effort even into tasks that required no heroism, and it seems clear that concern for his own position and reputation played a much larger role in his motivation than did any concern for the people he was expected to save. If DeVoto is right about this evidence, moreover, it seems reasonable that part of the explanation of his believing that Woodworth was no damned good is just that Woodworth *was* no damned good.

DeVoto writes of course with more moral intensity (and with more of a flourish) than academic historians usually permit themselves, but it would be difficult to find a serious work of biography, for example, in which actions are not explained by appeal to moral character: sometimes by appeal to specific virtues and vices, but often enough also by appeal to a more general assessment. A different question, and perhaps a more difficult one, concerns the sort of example on which Harman concentrates, the explanation of judgments of right and wrong. Here again Harman appears just to have overlooked explanations in terms of moral character: A judge's thinking that it would be wrong to sentence a particular offender to the maximum prison term the law allows, for example, may be due in part to her decency and fairmindedness, which I take to be moral facts if any are. But do moral features of the action or institution being judged ever play an explanatory role? Here is an example in which they appear to. An interesting historical question is why vigorous and reasonably widespread moral opposition to slavery arose for the first time in the eighteenth and nineteenth centuries, even though slavery was a very old institution; and why this opposition arose primarily in Britain, France, and in French- and English-speaking North America, even though slavery existed throughout the New World.[17] There is a standard answer to this question. It is that chattel slavery in British and French America, and then in the United States, was much *worse* than previous forms of slavery, and much worse than slavery in Latin America. This is, I should add, a controversial explanation. But as is often the case with historical explanations, its proponents do not claim it is the whole story, and many of its opponents grant that there may be some truth in these comparisons, and that they may after all form a small part of a larger explanation.[18] This latter concession is all I require for my example. Equally good for my purpose would be the more limited thesis that explains the growth of antislavery sentiment in the United States, between the Revolution and the Civil War, in part by saying that slavery in the United States became a more oppressive institution during that time. The appeal in these standard explanations is straightforwardly to moral facts.

What is supposed to be wrong with all these explanations? Harman says that assumptions about moral facts seem "completely irrelevant" in explaining moral observations and moral beliefs (p. 7), but on its more natural reading that claim seems pretty obviously mistaken about these examples. For it is natural to think that if a particular assumption is completely irrelevant to the explanation of a certain fact, then the fact would have obtained, and we could have explained it just as well, even if the assumption had been false.[19] But I do not believe that Hitler would have done all he did if he had not been morally depraved, nor, on the assumption that he was not depraved, can I think of any plausible alternative explanation for his doing things. Nor is it plausible that we would all have believed he was morally depraved even if he hadn't been. Granted, there is a tendency for writers who do not attach much weight to fascism as a social movement to want to blame its evils on a single maniacal leader, so perhaps some of them would have painted Hitler as a moral monster even if he had not been one. But this is only a tendency, and one for which many people know how to discount, so I doubt that our moral belief really is overdetermined in this way. Nor, similarly, do I believe that Woodworth's actions were overdetermined, so that he would have done just as he did even if he had been a more admirable person. I suppose one could have doubts about DeVoto's objectivity and reliability; it is obvious he dislikes Woodworth, so perhaps he would have thought him a moral loss and convinced his readers of this no matter what the man was really like. But is more plausible that the dislike is mostly based on the same evidence that supports DeVoto's moral view of him, and that very different evidence, at any rate, would have produced a different verdict. If so, then Woodworth's moral character is part of the explanation of DeVoto's belief about his moral character.

It is more plausible of course that serious moral opposition to slavery would have emerged in Britain, France, and the United States even if slavery hadn't been worse in the modern period than before, and worse in the United States than in Latin America, and that the American antislavery movement would have grown even if slavery had not become more oppressive as the nineteenth century progressed. But that is because these moral facts are offered as at best a partial explanation of these developments in moral opinion. And if they really *are* part of the explanation, as seems plausible, then it is also plausible that whatever effect they produced was not entirely overdetermined; that, for example, the growth of the antislavery movement in the United States would at least have been somewhat slower if slavery had been and remained less bad an institution. Here again it hardly seems "completely irrelevant" to the explanation whether or not these moral facts obtained.

It is more puzzling, I grant, to consider Harman's own example in which you see the children igniting a cat and react immediately with the thought that this is wrong. Is it true, as Harman claims, that the assumption that the children are really doing something wrong is "totally irrelevant" to any reasonable explanation of your making that judgment? Would you, for example, have reacted in just the same way, with the thought that the action is wrong, even if what they were doing *hadn't* been wrong, and could we explain your reaction equally well on this assumption? Now, there is more than one way to understand this counterfactual question, and I shall return below to a reading of it that might appear favorable to Harman's view. What I wish to point out for now is merely that there is a natural way of taking it, parallel to the way in which I have been understanding similar counterfactual questions about my own examples, on which the answer to it has to be simply: It depends. For to answer the question, I take it, we must consider a situation in which what the children are doing is not wrong, but which is otherwise as much like the actual situation as possible, and then decide what your reaction would be in that situation. But since what makes their action wrong, what its wrongness *consists* in, is presumably something like its being an act of gratuitous cruelty (or, perhaps we should add, of intense cruelty, and to a helpless victim), to imagine them not doing something wrong we are going to have to imagine their action different in this respect. More cautiously and more generally, if what they are actually doing is wrong, and if moral properties are, as many writers have held, supervenient on natural ones,[20] then in order to imagine them not doing something wrong we are

going to have to suppose their action different from the actual one in some of its natural features as well. So our question becomes: Even if the children had been doing something else, something just different enough not to be wrong, would you have taken them even so to be doing something wrong?

Surely there is no one answer to this question: It depends on a lot about you, including your moral views and how good you are at seeing at a glance what some children are doing. It probably depends also on a debatable moral issue; namely, just *how* different the children's action would have to be in order not to be wrong. (Is unkindness to animals, for example, also wrong?) I believe we can see how, in a case in which the answer was clearly affirmative, we might be tempted to agree with Harman that the wrongness of the action was no part of the explanation of your reaction. For suppose you are like this. You hate children. What you especially hate, moreover, is the sight of children enjoying themselves; so much so that whenever you see children having fun, you immediately assume they are up to no good. The more they seem to be enjoying themselves, furthermore, the readier you are to fasten on any pretext for thinking them engaged in real wickedness. Then it is true that even if the children had been engaged in some robust but innocent fun, you would have thought they were doing something wrong; and Harman is perhaps right[21] about you that the actual wrongness of the action you see is irrelevant to your thinking it wrong. This is because your reaction is due to a feature of the action that coincides only very accidentally with the ones that make it wrong.[22] But, of course, and fortunately, many people aren't like this (nor does Harman argue that they are). It isn't true of them that, in general, if the children had been doing something similar, although different enough not to be wrong, they would still have thought the children were doing something wrong. And it isn't true either, therefore, that the wrongness of the action is irrelevant to the explanation of why they think it wrong.

Now, one might have the sense from my discussion of all these examples—but perhaps especially from my discussion of this last one, Harman's own—that I have perversely been refusing to understand his claim about the explanatory irrelevance of moral facts in the way he intends. And perhaps I have not been understanding it as he wishes. In any case, I agree, I have certainly not been understanding the crucial counterfactual question, of whether we would have drawn the same moral conclusion even if the moral facts had been different, in the way he must intend. But I am not being perverse. I believe, as I said, that my way of taking the question is the more natural one. And more important, although there is, I grant, a reading of that question on which it will always yield the answer Harman wants—namely, that a difference in the moral facts would *not* have made a difference in our judgment—I do not believe this can support his argument. I must now explain why.

It will help if I contrast my general approach with his. I am addressing questions about the justification of belief in the spirit of what Quine has called "epistemology naturalized."[23] I take this to mean that we have in general no a priori way of knowing which strategies for forming and refining our beliefs are likely to take us closer to the truth. The only way we have of proceeding is to assume the approximate truth of what seems to us the best overall theory we already have of what we are like and what the world is like, and to decide in the light of *that* what strategies of research and reasoning are likely to be reliable in producing a more nearly true overall theory. One result of applying these procedures, in turn, is likely to be the refinement or perhaps even the abandonment of parts of the tentative theory with which we began.

I take Harman's approach, too, to be an instance of this one. He says we are justified in believing in those facts that we need to assume to explain why we observe what we do. But he does not think that our knowledge of this principle about justification is a priori. Furthermore, as he knows, we cannot decide whether one explanation is better than another without relying on beliefs we already have about the world. Is it really a better explanation of the vapor trail the physicist sees in the cloud chamber to suppose that a proton caused it, as Harman suggests in his example, rather than some other charged particle? Would there, for example, have been no vapor trail in the absence of that proton? There is obviously no hope of answering such questions without assuming at least the approximate truth of some quite far-reaching microphysical theory, and our knowledge of such theories is not a priori.

But my approach differs from Harman's in one crucial way. For among the beliefs in which I have enough confidence to rely on in evaluating explanations, at least at the outset, are some moral beliefs. And I have been relying on them in the following way.[24] Harman's thesis implies that the supposed moral fact of Hitler's being morally depraved is irrelevant to the explanation of Hitler's doing what he did. (For we may suppose that if it explains his doing what he did, it also helps explain, at greater remove, Harman's belief and mine in his moral depravity.) To assess this claim, we need to conceive a situation in which Hitler was *not* morally depraved and consider the question whether in that situation he would still have done what he did. My answer is that he would not, and this answer relies on a (not very controversial) moral view: that in any world at all like the actual one, only a morally depraved person could have initiated a world war, ordered the "final solution," and done any number of other things Hitler did. That is why I believe that, if Hitler hadn't been morally depraved, he wouldn't have done those things, and hence that the fact of his moral depravity is relevant to an explanation of what he did.

Harman, however, cannot want us to rely on any such moral views in answering this counterfactual question. This comes out most clearly if we return to his example of the children igniting the cat. He claims that the wrongness of this act is irrelevant to an explanation of your thinking it wrong, that you would have *thought* it wrong even if it wasn't. My reply was that in order for the action not to be wrong it would have had to lack the feature of deliberate, intense, pointless cruelty, and that if it had differed in this way you might very well *not* have thought it wrong. I also suggested a more cautious version of this reply: that since the action is in fact wrong, and since moral properties supervene on more basic natural ones, it would have had to be different in *some* further natural respect in order not to be wrong; and that we do not know whether if it had so differed you would still have thought it wrong. Both of these replies, again, rely on moral views, the latter merely on the view that there is *something* about the natural features of the action in Harman's example that makes it wrong, the former on a more specific view as to which of these features do this.

But Harman, it is fairly clear, intends for us *not* to rely on any such moral views in evaluating his counterfactual claim. His claim is not that if the action had not been one of deliberate cruelty (or had otherwise differed in whatever way would be required to remove its wrongness), you would still have thought it wrong. It is, instead, that if the action were one of deliberate, pointless cruelty, but this *did not make it wrong*, you would still have thought it was wrong. And to return to the example of Hitler's moral character, the counterfactual claim that Harman will need in order to defend a comparable conclusion about that case is not that if Hitler had been, for example, humane and fair-minded, free of nationalistic pride and racial hatred, he would still have done exactly as he did. It is, rather, that if Hitler's psychology, and anything else about his situation that could strike us as morally relevant, had been exactly as it in fact was, but this had *not constituted moral depravity*, he would still have done exactly what he did.

Now the antecedents of these two conditionals are puzzling. For one thing, both

are, I believe, necessarily false. I am fairly confident, for example, that Hitler really was morally depraved,[25] and since I also accept the view that moral features supervene on more basic natural properties,[26] I take this to imply that there is no possible world in which Hitler has just the personality he in fact did, in just the situation he was in, but is not morally depraved. Any attempt to describe such a situation, moreover, will surely run up against the limits of our moral concepts—what Harman calls our "moral sensibility"—and this is no accident. For what Harman is asking us to do, in general, is to consider cases in which absolutely *everything* about the nonmoral facts that could seem morally relevant to us, in light of whatever moral theory we accept and of the concepts required for our understanding of that theory, is held fixed, but in which the moral judgment that our theory yields about the case is nevertheless mistaken. So it is hardly surprising that, using that theory and those concepts, we should find it difficult to conceive in any detail what such a situation would be like. It is especially not surprising when the cases in question are as paradigmatic in light of the moral outlook we in fact have as is Harman's example or as is, even more so, mine of Hitler's moral character. The only way we could be wrong about this latter case (assuming we have the nonmoral facts right) would be for our whole moral theory to be hopelessly wrong, so radically mistaken that there could be no hope of straightening it out through adjustments from within.

But I do not believe we should conclude, as we might be temped to,[27] that we therefore know a priori that this is not so, or that we cannot understand these conditionals that are crucial to Harman's argument. Rather, now that we have seen how we have to understand them, we should grant that they are true: that if our moral theory were somehow hopelessly mistaken, but all the nonmoral facts remained exactly as they in fact are, then, since we do *accept* that moral theory, we would still draw exactly the moral conclusions we in fact do. But we should deny that any skeptical conclusion follows from this. In particular, we should deny that it follows that moral facts play no role in explaining our moral judgments.

For consider what follows from the parallel claim about microphysics, in particular about Harman's example in which a physicist concludes from his observation of a vapor trail in a cloud chamber, and from the microphysical theory he accepts, that a free proton has passed through the chamber. The parallel claim, notice, is *not* just that if the proton had not been there the physicist would have thought it was. This claim is implausible, for we may assume that the physicist's theory is generally correct, and it follows from that theory that if there hadn't been a proton there, then there wouldn't have been a vapor trail. But in a perfectly similar way it is implausible that if Hitler hadn't been morally depraved we would still have thought he was: for we may assume that our moral theory also is at least roughly correct, and it follows from the most central features of that theory that if Hitler hadn't been morally depraved, he wouldn't have done what he did. The *parallel* claim about the microphysical example is, instead, that if there hadn't been a proton there, but there *had* been a vapor trail, the physicist would still have concluded that a proton was present. More precisely, to maintain a perfect parallel with Harman's claims about the moral cases, the antecedent must specify that although no proton is present, absolutely *all* the nonmicrophysical facts that the physicist, in light of his theory, might take to be relevant to the question of whether or not a proton is present, are exactly as in the actual case. (These macrophysical facts, as I shall for convenience call them, surely include everything one would normally think of as an observable fact.) Of course, we shall be unable to imagine this without imagining that the physicist's theory is pretty badly mistaken,[28] but I believe we should grant that, *if* the physicist's theory were somehow this badly mistaken, but all the macrophysical facts (including all the observable facts) were held fixed, then the

physicist, since he does accept that theory, would still draw all the same conclusions that he actually does. That is, this conditional claim, like Harman's parallel claims about the moral cases, is true.

But no skeptical conclusions follow; nor can Harman, since he does not intend to be a skeptic about physics, think that they do. It does not follow, in the first place, that we have any reason to think the physicist's theory *is* generally mistaken. Nor does it follow, furthermore, that the hypothesis that a proton really did pass through the cloud chamber is not part of a good explanation of the vapor trail, and hence of the physicists thinking this has happened. This looks like a reasonable explanation, of course, only on the assumption that the physicist's theory is at least roughly true, for it is this theory that tells us, for example, what happens when charged particles pass through a supersaturated atmosphere, what other causes (if any) there might be for a similar phenomenon, and so on. But, as I say, we have not been provided with any reason for not trusting the theory to this extent.

Similarly, I conclude, we should draw no skeptical conclusions from Harman's claims about the moral cases. It is true, I grant, that if our moral theory were seriously mistaken, but we still believed it, and the nonmoral facts were held fixed, we would still make just the moral judgments we do. But *this* fact by itself provides us with no reason for thinking that our moral theory *is* generally mistaken. Nor, again, does it imply that the fact of Hitler's really having been morally depraved forms no part of a good explanation of his doing what he did and hence, at greater remove, of our thinking him depraved. This explanation will appear reasonable, of course, only on the assumption that our accepted moral theory is at least roughly correct, for it is this theory that assures us that only a depraved person could have thought, felt, and acted as Hitler did. But, as I say, Harman's argument has provided us with no reason for not trusting our moral views to this extent, and hence with no reason for

doubting that it is sometimes moral facts that explain our moral judgments.

I conclude with three comments about my argument.

(1) I have tried to show that Harman's claim—that we would have held the particular moral beliefs we do even if those beliefs were untrue—admits of two readings, one of which makes it implausible, and the other of which reduces it to an application of a general skeptical strategy, which could as easily be used to produce doubt about microphysical as about moral facts. The general strategy is this. Consider any conclusion C we arrive at by relying both on some distinguishable "theory" T and on some body of evidence not being challenged, and ask whether we would have believed C even if it had been false. The plausible answer, *if* we are allowed to rely on T, will often be no: for if C had been false, then (according to T) the evidence would have had to be different, and in that case we wouldn't have believed C. (I have illustrated the plausibility of this sort of reply for all my moral examples, as well as for the microphysical one.) But the skeptic intends us *not* to rely on T in this way, and so rephrases the question: Would we have believed C even if it were false *but* all the evidence had been exactly as it in fact was? Now the answer has to be yes, and the skeptic concludes that C is doubtful. (It should be obvious how to extend this strategy to belief in other minds, or in an external world.) I am of course not convinced: I do not think answers to the rephrased question show anything interesting about what we know or justifiably believe. But it is enough for my purposes here that no such *general* skeptical strategy could pretend to reveal any problems peculiar to belief in *moral* facts.

(2) My conclusion about Harman's argument, although it is not exactly the same as, is nevertheless similar to and very much in the spirit of the Duhemian point I invoked earlier against verificationism. There the question was whether typical moral assertions have testable implications, and the answer was that they do, so

long as you include additional moral assumptions of the right sort among the background theories on which you rely in evaluating these assertions. Harman's more important question is whether we should ever regard moral facts as relevant to the explanation of nonmoral facts, and in particular of our having the moral beliefs we do. But the answer, again, is that we should, so long as we are willing to hold the right sorts of *other* moral assumptions fixed in answering counterfactual questions. Neither answer shows morality to be on any shakier ground than, say, physics: for typical microphysical hypotheses, too, have testable implications, and appear relevant to explanations, only if we are willing to assume at least the approximate truth of an elaborate microphysical theory and to hold this assumption fixed in answering counterfactual questions.

(3) Of course, this picture of how explanations depend on background theories, and moral explanations in particular on moral background theories, does show why someone already tempted toward moral skepticism on other grounds (such as those mentioned at the beginning of this essay) might find Harman's claim about moral explanations plausible. To the extent that you already have pervasive doubts about moral theories, you will also find moral facts nonexplanatory. So I grant that Harman may have located a natural symptom of moral skepticism; but I am sure he has neither traced this skepticism to its roots nor provided any independent argument for it. His claim that we do not *in fact* cite moral facts in explanation of moral beliefs and observations cannot provide such an argument, for that claim is false. So, too, is the claim that assumptions about moral facts seem irrelevant to such explanations, for many do not. The claim that we *should* not rely on such assumptions because they *are* irrelevant, on the other hand, unless it is supported by some independent argument for moral skepticism, will just be question-begging: for the principal test of whether they are relevant, in any situation in which it appears they might be, is a

counterfactual question about what would have happened if the moral fact had not obtained, and how we answer that question depends precisely upon whether we *do* rely on moral assumptions in answering it.

A different concern, to which Harman only alludes in the passages I have discussed, is that belief in moral facts may be difficult to render consistent with a naturalistic world view. Since I share a naturalistic viewpoint, I agree that it is important to show that belief in moral facts need not be belief in anything supernatural or "nonnatural." I have of course not dealt with every argument from this direction, but I *have* argued for the important point that naturalism in ethics does not require commitment to reductive definitions for moral terms, any more than physicalism about psychology and biology requires a commitment to reductive definitions for the terminology of those sciences.

My own view I stated at the outset: that the only argument for moral skepticism with any independent weight is the argument from the difficulty of settling disputed moral questions. I have shown that anyone who finds Harman's claim about moral explanations plausible must already have been tempted toward skepticism by some other considerations, and I suspect that the other considerations will always just be the ones I sketched. So that is where discussion should focus. I also suggested that those considerations may provide less support for moral skepticism than is sometimes supposed, but I must reserve a thorough defense of that thesis for another occasion.[29]

Notes

1. As, for example, in Alan Gerwirth "Positive 'Ethics' and Normative 'Science'," *Philosophical Review* 69 (1960), 311–30, in which there are some useful remarks about the first of them.

2. Harman's title for the entire first section of his book.

3. This point is generally credited to Pierre Duhem, *The Aim and Structure of Physical Theory*, trans. Philip P. Wiener (Princeton, 1954). It is a prominent theme in the influential writings of W. V. O. Quine. For an especially clear application of it, see Hilary Putnam, "The 'Corroboration' of Theories," in *Mathematics, Matter, and Method. Philosophical Papers*, vol. I, 2d ed. (Cambridge, 1977).

4. Harman is careful always to say only that moral beliefs *appear* to play no such role; and since he eventually concludes that there *are* moral facts (p. 132), this caution may be more than stylistic. I shall argue that this more cautious claim, too, is mistaken (indeed, that is my central thesis), But to avoid issues about Harman's intent, I shall simply mean by "Harman's argument" the skeptical argument of his first two chapters, whether or not he means to endorse all of it. This argument surely deserves discussion in its own right in either case, especially since Harman himself never explains what is wrong with it.

5. He asks: "Can moral principles be tested in the same way [as scientific hypotheses can], out in the world? You can observe someone do something, but can you ever perceive the rightness or wrongness of what he does?" (p. 4).

6. The other is that Harman appears to use "observe" and ("perceive" and "see") in a surprising way. One would normally take observing (or perceiving, or seeing) something to involve knowing it was the case. But Harman apparently takes an observation to be *any* opinion arrived at as "a direct result of perception" (p. 5) or, at any rate (see next footnote), "immediately and without conscious reasoning" (p. 7). This means that observations need not even be true, much less known to be true. A consequence is that the existence of moral observations, in Harman's sense, would not be sufficient to show that moral theories can be tested against the world, or to show that there is moral knowledge, although this *would* be suffi-

cient if "observe" were being used in a more standard sense. What I argue in the text is that the existence of moral observations (in either Harman's or the standard sense) is not *necessary* for showing this about moral theories either.

7. This sort of case does not meet Harman's characterization of an observation as an opinion that is "a direct result of perception" (p. 5), but he is surely right that moral facts would be as well vindicated if they were needed to explain our drawing conclusions about hypothetical cases as they would be if they were needed to explain observations in the narrower sense. To be sure, Harman is still confining his attention to cases in which we draw the moral conclusion from our thought experiment "immediately and without conscious reasoning" (p. 7), and it is no doubt the existence of such cases that gives purchase to talk of a "moral sense." But this feature, again, can hardly matter to the argument: Would belief in moral facts be less justified if they were needed only to explain the instances in which we draw the moral conclusion *slowly*? Nor can it make any difference for that matter whether the case we are reflecting on is hypothetical. So my example in which we, quickly or slowly, draw a moral conclusion about Hitler from what we know of him, is surely relevant.

8. Thomas Nagel, "The Limits of Objectivity," in Sterling M. McMurrin, ed., *The Tanner Lectures on Human Values* (Salt Lake City and Cambridge, 1980), p. 114n. Nagel actually directs this reply to J. L. Mackie.

9. It is surprising that Harman does not mention the obvious intermediate possibility, which would occur to any instrumentalist: to cite the physicist's psychological set *and* the vapor trail, but say nothing about protons or other unobservables. It is *this* explanation that is most closely parallel to an explanation of beliefs about an external world in terms of sensory experience and psychological makeup, or of moral beliefs in terms of

nonmoral facts together with our "moral sensibility."

10. And it is hard to see how facts could be reducible to explanatory facts without being themselves explanatory. Opaque objects often look red to normally sighted observers in white light because they *are* red; it amplifies this explanation, but hardly undermines it, if their redness turns out to be an electronic property of the matter composing their surfaces.

11. Some of what I say could no doubt be appropriated by believers in supernatural facts, but I leave the details to them. For an account I could largely accept, if I believed any of the theology, see R. M. Adams, "Divine Command Metaethics as Necessary A Posteriori," in Paul Helm, ed., *Divine Commands and Morality* (Oxford, 1981), pp. 109–18.

12. Or, at any rate, a reductive scheme of translation. It surely needn't provide explicit term-by-term definitions. Since this qualification does not affect my argument, I shall henceforth ignore it.

13. *Nonmoral* because ethics (or large parts of it) will be trivially reducible to psychology and social theory if we take otherwise unreduced talk of moral character traits just to be *part* of psychology and take social theory to *include*, for example, a theory of justice. As an ethical naturalist, I see nothing objectionable or unscientific about conceiving of psychology and social theory in this way, but of course this is not usually how they are understood when questions about reduction are raised.

14. For more on this view of moral reasoning, see Nicholas L. Sturgeon, "Brandt's Moral Empiricism," *Philosophical Review* 91 (1982), 389–422. On scientific reasoning see Richard N. Boyd, *Realism and Scientific Epistemology* (Cambridge, forthcoming).

G. E. Moore, *Principia Ethica*, (Cambridge, 1903) thought that the *metaphysical* thesis that moral facts are natural facts entailed that moral theory would have a priori foundations. For he took the metaphysical thesis to require not merely that there be a reductive scheme of translation for moral terminology, but that this reduction include explicit property-identities (such as "goodness = pleasure and the absence of pain"); and these he assumed could be true only if analytic. I of course reject the view that naturalism requires any sort of reductive definitions; but even if it required this sort, it is by now widely acknowledged that reductive property-identities (such as "temperature = mean molecular kinetic energy") can be true without being analytic. See Hilary Putnam, "On Properties," in *Mathematics, Matter and Method. Philosophical Papers*, vol. I, 2d. ed. (Cambridge, 1977).

15. Nor does this view really promise that we can do without reference to moral facts; it merely says that we can achieve this reference without using moral terms. For we would surely have as much reason to think that the facts expressed by *these* nonmoral terms were moral facts as we would for thinking that our reductive definitions were correct.

16. DeVoto, *The Year of Decision: 1846* (Boston, 1942), p. 426; a quotation from the notebooks of Francis Parkman. The account of the entire rescue effort is on pp. 424–44.

17. What is being explained, of course, is not just why people came to think slavery wrong, but why people who were not themselves slaves or in danger of being enslaved came to think it so seriously wrong as to be intolerable. There is a much larger and longer history of people who thought it wrong but tolerable, and an even longer one of people who appear not to have got past the thought that the world would be a better place without it. See David Brion Davis, *The Problem of Slavery in Western Culture* (Ithaca, 1966).

18. For a version of what I am calling the standard view about slavery in the Americas, see Frank Tannenbaum, *Slave and Citizen* (New York, 1947). For an argument against both halves of the standard view, see Davis, esp. pp. 60–61, 223–25, 262–63.

19. This counterfactual test no doubt requires qualification. When there are concomitant effects that in the circumstances could each only have been brought about by their single cause, it may be true that if the one effect had not occurred, then neither would the other, but the occurrence of the one is not relevant to the explanation of the other. The test will also be unreliable if it employs backtracking or "that-would-have-had-to-be-because" counterfactuals. (I take these to include ones in which what is tracked back to is not so much a cause as a condition that partly constitutes another: as when someone's winning a race is part of what constitutes her winning five events in one day, and it is true that if she hadn't won five events, that would have had to be because she didn't win that particular race.) So it should not be relied on in cases of either of these sorts. But none of my examples falls into either of these categories.

20. What would be generally granted is just that *if* there are moral properties they supervene on natural properties. But, remember, we are assuming for the sake of argument that there are.

From my view that moral properties *are* natural properties, it of course follows trivially that they supervene on my natural properties: that, necessarily, nothing could differ in its moral properties without differing in some natural respect. But I also accept the more interesting thesis usually intended by the claim about supervenience—that there are more basic natural features such that, necessarily, once they are fixed, so are the moral properties. (In supervening on more basic facts of some sort, moral facts are like *most* natural facts. Social facts like unemployment, for example, supervene on complex histories of many individuals and their relations; and facts about the existence and properties of macroscopic physical objects—colliding billiard balls, say—

clearly supervene on the microphysical constitution of the situations that include them.)

21. Not *certainly* right, because there is still the possibility that your reaction is to some extent overdetermined and is to be explained partly by your sympathy for the cat and your dislike of cruelty, as well as by your hatred for children (although this last alone would have been sufficient to produce it).

We could of course rule out this possibility by making you an even less attractive character, indifferent to the suffering of animals and not offended by cruelty. But it may then be hard to imagine that such a person (whom I shall cease calling "you") could retain enough of a grip on moral thought for us to be willing to say he thought the action wrong, as opposed to saying that he merely pretended to do so. This difficulty is perhaps not insuperable, but it is revealing. Harman says that the actual wrongness of the action is "completely irrelevant" to the explanation of the observer's reaction. Notice that what is in fact true, however, is that it is *very hard* to imagine someone who reacts in the way Harman describes, but whose reaction is *not* due, at least in part, to the actual wrongness of the action.

22. Perhaps deliberate cruelty is worse the more one enjoys it (a standard counterexample to hedonism). If so, the fact that the children are enjoying themselves makes their action worse, but presumably isn't what makes it wrong to begin with.

23. W. V. O. Quine, "Epistemology Naturalized," in *Ontological Relativity and Other Essays* (New York, 1969), pp. 69–90. See also Quine, "Natural Kinds," in the same volume.

24. Harman of course allows us to assume the moral facts whose explanatory relevance is being assessed: that Hitler was depraved, or that what the children in his example are doing is wrong. But I have been assuming something more—something about what depravity *is*, and about what *makes* the children's action wrong. (At a minimum, in the more cautious version of my argument, I have been assuming that *something* about its more basic features makes it wrong, so that it could not have differed in its moral quality without differing in those other features as well.)

25. And anyway, remember, this is the sort of fact Harman allows us to assume in order to see whether, if we assume it, it will look explanatory.

26. It is about here that I have several times encountered the objection: but surely *supervenient* properties aren't needed to explain anything. It is a little hard, however, to see just what this objection is supposed to come to. If it includes endorsement of the conditional I here attribute to Harman, then I believe the remainder of my discussion is an adequate reply to it. If it is the claim that, because moral properties are supervenient, we can always exploit the insights in any moral explanations, however plausible they may seem, without resort to moral *language*, then I have already dealt with it in my discussion of reduction: The claim is probably false, but even if it is true, it is no support for Harman's view, which is not that moral explanations are plausible but reducible, but that they are totally implausible. And doubts about the causal efficacy of supervenient facts seem misplaced in any case, as attention to my earlier examples (note 20) illustrates. High unemployment causes widespread hardship, and can also bring down the rate of inflation. The masses and velocities of two colliding billiard balls causally influence the subsequent trajectories of the two balls. There is no doubt some sense in which these facts are causally efficacious *in virtue of* the way they supervene on—that is, are constituted out of, or causally realized by—more basic facts, but this hardly shows them *inefficacious*. (Nor does Harman appear to think it does: for his *favored* explanation of your moral belief about the burning cat, recall, appeals to psychological facts (about

your moral sensibility), a biological fact (that it's a cat), and macrophysical facts (that it's on fire)—supervenient facts all, on his physicalist view and mine.) If anyone does hold to a general suspicion of causation by supervenient facts and properties, however, as Jaegwon Kim appears to ("Causality, Identity and Supervenience in the Mind Body Problem," in *Midwest Studies* 4 (Morris 1979), pp. 47–48.), it is enough here to note that this suspicion cannot diagnose any special difficulty with *moral* explanations, any distinctive "problem with ethics." The "problem," arguably, will be with every discipline but fundamental physics. On this point, see Richard W. Miller, "Reason and Commitment in the Social Sciences," *Philosophy & Public Affairs*, 8 (1979), esp. 252–55.

27. And as I take it Philippa Foot, in *Moral Relativism*, the Lindley Lectures (Lawrence, Kans., 1978), for example, is still prepared to do, at least about paradigmatic cases.

28. If we imagine the physicist *regularly* mistaken in this way, moreover, we will have to imagine his theory not just mistaken but hopelessly so. And we can easily reproduce the other notable feature of Harman's claims about the moral cases, that what we are imagining is *necessarily* false, if we suppose that one of the physicist's (or better, chemist's) conclusions is about the microstructure of some common substance, such as water. For I agree with Saul Kripke that whatever microstructure water actually has is essential to it, that it has this structure in every possible world in which it exists. (S. A. Kripke, *Naming and Necessity* [Cam-bridge, Mass., 1980], pp. 115–44.) If we are right (as we have every reason to suppose) in thinking that water is actually H_2O, therefore, the conditional "If water were not H_2O, but all the observable, macrophysical facts were just as they actually are, chemists would still have come to *think* it was H_2O" has a necessarily false antecedent; just as, if we are

right (as we also have good reason to suppose) in thinking that Hitler was actually morally depraved, the conditional "If Hitler were just as he was in all natural respects, but not morally depraved, we would still have *thought* he was depraved" has a necessarily false antecedent. Of course, I am not suggesting that in either case our knowledge that the antecedent is false is a priori.

These counterfactuals, because of their impossible antecedents, will have to be interpreted over worlds that are (at best) only "epistemically" possible; and, as Richard Boyd has pointed out to me, this helps to explain why anyone who accepts a causal theory of knowledge (or any theory according to which the justification of our beliefs depends on what explains our holding them) will find their truth irrelevant to the question of how much we know, either in chemistry or in morals. For although there certainly are counterfactuals that are relevant to questions about what causes (and, hence, about what explains what), these have to be counterfactuals about real possibilities, not merely epistemic ones.

29. This essay has benefited from helpful discussion of earlier versions read at the University of Virginia, Cornell University, Franklin and Marshall College, Wayne State University, and the University of Michigan. I have been aided by a useful correspondence with Gilbert Harman; and I am grateful also for specific comments from Richard Boyd, David Brink, David Copp, Stephen Darwall, Terence Irwin, Norman Kretzmann, Ronald Nash, Peter Railton, Bruce Russell, Sydney Shoemaker, and Judith Slein.

Only after this essay had appeared in print did I notice that several parallel points about *aesthetic* explanations had been made by Michael Slote in "The Rationality of Aesthetic Value Judgments," *Journal of Philosophy* 68 (1971), 821–39: interested readers should see that paper.

Part V

VALUE AND OBLIGATION

25 / G. E. MOORE

RESULTS, THE TEST OF RIGHT AND WRONG

In our last chapter we began considering objections to one very fundamental principle, which is pre-supposed by the theory stated in the first two chapters—a principle which may be summed up in the two propositions (1) that the question whether an action is right or wrong always depends upon its *total* consequences, and (2) that if it is once right to prefer one set of *total* consequences, A, to another set, B, it must always be right to prefer any set precisely similar to A to any set precisely similar to B. The objections to this principle, which we considered in the last chapter, rested on certain views with regard to the meaning of the words 'right' and 'good'. But there remain several other quite independent objections, which may be urged against it even if we reject those views. That is to say, there are objections which may and would be urged against it by many people who accept both of the two propositions which I was trying to establish in the last chapter, namely (1) that to call an action 'right' or 'wrong' is not the same thing as to say that any being whatever has towards it any mental attitude whatever; and (2) that if any given whole is once intrinsically good or bad, any whole precisely similar to it must always be intrinsically good or bad in precisely the same degree. And in the present chapter I wish briefly to consider what seem to me to be the most important of these remaining objections.

All of them are directed against the view

Reprinted by permission of the publisher and copyright holder from G. E. Moore, *Ethics* (Oxford: Oxford University Press, 1912), pp. 72–83.

that right and wrong do always depend upon an action's *actual* consequences or results. This may be denied for several different reasons; and I shall try to state fairly the chief among these reasons, and to point out why they do not seem to be conclusive.

In the first place, it may be said that, by laying down the principle that right and wrong depend upon consequences, we are doing away with the distinction between what is a *duty* and what is merely *expedient*; and between what is *wrong* and what is merely *inexpedient*. People certainly do commonly make a distinction between duty and expediency. And it may be said that the very meaning of calling an action 'expedient' is to say that it will produce the best consequences possible under the circumstances. If, therefore, we also say that an action is a *duty*, whenever and only when it produces the best possible consequences, it may seem that nothing is left to distinguish duty from expediency.

Now, as against this objection, it is important to point out, first of all, that, even if we admit that to call an action expedient is the same thing as to say that it produces the best possible consequences, our principle still does not compel us to hold that to call an action expedient is *the same thing* as to call it a duty. All that it does compel us to hold is that whatever is expedient is always *also* a duty, and that whatever is a duty is always *also* expedient. That is to say, it *does* maintain that duty and expediency *coincide*; but it does *not* maintain that the meaning of the two words is the same. It is, indeed, quite plain, I think, that the meaning of the two words is *not* the same;

for, if it were, then it would be a mere tautology to say that it is always our duty to do what will have the best possible consequences. Our theory does not, therefore, do away with the distinction between the *meaning* of the words 'duty' and 'expediency'; it only maintains that both will always apply to the same actions.

But, no doubt, what is meant by many who urge this objection is to deny this. What they mean to say is not merely that to call an action expedient is a different thing from calling it a duty, but also that sometimes what is expedient is *wrong*, and what *is* a duty is inexpedient. This is a view which is undoubtedly often held; people often speak as if there often were an actual conflict between duty and expediency. But many of the cases in which it would be commonly held that there is such a conflict may, I think, be explained by supposing that when we call an action 'expedient' we do not always mean quite strictly that its *total* consequences, taking absolutely *everything* into account, are the best possible. It is by no means clear that we do always mean this. We may, perhaps, sometimes mean merely that the action is expedient for some particular purpose; and sometimes that it is expedient in the interests of the agent, though not so on the whole. But if we only mean this, our theory, of course, does *not* compel us to maintain that the expedient *is* always a duty, and duty always expedient. It only compels us to maintain this, if 'expedient' be understood in the strictest and fullest sense, as meaning that, when *absolutely all* the consequences are taken into account, they will be found to be the best possible. And if this be clearly understood, then most people, I think, will be reluctant to admit that it can ever be really inexpedient to do our duty, or that what is really and truly expedient, in this strict sense, can ever be wrong.

But, no doubt, some people may still maintain that it is or may be sometimes our duty to do actions which will *not* have the best possible consequences, and sometimes also positively wrong, to do actions which

will. And the chief reason why this is held is, I think, the following.

It is, in fact, very commonly held indeed that there are certain specific kinds of action which are absolutely always right, and others which are absolutely always wrong. Different people will, indeed, take different views as to exactly what kinds of action have this character. A rule which will be offered by one set of persons as a rule to which there is absolutely no exception will be rejected by others, as obviously admitting of exceptions; but these will generally, in their turn, maintain that some other rule, which they can mention, really has no exceptions. Thus there are enormous numbers of people who would agree that *some rule or other* (and generally more than one) ought *absolutely always* to be obeyed; although probably there is not one single rule which *all* the persons who maintain this would agree upon. Thus, for instance, some people might maintain that murder (defined in some particular way) is an act which ought absolutely *never* to be committed; or that to act *justly* is a rule which ought absolutely always to be obeyed; and similarly it might be suggested with regard to many other kinds of action, that they are actions, which it is either *always* our duty, or *always* wrong to do.

But once we assert with regard to any rule of this kind that it *is absolutely always* our duty to obey it, it is easy and natural to take one further step and to say that it *would* always be our duty to obey it, *whatever* the consequences might be. Of course, this further step does not necessarily and logically follow from the mere position that there are some kinds of action which ought, *in fact*, absolutely always to be done or avoided. For it is just possible that there are some kinds which do, as a matter of fact, absolutely always produce the best possible consequences, and other kinds which absolutely never do so. And there is a strong tendency among persons who hold the first position to hold that, as a matter of fact, this is the case: that right actions always do, as a matter of fact, produce the best possible results, and wrong actions never. Thus even those who would assent to the maxim that 'Justice should always be done, though the heavens should fall', will generally be disposed to believe that justice never will, in fact, cause the heavens to fall, but will rather be always the best means of upholding them. And similarly those who say that 'you should never do evil that good may come', though their maxim seems to imply that good *may* sometimes come from doing wrong, would yet be very loth to admit that, by doing wrong, you ever would *really* produce better consequences *on the whole* than if you had acted rightly instead. Or again, those who say 'that the end will never justify the means', though they certainly imply that certain ways of acting would be always wrong, *whatever* advantages might be secured by them, yet, I think, would be inclined to deny that the advantages to be obtained by acting wrongly ever do *really* outweigh those to be obtained by acting rightly, if we take into account absolutely *all* the consequences of each course.

Those, therefore, who hold that certain specific ways of acting are absolutely always right, and others absolutely always wrong, do, I think, generally hold that the former do also, as a matter of fact, absolutely always produce the best results, and the latter never. But, for the reasons given at the beginning of Chapter III, it is, I think, very unlikely that this belief can be justified. The total results of an action always depend, not merely on the specific nature of the action, but on the circumstances in which it is done; and the circumstances vary so greatly that it is, in most cases, extremely unlikely that any particular kind of action will *absolutely* always, in absolutely all circumstances, either produce or fail to produce the best possible results. For this reason, if we do take the view that right and wrong depend upon consequences, we must, I think, be prepared to doubt whether any particular kind of action whatever is absolutely always right or absolutely always wrong. For instance, however we define 'murder', it is unlikely that absolutely *no* case will ever

occur in which it would be right to commit a murder; and, however we define 'justice', it is unlikely that *no* case will ever occur in which it would be right to do an injustice. No doubt it may be possible to define actions of which it is true that, in an *immense* majority of cases, it is right or wrong to perform them; and perhaps *some* rules of this kind might be found to which there are really *no* exceptions. But in the case of most of the ordinary moral rules, it seems extremely unlikely that obedience to them will *absolutely always* produce the best possible results. And most persons who realize this would, I think, be disposed to give up the view that they ought absolutely *always* to be obeyed. They would be content to accept them as *general* rules, to which there are very few exceptions, without pretending that they are absolutely universal.

But, no doubt, there may be some persons who will hold, in the case of some particular rule or set of rules, that even if obedience to it does in some cases *not* produce the best possible consequences, yet we ought even in these cases to obey it. It may seem to them that they really do know certain rules, which ought *absolutely always* to be obeyed, *whatever* the consequences may be, and even, therefore, if the total consequences are not the best possible. They may, for instance, take quite seriously the assertion that justice ought to be done, even though the heavens should fall, as meaning that, *however* bad the consequences of doing an act of justice might in some circumstances be, yet it always would be our duty to do it. And such a view does necessarily contradict our principle; since, whether it be true or not that an act of injustice ever actually could in this world produce the best possible consequences, it is certainly possible to *conceive* circumstances in which it would do so. I doubt whether those who believe in the absolute universality of certain moral rules do generally thus distinguish quite clearly between the question whether disobedience to the rule ever *could* produce the best possible consequences, and the question whether, *if* it did, then disobedience would be wrong. They would generally be disposed to argue that it never really *could*. But some persons might perhaps hold that, even if it did, yet disobedience would be wrong. And if this view be quite clearly held, there is, so far as I can see, absolutely no way of refuting it except by appealing to the self-evidence of the principle that if we *knew* that the effect of a given action really would be to make the world, as a whole, *worse* than it would have been if we had acted differently, it certainly would be wrong for us to do that action. Those who say that certain rules ought *absolutely always* to be obeyed, *whatever* the consequences may be, are logically bound to deny this; for by saying '*whatever* the consequences may be', they do imply '*even if* the world as a whole were the worse because of our action'. It seems to me to be self-evident that knowingly to do an action which would make the world, on the whole, really and truly *worse* than if we had acted differently, must always be wrong. And if this be admitted, then it absolutely disposes of the view that there are any kinds of action whatever, which it *would* always be our duty to do or to avoid, *whatever* the consequences might be.

For this reason it seems to me we must reject this particular objection to the view that right and wrong always depend upon consequences; namely, the objection that there are certain *kinds* of action which ought absolutely always and quite unconditionally to be done or avoided. But there still remain two other objections, which are so commonly held, that it is worth while to consider them.

The first is the objection that right and wrong depend neither upon the nature of the action, nor upon its consequences, but partly, or even entirely, upon the *motive* or *motives* from which it is done. By the view that it depends *partly* upon the motives, I mean the view that no action can be *really* right, unless it be done from some one motive, or some one of a set of motives, which are supposed to be good; but that the being done from such a motive is not suffi-

cient, *by itself*, to make an action right: that the action, if it is to be right, must always *also* either produce the best possible consequences, or be distinguished by some other characteristic. And this view, therefore, will not necessarily contradict our principle so far as it asserts that no action can be right, *unless* it produces the best possible consequences: it only contradicts that part of it which asserts that *every* action which does produce them is right. But the view has sometimes been held, I think, that right and wrong depend *entirely* upon motives: that is to say, that not only is no action right, *unless* it be done from a good motive, but also that *any* action which is done from some one motive or some one of a set of motives is always right, whatever its consequences may be and whatever it may be like in other respects. And this view, of course, will contradict both parts of our principle; since it not only implies that an action, which produces the best possible consequences may be wrong, but also that an action may be right, in spite of failing to produce them.

In favour of both these views it may be urged that in our moral judgements we actually do, and ought to, take account of motives; and indeed that it marks a great advance in morality when men do begin to attach importance to motives and are not guided exclusively, in their praise or blame, by the 'external' nature of the act done or by its consequences. And all this may be fully admitted. It is quite certain that when a man does an action which has bad consequences from a good motive, we do tend to judge him differently from a man who does a similar action from a bad one; and also that when a man does an action which has good consequences from a bad motive, we may nevertheless think badly of him for it. And it may be admitted that, in some cases at least, it is right and proper that a man's motives should thus influence our judgement. But the question is: What *sort* of moral judgement is it right and proper that they should influence? Should it influence our view as to whether the action in question is right or wrong? It seems very doubtful whether, as a rule, it actually does affect our judgement on this particular point, for we are quite accustomed to judge that a man sometimes acts *wrongly* from the best of motives; and though we should admit that the good motive forms some excuse, and that the whole state of things is better than if he had done the same thing from a bad motive, it yet does not lead us to deny that the action *is* wrong. There is, therefore, reason to think that the kind of moral judgements which a consideration of motives actually *does* affect do not consist of judgements as to whether the action done from the motive is *right* or *wrong;* but are moral judgements of *some different kind;* and there is still more reason to think that it is only judgements of some different kind which *ought* to be influenced by it.

The fact is that judgements as to the rightness and wrongness of actions are by no means the only kind of moral judgements which we make; and it is, I think, solely because some of these other judgements are confused with judgements of right and wrong that the latter are ever held to depend upon the motive. There are three other kinds of judgements which are chiefly concerned in this case. In the first place it may be held that some motives are *intrinsically good* and others *intrinsically bad;* and though this is a view which is inconsistent with the theory of our first two chapters, it is not a view which we are at present concerned to dispute: for it is not at all inconsistent with the principle which we are at present considering—namely, that right and wrong always depend solely upon consequences. If we held this view, we might still hold that a man may act wrongly from a good motive, and rightly from a bad one, and that the motive would make no difference whatever to the rightness or wrongness of the action. What it would make a difference to is the goodness or badness of the whole state of affairs: for, if we suppose the same action to be done in one case from a good motive and in the

other from a bad one, then, so far as the consequences of the action are concerned, the goodness of the whole state of things will be the same, while the presence of the good motive will mean the presence of an *additional* good in the one case which is absent in the other. For this reason alone, therefore, we might justify the view that motives are relevant to *some* kinds of moral judgements, though not to judgements of right and wrong.

And there is yet another reason for this view, and this a reason which may be consistently held even by those who hold the theory of our first two chapters. It may be held, namely, that good motives have a *general* tendency to produce right conduct, though they do not *always* do so, and bad motives to produce wrong conduct; and this would be another reason which would justify us in regarding right actions done from a good motive differently from right actions done from a bad one. For though, in the case supposed, the bad motive would not *actually* have led to wrong action, yet, if it is true that motives of that kind do *generally* lead to wrong action, we should be right in passing this judgement upon it; and judgements to the effect that a motive is of a kind which generally leads to wrong action are undoubtedly moral judgements of a sort, and an important sort, though they do not prove that every action done from such a motive is wrong.

And finally motives seem also to be relevant to a third kind of moral judgement of great importance—namely, judgements as to whether, and in what degree, the agent *deserves* moral praise or blame for acting as he did. This question as to what is deserving of moral praise or blame is, I think, often confused with the question as to what is right or wrong. It is very natural, at first sight, to assume that to call an action morally praiseworthy is the same thing as to say that it is right, and to call it morally blameworthy the same thing as to say that it is wrong. But yet a very little reflection suffices to show that the two things are certainly distinct. When we say that an action *deserves* praise or blame, we imply that it is *right* to praise or blame it; that is to say, we are making a judgement *not* about the rightness of the original action, but about the rightness of the further action which we should take, if we praised or blamed it. And these two judgements are certainly not identical; nor is there any reason to think that what is right *always* also deserves to be praised, and what is wrong *always* also deserves to be blamed. Even, therefore, if the motive *is* relevant to the question whether an action deserves praise or blame, it by no means follows that it is *also* relevant to the question whether it is right or wrong. And there is some reason to think that the motive *is* relevant to judgements of the former kind: that we really *ought* sometimes to praise an action done from a bad motive less than if it had been done from a good one, and to blame an action done from a good motive less than if it had been done from a bad one. For one of the considerations upon which the question whether it is right to blame an action depends, is that our blame may tend to prevent the agent from doing similar wrong actions in future; and obviously, if the agent only acted wrongly from a motive which is not likely to lead him wrong in the future, there is less need to try to deter him by blame than if he had acted from a motive which was likely to lead him to act wrongly again. This is, I think, a very real reason why we *sometimes* ought to blame a man less when he does wrong from a good motive. But I do not mean to say that the question whether a man deserves moral praise or blame, or the degree to which he deserves it, depends *entirely* or *always* upon his motive. I think it certainly does not. My point is only that this *question* does *sometimes* depend on the motive in some degree; whereas the question whether his action was right or wrong *never* depends upon it at all.

There are, therefore, at least three different kinds of moral judgements, in making which it is at least plausible to hold that we ought to take account of motives; and if all these judgements are carefully distinguished from that particular kind which is solely concerned with the question whether an action is right or wrong, there ceases, I think, to be any reason to suppose that this last question ever depends upon the motive at all. At all events the mere fact that motives are and ought to be taken account of in *some* moral judgements does not constitute such a reason. And hence this fact cannot be urged as an objection to the view that right and wrong depend solely on consequences.

But there remains one last objection to this view, which is, I am inclined to think, the most serious of all. This is an objection which will be urged by people who strongly maintain that right and wrong do *not* depend either upon the nature of the action or upon its motive, and who will even go so far as to admit as self-evident the hypothetical proposition that *if* any being absolutely *knew* that one action would have better total consequences than another, then it *would* always be his duty to choose the former rather than the latter. But what such people would point out is that this hypothetical case is hardly ever, if ever, realized among us men. We hardly ever, if ever, *know for certain* which among the courses open to us *will* produce the best consequences. Some accident, which we could not possibly have foreseen, may always falsify the most careful calculations, and make an action, which we had every reason to think would have the best results, *actually* have worse ones than some alternative would have had. Suppose, then, that a man has taken all possible care to assure himself that a given course will be the best, and has adopted it for that reason, but that owing to some subsequent event, which he could not possibly have foreseen, it turns out *not* to be the best: are we for that reason to say that his action was wrong? It may seem outrageous to say so; and yet this is what we must say, if we are to hold that right and wrong depend upon the *actual* consequences. Or suppose that a man has deliberately chosen a course, which he has every reason to suppose will *not* produce the best consequences, but that some unforeseen accident defeats his purpose and makes it actually turn out to be the best: are we to say that such a man, because of this unforeseen accident, has acted rightly? This also may seem an outrageous thing to say; and yet we must say it, if we are to hold that right and wrong depend upon the *actual* consequences. For these reasons many people are strongly inclined to hold that they do *not* depend upon the *actual* consequences, but only upon those which were antecedently *probable*, or which the agent had *reason* to expect, or which it was *possible* for him to *foresee*. They are inclined to say that an action is *always* right, whatever its *actual* consequences may be, provided the agent had reason to expect that they would be the best possible; and *always* wrong, if he had reason to expect that they would not.

This, I think, is the most serious objection to the view that right and wrong depend upon the *actual* consequences. But yet I am inclined to think that even this objection can be got over by reference to the distinction between what is right or wrong, on the one hand, and what is morally praiseworthy or blameworthy on the other. What we should naturally say of a man whose action turns out badly owing to some unforeseen accident when he had every reason to expect that it would turn out well, is not that his action was right, but rather that *he is not to blame*. And it may be fully admitted that in such a case he really *ought* not to be blamed; since blame cannot possibly serve any good purpose, and would be likely to do harm. But, even if we admit that he was not to blame, is that any reason for asserting also that he acted rightly? I cannot see that it is; and therefore I am inclined to think that in all such cases the man really did act *wrongly*, although he is not to blame, and although, perhaps, he even deserves praise for acting as he did.

But the same difficulty may be put in another form, in which there may seem an even stronger case against the view that right and wrong depend on the *actual* consequences. Instead of considering what judgement we ought to pass on an action *after* it has been done, and when many of its results are already known, let us consider what judgement we ought to pass on it *beforehand*, and when the question is which among several courses still open to a man he *ought* to choose. It is admitted that he cannot *know for certain* beforehand which of them will actually have the best results; but let us suppose that he has every reason to think that one of them will produce decidedly better results than any of the others—that all probability is in favour of this view. Can we not say, in such a case, that he absolutely *ought* to choose that one? that he will be acting very *wrongly* if he chooses any other? We certainly *should* actually say so; and many people may be inclined to think that we should be right in saying so, no matter what the results may subsequently prove to be. There does seem to be a certain paradox in maintaining the opposite: in maintaining that, in such a case, it can possibly be true that he *ought* to choose a course, which he has every reason to think will *not* be the best. But yet I am inclined to think that even this difficulty is not fatal to our view. It may be admitted that we should say, and should be justified in saying, that he absolutely *ought* to choose the course, which he has reason to think will be the best. But we may be justified in saying many things, which we do not know to be true, and which in fact are not so, provided there is a strong probability that they are. And so in this case I do not see why we should not hold, that though we should be justified in saying that he *ought* to choose one course, yet it may not be really true that he ought. What certainly will be true is that he will deserve the strongest moral blame if he does not choose the course in question, even though it may be wrong. And we are thus committed to the paradox that a man may really deserve the strongest moral condemnation for choosing an action, which *actually* is right. But I do not see why we should not accept this paradox.

I conclude, then, that there is no conclusive reason against the view that our theory is right, so far as it maintains that the question whether an action is right or wrong *always* depends on its *actual* consequences. There seems no sufficient reason for holding either that it depends on the intrinsic nature of the action, or that it depends upon the motive, or even that it depends on the *probable* consequences.

26 / J. J. C. SMART

ACT-UTILITARIANISM AND RULE-UTILITARIANISM

The system of normative ethics which I am here concerned to defend is, as I have said earlier, *act*-utilitarianism. Act-utilitarianism is to be contrasted with rule-utilitarianism. Act-utilitarianism is the view that the rightness or wrongness of an action is to be judged by the consequences, good or bad, of the action itself. Rule-utilitarianism is the view that the rightness or wrongness of an action is to be judged by the goodness and badness of the consequences of a rule that everyone should perform the action in like circumstances. There are two sub-varieties of rule-utilitarianism according to whether one construes 'rule' here as 'actual rule' or 'possible rule'. With the former, one gets a view like that of S. E. Toulmin[1] and with the latter, one like Kant's.[2] That is, if it is permissible to interpret Kant's principle 'Act only on that maxim through which you can at the same time will that it should become a universal law' as 'Act only on that maxim which you as a humane and benevolent person would like to see established as a universal law.' Of course Kant would resist this appeal to human feeling, but it seems necessary in order to interpret his doctrine in a plausible way. A subtle version of the Kantian type of rule-utilitarianism is given by R. F. Harrod in his 'Utilitarianism Revised'.[3]

I have argued elsewhere[4] the objections to rule-utilitarianism as compared with act-utilitarianism.[5] Briefly they boil down to

the accusation of rule worship:[6] the rule-utilitarian presumably advocates his principle because he is ultimately concerned with human happiness: why then should he advocate abiding by a rule when he knows that it will not in the present case be most beneficial to abide by it? The reply that in most cases it is most beneficial to abide by the rule seems irrelevant. And so is the reply that it would be better that everybody should abide by the rule than that nobody should. This is to suppose that the only alternative to 'everybody does A' is 'no one does A'. But clearly we have the possibility 'some people do A and some don't'. Hence to refuse to break a generally beneficial rule in those cases in which it is not most beneficial to obey it seems irrational and to be a case of rule worship.

The type of utilitarianism which I shall advocate will, then, be act-utilitarianism, not rule-utilitarianism.

David Lyons has recently argued that rule-utilitarianism (by which, I think, he means the sort of rule-utilitarianism which I have called the Kantian one) collapses into act-utilitarianism.[7] His reasons are briefly as follows. Suppose that an exception to a rule R produces the best possible consequences. Then this is evidence that the rule R should be modified so as to allow this exception. Thus we get a new rule of the form 'do R except in circumstances of the sort C'. That is, whatever would lead the act-utilitarian to break a rule would lead the Kantian rule-utilitarian to modify the rule. Thus an adequate rule-utilitarianism would be extensionally equivalent to act-utilitarianism.

Lyons is particularly interested in what he calls 'threshold effects'. A difficulty for rule-utilitarianism has often appeared to be that of rules like 'do not walk on the grass' or 'do not fail to vote at an election'. In these cases it would seem that it is beneficial if some people, though not too many, break the rule. Lyons points out that we can distinguish the action of doing something (say, walking on the grass) after some largish number n other people have done it from the action of doing it when few or no people have done it. When these extra circumstances are written into the rule, Lyons holds that the rule will come to enjoin the same actions as would the act-utilitarian principle. However there seems to be one interesting sort of case which requires slightly different treatment. This is the sort of case in which not too many people must do action X, but each person must plan his action in ignorance of what the other person does. That is, what A does depends on what B does, and what B does depends on what A does. Situations possessing this sort of circularity will be discussed below.

I am inclined to think that an adequate rule-utilitarianism would not only be extensionally equivalent to the act-utilitarian principle (i.e. would enjoin the same set of actions as it) but would in fact consist of one rule only, the act-utilitarian one: 'maximize probable benefit'. This is because any rule which can be formulated must be able to deal with an indefinite number of unforeseen types of contingency. No rule, short of the act-utilitarian one, can therefore be safely regarded as extensionally equivalent to the act-utilitarian principle unless it is that very principle itself. I therefore suggest that Lyons' type of consideration can be taken even further, and that rule-utilitarianism of the Kantian sort must collapse into act-utilitarianism in an even stronger way: it must become a 'one-rule' rule-utilitarianism which is identical to act-utilitarianism. In any case, whether this is correct or not, it is with the defence of act-utilitarianism, and not with rule-utilitarianism (supposing that there are viable forms of rule-utilitarianism which may be

distinguished from act-utilitarianism) that this monograph is concerned. (Lyons himself rejects utilitarianism.)

Notes

1. *An Examination of the Place of Reason in Ethics* (Cambridge University Press, London, 1950).

2. Immanuel Kant, *Groundwork of the Metaphysic of Morals*. Translated from the German in *The Moral Law*, by H. J. Paton (Hutchinson, London, 1948).

3. *Mind* 45 (1936), 137–56.

4. In my article 'Extreme and restricted utilitarianism', *Philosophical Quarterly* 6 (1956) 344–54. This contains bad errors and a better version of the article will be found in Philippa Foot (ed.), *Theories of Ethics* (Oxford University Press, London, 1967), or Michael D. Bayles (ed.), *Contemporary Utilitarianism* (Doubleday, New York, 1968). In this article I used the terms 'extreme' and 'restricted' instead of Brandt's more felicitous 'act' and 'rule' which I now prefer.

5. For another discussion of what in effect is the same problem see A. K. Sout's excellent paper, 'But suppose everyone did the same', *Australasian Journal of Philosophy* 32 (1954) I–29.

6. On rule worship see I. M. Crombie, 'Social clockwork and utilitarian morality', in D. M. Mackinnon (ed.), *Christian Faith and Communist Faith* (Macmillan, London, 1953). See p. 109.

7. David Lyons, *The Forms and Limits of Utilitarianism* (Oxford University Press, London, 1965). Rather similar considerations have been put forward by R. M. Hare, *Freedom and Reason* (Oxford University Press, London, 1963), pp. 131–6, and R. B. Brandt, 'Toward a credible form of utilitarianism', in H. N. Castañeda and G. Nakhnikian, *Morality and the Language of Conduct* (Wayne State University, Detroit, 1963), esp. pp. 119–23.

27 / RICHARD BRANDT

THE REAL AND ALLEGED PROBLEMS OF UTILITARIANISM

Everybody believes that some actions, or types of action, are morally right or wrong; or that it is a person's moral obligation to do, or to avoid doing, these actions. Many philosophers, however, have wanted to introduce some order into this chaos of opinions, and have sought to find a small number of fundamental principles of right and wrong from which all justified moral beliefs can be deduced, given relevant factual information. A few philosophers—among them Immanuel Kant, with his famous "categorical imperative," and recently John Rawls, with his emphasis on justice—have thought that we can make do with just one fundamental principle. The oldest of such one-principle theories, which has shown vitality and appeal for philosophers for thousands of years, is utilitarianism, the view that the benefit or harm done by an act, or class of actions, or prohibition of an act-type, determines whether it is wrong or right morally. If acts of incest or homosexual contact or deceit are wrong, for example, it is because the acts or practice or traits of character they involve have impact for good or ill, happiness or unhappiness.

Unfortunately from the point of view of simplicity, there are different kinds of utilitarianism. One of them is "act-utilitarianism"—the thesis that a particular act is right if, and only if, no other act the agent could perform at the time would have, or probably would have (on the agent's evidence), better consequences. Such impor-

tant philosophers as G.E. Moore, Henry Sidgwick, and Bertrand Russell advocated this view at about the turn of the century. A second form, which is older and probably more influential among philosophers at present, is "rule-utilitarianism"; its thesis is roughly that an act is morally right if, and only if, it would be as beneficial to have a moral code permitting that act as to have any moral code that is similar but prohibits the act. There are other types of utilitarianism, but these two seem most important now.

Quite a few articulate philosophers are critical of utilitarianism. A recent article in the *Yale Law Review* speculated that a half-dozen adherents today are all that separates utilitarianism from extinction. This anticipation of the demise of utilitarianism seems decidedly premature; in my opinion some form of utilitarianism is probably convincing to the "silent majority" of philosophers. However that may be, non-philosophers widely employ the general utilitarian framework in thinking about moral issues. It is obvious that "cost-benefit analysis" is used (doubtless often misused, by construing it in a much oversimplified form) in evaluating government projects. The utilitarian conception appears to pervade the American Law Institute's recommendations for reform of the criminal law and it underlies the currently influential movement of "economic criticism" of the law. Indeed, in evaluating systems of "professional ethics" an assessment of the general costs and benefits of recognizing certain standards seems inescapable, although talk about "rights" is

Reprinted by permission of the publisher and copyright holder from *Hastings Center Report* 13 (1983): 37–43.

often introduced in this connection. (But J.S. Mill seems to have been correct in thinking that we can determine who has which rights only by utilitarian reflections.)

In particular, utilitarian reflection is prominent in the field of medicine; for instance, in the literature on the "autonomy" to be granted patients in decisions about treatment, or on what physicians should tell seriously ill patients about their prospects. (See the exchange between M. W. Martin and B. Freedman, for example, in the July 1981 issue of *Ethics*.) Utilitarian reflections, in fact, were important in the thinking of physicians and surgeons of the nineteenth century, as Martin S. Pernick brings out in his article in this issue of the *Hastings Center Report*; some of the debates he reports, incidentally, are still alive in the forthcoming report of the President's Commission for the Study of Ethical Problems in Medicine and Biomedical and Behavioral Research. Utilitarian reflections are also prominent in recent analyses of U.S. foreign policy, including policy about immigration, although of course some writers take different approaches. The recent report of a Congressional Select Committee on immigration policy is full of talk about the impact of a liberal policy on unemployment in the U.S., about the alleged long-range negative noneconomic cost of a society culturally more heterogeneous than at present, of the human cost of refusing admission to refugees or the poverty-stricken hoping for a better life in America, and so on. Some form of utilitarian-type thinking pervades most present reflection about public affairs and policy making in this country.

Philosophers who criticize utilitarianism usually center their fire on the first form of the theory (act-utilitarianism). Unfortunately they often imply, if not state, that this criticism disposes of utilitarianism in all its forms. This is a mistake. Adherents of rule-utilitarianism are themselves quite critical of act-utilitarianism, although the theories are fairly closely related, especially when evaluation of a long-range public policy is the issue.

In what follows I shall discuss rule-utilitarianism, since it seems to me more plausible. The choice is not eccentric; despite the number of thoughtful advocates today of act-utilitarianism I believe most philosophers who advocate utilitarianism today are in the rule-utilitarian camp. Another reason for concentrating on rule-utilitarianism is that some of its problems have not received comparable attention.

What is Rule-Utilitarianism?

One can argue that rule-utilitarianism goes back to Epicurus (341–270 B.C.), who was a utilitarian about laws. He said that "natural justice is a symbol or expression of expedience" and that "among the things accounted just by conventional law, whatever in the needs of mutual intercourse is attested to be expedient, is thereby stamped as just . . ." (*Sovran Maxims*, cited by Diogenes Laertius, nos. 31 and 57). One might also argue that St. Thomas's theory of natural law is utilitarian.

However, rule-utilitarianism as a theory of *action*—not of right laws—goes back at least as far as Richard Cumberland in 1672. Bishop Berkeley, in his *Passive Obedience* (1712), was the first to distinguish clearly between the two forms of utilitarianism, and he opted for the second. More specifically, he asserted that we are not morally bound to do whatever we believe will produce most good or happiness, but we are morally bound to follow certain moral laws, prohibiting or enjoining certain types of action—these being God's laws as identified by revelation or natural reason. These laws have been selected by God because, in his benevolence, he wants the happiness of mankind and knows that following these laws will maximize it. God, incidentally, also lets it be known that it will not be to the long-range interest of anyone to infringe his laws; so the theory provides motivation to do what is right. Now, if the part about God is deleted from Berkeley's view, what remains is the skeleton of much the kind of rule-utilitarianism I wish to discuss. This is the view roughly held by J.S. Mill; we of course have to flesh out the account a bit.

First, we have to think of the morality of a society: that is, of people in the society mostly sharing certain aversions to or desires for (partly as a matter of innate or learned benevolence, but partly as a result of a process of motivational learning we need not try to specify) certain types of actions. These presumably will include aversions to hurting others, telling lies, and breaking promises. But there are also learned dispositions to experience guilt in case we act contrary to these aversions, and disapproval of others when they act contrary. We also admire others who do what we say is above and beyond the call of duty. Further, we disapprove of, and are averse to, various kinds of acts in different degrees: we would not commit murder and we disapprove intensely of anyone who does (without excuse); we also don't like it very much when a person brushes off a request for a match, but our disapproval is slight, and we feel only mild aversion to doing the same thing. Consciences are also equipped with a system of excuses; we don't feel guilty, or at least don't disapprove so vigorously of others, if we believe infractions are the result of certain conditions, say, ignorance, insanity, extreme fear, and so on.

This motivational description of conscience may not be appealing, but most of it appears in Mill's third chapter, and to some extent in the fifth chapter, of *Utilitarianism*. To my mind that *is* conscience, and the morality of a society is nothing more than the consciences of its members; or, if you like, the conscience of the average person.

If this is what a morality—or moral code—is, what is a "rule-utilitarian"? A rule-utilitarian thinks that right actions are the kind permitted by the moral code optimal for the society of which the agent is a member. An optimal code is one designed to maximize welfare or what is good (thus, utility). This leaves open the possibility that a particular right act by itself may not maximize benefit.

This definition does not imply anything about what a utilitarian means by "right" or "optimal,'; or about how a utilitarian will justify the main thesis. Utilitarians need not have any particular account of the meaning of these terms, and they need not cffer any particular justification of their thesis; they can simply advocate the utilitarian principle.

On the rule-utilitarian view, then, to find what is morally right or wrong we need to find which actions would be permitted by a moral system that is "optimal" for the agent's society.

The First Real Puzzle

The last phrase in this definition raises the first "problem" or "puzzle" I wish to discuss—for an agent's society will comprise various subgroups, and it could be that the moral code optimal for one may not be optimal for others. For instance, perhaps the moral code comprising the consciences of physicians and lawyers should be more clearly articulated in certain areas than the moral code of the general public. There is no reason to burden the general public with, say, aversion to refusing to treat patients who cannot pay, or breaches of confidentiality. Remember that we have to include the learning-costs in a cost-benefit analysis of a moral system. That being so, perhaps the rule-utilitarian must recognize special moralities for groups like physicians who, unlike the general public, meet certain problems regularly and need to respond to them intuitively without long inference from general principles. Similarly, it is possible that the morality optimal for children is not the morality optimal for adults. Rule-utilitarians, then, may be free to think that the moral codes justified for physicians, lawyers, children, bishops, and university students will differ. The identification of such possible special codes is part of the subject matter of "professional ethics."

This conception raises a difficult question that I shall not try to answer. Could the optimal moral code for a physician or a politician or an army officer direct a person to do something incompatible with what the optimal code for the general public would prescribe for the same situation? Presumably we *do* think that the optimal code for one society might lead to behavior incompatible with behavior required by the optimal code for another society. If that is possible, what is the really right thing to do when these codes conflict? For a rule-utilitarian who thinks that the actions of governments may be morally right or wrong, there is a related question. Must we talk of an "optimal moral code" for governments? Can we think of governments as quasi-persons, and talk of an optimal conscience for them? Or may we talk not of the acts of governments being right or wrong, but only of the morally right or wrong acts of office-holders or politicians? Rule-utilitarians should think more about this.

There is another complication that I shall only mention. Suppose a law—but we might generalize to any institution—is less than optimal, by the utilitarian standard. Might it still be morally acceptable? Or suppose it is optimal. Is it then necessarily also morally acceptable? Writers like Rawls would say "no" to both questions; there is no necessary correlation between optimality and moral acceptability. But what would rule-utilitarians say? They might take either option. They might just identify the moral acceptability of an institution, say a law, with its optimality, in the context of other institutions in the society. Or they might deny this, and say that what makes an institution morally acceptable is not *its* optimality, but whether an optimal moral code would require persons to work to change it or work to preserve it. So some utilitarians might say that the tax law, or welfare system, might be optimal but not morally acceptable, because morality requires more equality. Thus the utilitarian might say that the optimality of the moral code is dispositive for the moral acceptability of an institution, not the optimality of the institution itself. Very likely, of course, there will be a close connection between the two.

One might ask: how should a utilitarian decide which of these lines to take? I shall not try to answer this question[1] but will shortly consider how the rule-utilitarian must go about resolving such difficulties.

The Second Puzzle

The rule-utilitarian, then, says that right action is action permitted by the moral code for society that would maximize net-benefit or utility. But what is meant to count as benefit or utility? The traditional answer has been: pleasure, hedonic tone (positive or negative), or happiness. So said Bentham, Mill, and the earlier theological utilitarians. Now many philosophers argue that this is not what we should try to maximize, and that anyone who thinks this way is taking a crude view of human nature. What then should we add? J.L. Mackie suggests in *Ethics: Inventing Right and Wrong* (1977): "Liberty of thought and discussion, thought and discussion themselves, understanding of all sorts of things, including ourselves and other human beings, a self-reliant, enterprising, and experimental spirit and way of life, artistic creation and craftsmanship of any sort, the enjoyment and appreciation of beauty, and general participatory self-government both in smaller institutions and in the determination of large scale social policies and laws" (p. 150). He says this in criticism of utilitarianism of all kinds. Is utilitarianism in all its forms committed to a hopelessly narrow view of what is good?

There is no *logical* connection between either act- or rule-utilitarianism and hedonism, and none between a deontological ethics and nonhedonism. True, the utilitarian says we are to identify right action by appeal to maximizing net benefit or utility, but he leaves the definition of these terms open. Indeed, one can say: we should maximize what is intrinsically good, and go on to say, as "ideal utilitarians" like Moore and Rashdall did, that various states of affairs quite different from pleasure are intrinsically good—say, knowledge, virtue, and friendship. One could then say, as these ideal utilitarians did, that the right action is fixed by maximizing the intrinsically good, and then propose that one can make justified comparative judgments about the intrinsic worth of knowledge, virtue, and the like so as to determine, roughly, when the good is being maximized.

However, this heterogeneity of intrinsic goods should surely be avoided, if possible. For different persons, with different intuitions about how intrinsically good some of these things are, can come out in very different places in their estimates of the total goodness that one action or moral code is likely to produce, as compared with another. So philosophers have wanted to find a view that does not rely so much on intuitions. This is one consideration that makes hedonism attractive; for the hedonist holds that only one sort of thing is good in itself, so the question of which code or action maximizes the good can be reduced to a factual question of how much enjoyment is produced. But there is another theory that avoids both reliance on intuitions and the alleged narrowness of the hedonist view. This is the view that "utility" is to be defined not in terms of pleasure, but of *satisfaction of desires* or *interest*. Whereas the hedonist says state of affairs X is better than state of affairs Y if it contains more pleasure, the desire-satisfactionist says X is better than Y if there is more preference for X over Y than for Y over X. This last sounds a bit complex, but many people who have observed betting behavior think that cardinal numbers can be assigned to a person's desires: if so, then, if the strengths among different persons' desires can be compared and we can determine how many people prefer X over Y (or Y over X) and by how much, we have a way to aggregate preferences of a society. So, ideally (just as does the traditional hedonist view, assuming pleasures can be measured) the interest-satisfaction theory provides a way to identify which policy or behavior would maximize desire-satisfaction.

Thus hedonism and the desire theory have emerged as leading contenders for a

conception of utility suited for a simple maximizing theory of right and wrong conduct—simple in the sense that essentially there is only one sort of thing that is good in itself. The second theory is probably more popular today, for one or more of three reasons. First, it allows many things to be good—anything wanted for itself. Second, it seems easier to measure the strength of desires than an amount of pleasure. Third, the desire theory may seem more democratic; it goes on the basis of what people actually want, not on the basis of what will give them happiness we are not to deny people what they want just because we think it will make them happier in the long run.[2]

From a practical point of view, the two theories are not all that different, since there is a close relation between desire and pleasure. People want to attain pleasant states and avoid unpleasant ones; other things being equal. Further, other things being equal, getting what one wants is pleasant and not getting it is unpleasant. So there is a close connection between desire and pleasure, but the implications of the two theories are not identical.

Though I shall not attempt here to adjudicate between these theories, I want to make three remarks. First, to avoid misunderstanding, the hedonistic theory must obviously make up its mind what pleasure is. I myself think that some element of experience or activity is pleasant if it makes the person, at the time, want to continue or repeat it, simply for itself and not for extraneous reasons. This view has been called a "motivational" theory of pleasure. If we accept this, we will recognize that not only physical sensations are pleasant: a person can thoroughly enjoy reading a book, solving a crossword puzzle, or even writing a philosophy paper. This leads to my second point. Some critics like Mackie have argued that utilitarianism, in its hedonist form, is very narrow in its conclusions about what is to be maximized, or what is good. But when we start surveying the various items philosophers have characterized as good, like knowledge, or friendship and love, or relationships of trust, or qualities of character like courage or fairmindedness, we need to ask whether all of these do not make life more pleasant, and whether we would be much interested in them if they didn't. The critic may reply that of course all these things add to happiness, but they would be worthwhile in themselves even if they didn't. But if the critic takes this line the point is much harder to establish, and one is left feeling that the happiness theory is not so narrow after all.

Such criticisms are, of course, blunted if we adopt the desire theory of utility, for then the utilitarian can say that anything judged intrinsically good by the antihedonist is something people desire. Hence the utilitarian will consider it one of the things to be maximized.

My third comment refers to some difficulties in the desire theory. I don't think we really want to maximize satisfaction of desire in general. People desire all sorts of things that it is idiotic to desire. At most we should want to maximize the satisfaction of those desires that people *would* have if they were fully informed about everything that might make them change their desires. Call this the "informed desire" theory. Even so, I doubt that we want to maximize desire-satisfaction as such; mostly we are concerned to help people get what they want because we think it will make them happy, whereas not getting it will sadden or frustrate them. There is a further complicated point that I cannot develop. People's desires are continually changing. So which desires should one try to satisfy at any time? Only the unchanging desires? The desires the person has now but won't have later? Desires the person will have at the time he is to get what he now wants? It is very difficult to find any convincing formulation.

The utilitarian, then, has to decide upon his conception of the "utility" which, when maximized, is the test of right and wrong. He ought to think more about this choice. But the charge that the utilitarian is committed to a crude or narrow view of what is good seems manifestly mistaken.

The Third Puzzle

For the sake of simplicity let us assume from here on that we are opting for a hedonist conception of "utility." Let us think of pleasure as being measurable, so that the basic unit is a "hedon-moment"—an experience, for one minute, with a pleasure level of plus one. We shall speak of "hedon-moments" having a negative value when the pleasure level is negative. An experience for one minute with a hedonic tone of level plus two would be two hedon-moments, just as an experience for two minutes with hedonic tone or level plus one. And so on.

Given these concepts, we might say that moral system A produces more utility than moral system B if and only if the net balance of hedon-moments from getting A current in the society and keeping it there would be, or would probably be, greater than the net balance from getting B into place and keeping it there. When a system A is more satisfactory in this sense than any other system, we can say that A is the optimal moral system, and that its content fixes which acts are morally right or wrong.

Some utilitarians, however, would like to see this conception modified in certain ways. I shall consider three of these.

The first concerns the implications for population control. Some utilitarians believe that one way to increase the total net hedon-moments in the world would be to increase the number of people in the world, even at the cost of some reduction in standards of living. The premise is that people are mostly happy even when not very well off, so the production of a million extra babies, with economic resources held constant, could add more than enough to the net hedon-moment balance to offset the loss to everyone else from the reduction in available income. Some writers find this thinking highly objectionable. Hence they wish to change the general principle so that the "optimal" system is not one that produces the greatest net balance of hedon moments, but one that produces the greatest average net balance. This seems to imply that a moral system ought to regulate the production of infants so as to maximize the average net utility per person. Such proposal might open a Pandora's box: for instance, do we wish to forbid persons whose genes are likely to produce offspring with an I.Q. less than 140 to have children?

This problem has principally agitated act-utilitarians. Quite possibly, it is much easier to solve within the framework of a rule-utilitarian theory. To my knowledge, population control has not been thoroughly discussed by any rule-utilitarian; it is on the agenda for the future.

A second problem, which I shall only mention, is whether the hedon-moments of animals are to be weighted equally with those of rational human beings. And if not, why not? (Or, within the desire-satisfaction definition of "utility," is the satisfaction of an animal's desire to be weighted less heavily than that of a human being, provided the desires are of equal intensity? And if so, why?) This issue clearly has many practical implications and rule-utilitarians ought to think more about it.

Still a third problem about which rule-utilitarians ought to think is raised by some philosophers who are mostly sympathetic to act-utilitarianism. These writers believe that we have more of an obligation to avoid harming another person by an amount A, than we have to do something that would raise the utility level of another person by the same amount A. They also believe that we have some obligation to act to reduce the misery of another, at least when the cost to ourselves is not very great; but we do not have a comparable obligation to bring about an equal improvement in the well-being of another who is already above the misery-range. In the latter case there is *no* obligation to act at all, or at most a weak one. It is generally thought that an act-utilitarian theory cannot recognize such distinctions. How about a rule-utilitarian theory? This issue has been far from adequately discussed; it belongs on the agenda for the future.

The notion that rule-utilitarianism is not beyond refinement may be discouraging, especially for those who believe that at last we have produced a form of utilitarianism which is invulnerable to major objections. Perhaps the theory *is* invulnerable to major objections. But it does look as if more thinking needs to be done. From my point of view that is a good thing. How boring it would be if rule-utilitarianism were already so well stated and firmly established that the only thing left to do in moral philosophy were to work out the practical implications!

If we have to change our form of rule-utilitarianism, how are we to decide which form to prefer? Here we have to go back to the theory of justification, which I have been avoiding. I think we have to inquire what kind of moral code a person would support for the society in which he or she expects to live. Here I am talking about a person who is fully rational, fully informed, and has that degree of benevolence a fully informed person would have. Others might say we have to find the moral principles that fully informed, impartial, but otherwise normal people would subscribe to. Still others might say we have to find the principles that reflect our carefully considered moral "intuitions." The reader may object that thinking all this out would require a lifetime, but the form of rule-utilitarianism stated above may not need any amendment for the range of cases about which the reader has to make practical decisions.

The First Alleged Problem

I now take leave of puzzles, thought about which might lead us to some refinements of rule-utilitarianism, and turn to just plain objections that have been raised against rule-utilitarianism in any form. The ones I shall discuss are related, and together they may be viewed as variations on a charge of Utopianism.

In order to appraise these objections, I must expand still more the conception of an "optimal" moral code. The term does not refer to a set of rules that would do most good if everyone conformed to them all the time. The meaning is more complex. Recall that "a moral code" is a set of desires or aversions directed at certain types of acts, and the disposition to feel guilty about not conforming to these desires or aversions, as well as to disapprove of such failure to conform on the part of others when they have no excuse. Now these dispositions may vary both in their intensity, and in their prevalence in a given society. The more intense and widespread an aversion to a certain sort of behavior, the less frequent the behavior is apt to be. But the more intense and widespread, the greater the cost of teaching the rule and keeping it alive, the greater the burden on the individual, and so on.

The "optimality" of a moral code encompasses both the benefits of reduced objectionable behavior and the long-term cost. So the moral code optimal for a given society is that whole system, with a given degree of average intensity, and spread among the population, for each of its components, that comes out best in a cost-benefit analysis. Needless to say, like the law, the optimal moral code normally will not produce 100 percent compliance with all its rules; that would be too costly. It may do so in small homogeneous populations: physical violence is unheard of on the Hopi reservation. But mostly not. According to our conception, the rule-utilitarian believes that an act is prima facie obligatory if and only if (and to the degree that) such an optimal code would build in some degree of moral aversion to not performing it.

The first objection to this view is that it would be harmful for some people to live according to the optimal code, in a society where the optimal code is not widespread, for so doing could be either pointless or injurious. For instance, the optimal moral code might call for no one ever to carry a lethal weapon, whereas living by such a code would not be a good idea, these critics say, in a society where most persons are trigger-happy gun-carrying demons. Furthermore, it is especially incoherent for a utilitarian to advocate behaving in such a counterproductive way; his basic thesis is

that utility is the point of morality, but here the rule-utilitarian seems to be advocating behavior that is likely to be harmful.

There is an adequate reply to this objection: it has not been shown that such harmful requirements would ever appear in an optimal moral code. In the gun-carrying society, an optimal moral code would surely give directions to be prepared to defend one's self and one's family, but of course to defend only. The rule might be: "Never carry a gun when it can be done at no personal risk; otherwise carry a gun but use it only in self-defense." (An actual moral code would rarely include injunctions as specific as this but it might, if a rule were aimed at meeting a specific problem about which more abstract principles were not much help.) An optimal moral code may not always provide for doing the very best possible thing in every situation; morality is a blunt instrument, like the law. But no proof has been offered that an optimal code would prescribe doing seriously harmful things as a result of the optimal moral code not being widely accepted in the society. True, an optimal code might well tell one to keep a promise when few others are doing so, and this might do little immediate good; but at least it would be a step in building a convention of promise-keeping.

The second objection is that it would cause more than a little chaos for people to be advised to live in accordance with an optimal moral code, when nobody has yet decided precisely what that code is and certainly the average person has no idea. Act-utilitarianism has often been criticized on the ground that it would be chaotic if every individual felt morally obligated to do what seemed to him likely to have the best consequence; wouldn't it be even more chaotic if every individual really felt morally obligated to do what seemed to be required by an optimal moral code? How much has any individual thought about the optimal moral code, and how nearly would any two individuals come to agreement about what it is? It is, however, true that, if one is to advocate living by an optimal moral code, it would be absurd merely to advise living by such a code, with no explanation of the conception of a moral code, the value of moral codes, and the point of living by an optimal one.

An advocate of an optimal morality would presumably offer some explanation of how nearly the *actual* moral code is apt to approximate to the optimal one, and we can anticipate that intelligent people will be incrementalists in their moral thinking, not wild-eyed utopians. If people stop to reflect, they can see that this or that provision in the traditional morality has outlived its function and be willing to forget it. On the other hand, presumably they will see that new problems—say of an organized metropolitan society rapidly using up natural resources—demand novel features in the moral code. To say this is to speculate what would happen if intelligent people become convinced that they ought to live by an optimal moral code, and try to think through what it would be like. I have not seen proof that the results of this would be disastrous.

A third objection has been raised: whereas it might be nice for people to act in accordance with an optimal moral code when that code is not widely accepted, one cannot seriously claim that it is their moral obligation. Some critics say it may be morally obligatory to do what will in fact do most good in an actual situation even when the conventional moral code doesn't call for that, and that it may even be obligatory to act in accordance with an optimal moral code if there is good reason to think that so doing would seriously tend to usher the optimal code into the status of being conventional. But, these critics say, just to live by an optimal moral code for no further reason is not one's moral obligation. To this objection there are adequate retorts. We may begin by asking what the ground rules are supposed to be for deciding that one does or doesn't really have a moral obligation to do something. Doubtless answering this question adequately would lead us back to the theory of the meaning and justification of moral beliefs. But suppose it can be shown that what one is

morally obligated to do is what an impartial, informed, otherwise normal person would demand of one morally, or what would be demanded by a moral system that rational, fully informed people with a rational degree of benevolence would support in preference to other moral systems and to no system at all. And suppose that these conceptions lead to the conclusion that it is obligatory to follow an optimal moral code. Then it is hard to see why one must then start over and do something more in order to show that it is morally obligatory to follow the requirements of the optimal code.

Furthermore, we do not believe that a person has no obligation to do things which the moral code current in his society does not demand. We do not believe that a person has no obligation to be kind to suffering animals, or to prisoners in a prison camp in wartime, just because other people don't or because conventional morality doesn't demand it. Are moral reformers never correct when they martyr themselves, in order to discharge their moral obligations as they see them? We must make at least two concessions. First, we must agree that if one lives according to a moral code that demands more than the traditional moral codes, one is doing something that it would not be disgraceful not to do—assuming that to act disgracefully is to fall a bit below the normal level. Second, I agree that the normal social sanctions for behaving morally are absent if one is living up to a standard that conventional morality does not require. Indeed, one may sometimes *incur* moral sanctions for living in accordance with an optimal code, for instance if one insists on treating persons of another race as social equals in a place where such behavior is frowned upon.

Some of the reasons we ordinarily have for acting morally will be absent in such a case. But some of the reasons we ordinarily have for acting morally will also be present. For one thing, as often has been pointed out, one common reason for acting morally is our own sympathy or benevolence; and it would appear that sympathy or benevolence will always, or virtually always, be engaged on behalf of an optimal moral code. For another, most of us have somehow acquired a desire to do what we consider the morally right thing for no further reason. And this desire will move us to act according to the provisions of an optimal code, if we are convinced that we ought morally to conform our conduct to those provisions. When all these considerations are taken into account, the claim that we have no moral obligation to live according to what we think is the optimal code, or according to what we think we ought to do, even when that code or standard is not in place in our society, seems to evaporate.

Two Final Alleged Problems

Thus far I have said nothing about two rocks upon which many philosophers think utilitarianism in all its forms must necessarily founder: the moral demand for economic equality, and the moral requirement for legal punishment only where and to the extent it is deserved. Philosophical critics of utilitarianism suppose that there are here certain well-founded moral injunctions about both distributive and retributive justice and that these are inconsistent with the implications of utilitarianism in all its forms.

I shall limit my comments to the first charge, which strikes me as the more serious, but what I say about the first can in principle be transposed to a discussion about the second.

If we look at present legislation regarding the welfare of the poor or underprivileged in the United States, we find aid to dependent children, the food stamp program, a limited program of negative income tax, a Medicaid program to take care of the health of those who are less well off, and an assistance program for the aged, the blind, and the disabled. How is all this paid for? Mostly out of general funds: from a progressive income tax on those who are more well off. Now I do not suggest that

this system is perfect; far from it. But every one of the provisions of the system—which after all is a system for the redistribution of income can be defended on utilitarian grounds. The utilitarian justification for all this is that a dollar taken in taxes from the wealthy would have done the wealthy far less good than the same dollar spent providing food stamps, medical care, and so on for the poor or handicapped. All this the utilitarian can defend, and it is easy to see that application of the utilitarian criterion for optimal institutions moves in the direction of economic equality for all.

True, utilitarians do not take equality as an end in itself; the move in the direction of equality is advocated only because maximizing the general welfare can be attained only by more equality. Utilitarians also do not favor taking steps that would diminish the general welfare just for the sake of equality—for instance, perhaps, giving a great deal of extra income to a disabled person in order to make up for a natural disability. (Neither, incidentally, as far as I can see, does Rawls's theory.) But when we see how far a utilitarian theory does take us toward economic equality, we can well wonder how much farther the critics of utilitarianism would like to go. How large a percentage of the gross national product would they want diverted for the achievement of more equality than the utilitarian would ask for, and exactly how would they want it distributed? I suggest that when we reflect on how much economic equality we want in society, we shall not think that the implications of utilitarianism fall short. Many attacks on utilitarianism suppose that we are in a position to distribute happiness, not money, and it is said that a utilitarian must be oblivious of any inequalities in happiness, however great, so long as the maximum amount of happiness has been produced. But this charge, while true, ignores the fact that the utilitarian theory does provide against severe deprivation of happiness, as in the case of a disabled person, on the ground that such provision is the best investment of national resources. As far as I can see, the response of the utilitarian to the charge of an unsatisfactory theory of distributive justice comes off very well.

Notes

1. Mill seems not to have reflected on these puzzles as much as he should have. He says an act is wrong only if it is desirable that it be penalized somehow, either by law, or public opinion, or the individual's own conscience. He threw all three of these in together, as if he did not have to worry about conflicts. But it might be expedient for the law to impose a fine for overparking, or for failing to make a certain type of report about the assets of one's company, but it is far from clear that we would want to make these requirements of conscience, except in so far as conscience may tell us that there is a presumption that the law is to be obeyed. At any rate, overparking and failing to make required reports do not ap-

pear to be immoral i
Mill should have said, I t
thing is morally wrong if it i
act-type for which it is desirab
agent be penalized by his own con
or is one which his own conscience s
motivate him to avoid, or disapprove of i
others, on utilitarian grounds.

2. Actually, one could argue with some force that Mill, who is supposed to be a hedonist, was straddling the two. For he takes the odd view that virtue and wealth are *parts* of happiness. He has often been accused of confusion here, and doubtless he was confused. What he had good reason for saying was only that people *want* things like money and virtue, and may be made unhappy by not obtaining them. Could he have confused being desired and being pleasant? On a later page he seems to confirm such a confusion by saying that "desiring a thing and finding it pleasant . . . are two different modes of naming the same psychological fact" (*Utilitarianism*, Ch. 4).

/ W. D. ROSS

ᴀKES RIGHT ACTS RIGHT?

The real point at issue between hedonism and utilitarianism on the one hand and their opponents on the other is not whether 'right' means 'productive of so and so'; for it cannot with any plausibility be maintained that it does. The point at issue is that to which we now pass, viz. whether there is any general character which makes right acts right, and if so, what it is. Among the main historical attempts to state a single characteristic of all right actions which is the foundation of their rightness are those made by egoism and utilitarianism. But I do not propose to discuss these, not because the subject is unimportant, but because it has been dealt with so often and so well already, and because there has come to be so much agreement among moral philosophers that neither of these theories is satisfactory. A much more attractive theory has been put forward by Professor Moore: that what makes actions right is that they are productive of more *good* than could have been produced by any other action open to the agent.[1]

This theory is in fact the culmination of all the attempts to base rightness on productivity of some sort of result. The first form this attempt takes is the attempt to base rightness on conduciveness to the advantage or pleasure of the agent. This theory comes to grief over the fact, which stares us in the face, that a great part of duty consists in an observance of the rights and a furtherance of the interests of others,

whatever the cost to ourselves may be. Plato and others may be right in holding that a regard for the rights of others never in the long run involves a loss of happiness for the agent, that 'the just life profits a man'. But this, even if true, is irrelevant to the rightness of the act. As soon as a man does an action *because* he thinks he will promote his own interests thereby, he is acting not from a sense of its rightness but from self-interest.

To the egoistic theory hedonistic utilitarianism supplies a much-needed amendment. It points out correctly that the fact that a certain pleasure will be enjoyed by the agent is no reason why he *ought* to bring it into being rather than an equal or greater pleasure to be enjoyed by another, though, human nature being what it is, it makes it not unlikely that he *will* try to bring it into being. But hedonistic utilitarianism in its turn needs a correction. On reflection it seems clear that pleasure is not the only thing in life that we think good in itself, that for instance we think the possession of a good character, or an intelligent understanding of the world, as good or better. A great advance is made by the substitution of 'productive of the greatest good' for 'productive of the greatest pleasure.'

Not only is this theory more attractive than hedonistic utilitarianism, but its logical relation to that theory is such that the latter could not be true unless *it* were true, while it might be true though hedonistic utilitarianism were not. It is in fact one of the logical bases of hedonistic utilitarianism. For the view that what produces the maximum pleasure is right has for its bases

Reprinted by permission of the publisher and copyright holder from W. D. Ross, *The Right and the Good* (Oxford: Clarendon Press, 1930), pp. 16–36, 38–42.

the views (1) that what produces the maximum good is right, and (2) that pleasure is the only thing good in itself. If they were not assuming that what produces the maximum *good* is right, the utilitarians' attempt to show that pleasure is the only thing good in itself, which is in fact the point they take most pains to establish, would have been quite irrelevant to their attempt to prove that only what produces the maximum *pleasure* is right. If, therefore, it can be shown that productivity of the maximum good is not what makes all right actions right, we shall a *fortiori* have refuted hedonistic utilitarianism.

When a plain man fulfils a promise because he thinks he ought to do so, it seems clear that he does so with no thought of its total consequences, still less with any opinion that these are likely to be the best possible. He thinks in fact much more of the past than of the future. What makes him think it right to act in a certain way is the fact that he has promised to do so—that and, usually, nothing more. That his act will produce the best possible consequences is not his reason for calling it right. What lends colour to the theory we are examining, then, is not the actions (which form probably a great majority of our actions) in which some such reflection as 'I have promised' is the only reason we give ourselves for thinking a certain action right, but the exceptional cases in which the consequences of fulfilling a promise (for instance) would be so disastrous to others that we judge it right not to do so. It must of course be admitted that such cases exist. If I have promised to meet a friend at a particular time for some trivial purpose, I should certainly think myself justified in breaking my engagement if by doing so I could prevent a serious accident or bring relief to the victims of one. And the supporters of the view we are examining hold that my thinking so is due to my thinking that I shall bring more good into existence by the one action than by the other. A different account may, however, be given of the matter, an account which will, I believe, show itself to be the true one. It may be said

that besides the duty of fulfilling promises I have and recognize a duty of relieving distress,[2] and that when I think it right to do the latter at the cost of not doing the former, it is not because I think I shall produce more good thereby but because I think it the duty which is in the circumstances more of a duty. This account surely corresponds much more closely with what we really think in such a situation. If, so far as I can see, I could bring equal amounts of good into being by fulfilling my promise and by helping some one to whom I had made no promise, I should not hesitate to regard the former as my duty. Yet on the view that what is right is right because it is productive of the most good I should not so regard it.

There are two theories, each in its way simple, that offer a solution of such cases of conscience. One is the view of Kant, that there are certain duties of perfect obligation, such as those of fulfilling promises, of paying debts, of telling the truth, which admit of no exception whatever in favour of duties of imperfect obligation, such as that of relieving distress. The other is the view of, for instance, Professor Moore and Dr. Rashdall, that there is only the duty of producing good, and that all 'conflicts of duties' should be resolved by asking 'by which action will most good be produced?' But it is more important that our theory fit the facts than that it be simple, and the account we have given above corresponds (it seems to me) better than either of the simpler theories with what we really think, viz. that normally promise-keeping, for example, should come before benevolence, but that when and only when the good to be produced by the benevolent act is very great and the promise comparatively trivial, the act of benevolence becomes our duty.

In fact the theory of 'ideal utilitarianism', if I may for brevity refer so to the theory of Professor Moore, seems to simplify unduly our relations to our fellows. It says, in effect, that the only morally significant relation in which my neighbours stand to me is that of being possible beneficiaries by my action.[3] They do stand in this relation to me, and this relation is morally significant. But they may also stand to me in the relation of promisee to promiser, of creditor to debtor, of wife to husband, of child to parent, of friend to friend, of fellow countryman to fellow countryman, and the like; and each of these relations is the foundation of a *prima facie* duty, which is more or less incumbent on me according to the circumstances of the case. When I am in a situation, as perhaps I always am, in which more than one of these *prima facie* duties is incumbent on me, what I have to do is to study the situation as fully as I can until I form the considered opinion (it is never more) that in the circumstances one of them is more incumbent than any other; then I am bound to think that to do this *prima facie* duty is my duty *sans phrase* in the situation.

I suggest '*prima facie* duty' or 'conditional duty' as a brief way of referring to the characteristic (quite distinct from that of being a duty proper) which an act has, in virtue of being of a certain kind (e.g. the keeping of a promise), of being an act which would be a duty proper if it were not at the same time of another kind which is morally significant. Whether an act is a duty proper or actual duty depends on *all* the morally significant kinds it is an instance of. The phrase '*prima facie* duty' must be apologized for, since (1) it suggests that what we are speaking of is a certain kind of duty, whereas it is in fact not a duty, but something related in a special way to duty. Strictly speaking, we want not a phrase in which duty is qualified by an adjective, but a separate noun. (2) '*Prima*' *facie* suggests that one is speaking only of an appearance which a moral situation presents at first sight, and which may turn out to be illusory; whereas what I am speaking of is an objective fact involved in the nature of the situation, or more strictly in an element of its nature, though not, as duty proper does, arising from its *whole* nature. I can, however, think of no term which fully meets the case. 'Claim' has been suggested by Professor Prichard. The word 'claim' has

the advantage of being quite a familiar one in this connexion, and it seems to cover much of the ground. It would be quite natural to say, 'a person to whom I have made a promise has a claim on me', and also, 'a person whose distress I could relieve (at the cost of breaking the promise) has a claim on me'. But (1) while 'claim' is appropriate from *their* point of view, we want a word to express the corresponding fact from the agent's point of view—the fact of his being subject to claims that can be made against him; and ordinary language provides us with no such correlative to 'claim'. And (2) (what is more important) 'claim' seems inevitably to suggest two persons, one of whom might make a claim on the other; and while this covers the ground of social duty, it is inappropriate in the case of that important part of duty which is the duty of cultivating a certain kind of character in oneself. It would be artificial, I think, and at any rate metaphorical, to say that one's character has a claim on oneself.

There is nothing arbitrary about these *prima facie* duties. Each rests on a definite circumstance which cannot seriously be held to be without moral significance. Of *prima facie* duties I suggest, without claiming completeness or finality for it, the following division.[4]

(1) Some duties rest on previous acts of my own. These duties seem to include two kinds, (*a*) those resting on a promise or what may fairly be called an implicit promise, such as the implicit undertaking not to tell lies which seems to be implied in the act of entering into conversation (at any rate by civilized men), or of writing books that purport to be history and not fiction. These may be called the duties of fidelity. (*b*) Those resting on a previous wrongful act. These may be called the duties of reparation. (2) Some rest on previous acts of other men, i.e. services done by them to me. These may be loosely described as the duties of gratitude.[5] (3) Some rest on the fact or possibility of a distribution of pleasure or happiness (or of the means thereto) which is not in accordance with the merit of the persons con-

cerned; in such cases there arises a duty to upset or prevent such a distribution. These are the duties of justice. (4) Some rest on the mere fact that there are other beings in the world whose condition we can make better in respect of virtue, or of intelligence, or of pleasure. These are the duties of beneficence. (5) Some rest on the fact that we can improve our own condition in respect of virtue or of intelligence. These are the duties of self-improvement. (6) I think that we should distinguish from (4) the duties that may be summed up under the title of 'not injuring others'. No doubt to injure others is incidentally to fail to do them good; but it seems to me clear that non-maleficence is apprehended as a duty distinct from that of beneficence, and as a duty of a more stringent character. It will be noticed that this alone among the types of duty has been stated in a negative way. An attempt might no doubt be made to state this duty, like the others, in a positive way. It might be said that it is really the duty to prevent ourselves from acting either from an inclination to harm others or from an inclination to seek our own pleasure, in doing which we should incidentally harm them. But on reflection it seems clear that the primary duty here is the duty not to harm others, this being a duty whether or not we have an inclination that if followed would lead to our harming them; and that when we have such an inclination the primary duty not to harm others gives rise to a consequential duty to resist the inclination. The recognition of this duty of non-maleficence is the first step on the way to the recognition of the duty of beneficence; and that accounts for the prominence of the commands 'thou shalt not kill', 'thou shalt not commit adultery', 'thou shalt not steal', 'thou shalt not bear false witness', in so early a code as the Decalogue. But even when we have come to recognize the duty of beneficence, it appears to me that the duty of non-maleficence is recognized as a distinct one, and as *prima facie* more binding. We should not in general consider it justifiable to kill one person in or-

der to keep another alive, or to steal from one in order to give alms to another.

The essential defect of the 'ideal utilitarian' theory is that it ignores, or at least does not do full justice to, the highly personal character of duty. If the only duty is to produce the maximum of good, the question who is to have the good—whether it is myself, or my benefactor, or a person to whom I have made a promise to confer that good on him, or a mere fellow man to whom I stand in no such special relation—should make no difference to my having a duty to produce that good. But we are all in fact sure that it makes a vast difference.

One or two other comments must be made on this provisional list of the divisions of duty. (1) The nomenclature is not strictly correct. For by 'fidelity' or 'gratitude' we mean, strictly, certain states of motivation; and, as I have urged, it is not our duty to have certain motives, but to do certain acts. By 'fidelity', for instance, is meant, strictly, the disposition to fulfil promises and implicit promises *because we have made them*. We have no general word to cover the actual fulfilment of promises and implicit promises *irrespective of motive*; and I use 'fidelity', loosely but perhaps conveniently, to fill this gap. So too I use 'gratitude' for the returning of services, irrespective of motive. The term 'justice' is not so much confined, in ordinary usage, to a certain state of motivation, for we should often talk of a man as acting justly even when we did not think his motive was the wish to do what was just simply for the sake of doing so. Less apology is therefore needed for our use of 'justice' in this sense. And I have used the word 'beneficence' rather than 'benevolence', in order to emphasize the fact that it is our duty to do certain things, and not to do them from certain motives.

(2) If the objection be made, that this catalogue of the main types of duty is an unsystematic one resting on no logical principle, it may be replied, first, that it makes no claim to being ultimate. It is a *prima facie* classification of the duties which reflection on our moral convictions seems actu-

ally to reveal. And if these convictions are, as I would claim that they are, of the nature of knowledge, and if I have not misstated them, the list will be a list of authentic conditional duties, correct as far as it goes though not necessarily complete. The list of *goods* put forward by the rival theory is reached by exactly the same method—the only sound one in the circumstances—viz. that of direct reflection on what we really think. Loyalty to the facts is worth more than a symmetrical architectonic or a hastily reached simplicity. If further reflection discovers a perfect logical basis for this or for a better classification, so much the better.

(3) It may, again, be objected that our theory that there are these various and often conflicting types of *prima facie* duty leaves us with no principle upon which to discern what is our actual duty in particular circumstances. But this objection is not one which the rival theory is in a position to bring forward. For when we have to choose between the production of two heterogeneous goods, say knowledge and pleasure, the 'ideal utilitarian' theory can only fall back on an opinion, for which no logical basis can be offered, that one of the goods is the greater; and this is no better than a similar opinion that one of two duties is the more urgent. And again, when we consider the infinite variety of the effects of our actions in the way of pleasure, it must surely be admitted that the claim which *hedonism* sometimes makes, that it offers a readily applicable criterion of right conduct, is quite illusory.

I am unwilling, however, to content myself with an *argumentum ad hominem*, and I would contend that in principle there is no reason to anticipate that every act that is our duty is so for one and the same reason. Why should two sets of circumstances, or one set of circumstances, *not* possess different characteristics, any one of which makes a certain act our *prima facie* duty? When I ask what it is that makes me in certain cases sure that I have a *prima facie* duty to do so and so, I find that it lies in the fact that I have made a promise; when I ask the

same question in another case, I find the answer lies in the fact that I have done a wrong. And if on reflection I find (as I think I do) that neither of these reasons is reducible to the other, I must not on any *a priori* ground assume that such a reduction is possible.

An attempt may be made to arrange in a more systematic way the main types of duty which we have indicated. In the first place it seems self-evident that if there are things that are intrinsically good, it is *prima facie* a duty to bring them into existence rather than not to do so, and to bring as much of them into existence as possible. It will be argued in our fifth chapter that there are three main things that are intrinsically good—virtue, knowledge, and, with certain limitations, pleasure. And since a given virtuous disposition, for instance, is equally good whether it is realized in myself or in another, it seems to be my duty to bring it into existence whether in myself or in another. So too with a given piece of knowledge.

The case of pleasure is difficult; for while we clearly recognize a duty to produce pleasure for others, it is by no means so clear that we recognize a duty to produce pleasure for ourselves. This appears to arise from the following facts. The thought of an act as our duty is one that presupposes a certain amount of reflection about the act; and for that reason does not normally arise in connexion with acts towards which we are already impelled by another strong impulse. So far, the cause of our not thinking of the promotion of our own pleasure as a duty is analogous to the cause which usually prevents a highly sympathetic person from thinking of the promotion of the pleasure of others as a duty. He is impelled so strongly by direct interest in the well-being of others towards promoting their pleasure that he does not stop to ask whether it is his duty to promote it; and we are all impelled so strongly towards the promotion of our own pleasure that we do not stop to ask whether it is a duty or not. But there is a further reason why even when we stop to think about the matter it does not usually present itself as a duty:

viz. that, since the performance of most of our duties involves the giving up of some pleasure that we desire, the doing of duty and the getting of pleasure for ourselves come by a natural association of ideas to be thought of as incompatible things. This association of ideas is in the main salutary in its operation, since it puts a check on what but for it would be much too strong, the tendency to pursue one's own pleasure without thought of other considerations. Yet if pleasure is good, it seems in the long run clear that it is right to get it for ourselves as well as to produce it for others, when this does not involve the failure to discharge some more stringent *prima facie* duty. The question is a very difficult one, but it seems that this conclusion can be denied only on one or other of three grounds: (1) that pleasure is not *prima facie* good (i.e. good when it is neither the actualization of a bad disposition nor undeserved), (2) that there is no *prima facie* duty to produce as much that is good as we can, or (3) that though there is a *prima facie* duty to produce other things that are good, there is no *prima facie* duty to produce pleasure which will be enjoyed by ourselves. I give reasons later[6] for not accepting the first contention. The second hardly admits of argument but seems to me plainly false. The third seems plausible only if we hold that an act that is pleasant or brings pleasure to ourselves must for that reason not be a duty; and this would lead to paradoxical consequences, such as that if a man enjoys giving pleasure to others or working for their moral improvement, it cannot be his duty to do so. Yet it seems to be a very stubborn fact, that in our ordinary consciousness we are not aware of a duty to get pleasure for ourselves; and by way of partial explanation of this I may add that though, as I think, one's own pleasure is a good and there is a duty to produce it, it is only if we *think* of our own pleasure not as simply our own pleasure, but as an objective good, something that an impartial spectator would approve, that we can think of the getting it as a duty; and we do not habitually think of it in this way.

If these contentions are right, what we have called the duty of beneficence and the duty of self-improvement rest on the same ground. No different principles of duty are involved in the two cases. If we feel a special responsibility for improving our own character rather than that of others, it is not because a special principle is involved, but because we are aware that the one is more under our control than the other. It was on this ground that Kant expressed the practical law of duty in the form 'seek to make yourself good and other people happy'. He was so persuaded of the internality of virtue that he regarded any attempt by one person to produce virtue in another as bound to produce, at most, only a counterfeit of virtue, the doing of externally right acts not from the true principle of virtuous action but out of regard to another person. It must be admitted that one man cannot compel another to be virtuous; compulsory virtue would just not be virtue. But experience clearly shows that Kant overshoots the mark when he contends that one man cannot do anything to *promote* virtue in another, to bring such influences to bear upon him that his own response to them is more likely to be virtuous than his response to other influences would have been. And our duty to do this is not different in kind from our duty to improve our own characters.

It is equally clear, and clear at an earlier stage of moral development, that if there are things that are bad in themselves we ought, *prima facie*, not to bring them upon others; and on this fact rests the duty of non-maleficence.

The duty of justice is particularly complicated, and the word is used to cover things which are really very different—things such as the payment of debts, the reparation of injuries done by oneself to another, and the bringing about of a distribution of happiness between other people in proportion to merit. I use the word to denote only the last of these three. In the fifth chapter I shall try to show that besides the three (comparatively) simple goods, virtue, knowledge, and pleasure, there is a more complex good, not reducible to these, consisting in the proportionment of happiness to virtue. The bringing of this about is a duty which we owe to all men alike, though it may be reinforced by special responsibilities that we have undertaken to particular men. This, therefore, with beneficence and self-improvement, comes under the general principle that we should produce as much good as possible, though the good here involved is different in kind from any other.

But besides this general obligation, there are special obligations. These may arise, in the first place, incidentally, from acts which were not essentially meant to create such an obligation, but which nevertheless create it. From the nature of the case such acts may be of two kinds—the infliction of injuries on others, and the acceptance of benefits from them. It seems clear that these put us under a special obligation to other men, and that only these acts can do so incidentally. From these arise the twin duties of reparation and gratitude.

And finally there are special obligations arising from acts the very intention of which, when they were done, was to put us under such an obligation. The name for such acts is 'promises'; the name is wide enough if we are willing to include under it implicit promises, i.e. modes of behaviour in which without explicit verbal promise we intentionally create an expectation that we can be counted on to behave in a certain way in the interest of another person.

These seem to be, in principle, all the ways in which *prima facie* duties arise. In actual experience they are compounded together in highly complex ways. Thus, for example, the duty of obeying the laws of one's country arises partly (as Socrates contends in the *Crito*) from the duty of gratitude for the benefits one has received from it; partly from the implicit promise to obey which seems to be involved in permanent residence in a country whose laws we know we are *expected* to obey, and still more clearly involved when we ourselves invoke the protection of its laws (this is the truth underlying the doctrine of the social

contract); and partly (if we are fortunate in our country) from the fact that its laws are potent instruments for the general good.

Or again, the sense of a general obligation to bring about (so far as we can) a just apportionment of happiness to merit is often greatly reinforced by the fact that many of the existing injustices are due to a social and economic system which we have, not indeed created, but taken part in and assented to; the duty of justice is then reinforced by the duty of reparation.

It is necessary to say something by way of clearing up the relation between *prima facie* duties and the actual or absolute duty to do one particular act in particular circumstances. If, as almost all moralists except Kant are agreed, and as most plain men think, it is sometimes right to tell a lie or to break a promise, it must be maintained that there is a difference between *prima facie* duty and actual or absolute duty. When we think ourselves justified in breaking, and indeed morally obliged to break, a promise in order to relieve some one's distress, we do not for a moment cease to recognize a *prima facie* duty to keep our promise, and this leads us to feel, not indeed shame or repentance, but certainly compunction, for behaving as we do; we recognize, further, that it is our duty to make up somehow to the promise for the breaking of the promise. We have to distinguish from the characteristic of being our duty that of tending to be our duty. Any act that we do contains various elements in virtue of which it falls under various categories. In virtue of being the breaking of a promise, for instance, it tends to be wrong; in virtue of being an instance of relieving distress it tends to be right. Tendency to be one's duty may be called a parti-resultant attribute, i.e. one which belongs to an act in virtue of some one component in its nature. *Being* one's duty is a toti-resultant attribute, one which belongs to an act in virtue of its whole nature and of nothing less than this.[7] This distinction between parti-resultant and toti-resultant attributes is one which we shall meet in another context also.[8]

Another instance of the same distinction may be found in the operation of natural laws. *Qua* subject to the force of gravitation towards some other body, each body tends to move in a particular direction with a particular velocity; but its actual movement depends on *all* the forces to which it is subject. It is only by recognizing this distinction that we can preserve the absoluteness of laws of nature, and only by recognizing a corresponding distinction that we can preserve the absoluteness of the general principles of morality. But an important difference between the two cases must be pointed out. When we say that in virtue of gravitation a body tends to move in a certain way, we are referring to a causal influence actually exercised on it by another body or other bodies. When we say that in virtue of being deliberately untrue a certain remark tends to be wrong, we are referring to no causal relation, to no relation that involves succession in time, but to such a relation as connects the various attributes of a mathematical figure. And if the word 'tendency' is thought to suggest too much a causal relation, it is better to talk of certain types of act as being *prima facie* right or wrong (or of different persons as having different and possibly conflicting claims upon us), than of their tending to be right or wrong.

Something should be said of the relation between our apprehension of the *prima facie* rightness of certain types of act and our mental attitude towards particular acts. It is proper to use the word 'apprehension' in the former case and not in the latter. That an act, *qua* fulfilling a promise, or *qua* effecting a just distribution of good, or *qua* returning services rendered, or *qua* promoting the good of others, or *qua* promoting the virtue or insight of the agent, is *prima facie* right, is self-evident; not in the sense that it is evident from the beginning of our lives, or as soon as we attend to the proposition for the first time, but in the sense that when we have reached sufficient mental maturity and have given sufficient attention to the proposition it is evident without any need of proof, or of evidence

beyond itself. It is self-evident just as a mathematical axiom, or the validity of a form of inference, is evident. The moral order expressed in these propositions is just as much part of the fundamental nature of the universe (and, we may add, of any possible universe in which there were moral agents at all) as is the spatial or numerical structure expressed in the axioms of geometry or arithmetic. In our confidence that these propositions are true there is involved the same trust in our reason that is involved in our confidence in mathematics; and we should have no justification for trusting it in the latter sphere and distrusting it in the former. In both cases we are dealing with propositions that cannot be proved, but that just as certainly need no proof.

Some of these general principles of *prima facie* duty may appear to be open to criticism. It may be thought, for example, that the principle of returning good for good is a falling off from the Christian principle, generally and rightly recognized as expressing the highest morality, of returning good for evil. To this it may be replied that I do not suggest that there is a principle commanding us to return good for good and forbidding us to return good for evil, and that I do suggest that there is a positive duty to seek the good of all men. What I maintain is that an act in which good is returned for good is recognized as *specially* binding on us just because it is of that character, and that *ceteris paribus* any one would think it his duty to help his benefactors rather than his enemies, if he could not do both; just as it is generally recognized that *ceteris paribus* we should pay our debts rather than give our money in charity, when we cannot do both. A benefactor is not only a man, calling for our effort on his behalf on that ground, but also our benefactor, calling for our *special* effort on *that* ground.

Our judgements about our actual duty in concrete situations have none of the certainty that attaches to our recognition of the general principles of duty. A statement is certain, i.e. is an expression of knowledge, only in one or other of two cases: when it is either self-evident, or a valid conclusion from self-evident premisses. And our judgements about our particular duties have neither of these characters. (1) They are not self-evident. Where a possible act is seen to have two characteristics, in virtue of one of which it is *prima facie* right, and in virtue of the other *prima facie* wrong, we are (I think) well aware that we are not certain whether we ought or ought not to do it; that whether we do it or not, we are taking a moral risk. We come in the long run, after consideration, to think one duty more pressing than the other, but we do not feel certain that it is so. And though we do not always recognize that a possible act has two such characteristics, and though there *may* be cases in which it has not, we are never certain that any particular possible act has not, and therefore never certain that it is right, nor certain that it is wrong. For, to go no further in the analysis, it is enough to point out that any particular act will in all probability in the course of time contribute to the bringing about of good or of evil for many human beings, and thus have a *prima facie* rightness or wrongness of which we know nothing. (2) Again, our judgements about our particular duties are not logical conclusions from self-evident premisses. The only possible premisses would be the general principles stating their *prima facie* rightness or wrongness *qua* having the different characteristics they do have; and even if we could (as we cannot) apprehend the extent to which an act will tend on the one hand, for example, to bring about advantages for our benefactors, and on the other hand to bring about disadvantages for fellow men who are not our benefactors, there is no principle by which we can draw the conclusion that it is on the whole right or on the whole wrong. In this respect the judgement as to the rightness of a particular act is just like the judgement as to the beauty of a particular natural object or work of art. A poem is, for instance, in respect of certain qualities beautiful and in respect of certain others not beautiful; and our judgement as to the degree of

beauty it possesses on the whole is never reached by logical reasoning from the apprehension of its particular beauties or particular defects. Both in this and in the moral case we have more or less probable opinions which are not logically justified conclusions from the general principles that are recognized as self-evident.

There is therefore much truth in the description of the right act as a fortunate act. If we cannot be certain that it is right, it is our good fortune if the act we do is the right act. This consideration does not, however, make the doing of our duty a mere matter of chance. There is a parallel here between the doing of duty and the doing of what will be to our personal advantage. We never *know* what act will in the long run be to our advantage. Yet it is certain that we are more likely in general to secure our advantage if we estimate to the best of our ability the probable tendencies of our actions in this respect, than if we act on caprice. And similarly we are more likely to do our duty if we reflect to the best of our ability on the *prima facie* rightness or wrongness of various possible acts in virtue of the characteristics we perceive them to have, than if we act without reflection. With this greater likelihood we must be content.

Many people would be inclined to say that the right act for me is not that whose general nature I have been describing, viz. that which if I were omniscient I should see to be my duty, but that which on all the evidence available to me I should think to be my duty. But suppose that from the state of partial knowledge in which I think act *A* to be my duty, I could pass to a state of perfect knowledge in which I saw act *B* to be my duty, should I not say 'act *B* was the right act for me to do'? I should no doubt add 'though I am not to be blamed for doing act *A*'. But in adding this, am I not passing from the question 'what is right' to the question 'what is morally good'? At the same time I am not making the *full* passage from the one notion to the other; for in order that the act should be morally good, or an act I am not to be blamed for doing, it must not merely be the act which it is reasonable for me to think my duty; it must also be done for that reason, or from some other morally good motive. Thus the conception of the right act as the act which it is reasonable for me to think my duty is an unsatisfactory compromise between the true notion of the right act and the notion of the morally good action.

The general principles of duty are obviously not self-evident from the beginning of our lives. How do they come to be so? The answer is, that they come to be self-evident to us just as mathematical axioms do. We find by experience that this couple of matches and that couple make four matches, that this couple of balls on a wire and that couple make four balls: and by reflection on these and similar discoveries we come to see that it is of the nature of two and two to make four. In a precisely similar way, we see the *prima facie* rightness of an act which would be the fulfilment of a particular promise, and of another which would be the fulfilment of another promise, and when we have reached sufficient maturity to think in general terms, we apprehend *prima facie* rightness to belong to the nature of any fulfilment of promise. What comes first in time is the apprehension of the self-evident *prima facie* rightness of an individual act of a particular type. From this we come by reflection to apprehend the self-evident general principle of *prima facie* duty. From this, too, perhaps along with the apprehension of the self-evident *prima facie* rightness of the same act in virtue of its having another characteristic as well, and perhaps in spite of the apprehension of its *prima facie* wrongness in virtue of its having some third characteristic, we come to believe something not self-evident at all, but an object of probable opinion, viz. that this particular act is (not *prima facie* but) actually right.

In this respect there is an important difference between rightness and mathematical properties. A triangle which is isosceles necessarily has two of its angles equal, whatever other characteristics the triangle may have—whatever, for instance, be its area, or the size of its third angle. The equality of the two angles is a parti-resultant attribute.[9] And the same is true of all mathematical attributes. It is true, I may add, of *prima facie* rightness. But no act is ever, in virtue of falling under some general description, necessarily actually right; its rightness depends on its whole nature[10] and not on any element in it. The reason is that no mathematical object (no figure, for instance, or angle) ever has two characteristics that tend to give it opposite resultant characteristics, while moral acts often (as every one knows) and indeed always (as on reflection we must admit) have different characteristics that tend to make them at the same time *prima facie* right and *prima facie* wrong; there is probably no act, for instance, which does good to any one without doing harm to some one else, and *vice versa*.

Supposing it to be agreed, as I think on reflection it must, that no one *means* by 'right' just 'productive of the best possible consequences', or 'optimific', the attributes 'right' and 'optimific' might stand in either of two kinds of relation to each other. (1) They might be so related that we could apprehend *a priori*, either immediately or deductively, that any act that is optimific is right and any act that is right is optimific, as we can apprehend that any triangle that is equilateral is equiangular and *vice versa*. Professor Moore's view is, I think, that the coextensiveness of 'right' and 'optimific' is apprehended immediately.[11] He rejects the possibility of any proof of it. Or (2) the two attributes might be such that the question whether they are invariably connected had to be answered by means of an inductive inquiry. Now at first sight it might seem as if the constant connexion of the two attributes could be immediately apprehended. It might seem absurd to suggest that it could be right for any one to do an act which would produce consequences less good than those which would be produced by some other act in his power. Yet a little thought will convince us that this is not absurd. The type of case in which it is easiest to see that this is so is, perhaps, that in which one has made a promise. In such a case we all think that *prima facie* it is our duty to fulfil the promise irrespective of the precise goodness of the total consequences. And though we do not think it is necessarily our actual or absolute duty to do so, we are far from thinking that any, even the slightest, gain in the value of the total consequences will necessarily justify us in doing something else instead. Suppose, to simplify the case by abstraction, that the fulfilment of a promise to A would produce 1,000 units of good[12] for him, but that by doing some other act I could produce 1,001 units of good for B, to whom I have made no promise, the other consequences of the two acts being of equal value; should we really think it self-evident that it was our duty to do the second act and not the first? I think not. We should, I fancy, hold that only a much greater disparity of value between the total consequences would justify us in failing to discharge our *prima facie* duty to A. After all, a promise is a promise, and is not to be treated so lightly as the theory we are examining would imply. What, exactly, a promise is, is not so easy to determine, but we are surely agreed that it constitutes a serious moral limitation to our freedom of action. To produce the 1,001 units of good for B rather than fulfil our promise to A would be to take, not perhaps our duty as philanthropists too seriously, but certainly our duty as makers of promises too lightly.

Or consider another phase of the same problem. If I have promised to confer on A a particular benefit containing 1,000 units of good, is it self-evident that if by doing some different act I could produce 1,001 units of good for A himself (the other consequences of the two acts being supposed equal in value), it would be right for me to do so? Again, I think not. Apart from my general *prima facie* duty to do A what good I can, I have another *prima facie* duty to do him the particular service I have promised to do him, and this is not to be set aside in consequence of a disparity of good of the order of 1,001 to 1,000, though a much

greater disparity might justify me in so doing.

Or again, suppose that A is a very good and B a very bad man, should I then, even when I have made no promise, think it self-evidently right to produce 1,001 units of good for B rather than 1,000 for A? Surely not. I should be sensible of a *prima facie* duty of justice, i.e. of producing a distribution of goods in proportion to merit, which is not outweighed by such a slight disparity in the total goods to be produced.

Such instances—and they might easily be added to—make it clear that there is no self-evident connexion between the attributes 'right' and 'optimific'. The theory we are examining has a certain attractiveness when applied to our decision that a particular act is our duty (though I have tried to show that it does not agree with our actual moral judgements even here). But it is not even plausible when applied to our recognition of *prima facie* duty. For if it were self-evident that the right coincides with the optimific, it should be self-evident that what is *prima facie* right is *prima facie* optimific. But whereas we are certain that keeping a promise is *prima facie* right, we are not certain that it is *prima facie* optimific (though we are perhaps certain that it is *prima facie* bonific). Our certainty that it is *prima facie* right depends not on its consequences but on its being the fulfilment of a promise. The theory we are examining involves too much difference between the evident ground of our conviction about *prima facie* duty and the alleged ground of our conviction about actual duty.

The coextensiveness of the right and the optimific is, then, not self-evident. And I can see no way of proving it deductively; nor, so far as I know, has any one tried to do so. There remains the question whether it can be established inductively. Such an inquiry, to be conclusive, would have to be very thorough and extensive. We should have to take a large variety of the acts which we, to the best of our ability, judge to be right. We should have to trace as far as possible their consequences, not only for the persons directly affected but also for those indirectly affected, and to these no limit can be set. To make our inquiry thoroughly conclusive, we should have to do what we cannot do, viz. trace these consequences into an unending future. And even to make it reasonably conclusive, we should have to trace them far into the future. It is clear that the most we could possibly say is that a large variety of typical acts that are judged right appear, so far as we can trace their consequences, to produce more good than any other acts possible to the agents in the circumstances. And such a result falls far short of proving the constant connexion of the two attributes. But it is surely clear that no inductive inquiry justifying even this result has ever been carried through. The advocates of utilitarian systems have been so much persuaded either of the identity or of the self-evident connexion of the attributes 'right' and 'optimific' (or 'felicific') that they have not attempted even such an inductive inquiry as is possible. . . .

To put the matter otherwise, utilitarians say that when a promise ought to be kept it is because the total good to be produced by keeping it is greater than the total good to be produced by breaking it, the former including as its main element the maintenance and strengthening of general mutual confidence, and the latter being greatly diminished by a weakening of this confidence. They say, in fact, that the case I put some pages back[13] never arises—the case in which by fulfilling a promise I shall bring into being 1,000 units of good for my promisee, and by breaking it 1,001 units of good for some one else, the other effects of the two acts being of equal value. The other effects, they say, never are of equal value. By keeping my promise I am helping to strengthen the system of mutual confidence; by breaking it I am helping to weaken this; so that really the first act produces $1,000 + x$ units of good, and the second $1,001 - y$ units, and the difference between $+x$ and $-y$ is enough to outweigh the slight superiority in the *immediate* effects of the second act. In answer to this it may be pointed out that there must be *some*

amount of good that exceeds the difference between $+x$ and $-y$ (i.e. exceeds $x + y$); say, $x + y + z$. Let us suppose the *immediate* good effects of the second act to be assessed not at 1,001 but at $1,000 + x + y + z$. Then its *net* good effects are $1,000 + x + z$, i.e. greater than those of the fulfilment of the promise; and the utilitarian is bound to say forthwith that the promise should be broken. Now, we may ask whether that is really the way we think about promises? Do we really think that the production of the slightest balance of good, no matter who will enjoy it, by the breach of a promise frees us from the obligation to keep our promise? We need not doubt that a system by which promises are made and kept is one that has great advantages for the general well-being. But that is not the whole truth. To make a promise is not merely to adapt an ingenious device for promoting the general well-being; it is to put oneself in a new relation to one person in particular, a relation which creates a specifically new *prima facie* duty to him, not reducible to the duty of promoting the general well-being of society. By all means let us try to foresee the net good effects of keeping one's promise and the net good effects of breaking it, but even if we assess the first at $1,000 + x$ and the second at $1,000 + x + z$, the question still remains whether it is not our duty to fulfil the promise. It may be suspected, too, that the effect of a single keeping or breaking of a promise in strengthening or weakening the fabric of mutual confidence is greatly exaggerated by the theory we are examining. And if we suppose two men dying together alone, do we think that the duty of one to fulfil before he dies a promise he has made to the other would be extinguished by the fact that neither act would have any effect on the general confidence? Any one who holds this may be suspected of not having reflected on what a promise is.

I conclude that the attributes 'right' and 'optimific' are not identical, and that we do not know either by intuition, by deduction, or by induction that they coincide in their application, still less that the latter is the foundation of the former. It must be added, however, that if we are ever under no special obligation such as that of fidelity to a promisee or of gratitude to a benefactor, we ought to do what will produce most good; and that even when we are under a special obligation the tendency of acts to promote general good is one of the main factors in determining whether they are right.

In what has preceded, a good deal of use has been made of 'what we really think' about moral questions; a certain theory has been rejected because it does not agree with what we really think. It might be said that this is in principle wrong; that we should not be content to expound what our present moral consciousness tells us but should aim at a criticism of our existing moral consciousness in the light of theory. Now I do not doubt that the moral consciousness of men has in detail undergone a good deal of modification as regards the things we think right, at the hands of moral theory. But if we are told, for instance, that we should give up our view that there is a special obligatoriness attaching to the keeping of promises because it is self-evident that the only duty is to produce as much good as possible, we have to ask ourselves whether we really, when we reflect, *are* convinced that this is self-evident, and whether we really *can* get rid of our view that promise-keeping has a bindingness independent of productiveness of maximum good. In my own experience I find that I cannot, in spite of a very genuine attempt to do so; and I venture to think that most people will find the same, and that just because they cannot lose the sense of special obligation, they cannot accept as self-evident, or even as true, the theory which would require them to do so. In fact it seems, on reflection, self-evident that a promise, simply as such, is something that *prima facie* ought to be kept, and it does *not*, on reflection, seem self-evident that production of maximum good is the only thing that makes an act obligatory. And to ask us to give up at the bidding of a theory our

actual apprehension of what is right and what is wrong seems like asking people to repudiate their actual experience of beauty, at the bidding of a theory which says 'only that which satisfies such and such conditions can be beautiful.' If what I have called our actual apprehension is (as I would maintain that it is) truly an apprehension, i.e. an instance of knowledge, the request is nothing less than absurd.

I would maintain, in fact, that what we are apt to describe as 'what we think' about moral questions contains a considerable amount that we do not think but know, and that this forms the standard by reference to which the truth of any moral theory has to be tested, instead of having itself to be tested by reference to any theory. I hope that I have in what precedes indicated what in my view these elements of knowledge are that are involved in our ordinary moral consciousness.

It would be a mistake to found a natural science on 'what we really think', i.e. on what reasonably thoughtful and well-educated people think about the subjects of the science before they have studied them scientifically. For such opinions are interpretations, and often misinterpretations, of sense-experience; and the man of science must appeal from these to sense-experience itself, which furnishes his real data. In ethics no such appeal is possible. We have no more direct way of access to the facts about rightness and goodness and about what things are right or good, than by thinking about them; the moral convictions of thoughtful and well-educated people are the data of ethics just as sense-perceptions are the data of a natural science. Just as some of the latter have to be rejected as illusory, so have some of the former; but as the latter are rejected only when they are in conflict with other more accurate sense-perceptions, the former are rejected only when they are in conflict with other convictions which stand better the test of reflection. The existing body of moral convictions of the best people is the cumulative product of the moral reflection of many generations, which has developed an extremely delicate power of appreciation of moral distinctions; and this the theorist cannot afford to treat with anything other than the greatest respect. The verdicts of the moral consciousness of the best people are the foundation on which he must build; though he must first compare them with one another and eliminate any contradictions they may contain.

It is worth while to try to state more definitely the nature of the acts that are right. We may try to state first what (if anything) is the universal nature of *all* acts that are right. It is obvious that any of the acts that we do has countless effects, directly or indirectly, on countless people, and the probability is that any act, however right it be, will have adverse effects (though these may be very trivial) on some innocent people. Similarly, any wrong act will probably have beneficial effects on some deserving people. Every act therefore, viewed in some aspects, will be *prima facie* right, and viewed in others, *prima facie* wrong, and right acts can be distinguished from wrong acts only as being those which, of all those possible for the agent in the circumstances, have the greatest balance of *prima facie* rightness, in those respects in which they are *prima facie* right, over their *prima facie* wrongness, in those respects in which they are *prima facie* wrong—*prima facie* rightness and wrongness being understood in the sense previously explained. For the estimation of the comparative stringency of these *prima facie* obligations no general rules can, so far as I can see, be laid down. We can only say that a great deal of stringency belongs to the duties of 'perfect obligation'—the duties of keeping our promises, of repairing wrongs we have done, and of returning the equivalent of services we have received. For the rest, ἐν τῇ αἰσθήσει ἡ κρίσις.[14] This sense of our particular duty in particular circumstances, preceded and informed by the fullest reflection we can bestow on the act in all its bearings, is highly fallible, but it is the only guide we have to our duty.

Notes

1. I take the theory which, as I have tried to show, seems to be put forward in *Ethics* rather than the earlier and less plausible theory put forward in *Principia Ethica*.

2. These are not strictly speaking duties, but things that tend to be our duty, or *prima facie* duties. Cf. *The Right and the Good*, pp. 19–20.

3. Some will think it, apart from other considerations, a sufficient refutation of this view to point out that I also stand in that relation to myself, so that for this view the distinction of oneself from others is morally insignificant.

4. I should make it plain at this stage that I am *assuming* the correctness of some of our main convictions as to *prima facie* duties, or, more strictly, am claiming that we *know* them to be true. To me it seems as self-evident as anything could be, that to make a promise, for instance, is to create a moral claim on us in someone else. Many readers will perhaps say that they do *not* know this to be true. If so, I certainly cannot prove it to them; I can only ask them to reflect again, in the hope that they will ultimately agree that they also know it to be true. The main moral convictions of the plain man seem to me to be, not opinions which it is for philosophy to prove or disprove, but knowledge from the start; and in my own case I seem to find little difficulty in distinguishing these essential convictions from other moral convictions which I also have, which are merely fallible opinions based on an imperfect study of the working for good or evil of certain institutions or types of action.

5. For a needed correction of this statement, cf. *The Right and the Good*, pp. 22–3.

6. *The Right and the Good*, pp. 135–8.

7. But cf. the qualification in *The Right and the Good*, p. 33, n. 2.

8. Cf. *The Right and the Good*, pp. 122–3.

9. Cf. *The Right and the Good*, pp. 28, 122–3.

10. To avoid complicating unduly the statement of the general view I am putting forward, I have here rather overstated it. Any act is the origination of a great variety of things many of which make no difference to its rightness or wrongness. But there are always many elements in its nature (i.e. in what it is the origination of) that make a difference to its rightness or wrongness, and no elements in its nature can be dismissed without consideration as indifferent.

11. *Ethics*, 181.

12. I am assuming that good is objectively quantitative, but not that we can accurately assign an exact quantitative measure to it. Since it is of a definite amount, we can make the *supposition* that its amount is so-and-so, though we cannot with any confidence *assert* that it is. Cf. *The Right and the Good*, pp. 142–4.

13. *The Right and the Good*, p. 34.

14. 'The decision rests with perception'. Arist. *Nic. Eth.* 1109 b 23, 1126 b 4.

29 / WILLIAM K. FRANKENA

Obligation and Motivation in Recent Moral Philosophy

This paper will be concerned with a problem about the analysis of judgments of moral obligation, that is, of judgments in which an agent is said, by himself or others, to have a certain moral duty or obligation in a certain situation or kind of situation. It will not offer an analysis of such judgments, but will occupy itself with a study of a particular opposition between two points of view as to their analysis. The character of this opposition may be indicated as follows. Many moral philosophers have said or implied that it is in some sense logically possible for an agent to have or see that he has an obligation even if he has no motivation, actual or dispositional, for doing the action in question; many others have said or implied that this is paradoxical and not logically possible. The former are convinced that no reference to the existence of motives in the agent involved need be made in the analysis of a moral judgment; the latter are equally convinced that such a reference is necessary there.

Roughly, the opposition in question is between those who regard motivation as external and those who regard it as internal to obligation. We may, therefore, borrow W. D. Falk's labels and call the two points of view externalism and internalism, respectively.[1] It should be noted, then, that the question is not whether or not moral philosophers may or must introduce the topic of motivation. Externalists have gen-erally been concerned about motivation as well as about obligation; they differ from their opponents only about the reason for this concern. Internalists hold that motivation must be provided for because it is involved in the analysis of moral judgments and so is essential for an action's being or being shown to be obligatory. Externalists insist that motivation is not part of the analysis of moral judgments or of the justification of moral claims; for them motivation is an important problem, but only because it is necessary to persuade people to act in accordance with their obligations.

Again, the issue is not whether morality is to be practical. Both parties agree that it is to be practical in the sense of governing and guiding human behavior. That is, it should supply the rules of human practice, and it should not do this out of idle curiosity, but with a real concern for their being followed. But the one party insists that judgments of obligation must be practical in the further sense that their being efficacious in influencing behavior is somehow logically internal to them, and the other denies this. The question is whether motivation is somehow to be "built into" judgments of moral obligation, not whether it is to be taken care of in some way or other.[2]

Here is an old and basic issue. It may be regarded as involved in Aristotle's critique of Plato's Idea of the Good, and is certainly present in Hume's polemic against cognitivists and rationalists in ethics. It is different from, and to a considerable extent cuts across, the issues which have been discussed so much recently (intuitionism versus naturalism, cognitivism versus noncog-

nitivism, humanism versus supernatural-
ism, relativism versus absolutism, deontol-
ogism versus teleologism), for proponents
of almost every one of these embattled
points of view can be found on either side
in this controversy. Indeed, I am disposed
to think that it is more basic than most of
these other issues, since answers to it are
often taken as premises for settling them,
for example they are frequently taken by
naturalists and noncognitivists as premises
for refuting intuitionism.

Yet, ancient and fundamental as it may
be, this opposition has seldom been made
explicit or studied in its own right, even in
recent times when so many of the other op-
positions which were latent in earlier moral
philosophy have been underlined and debated. Its ghost was raised and given something like form by H. A. Prichard, but only,
as he vainly hoped, to be laid forever.[3]
R. M. Blake and Falk are perhaps the only
others to make a separate study of it.[4] For
the rest, however, the opposing positions
involved have simply been assumed, it
seems to me, without adequate analysis or
defense. Hence it is my purpose here to call
attention once more to this issue, to consider its present status, and to do something to clarify it and the methods by which
it is to be settled.

My sympathies have always been with
the first of the two positions described. It
has not seemed to me inconceivable that
one should have an obligation and recognize that one has it and yet have no motivation to perform the required act. But I am
less sure of this than I used to be, and shall
therefore explore the problem now with
the goal, not of arriving at any final conclusions, but of taking some steps in that
direction. I shall not proceed, however, by
making an independent study of the matter, but by reviewing analytically and critically a number of passages and discussions in the literature of the last two or
three decades.

Externalism may take various forms, as
has been indicated. Intuitionism, holding
that obligation is indefinable and nonnatural, is the most striking example of it, and

internalism has cropped out most frequently in refutations of intuitionism. But
many other views have held that moral
judgments can be analyzed without any
reference to the conations of the agent involved,[5] for instance, any form of naturalism which regards "I ought to do B" as
equivalent to "B is approved by most people" or "B is conducive to the greatest
general happiness," and any form of
noncognitivism which identifies moral requirements with social or divine imperatives.[6] For all such theories, obligation represents a fact or requirement which is
external to the agent in the sense of being
independent of his desires or needs.

Against them, internalists have a number of arguments which are more or less related and which they usually attribute to
Hume, sometimes correctly. It is to a study
of these arguments that the first main part
of this paper will be devoted. In all of them
the theme is that externalism has a problem about motivation, and is therefore
false. The first to be considered is an argument by G. C. Field to the effect that, if an
obligation represents an external fact about
an agent in the sense explained above, then
its presence entails no "reason for action."[7]
But it is "one of the most deeply recognized
characteristics of the moral fact" that it is
in itself and necessarily "a reason for acting." Therefore the views of Kant, Moore,
and other externalists are false.

We need not question Field's claim (1)
that, if an action is obligatory, this is a reason for doing it, since an externalist can accept it. But Field assumes in his discussion
(2) that a reason for action is a motive, and
this may well be doubted. It seems to me,
at any rate, that we must distinguish two
kinds of reasons for action, "exciting reasons" and "justifying reasons," to use
Hutcheson's terms.[8] When A asks, "Why
should I give Smith a ride?" B may give answers of two different kinds. He may say,
"Because you promised to," or he may say,
"Because, if you do, he will remember you
in his will." In the first case he offers a justification of the action, in the second a motive for doing it. In other words, A's "Why

should I . . . ?" and "Why ought I . . . ?" are ambiguous questions. They may be asking for an ethical justification of the action proposed, or they may be asking what motives there are for his doing it. "Should" and "ought" likewise have two meanings (at least) which are prima facie distinct: a moral one and a motivational one.

Thus a motive is one kind of reason for action, but not all reasons for action are motives. Perhaps we should distinguish between reasons for acting and reasons for regarding an action as right or justified. It is plausible to identify reasons for acting with motives, i.e., with considerations which will or may move one to action, and perhaps this is why Field assumes that all reasons are motives, but it is not plausible to identify motives with reasons for regarding an action as morally right or obligatory. At any rate there is a prima facie distinction to be made between two senses of "ought" and two kinds of reasons, and, if this distinction is valid, then Field's case as he states it collapses. For then an externalist can reply that (1) is obviously true only if "reason" means "justifying reason" and not "motivating reason," and that (2) is true only if "reason" means "motivating reason"; and he may go on to claim that "obligation" is ambiguous, being indeed susceptible of an internalist analysis in its motivational sense, but not in its moral sense. He may even contend that the plausibility of internalism rests on a failure to make this distinction.

The internalist, then, must either show that the above distinction is invalid, which Field does not do, shift to a different argument, or move the entire discussion to another level.

II

W. T. Stace and others use a similar argument against intuitionism and Platonism, contending boldly that, on any such analysis of "A ought to do B," A can admit that he ought to do B without its following that he has an *obligation* to *do* B. Stace's version

of this contention may be paraphrased as follows.[9] On an externalist analysis of judgments of obligation, such a judgment merely asserts a kind of fact, simple or complex, natural or nonnatural. Then, even if the judgment "A ought to do B" is true, it does not follow that A has any obligation to *act*, any *practical* obligation, but only an obligation to *believe*. Why should he do anything about B? An obligation to act follows only if A desires to do something about it, and then it follows from this desire alone. Moreover, he may not desire to do anything about it, and then he has no obligation of any sort to act. But a moral judgment necessarily entails an obligation to act: therefore externalist theories are false.

This argument, which seems so plausible to Stace, has always been puzzling to me. Let us begin, as he does, by supposing that a moral judgment *is* just a statement of some kind of "external" fact. Then one cannot admit such a fact about oneself, and still ask sensibly if one has a moral obligation to act. For to admit the fact is then to admit the obligation. One cannot in that case ask, "Why morally ought I do the act in question?" except to gain an insight into the *grounds* of the admitted obligation. One can still ask, "Why should I do the act?" but only if one is using "should" in the sense in which one is asking for motivation, or in some third sense. No doubt, as Stace says, one *will* do it only if he desires to do what has the given kind of "external" characteristic. Then one's desire obliges him in the sense of moving him. But the admitted moral judgment asserts a *moral* obligation nonetheless, and whether one will in fact perform the act in question or not does not bear on his having this obligation. Even if one may not desire to do what is right (i.e., what has the characteristic referred to by "right" on our hypothesis),[10] this does not change the fact that one has a moral obligation; it means only that one has no motivation, at least occurrently. That one has no moral obligation does not follow unless having an obligation entails having a motive. But this Stace does not show, and it is obviously true only in one sense of "obligation."

In fact, it is clear that Stace is assuming that to have an obligation is to have a motive, just as Field did, and his argument is essentially the same, though verbally different. And again the answer is that, until the contrary is shown, one must distinguish between two senses of "should" or "ought." For, if this distinction is valid, it can be claimed that Stace's argument reduces to this: even if I ought in one sense, it does not follow that I ought in the other sense, which is true but refutes no one. Stace, like Field, has failed to observe or consider the possible ambiguity of "should."

What he has noticed is that one apparently can ask, "Why should I do what I morally ought to do (if this represents some fact independent of my interests)?" But one can ask this sensibly only if "should" and "morally ought" are used in different senses. One cannot ask, "Why morally ought I to do what I morally ought to do?" even if "morally ought" does stand for an objective property. But neither can one ask, "Why should I do what I morally ought to do?" if "I should" and "I morally ought" *both* mean "I have a motive" or "It is necessary for my happiness," as they do on Stace's own view. For the question to be sensible, "I should" and "I morally ought" must have distinct meanings, whatever these are; and, while one may entail motivation, the other need not.

III

The fullest and most recent version of this argument is to be found in P. H. Nowell-Smith's book.[11] He remarks with interest that the intuitionists "have but repeated Hume's argument" about the gap between the *is* and the *ought* in refuting naturalistic theories.[12] Then he goes on to contend that intuitionism itself may be disposed of by essentially the same argument, namely, that it likewise fails to bridge the gap; and in making this striking contention good he elaborates the argument that, no matter what "fact," natural, metaphysical, or non-natural, one may establish about an action, it will still not follow that one ought to do the action.

The intuitionist's answer to the question "Why should I be moral?"—unless, like Prichard, he rejects it as a senseless question—is that, if you reflect carefully, you will notice that a certain act has two characteristics, (a) that of being obligatory and (b) that of producing a maximum of good or of being a fulfilment of a promise ... etc. ... But suppose all this has taken place.... Does it follow that I ought to do the action ...? ... a world of non-natural characteristics is revealed to us by a ... faculty called *"intuition."* ... And from statements to the effect that these exist no conclusions follow about what I *ought to do*. A new world is revealed for our inspection ... it is mapped and described in elaborate detail. No doubt it is all very interesting. If I happen to have a thirst for knowledge, I shall read on.... But what if I am not interested? Why should I do anything about these newly-revealed objects? Some things, I have now learnt, are right and others wrong; but why should I do what is right and eschew what is wrong? ...

Of course the question "Why should I do what I see to be right?" is ... an absurd one.... But ... [this question], which [is] absurd when words are used in the ordinary way, would not be absurd if moral words were used in the way that intuitionists suppose ... if "X is right" and "X is obligatory" are construed as statements to the effect that X has the non-natural characteristic of rightness or obligatoriness, which we just "see" to be present, it would seem that we can no more deduce "I ought to do X" from these premises than we could deduce it from "X is pleasant" or "X is in accordance with God's will."

This passage needs discussion here, even at the risk of some repetition. To begin with, it seems to me that Nowell-Smith is confusing two arguments, both suggested by Hume.[13] One says that conclusions involving "ought" cannot be derived from premises involving only "is" and not "ought." The other says something like this: conclusions involving "ought" cannot be derived from premises stating only *truths*, natural or nonnatural, even if one of these truths is what is meant by an ought-statement. Now it is the first of these which is used by the intuitionists against their opponents, and *it* cannot be turned against them. For its point is valid even if ought-statements assert truths as the intuitionists claim, provided only that the truths they assert are different from those asserted by any is-statements. Insofar, then, as Nowell-Smith is trading on whatever validity this argument possesses, his case against intuitionism breaks down. It is the other argument on which he must rely.

This one is harder to deal with. We must first eliminate another point on which Nowell-Smith seems to trade. He supposes that "X is obligatory" stands for a nonnatural property and then argues that it does not follow that I ought to do X. Of course, it does not follow that *I* ought to do X, since it was not specified for whom X is obligatory. Let us take "I have an obligation to do X" instead, and let us suppose that it asserts a fact about me and X, natural or nonnatural. Then the argument is that, even if it is true, it does not follow that I have an obligation to do X. Whether this is correct or not, however, depends on the meaning of "I have an obligation to do X" when it appears after the words "it does not follow."[14] If it here also stands for the fact in question, as cognitivists hold and as we are for the moment supposing, then it does follow that I have an obligation to do X, for the "conclusion" simply repeats the "premise."

Nowell-Smith may, of course, reply that no truth, natural or nonnatural, can entail an *obligation*. My point has been that it can *if* an obligation is a certain fact, as cognitivists claim. Nowell-Smith may go on to contend that an obligation is not identical with *any* such fact, but then he must show this independently, and cannot do so by the present argument. His contention may seem plausible when it is applied to naturalistic theories, as intuitionists have al-

ways thought. But it is not obviously true, if one does not identify obligation and motivation, that an obligation cannot be identical with any peculiar kind of "fact" such as the intuitionist believes in, for he claims that it is such a peculiar "fact" precisely to account for its obligatoriness. He has, as it were, built obligatoriness into his "fact." Possibly this cannot be done or is too pat a solution, as Nowell-Smith suggests. But this must be shown independently; Nowell-Smith must argue directly that such a fact is inconceivable or is not what is meant by "obligation," remembering as he does so the prima facie distinction introduced above. For if it is conceivable and is what is meant by "obligation," his present argument is not cogent.

The real reason why Nowell-Smith thinks that no set of truths or facts entails my having an obligation to act is, of course, the fact that he implicitly assumes that my having an obligation implies my having a motive. This comes out when he says about the intuitionist's brave nonnatural world: "But what if I am not interested?" And again the answer is that, while there is a sense in which having an obligation equals having an interest, there is prima facie another sense in which it may stand for a truth of another kind, natural or not. It is true that motivation will not follow logically from this truth (though it may follow casually from a recognition of it);[15] it will not follow any more than "Y is a fellow traveler" follows from "Y is tickled pink." In this sense Nowell-Smith's point is correct. I can contemplate all the facts pointed out by the intuitionists and externalists and still ask sensibly, "Ought I?" if I am asking about motivation. But it may still be nonsense to ask, "Ought I?" in the moral sense, as the cognitivist would claim.

Here Nowell-Smith insists that, when words are used in the ordinary way, it is absurd to ask of an act which it is admittedly right for me to do, "Why should I do it?" And of course it is, if "should" is used in its moral sense. But in this sense, the intuitionist may contend, his usage involves no gap either, as we have been seeing. It is only if "should" is used in its motivation-seeking sense that he must allow that there is a gap, and in this sense, he may claim, there really is a gap, which is not noticed because of an ambiguity in the word "should" as it is ordinarily used.

Again, then, it becomes apparent that the internalist must either challenge this distinction between two uses of "should," or show independently that "should" implies motivation even in its moral use.

IV

The internalist arguments discussed above depend on the claim that obligation and its recognition entail the existence of motivation, but they depend on it indirectly, through an identification of a reason for acting, or of an obligation to act, with a motive for doing so. Frequently, however, the internalists make this claim in so many words, and conclude directly that externalistic theories are mistaken. Thus Field argues against Moore that "the moral fact" is in itself and necessarily of interest to us when apprehended, but this it cannot be on Moore's view, and therefore Moore's view is false.[16] Likewise for all forms of externalism. Suppose we take Field's first premise in a psychological sense, as asserting (1) that, if one acknowledges an obligation to do something, then it is psychologically impossible for him not to have some tendency to do it, and (2) that his recognizing his obligation by itself produces this tendency. Then it can be denied with some plausibility, for not everyone's moral experience witnesses to the truth of either of these assertions, let alone of both of them. But suppose it is true. Must an externalist give up his position? Only if we can add two further premises: (3) that, no matter what external fact we may become acquainted with, it is always psychologically possible for us to be indifferent to it, and (4) that "the bare knowledge of anything can never move us to action." Now (4) is plausible, as Field shows at some length in attacking "the Kantian fallacy."

But most externalists would admit that knowledge can move us to action only by awakening an already existing desire, in this case, perhaps, a desire to do the right.[17] As for (3), it is obviously false, since there are external facts to which, given the conative natures we have, we cannot remain wholly indifferent. And, this being the case, an externalist like Moore might insist that we are so constituted that we cannot be wholly cold in the presence of the particular external fact which he regards as constituting obligation—a claim which Field does nothing to disprove.

However this may be, Field gives us no grounds for accepting his premise that the recognition of an obligation is by itself and necessarily a motive. He seems simply to infer this from the fact that such recognition is by itself necessarily a reason for action. But we have seen that, at least prima facie, "reason" is ambiguous here, and something may be a reason without thereby being a motive. Field must then show that his assertion is true independently of any possible confusion between two senses of "reason," which he does not do. And, if he is not going in for the longer kind of reasoning to be described in our last section, he must show that it is true in a logical sense, as asserting that it is logically impossible to have an obligation to which one is indifferent.

Another use of the argument occurs in C. L. Stevenson's important first article,[18] where he employs it against "any attempt to define ethical terms without reference to the interests of the speaker"—in favor, not of an internalistic cognitive theory, as in Field and Stace, but of an emotive one. Stevenson contends, among other things, that ethical terms "must have, so to speak, a magnetism," and that any analysis of them must provide for this. By saying they have magnetism he means that "a person who recognizes X to be 'good' [or 'obligatory'] must *ipso facto* acquire a stronger tendency to act in its favor than he otherwise would have had." He then writes:

This rules out the Humian type of definition. For according to Hume, to recognize that something is "good" is simply to recognize that the majority approve of it. Clearly, a man may see that the majority approve of X without having, himself, a stronger tendency to favour it.

The same reasoning, of course, will rule out intuitionism and other forms of externalism. On all such views, to assent to a moral judgment is to assent to a fact which involves no reference to one's interests; therefore this assent does not *ipso facto* or necessarily lead to a stronger tendency to favor the action in question.

This is essentially Field's argument over again, as Stevenson himself recognizes. The crucial premises are two: (1) that anyone who assents to a moral judgment must *ipso facto* or necessarily acquire a stronger tendency to do the action in question, and (2) that assenting to a fact which involves no reference to one's own interests will in no case *ipso facto* or necessarily produce such a tendency. Now these statements may be understood in a *causal* or psychological sense. But, if so, they should be shown to be true before they are used to rule out entire theories. The first is certainly not obvious in the case of all kinds of ethical judgments; it may be true of value-judgments but is it true of all ought-judgments? That it is seems particularly doubtful if we must distinguish between two kinds of ought-statements, for then one kind might be incitive in tendency and the other not; yet Stevenson takes no account of the possibility of such a distinction. Again, as was just said, it is hard to believe that in the case of every "external fact" about an action it is *psychologically* possible for us to be indifferent to it. If this were so we could have no "primary appetites" in Butler's sense; all of our interests would be washing-women taking in each others' laundry. But, if there are interests whose objects are "external," then Hume can plausibly claim that it is a psychological law of human nature that we invariably feel *some* tendency to do what we believe the majority to approve, or an intuitionist that it is psychologically necessary that we pursue a nonnatural right or good, as Plato thought.

Now Stevenson does nothing to refute such psychological theories. He must, then, be thinking that assenting to a moral judgment in some sense *logically* entails its having a tendency to affect one's action—that an analysis of a person's moral judgment or recognition that something is obligatory must in some way involve a reference to his tendencies to do the action in question. That is, motivation must be "built into" the analysis of ethical utterances. This dictum, however, cannot simply be assumed, if the issue is not to be begged, especially if the distinction referred to earlier holds. Moreover, it is ambiguous. It may mean that a reference to the agent's desires is to be built into the *descriptive* meaning of ethical judgments, or it may mean that part of what is meant by *assenting* to a moral judgment is a disposition to respond accordingly. The first of these alternatives is taken by Field and Falk[19] but rejected by Stevenson. The second, as we shall see in a later section, can be accepted by an externalist.

V

A somewhat novel form of the present argument has been advanced by H. D. Aiken in a well-known article.[20] He maintains (1) that judgments of obligation are normative in the sense that they influence the will and determine conduct, and (2) that "the relation between cognition and motivation, on any theory of motivation whatever, is a causal, not a logical, relation"; and he concludes that all "descriptivist" analyses of judgments of obligation are therefore mistaken, whether naturalistic or nonnaturalistic (including internalistic forms of naturalism such as those of Field and Stace). (2) is an important point and needed to be made, but it may be admitted. (1) is a premise already familiar to us in other forms, but, whereas his predecessors regard it as empirical, Aiken makes it analytic. He defines a judgment of obligation as one which influences conduct "by whatever means." This, however, has a curious effect, namely, that what are usually called ethical judgments may not be judgments of obligation in his sense, since they will be so only if they influence the will. But then, even if his argument shows that his "judgments of obligation" cannot be descriptively analyzed, it proves nothing about the so-called moral judgments with which the rest of us have been concerned.

Aiken is tacitly assuming that judgments of the form "A should . . . ," "B ought . . . ," and so forth, in the uses with which we are concerned, are all causally efficacious, at least normally, and so fall under what he calls "judgments of obligation." This may be doubted, especially if we keep in mind our distinction between two kinds of "should" sentences, but let us accept it for the sake of the argument. Then his conclusion still does not follow. For a judgment that causally affects behavior may be susceptible of a cognitivist analysis, and even of an externalistic one. That is, a statement may be a "judgment of obligation" and yet be descriptive. For its moving power may be due wholly to the information, natural or nonnatural, which it conveys to our desires. If I say to you as we cross the street, "There is a car coming," my statement will influence your actions, and it may do so simply in its informative capacity (given your desire to live). Then it will be a "judgment of obligation" and yet be capable of a descriptivist and externalist analysis.

The matter may be put thus. Consider "I ought to do X" in any safely ethical use. The question is whether or not this is to be given an internalistic analysis. Aiken does give us such an analysis of the meta-sentence, "'I ought to do X' is normative." But this is not an analysis of the sentence, "I ought to do X," itself, and so all of the standard theories about its analysis remain open. It is, however, this sentence which constitutes our problem; we want to know the function or meaning of "obligatory" as it is used in, "It is obligatory on me to do X," not in, "'It is obligatory on me to do X' is obligatory." Aiken's attempt to sidestep the dispute about ethical sentences is no doubt a laudable one; the moral of my critique is only that, if one does sidestep it,

one must not draw any conclusions about it, as he seems to do.

VI

The above kinds of argument against externalism all depend on the claim that obligation or judgments of obligation somehow entail motivation, perhaps directly, perhaps by identifying motivation and reasons for acting or by identifying motivation and obligation to act. I have tried to dispose of each argument individually, but my main point has been that there is a prima facie distinction to be made between moral or justifying reasons and exciting or motivating ones, or between moral and nonmoral obligation; that this distinction is usually neglected by internalists when they use such arguments; and that if this distinction is valid the arguments lose their cogency. For then the externalist can reply that, while there is a motivational sense of "ought" which *is* "internal," there is another sense of "ought" which is moral and which may be "external" for all that has been shown so far.

In making this point I have but echoed an old intuitionist refrain, which to my knowledge was first sung by Samuel Clarke and last by R. M. Blake, but which may also be sung by nonintuitionists. Clarke, observing the rising conflict between internalism and externalism of his day, distinguishes "the truest and formallest obligation," which is moral, from "the Dread of Superior Power and Authority, and the Sanction of Rewards and Punishments . . . which is . . . really in itself only a *secondary* and *additional* Obligation, or *Inforcement* of the first." Then he remarks that a failure to notice this ambiguity of the term "obligation" has blinded some writers to the (externalist) truth that "the original *Obligation* of all . . . is the eternal *Reason* of Things. . . ." He says drily, in parentheses, ". . . the ambiguous use of which word [Obligation], as a *Term of Art*, has caused some Perplexity and Confusion in this Matter"—the perplexity and confusion being, of course, in the minds of the internalists.[21] It seems to me, as it seemed to him and to Blake, that neglect of this ambiguity has been a serious mistake in recent moral philosophy.

Even if the distinction is valid, however, it does not follow that internalism is false, but only that externalism may be true if it cannot be refuted on grounds other than those so far considered. One may admit the distinction and still claim that both kinds of judgment of obligation, the moral as well as the nonmoral, are susceptible of an internalistic analysis. In fact, some recent internalists do distinguish moral from nonmoral obligation in one way or another, though apparently without seeing that the above kind of argument does not establish the internality of the moral ought, when this is distinguished from the nonmoral one. It may then be held that, independently of such a distinction and of the above arguments, it can be shown that moral obligation is internal. We must now in the second main part of this paper take up some considerations that seem calculated to show this.

It will be helpful, first, to sort out a number of propositions that internalists have held or may be holding, particularly since they have rarely been distinguished in the literature. All of the above writers, and many others, are convinced that having or acknowledging an obligation to do something involves having, either occurrently or dispositionally, some motivation for doing it; and they infer that externalism is false. But this proposition can be taken to assert several things, namely: (1) that the state of having an obligation includes or is identical with that of being motivated in a certain way; (2) that the statement. "I have an obligation to do B," means or logically entails the statement, "I have, actually or potentially, some motivation for doing B";[22] (3) that the reasons that justify a judgment of obligation include or are identical with the reasons that prove the existence of motivation to act accordingly; (4) that the reasons that justify a judgment of obligation include or are identical with those that

bring about the existence of motivation to act accordingly; (5) that, although justifying a moral judgment does not include giving exciting reasons for acting on it, it presupposes the existence, at least potentially, of such excitement; (6) that *saying* or being *said* to have an obligation presupposes one's having motives for doing the action in question; (7) that *assenting* to an obligation entails feeling or having a disposition to feel at least some inclination to act in the way prescribed; or (8) that one can know or "see" or think that one has a certain obligation only when one is in a favorable conative state with respect to performing the act in question.

Even these formulations are not very rigorous, but perhaps they will suffice to make clearer the opposition we are discussing. The externalist is concerned to deny (1) through (4), which the internalist will assert. If they are true, externalism is untenable. However, as far as I can see, the internalists have not shown them to be true to such a degree that they can be safely used as premises for refuting externalism; indeed, they are plausible only when the distinction between two senses of "ought" and "reason" that we have been stressing is not borne in mind.

As for (5) through (8), an externalist may accept them, though they may also be denied with some plausibility (and would be denied by a really "compleat" externalist). It is obvious that he can admit (8), for it makes only a psychological assertion about the conditions of moral insight; in fact, (8) is maintained by such externalists as Scheler and Hartmann.[23] (5), as we shall see, may also be agreed to by an externalist, though only if "presupposes" is understood in some psychological or "contextual" sense, and not in a strictly logical one.

The arguments to be dealt with here generally involve (1), (6), or (7), and we may take first those that use (1) in some form or other. In one of them Falk appeals to the familiar principle that "I morally ought" implies "I can," adding that "I can" implies "I want to (in the sense that I have, at least dispositionally, some motivation for doing)," and then drawing an internalist con-clusion.[24] Suppose we admit, though both claims may be disputed, that "I morally ought" in all its sense implies "I can," and that "I can" implies "I want to." Even then this argument will be cogent only if the "implies" involved is a logical one in both cases. But is it in "'I can' implies 'I want to'"? To say, "I cannot whistle a tune while standing on my head, unless I feel some in-clination to do so," is perhaps an odd thing to say about an odd bit of behavior, but it seems at most to state a physical fact, not a logical necessity. One may, of course, so define "I can" as to include "I have some impulse to," but it is not obvious that one should, and it is not clear that "ought" im-plies "can" as so defined.

But *ought* implies *can* need not be con-strued as asserting a strict logical implica-tion. It may plausibly be understood as say-ing: (a) moral judgments "presuppose," "contextually imply," or "pragmatically imply" that the agent is able to act as pro-posed or is believed to be, but do not as-sert or state that he is; or (b) the *point of ut-tering* moral judgments disappears if the agents involved are not able to act as pro-posed or at least believed to be; or (c) it would be morally wrong to insist that an agent ought to do a certain action, if he is or is thought to be unable to do it. If Kant's dictum is interpreted in one of these ways the externalist need have no fear, for then it will not serve to refute him.

VII

In a somewhat similar argument, Aiken reasons that obligation presupposes re-sponsibility and that this presupposes mo-tivation:

> Hume's argument can be stated in another . . . way. We assume that no person can be held morally responsible for actions which he did not willingly perform. We do not address such judgments as "Killing is wrong" to cyclones. . . . In short, we regard only responsible beings as moral or im-moral. But . . . responsibility *presupposes* a

motive for or interest in any act for which a person is held "responsible." If this is so, the very notions of "moral" and "im-moral" involve a reference to feeling or sentiment; and every moral judgment states or implies such a reference.

Aiken then asserts that this argument "dis-qualifies all theories whatever which . . . deny that moral categories are to be con-strued in terms of human feeling or inter-est. . . ."[25] In another place he claims that obligation and desire are intimately re-lated, "For . . . it is doubtful whether the term ['ought'] is ever properly applied to anything save motivated activity." Here too he takes this conviction as a criterion to be met "by any adequate analysis of 'ought'."[26]

Now, the argument from obligation to responsibility to motivation is like the ar-gument from obligation to ability to moti-vation, and the same points hold about it. Instead of repeating, then, let us take up the conviction that moral obligation and judgment presuppose motivation. It does seem correct to say that my having moral duties implies that *others* have desires and feelings, but this externalists need not deny. It is also plausible to hold that my having duties, or being a moral agent whose acts are right or wrong, presupposes *my* having interests and motives. To this extent Aiken is, in my opinion, correct. But an externalist can agree, and still insist that, although one can ascribe obligation only to a motivated being, to ascribe an obligation to such a being is not to talk about his mo-tives but to assert some external fact about him.

More crucial is Aiken's further claim that A's having an obligation to do B presup-poses his having not only interests *über-haupt* but, directly or indirectly, an interest in doing B (though not necessarily a pre-dominant one). If this means that A's hav-ing a duty to do B logically entails his hav-ing an interest in doing B, or that establishing his obligation to do B logically entails showing him that he has such an in-terest or producing such an interest in him, it may be denied. A man who is seeking to determine if he has a duty to do a certain deed need not look to see if he has any motives for doing it, and he cannot claim that he does not have the duty simply on the ground that he finds no supporting motivation. Aiken may reply that, nevertheless, A's having an obligation to do B in some sense presupposes his having a concern to do B, at least dispositionally, and I am inclined to agree that it does, but only in the sense that *ascribing* this duty to A "contextually" or pragmatically implies that, if A sees he has it, he will have some concern to perform it (6). This, however, does not mean that A's having this concern is a condition of his having a duty to do B, and it can be admitted by an externalist. In *Principia Ethica* Moore says, "If I ask whether an action is *really* my duty or *really* expedient, the predicate of which I question the applicability to the action in question is precisely the same. In both cases I am asking, 'Is this event the best on the whole that I can effect?'" Yet, although "duty" and "expedient" have the same conceptual meaning for Moore, he maintains that there is a difference in their use, "duty" being applied to those useful actions "which it is more useful to praise and to enforce by sanctions, since they are actions which there is a temptation to omit."[27] Then "B is A's duty" *means*, "B is the best thing on the whole that A can do," but it *presupposes* that A is tempted not to do it. Perhaps moral judgments only presuppose motivation in a similar sense.

VIII

Two other considerations seem to have been regarded as showing that having an obligation entails having a corresponding motivation. One is a conviction that a man cannot have an obligation unless he accepts it as such and "beats responsive and not irresponsive to the claim" in what James calls the "everlasting ruby vaults" of his heart.[28] This is expressed in the following quotation from Falk: ". . . Even the commands of God could only constitute moral obliga-tions for somebody who considered it a *law unto himself* to respect what God bids him to do."[29] Now it does seem in some sense correct to say that a man cannot actually have a moral duty if he does not see and accept it. At the same time, this is an odd thing to say unless we are using "duty" in two senses, for we are saying that A has no duty to do B if he does not recognize that he has a duty to do B. The same double usage occurs in the sentence, "You ought to do what you think you ought to do." The matter can be cleared up using the distinction, long accepted by externalists, between what one *subjectively* ought to do and what one *objectively* ought to do. The point, then, is that A subjectively ought to do B only if he accepts this as his obligation. It still may be, however, that B would be objectively right for him to do anyway. In fact, when a man thinks that something is his duty, what he thinks is that it is a duty independently of his thinking so (and independently of his wanting to do it); and when he asks what his duty is, he implies that he has a duty that he does not yet recognize, and what he is seeking to know, as it were, is what it would have been his duty to do even if he had not discovered it. Thus there is a sense in which one has a moral obligation even if one does not recognize it as such.

It has also been insisted by internalists that the moral will is autonomous, and R. M. Blake believed that this doctrine should be repudiated by externalists as incompatible with the existence of any categorical imperative. Nowell-Smith is especially persistent in asserting such autonomy. ". . . The feature which distinguishes moral obligations from all others is that they are self-imposed. . . ." "The questions 'what shall I do?' and 'what moral principles should I adopt?' must be answered by each man for himself; that at least is part of the connotation of the word 'moral'."[30] In spite of what Blake says, it is hard entirely to reject this "moral protestantism," as Margaret Macdonald has called it.[31] common as it is to Kant, existentialism, and Nowell-Smith. But I am not persuaded that a recognition of autonomy necessarily leads to internalism. In areas outside of ethics we also believe in autonomy, e.g., in our scientific beliefs, and, in "religious protestantism," in our theological beliefs. Yet here the "facts" in which we freely believe or disbelieve are "external" ones—facts which are independent of us but about which we are nevertheless left to make up our own minds. It may then be that obligations are external facts of a similar sort. Certainly intuitionists and naturalists can allow us the same kind of autonomy in ethics that we claim in science and religion, without thereby going over to the enemy. They may hold that what we objectively ought to do is self-imposed only in the sense of being self-discovered or self-recognized, as scientific facts are, and that only what we subjectively ought to do is self-imposed in the more radical manner indicated earlier.

IX

However, even if *having* a moral obligation does not always and in every sense depend on the agent's accepting it and feeling motivated to do it, it may nevertheless be maintained that *assenting to* a moral obligation entails a feeling of motivation on his part. This brings us to (7), which is widely insisted on by internalists.[32] It may be put in various ways, but the essential point of it is either (a) that one cannot assent to or be convinced of an obligation of one's own without having some disposition to act accordingly, or (b) that we should regard it as odd or paradoxical if someone were to assent to an obligation without feeling any motivation whatever for fulfilling it. In the first case, there is a direct assertion that a certain sequence of events is not possible; in the second, there is only a claim that we should be puzzled if we observed such a sequence or, rather, do not believe that one can occur.

Now, taken in its first form, (7) does not seem to me to be obviously true. In any case, as we have noticed, it is ambiguous

in a way that its proponents do not recognize. Taken as an assertion of a psychological law, it can be admitted by any externalist who does not hold our conative nature to be *totally* depraved.[33] It must then be regarded as asserting a logical truth, if it is to say anything inconsistent with externalism. Here again there are two alternatives. (m) It may be meant that part of what a judgment of obligation *asserts* or *states* is that the agent referred to feels a responsive beat in his heart. Then (7) is identical with (2), and simply to assume it is a *petitio*. (n) The other alternative is that motivation is to be built, not into the content of a moral judgment, but into the process of assenting to it. On this view, it is not "A ought to do B" that logically implies his having some tendency to do B, but "A is convinced that he ought to do B." That is to say, part of what is meant by "assenting to an obligation" is that one feels a responsive stirring.

Most recent internalists, I believe, would prefer this formulation of (7) to that represented by (m). I am not at all sure that (7), so interpreted, is true, but I should like to suggest that an externalist can accept it if it is. An externalist may agree, it seems to me, that we cannot, in the sense in which we use these words in connection with moral judgments, "accept," "recognize," or "be convinced of" an obligation without thereby having at least some motivation to fulfill it. He may hold, for example, that judgments of obligation have a conceptual content of an "external" kind, but add that we do not speak of a man's *assenting* or *sincerely assenting* to them unless he not only apprehends the truth of their conceptual content but is at least to some extent moved to conform to it. He would then admit that it is *logically* possible that one might have a "mere intellectual apprehension," as Field calls it, of their truth, but he would recognize the generally practical function of language (which his opponents have made so much of), especially moral discourse. There is no reason why he cannot change his ways enough to do this; even an intuitionist need not insist that the *actual* use of moral language is merely to report the news of a non-natural world and is in no way adapted to the interests of the reader. It may be part of the ordinary "grammar" of such words as "assent," when used in connection with ethical judgments, that they are not to be employed except when "mere intellectual apprehension" is accompanied by a responsive beating of the heart. Even in the case of nonethical judgments it has been held that one does not believe unless one is in some sense disposed to act accordingly in appropriate circumstances. But, even if this is not so, it might be argued that because ethical discourse is more particularly concerned to guide human action than is nonethical discourse, such terms as "believe" may be presumed to obey different rules here.

Of course, the internalist may still complain that on his opponent's view it is logically, if not actually, possible to have a "mere intellectual apprehension" of an obligation. But, if the position just described is tenable, then he cannot support his complaint by appealing to the dictum that we cannot really assent to an obligation without having a disposition to respond. And simply to assume that it is not even logically possible to have a "mere intellectual apprehension" of an obligation is a *petitio*.

Consider now (7) in form (b). Here there is an appeal to certain data about our ordinary moral consciousness and its ways of thinking; these data are supposed to show that internalism is true or at least is embedded in moral common sense. Thus Falk has argued that externalism fails to account for such facts as the following:[34] (p) that "we commonly expect that in thinking ourselves obliged we *ipso facto* feel some constraint to do what we think we ought to do"; (q) that, "when we try to convince another that he ought to pay his bills, we expect our argument if accepted to effect some change of heart in him"; (r) that "we should think it odd to receive the answer: 'Yes, I know now *that* and *why* I ought to pay my bills, but I am still without any incentive for doing so.'"

I am not so much concerned to question these facts, though I do not myself find the answer in (r) entirely odd, as to point out that they do not, as stated, prove obligation and motivation to be *logically* connected. If we have the expectations and feelings of oddity described, this may only mean that we commonly believe that all men are *psychologically* so constituted as to be moved by the recognition that something is right. It need not mean that this is *logically* necessary or even that we believe it to be so. And we have already seen that one may hold rightness to be an external characteristic and yet claim that we are so made as necessarily (causal) to take an interest in it.

Falk's facts may also be explained in another way by the externalist. For, until evidence is given to the contrary, the externalist can argue that the common moral consciousness feels the expectations and oddities mentioned only because it does not distinguish at all clearly or consistently in its thinking between two senses in which one may be obliged, so that it links to the one feelings and thoughts appropriate to the other. This seems to me plausible, for we do frequently fail to see any difference between the two kinds of reasons for action, and often shift from one to the other without noticing.

Still a third explanation is possible. As we have indicated before, when one asks what he ought to do, he is not or at least need not be asking what he already accepts as his duty, but what is his duty although it is not yet accepted as such; and he is not or need not be asking what he has or may have a motive for doing, but what he is morally required to do and may not have any motive for doing until after he sees that it is his duty. But, of course, one would not normally ask the question unless one was concerned about the answer and felt some motivation to do his duty, whatever that might turn out to be. And so, when one concludes that such and such is what he ought to do, he can be expected to feel some motivation to do such and such and even to decide to do it. The whole process of moral question and answer normally takes place in this atmosphere of moral concern. This is all that such facts as those mentioned prove, and this much an externalist may and no doubt should admit, though he may add that it is logically possible that the case should be otherwise. Normally, then, when assent occurs in the course of a moral inquiry, it can be expected to involve commitment. But it does not follow that it is a condition of one's having an obligation to do a certain action that he should have a motive for doing it apart from discovering that it is his duty, nor that discovering it to be his duty logically entails his having a motive for doing it.

It has been argued that, if a man says he believes that he has a duty to do a certain action but feels no conation at all in favor of it, then he does not understand the sentence, "I have a duty," or its use.[35] If by this it is meant that he does not understand what an obligation is, then simply to assert this is to beg the question against the externalist. If it is meant that he does not understand what it is to *assent* to an obligation, the externalist can agree and give the explanation indicated above in our discussion of (7). But it may be that what is intended is that he just does not know in what circumstances to *say*, "I ought to do so and so," and this an externalist may also concede.

X

This brings up a number of points made by internalists, not so much about *having* an obligation or *assenting* to one, as about *uttering* sentences to the effect that one has an obligation or that someone else has—in short, (6). For example, it is said (a) that my uttering a sentence beginning with "I ought" always or normally "expresses" a pro-attitude or decision on my part or "contextually implies" one.[36] But this an externalist may grant even if he holds that such a sentence "asserts" an external fact. The sentence, "There are flying saucers," expresses the speaker's belief, but for all that it purports to assert an external fact.

Thus, W. D. Ross, who holds that "good" *means* an external characteristic, is "inclined to think" that we *use* or *apply* the term in such a way "that in each case the *judge* has some feeling of approval or interest towards what he calls good."[37] It is also said (b) that my uttering a sentence starting with "You ought" expresses or contextually implies a pro-attitude on my part toward your doing the act specified, as well as one on yours.[38] But Ross could admit this too. If I say, "There is a tidal wave coming up behind you," I "express" a concern about your welfare and "presuppose" that you also have one, but what I assert is still an external fact or purports to be.

In a similar vein internalists contend (c) that it would be absurd, odd, or "logically odd" to say things like: "You ought to do A, but don't"; "I ought to do A, but shall I?"; "I ought to do A, but I shall not."[39] Now these would, perhaps, be unusual uses of language, but are they logically impossible? "There are flying saucers, but I don't believe it" would be an unusual contribution to any serious and sober conversation, but it is not a logically self-contradictory one, since both parts of what is asserted may be true together; the apparent conflict is not between parts of what is asserted but between part of what is asserted and one of the presuppositions of asserting the rest.

Logically, as far as I can see, "I should" and "I shall" are distinct, and one can admit that he ought and still not resolve to do. One would not then be very likely to say, "I ought but I shall not," for one probably would not be that interested in the morality of what one was doing, but logically the situation would be such as to be describable in those terms. No doubt, as Nowell-Smith and P. B. Rice claim, a firsthand "I ought" does normally express commitment or decision on the speaker's part, for one would not normally go through the process of moral deliberation that concludes with "I ought" if he were not sufficiently devoted to the moral enterprise for this conclusion to coincide with his decision. This does not mean, however, that "I ought" logically entails "I shall"; it may only pragmatically presuppose or contextually imply this.

Nowell-Smith's discussion of "I ought" and "I shall" is interesting in this connection.[40] According to him, "I (morally) ought" expresses a decision, just as "I shall" does, although it is a decision based on rules, and therefore "I ought but shall I?" is logically odd unless "shall I?" is used in a predictive sense. Yet he admits that "I ought" is "also used, not to express a decision, but in the course of making up one's mind before a decision has been reached," and it is this use that interests me. It seems to me that in this use one *could* say, "I ought but shall I?" and one might go on thinking he ought and yet decide not to. Nowell-Smith seeks to avoid this conclusion by turning the "I ought" here into the Voice of Conscience or "self-hortatory 'you ought'"—a neat device but question-begging in this context. The main point, however, is that there is an "I ought" which does not express decision. It is true that this "I ought" is normally replaced by "the verdict-giving 'I ought'" *if* desire does not win out over conscience. But desire may win, and then there is a situation which can be described by "I ought, but I shall not," where "shall" is not predictive but decisive, though if one is in this situation one is not likely so to describe it until later, and then in the past tense.

XI

So far our study of the opposition between internalism and externalism in moral philosophy has fallen into two main parts. In the first (sections I through V) we reviewed one family of arguments against externalism and saw that they are not successful, mainly because they can for the most part be answered by distinguishing two senses of "obligation," corresponding to two meanings of, "Why should I?" In the second (sections VI through X) we found that another set of considerations that are rela-

tively independent of this distinction can, insofar as they are valid at all, be met or accepted if certain other distinctions are made—between what we objectively and what we subjectively ought to do; between having an obligation, assenting to an obligation, and saying one has an obligation; between what is stated or logically implied and what is "presupposed" or "implied" in some not strictly logical sense by a moral judgment, and so forth. In short, we have seen that externalism is not refuted by these arguments and considerations and can be maintained if there are not yet other grounds on which it must be given up.

We might now go on to consider corresponding arguments against internalism. It is, however, difficult to find such arguments explicitly set forth in recent literature, and perhaps we may assume that they too would turn out to be inconclusive. The distinction between two senses of "should" and "ought" to which we have appealed, for example, cannot, even if it is valid, be used as an argument to refute internalism, although it disposes of some arguments used in its support.[41] For it is possible to admit this distinction and still maintain a kind of internalism. One might hold, for instance, that moral judgments are expressions of some specifically moral attitude, such as love, sympathy, an internalized sense of social demand, an attitude of impartial spectatorship, and so forth, and regard justifying reasons as reasons calculated to appeal to this attitude, exciting reasons as those that appeal to other attitudes and desires. One would then regard this attitude as conative (unlike Hutcheson's moral sense), and moral judgments as *ipso facto* to some extent motivating. But one would not claim that this attitude is always dominant, and so could admit that I may agree that I ought to do a certain action and yet say, "But I shall not!" In this very important respect one's position, though a form of internalism, would be like externalism.

The main result yielded by our discussion, then, is that the opposition we are studying cannot be resolved, as so many seem to think, by such relatively small-scale logical or semi-logical arguments as we have been dealing with. But we have also achieved some clarity about the exact points at issue. The externalist can admit that there is a nonmoral obligation and even a "subjective" moral obligation that logically entails motivation. He can accept any statement that says that having an obligation, assenting to one, or being said to have one causally or *psychologically* involves the existence of a corresponding motivation. He may also agree that assenting to an obligation *logically* entails the existence of motivation for acting accordingly. He may even allow, and perhaps should, that having or being said to have an obligation presupposes in some not strictly logical sense the existence of such motivation. What he must deny, and the internalist assert, is that having objectively a certain moral obligation logically entails having some motivation for fulfilling it, that justifying a judgment of objective moral obligation logically implies establishing or producing a motivational buttress, and that it is logically impossible that there should be a state of apprehending a moral obligation of one's own which is not accompanied by such a buttress (even if this "mere intellectual apprehension" is never actual and does not amount to what is called "assenting to" or "acknowledging" an obligation).

Now one may, if sufficiently hardy, choose to defend a form of externalism that does not make any of the concessions just indicated, or a form of internalism that does not incorporate the distinction between two senses of "Why should I?" or between exciting and justifying reasons. Personally, it seems to me that the choice must in practice be between an externalism that makes such concessions and an internalism that recognizes such a distinction. But, in any case, how is the issue to be settled? If arguments of the kind we have been reviewing are inadequate, are we then at an impasse here, too, as so many think we are on other questions? This does not follow. It does follow that neither kind of

moral philosophy can be decisively refuted by the other, and that we must give up the quest for certainty in the sense of no longer hoping for such refutations. But it does not follow that nothing can be said for one view as against the other. What does follow is that the whole discussion must consciously move to another level.[42]

This does not mean that it must become even more "meta" than it already is. What this shift involves, and that it is necessary, can best be made clear by taking a look at Falk's best-known paper.[43] Here he first seems to argue very much as he does in the earlier articles already dealt with. But soon it becomes apparent that something different is going on. Falk finds in the controversy between Prichard and his opponents and in moral common sense a tension between two positions, namely, "that morality needs some additional psychological sanction" and "that what sanction it requires, it necessarily carries with it." That is, moral philosophy and ordinary moral thinking have been a confused combination of, or alternation between, externalism and internalism. Falk suggests that this situation "has its origin in uncertainties and contradictions in the common use of words like 'ought' or 'duty'; in an unnoticed juxtaposition of meanings each of which entails a different relation to motivation." It is due to the fact that "ought" is used in both an externalist and an internalist sense, which "remain undifferentiated and are imperceptibly juxtaposed and confused," so that "there may be an unnoticed switch from the one use of 'ought' to the other." This is why the questioner's "Why should I be moral?" has been so puzzling. In one sense of "ought" it is "legitimate and in need of some factual answer," in the other it is absurd; and where the two senses are confused "no answer can satisfy," and the way is open for the skeptic to draw his disturbing conclusion.

In other words, Falk, although he is an internalist, is explicitly recognizing the ambiguity we have made so much of—indeed, he goes further and says that one of the senses involved *is* external, a claim we have not made. He uses this ambiguity to explain the rise of our two points of view and their juxtaposition in moral common sense and philosophy. All this I cannot but approve. I have only wanted to add that it is the internalists rather than the externalists who have failed to notice the ambiguity, and that this failure vitiates much of their argument. Falk does not deny this; he simply does not repeat his earlier arguments for internalism, apparently recognizing their insufficiency. Instead, he proceeds to a new line of attack.

Falk contends that we cannot be satisfied, as an externalist would be, with uncovering the confusion and replacing it with an avowed use of "ought" in two senses, one external and one internal, one moral and the other motivational. In fact, he insists that the external use of "ought" cannot be accepted by a mature reflective person who is "aware of a capacity of reasoned choice and intent on using it," because such a person cannot "easily agree to a use of [moral] words for any demand on him that still left him to ask whether he also had a sufficient reason for doing the act." He then argues that one internal use of "ought" bears "at least a sufficient resemblance to what ordinary usage expects of a normative term" for it to qualify as moral.[44] He calls this "the purely formal motivational 'ought.'" To say one ought in this sense is to say he has a reason or motive for acting with regard to which no further question can be asked, or which is compelling no matter what considerations reason may advance, and so is "formally sufficient." This "ought," Falk holds, can be identified with the moral "ought," since it is normative in the sense of influencing "the direction of people's volitional attitudes and actions," it is not simply a function of occurrent wants, and it is categorical, not hypothetical. It is, in fact, confused with the external moral "ought" in ordinary thinking. It *should* be taken as *the* moral "ought" because it must be recognized in any case, and because "in using moral language we mean to denote something that when known, can conclusively

serve to direct what we do, and we cannot obey two masters."

Now I am not convinced by what Falk says, all too briefly, even here. He says that "we cannot avowedly use 'moral ought' both for an external and an internal state of affairs, as if a man might have one but not another sort of moral duty in respect of the same act." Yet he has not shown that we ever do use the *moral* "ought" for an internal state of affairs, but at most that we ought to. Besides, in the distinction between a subjective and an objective "ought" it seems to be possible to use even "morally ought" in two senses, one more internal and one more external, without thereby having to serve two masters. Moreover, it does not appear that his substitute will do as the moral "ought." As far as I can see, an act may be morally wrong even though I am impelled to do it after full reflection. What one is impelled to do even after reason has done its best is still dependent on the vagaries of one's particular conative disposition, and I see no reason for assuming that it will always coincide with what is in fact right or regarded as right. As for Falk's assertion that "in using moral language we mean to denote something that when known, can conclusively serve to direct what we do"—this is ambiguous. It may mean that moral judgments are intended to serve as conclusive *guides* or that they are meant to serve as conclusive *goads*. In the first case Falk is clearly right, but an externalist can agree. In the second he is either forgetting his own admission that there is an external use of "ought" in ordinary discourse or begging the question. His further claim that a reflective person cannot accept as a moral duty anything which he does not have a "formally sufficient" motive for doing seems to me to beg the question as it stands.

What interests me here about Falk's paper, however, is the fact that he has moved the controversy to another level, a less merely logical and larger scale level. The issue, he says in conclusion, is not settled merely by distinguishing "between normative facts of different kinds, confusedly referred to by the same name"; ultimately what is necessary is "clarity and decision about what fact would most nearly correspond to our intentions in the use of moral language and which words like 'ought' and 'duty' should be made to denote." This is the problem as it shapes itself at the end of our study. Externalism versus internalism, yes, but on a macroscopic rather than a microscopic plane. These are not small positions that may be decisively established or taken in a brief action recorded in a page or two. They are whole theories of "our intentions in the use of moral language," past, present, and future.

To see this let us glance at the internalist case, as it must be made if the above discussion has been correct. Central in it must be the contention that externalism leaves a gap between perceived obligation and motivation. Now, we have seen that externalism does not *logically* entail the existence of a *psychological* gap here. By itself it entails only that it is logically possible that one should in some sense perceive (though perhaps without giving a full-fledged *assent*) that one has an obligation and yet have no disposition to fulfill it. That is, the argument that externalism logically involves a gap does not come off; externalism implies only that there is a logical gap or that it is logically possible there is a psychological gap, and it is simply begging the question to begin with the opposite premise. But instead of reasoning in this way, as in effect the writers we have dealt with do, the internalist may and should elaborate his case as follows.

1. Externalism does not by itself logically imply that there may (psychologically) be a gap between perceived obligation and motivation, but it implies that such a gap is logically possible. This is true in the qualified sense just indicated.

2. An externalist may claim that there is in fact no gap—that actually there is always some possibly adequate motivation for doing what one perceives to be right—and he may offer various psychological theories in his support. He may hold that a "mere intellectual apprehension" of one's duty is it-

self moving, that there is in human nature a desire to do what is right, that the sentiment of benevolence is always on hand to support the call of duty, and so forth. But all such theories are false; there is no external fact which the externalist may plausibly identify with obligation which is also such that its apprehension is always, let alone by a psychological necessity, accompanied by a responsive beating of the heart. Therefore, there is in fact a psychological gap between obligation and motivation if any form of externalism is true, in the sense that then one actually might perceive an obligation and have no corresponding motivation.

3. At this point the internalist may argue either that there is in fact no psychological gap, that the existence of such a gap is intolerable from the point of view of morality, or that our moral common sense does not believe there is such a gap, concluding that externalism is false or inconsistent with common sense.

Such a line of reasoning involves first establishing (2), and this requires a full-scale psychological inquiry, which is more than internalists have yet gone in for. Suppose that it is established. All that follows is that, if externalism is true, human beings may sometimes lack all motivation to do what they apprehend as right. One who is willing to admit this need follow the argument no farther. This brings us to (3). To argue here that there is no gap is to make a factual, psychological claim, the establishing of which again calls for an empirical inquiry, one as difficult to handle as the question whether Socrates was correct in believing that we always do what we think is right. It is hard to see how it could be carried out without taking some position with respect to the definition of obligation, assenting, and so forth, and it is just this that constitutes our problem. In any case, the record of human conduct is not such as to make it obvious that human beings always do have some tendency to do what they regard as their duty. The contention that our common moral consciousness supposes that there can be no gap will be met by conflicting evidence, as Falk admits, and, in any event, one may reply that common sense may be mistaken, thus opening the whole question again. If the contention is only that it is a rule of ordinary moral discourse that a person shall not be *said* to have an obligation unless there is or may be presumed to be in him some disposition to respond favorably, then, as we have seen, the externalist may admit it, but he may also contest it or argue for a change in the rules.

It seems to me, therefore, that in the end the internalist must argue, as Falk does, not only that externalism involves a gap between obligation and motivation, but that such a gap cannot be tolerated, given morality's task of guiding human conduct autonomously. Then, however, the externalist will counter by pointing out that internalism also entails a danger to morality. Externalism, he will say, in seeking to keep the obligation to act in certain ways independent of the vagaries of individual motivation, runs the risk that motivation may not always be present, let alone adequate, but internalism, in insisting on building in motivation, runs the corresponding risk of having to trim obligation to the size of individual motives.

Here the true character of the opposition appears. Each theory has strengths and weaknesses, and deciding between them involves determining their relative total values as accounts of morality. But such a determination calls for a very broad inquiry. It cannot be based on individual preference. We must achieve "clarity and decision" about the nature and function of morality, of moral discourse, and of moral theory, and this requires not only small-scale analytical inquiries but also studies in the history of ethics and morality, in the relation of morality to society and of society to the individual, as well as in epistemology and in the psychology of human motivation.[45]

The battle, if war there be, cannot be contained; its field is the whole human world, and a grand strategy with a total commitment of forces is demanded of each of its participants. What else could a philosopher expect?

Notes

1. See W.D. Falk, " 'Ought' and Motivation," *Proceedings of the Aristotelian Society*, N.S. XLVIII (1947–48), 137, reprinted in *Readings in Ethical Theory*, ed. W. S. Sellars and J. Hospers (New York: Appleton-Century-Crofts, 1952). The older term "rigorism" would do for externalism, but it has no good opposite for present purposes.

2. I owe this use of the phrase "built into" to my colleague C. L. Stevenson.

3. *Duty and Interest* (Oxford: Oxford University Press, 1928).

4. R. M. Blake, "The Ground of Moral Obligation," *International Journal of Ethics*, XXXVIII (1928), 129–40. Blake was especially concerned about the "internalism," as I call it, of the idealistic ethics of self-realization. See also Falk, " 'Ought' and Motivation," and articles cited below. H. Reiner in *Pflicht und Neigung* (Meisenheim: Westkulturverlag A. Hain, 1951) is dealing with a somewhat different problem.

5. Notice, the question here is about a reference to the interests of the *agent* spoken of, not the interests of the *speaker*.

6. Not all theological theories of obligations are externalistic, for theologies often hold or imply that "the moral law" is law or is obligatory because it is divinely *sanctioned* (i.e., because it is made to our interest to obey), not merely because it is commanded by God.

7. *Moral Theory* (London: Methuen & Co., 1921), pp. 51, 52, 56 f.

8. Cf. F. Hutcheson, "Illustrations on the Moral Sense" (1728), section 1, in *British Moralists*, ed. L. A. Selby-Bigge (2 vols.; Oxford: Clarendon Press, 1897), 1, 403 f.

9. W. T. Stace, *The Concept of Morals* (New York: Macmillan Co., 1937), pp. 41–43.

10. That one may fail to feel any disposition

whatsoever to do what is right cannot simply be asserted, for it is to make an important claim about human nature even on an externalist view.

11. *Ethics* (London: Penguin Books, 1954), pp. 36–43. Nowell-Smith is a non-cognitivist, not a cognitivist as Field and Stace are. There are similar arguments in A. J. Ayer, "On the Analysis of Moral Judgments," *Horizon*, IX (1949), 171 ff.; Alf Ross, "The Logical Status of Value Judgments," *Theoria*, XI (1945), 203–8; R. C. Cross, "Virtue and Nature," *Proceedings of the Aristotelian Society*, N.S. L (1949–50), 123–37; H. Reichenbach, *The Rise of Scientific Philosophy* (Berkeley and Los Angeles: University of California Press, 1954), chap. xvii; R. M. Hare, *The Language of Morals* (Oxford: Clarendon Press, 1952), pp. 30, 79–93, 171; and elsewhere. I do not discuss these writers, however, because they may not be advancing quite the same argument; they seem to be insisting not so much that moral judgments are motivating, as that they are prescriptive. Hence they may not be internalists. But, if they are, then what I say will apply to them, too.

12. A. N. Prior says that Hume was but repeating Cudworth! Cf. *Logic and the Basis of Ethics* (Oxford: Clarendon Press, 1949), p. 33.

13. The famous passage in Hume (*Treatise*, Bk. III, Pt. 1, section 1), often appealed to lately, can be read as stating either of these arguments, but they must not be confused. He himself seems to distinguish it from the more obviously internalistic argument given a few pages earlier; hence he may intend it only in the first sense.

14. As G. E. Moore pointed out in his reply to me, *The Philosophy of G. E. Moore*, ed. P. A. Schilpp (Evanston and Chicago: Northwestern University, 1942), pp. 567 ff.

15. As H. D. Aiken has pointed out. See below.

16. *Moral Theory*, pp. 56 f.

17. Cf. e.g., W. D. Ross, *The Right and the Good* (Oxford: Clarendon Press, 1930), pp. 157 f.

18. "The Emotive Meaning of Ethical Terms," *Mind*, N.S. XL VI (1937), 16.

19. Cf. Also D. C. Williams, "The Meaning of Good," *Philosophical Review*, XLVI (1937), 416–23.

20. "Evaluation and Obligation," *Journal of Philosophy*, XLVII (1950), 5–22, reprinted in *Readings in Ethical Theory*. See also "The Authority of Moral Judgments," *Philosophy and Phenomenological Research*, XII (1951–52), 513. A similar view is present in A. Moore, "A Categorical Imperative?" *Ethics*, LXIII (1952–53), 235–50, to which my criticisms also apply.

21. Cf. *British Moralists*, II, 16.

22. Or, "It is to my interest to do B," or, "B is conducive to my self-realization."

23. Cf. also H. Reiner, *Pflicht und Neigung*.

24. Cf. "Morals without Faith," *Philosophy*, XIX (1944), 7; "Obligation and Rightness," *Philosophy*, XX (1945), 139.

25. *Hume's Moral and Political Philosophy* (New York: Hafner Publishing Co., 1948), p. xxxi.

26. "A Pluralistic Analysis of the Ethical 'Ought,' " *Journal of Philosophy*, XLVIIII (1951), 497.

27. See G. E. Moore, *Principia Ethica* (Cambridge: Cambridge University Press, 1903), pp. 169–70.

28. W. James, "The Moral Philosopher and the Moral Life," in *The Will to Believe* (New York: Longmans, Green & Co., 1897), p. 196. James is inconsistent on this point, for he also says that a man has an obligation as soon as someone else makes a demand on him.

29. "Obligation and Rightness," p. 147.

30. *Ethics*, pp. 210, 320.

31. Cf. *Philosophical Analysis*, ed. M. Black (Ithaca: Cornell University Press, 1950), p. 220.

32. See H. J. N. Horsburgh, "The Criteria of Assent to a Moral Rule," *Mind*, N.S. LXIII

(1954), 345–58; Hare, *The Language of Morals*, pp. 20, 169.

33. Cf. Plato, *Symposium:* R. Price, *Review of the Principal Questions of Morals* (Oxford: Clarendon Press, 1948), chap. iii; W. D. Ross. *The Right and the Good*, pp. 157 f. If the doctrine of total depravity does not imply that we have naturally no disposition *whatsoever* to do what is right, but only that such a disposition as we have to do what is right is always overcome by other desires when it comes into conflict with them, except by the grace of God, then even its proponents can accept (7) as a psychological statement.

34. "Obligation and Rightness," pp. 139–41. Falk also recognizes, however, that externalism "finds some support in common usage" (p. 138).

35. E.g., A. Moore, "A Categorical Imperative?" pp. 237 f.; I discuss a similar claim by S. M. Brown, Jr., in "Natural and Inalienable Rights," *Philosophical Review*, LXIV (1955), 222 f.

36. Cf. Nowell-Smith, *Ethics*, pp. 186 ff., 261; W. S. Sellars, "Obligation and Motivation," in *Readings in Ethical Theory*, p. 516; H. D. Aiken, "Emotive Meanings and Ethical Terms," *Journal of Philosophy*, XLI (1944), 461 ff.; P. B. Rice, *On the Knowledge of Good and Evil* (New York: Random House, 1955), pp. 108 ff., 113, 231 f.

37. *The Right and the Good*, p. 90.

38. Nowell-Smith, *Ethics*, p. 199 (the phrase "contextually implies" is owed to Nowell-Smith); Aiken, "Emotive Meanings and Ethical Terms," pp. 461 ff.

39. Cf. Nowell-Smith, *Ethics*, pp. 146, 152, 178, 261. Note: "I *ought* implies I *shall*" is much stronger than "I *ought* implies I *feel*

some disposition to," and an internalist need not hold the former.

40. *Ibid.*, pp. 261–63, 267 f.

41. It seems to me also to refute *egoistic* forms of internalism.

42. In "The Naturalistic Fallacy," *Mind*, N.S. XLVIII (1939), 464–77, I made a similar point about the issue between naturalism and nonnaturalism, but I then had rather simple-minded views about an appeal to "inspection" which was to decide it.

43. " 'Ought' and Motivation."

44. In "Morals without Faith," Falk distinguished four senses of "should" or "ought," one "moral" but all "internal."

45. Suggestions of such "macroscopic" considerations as I describe here may be found in Nowell-Smith, *Ethics*, chap. i and p. 267; C. L. Stevenson, "The Emotive Conception of Ethics and Its Cognitive Implications." *Philosophical Review*, L (1950), 294 f.; H. D. Aiken, "A Pluralistic Analysis of the Ethical 'Ought' " and "The Authority of Moral Judgments"; and in two less technical works: W. T. Stace, *The Destiny of Western Man* (New York: Reynal & Hitchcock, 1942), and Erich Fromm, *Man for Himself* (New York: Rinehart & Co., 1947). In fact, Field, *Moral Theory*, pp. 51, 52, 56 f., broaches the line of argument sketched in this last section, but in a very incomplete way. Such a macroscopic line of reasoning must also be in W. S. Sellars' mind in "Obligation and Motivation," note 36, as a support for his identification of moral obligation with a certain kind of motivation, though he appears to expound only this conclusion without the supporting argumentation.

30 / ROBERT M. ADAMS

A Modified Divine Command Theory of Ethical Wrongness*

I

It is widely held that all those theories are indefensible which attempt to explain in terms of the will or commands of God what it is for an act to be ethically right or wrong. In this paper I shall state such a theory, which I believe to be defensible; and I shall try to defend it against what seem to me to be the most important and interesting objections to it. I call my theory a *modified* divine command theory because in it I renounce certain claims that are commonly made in divine command analyses of ethical terms. (I should add that it is *my* theory only in that I shall state it, and that I believe it is defensible—not that I am sure it is correct.) I present it as a theory of ethical *wrongness* partly for convenience. It could also be presented as a theory of the nature of ethical obligatoriness or of ethical permittedness. Indeed, I will have occasion to make some remarks about the concept of ethical permittedness. But as we shall see (in section IV) I am not prepared to claim that the theory can be extended to all ethical terms; and it is therefore important that it not be presented as a theory about ethical terms in general.

It will be helpful to begin with the statement of a simple, *unmodified* divine command theory of ethical wrongness. This is the theory that ethical wrongness *consists in* being contrary to God's commands, or that the word 'wrong' in ethical contexts *means* 'contrary to God's commands'. It implies that the following two statement forms are logically equivalent.

(1) It is wrong (for A) to do X.

(2) It is contrary to God's commands (for A) to do X.

Of course that is not all that the theory implies. It also implies that (2) is conceptually prior to (1), so that the meaning of (1) is to be explained in terms of (2), and not the other way around. It might prove fairly difficult to state or explain in what that conceptual priority consists, but I shall not go into that here. I do not wish ultimately to defend the theory in its unmodified form, and I think I have stated it fully enough for my present purposes.

I have stated it as a theory about the meaning of the word 'wrong' in ethical contexts. The most obvious objection to the theory is that the word 'wrong' is used in ethical contexts by many people who cannot mean by it what the theory says they must mean, since they do not believe that there exists a God. This objection seems to me sufficient to refute the theory if it is presented as an analysis of what *everybody* means by 'wrong' in ethical contexts. The theory cannot reasonably be offered except as a theory about what the word 'wrong' means as used by *some but not all* people in ethical contexts. Let us say that the theory

Reprinted by permission of the publisher and copyright holder from Robert. M. Adams, *The Virtue of Faith* (New York: Oxford University Press, 1987), pp. 97–127.
*I am indebted to many who have read, or heard, and discussed versions of this essay, and particularly to Richard Brandt, William Frankena, John Reeder, and Stephen Stich, for helpful criticisms.

offers an analysis of the meaning of 'wrong' in Judeo-Christian religious ethical discourse. This restriction of scope will apply to my modified divine command theory too. This restriction obviously gives rise to a possible objection. Isn't it more plausible to suppose that Judeo-Christian believers use 'wrong' with the same meaning as other people do? This problem will be discussed in section VI.

In section II, I will discuss what seems to me the most important objection to the unmodified divine command theory, and suggest how the theory can be modified to meet it. Section III will be devoted to a brief but fairly comprehensive account of the use of 'wrong' in Judeo-Christian ethical discourse, from the point of view of the modified divine command theory. The theory will be further elaborated in dealing with objections in sections IV to VI. In a seventh and final section, I will note some problems arising from unresolved issues in the general theory of analysis and meaning, and briefly discuss their bearing on the modified divine command theory.

II

The following seems to me to be the gravest objection to the divine command theory of ethical wrongness, in the form in which I have stated it. Suppose God should command me to make it my chief end in life to inflict suffering on other human beings, for no other reason than that he commanded it. (For convenience I shall abbreviate this hypothesis to 'Suppose God should command cruelty for its own sake'.) Will it seriously be claimed that in that case it would be wrong for me not to practice cruelty for its own sake? I see three possible answers to this question.

(1) It might be claimed that it is logically impossible for God to command cruelty for its own sake. In that case, of course, we need not worry about whether it would be wrong to disobey if he did command it. It is senseless to agonize about what one should do in a logically impossible situa-

tion. This solution to the problem seems unlikely to be available to the divine command theorist, however. For why would he hold that it is logically impossible for God to command cruelty for its own sake? Some theologians (for instance, Thomas Aquinas) have believed (a) that what is right and wrong is independent of God's will, *and* (b) that God always does right by the necessity of his nature. Such theologians, if they believe that it would be wrong for God to command cruelty for its own sake, have reason to believe that it is logically impossible for him to do so. But the divine command theorist, who does not agree that what is right and wrong is independent of God's will, does not seem to have such a reason to deny that it is logically possible for God to command cruelty for its own sake.

(2) Let us assume that it is logically possible for God to command cruelty for its own sake. In that case the divine command theory seems to imply that it would be wrong not to practice cruelty for its own sake. There have been at least a few adherents of divine command ethics who have been prepared to accept this consequence. William Ockham held that those acts which we call "theft," "adultery," and "hatred of God" would be meritorious if God had commanded them.[1] He would surely have said the same about what I have been calling the practice of "cruelty for its own sake."

This position is one which I suspect most of us are likely to find somewhat shocking, even repulsive. We should therefore be particularly careful not to misunderstand it. We need not imagine that Ockham disciplined himself to be ready to practice cruelty for its own sake if God should command it. It was doubtless an article of faith for him that God is unalterably opposed to any such practice. The mere logical possibility that theft, adultery, and cruelty might have been commanded by God (and therefore meritorious) doubtless did not represent in Ockham's view any real possibility.

(3) Nonetheless, the view that if God commanded cruelty for its own sake it would be wrong not to practice it seems

unacceptable to me; and I think many, perhaps most, other Jewish and Christian believers would find it unacceptable too. I must make clear the sense in which I find it unsatisfactory. It is not that I find an internal inconsistency in it. And I would not deny that it may reflect, accurately enough, the way in which some believers use the word 'wrong'. I might as well frankly avow that I am looking for a divine command theory which at least might possibly be a correct account of how *I* use the word 'wrong'. I do not use the word 'wrong' in such a way that I would say that it would be wrong not to practice cruelty if God commanded it, and I am sure that many other believers agree with me on this point.

But now have I not rejected the divine command theory? I have assumed that it would be logically possible for God to command cruelty for its own sake. And I have rejected the view that if God commanded cruelty for its own sake, it would be wrong not to obey. It seems to follow that I am committed to the view that in certain logically possible circumstances it would not be wrong to disobey God. This position seems to be inconsistent with the theory that 'wrong' means 'contrary to God's commands'.

I want to argue, however, that it is still open to me to accept a modified form of the divine command theory of ethical wrongness. According to the modified divine command theory, when I say, 'It is wrong to do X', (at least part of) what I *mean* is that it is contrary to God's commands to do X. 'It is wrong to do X' *implies* 'It is contrary to God's commands to do X'. But 'It is contrary to God's commands to do X' implies 'It is wrong to do X' only if certain conditions are assumed—namely, only if it is assumed that God has the character which I believe him to have, of loving his human creatures. If God were really to command us to make cruelty our goal, then he would not have that character of loving us, and I would not say it would be wrong to disobey him.

But do I say that it would be wrong to obey him in such a case? This is the point

at which I am in danger of abandoning the divine command theory completely. I do abandon it completely if I say both of the following things.

(A) It would be wrong to obey God if he commanded cruelty for its own sake.

(B) In (A), 'wrong' is used in what is for me its normal ethical sense.

If I assert both (A) and (B), it is clear that I cannot consistently maintain that 'wrong' in its normal ethical sense for me means or implies 'contrary to God's commands'.

But from the fact that I deny that it would be wrong to disobey God if He commanded cruelty for its own sake, it does not follow that I must accept (A) and (B). Of course someone might claim that obedience and disobedience would both be ethically permitted in such a case; but that is not the view that I am suggesting. If I adopt the modified divine command theory as an analysis of my present concept of ethical wrongness (and if I adopt a similar analysis of my concept of ethical permittedness), I will not hold either that it would be wrong to disobey, or that it would be ethically permitted to disobey, or that it would be wrong to obey, or that it would be ethically permitted to obey, if God commanded cruelty for its own sake. For I will say that my concept of ethical wrongness (and my concept of ethical permittedness) would "break down" if I really believed that God commanded cruelty for its own sake. Or to put the matter somewhat more prosaically, I will say that my concepts of ethical wrongness and permittedness could not serve the functions they now serve, because using those concepts I could not call any action ethically wrong or ethically permitted, if I believed that God's will was so unloving. This position can be explained or developed in either of two ways, each of which has its advantages.

I could say that by 'X is ethically wrong' I mean 'X is contrary to the commands of a *loving* God' (i.e., 'There is a *loving* God and X is contrary to his commands') and by 'X is ethically permitted' I mean 'X is in accord with the commands of a *loving* God' (i.e., 'There is a *loving* God and X is not contrary to his commands'). On this analysis we can reason as follows. If there is only one God and he commands cruelty for its own sake, then presumably there is not a *loving* God. If there is not a loving God then neither 'X is ethically wrong' nor 'X is ethically permitted' is true of any X. Using my present concepts of ethical wrongness and permittedness, therefore, I could not (consistently) call any action ethically wrong or permitted if I believed that God commanded cruelty for its own sake. This way of developing the modified divine command theory is the simpler and neater of the two, and that might reasonably lead one to choose it for the construction of a theological ethical theory. On the other hand, I think it is also simpler and neater than ordinary religious ethical discourse, in which (for example) it may be felt that the statement that a certain act is wrong is *about* the will or commands of God in a way in which it is not about his love.

In this essay I shall prefer a second, rather similar, but somewhat untidier, understanding of the modified divine command theory, because I think it may lead us into some insights about the complexities of actual religious ethical discourse. According to this second version of the theory, the statement that something is ethically wrong (or permitted) says something about the will or commands of God, but not about his love. Every such statement, however, *presupposes* that certain conditions for the applicability of the believer's concepts of ethical right and wrong are satisfied. Among these conditions is that God does not command cruelty for its own sake—or, more generally, that God loves his human creatures. It need not be assumed that God's love is the only such condition.

The modified divine command theorist can say that the possibility of God commanding cruelty for its own sake is not provided for in the Judeo-Christian religious ethical system as he understands it. The

possibility is not provided for, in the sense that the concepts of right and wrong have not been developed in such a way that actions could be correctly said to be right or wrong if God were believed to command cruelty for its own sake. The modified divine command theorist agrees that it is logically possible[2] that God should command cruelty for its own sake; but he holds that it is unthinkable that God should do so. To have *faith* in God is not just to believe that he exists, but also to trust in his love for mankind. The believer's concepts of ethical wrongness and permittedness are developed within the framework of his (or the religious community's) religious life, and therefore within the framework of the assumption that God loves us. The concept of the will or commands of God has a certain function in the believer's life, and the use of the words 'right' (in the sense of 'ethically permitted') and 'wrong' is tied to that function of that concept. But one of the reasons why the concept of the will of God can function as it does is that the love which God is believed to have toward men arouses in the believer certain attitudes of love toward God and devotion to his will. If the believer thinks about the unthinkable but logically possible situation in which God commands cruelty for its own sake, he finds that in relation to that kind of command of God he cannot take up the same attitude, and that the concept of the will or commands of God could not then have the same function in his life. For this reason he will not say that it would be wrong to disobey God, or right to obey him, in that situation. At the same time he will not say that it would be wrong to obey God in that situation, because he is accustomed to use the word 'wrong' to say that something is contrary to the will of God, and it does not seem to him to be the right word to use to express his own personal revulsion toward an act against which there would be no divine authority. Similarly, he will not say that it would be "right" in the sense of 'ethically permitted', to disobey God's command of cruelty; for that does not seem to him to be the right way to express his own personal attitude toward an act which would not be in accord with a divine authority. In this way the believer's concepts of ethical rightness and wrongness would break down in the situation in which he believed that God commanded cruelty for its own sake; that is, they would not function as they now do, because he would not be prepared to use them to say that any action was right or wrong.

III

It is clear that according to this modified divine command theory, the meaning of the word 'wrong' in Judeo-Christian ethical discourse must be understood in terms of a complex of relations which believers' use of the word has, not only to their beliefs about God's commands, but also to their attitudes toward certain types of action. I think it will help us to understand the theory better if we can give a brief but fairly comprehensive description of the most important features of the Judeo-Christian ethical use of 'wrong', from the point of view of the modified divine command theory. That is what I shall try to do in this section.

(1) 'Wrong' and 'contrary to God's commands' at least contextually imply each other in Judeo-Christian ethical discourse. 'It is wrong to do X' will be assented to by the sincere Jewish or Christian believer if and only if he assents to 'It is contrary to God's commands to do X'. This is a fact sufficiently well known that the known believer who says the one commits himself publicly to the other.

Indeed 'wrong' and such expressions as 'against the will of God' seem to be used interchangeably in religious ethical discourse. If a believer asks his pastor, "Do you think it's always against the will of God to use contraceptives?" and the pastor replies, "I don't see anything wrong with the use of contraceptives in many cases," the pastor has answered the same question the inquirer asked.

(2) In ethical contexts, the statement that a certain action is wrong normally expresses certain volitional and emotional attitudes toward that action. In particular it normally expresses an intention, or at least an inclination, not to perform the action, and/or dispositions to feel guilty if one has performed it, to discourage others from performing it, and to react with anger, sorrow, or diminished respect toward others if they have performed it. I think this is true of Judeo-Christian ethical discourse as well as of other ethical discourse.

The interchangeability of 'wrong' and 'against the will of God' applies in full force here. It seems to make no difference to the expressive function of an ethical statement in a Judeo-Christian context which of these expressions is used. So far as I can see, the feelings and dispositions normally expressed by 'It is wrong to commit suicide' in a Judeo-Christian context are exactly the same as those normally expressed by 'It is against God's will to commit suicide', or by 'Suicide is a violation of the commandments of God'.

I am speaking of attitudes *normally* expressed by statements that it is wrong to do a certain thing, or that it would be against God's will or commands to do that thing. I am not claiming that such attitudes are *always* expressed by statements of those sorts. Neither am I now suggesting any analysis of the *meaning* of the statements in terms of the attitudes they normally express. The relation between the meaning of the statements and the attitudes expressed is a matter about which I shall have somewhat more to say, later in this section and in section VI. At this point I am simply observing that in fact statements of the forms 'It is wrong to do X', 'It is against God's will to do X', 'X is a violation of the commandments of God', normally do express certain attitudes, and that in Judeo-Christian ethical discourse they all typically express the same attitudes.

Of course these attitudes can be specified only within certain very wide limits of normality. The experience of guilt, for instance, or the feelings that one has about conduct of others of which one disapproves, vary greatly from one individual to another, and in the same individual from one occasion to another.

(3) In a Judeo-Christian context, moreover, the attitudes expressed by a statement that something is wrong are normally quite strongly affected and colored by specifically religious feelings and interests. They are apt to be motivated in various degrees by, and mixed in various proportions with, love, devotion, and loyalty toward God, and/or fear of God. Ethical wrongdoing is seen and experienced as *sin*, as rupture of personal or communal relationship with God. The normal feelings and experience of guilt for Judeo-Christian believers surely cannot be separated from beliefs, and ritual and devotional practices, having to do with God's judgment and forgiveness.

In all sin there is offense against a person (God), even when there is no offense against any other human person—for instance, if I have a vice which harms me but does not importantly harm any other human being. Therefore in the Judeo-Christian tradition reactions which are appropriate when one has offended another person are felt to be appropriate reactions to any ethical fault, regardless of whether another human being has been offended. I think this affects rather importantly the emotional connections of the word 'wrong' in Judeo-Christian discourse.

(4) When a Judeo-Christian believer is trying to decide, in an ethical way, whether it would be wrong for him to do a certain thing, he typically thinks of himself as trying to determine whether it would be against God's will for him to do it. His deliberations may turn on the interpretation of certain religiously authoritative texts. They may be partly carried out in the form of prayer. It is quite possible, however, that his deliberations will take forms more familiar to the nonbeliever. Possibly his theology will encourage him to give some weight to his own intuitions and feelings about the matter, and those of other people. Such encouragement might be provided, for instance, by a doctrine of the leading of the Holy Spirit. Probably the be-

liever will accept certain very general ethical principles as expressing commandments of God, and most of these may be principles which many nonbelievers would also accept (for instance, that it is always, or with very few exceptions, wrong to kill another human being). The believer's deliberation might consist entirely of reasoning from such general principles. But he would still regard it as an attempt to discover God's will on the matter.

(5) Typically, the Judeo-Christian believer is a nonnaturalist objectivist about ethical wrongness. When he says that something is (ethically) wrong, he means to be stating what he believes to be a fact of a certain sort—what I shall call a "nonnatural objective fact." Such a fact is objective in the sense that whether it obtains or not does not depend on whether any human being thinks it does. It is harder to give a satisfactory explanation of what I mean by 'nonnatural' here. Let us say that a nonnatural fact is one which does not consist simply in any fact or complex of facts which can be stated entirely in the languages of physics, chemistry, biology, and human psychology. That way of putting it obviously raises questions which it leaves unanswered, but I hope it may be clear enough for present purposes.

That ethical facts are objective and nonnatural has been believed by many people, including some famous philosophers—for instance, Plato and G. E. Moore. The term 'nonnaturalism' is sometimes used rather narrowly, to refer to a position held by Moore, and positions closely resembling it. Clearly, I am using 'nonnaturalist' in a broader sense here.

Given that the facts of wrongness asserted in Judeo-Christian ethics are nonnatural in the sense explained above, and that they accordingly do not consist entirely in facts of physics, chemistry, biology, and human psychology, the question arises, in what they do consist. According to the divine command theory (even the modified divine command theory), insofar as they are nonnatural and objective, they consist in facts about the will or commands of God. I think this is really the central point in a divine command theory of ethical wrongness. This is the point at which the divine command theory is distinguished from alternative theological theories of ethical wrongness, such as the theory that facts of ethical rightness and wrongness are objective, nonnatural facts about ideas or essences subsisting eternally in God's understanding, not subject to his will but guiding it.

The divine command account of the non-natural fact-stating function of Judeo-Christian ethical discourse has at least one advantage over its competitors. It is clear, I think, that in stating that X is wrong a believer normally commits himself to the view that X is contrary to the will or commands of God. And the fact (if it is a fact) that X is contrary to the will or commands of God is surely a nonnatural objective fact. But it is not nearly so clear that in saying that X is wrong, the believer normally commits himself to belief in any *other* nonnatural objective fact. (The preceding sentence presupposes the rejection of the Moorean view that the fact that X is wrong[3] is an objective nonnatural fact which cannot and should not be analyzed in terms of other facts, natural or nonnatural.)

(6) The modified divine command theorist cannot consistently claim that 'wrong' and 'contrary to God's commands' have exactly the same meaning for him. For he admits that there is a logically possible situation which he would describe by saying, 'God commands cruelty for its own sake', but not by saying, 'It would be wrong not to practice cruelty for its own sake'. If there were not at least some little difference between the meanings with which he actually, normally uses the expressions 'wrong' and 'contrary to God's commands', there would be no reason for them to differ in their applicability or inapplicability to the far-out unthinkable case. We may now be in a position to improve somewhat our understanding of what the modified divine command theorist can suppose that difference in meaning to be, and of why he supposes that the believer is unwilling to say

that disobedience to a divine command of cruelty for its own sake would be wrong.

We have seen that the expressions 'It is wrong' and 'It is contrary to God's commands' or 'It is against the will of God' have virtually the same uses in religious ethical discourse, and the same functions in the religious ethical life. No doubt they differ slightly in the situations in which they are most likely to be used and the emotional overtones they are most apt to carry. But in all situations experienced or expected by the believer as a believer they at least contextually imply each other, and normally express the same or extremely similar emotional and volitional attitudes.

There is also a difference in meaning, however: a difference which is normally of no practical importance. All three of the following are aspects of the normal use of 'It is wrong' in the life and conversation of believers. (a) It is used to state what are believed to be facts about the will or commands of God. (b) It is used in formulating decisions and arguments about what to do (i.e., not just in deciding what one *ought* to do, but in deciding *what to do*). (c) It expresses certain emotional and volitional attitudes toward the action under discussion. 'It is wrong' is commonly used to do all three of those things at once.

The same is true of 'It is contrary to God's commands' and 'It is against the will of God'. They are commonly used by believers to do the same three things, and to do them at once. But because of their grammatical form and their formal relationships with other straightforwardly descriptive expressions about God, they are taken to be, first and last, descriptive expressions about God and his relation to whatever actions are under discussion. They can therefore be used to state what are supposed to be facts about God, even when one's emotional and decision-making attitude toward those supposed facts is quite contrary to the attitudes normally expressed by the words 'against the will of God'.

In the case of 'It is wrong', however, it is not clear that one of its functions, or one of the aspects of its normal use, is to be preferred in case of conflict with the others. I am not willing to say, 'It would be wrong not to do X', when both my own attitude and the attitude of most other people toward the doing of X under the indicated circumstances is one of unqualified revulsion. On the other hand, neither am I willing to say, 'It would be wrong to do X', when I would merely be expressing my own personal revulsion (and perhaps that of other people as well) but nothing that I could regard as clothed in the majesty of a divine authority. The believer's concept of ethical wrongness therefore breaks down if one tries to apply it to the unthinkable case in which God commands cruelty for its own sake.

None of this seems to me inconsistent with the claim that part of what the believer normally means in saying 'X is wrong' is that X is contrary to God's will or commands.

IV

The modified divine command theory clearly conceives of believers as valuing some things independently of their relation to God's commands. If the believer will not say that it would be wrong not to practice cruelty for its own sake if God commanded it, that is because he values kindness, and has a revulsion for cruelty, in a way that is at least to some extent independent of his belief that God commands kindness and forbids cruelty. This point may be made the basis of both philosophical and theological objections to the modified divine command theory, but I think the objections can be answered.

The philosophical objection is, roughly, that if there are some things I value independently of their relation to God's commands, then my value concepts cannot rightly be analyzed in terms of God's commands. According to the modified divine command theory, the acceptability of divine command ethics depends in part on the believer's independent positive valuation of the sorts of things that God is believed to command. But then, the philosophical critic objects, the believer must have a prior, nontheological conception of ethical right and wrong, in terms of which he judges God's commandments to be acceptable—and to admit that the believer has a prior, nontheological conception of ethical right and wrong is to abandon the divine command theory.

The weakness of this philosophical objection is that it fails to note the distinctions that can be drawn among various value concepts. From the fact that the believer values some things independently of his beliefs about God's commands, the objector concludes, illegitimately, that the believer must have a conception of ethical right and wrong that is independent of his beliefs about God's commands. This inference is illegitimate because there can be valuations which do not imply or presuppose a judgment of ethical right or wrong. For instance, I may simply like something, or want something, or feel a revulsion at something.

What the modified divine command theorist will hold, then, is that the believer values some things independently of their relation to God's commands, but that these valuations are not judgments of ethical right and wrong and do not of themselves imply judgments of ethical right and wrong. He will maintain, on the other hand, that such independent valuations are involved in, or even necessary for, judgments of ethical right and wrong which also involve beliefs about God's will or commands. The adherent of a divine command ethics will normally be able to give reasons for his adherence. Such reasons might include: "Because I am grateful to God for his love"; "Because I find it the most satisfying form of ethical life"; "Because there's got to be an objective moral law if life isn't to fall to pieces, and I can't understand what it would be if not the will of God."[4] As we have already noted, the modified divine command theorist also has reasons why he would not accept a divine command ethics in certain logically possible situations which he believes not to be actual. All of these reasons seem to me to involve valuations that are independent of divine command ethics. The person who has such reasons wants certain things—happiness, certain satisfactions—for himself and others; he hates cruelty and loves kindness; he has perhaps a certain unique and "numinous" awe of God. And these are not attitudes which he has simply because of his beliefs about God's commands.[5] They are not attitudes, however, which presuppose judgments of moral right and wrong.

It is sometimes objected to divine command theories of moral obligation, or of ethical rightness and wrongness, that one must have some reason for obeying God's commands or for adopting a divine command ethics, and that therefore a nontheological concept of moral obligation or of ethical rightness and wrongness must be presupposed, in order that one may judge that one ought to obey God's commands.[6] This objection is groundless. For one can certainly have reasons for doing something which do not involve believing one morally ought to do it or believing it would be ethically wrong not to do it.

I grant that in giving reasons for his attitudes toward God's commands the believer will probably use or presuppose concepts which, in the context, it is reasonable to count as nontheological value concepts (e.g., concepts of satisfactoriness and repulsiveness). Perhaps some of them might count as moral concepts. But all that the defender of a divine command theory of ethical wrongness has to maintain is that the concept of ethical wrongness which occurs in the ethical thought and discourse of believers is not one of the concepts which are used or presupposed in this way. Divine command theorists, including the modified divine command theorist, need not maintain that *all* value concepts, or even all moral concepts, must be understood in terms of God's commands.

In fact some well-known philosophers have held forms of divine command theory which quite explicitly presuppose some nontheological value concepts. Locke, for instance, says in his *Essay,*

> Good and evil . . . are nothing but pleasure or pain, or that which occasions or procures pleasure or pain to us. *Morally good and evil,* then, is only the conformity or disagreement of our voluntary actions to some law, whereby good or evil is drawn on us from the will and power of the lawmaker . . . (*Essay,* II, xxviii, 5)[7].

Locke goes on to distinguish three laws, or types of law, by reference to which actions are commonly judged as to moral good and evil: "(1) The *divine* law. (2) The *civil* law. (3) The law of *opinion* or *reputation*, if I may so call it" (*Essay,* II, xxviii, 7). Of these three Locke says that the third is "the common *measure of virtue and vice*" (*Essay,* II, xxviii, 11). In Locke's opinion the terms 'virtue' and 'vice' are particularly closely attached to the praise and blame of society. But the terms 'duty' and 'sin' are connected with the commandments of God. About the divine law Locke says,

> This is the only true touchstone of *moral rectitude;* and by comparing them to this law, it is that men judge of the most considerable *moral good* or *evil* of their actions: that is, whether, as *duties or sins,* they are like to procure them happiness or misery from the hands of the ALMIGHTY (*Essay,* II, xxviii, 8).

The structure of Locke's analysis is clear enough. By 'good' and 'evil' we *mean* (nontheologically enough) pleasurable and painful. By 'morally good' and 'morally evil' we *mean* that the actions so described agree or disagree with some law under which the agent stands to be rewarded or punished. By 'duty' and 'sin', which denote the most important sort of moral good and evil, we *mean* (theologically now) actions which are apt to cause the agent good or evil (in the nontheological sense) because they agree or disagree with the law of God. I take it that the divine command theory advocated by Peter Geach,[8] and hinted at by G.E.M. Anscombe,[9] is similar in structure, though not in all details, to Locke's.

The modified divine command theory that I have in mind does not rely as heavily as Locke's theory does on God's power to reward and punish, nor do I wish to assume Locke's analysis of 'good' and 'evil'. The point I want to make by discussing Locke here is just that there are many different value concepts and it is clearly possible to give one or more of them a theological analysis while giving others a nontheological analysis. And I do assume that the modified divine command theorist will give a nontheological analysis of some value concepts although he gives a theological analysis of the concept of ethical wrongness. For instance, he may give a nontheological analysis, perhaps a naturalistic one or a noncognitivist one, of the meaning of 'satisfactory' and 'repulsive', as he uses them in some contexts. He may even regard as *moral* concepts some value concepts of which he gives a nontheological analysis.

For it is not essential to a divine command theory of ethical wrongness to maintain that all valuing, or all value concepts, or even all moral concepts, depend on beliefs about God's commands. What is essential to such a theory is to maintain that when a believer says something is (ethically) *wrong*, at least part of what he means is that the action in question is contrary to God's will or commands. Another way of putting the matter is this. What depends on beliefs about God and his will is not all of the religious person's value concepts, nor in general his ability to value things, but only his ability to appraise actions (and possible actions) in terms of their relation to a superhuman, nonnaturally objective, law. Indeed, it is obvious that Judeo-Christian ethics presupposes concepts that have at least ethical overtones and that are not essentially theological but have their background in human social relations and political institutions—such as the concepts of promise, kindness, law, and command. What the specifically theological doctrines introduce into Judeo-Christian ethics, according to the divine command theory, is the belief in a law that is superior to all human laws.

This version of the divine command theory may seem *theologically* objectionable to some believers. One of the reasons, surely, why divine command theories of ethics have appealed to some theologians is that such theories seem especially congruous with the religious demand that God be the object of our highest allegiance. If our supreme commitment in life is to doing what is right just because it is right, and if what is right is right just because God wills or commands it, then surely our highest allegiance is to God. But the modified divine command theory seems not to have this advantage. For the modified divine command theorist is forced to admit, as we have seen, that he has reasons for his adherence to a divine command ethics, and that his having these reasons implies that there are some things which he values independently of his beliefs about God's commands. It is therefore not correct to say of him that he is committed to doing the will of God *just* because it is the will of God; he is committed to doing it partly because of other things which he values independently. Indeed it appears that there are certain logically possible situations in which his present attitudes would not commit him to obey God's commands (for instance, if God commanded cruelty for its own sake). This may even suggest that he values some things, not just independently of God's commands, but more than God's commands.

We have here a real problem in religious ethical motivation. The Judeo-Christian believer is supposed to make God the supreme focus of his loyalties; that is clear. One possible interpretation of this fact is the following. Obedience to whatever God may command is (or at least ought to be) the one thing that the believer values for its own sake and more than anything and everything else. Anything else that he values, he values (or ought to) only to a lesser degree and as a means to obedience to God. This conception of religious ethical motivation is obviously favorable to an *un*modified divine command theory of ethical wrongness.

But I think it is not a realistic conception. Loyalty to God, for instance, is very often explained, by believers themselves, as motivated by gratitude for benefits conferred. And I think it is clear in most cases that the gratitude presupposes that the benefits are valued, at least to some extent, independently of loyalty to God. Similarly, I do not think that most devout Judeo-Christian believers would say that it would be wrong to disobey God if he commanded cruelty for its own sake. And if I am right about that I think it shows that their positive valuation of (emotional/volitional pro-attitude toward) doing *whatever* God may command is not clearly greater than their independent negative valuation of cruelty.

In analyzing ethical motivation in general, as well as Judeo-Christian ethical motivation in particular, it is probably a mistake to suppose that there is (or can be expected to be) one only thing that is valued supremely and for its own sake, with nothing else being valued independently of it. The motivation for a person's ethical orientation in life is normally much more complex than that, and involves a plurality of emotional and volitional attitudes of different sorts which are at least partly independent of each other. At any rate, I think the modified divine command theorist is bound to say that that is true of his ethical motivation.

In what sense, then, can the modified divine command theorist maintain that God is the supreme focus of his loyalties? I suggest the following interpretation of the single-hearted loyalty to God which is demanded in Judeo-Christian religion. In this interpretation the crucial idea is *not* that some one thing is valued for its own sake and more than anything else, and nothing else valued independently of it. It is freely admitted that the religious person will have a plurality of motives for his ethical position, and that these will be at least partly independent of each other. It is admitted further that a desire to obey the commands of God (*whatever* they may be) may not be the strongest of these motives. What will be claimed is that certain beliefs

about God enable the believer to integrate or focus his motives in a loyalty to God and his commands. Some of these beliefs are about what God commands or wills (contingently: that is, although he could logically have commanded or willed something else instead).

Some of the motives in question might be called egoistic; they include desires for satisfactions for oneself—which God is believed to have given or to be going to give. Other motives may be desires for satisfaction for other people—these may be called altruistic. Still other motives might not be desires for anyone's satisfaction, but might be valuations of certain kinds of action for their own sakes—these might be called idealistic. I do not think my argument depends heavily on this particular classification, but it seems plausible that all of these types, and perhaps others as well, might be distinguished among the motives for a religious person's ethical position. Obviously such motives might pull one in different directions, conflicting with one another. But in Judeo-Christian ethics beliefs about what God does in fact will (although he could have willed otherwise) are supposed to enable one to *fuse* these motives, so to speak, into one's devotion to God and his will, so that they all pull together. Doubtless the believer will still have some motives which conflict with his loyalty to God. But the religious ideal is that these should all be merely momentary desires and impulses, and kept under control. They ought not to be allowed to influence voluntary action. The deeper, more stable, and controlling desires, intentions, and psychic energies are supposed to be fused in devotion to God. As I interpret it, however, it need not be inconsistent with the Judeo-Christian ethical and religious ideal that this fusion of motives, this integration of moral energies, depends on belief in certain propositions which are taken to be contingent truths about God.

Lest it be thought that I am proposing unprecedented theological positions, or simply altering Judeo-Christian religious beliefs to suit my theories, I will call to my aid on this point a theologian known for his insistence on the sovereignty of God. Karl Barth seems to me to hold a divine command theory of ethics. But when he raises the question of why we should obey God, he rejects with scorn the suggestion that God's *power* provides the basis for his claim on us. "By deciding for God [man] has definitely decided not to be obedient to power as power."[10] God's claim on us is based rather on his grace. "God calls us and orders us and claims us by being gracious to us in Jesus Christ."[11] I do not mean to suggest that Barth would agree with everything I have said about motivation, or that he offers a lucid account of a divine command theory. But he does agree with the position I have proposed on this point, that the believer's loyalty is not to be construed as a loyalty to God *as* all-powerful, nor to God *whatever* he might conceivably have willed. It is a loyalty to God *as* having a certain attitude toward us, a certain will for us, which God was free not to have, but to which, in Barth's view, he has committed himself irrevocably in Jesus Christ. The believer's devotion is not to merely possible commands of God as such, but to God's actual (and gracious) will.

V

The ascription of moral qualities to God is commonly thought to cause problems for divine command theories of ethics. It is doubted that God, as an agent, can properly be called 'good' in the moral sense if he is not subject to a moral law that is not of his own making. For if he is morally good, mustn't he do what is right *because* it is right? And how can he do that, if what's right is right because he wills it? Or it may be charged that divine command theories trivialize the claim that God is good. If 'X is (morally) good' means roughly 'X does what God wills', then 'God is (morally) good' means only that God does what he wills—which is surely much less than people are normally taken to mean when they say that God is (morally) good. In this sec-

tion I will suggest an answer to these objections.

Surely no analysis of Judeo-Christian ethical discourse can be regarded as adequate which does not provide for a sense in which the believer can seriously assert that God is good. Indeed an adequate analysis should provide a plausible account of what believers do in fact mean when they say, 'God is good'. I believe that a divine command theory of ethical (rightness and) wrongness can include such an account. I will try to indicate its chief features.

(1) In saying 'God is good' one is normally expressing a favorable emotional attitude toward God. I shall not try to determine whether or not this is part of the meaning of 'God is good'; but it is normally, perhaps almost always, at least one of the things one is doing if one says that God is good. If we were to try to be more precise about the type of favorable emotional attitude normally expressed by 'God is good', I suspect we would find that the attitude expressed is most commonly one of *gratitude*.

(2) This leads to a second point, which is that when God is called 'good' it is very often meant that he is *good to us*, or *good to* the speaker. 'Good' is sometimes virtually a synonym for 'kind'. And for the modified divine command theorist it is not a trivial truth that God is kind. In saying that God is good in the sense of 'kind', one presupposes, of course, that there are some things which the beneficiaries of God's goodness value. We need not discuss here whether the beneficiaries must value them independently of their beliefs about God's will. For the modified divine command theorist does admit that there are some things which believers value independently of their beliefs about God's commands. Nothing that the modified divine command theorist says about the meaning of ('right' and) 'wrong' implies that it is a trivial truth that God bestows on his creatures things that they value.

(3) I would not suggest that the descriptive force of 'good' as applied to God is exhausted by the notion of kindness.

'God is good' must be taken in many contexts as ascribing to God, rather generally, qualities of character which the believing speaker regards as virtues in human beings. Among such qualities might be faithfulness, ethical consistency, a forgiving disposition, and, in general, various aspects of love, as well as kindness. Not that there is some definite list of qualities, the ascription of which to God is clearly implied by the claim that God is good. But saying that God is good normally commits one to the position that God has some important set of qualities which one regards as virtues in human beings.

(4) It will not be thought that God has *all* the qualities which are virtues in human beings. Some such qualities are logically inapplicable to a being such as God is supposed to be. For example, aside from certain complications arising from the doctrine of the incarnation, it would be logically inappropriate to speak of God as controlling his sexual desires. (He doesn't have any.) And given some widely held conceptions of God and his relation to the world, it would hardly make sense to speak of him as *courageous*. For if he is impassible and has predetermined absolutely everything that happens, he has no risks to face and cannot endure (because he cannot suffer) pain or displeasure.[12]

Believers in God's goodness also typically think he lacks some human virtues which would *not* be logically inapplicable to a being like him. A virtuous man, for instance, does not intentionally cause the death of other human beings, except under exceptional circumstances. But God has intentionally brought it about that all men die. There are agonizing forms of the problem of evil; but I think that for most Judeo-Christian believers (especially those who believe in life after death), this is not one of them. They believe that God's making men mortal and his commanding them not to kill each other, fit together in a larger pattern of harmonious purposes. How then can one distinguish between human virtues which God must have if he is good and human virtues which God may lack

and still be good? This is an interesting and important question, but I will not attempt here to formulate a precise or adequate criterion for making the distinction. I fear it would require a lengthy digression from the issues with which we are principally concerned.

(5) If we accept a divine command theory of ethical rightness and wrongness, I think we shall have to say that *dutifulness* is a human virtue which, like sexual chastity, is logically inapplicable to God. God cannot either do or fail to do his duty, since he does not have a duty—at least not in the most important sense in which human beings have a duty. For he is not subject to a moral law not of his own making. Dutifulness is one virtuous disposition which men can have that God cannot have. But there are other virtuous dispositions which God can have as well as men. Love, for instance. It hardly makes sense to say that God does what he does *because* it is right. But it does not follow that God cannot have any reason for doing what he does. It does not even follow that he cannot have reasons of a type on which it would be morally virtuous for a man to act. For example, he might do something because he knew it would make his creatures happier.

(6) The modified divine command theorist must deny that in calling God 'good' one presupposes a standard of moral rightness and wrongness superior to the will of God, by reference to which it is determined whether God's character is virtuous or not. And I think he can consistently deny that. He can say that morally virtuous and vicious qualities of character are those which agree and conflict, respectively, with God's commands, and that it is their agreement or disagreement with God's commands that makes them virtuous or vicious. But the believer normally thinks he has at least a general idea of what qualities of character are in fact virtuous and vicious (approved and disapproved by God). Having such an idea, he can apply the word 'good' descriptively to God, meaning that (with some exceptions, as I have noted) God has

the qualities which the believer regards as virtues, such as faithfulness and kindness.

I will sum up by contrasting what the believer can mean when he says, 'Moses is good', with what he can mean when he says, 'God is good', according to the modified divine command theory. When the believer says, 'Moses is good', (a) he normally is expressing a favorable emotional attitude toward Moses (normally, though perhaps not always—sometimes a person's moral goodness displeases us). (b) He normally implies that Moses possesses a large proportion of those qualities of character which are recognized in the religious-ethical community as virtues, and few if any of those which are regarded as vices. (c) He normally implies that the qualities of Moses' character on the basis of which he describes Moses as good are qualities approved by God.

When the believer says, 'God is good', (a) he normally is expressing a favorable emotional attitude toward God, and I think exceptions on this point would be rarer than in the case of statements that a man is good. (b) He normally is ascribing to God certain qualities of character. He may mean primarily that God is kind or benevolent, that he is *good* to human beings or certain ones of them. Or he may mean that God possesses (with some exceptions) those qualities of character which are regarded as virtues in the religious-ethical community. (c) Whereas in saying, 'Moses is good', the believer was stating or implying that the qualities of character which he was ascribing to Moses conform to a standard of ethical rightness which is independent of the will of Moses, he is not stating or implying that the qualities of character which he ascribes to God conform to a standard of ethical rightness which is independent of the will of God.

VI

As I noted at the outset, the divine command theory of ethical wrongness, even in its modified form, has the consequence that

believers and nonbelievers use the word 'wrong' with different meanings in ethical contexts, since it will hardly be thought that nonbelievers mean by 'wrong' what the theory says believers mean by it. This consequence gives rise to an objection. For the phenomena of common moral discourse between believers and nonbelievers suggest that they mean the same thing by 'wrong' in ethical contexts. In the present section I shall try to explain how the modified divine command theorist can account for the facts of common ethical discourse.

I will first indicate what I think the troublesome facts are. Judeo-Christian believers enter into ethical discussions with people whose religious or antireligious beliefs they do not know. It seems to be possible to conduct quite a lot of ethical discourse, with apparent understanding, without knowing one's partner's views on religious issues. Believers also discuss ethical questions with persons who are known to them to be nonbelievers. They agree with such persons, disagree with them, and try to persuade them, about what acts are morally wrong. (Or at least it is normally *said*, by the participants and others, that they agree and disagree about such issues.) Believers ascribe, to people who are known not to believe in God, beliefs that certain acts are morally wrong. Yet surely believers do not suppose that nonbelievers, in calling acts wrong, mean that they are contrary to the will or commandments of God. Under these circumstances how can the believer really mean 'contrary to the will or commandments of God' when he says 'wrong'? If he agrees and disagrees with nonbelievers about what is wrong, if he ascribes to them beliefs that certain acts are wrong, must he not be using 'wrong' in a nontheological sense?

What I shall argue is that in some ordinary (and I fear imprecise) sense of 'mean', what believers and nonbelievers mean by 'wrong' in ethical contexts may well be partly the same and partly different. There are agreements between believers and nonbelievers which make common moral discourse between them possible. But these agreements do not show that the two groups mean exactly the same thing by 'wrong'. They do not show that 'contrary to God's will or commands' is not part of what believers mean by 'wrong'.

Let us consider first the agreements which make possible common moral discourse between believers and nonbelievers.

(1) One important agreement, which is so obvious as to be easily overlooked, is that they use many of the same ethical terms—'wrong', 'right', 'ought', 'duty', and others. And they may utter many of the same ethical sentences, such as 'Racial discrimination is morally wrong'. In determining what people believe we rely very heavily on what they say (when they seem to be speaking sincerely)—and that means, in large part, on the words that they use and the sentences they utter. If I know that somebody says, with apparent sincerity, 'Racial discrimination is morally wrong', I will normally ascribe to him the belief that racial discrimination is morally wrong, even if I also know that he does not mean *exactly* the same thing as I do by 'racial discrimination' or 'morally wrong'. Of course if I know he means something *completely* different, I would not ascribe the belief to him without explicit qualification.

I would not claim that believers and nonbelievers use *all* the same ethical terms. 'Sin', 'law of God', and 'Christian', for instance, occur as ethical terms in the discourse of many believers, but would be much less likely to occur in the same way in nonbelievers' discourse.

(2) The shared ethical terms have the same basic grammatical status for believers as for nonbelievers, and at least many of the same logical connections with other expressions. Everyone agrees, for instance, in treating 'wrong' as an adjective and 'Racial discrimination is morally wrong' as a declarative sentence. '(All) racial discrimination is morally wrong' would be treated by all parties as expressing an A-type (universal affirmative) proposition, from which consequences can be drawn by syllogistic reasoning or the predicate calculus. All agree that if X is morally wrong,

then it isn't morally right and refraining from X is morally obligatory. Such grammatical and formal agreements are important to common moral discourse.

(3) There is a great deal of agreement, among believers and nonbelievers, as to what types of action they call 'wrong' in an ethical sense and I think that that agreement is one of the things that make common moral discourse possible.[13] It is certainly not complete agreement. Obviously there is a lot of ethical disagreement in the world. Much of it cuts right across religious lines, but not all of it does. There are things which are typically called 'wrong' by members of some religious groups, and not by others. Nonetheless there are types of action which everyone or almost everyone would call morally wrong, such as torturing someone to death because he accidentally broke a small window in your house. Moreover any two people (including any one believer and one nonbeliever) are likely to find some actions they both call wrong that not everyone does. I imagine that most ethical discussion takes place among people whose area of agreement in what they call wrong is relatively large.

There is probably much less agreement about the most basic issues in moral theory than there is about many ethical issues of less generality. There is much more unanimity in what people (sincerely) say in answer to such questions as 'Was what Hitler did to the Jews wrong'? or 'Is it normally wrong to disobey the laws of one's country'? than in what they (sincerely) say in answer to such questions as 'Is it always right to do the act which will have the best results'? or 'Is pleasure the only thing that is good for its own sake'? The issue between adherents and nonadherents of divine command ethics is typical of basic issues in ethical and metaethical theory in this respect.

(4) The emotional and volitional attitudes normally expressed by the statement that something is 'wrong' are similar in believers and nonbelievers. They are not exactly the same; the attitudes typically expressed by the believer's statement that

something is 'wrong' are importantly related to his religious practice and beliefs about God, and this doubtless makes them different in some ways from the attitudes expressed by nonbelievers uttering the same sentence. But the attitudes are certainly similar, and that is important for the possibility of common moral discourse.

(5) Perhaps even more important is the related fact that the social functions of a statement that something is (morally) 'wrong' are similar for believers and nonbelievers. To say that something someone else is known to have done is 'wrong' is commonly to attack him. If you say that something you are known to have done is 'wrong', you abandon certain types of defense. To say that a public policy is 'wrong' is normally to register oneself as opposed to it, and is sometimes a signal that one is willing to be supportive of common action to change it. These social functions of moral discourse are extremely important. It is perhaps not surprising that we are inclined to say that two people agree with each other when they both utter the same sentence and thereby indicate their readiness to take the same side in a conflict.

Let us sum up these observations about the conditions which make common moral discourse between believers and nonbelievers possible. (1) They use many of the same ethical terms, such as 'wrong'. (2) They treat those terms as having the same basic grammatical and logical status, and many of the same logical connections with other expressions. (3) They agree to a large extent about what types of action are to be called 'wrong'. To call an action 'wrong' is, among other things, to classify it with certain other actions, and there is considerable agreement between believers and nonbelievers as to what actions those are. (4) The emotional and volitional attitudes which believers and nonbelievers normally express in saying that something is 'wrong' are similar, and (5) saying that something is 'wrong' has much the same social functions for believers and nonbelievers.

So far as I can see, none of this is inconsistent with the modified divine command theory of ethical wrongness. According to that theory there are several things which are true of the believer's use of 'wrong' which cannot plausibly be supposed to be true of the nonbeliever's. In saying 'X is wrong', the believer commits himself (subjectively, at least, and publicly if he is known to be a believer) to the claim that X is contrary to God's will or commandments. The believer will not say that anything would be wrong, under any possible circumstances, if it were not contrary to God's will or commandments. In many contexts he uses the term 'wrong' interchangeably with 'against the will of God' or 'against the commandments of God'. The heart of the modified divine command theory, I have suggested, is the claim that when the believer says, 'X is wrong', one thing he means to be doing is stating a nonnatural objective fact about X, and the nonnatural objective fact he means to be stating is that X is contrary to the will or commandments of God. This claim may be true even though the uses of 'wrong' by believers and nonbelievers are similar in all five of the ways pointed out above.

Suppose these contentions of the modified divine command theory are correct. (I think they are very plausible as claims about the ethical discourse of at least some religious believers.) In that case believers and nonbelievers surely do not mean exactly the same thing by 'X is wrong' in ethical contexts. But neither is it plausible to suppose that they mean entirely different things, given the phenomena of common moral discourse. We must suppose, then, that their meaning is partly the same and partly different. 'Contrary to God's will or commands' must be taken as expressing only part of the meaning with which the believer uses 'wrong'. Some of the similarities between believers' and nonbelievers' use of 'wrong' must also be taken as expressing parts of the meaning with which the believer uses 'wrong'. This view of the matter agrees with the account of the modified divine command theory in section III, where I pointed out that the modified divine command theorist cannot mean exactly the same thing by 'wrong' that he means by 'contrary to God's commands'.

We have here a situation which commonly arises when some people hold, and others do not hold, a given theory about the nature of something which everyone talks about. The chemist, who believes that water is a compound of hydrogen and oxygen, and the man who knows nothing of chemistry, surely do not use the word 'water' in entirely different senses, but neither is it very plausible to suppose that they use it with exactly the same meaning. I am inclined to say that in some fairly ordinary sense of 'mean', a phenomenalist, and a philosopher who holds some conflicting theory about what it is for a physical object to exist, do not mean exactly the same thing by 'There is a bottle of milk in the refrigerator'. But they certainly do not mean entirely different things, and they can agree that there is a bottle of milk in the refrigerator.

VII

These remarks bring us face to face with some important issues in the general theory of analysis and meaning. What are the criteria for determining whether two utterers of the same expression mean exactly the same thing by it, or something partly different, or something entirely different? What is the relation between philosophical analyses, and philosophical theories about the natures of things, on the one hand, and the meanings of terms in ordinary discourse on the other hand? I have permitted myself the liberty of speaking as if these issues did not exist. But their existence is notorious, and I certainly cannot resolve them in this essay. Indeed, I do not have resolutions to offer.

In view of these uncertainties in the theory of meaning, it is worth noting that much of what the modified divine command theorist wants to say can be said without making claims about the *meaning* of ethical terms. He wants to say, for instance, that believers' claims that certain acts are wrong normally express certain attitudes toward those acts, whether or not that is part of their meaning; that an act is wrong if and only if it is contrary to God's will or commands (assuming God loves us); that nonetheless, if God commanded cruelty for its own sake, neither obedience nor disobedience would be ethically wrong or ethically permitted; that if an act is contrary to God's will or commands that is a nonnatural objective fact about it; and that that is the only nonnatural objective fact which obtains if and only if the act is wrong. These are among the most important claims of the modified divine command theory—perhaps they include the very most important. But in the form in which I have just stated them, they are not claims about the *meaning* of ethical terms.

I do not mean to reject the claims about the meanings of terms in religious ethical discourse which I have included in the modified divine command theory. In the absence of general solutions to general problems in the theory of meaning, we may perhaps say what seems to us intuitively plausible in particular cases. That is presumably what the modified divine command theorist is doing when he claims that 'contrary to the will or commands of God' is part of the meaning of '(ethically) wrong' for many Judeo-Christian believers. And I think it is fair to say that if we have found unresolved problems about meaning in the modified divine command theory, they are problems much more about what we mean in general by 'meaning' than about what Judeo-Christian believers mean by 'wrong'.

Notes

1. Guillelmus de Occam, *Super 4 libros sententiarum*, bk. II, qu. 19, O, in vol. IV of his *Opera plurima* (Lyon, 1494–6; réimpression en fac-similé, Farnborough, Hants., England: Gregg Press, 1962). I am not claiming that Ockham held a divine command theory of exactly the same sort that I have been discussing.

2. Perhaps he will even think it is causally possible, but I do not regard any view on that issue as an integral part of the theory. The question whether it is causally possible for God to act 'out of character' is a difficult one, which we need not go into here.

3. Moore took goodness and badness as primitive, rather than rightness and wrongness; but that need not concern us here.

4. The mention of moral law in the last of these reasons may presuppose the ability to *mention* concepts of moral right and wrong, which may or may not be theological and which may or may not be concepts one uses oneself to make judgments of right and wrong. So far as I can see, it does not *presuppose* the *use* of such concepts to make judgments of right and wrong, or one's adoption of them for such use, which is the crucial point here.

5. The independence ascribed to these attitudes is not a *genetic* independence. It may be that the person would not have come to have some of them had it not been for his religious beliefs. The point is that he has come to hold them in such a way that his holding them does not now depend entirely on his beliefs about God's commands.

6. I take A. C. Ewing to be offering an objection of this type on p. 112 of his book *Ethics* (London: English Univs. Press, 1953).

7. I quote from John Yolton's edition of *An Essay Concerning Human Understanding*, 2 vols. (London and New York: Everyman's Library, 1967).

8. In *God and the Soul* (London: Routledge, 1969), ch. 9.

9. In "Modern Moral Philosophy," *Philosophy*, 33 (1958), pp. 1–19.

10. Karl Barth, *Church Dogmatics*, vol. II, pt. 2, trans. G. W. Bromiley and others (Edinburgh: T. & T. Clark, 1957), p. 553.

11. Ibid., p. 560.

12. The argument here is similar to one which is used for another purpose by Ninian Smart in "Omnipotence, Evil, and Superman," *Philosophy*, 36 (1961), reprinted in Nelson Pike, ed., *God and Evil* (Englewood Cliffs, N.J.: Prentice-Hall, 1964), pp. 103–12.

I do not mean to endorse the doctrines of divine impassibility and theological determinism.

13. Cf. Ludwig Wittgenstein, *Philosophical Investigations*, 2d ed. (Oxford: Blackwell, 1958), pt. I, sec. 242: "If language is to be a means of communication there must be agreement not only in definitions but also (queer as this may sound) in judgments." In contemporary society I think it may well be the case that because there is not agreement in ethical definitions, common ethical discourse requires a measure of agreement in ethical judgments. (I do not mean to comment here more broadly on the truth or falsity of Wittgenstein's statement as a statement about the conditions of linguistic communication in general.)

PART VI

THE VALUE
AND MEANING
OF LIFE

31 / LEO TOLSTOY

My Confession

Although I regarded authorship as a waste of time, I continued to write during those fifteen years. I had tasted of the seduction of authorship, of the seduction of enormous monetary remunerations and applauses for my insignificant labour, and so I submitted to it, as being a means for improving my material condition and for stifling in my soul all questions about the meaning of my life and life in general.

In my writings I advocated, what to me was the only truth, that it was necessary to live in such a way as to derive the greatest comfort for oneself and one's family.

Thus I proceeded to live, but five years ago something very strange began to happen with me: I was overcome by minutes at first of perplexity and then of an arrest of life, as though I did not know how to live or what to do, and I lost myself and was dejected. But that passed, and I continued to live as before. Then those minutes of perplexity were repeated oftener and oftener, and always in one and the same form. These arrests of life found their expression in ever the same questions: "Why? Well, and then?"

At first I thought that those were simply aimless, inappropriate questions. It seemed to me that that was all well known and that if I ever wanted to busy myself with their solution, it would not cost me much

labour,—that now I had no time to attend to them, but that if I wanted to I should find the proper answers. But the questions began to repeat themselves oftener and oftener, answers were demanded more and more persistently, and, like dots that fall on the same spot, these questions, without any answers, thickened into one black blotch.

There happened what happens with any person who falls ill with a mortal internal disease. At first there appear insignificant symptoms of indisposition, to which the patient pays no attention; then these symptoms are repeated more and more frequently and blend into one temporally indivisible suffering. The suffering keeps growing, and before the patient has had time to look around, he becomes conscious that what he took for an indisposition is the most significant thing in the world to him,—is death.

The same happened with me. I understood that it was not a passing indisposition, but something very important, and that, if the questions were going to repeat themselves, it would be necessary to find an answer for them. And I tried to answer them. The questions seemed to be so foolish, simple, and childish. But the moment I touched them and tried to solve them, I became convinced, in the first place, that they were not childish and foolish, but very important and profound questions in life, and, in the second, that, no matter how much I might try, I should not be able to answer them. Before attending to my Samára estate, to my son's education, or to the writing of a book, I ought to know why I should do that. So long as I did not

Reprinted by permission of the publisher and copyright holder from Leo Tolstoy, *My Confession*, trans. Leo Weiner (London: J. M. Dent & Sons, 1905). The following selection follows that in Steven Sanders and David R. Cheney, *The Meaning of Life: Questions, Answers and Analysis* (Englewood Cliffs, N.J.: Prentice-Hall, 1980).

know why, I could not do anything. I could not live. Amidst my thoughts of farming, which interested me very much during that time, there would suddenly pass through my head a question like this: "All right, you are going to have six thousand desyatínas of land in the Government of Samára, and three hundred horses,—and then?" And I completely lost my senses and did not know what to think farther. Or, when I thought of the education of my children, I said to myself: "Why?" Or, reflecting on the manner in which the masses might obtain their welfare, I suddenly said to myself: "What is that to me?" Or, thinking of the fame which my works would get me, I said to myself: "All right, you will be more famous than Gógol, Púshkin, Shakespeare, Moliére, and all the writers in the world,— what of it?" And I was absolutely unable to make any reply. The questions were not waiting, and I had to answer them at once; if I did not answer them, I could not live.

I felt that what I was standing on had given way, that I had no foundation to stand on, that that which I lived by no longer existed, and that I had nothing to live by. . . .

All that happened with me when I was on every side surrounded by what is considered to be complete happiness. I had a good, loving, and beloved wife, good children, and a large estate, which grew and increased without any labour on my part. I was respected by my neighbours and friends, more than ever before, was praised by strangers, and, without any self-deception, could consider my name famous. With all that, I was not deranged or mentally unsound,—on the contrary, I was in full command of my mental and physical powers, such as I had rarely met with in people of my age: physically I could work in a field, mowing, without falling behind a peasant; mentally I could work from eight to ten hours in succession, without experiencing any consequences from the strain. And while in such condition I arrived at the conclusion that I could not live, and, fearing death, I had to use cunning against myself, in order that I might not take my life.

This mental condition expressed itself to me in this form: my life is a stupid, mean trick played on me by somebody. Although I did not recognize that "somebody" as having created me, the form of the conception that some one had played a mean, stupid trick on me by bringing me into the world was the most natural one that presented itself to me.

Involuntarily I imagined that there, somewhere, there was somebody who was now having fun as he looked down upon me and saw me, who had lived for thirty or forty years, learning, developing, growing in body and mind, now that I had become strengthened in mind and had reached that summit of life from which it lay all before me, standing as a complete fool on that summit and seeing clearly that there was nothing in life and never would be. And that was fun to him—

But whether there was or was not that somebody who made fun of me, did not make it easier for me. I could not ascribe any sensible meaning to a single act, or to my whole life. I was only surprised that I had not understood that from the start. All that had long ago been known to everybody. Sooner or later there would come diseases and death (they had come already) to my dear ones and to me, and there would be nothing left but stench and worms. All my affairs, no matter what they might be, would sooner or later be forgotten, and I myself should not exist. So why should I worry about all these things? How could a man fail to see that and live,—that was surprising! A person could live only so long as he was drunk; but the moment he sobered up, he could not help seeing that all that was only a deception, and a stupid deception at that! Really, there was nothing funny and ingenious about it, but only something cruel and stupid.

Long ago has been told the Eastern story about the traveller who in the steppe is overtaken by an infuriated beast. Trying to save himself from the animal, the traveller jumps into a waterless well, but at its bottom he sees a dragon who opens his jaws in order to swallow him. And the unfortunate man does not dare climb out, lest he perish from the infuriated beast, and does not dare jump down to the bottom of the well, lest he be devoured by the dragon, and so clutches the twig of a wild bush growing in a cleft of the well and holds on to it. His hands grow weak and he feels that soon he shall have to surrender to the peril which awaits him at either side; but he still holds on and sees two mice, one white, the other black, in even measure making a circle around the main trunk of the bush to which he is clinging, and nibbling at it on all sides. Now, at any moment, the bush will break and tear off, and he will fall into the dragon's jaws. The traveller sees that and knows that he will inevitably perish; but while he is still clinging, he sees some drops of honey hanging on the leaves of the bush, and so reaches out for them with his tongue and licks the leaves. Just so I hold on to the branch of life, knowing that the dragon of death is waiting inevitably for me, ready to tear me to pieces, and I cannot understand why I have fallen on such suffering. And I try to lick that honey which used to give me pleasure; but now it no longer gives me joy, and the white and the black mouse day and night nibble at the branch to which I am holding on. I clearly see the dragon, and the honey is no longer sweet to me. I see only the inevitable dragon and the mice, and am unable to turn my glance away from them. That is not a fable, but a veritable, indisputable, comprehensible truth.

The former deception of the pleasures of life, which stifled the terror of the dragon, no longer deceives me. No matter how much one should say to me, "You cannot understand the meaning of life, do not think, live!" I am unable to do so, because I have been doing it too long before. Now I cannot help seeing day and night, which run and lead me up to death. I see that alone, because that alone is the truth. Everything else is a lie.

The two drops of honey that have longest turned my eyes away from the cruel truth, the love of family and of authorship, which I have called an art, are no longer sweet to me.

"My family—" I said to myself, "but my family, my wife and children, they are also human beings. They are in precisely the same condition that I am in: they must either live in the lie or see the terrible truth. Why should they live? Why should I love them, why guard, raise, and watch them? Is it for the same despair which is in me, or for dulness of perception? Since I love them, I cannot conceal the truth from them,—every step in cognition leads them up to this truth. And the truth is death."

"Art, poetry?" For a long time, under the influence of the success of human praise, I tried to persuade myself that that was a thing which could be done, even though death should come and destroy everything, my deeds, as well as my memory of them; but soon I came to see that that, too, was a deception. It was clear to me that art was an adornment of life, a decoy of life. But life lost all its attractiveness for me. How, then, could I entrap others? So long as I did not live my own life, and a strange life bore me on its waves; so long as I believed that life had some sense, although I was not able to express it,—the reflections of life of every description in poetry and in the arts afforded me pleasure, and I was delighted to look at life through this little mirror of art; but when I began to look for the meaning of life, when I experienced the necessity of living myself, that little mirror became either useless, superfluous, and ridiculous, or painful to me. I could no longer console myself with what I saw in the mirror, namely, that my situation was stupid and desperate. It was all right for me to rejoice so long as I believed in the depth of my soul that life had some sense. At that time the play of lights—of the comical, the tragical, the touching, the beautiful, the terrible in life—afforded me amusement. But when I knew that life was meaningless and terrible, the play in the little mirror could no longer amuse me. No sweetness of honey could be sweet to me, when, I saw the dragon and the mice that were nibbling down my support. . . .

In my search after the question of life I experienced the same feeling which a man who has lost his way in the forest may experience.

He comes to a clearing, climbs a tree, and clearly sees an unlimited space before him; at the same time he sees that there are no houses there, and that there can be none; he goes back to the forest, into the darkness, and he sees darkness, and again there are no houses.

Thus I blundered in this forest of human knowledge, between the clearings of the mathematical and experimental sciences, which disclosed to me clear horizons, but such in the direction of which there could be no house, and between the darkness of the speculative sciences, where I sunk into a deeper darkness, the farther I proceeded, and I convinced myself at last that there was no way out and could not be.

By abandoning myself to the bright side of knowledge I saw that I only turned my eyes away from the question. No matter how enticing and clear the horizons were that were disclosed to me, no matter how enticing it was to bury myself in the infinitude of this knowledge, I comprehended that these sciences were the more clear, the less I needed them, the less they answered my question.

"Well, I know," I said to myself, "all which science wants so persistently to know, but there is no answer to the question about the meaning of my life." But in the speculative sphere I saw that, in spite of the fact that the aim of the knowledge was directed straight to the answer of my question, or because of that fact, there could be no other answer than what I was giving to myself: "What is the meaning of my life?"—"None." Or, "What will come of my life?"—"Nothing." Or, "Why does everything which exists exist, and why do I exist?"—"Because it exists."

Putting the question to the one side of human knowledge, I received an endless quantity of exact answers about what I did not ask: about the chemical composition of the stars, about the movement of the sun toward the constellation of Hercules, about the origin of species and of man, about the forms of infinitely small, imponderable particles of ether; but the answer in this sphere of knowledge to my question what the meaning of my life was, was always: "You are what you call your life; you are a temporal, accidental conglomeration of particles. The interrelation, the change of these particles, produces in you that which you call life. This congeries will last for some time; then the interaction of these particles will cease, and that which you call life and all your questions will come to an end. You are an accidentally cohering globule of something. The globule is fermenting. This fermentation the globule calls its life. The globule falls to pieces, and all fermentation and all questions will come to an end." Thus the clear side of knowledge answers, and it cannot say anything else, if only it strictly follows its principles.

With such an answer it appears that the answer is not a reply to the question. I want to know the meaning of my life, but the fact that it is a particle of the infinite not only gives it no meaning, but even destroys every possible meaning.

Those obscure transactions, which this side of the experimental, exact science has with speculation, when it says that the meaning of life consists in evolution and the coöperation with this evolution, because of their obscurity and inexactness cannot be regarded as answers.

The other side of knowledge, the speculative, so long as it sticks strictly to its fundamental principles in giving a direct answer to the question, everywhere and at all times has answered one and the same: "The world is something infinite and incomprehensible. Human life is an incomprehensible part of this incomprehensible all. . . ."

I lived for a long time in this madness, which, not in words, but in deeds, is particularly characteristic of us, the most liberal and learned of men. But, thanks either to my strange, physical love for the real working class, which made me understand it and see that it is not so stupid as we suppose, or to the sincerity of my conviction, which was that I could know nothing and that the best that I could do was to hang myself,—I felt that if I wanted to live and understand the meaning of life, I ought naturally to look for it, not among those who had lost the meaning of life and wanted to kill themselves, but among those billions departed and living men who had been carrying their own lives and ours upon their shoulders. And I looked around at the enormous masses of deceased and living men,—not learned and wealthy, but simple men,—and I saw something quite different. I saw that all these billions of men that lived or had lived, all, with rare exceptions, did not fit into my subdivisions, and that I could not recognize them as not understanding the question, because they themselves put it and answered it with surprising clearness. Nor could I recognize them as Epicureans, because their lives were composed rather of privations and suffering than of enjoyment. Still less could I recognize them as senselessly living out their meaningless lives, because every act of theirs and death itself was explained by them. They regarded it as the greatest evil to kill themselves. It appeared, then, that all humanity was in possession of a knowledge of the meaning of life, which I did not recognize and which I contemned. It turned out that rational knowledge did not give any meaning to life, excluded life, while the meaning which by billions of people, by all humanity, was ascribed to life was based on some despised, false knowledge.

The rational knowledge in the person of the learned and the wise denied the meaning of life, but the enormous masses of men, all humanity, recognized this meaning in an irrational knowledge. This irrational knowledge was faith, the same that I could not help but reject. That was God as one and three, the creation in six days, devils and angels, and all that which I could not accept so long as I had not lost my senses.

My situation was a terrible one. I knew that I should not find anything on the path of rational knowledge but the negation of life, and there, in faith, nothing but the negation of reason, which was still more impossible than the negation of life. From the rational knowledge it followed that life was an evil and men knew it,—it depended on men whether they should cease living, and yet they lived and continued to live, and I myself lived, though I had known long ago that life was meaningless and an evil. From faith it followed that, in order to understand life, I must renounce reason, for which alone a meaning was needed.

There resulted a contradiction, from which there were two ways out: either what I called rational was not so rational as I had thought; or that which to me appeared irrational was not so irrational as I had thought. And I began to verify the train of thoughts of my rational knowledge.

In verifying the train of thoughts of my rational knowledge, I found that it was quite correct. The deduction that life was nothing was inevitable; but I saw a mistake. The mistake was that I had not reasoned in conformity with the question put by me. The question was, "Why should I live?" that is, "What real, indestructible essence will come from my phantasmal; destructible life? What meaning has my finite existence in this infinite world?" And in order to answer this question, I studied life.

The solutions of all possible questions of life apparently could not satisfy me, because my question, no matter how simple it appeared in the beginning, included the necessity of explaining the finite through the infinite, and vice versa.

I asked, "What is the extra-temporal, extra-causal, extra-spatial meaning of life?" But I gave an answer to the question, "What is the temporal, causal, spatial meaning of my life?" The result was that after a long labour of mind I answered, "None."

In my reflections I constantly equated, nor could I do otherwise, the finite with the finite, the infinite with the infinite, and so from that resulted precisely what had to result: force was force, matter was matter, will was will, infinity was infinity, nothing was nothing,—and nothing else could come from it.

There happened something like what at times takes place in mathematics: you think you are solving an equation, when you have only an identity. The reasoning is correct, but you receive as a result the answer: $a = a$, or $x = x$, or $0 = 0$. The same happened with my reflection in respect to the question about the meaning of my life. The answers given by all science to that question are only identities.

Indeed, the strictly scientific knowledge, that knowledge which, as Descartes did, begins with a full doubt in everything, rejects all knowledge which has been taken on trust, and builds everything anew on the laws of reason and experience, cannot give any other answer to the question of life than what I received,—an indefinite answer. It only seemed to me at first that science gave me a positive answer,—Schopenhauer's answer: "Life has no meaning, it is an evil." But when I analyzed the matter, I saw that the answer was not a positive one, but that it was only my feeling which expressed it as such. The answer, strictly expressed, as it is expressed by the Brahmins, by Solomon, and by Schopenhauer, is only an indefinite answer, or an identity, $0 = 0$, life is nothing. Thus the philosophical knowledge does not negate anything, but only answers that the question cannot be solved by it, that for philosophy the solution remains insoluble.

When I saw that, I understood that it was not right for me to look for an answer to my question in rational knowledge, and that the answer given by rational knowledge was only an indication that the answer might be got if the question were differently put, but only when into the discussion of the question should be introduced the question of the relation of the finite to the infinite. I also understood that, no matter how irrational and monstrous the answers might be that faith gave, they had this advantage that they introduced into each answer the relation of the finite

to the infinite, without which there could be no answer.

No matter how I may put the question, "How must I live?" the answer is, "According to God's law." "What real result will there be from my life?"—"Eternal torment or eternal bliss." "What is the meaning which is not destroyed by death?"—"The union with infinite God, paradise."

Thus, outside the rational knowledge, which had to me appeared as the only one, I was inevitably led to recognize that all living humanity had a certain other irrational knowledge, faith, which made it possible to live.

All the irrationality of faith remained the same for me, but I could not help recognizing that it alone gave to humanity answers to the questions of life, and, in consequence of them, the possibility of living.

The rational knowledge brought me to the recognition that life was meaningless,—my life stopped, and I wanted to destroy myself. When I looked around at people, at all humanity, I saw that people lived and asserted that they knew the meaning of life. I looked back at myself: I lived so long as I knew the meaning of life. As to other people, so even to me, did faith give the meaning of life and the possibility of living.

Looking again at the people of other countries, contemporaries of mine and those passed away, I saw again the same. Where life had been, there faith, ever since humanity had existed, had given the possibility of living, and the chief features of faith were everywhere one and the same.

No matter what answers faith may give, its every answer gives to the finite existence of man the sense of the infinite,—a sense which is not destroyed by suffering, privation, and death. Consequently in faith alone could we find the meaning and possibility of life. What, then, was faith? I understood that faith was not merely an evidence of things not seen, and so forth, not revelation (that is only the description of one of the symptoms of faith), not the relation of man to man (faith has to be defined, and then God, and not first God, and faith through him), not merely an agreement with what a man was told, as faith was generally understood,—that faith was the knowledge of the meaning of human life, in consequence of which man did not destroy himself, but lived. Faith is the power of life. If a man lives he believes in something. If he did not believe that he ought to live for some purpose, he would not live. If he does not see and understand the phantasm of the finite, he believes in that finite; if he understands the phantasm of the finite, he must believe in the infinite. Without faith one cannot live. . . .

In order that all humanity may be able to live, in order that they may continue living, giving a meaning to life, they, those billions, must have another, a real knowledge of faith, for not the fact that I, with Solomon and Schopenhauer, did not kill myself convinced me of the existence of faith, but that these billions had lived and had borne us, me and Solomon, on the waves of life.

Then I began to cultivate the acquaintance of the believers from among the poor, the simple and unlettered folk, of pilgrims, monks, dissenters, peasants. The doctrine of these people from among the masses was also the Christian doctrine that the quasi-believers of our circle professed. With the Christian truths were also mixed in very many superstitions, but there was this difference: the superstitions of our circle were quite unnecessary to them, had no connection with their lives, were only a kind of an Epicurean amusement, while the superstitions of the believers from among the labouring classes were to such an extent blended with their life that it would have been impossible to imagine it without these superstitions,—it was a necessary condition of that life. I began to examine closely the lives and beliefs of these people, and the more I examined them, the more did I become convinced that they had the real faith, that their faith was necessary for them, and that it alone gave them a meaning and possibility of life. In con-

tradistinction to what I saw in our circle, where life without faith was possible, and where hardly one in a thousand professed to be a believer, among them there was hardly one in a thousand who was not a believer. In contradistinction to what I saw in our circle, where all life passed in idleness, amusements, and tedium of life, I saw that the whole life of these people was passed in hard work, and that they were satisfied with life. In contradistinction to the people of our circle, who struggled and murmured against fate because of their privations and their suffering, these people accepted diseases and sorrows without any perplexity or opposition, but with the calm and firm conviction that it was all for good. In contradistinction to the fact that the more intelligent we are, the less do we understand the meaning of life and the more do we see a kind of a bad joke in our suffering and death, these people live, suffer, and approach death, and suffer in peace and more often in joy. In contradistinction to the fact that a calm death, a death without terror or despair, is the greatest exception in our circle, a restless, insubmissive, joyless death is one of the greatest exceptions among the masses. And of such people, who are deprived of everything which for Solomon and for me constitutes the only good of life, and who withal experience the greatest happiness, there is an enormous number. I cast a broader glance about me. I examined the life of past and present vast masses of men, and I saw people who in like manner had understood the meaning of life, who had known how to live and die, not two, not three, not ten, but hundreds, thousands, millions. All of them, infinitely diversified as to habits, intellect, culture, situation, all equally and quite contrary to my ignorance knew the meaning of life and of death, worked calmly, bore privations and suffering, lived and died, seeing in that not vanity, but good.

I began to love those people. The more I penetrated into their life, the life of the men now living, and the life of men departed, of whom I had read and heard, the more did I love them, and the easier it became for me to live. Thus I lived for about two years, and within me took place a transformation, which had long been working within me, and the germ of which had always been in me. What happened with me was that the life of our circle,—of the rich and the learned,—not only disgusted me, but even lost all its meaning. All our acts, reflections, sciences, arts,—all that appeared to me in a new light. I saw that all that was mere pampering of the appetites, and that no meaning could be found in it; but the life of all the working masses, of all humanity, which created life, presented itself to me in its real significance. I saw that there was life itself and that the meaning given to this life was truth, and I accepted it.

32 / PAUL EDWARDS

MEANING AND VALUE OF LIFE

To the questions "Is human life ever worthwhile?" and "Does (or can) human life have any meaning?" many religious thinkers have offered affirmative answers with the proviso that these answers would not be justified unless two of the basic propositions of most Western religions were true—that human life is part of a divinely ordained cosmic scheme and that after death at least some human beings will be rewarded with eternal bliss. Thus, commenting on Bertrand Russell's statement that not only must each individual human life come to an end but that life in general will eventually die out, C. H. D. Clark contrasts this "doctrine of despair" with the beauty of the Christian scheme. "If we are asked to believe that all our striving is without final consequence," then "life is meaningless and it scarcely matters how we live if all will end in the dust of death." According to Christianity, on the other hand, "each action has vital significance." Clark assures us that "God's grand design is life eternal for those who walk in the steps of Christ. Here is the one grand incentive to good living. . . . As life is seen to have purpose and meaning, men find release from despair and the fear of death" (*Christianity and Bertrand Russell*, p. 30). In a similar vein, the Jewish existentialist Emil Fackenheim claims that "whatever meaning life acquires" is derived from the encounter between God and man. The meaning thus

Reprinted by permission of the publisher and copyright holder from *The Encyclopedia of Philosophy*, vol. 4, ed. Paul Edwards (New York: Macmillan, 1967), pp. 467–477.

conferred upon human life "cannot be understood in terms of some finite human purpose, supposedly more ultimate than the meeting itself. For what could be more ultimate than the Presence of God?" It is true that God is not always "near," but "times of Divine farness" are by no means devoid of meaning. "Times of Divine nearness do not light up themselves alone. Their meaning extends over all of life." There is a "dialectic between Divine nearness and Divine farness," and it points to "an eschatological future in which it is overcome" ("Judaism and the Meaning of Life").

Among unbelievers not a few maintain that life can be worthwhile and have meaning in some humanly important sense even if the religious world view is rejected. Others, however, agree with the religious theorists that our two questions must be given negative answers if there is no God and if death means personal annihilation. Having rejected the claims of religion, they therefore conclude that life is not worthwhile and that it is devoid of meaning. These writers, to whom we shall refer here as "pessimists," do not present their judgments as being merely expressions of certain moods or feelings but as conclusions that are in some sense objectively warranted. They offer reasons for their conclusions and imply that anybody reaching a contradictory conclusion is mistaken or irrational. Most pessimists do not make any clear separation between the statements that life is not worthwhile and that life is without meaning. They usually speak of the "futility" or the "vanity" of life, and presumably they mean by this both that life is not worth living and that it has no meaning. For the time being we, too, shall treat these statements as if they were equivalent. However, later we shall see that in certain contexts it becomes important to distinguish between them.

Our main concern in this article will be to appraise pessimism as just defined. We shall not discuss either the question whether life is part of a divinely ordained plan or the question whether we survive our bodily death. Our question will be whether the pessimistic conclusions are justified if belief in God and immortality are rejected.

Schopenhauer's Arguments

Let us begin with a study of the arguments offered by the pessimists, remembering that many of these are indirectly endorsed by religious apologists. The most systematic and probably the most influential, though in fact not the gloomiest, of the pessimists was Schopenhauer. The world, he wrote, is something which ought not to exist: the truth is that "we have not to rejoice but rather to mourn at the existence of the world; that its non-existence would be preferable to its existence; that it is something which ought not to be." It is absurd to speak of life as a gift, as so many philosophers and thoughtless people have done. "It is evident that everyone would have declined such a gift if he could have seen it and tested it beforehand." To those who assure us that life is only a lesson, we are entitled to reply: "For this very reason I wish I had been left in the peace of the all-sufficient nothing, where I would have no need of lessons or of anything else" (*The World as Will and Idea*, Vol. III, p. 390).

Schopenhauer offers numerous arguments for his conclusion. Some of these are purely metaphysical and are based on his particular system. Others, however, are of a more empirical character and are logically independent of his brand of metaphysical voluntarism. Happiness, accord-

ing to Schopenhauer, is unobtainable for the vast majority of mankind. "Everything in life shows that earthly happiness is destined to be frustrated or recognized as illusion." People either fail to achieve the ends they are striving for or else they do achieve them only to find them grossly disappointing. But as soon as a man discovers that a particular goal was not really worth pursuing, his eye is set on a new one and the same illusory quest begins all over again. Happiness, accordingly, always lies in the future or in the past, and "the present may be compared to a small dark cloud which the wind drives over the sunny plain: before and behind it all is bright, only it itself always casts a shadow. The present is therefore always insufficient; but the future is uncertain, and the past is irrevocable" (*ibid.*, p. 383). Men in general, except for those sufficiently rational to become totally resigned, are constantly deluded—"now by hope, now by what was hoped for." They are taken in by "the enchantment of distance," which shows them "paradises." These paradises, however, vanish like "optical illusions when we have allowed ourselves to be mocked by them." The "fearful envy" excited in most men by the thought that somebody else is genuinely happy shows how unhappy they really are, whatever they pretend to others or to themselves. It is only "because they feel themselves unhappy" that "men cannot endure the sight of one whom they imagine happy."

On occasions Schopenhauer is ready to concede that some few human beings really do achieve "comparative" happiness, but this is not of any great consequence. For aside from being "rare exceptions," these happy people are really like "decoy birds"—they represent a possibility which must exist in order to lure the rest of mankind into a false sense of hope. Moreover, happiness, insofar as it exists at all, is a purely "negative" reality. We do not become aware of the greatest blessings of life—health, youth, and freedom—until we have lost them. What is called pleasure or satisfaction is merely the absence of craving or pain. But craving and pain are positive. As for the few happy days of our life—if there are any—we notice them only "after they have given place to unhappy ones."

Schopenhauer not infrequently lapsed from his doctrine of the "negative" nature of happiness and pleasure into the more common view that their status is just as "positive" as that of unhappiness and pain. But he had additional arguments which do not in any way depend on the theory that happiness and pleasure are negative. Perhaps the most important of these is the argument from the "perishableness" of all good things and the ultimate extinction of all our hopes and achievements in death. All our pleasures and joys "disappear in our hands, and we afterwards ask astonished where they have gone." Moreover, a joy which no longer exists does not "count"—it counts as little as if it had never been experienced at all:

> That which *has been* exists no more; it exists as little as that which has *never* been. But of everything that exists you may say, in the next moment, that it has been. Hence something of great importance in our past is inferior to something of little importance in our present, in that the latter is a *reality*, and related to the former as something to nothing. ("The Vanity of Existence," in *The Will to Live,* p. 229)

Some people have inferred from this that the enjoyment of the present should be "the supreme object of life." This is fallacious; for "that which in the next moment exists no more, and vanishes utterly, like a dream, can never be worth a serious effort."

The final "judgment of nature" is destruction by death. This is "the last proof" that life is a "false path," that all man's wishing is "a perversity," and that "nothing at all is worth our striving, our efforts and struggles." The conclusion is inescapable: "All good things are vanity, the world in all its ends bankrupt, and life a business which does not cover its ex-

penses" (*The World as Will and Idea,* Vol. III p. 383).

The Pointlessness Of It All

Some of Schopenhauer's arguments can probably be dismissed as the fantasies of a lonely and embittered man who was filled with contempt for mankind and who was singularly incapable of either love or friendship. His own misery, it may be plausibly said, made Schopenhauer overestimate the unhappiness of human beings. It is frequently, but not universally, true that what is hoped for is found disappointing when it is attained, and while "fearful envy" of other people's successes is common enough, real sympathy and generosity are not quite so rare as Schopenhauer made them out to be. Furthermore, his doctrine that pleasure is negative while pain is positive, insofar as one can attach any clear meaning to it, seems glaringly false. To this it should be added, however, that some of Schopenhauer's arguments are far from idiosyncratic and that substantially the same conclusions have been endorsed by men who were neither lonely nor embittered and who did not, as far as one can judge, lack the gift of love or friendship.

Darrow

Clarence Darrow, one of the most compassionate men who ever lived, also concluded that life was an "awful joke." Like Schopenhauer, Darrow offered as one of his reasons the apparent aimlessness of all that happens. "This weary old world goes on, begetting, with birth and with living and with death," he remarked in his moving plea for the boy-murderers Loeb and Leopold, "and all of it is blind from the beginning to the end" (*Clarence Darrow—Attorney for the Damned,* A. Weinberg, ed., New York, 1957). Elsewhere he wrote: "Life is like a ship on the sea, tossed by every wave and by every wind; a ship headed for no port and no harbor, with no rudder, no compass, no pilot; simply floating for a time, then lost in the waves" ("Is Life

Worth Living?," p. 43). In addition to the aimlessness of life and the universe, there is the fact of death. "I love my friends," wrote Darrow, "but they all must come to a tragic end." Death is more terrible the more one is attached to things in the world. Life, he concludes, is "not worth while," and he adds (somewhat inconsistently, in view of what he had said earlier) that "it is an unpleasant interruption of nothing, and the best thing you can say of it is that it does not last long" ("Is the Human Race Getting Anywhere?," p. 53).

Tolstoy

Tolstoy, unlike Darrow, eventually came to believe in Christianity, or at least in his own idiosyncratic version of Christianity, but for a number of years the only position for which he could see any rational justification was an extreme form of pessimism. During that period (and there is reason to believe that in spite of his later protestations to the contrary, his feelings on this subject never basically changed) Tolstoy was utterly overwhelmed by the thought of his death and the death of those he cared for and, generally, by the transitory nature of all human achievements. "Today or tomorrow," he wrote in "A Confession," "sickness and death will come to those I love or to me; nothing will remain but stench and worms. Sooner or later my affairs, whatever they may be, will be forgotten, and I shall not exist. Then why go on making any effort?" Tolstoy likened the fate of man to that of the traveler in the Eastern tale who, pursued by an enraged beast, seeks refuge in a dry well. At the bottom of the well he sees a dragon that has opened its jaws to swallow him. To escape the enraged beast above and the dragon below, he holds onto a twig that is growing in a crack in the well. As he looks around he notices that two mice are gnawing at the stem of the twig. He realizes that very soon the twig will snap and he will fall to his doom, but at the same time he sees some drops of honey on the leaves of the branch and reaches out with his tongue to lick

them. "So I too clung to the twig of life, knowing that the dragon of death was inevitably awaiting me, ready to tear me to pieces. . . . I tried to lick the honey which formerly consoled me, but the honey no longer gave me pleasure. . . . I only saw the unescapable dragon and the mice, and I could not tear my gaze from them. And this is not a fable but the real unanswerable truth."

These considerations, according to Tolstoy, inevitably lead to the conclusion that life is a "stupid fraud," that no "reasonable meaning" can be given to a single action or to a whole life. To the questions "What is it for?" "What then?" "Why should I live?" the answer is "Nothing can come of it," "Nothing is worth doing," "Life is not worthwhile."

What ways out are available to a human being who finds himself in this "terrible position"? Judging by the conduct of the people he observed, Tolstoy relates that he could see only four possible "solutions." The first is the way of ignorance. People who adopt this solution (chiefly women and very young and very dull people) have simply not or not yet faced the questions that were tormenting him. Once a person has fully realized what death means, this solution is not available to him. The second way is that of "Epicureanism," which consists in admitting the "hopelessness of life" but seizing as many of life's pleasures as possible while they are within reach. It consists in "disregarding the dragon and the mice and licking the honey in the best way, especially if much of it is around." This, Tolstoy adds, is the solution adopted by the majority of the people belonging to his "circle," by which he presumably means the well-to-do intellectuals of his day. Tolstoy rejects this solution because the vast majority of human beings are not well-to-do and hence have little or no honey at their disposal and also because it is a matter of accident whether one is among those who have honey or those who have not. Moreover, Tolstoy observes, it requires a special "moral dullness," which he himself lacked, to enjoy the honey while knowing the truth about death and the deprivations of the great majority of men. The third solution is suicide. Tolstoy calls this the way of "strength and energy." It is chosen by a few "exceptionally strong and consistent people." After they realize that "it is better to be dead than to be alive, and that it is best of all not to exist," they promptly end the whole "stupid joke." The means for ending it are readily at hand for everybody, but most people are too cowardly or too irrational to avail themselves of them. Finally, there is the way of "weakness." This consists in seeing the dreadful truth and clinging to life nevertheless. People of this kind lack the strength to act rationally and Tolstoy adds that he belonged to this last category.

Strengths of the Pessimist Position

Is it possible for somebody who shares the pessimists' rejection of religion to reach different conclusions without being plainly irrational? Whatever reply may be possible, any intelligent and realistic person would surely have to concede that there is much truth in the pessimists' claims. That few people achieve real and lasting happiness, that the joys of life (where there are any) pass away much too soon, that totally unpredictable events frequently upset the best intentions and wreck the noblest plans—this and much more along the same lines is surely undeniable. Although one should not dogmatize that there will be no significant improvements in the future, the fate of past revolutions, undertaken to rid man of some of his apparently avoidable suffering, does not inspire great hope. The thought of death, too, even in those who are not so overwhelmed by it as Tolstoy, can be quite unendurable. Moreover, to many who have reflected on the implications of physical theory it seems plain that because of the constant increase of entropy in the universe all life anywhere will eventually die out. Forebodings of this kind moved Bertrand Russell to write his famous essay "A Free Man's Worship," in which he concluded that "all the labors of the ages, all the devotion, all the inspiration, all the noonday brightness of human genius, are destined to extinction in the vast death of the solar system, and the whole temple of man's achievement must inevitably be buried beneath the debris of a universe in ruins." Similarly, Wilhelm Ostwald observed that "in the longest run the sum of all human endeavor has no recognizable significance." Although it is disputed whether physical theory really has such gloomy implications, it would perhaps be wisest to assume that the position endorsed by Russell and Ostwald is well-founded.

Comparative Value Judgments About Life and Death

Granting the strong points in the pessimists' claims, it is still possible to detect certain confusions and dubious inferences in their arguments. To begin with, there is a very obvious inconsistency in the way writers like Darrow and Tolstoy arrive at the conclusion that death is better than life. They begin by telling us that death is something terrible because it terminates the possibility of any of the experiences we value. From this they infer that nothing is really worth doing and that death is better than life. Ignoring for the moment the claim that in view of our inevitable death nothing is "worth doing," there very plainly seems to be an inconsistency in first judging death to be such a horrible evil and in asserting later on that death is better than life. Why was death originally judged to be an evil? Surely because it is the termination of life. And if something, y, is bad because it is the termination of something, x, this can be so only if x is good or has positive value. If x were not good, the termination of x would not be bad. One cannot consistently have it both ways.

To this it may be answered that life did have positive value prior to one's realization of death but that once a person has become aware of the inevitability of his destruction life becomes unbearable and that this is the real issue. This point of view is well expressed in the following exchange between Cassius and Brutus in Shakespeare's *Julius Caesar* (III.i. 102–105):

CASSIUS. Why he that cuts off twenty years of life
Cuts off so many years of fearing death.
BRUTUS. Grant that, and then is death a benefit:
So are we Caesar's friends that have abridged
His time of fearing death.

There is a very simple reply to this argument. Granting that some people after once realizing their doom cannot banish the thought of it from their minds, so much so that it interferes with all their other activities, this is neither inevitable nor at all common. It is, on the contrary, in the opinion of all except some existentialists, morbid and pathological. The realization that one will die does not in the case of most people prevent them from engaging in activities which they regard as valuable or from enjoying the things they used to enjoy. To be told that one is not living "authentically" if one does not brood about death day and night is simply to be insulted gratuitously. A person who knows that his talents are not as great as he would wish or that he is not as handsome as he would have liked to be is not usually judged to live "inauthentically," but on the contrary to be sensible if he does not constantly brood about his limitations and shortcomings and uses whatever talents he does possess to maximum advantage.

There is another and more basic objection to the claim that death is better than life. This objection applies equally to the claim that while death is better than life it would be better still not to have been born in the first place and to the judgment that life is better than death. It should be remembered that we are here concerned with such pronouncements when they are intended not merely as the expression of certain moods but as statements which are in some sense true or objectively warranted. It may be argued that a value compari-

son—any judgment to the effect that *A* is better or worse than *B* or as good as *B*— makes sense only if both *A* and *B* are, in the relevant respect, in principle open to inspection. If somebody says, for example, that Elizabeth Taylor is a better actress than Betty Grable, this seems quite intelligible. Or, again, if it is said that life for the Jews is better in the United States than it was in Germany under the Nazis, this also seems readily intelligible. In such cases the terms of the comparison are observable or at any rate describable. These conditions are fulfilled in some cases when value comparisons are made between life and death, but they are not fulfilled in the kind of case with which Tolstoy and the pessimists are concerned. If the conception of an afterlife is intelligible, then it would make sense for a believer or for somebody who has not made up his mind to say such things as "Death cannot be worse than this life" or "I wonder if it will be any better for me after I am dead." Achilles, in the *Iliad*, was not making a senseless comparison when he exclaimed that he would rather act

. . . as a serf of another,
A man of little possessions, with scanty means of subsistence,
Than rule as a ghostly monarch the ghosts of all the departed.

Again, the survivors can meaningfully say about a deceased individual "It is better (for the world) that he is dead" or the opposite. For the person himself, however, if there is no afterlife, death is not a possible object of observation or experience, and statements by him that his own life is better than, as good as, or worse than his own death, unless they are intended to be no more than expressions of certain wishes or moods, must be dismissed as senseless. At first sight the contention that in the circumstances under discussion value comparisons between life and death are senseless may seem implausible because of the widespread tendency to think of death as a shadowy kind of life—as sleep, rest, or some kind of home-coming. Such "descriptions" may be admirable as poetry or consolation, but taken literally they are simply false.

Irrelevance of the Distant Future

These considerations do not, however, carry us very far. They do not show either that life is worth living or that it "has meaning." Before tackling these problems directly, something should perhaps be said about the curious and totally arbitrary preference of the future to the present, to which writers like Tolstoy and Darrow are committed without realizing it. Darrow implies that life would not be "futile" if it were not an endless cycle of the same kind of activities and if instead it were like a journey toward a destination. Tolstoy clearly implies that life would be worthwhile, that some of our actions at least would have a "reasonable meaning," if the present life were followed by eternal bliss. Presumably, what would make life no longer futile as far as Darrow is concerned is some feature of the destination, not merely the fact that it is a destination; and what would make life worthwhile in Tolstoy's opinion is not merely the eternity of the next life but the "bliss" which it would confer—eternal misery and torture would hardly do. About the bliss in the next life, if there is such a next life, Tolstoy shows no inclination to ask "What for?" or "So what?" But if bliss in the next life is not in need of any further justification, why should any bliss that there might be in the present life need justification?

The Logic of Value Judgments

Many of the pessimists appear to be confused about the logic of value judgments. It makes sense for a person to ask about something "Is it really worthwhile?" or "Is it really worth the trouble?" if he does not regard it as intrinsically valuable or if he is weighing it against another good with which it may be in conflict. It does not make sense to ask such a question about something he regards as valuable in its own right and where there is no conflict with the attainment of any other good. (This observation, it should be noted, is quite independent of what view one takes of the logical status of intrinsic value judgments.) A person driving to the beach on a crowded Sunday, may, upon finally getting there, reflect on whether the trip was really worthwhile. Or, after undertaking a series of medical treatments, somebody may ask whether it was worth the time and the money involved. Such questions make sense because the discomforts of a car ride and the time and money spent on medical treatments are not usually judged to be valuable for their own sake. Again, a woman who has given up a career as a physician in order to raise a family may ask herself whether it was worthwhile, and in this case the question would make sense not because she regards the raising of a family as no more than a means, but because she is weighing it against another good. However, if somebody is very happy, for any number of reasons—because he is in love, because he won the Nobel prize, because his child recovered from a serious illness—and if this happiness does not prevent him from doing or experiencing anything else he regards as valuable, it would not occur to him to ask "Is it worthwhile?" Indeed, this question would be incomprehensible to him, just as Tolstoy himself would presumably not have known what to make of the question had it been raised about the bliss in the hereafter.

It is worth recalling here that we live not in the distant future but in the present and also, in a sense, in the relatively near future. To bring the subject down to earth, let us consider some everyday occurrences: A man with a toothache goes to a dentist, and the dentist helps him so that the toothache disappears. A man is falsely accused of a crime and is faced with the possibility of a severe sentence as well as with the loss of his reputation; with the help of a devoted attorney his innocence is established, and he is acquitted. It is true that a hundred years later all of the participants in these events will be dead and none of them will *then* be able to enjoy the fruits of any of the efforts involved. But this most emphatically does not imply that the dentist's efforts were not worthwhile or that the attorney's work was not worth doing. To bring in considerations of what will or will not happen in the remote future is, in such and many other though certainly not in all human situations, totally irrelevant. Not only is the finality of death irrelevant here; equally irrelevant are the facts, if they are facts, that life is an endless cycle of the same kind of activities and that the history of the universe is not a drama with a happy ending.

This is, incidentally, also the answer to religious apologists like C. H. D. Clark who maintain that all striving is pointless if it is "without final consequence" and that "it scarcely matters how we live if all will end in the dust of death." Striving is not pointless if it achieves what it is intended to achieve even if it is without *final* consequence, and it matters a great deal how we live if we have certain standards and goals, although we cannot avoid "the dust of death."

The Vanished Past

In asserting the worthlessness of life Schopenhauer remarked that "what has been exists as little as what has never been" and that "something of great importance now past is inferior to something of little importance now present." Several comments are in order here. To begin with, if Schopenhauer is right, it must work both ways: if only the present counts, then past sorrows no less than past pleasures do not "count." Furthermore, the question whether "something of great importance now past is inferior to something of little importance now present" is not, as Schopenhauer supposed, a straightforward question of fact but rather one of valuation, and different answers, none of which can be said to be mistaken, will be given by different people according to their circumstances and interests. Viktor Frankl, the

founder of "logotherapy," has compared the pessimist to a man who observes, with fear and sadness, how his wall calendar grows thinner and thinner as he removes a sheet from it every day. The kind of person whom Frankl admires, on the other hand, "files each successive leaf neatly away with its predecessors" and reflects "with pride and joy" on all the richness represented by the leaves removed from the calendar. Such a person will not in old age envy the young. "'No, thank you,' he will think. 'Instead of possibilities, I have realities in my past'" (*Man's Search for Meaning*, pp. 192–193). This passage is quoted not because it contains any great wisdom but because it illustrates that we are concerned here not with judgments of fact but with value judgments and that Schopenhauer's is not the only one that is possible. Nevertheless, his remarks are, perhaps, a healthy antidote to the cheap consolation and the attempts to cover up deep and inevitable misery that are the stock in trade of a great deal of popular psychology. Although Schopenhauer's judgments about the inferior value of the past cannot be treated as objectively true propositions, they express only too well what a great many human beings are bound to feel on certain occasions. To a man dying of cancer it is small consolation to reflect that there was a time when he was happy and flourishing; and while there are undoubtedly some old people who do not envy the young, it may be suspected that more often the kind of talk advocated by the prophets of positive thinking is a mask for envy and a defense against exceedingly painful feelings of regret and helplessness in the face of aging and death and the now-unalterable past.

The Meanings of the "Meaning of Life"

Let us now turn to the question whether, given the rejection of belief in God and immortality, life can nevertheless have any "meaning" or "significance." Kurt Baier has called attention to two very different senses in which people use these expressions and to the confusions that result when they are not kept apart. Sometimes when a person asks whether life has any meaning, what he wants to know is whether there is a superhuman intelligence that fashioned human beings along with other objects in the world to serve some end—whether their role is perhaps analogous to the part of an instrument (or its player) in a symphony. People who ask whether history has a meaning often use the word in the same sense. When Macbeth exclaimed that life "is a tale/Told by an idiot, full of sound and fury,/Signifying nothing," he was answering this cosmic question in the negative. His point evidently was not that human life is part of a scheme designed by a superhuman idiot but that it is not part of any design. Similarly, when Fred Hoyle, in his book *The Nature of the Universe* (rev. ed., New York, 1960), turns to what he calls "the deeper issues" and remarks that we find ourselves in a "dreadful situation" in which there is "scarcely a clue as to whether our existence has any real significance," he is using the word "significance" in this cosmic sense.

On the other hand, when we ask whether a *particular* person's life has or had any meaning, we are usually concerned not with cosmic issues but with the question whether certain purposes are to be found *in* his life. Thus, most of us would say without hesitation that a person's life had meaning if we knew that he devoted himself to a cause (such as the spread of Christianity or communism or the reform of mental institutions), or we would at least be ready to say that it "acquired meaning" once he became sufficiently attached to his cause. Whether we approve of what they did or not, most of us would be ready to admit—to take some random examples—that Dorothea Dix, Pasteur, Lenin, Margaret Sanger, Anthony Comstock, and Winston Churchill led meaningful lives. We seem to mean two things in characterizing such lives as meaningful: we assert, first, that the life in question had some dominant, over-all goal or goals which gave direction to a great many of the individual's actions and, second, that these actions and possibly others not immediately related to the overriding goal were performed with a special zest that was not present before the person became attached to his goal or that would not have been present if there had been no such goal in his life. It is not necessary, however, that a person should be devoted to a cause, in the sense just indicated, before we call his life meaningful. It is sufficient that he should have some attachments that are not too shallow. This last expression is of course rather vague, but so is the use of the word "meaning" when applied to human lives. Since the depth or shallowness of an attachment is a matter of degree, it makes perfectly good sense to speak of degrees of meaning in this context. Thus, C. G. Jung writes that in the lives of his patients there never was "sufficient meaning" (*Memories, Dreams, Reflections*, New York and Toronto, 1963, p. 140). There is nothing odd in such a location, and there is equally nothing odd in saying about a man who has made a partial recovery from a deep depression that there is now again "some" meaning in his life.

Although frequently when people say about somebody that his life has or had meaning, they evidently regard this as a good thing, this is not invariably the case. One might express this point in the following way: saying that attachment to a certain goal has made a man's life meaningful is *not* tantamount to saying that the acts to which the goal has given direction are of positive value. A man might himself observe—and there would be nothing logically odd about it—"As long as I was a convinced Nazi (or communist or Christian or whatever) my life had meaning, my acts had a zest with which I have not been able to invest them since, and yet most of my actions were extremely harmful." Even while fully devoted to his cause or goal the person need not, and frequently does not, regard it as *intrinsically* valuable. If challenged he will usually justify the attachment to his goal by reference to more fundamental value judgments. Thus, somebody devoted to communism or to medical research or to the dissemination of birth-control information will in all likelihood justify his devotion in terms of the production of happiness and the reduction of suffering, and somebody devoted to Christianity will probably justify his devotion by reference to the will of God.

Let us refer to the first of the two senses we have been discussing as the "cosmic" sense and to the second as the "terrestrial" sense. (These are by no means the only senses in which philosophers and others have used the word "meaning" when they have spoken of the meaning or meaninglessness of life, but for our purposes it is sufficient to take account of these two senses.) Now if the theory of cosmic design is rejected it immediately follows that human life has no meaning in the first or cosmic sense. It does not follow in the least, however, that a particular human life is meaningless in the second, or terrestrial, sense. This conclusion has been very clearly summarized by Baier: "Your life or mine may or may not have meaning (in one sense)," he writes, "even if life as such has none (in the other). . . . The Christian view guarantees a meaning (in one sense) to every life, the scientific view [what we have simply been calling the unbeliever's position] does not in any sense" (*The Meaning of Life*, p. 28). In the terrestrial sense it will be an open question whether an individual's life has meaning or not, to be decided by the particular circumstances of his existence. It may indeed be the case that once a person comes to believe that life has no meaning in the cosmic sense his attachment to terrestrial goals will be undermined to such an extent that his life will cease to be meaningful in the other sense as well. However, it seems very plain that this is by no means what invariably happens, and even if it did invariably happen the meaninglessness of a given person's life in the terrestrial sense would not *logically* follow from the fact, if it is a fact, that life is meaningless in the cosmic sense.

This is perhaps the place to add a few words of protest against the rhetorical exaggerations of certain theological writers. Fackenheim's statement, quoted earlier, that "whatever meaning life acquires, it derives from the encounter between God and man" is typical of many theological pronouncements. Statements of this kind are objectionable on several grounds. Let us assume that there is a God and that meetings between God and certain human beings do take place; let us also grant that activities commanded by God in these meetings "acquire meaning" by being or becoming means to the end of pleasing or obeying God. Granting all this, it does not follow that obedience of God is the only possible unifying goal. It would be preposterous to maintain that the lives of *all* unbelievers have been lacking in such goals and almost as preposterous to maintain that the lives of believers never contain unifying goals other than obedience of God. There have been devout men who were also attached to the advance of science, to the practice of medicine, or to social reform and who regarded these ends as worth pursuing independently of any divine commandments. Furthermore, there is really no good reason to grant that the life of a particular person becomes meaningful in the terrestrial sense just because human life in general has meaning in the cosmic sense. If a superhuman being has a plan in which I am included, this fact will make (or help to make) my life meaningful in the terrestrial sense only if I know the plan and approve of it and of my place in it, so that working toward the realization of the plan gives direction to my actions.

Is Human Life Ever Worthwhile?

Let us now turn to the question of whether life is ever worth living. This also appears to be denied by the pessimists when they speak of the vanity or the futility of human life. We shall see that in a sense it cannot be established that the pessimists are "mistaken," but it is also quite easy to show that in at least two senses which seem to be of importance to many people, human lives frequently are worth living. To this end, let us consider under what circumstances a person is likely to raise the question "Is my life (still) worthwhile?" and what is liable to provoke somebody into making a statement like "My life has ceased to be worth living." We saw in an earlier section that when we say of certain acts, such as the efforts of a dentist or a lawyer, that they were worthwhile we are claiming that they achieved certain goals. Something similar seems to be involved when we say that a person's life is (still) worthwhile or worth living. We seem to be making two assertions: first, that the person has some goals (other than merely to be dead or to have his pains eased) which do not seem to him to be trivial and, second, that there is some genuine possibility that he will attain these goals. These observations are confirmed by various systematic studies of people who contemplated suicide, of others who unsuccessfully attempted suicide, and of situations in which people did commit suicide. When the subjects of these studies declared that their lives were no longer worth living they generally meant either that there was nothing left in their lives about which they seriously cared or that there was no real likelihood of attaining any of the goals that mattered to them. It should be noted that in this sense an individual may well be mistaken in his assertion that his life is or is not worthwhile any longer: he may, for example, mistake a temporary indisposition for a more permanent loss of interest, or, more likely, he may falsely estimate his chances of achieving the ends he wishes to attain.

Different Senses of "Worthwhile"

According to the account given so far, one is saying much the same thing in declaring a life to be worthwhile and in asserting that it has meaning in the "terrestrial" sense of the word. There is, however, an interesting difference. When we say that a person's life has meaning (in the terrestrial sense) we are not committed to the claim that the goal or goals to which he is devoted have any positive value. (This is a slight oversimplification, assuming greater uniformity in the use of "meaning of life" than actually exists, but it will not seriously affect any of the controversial issues discussed here.) The question "As long as his life was dedicated to the spread of communism it had meaning *to him*, but was it really meaningful?" seems to be senseless. We are inclined to say, "If his life had meaning to him, then it had meaning—that's all there is to it." We are not inclined (or we are much less inclined) to say something of this kind when we speak of the worth of a person's life. We might say—for example, of someone like Eichmann—"While he was carrying out the extermination program, his life *seemed* worthwhile to him, but since his goal was so horrible, his life *was not* worthwhile." One might perhaps distinguish between a "subjective" and an "objective" sense of "worthwhile." In the subjective sense, saying that a person's life is worthwhile simply means that he is attached to some goals which he does not consider trivial and that these goals are attainable for him. In declaring that somebody's life is worthwhile in the objective sense, one is saying that he is attached to certain goals which are both attainable and of positive value.

It may be held that unless one accepts some kind of rationalist or intuitionist view of fundamental value judgments one would have to conclude that in the objective sense of "worthwhile" no human life (and indeed no human action) could ever be shown to be worthwhile. There is no need to enter here into a discussion of any controversial questions about the logical status of fundamental value judgments. But it may be pointed out that somebody who favors a subjectivist or emotivist account can quite consistently allow for the distinction between ends that only seem to have positive value and those that really do. To mention just one way in which this could be done: one may distinguish between ends that would be approved by rational and sympathetic human beings and those that do not carry such an endorsement. One may then argue that when we condemn such a life as Eichmann's as not being worthwhile we mean not that the ends to which he devoted himself possess some non-natural characteristic of badness but that no rational or sympathetic person would approve of them.

The Pessimists' Special Standards

The unexciting conclusion of this discussion is that some human lives are at certain times not worthwhile in either of the two senses we have distinguished, that some are worthwhile in the subjective but not in the objective sense, some in the objective but not in the subjective sense, and some are worthwhile in both senses. The unexcitingness of this conclusion is not a reason for rejecting it, but some readers may question whether it meets the challenge of the pessimists. The pessimist, it may be countered, surely does not deny the plain fact that human beings are on occasions attached to goals which do not seem to them trivial, and it is also not essential to his position to deny (and most pessimists do not in fact deny) that these goals are sometimes attainable. The pessimist may even allow that in a superficial ("immediate") sense the goals which people try to achieve are of positive value, but he would add that because our lives are not followed by eternal bliss they are not "really" or "ultimately" worthwhile. If this is so, then the situation may be characterized by saying that the ordinary man and the pessimist do not mean the same by "worthwhile," or that they do mean the same in that both use it as a positive value expression but that their standards are different: the standards of the pessimist are very much more demanding than those of most ordinary people.

Anybody who agrees that death is final will have to concede that the pessimist is not mistaken in his contention that judged by *his* standards, life is never worthwhile. However, the pessimist is mistaken if he concludes, as frequently happens, that life

is not worthwhile by ordinary standards because it is not worthwhile by his standards. Furthermore, setting aside the objection mentioned earlier (that there is something arbitrary about maintaining that eternal bliss makes life worthwhile but not allowing this role to bliss in the present life), one may justifiably ask why one should abandon ordinary standards in favor of those of the pessimist. Ordinarily, when somebody changes standards (for example, when a school raises or lowers its standards of admission) such a change can be supported by reasons. But how can the pessimist justify his special standards? It should be pointed out here that our ordinary standards do something for us which the pessimist's standards do not: they guide our choices, and as long as we live we can hardly help making choices. It is true that in one type of situation the pessimist's standards also afford guidance—namely, in deciding whether to go on living. It is notorious, however, that whether or not they are, by their own standards, rational in this, most pessimists do not commit suicide. They are then faced with much the same choices as other people. In these situations their own demanding standards are of no use, and in fact they avail themselves of the ordinary standards. Schopenhauer, for example, believed that if he had hidden his antireligious views he would have had no difficulty in obtaining an academic appointment and other worldly honors. He may have been mistaken in this belief, but in any event his actions indicate that he regarded intellectual honesty as worthwhile in a sense in which worldly honors were not. Again, when Darrow had the choice between continuing as counsel for the Chicago and North Western Railway and taking on the defense of Eugene V. Debs and his harassed and persecuted American Railway Union, he did not hesitate to choose the latter, apparently regarding it as worthwhile to go to the assistance of the suppressed and not worthwhile to aid the suppressor. In other words, although no human action is worthwhile, some human actions and presumably some human lives are less unworthwhile than others.

Is the Universe Better With Human Life Than Without It?

We have not—at least not explicitly—discussed the claims of Schopenhauer, Eduard von Hartmann, and other pessimists that the nonexistence of the world would be better than its existence, by which they mean that a world without human life would be better than one with it.

Arguments of a Phenomenologist

Some writers do not think that life can be shown to have meaning in any philosophically significant sense unless an affirmative answer to this question can be justified. Thus, in his booklet *Der Sinn unseres Daseins* the German phenomenologist Hans Reiner distinguishes between the everyday question about what he calls the "need-conditioned" meaning of life, which arises only for a person who is already in existence and has certain needs and desires, and the question about the meaning of human life in general. The latter question arises in concrete form when a responsible person is faced with the *Zeugungsproblem*—the question whether he should bring a child into the world. Reiner allows that a person's life has meaning in the former or "merely subjective" sense as long as his ordinary goals (chiefly his desire for happiness) are attained. This, however, does not mean that his life has an "objective" or "existential" (*seinshaft*) meaning—a significance or meaning which "attaches to life as such" and which, unlike the need-conditioned meaning, cannot be destroyed by any accident of fate. The philosopher, according to Reiner, is primarily concerned with the question of whether life has meaning in this objective or existential sense. "Our search for the meaning of our life," Reiner writes, "is identical with the search for a logically

compelling reason (*einen einsichtigen Grund*) why it is better for us to exist than not to exist" (*Der Sinn unseres Daseins*, p. 27). Again, the real question is "whether it is better that mankind should exist than that there should be a world without any human life" (*ibid.*, p. 31). It may be questioned whether this is what anybody normally means when he asks whether life has any meaning, but Reiner certainly addresses himself to one of the questions raised by Schopenhauer and other pessimists that ought to be discussed here.

Reiner believes that he can provide a "logically compelling reason" why a world with human life is better than one without it. He begins by pointing out that men differ from animals by being, among other things, "moral individuals." To be a moral individual is to be part of the human community and to be actively concerned in the life of other human beings. It is indeed undeniable that people frequently fail to bring about the ends of morally inspired acts or wishes, but phenomenological analysis discloses that "the real moral value and meaning" of an act does not depend on the attainment of the "external goal." As Kant correctly pointed out, the decisive factor is "the good will," the moral intent or attitude. It is here that we find the existential meaning of life: "Since that which is morally good contains its meaning and value within itself, it follows that it is intrinsically worth while. The existence of what is morally good is therefore better than its nonexistence." (*ibid.*, pp. 54–55). But the existence of what is morally good is essentially connected with the existence of free moral individuals, and hence it follows that the existence of human beings as moral agents is better than their nonexistence.

Unlike happiness, which constitutes the meaning of life in the everyday or need-conditioned sense, the morally good does not depend on the accidents of life. It is not within a person's power to be happy, but it is "essentially" (*grundsätzlich*) in everybody's power to do what is good. Furthermore, while all happiness is subjective and transitory, leaving behind it no more than a "melancholy echo," the good has eternal value. Nobody would dream of honoring and respecting a person for his happiness or prosperity. On the other hand, we honor every good deed and the expression of every moral attitude, even if it took place in a distant land and among a foreign people. If we discover a good act or a good attitude in an enemy we nevertheless respect it and cannot help deriving a certain satisfaction from its existence. The same is true of good deeds carried out in ages long past. In all this the essentially timeless nature of morality becomes evident. Good deeds cease to exist as historical events only; their value, on the other hand, has eternal reality and is collected as an indestructible "fund." This may be a metaphysical statement, but it is not a piece of "metaphysical speculation." It simply makes explicit what the experience of the morally good discloses to phenomenological analysis (*ibid.*, pp. 55–57).

Replies to Reiner

There is a great deal in this presentation with which one could take issue. If one is not misled by the image of the ever-growing, indestructible "fund," one may wonder, for example, what could be meant by claiming that the value of a good deed is "eternal," other than that most human beings tend to approve of such an action regardless of when or where it took place. However, we are here concerned primarily with the question whether Reiner has met the challenge of the pessimists, and it seems clear that he has not. A pessimist like Schopenhauer or Darrow might provisionally grant the correctness of Reiner's phenomenological analysis of morality but still offer the following rejoinder: The inevitable misery of all or nearly all human beings is so great that even if in the course of their lives they have a chance to preserve their inner moral natures or their good will, the continued torture to which their lives condemn them would not be justified. Given the pessimist's estimate of human

life, this is surely not an unreasonable rejoinder. Even without relying on the pessimist's description of human life, somebody while accepting Reiner's phenomenological analysis might reach the opposite conclusion. He might, for example, share the quietist strain of Schopenhauer's teachings and object to the whole hustle and bustle of life, concluding that the "peace of the all-sufficient nothing"—or, more literally, a universe without human life—was better in spite of the fact that moral deeds could not then be performed. Since he admits the "facts" of morality on which Reiner bases his case but considers the peace of the all-sufficient nothing more valuable than morality, it is not easy to see how an appeal to the latter would show him to be mistaken. What phenomenological analysis has not disclosed, to Reiner or, as far as is known, to anybody else, is that doing good is the only or necessarily the greatest value.

Why the Pessimist Cannot Be Answered

The conclusion suggests itself that the pessimist cannot here be refuted, not because what he says is true or even because we do not know who is right and who is wrong but because the question whether a universe with human life is better than one without it does not have any clear meaning unless it is interpreted as a request for a statement of personal preference. The situation seems to be somewhat similar to what we found in the case of the question "Is my life better than my death?" when asked in certain circumstances. In some contexts indeed when we talk about human life in general, the word "better" has a reasonably clear meaning. Thus, if it is maintained that life for the human race will be better than it is now after cancer and mental illness have been conquered, or that human life will be better (or worse) after religion has disappeared, we understand fairly well what is meant, what facts would decide the issue either way. However, we do not really know what would count as evidence for or against the statement "The existence of human life as such is better than its nonexistence." Sometimes it is claimed that the question has a fairly clear meaning, namely, whether happiness outweighs unhappiness. Thus, von Hartmann supports his answer that the nonexistence of human life is better than its existence, that in fact an inanimate world would be better than one with life, with the argument that as we descend the scale of civilization and "sensitivity," we reach ever lower levels of misery. "The individuals of the lower and poorer classes and of ruder nations," he writes, "are happier than those of the elevated and wealthier classes and of civilized nations, not indeed because they are poorer and have to endure more want and privations, but because they are coarser and duller" (*Philosophy of the Unconscious*, Vol. III, p. 76). The "brutes," similarly, are "happier (i.e., less miserable)" than man, because "the excess of pain which an animal has to bear is less than that which a man has to bear." The same principle holds within the world of animals and plants:

How much more painful is the life of the more finely-feeling horse compared with that of the obtuse pig, or with that of the proverbially happy fish in the water, its nervous system being of a grade so far inferior! As the life of a fish is more enviable than that of a horse, so is the life of an oyster than that of a fish, and the life of a plant than that of an oyster. (*Ibid.*)

The conclusion is inevitable: the best or least undesirable form of existence is reached when, finally, we "descend beneath the threshold of consciousness"; for only there do we "see individual pain entirely disappear" (*Philosophy of the Unconscious*, Vol. III, pp. 76–77). Schopenhauer, also, addressing himself directly to the *"Zeugungsproblem,"* reaches a negative answer on the ground that unhappiness usually or necessarily outweighs happiness. "Could the human race continue to exist," he asks (in *Parerga und Paralipomena*, Vol. II, pp. 321–322), if "the generative act were . . . an affair of pure rational reflection? Would not rather everyone have so much compassion for the coming

generation as to prefer to spare it the burden of existence, or at least be unwilling to take on himself the responsibility of imposing such a burden in cold blood?" In these passages Schopenhauer and von Hartmann assume that in the question "Is a world with human life better than one without human life?" the word "better" must be construed in a hedonistic or utilitarian sense—and the same is true of several other philosophers who do not adopt their pessimistic answer. However, while one may *stipulate* such a sense for "better" in this context, it is clear that this is not what is meant prior to the stipulation. Spinoza, for example, taught that the most miserable form of existence is preferable to nonexistence. Perhaps few who have directly observed the worst agonies and tortures that may be the lot of human beings or of animals would subscribe to this judgment, but Spinoza can hardly be accused of a self-contradictory error. Again, Nietzsche's philosophy is usually and quite accurately described as an affirmation of life, but Nietzsche was very careful not to play down the horrors of much of life. While he did not endorse Schopenhauer's value judgments, he thought that, by and large, Schopenhauer had not been far wrong in his description of the miseries of the human scene. In effect Nietzsche maintained that even though unhappiness is more prevalent than happiness, the existence of life is nevertheless better than its nonexistence, and this surely is not a self-contradiction.

It is important to point out what does not follow from the admission that in a nonarbitrary sense of "better," the existence of the human race cannot be shown to be better than its nonexistence: It does not follow that I or anybody else cannot or should not prefer the continued existence of the human race to its nonexistence or my own life to my death, and it does not follow that I or anybody else cannot or should not enjoy himself or that I or anybody else is "irrational" in any of these preferences. It is also impossible to prove that in some nonarbitrary sense of "better," coffee with cream is better than black coffee, but it does not follow that I cannot or should not prefer or enjoy it or that I am irrational in doing so. There is perhaps something a trifle absurd and obsessive in the need for a "proof" that the existence of life is better than its nonexistence. It resembles the demand to have it "established by argument" that love is better than hate.

Perhaps it would be helpful to summarize the main conclusions reached in this essay:

(1) In certain familiar senses of "meaning," which are not usually regarded as trivial, an action or a human life can have meaning quite independently of whether there is a God or whether we shall live forever.

(2) Writers like Tolstoy, who, because of the horror that death inspires, conclude that death is better than life, are plainly inconsistent. Moreover, the whole question of whether my life is better than my death, unless it is a question about my preference, seems to be devoid of sense.

(3) Those who argue that no human action can be worthwhile because we all must eventually die ignore what may be called the "short-term context" of much of our lives.

(4) Some human lives are worthwhile in one or both of the two senses in which "worthwhile" is commonly used, when people raise the question of whether a given person's life is worthwhile. The pessimists who judge human life by more demanding standards are not mistaken when they deny that by *their* standards no human life is ever worthwhile. However, they are guilty of a fallacious inference if they conclude that for this reason no human life can be worthwhile by the usual standards. Nor is it clear why anybody should embrace their standards in the place of those commonly adopted.

(5) It appears that the pessimists cannot be answered if in order to answer them one has to be able to prove that in some nonarbitrary sense of the word "better," the existence of life is better than its nonexistence. But this admission does not have any of the gloomy consequences which it is sometimes believed to entail.

Bibliography

The position that human life cannot be meaningful without religious belief is defended in James Martineau, *Modern Materialism and Its Relation to Religion and Theology* (New York, 1877), and more recently in C. H. D. Clark, *Christianity and Bertrand Russell* (London, 1958), and in E. L. Fackenheim, "Judaism and the Meaning of Life," in *Commentary*, Vol. 39 (1965), 49–55. Substantially similar views are expounded in Paul Althaus, "The Meaning and Purpose of History in the Christian View," in *Universitas*, Vol. 7 (1965), 197–204, and in various publications by Viktor Frankl. Frankl's *Man's Search for Meaning* (New York, 1963) contains a full list of his own writings as well as those of his followers, most of whom may be described as practicing "pastoral psychology." A proreligious position is also advocated by William James in "Is Life Worth Living?," in *The Will To Believe and Other Essays in Popular Philosophy* (New York, 1897), and *The Varieties of Religious Experience* (New York, 1902), Chs. 6 and 7. A milder version of the same position is presented in Chad Walsh, *Life Is Worth Living* (Cincinnati, no date).

Schopenhauer's views about the "vanity" of life are stated in Vol. I, Bk. IV, of *Die Welt als Wille und Vorstellung* (Leipzig, 1818), translated by R. B. Haldane and J. Kemp as *The World as Will and Idea*, 3 vols. (London, 1883), and in several of his pieces included in *Parerga und Paralipomena*, 6th ed., ed. J. Frauenstädt, 2 vols. (Berlin, 1851). Three of his essays that bear most closely on the subject of the present article—"On the Vanity and Suffering of Life," "On the Sufferings of the World," and "The Vanity of Existence"—are available in an English translation by T. Bailey Saunders in Richard Taylor, ed., *The Will to Live—Selected Writings of Arthur Schopenhauer* (New York, 1962).

Eduard von Hartmann's position is stated in Vol. III of *Die Philosophie des Unbewussten*, 3 vols. (Berlin, 1869), translated by W. C. Coupland as *Philosophy of the Unconscious* (London, 1884), in *Zur Geschichte und Begründung des Pessimismus* (Berlin, 1892), and in *Philosophische Fragen der Gegenwart* (Leipzig and Berlin, 1885), Ch. 5. Clarence Darrow's pessimism is expounded in *The Story of My Life* (New York, 1932) and in two pamphlets, "Is Life Worth Living?" and "Is the Human Race Getting Anywhere?"

(Girard, Kansas, no date). Tolstoy's views are stated in "A Confession," in *A Confession, The Gospel in Brief and What I Believe*, translated by Aylmer Maude (London, 1940). Gloomy implications are derived from the second law of thermodynamics by Bertrand Russell in "A Free Man's Worship" (1903), which is available in several books, perhaps most conveniently in Russell's *Mysticism and Logic* (New York and London, 1918), and by Wilhelm Ostwald, *Die Philosophie der Werte* (Leipzig, 1913). F. P. Ramsey, in "How I Feel," in *The Foundations of Mathematics and Other Logical Essays* (London, 1931), agrees with Russell and Ostwald about the physical consequences of the second law but does not share their gloomy response. Stephen Toulmin, "Contemporary Scientific Mythology," in Toulmin et al., *Metaphysical Beliefs* (London, 1957), questions whether the second law has the physical consequences attributed to it by Russell, Ostwald, and many others. L. J. Russell, "The Meaning of Life," *Philosophy*, Vol. 28 (1953), pp. 30–40, contains some interesting criticisms of the view that eternal existence could render any human actions meaningful.

The fullest discussions of the questions of the meaning and value of life by contemporary analytic philosophers are Kurt Baier, *The Meaning of Life* (Canberra, 1957), parts of which are reprinted in Morris Weitz, ed., *Twentieth Century Philosophy—The Analytic Tradition* (New York, 1966); Ronald W. Hepburn, *Christianity and Paradox* (London, 1958), Ch. 8; and Antony Flew, "Tolstoi and the Meaning of Life," in *Ethics*, Vol. 73 (1963), 110–118. Baier, Hepburn, and Flew support the position that life can be meaningful even if there is no God and no afterlife. This position is also defended in Eugen Dühring, *Der Werth des Leben* (Leipzig, 1881), Chs. 6–7, and more recently in Bertrand Russell, *The Conquest of Happiness* (London and New York, 1930), Ch. 2; Ernest Nagel, "The Mission of Philosophy," in Lyman Bryson, ed., *An Outline of Man's Knowledge of the Modern World* (New York, 1960); Sidney Hook, "Pragmatism and the Tragic Sense of Life," in *Proceedings and Addresses of the American Philosophical Association*, Vol. 33 (1960), 5–26; Karl R. Popper, *The Open Society and Its Enemies*, 2 vols. (5th rev. ed., London, 1966), Vol. II, Ch. 25; and Kai Nielsen, "Examination of an Alleged Theological Basis of Morality," in *The Iliff Review*, Vol. 21 (1964), 39–49. Sartre and Camus are frequently (and rather inaccurately) described as "nihilists," but in effect they also take the position that although the universe is "absurd," human life can be meaningful. Sartre's views are found in *Being and Nothingness*, translated by Hazel E. Barnes (New York, 1956), Pt. 4. Camus's views are stated in *The Myth of Sisyphus and Other Essays*, translated by Justin O'Brien (New York, 1955). Views very similar to those of Sartre and Camus are advocated by Flew and R. W. Hepburn in their BBC discussion "Problems of Perspective," which is printed in *The Plain View*, Vol. 10 (1955), 151–166. C. D. McGee, *The Recovery of Meaning—An Essay on the Good Life* (New York, 1966), Ch. 1, contains a lively and detailed discussion of some of the issues treated in the present article. The author reaches similar conclusions but devotes far more attention to the "malaise" which inspires questions about the meaning of life. In a similar vein, Ilham Dilman, "Life and Meaning," in *Philosophy*, Vol. 40 (1965), 320–333, concentrates on the psychological situations that prompt people to ask whether their own lives or the lives of others have meaning. Moritz Schlick, *Vom Sinn des Lebens* (Berlin, 1927), is concerned primarily with psychological questions, arguing that modern life tends to be spoiled by overemphasis on the achievement of distant goals. Freud in several places alludes to the question of the meaning of life and usually dismisses it as senseless and pathological. "The moment a man questions the meaning and value of life," he wrote in a letter to Marie Bonaparte, "he is sick. . . . By asking this question one is merely admitting to a store of unsatisfied libido to which something else must have happened, a kind of fermentation leading to sadness and depression" (*Letters of Sigmund Freud*, translated by James Stern and Tania Stern, E. L. Freud, ed., New York, 1960, p. 436).

The Polish Marxist Adam Schaff deals with some of the issues discussed in the present article in his *A Philosophy of Man* (London, 1963). Schaff's views are criticized from a Christian point of view in Christopher Hollis. "What Is the Purpose of Life?," in *The Listener*, Vol. 70 (1961), 133–136. There is a discussion of the "meaning of life" from the point of view of fascism in Mario Palmieri, *The Philosophy of Fascism* (Chicago, 1936). The "phenomenological" position of Hans Reiner, which was discussed in the final section of this article, is stated in his *Der Sinn unseres Daseins*

(Tübingen, 1960). Other recent German works include Richard Wisser, ed., *Sinn und Sein* (Tübingen, 1960); Reinhart Lauth, *Die Frage nach den Sinn des Daseins* (Munich, 1953); and Johannes Hessen, *Der Sinn des Lebens* (Cologne, 1933).

Psychological studies of people who attempted or who committed suicide are contained in Margarite von Andies, *Suicide and the Meaning of Life* (London, 1947); Louis I. Dublin and Bessie Bunzel, *To Be or Not To Be* (New York, 1933); and E. Stengel, *Suicide and Attempted Suicide* (Harmondsworth, England, 1964).

Will Durant, *On the Meaning of Life* (New York, 1932), consists of answers by various eminent men, including Gandhi, H. L. Mencken, Russell, and George Bernard Shaw, to the question of what they take to be the meaning of life.

33 / NORMAN DAHL

MORALITY AND THE MEANING OF LIFE: SOME FIRST THOUGHTS*

Although there may be many questions about the meaning of life that will ultimately prove intractable, I think that there are some questions that can be answered. Furthermore, I think that progress towards answering them can be made through work that has and will be done in moral philosophy. In support of this I shall articulate a set of questions that I think are often at issue when people ask about the meaningfulness of life. These questions give rise to a set of conditions that a fully adequate answer must satisfy. Among other things, these conditions explain why a familiar theological answer to the meaningfulness of life seems so attractive. However, they also create problems for this answer, as well as for an answer that has appeared attractive to a number of contemporary philosophers, that the meaning of life is created by the choices that people make and the desires that they have. I shall suggest that work in moral philosophy may provide an answer that falls between these two camps that a moral life is a meaningful life. I shall sketch a theory of morality that satisfies the conditions that have

*Earlier drafts of this paper were read at Bethel College, Pacific Lutheran University, the University of California at Santa Cruz, and the University of Minnesota. I am grateful to all those who took part in the discussion on those occasions. William Hanson, Phillip Kitcher, and Takashi Yagisawa were kind enough to provide me with comments on a penultimate draft. I have also profited from the comments of referees of this journal. Reprinted by permission of the publisher and copyright holder from *Canadian Journal of Philosophy* 17 (1987): 1–22.

been set out. If this sketch can be filled out, then a moral life will be at least part of what can make a life meaningful. Whether this account of the moral life leaves out anything important for the meaningfulness of life will be the subject of some concluding remarks.

I

To see what questions are being raised when people wonder what makes life meaningful, it will be useful to look at two extremes: the first, the view that life is made meaningful by its relation to some transcendent purpose; the second, that life is not meaningful at all.

As an example of the first extreme, I shall take a familiar theological answer to the question of the meaningfulness of life, that of orthodox Christianity. Human life was created by God for a purpose, to stand in a relationship of fellowship or communion with God. In order for this relationship to be of the sort that fits God's purpose, it must be freely entered into. But people invariably abuse this freedom, turning away from God and undermining their chances for fellowship with Him. God in His mercy has provided a remedy for this abuse, in the form of His son Jesus Christ. All people have to do is repent of their abuse, receive God's forgiveness, and this relationship with God will be restored. Full and complete restoration can occur only after death, but until that time people have a mission to fulfill on earth. They are to obey God's commands, acting towards others in ways that respect their dignity as creatures of God, and displaying towards them the same compassion that God has Himself shown towards human beings. To someone who has acknowledged all of this, has asked God's forgiveness, and with the help of God is trying to carry out God's mission in her life, life can be lived with a new sense of purpose, one that allows her to approach her daily tasks both with a sense of tranquility and with enthusiasm. Whatever sufferings or misfortunes befall her, she knows that her relationship with God makes it all worthwhile. Here, is a set of claims which if true seem to provide life with a meaning in a sense in which people have often looked for it.

In contrast, the denial of the meaningfulness of life has taken a more and a less extreme form. In its more extreme form it holds that not only is there no such purpose to life as that outlined above, life is not worth living at all. If a person were rational, he would simply end his life.[1] People are in a no-win situation. Whatever desires they have are hardly ever satisfied. When they are satisfied, whatever significance this has is wiped away by the sands of time. Even if they are satisfied, that is not the end of the matter. New desires arise again, most of which also remain unsatisfied. The apparent point of all of this even seems to turn against itself. Complete satisfaction of desire turns out to be boring, a boredom whose tedium can be relieved only by a new outbreak of desires, most of which, again, are bound to be frustrated. Taken all in all, the suffering and anguish in life outweigh whatever pleasures are experienced. Even if there were a God who put us into this predicament, the character of our predicament shows that his purposes aren't worth achieving. If we were rational, we would spite him and put an end to the whole irrational show. Life is not just meaningless; it is better not to be lived at all.

The less extreme form acknowledges that a person's life may exhibit more pleasure on the whole than pain or suffering, but maintains that without some further point to which these pleasures contribute, there is no reason to go on living.[2] Faced with the inevitability of death, even a person like Tolstoy, whose life was filled with the pleasures of art, the love of family, and the attainment of success, can wonder whether her life has any meaning. Given death as its end, given that her pleasures and accomplishments will be of little or no consequence to future generations and certainly of no consequence when human life itself is extinguished from the earth, her life appears to be without meaning. Without some further point to which her pleasures and successes are related, a point of some more enduring quality than those pleasures themselves, it would seem to make no difference how her life has been spent or, indeed, whether it was spent at all. Had her life been spent in a different way, it would be of as much (and that is to say of as little) consequence as the way it was spent. Since there is no good reason to live her life one way rather than another, she might just as well end it. Life of any sort appears to be bleak and meaningless.

One does not have to grant the cogency of any of these views to see what some of the questions are that are being raised when it is asked whether life is meaningful and these views are taken as possible answers. To ask whether life is meaningful is at least to ask whether there isn't a certain way of living that gives one's life *value*, a value that outweighs whatever disvalue there may be in the suffering or misfortune contained in that life, a value it would lack if it were led in some other way. I.e., to ask whether life is meaningful is to ask whether there isn't a way of living one's life that in retrospect allows one to say that it was *good* that one lived it in that way, *better* than had one lived it in some other way, and *better* than had one not lived it at all.

The importance of bringing in a purpose to life in the theological view that we have considered is that fulfillment of a purpose is something that can be seen as *good*. Things do seem to be good to the extent to which they fulfill a purpose, and a purpose provided by someone with the credentials of the God of Christianity does seem worth fulfilling. Furthermore, the fact that full attainment of this purpose occurs after a person's death prevents whatever misfortune a person may suffer from interfering with the fulfillment of this purpose. The character of the relationship that constitutes fulfillment of this purpose, perfect fellowship with God, makes it outweigh the disvalue of any such suffering. Finally, according to this view, it makes a difference what kind of life one lives. Not only must one repent and ask God's forgiveness to achieve the purpose of human life, it is part of God's plan that people act in certain ways towards one another. Not any and every sort of life can fulfill these purposes.

This is confirmed by the two views we have considered that deny the meaningfulness of life. According to the more extreme view, there is nothing in human life that can make up for the suffering and frustration found in it. Life is on the whole *bad*. Like a cruel joke it ought to be ended rather than played out to its conclusion. On the less extreme view, life is not held out as something bad in itself. Rather, without some further point or purpose of the sort mentioned in the theological view we have considered, there is nothing in any way of life to single it out as *good*, allowing it to overcome whatever pain or misfortune that may occur, nothing that on balance would make it preferable to some other way of life.

Thus, to ask whether life is meaningful is at least to ask whether there is a way of lving one's life that will make it overall good, good in spite of the existence of suffering or misfortune, and good in a way in which it would not be had it been led in a different way. Given that this is so, one can see why one might look to moral philosophy for some help in seeing what makes life meaningful. One of the things that has occupied the attention of moral philosophers is what it is that brings value into a life. That one should look to moral philosophy for such help is, perhaps, not so surprising. Its importance is that once it is rec-

ognized, there is a chance of finding life to be meaningful without having to bring in the kind of transcendent purpose mentioned in the theological view. Not everything that has been thought to be good has been thought to be good in virtue of some purpose external to it. Some things appear to be worth doing for their own sakes. Indeed, if this weren't so, one could not claim that achieving fellowship with God by itself gives value to human life. On the face of it, there is no reason why such intrinsically valuable activities can't occur within human life itself.

II

However, there is more to an adequate answer to the meaningfulness of life than simply an answer to the question I have just articulated. There is some reason to think that any adequate answer must meet at least two further sets of conditions.

The first member of the first set of conditions is that whatever the value life is said to have that makes it worth living, it must be something that, once its nature is understood, a person will want to realize. Ronald Hepburn puts the point this way:

To give life meaning cannot be just a matter of pursuing worthy projects, . . . it is quite possible to make various value-judgments in cold blood, while yet suffering from a sense of meaninglessness. One may fill one's days with honest, useful and charitable deeds, not doubting them to be of value, but without feeling that these give one's life meaning or purpose. It may be profoundly boring. To seek meaning is not just a matter of seeking justification for one's policies, but of trying to discover how to organise one's vital resources and energies around these policies. To find meaning is not a matter of judging these to be worthy, but of seeing their pursuit as in some sense a fulfillment, as involving self-realisation as opposed to self-violation, and as not less opposed to the performance of a dreary task. . . . The author is asking how he can relate the pursuit of various valuable ends to the realising of a certain kind of form of life, the thought of which evokes in him the response; "The pursuit of these goals really concerns me, matters to me."[3]

If Hepburn is right, then any attempt to understand the meaningfulness of life in terms of value that might be realized within a life will have to meet the condition that this value is of the sort that when its nature is understood, a person will want to realize it. I shall call this the *internalist* condition, since it makes desire or motivation internal to what is said to be valuable.

The second member of this set of conditions is that value judgments of the appropriate sort turn out to be *objective*. As I am using the term 'objective,' value judgments are objective just in case for any two people if they were to disagree over a particular evaluative matter, one of them must be mistaken. I.e., to say that value judgments are objective is to say that there is a single correct answer to particular evaluative disputes. There are three conditions that suggest that judgments about a value must be objective if it is to contribute to the meaningfulness of life.

The first comes from considerations that lead Thomas Nagel to the conclusion that life is absurd.[4] According to Nagel, the absurdity of life arises from the recognition that there is no way of justifying a single conception of what it is that is valuable. Whatever standpoint it is from which a given conception of value may appear to be justified, there is another perspective from which the original standpoint appears to be arbitrary or unjustified. However, to say this is to say that the objectivity condition fails. Thus, a plausible condition on the meaningfulness of life seems to be that judgments about the value that is supposed to contribute to the meaningfulness of life be objective.

The second consideration arises from a discussion of Richard Hare of the thesis that nothing matters.[5] A young acquaintance of Hare's has been convinced by reading a novel of Camus' that nothing matters. Hare tries to help him by calling

attention to the logic of the concept 'mattering.' Hare argues that what matters always matters to someone, and that to say that something matters is to express one's concern. If this is right, then to be in a position to say that nothing matters would be to be completely detached, to have no concerns whatsoever. Since it is rare, if even a genuine possibility, that people will be so completely detached, it looks as if it is safe to reject the thesis that nothing matters.

The problem is that if all there is to mattering is what Hare says there is, then I think that there is still a sense in which nothing would matter. One of the things I think people have in mind when they ask whether anything matters is whether the fact that something matters to them is enough to make it really matter. Suppose, e.g. that one were to wake up one day with a new set of concerns. What matters to one on that day is different from what mattered the day before. Would this make any difference to what matters? If it wouldn't then it looks as if *what* matters to a person isn't important. But if this is so, then I think that there is a sense in which nothing really matters. For something to really matter, it must matter that it matters. If this is right, then in order for life to be meaningful it must make a difference *what* we take to be valuable. A necessary condition of this is that not any and every value judgment can be as good as any other. This in turn will be true if judgments about the values that are supposed to make life meaningful are objective.[6]

The third reason for accepting this objectivity condition arises from a challenge that one would expect an adequate answer to the meaningfulness of life to be able to meet. Suppose a person has devoted most of her life to her work, recognizing the challenges that lay in front of her, throwing herself eagerly into meeting them, and succeeding by dint of concentration and sustained effort. In the process she has had to sacrifice a number of personal relationships. At the time she thought it was worth it, but on reflection she wonders whether it was. Is a life spent in pursuit of this kind of success worth it when it was achieved at the expense of personal relationships? One would expect an adequate account of the meaningfulness of life to be able to answer such a question. This does not mean that the answer must be affirmative. There need be no guarantee that a given life is meaningful. But the question should be answerable. Such an answer will be forthcoming if the value judgments in question are objective, for to say that they are objective is to say that there is a single correct answer to questions like 'Is the life described above worth living?' If the value judgments in question turn out not to be objective, then any proposed answer to such a question would seem to be undermined by the fact that its denial can also be correct.

These last two considerations suggest a third condition, that what matters to a person must have a certain *kind* of value. Stephen Darwall has argued recently that what makes a life meaningful must have a certain kind of *importance.*[7] If, e.g., I enjoy building model airplanes, then it may be valuable for me to spend some of my time building them. But this kind of activity hardly seems important enough to insure that my life will be meaningful. For one thing, it is not the sort of thing that would be valuable for everyone else to spend their time at. The value that it has in my life seems to depend on the mere fact that I like building model airplanes. Not everyone else will share this desire. As one way of expressing this third condition, one might suggest that for something to have the kind of importance it needs to make a person's life meaningful, its value must not depend on particular desires a particular person or a particular subset of persons happen to have.[8]

The second set of conditions includes the condition that the meaningfulness of a particular life depends on contingent features of that life. It is not something that will hold necessarily of every life. If I am right in saying that what makes life meaningful makes one kind of life meaningful rather than other kinds and that it makes continuing to live preferable to ending one's life, then it can't be true that no matter what kind of life a person lives it will turn out to be meaningful. That is why an attempt to spell out the meaning of life in terms of a good end that the world is inevitably moving towards will ultimately fail to provide the kind of meaning that I am concerned with. If this purpose will be achieved no matter what kind of life one has lived, then it can not provide one with a reason for living one kind of life rather than another. If there is something that makes life meaningful in the way that most people have hoped for, then it must be something which may or may not be realized in a given life. The meaningfulness of a life must depend on contingent features of that life.[9]

The second member of this second set of conditions is that a meaningful life be within the grasp of most people. Unlike the previous conditions, this is not a necessary condition for life's being meaningful in the sense we are looking for. One can grant that a person who spends his life developing a cure for cancer, or achieving the artistic output of a Bach, will lead a meaningful life. A life of this sort of achievement will not be within the average person's grasp. Nevertheless, this appears to be a reasonable condition to accept given what we are looking for. When most people ask what makes life meaningful, they seem to be asking for something that could characterize *their* lives, making *those* lives worth living. If this is right, then for life to be meaningful in the way that most people have hoped for, what makes life meaningful should be within the average person's grasp.

There are, however, tensions that arise within both of these sets of conditions. The greatest tension occurs within the first set of conditions. If a value that makes life meaningful must meet the objectivity condition, then if someone denies that a life that displays this value is meaningful, that person will have to be mistaken. There would then seem to be something about this correct conception of value that in principle she could recognize that would make her realize that she was mistaken.[10] If the relevant value also meets the condition of internalism, then the recognition of its nature should also make her want to realize it. But if what moves people to act varies from person to person, a recognition of the nature of this purported value may fail to produce the relevant desire. Relying on the condition of internalism, the person can then deny that she is mistaken in rejecting the value in question, since an understanding of its nature fails to move her. Given the variability of what moves people to act, the condition of internalism threatens to undermine the objectivity of value judgments. But if both of these conditions can not be met, then it looks as if life can not be meaningful in the way that most people have hoped for.

This tension is only increased if we add in the third member of this set of conditions. If what makes life valuable is independent of the particular desires that particular people happen to have, then for any person, it looks as if it will be possible for something to be valuable without its being the object of any of the particular desires that the person happens to have. But if what moves people are just those particular desires, then it looks as if for any person it will be possible for something to be valuable without the recognition of its nature making him want to realize it. That is, it looks as if one will not be able to satisfy both the internalist condition and the importance condition.

There is also some tension between the members of the second set of conditions. If life can be meaningful only if it exhibits values that depend on contingent features of a person's life, then it may turn out that in most human lives external factors will prevent these values from being realized. The person may not have the right sorts of values in the first place. And even if she does, a premature death or circumstances beyond her control may prevent their realization. If realizing them depends at all on the success of a long-term project, then the possibilities of this project's being interrupted raise the question of whether a meaningful life will be within the grasp of the average person.

Whether life can be meaningful, thus, depends in part on whether there is a conception of value that satisfies all of these conditions. Given the tensions that arise between them, it is by no means clear that life can be meaningful. However, given these conditions, a large part of the question of whether life can be meaningful or not falls squarely within the provence of moral philosophy. E.g., one of the central problems in recent moral philosophy has been whether moral judgments can meet both the conditions of internalism and objectivity.

III

That an adequate conception of what makes life meaningful should satisfy the conditions set out above explains in part why the kind of theological answer to the meaningfulness of life summarized earlier has appeared so attractive. This in turn provides additional confirmation that these conditions are reasonable conditions for the meaningfulness of life.

Given God's nature, a perfect union with God does seem sufficient to outweigh whatever suffering a particular life might contain. His nature also seems to provide an objective basis for the evaluative judgments in question. What is valuable is to do what God desires or commands; and, given His goodness, it should be valuable to satisfy those desires and carry out those commands. Since what God commands does not seem to depend on any particular desires that people happen to have, it looks as if the importance condition will be satisfied. Once people understand their own nature and what God has done for them, they will be filled with love for God. Not only will this lead to the right sort of relationship between them and God, it will also provide the necessary motivation for them to live the kind of life they ought to live towards others, and to live it cheerfully and with enthusiasm. Thus, the internalist condition seems to be met. Furthermore, since whether a person achieves the right sort of relationship with God depends on whether he asks for God's forgiveness, and since it will only be by being filled with God's love that a person will be enabled to live properly towards others, the kind of value that makes life meaningful will depend on contingent features of that person's life. Nevertheless, because of the grace of God, a meaningful life is within everyone's grasp.

However, despite the way these conditions explain the appeal of this theological answer, they also provide part of the basis for some serious problems for it. If the value that makes a life meaningful can not be one that is realized in any sort of life, then there is some reason for thinking that the desires, purposes, and commands of God, fulfillment of which are supposed to make a person's life meaningful, can not themselves be arbitrary. If they were, then it looks as if any sort of life could turn out to be meaningful. All that would be required would be for God to command that people engage in it; and God could command this since His commands are arbitrary. If God's commands were arbitrary, this would also raise the question of whether the importance condition would be satisfied. If His commands were arbitrary, then it looks as if the value of obeying them would depend on particular desires that God happens to have. Of course, it is not ordinarily thought that God's commands are arbitrary, or that He would command just any old way of life. God is *good*, and His commands flow from that goodness. But if this is correct, then there are conditions that God's commands and desires must meet that make them the commands of a good God, conditions which if they aren't met cast doubt on God's goodness. Once this is granted, the sort of problems I have in mind arise.

Fellowship with God and obedience to His commands may have value if God is good, but the existence of evil in the world raises the question of whether God is good. If God is omnipotent and some of the evil we find in our world is avoidable, how can God be good? Wouldn't a good God pre-

vent avoidable evil? The situation in which people find themselves needing God's forgiveness also leaves God's goodness open to question. If the need for forgiveness is due to original sin, a condition that people can not avoid, then how can it be fair to demand that they avoid it and that they ask forgiveness for not avoiding it? Would a good God make demands that are beyond people's nature, especially when He as their creator was at least partly responsible for that nature? But if God is not good, then how can His nature provide an objective basis for the goodness of union with Him and obedience to His commands? Furthermore, if God is not good, then there is no reason for thinking that when people recognize God's nature they will want to enjoy union with Him or want to carry out those commands.[11] There is, thus, some reason to wonder whether the theological answer we have been considering can be an adequate answer to the meaningfulness of life.

There is also reason to wonder whether an answer suggested by a good number of contemporary philosophers, that the meaning of life is created rather than discovered, is an adequate answer to the meaningfulness of life.[12] The problem that arises here is essentially the problem that arises in the tension between the conditions of internalism and objectivity. According to the view in question, meaning is created because what is valuable is ultimately a matter of a person's basic *decisions* or *desires*. It is by wanting certain sorts of things or by making certain decisions that certain activities *become* valuable. They become valuable because one *takes* them to be valuable. There is no fixed pattern of life that anyone must live in order for their life to be valuable. To insist that there is, is to intrude on a person's autonomy as a moral agent. It should be clear that this conception of the meaningfulness of life meets the internalist condition. Whatever it is that makes life meaningful will be something that a person will want to achieve, because what makes life meaningful just is the object of one of her basic wants or decisions. The difficulty comes in meeting the objectivity condition. To take the most obvious example, how is one to deal with someone whose chosen way of life essentially involves interference with the chosen ways of life of others? How can something be valuable when by its very nature its existence prevents the existence of value in the lives of others? But there appears to be no way of ruling out as incorrect the claim that such a life is valuable, since it can be the object of someone's basic desires or decisions.

For similar reasons the importance condition fails to be satisfied. On the view in question what is valuable is what is taken to be valuable, and what is taken to be valuable depends on the particular desires that a person happens to have. But how important is it to be engaged in behavior that merely satisfies desires that a person happens to have, especially if in doing so the person prevents value from being realized in the lives of others? Won't the importance of a life at least depend on what a person's basic desires are desires for?

IV

The question remains whether there is a chance for a position that falls between these two camps, one that finds the value that makes life worthwhile in something other than a transcendent purpose and yet satisfies all of the conditions that have been set out. In what follows I shall sketch a view which, if the sketch can be filled out, shows that there is such a possibility. The view is that life is meaningful if it exhibits moral behavior, where moral behavior is understood as one species of rational behavior.

The central feature of this view is that it bases the value that is supposed to make life meaningful on people's rational nature. There are certain desires or motives that a person will come to have if she exercises reason correctly. These are *rational* desires. Action in accord with them is rational. Action contrary to them is irrational. What is valuable is to act in accord with them.

This conception of value seems to satisfy all of the conditions that have been set out. Since there are only certain ways in which reason can be exercised if it is to be exercised correctly, there are only certain desires or motives that one can have and act in accordance with if one is to be rational. This provides a basis for the objectivity of the value judgments in question. Second, in so far as the correct exercise of reason carries with it certain desires or motives, the kind of value in question is one that if recognized (i.e. if reason *is* exercised correctly) will lead one to want to realize it. Third, since what is valuable depends only on its being the object of rational desires, and since rational desires arise from people's common rational nature, the value in question does not depend on particular desires that particular people happen to have. Thus, the importance condition is satisfied. Fourth, in so far as the mere capacity for rational desires doesn't guarantee that one will have them, let alone act in accord with them, the contingency condition is met. Finally, in so far as a person's rational nature gives her the capacity both to have and to act in accord with rational desires, the kind of value in question is accessible to the average person.

Two key questions need to be answered if this view about the meaningfulness of life is to be at all plausible. Are there rational desires of the sort this view says there are? Can such rational desires provide the basis for moral behavior? Let us begin with the first of these.

Can the correct exercise of reason contribute to a person's having certain desires? To see that it is not wildly implausible to say that reason can play this role one need only consider theoretical rationality. It seems plausible to say that when a person recognizes an inconsistency in his beliefs, not only will he want to remove it, but that the desire to remove it is a result of his recognition of that inconsistency. It is because one's rational nature leads one to want to revise an inconsistent set of beliefs that we say that it is *irrational* to hang on to such a set. It will be plausible to talk about rational *behavior*, if reason can play a role in contributing to *desires* similar to the one it plays in contributing to beliefs.

The most plausible candidate for reason's playing such a role is its contribution to the desire to adopt means to already existing ends. Acknowledging such a role would explain, e.g., why imprudence is regarded as a species of irrationality. Imprudence can at least initially be thought of as the failure to adopt appropriate means to one's longterm ends. However, if reason's role in contributing to desire were confined to the recognition of means to already existing ends, it is doubtful that one could give an affirmative answer to the second of our two key questions, allowing rational desires to provide a basis for moral behavior. If it were so confined any form of behavior could turn out to be rational, provided a person held an end to which the behavior in question would be an appropriate means. If there are to be certain sorts of behavior that will be moral for anyone to pursue because it would be irrational not to act in those ways, then it looks as if there must be certain *ends* that are rational to pursue and irrational not to pursue. But how is one to make sense of such rational ends?

There are at least two ways in which the exercise of reason might play a role in the acquisition of ends. The first is by providing people with certain specific ends. The second is by limiting or expanding the pursuit of already existing ends.

An example of the first way can, I think, be found in Aristotle.[13] According to this view, there are certain ends that people aim at by nature. These are ends that people 're-ally want,' in the sense that their conscious desires and dispositions can be seen as more or less successful attempts at securing them. By reflecting on their own actions and the actions of others, people can make an inductive inference to what it is that they are aiming at by nature, and thus to what ends they should have. This inductive inference leads to a desire to have one's conscious desires and dispositions in accord with these ends. Although such self-conscious determination of what ends a person should aim at may be atypical, the more common modification of one's ends in the light of satisfaction or dissatisfaction obtained from the pursuit of them can be seen as the unreflective analogue of this self-conscious determination of ends. If asked for an example of what one such rational end would look like, I would suggest the ability to determine what happens to one by means of one's own decisions or choices (i.e. a desire for one's own autonomy). According to this suggestion, one of the things people 'really want' is not just that their actions turn out well in some sense of 'well,' but that whatever success they have, that success is due to them. People want their actions to turn out well because of decisions *they* have made. *They* want to determine what happens to them.

If asked where this capacity for rational desire comes from, one can say that people are not simply creatures who want certain things. They are creatures who can reflect on what they want and determine whether they want to have certain desires or not. It is this capacity to reflect on what desires one has that is at the basis of one's capacity to make value judgments.[14] E.g., we evaluate certain desires (and the actions they prompt us to perform) in terms of how well they promote our long-range ends. If the suggestion I have drawn from Aristotle is correct, this reflective capacity extends to our long-range ends as well. We have a way of reflecting on our ends to see if they are ones that we 'really want.'

However, to the extent to which one is looking for a theory of rational ends to provide a basis for morality, the above won't do by itself. It says only that each person ought to pursue her own rational ends. What happens if different people's ends come in conflict with one another? If morality has anything to say, it would seem to have something to say about how such conflicts are to be resolved or minimized. This brings us to the second way in which ends might be said to be rational. Besides views according to which specific ends are rational, there are views that set out *formal* principles of rationality, principles that limit or expand the pursuit of a person's ends, including her rational ends. They are *formal* principles because they require the existence of specific rational desires to serve as their *matter*. The best example of such a formal principle is Kant's categorical imperative.[15] As I interpret the categorical imperative, it attempts to set out what is rational to do independently of any particular ends a person might happen to have. It says that it is irrational to pursue a given end if the universalization of that pursuit can not consistently be willed to be a universal law.[16] As I interpret what it is to be able consistently to will something to be a universal law, it is for that universalization to be compatible with what one must want in so far as one is rational. This includes whatever rational ends there are. The categorical imperative, thus, restricts pursuit of a given end if everyone's pursuing that end would be incompatible with one of one's own rational ends.

If, e.g., the ability to determine what happens to me by my own choices is a rational end, and if I am contemplating promoting this ability by infringing on someone else's ability to determine what happens to him by means of his own choices, then the categorical imperative prohibits such an action. It says that it is irrational to want to pursue that end under these circumstances, because were others to behave in the same way (i.e. promote their autonomy at the expense of mine) this would be incompatible with what I must want in so far as I am rational. If it also leads to promoting others' rational ends (e.g. on the grounds that willing the universalization of not promoting others' rational ends would be incompatible with my rational ends), then the categorical imperative produces a new set of rational desires, one obtained by in a sense expanding on and in a sense restricting the previous set of rational desires. One is provided with the desire to promote anyone's rational ends provided that doing so isn't incompatible with the rational ends of others. Put in terms of the ability to determine what

happens to one by means of one's own choices, one ought to promote people's ability to determine what happens to them by means of their own choices, provided this is compatible with a similar ability for others. This, at least, has the beginning of the ring of a moral principle.

If asked where the capacity for this new set of rational ends comes from, one might as a beginning adopt a suggestion of Thomas Nagel.[17] People have the capacity to step back and reflect on themselves as one rational being among others. To the extent to which from this perspective our own rational desires still matter (i.e. are still ones we want ourselves to have), to that extent the rational desires of other rational beings must also matter. If my rational desires still matter from this perspective, then they must matter simply because they are the rational desires of a rational being. But then the recognition of others as rational beings must also make their rational desires matter. The exercise of my capacity to step back and view myself as one rational being among others will, thus, make me want not to interfere with the rational ends of others. This in itself is not enough to make me want to limit the pursuit of my own rational ends when they interfere with the rational ends of others, for from the same perspective I will also want to pursue my rational ends. But it is at least a beginning.

If all of this can be filled out (i.e. if one can see that the correct exercise of reason will lead to certain ends, and to the expansion and restriction of these ends, if one can identify what these ends are and what the expansions and restrictions on them are, and if finally the result of all this yields anything like a plausible set of moral principles), then it looks as if there will be a way of spelling out a moral value that can be exhibited in human life that is objective, independent of particular desires that people happen to have, and one whose recognition would lead a person to want to exhibit it. If what results are things like the demand that we promote people's ability to determine what happens to them by means of their own choices without thereby restricting a similar ability in others, then it appears to be a demand that can be achieved, without the guarantee that it will be achieved. Thus, there appears to be a way of understanding moral value according to which it does satisfy all of the conditions I have set out for a meaningful life.[18]

One further comment is needed before my suggestion about what would make a life meaningful is complete. There are two kinds of value that are associated with moral behavior, the value of doing what is right or ought to be done, and the value of being a morally worthy person. This latter can be understood in terms of being an appropriate object of moral praise or respect. In suggesting that life can be meaningful if it embodies moral behavior, I have in mind both of these sorts of values, both behaving as one ought and being a fitting object for moral praise or respect. I take the latter to involve not only doing the right sorts of things, but doing them for the right sorts of reasons. E.g., if a certain action is wrong because it takes unfair advantage of others, then the agent will display moral worth if she foregoes taking advantage of others because she doesn't want to treat people unfairly. One reason this is important is that if a person's life exhibits both the value of having done the right thing and the value of having done it for the right reasons, then it will increase the chances that this value will outweigh whatever suffering or misfortune that may occur in that life.

Here then is one suggestion about what will make life meaningful that falls between the two camps that we have previously considered. A moral life will be a meaningful life, where moral behavior is understood as one species of rational behavior.[19]

V

Strictly speaking, it would be premature to conclude that a moral life is a meaningful life, even if the theory of morality sketched above can be filled out. What follows so far from that theory is that a moral life satisfies a set of conditions necessary for life's being meaningful. Unless one can be assured that nothing important for the meaningfulness of life has been left out, all one is entitled to conclude is that a moral life will be part of what can make a life meaningful. In what follows I shall consider three candidates for what this theory might have left out. We shall see that at least one of them requires further investigation.

One of the consequences of the view I have sketched is that it is possible for a person to be mistaken about whether his life is meaningful or not. This, it has been suggested, is odd if not mistaken.[20] One thing, then, that this theory might have left out is something that will prevent a person who leads a moral life from being mistaken about whether his life is meaningful or not.

The first thing to say is that taking it to be impossible for a person to be mistaken about whether her life is meaningful concedes far too much to one who would argue that life is meaningless. Given this condition, all such a person would have to do would be to raise doubts about the meaningfulness of life. He would not have to provide any further justification for those doubts. This makes his task far too simple. Nevertheless, there does seem to be something odd about a person's being mistaken about her life being meaningful. This can be explained, I think, if we return to the reasons given for accepting the condition of internalism. Someone who recognizes the value of what makes her life meaningful will recognize that achieving that value is something that matters to her. In achieving it she will be 'caught up' in what she does, feeling at that time that it does make her life meaningful. This certainly holds true on the theory of morality that I have sketched. A person whose life exhibits the value of moral worth will do what she ought to do for the right reasons. What moves her will be just what makes her actions right. She will typically be 'caught up' in performing those actions, and, at the time, feel that they are important enough to make her life meaningful. However, all of this is still compatible with a person's being mistaken about her life's being meaningful. A person can take something to be valuable enough to make her life meaningful when in fact it isn't valuable enough. A person can exhibit a given value in her life that makes it meaningful without recognizing its nature in such a way that achieving it does matter that much to her. And even if she does recognize its nature in this way, she can stop to reflect on what she takes to be valuable, entertaining doubts about whether it is important enough to make her life meaningful. If these doubts persist, they can infect her active life, robbing it of a good deal of the vitality that allowed her to feel that her life was meaningful. Each of these carries with it the possibility of a person's being mistaken about whether her life is meaningful or not. Thus, in allowing people to be mistaken about whether their lives are meaningful, the theory I have sketched has not left out something important for the meaningfulness of life.

A second reason for thinking that this theory has left something out is that it looks as if according to this theory a person who spends his life working at a Coca-Cola bottling factory, never giving moral offense to anyone but never doing anything else of importance, can still lead a moral life. Such a life doesn't seem important enough to be a meaningful life.[21] This suggestion ignores two important points. A person's life involves much more than his work. And the theory I have sketched does require actions that positively affect others through the requirement that one promote other people's pursuit of their rational ends. E.g., a person who spends his life working at a Coca-Cola bottling factory may, when it comes his turn to schedule overtime, refrain from acting vindictively towards a co-worker, thereby earning the respect and trust of his other co-workers. Or he may have been the first to offer help when a tragedy struck his neighbor, his confident disclaimer that the neighbor would have done the same thing in a similar situation assuring what might

not have been true up to that time, that his neighbor would so act. The theory I have sketched does seem to be able to account for the value of these sorts of actions. And a person who affects others in these ways does, I think, lead a life that is important enough to be called meaningful. Given the way people's lives do impinge on one another, a moral life does seem important enough to be called meaningful.

The final consideration for thinking that the theory I have sketched has left out something important arises from a closer look at what is involved in exhibiting moral worth. If there is anyone who displays moral worth, it seems to me to be someone who acts out of compassionate concern for other individuals. It is someone who perceives their particular needs, who provides words of consolation when they are most needed and words of encouragement when they are needed. It is someone who goes out of her way to make a gesture that only the person involved would appreciate, someone who knows how to make others feel that they, with all of their personal peculiarities, are special and worth attention. I am far more confident that someone who acts in this way throughout her lifetime has led a meaningful life, than I am that any adequate answer to the meaningfulness of life must satisfy the conditions I have set down, or that the view I have sketched above has a chance of providing an adequate basis for moral behavior. The question is whether the recognition of the value of this kind of compassionate concern will fit with the kind of moral theory that I have sketched. The kind of compassionate concern I have in mind doesn't seem to arise from a rational desire based on the recognition of another person as one rational being among others. It seems quite different from the kind of respect for others that would lead one not to treat someone unfairly. It is focused on *them* and their *particular* needs and concerns, things that seem to arise from something other than their rational natures.[22]

The problem is not so much whether the kind of moral theory I have sketched can't make room for the value of fostering and acting on such personal attitudes. It can. The problem is whether it acknowledges sufficient scope and weight to this value. Just as Kant argued for a duty of benevolence on the grounds that, given the conditions of human life, there will always be the possibility that one will need the help of others to achieve one's rational ends; so it might be argued that circumstances under which being the object of such personal attitudes will be necessary for the kind of self-respect needed to exercise one's autonomy will give rise to an obligation to foster and act on personal attitudes. Nevertheless, it is not clear that this will be sufficient to explain the value of having and acting on such attitudes on all occasions on which we take them to be valuable. Nor is it clear that this theory will end up giving the proper weight to the value of acting on such attitudes when they come in conflict with other morally relevant concerns, such as the desire to treat people fairly.[23] If it fails in either of these tasks, then there is good reason for thinking that this theory does leave out something important both for morality and for the meaningfulness of life.[24]

That is why these first thoughts that I have on the meaningfulness of life require second thoughts. And these second thoughts undoubtedly will require still further thoughts. But, then, that *is* life.

Notes

1. This view is drawn from Arthur Schopenhauer. See, e.g., his 'On the Suffering of the World,' and 'On the Vanity of Existence,' in *Essays and Aphorisms*, translated by R.J. Hollingdale (Harmondsworth, England: Penguin Books 1970), 41–50, 51–4. These essays are reprinted in Steven Sanders and David R. Cheney, eds., *The Meaning of Life* (Englewood Cliffs, NJ: Prentice-Hall 1980), 25–32, 33–6.

2. What follows is taken from Leo Tolstoy, *My Confession*, translated by Leo Wiener,

(London: J.M. Dent & Sons 1905), excerpts of which are reprinted in Sanders and Cheney, 15–24, and in E. D. Klemke, ed., *The Meaning of Life* (New York: Oxford University Press 1981), 9–19.

3. R.W. Hepburn, 'Questions about the Meaning of Life,' Klemke, 212–13, Sanders and Cheney, 116–17.

4. Thomas Nagel, 'The Absurd,' *Journal of Philosophy* 63 (1971) 716–27, reprinted in Klemke, 151–61, and in Sanders and Cheney, 155–65.

5. R.M. Hare, 'Nothing Matters,' *Applications of Moral Philosophy* (London: Macmillan 1972) 32–9, reprinted in Klemke, 241–7, and in Sanders and Cheney, 97–103.

6. Note that I am not claiming that acknowledging the objectivity of value judgments is the only way of adding what Hare's account seems to have left out. I am only claiming that it is one such way. Nevertheless, this together with the other two considerations I offer does. I think, provide grounds for taking the objectivity of certain value judgments to be a necessary condition for the value in question to contribute to the meaningfulness of life.

7. Stephen Darwall, *Impartial Reason* (Ithaca, NY: Cornell University Press 1983), 164–6.

8. Two other points might be noted in connection with this third condition.

First, there is some question as to whether it is independent of the first two. The mere objectivity of value judgments will not insure its satisfaction; but on one understanding of the internalist condition, it looks as if it together with objectivity will insure the importance of the values in question. If one takes the internalist condition to say that whatever it is that makes something valuable, the recognition of it will make anyone want to realize that value, then it looks as if what makes something valuable will be independent of the particular desires that any given person might happen to have.

If it weren't, then someone without the relevant desires wouldn't want to realize the value in question. However, on another understanding of the internalist condition, it together with objectivity does not yield this third condition. Suppose that my spending my time building model airplanes has objective value because I enjoy spending my time that way. If the internalist condition only implies that anyone would want to spend their time building model airplanes *if they too enjoyed it*, then the importance condition will not be satisfied. The value of building model airplanes under these circumstances does depend on desires that are peculiar to certain people.

Second, it might be suggested that this formulation of the importance condition is too weak, and that a substantive account of what makes a value important should be included within it. It is, I think, premature to respond to this suggestion at this stage of the argument. For more on this see Section V below, including nos. 22 and 25.

9. It may be that on some occasions when people have asked about the meaning of life they have been looking for something that would provide their life with meaning no matter how their life might be lived. But if so, all this shows is that one will not be able to give a single answer to all of the questions people have in mind when they have asked about the meaning of life. That is one of the reasons why I have concerned myself with just one set of questions that people have asked when they have wondered about the meaning of life.

10. This carries with it the epistemological assumption that the value of whatever makes life meaningful can be recognized. But it seems to me that this assumption is one that one should be argued out of rather than into, if for no other reason than that it is what one would expect of the kind of value that would make life meaningful.

11. These are, of course, familiar problems, and various solutions to them have been proposed. The points I want to make here are that without solutions to them the theological view summarized above will not provide an adequate answer to the meaningfulness of life, and that the conditions I set out in Section II provide an important part of the explanation of why this is so.

12. See, e.g., Hazel Barnes, *An Existentialist Ethics* (New York: Alfred A. Knopf 1967), excerpts of which are reprinted in Sanders and Cheney, 105–12, along with Hare, 'Nothing Matters.' To a large extent this answer can also be found in Paul Edwards, 'Meaning and Value of Life,' *The Encyclopedia of Philosophy*, Paul Edwards, Editor in Chief (New York: Macmillan 1967), 467–77, reprinted in Klemke, 118–40, an abridged version of which is reprinted in Sanders and Cheney, 87–96, and in Kai Nielsen, 'Linguistic Philosophy and the Meaning of Life,' *Cross Currents* 14 (1964) 313–34, revised versions of which are reprinted in Klemke, 177–204, and in Sanders and Cheney, 129–54.

13. See, e.g, Norman O. Dahl, *Practical Reason, Aristotle, and Weakness of the Will* (Minneapolis, MN: University of Minnesota Press 1984), Chs. 3–6.

14. See, e.g., Harry Frankfurt, 'Freedom of the Will and the Concept of a Person,' *Journal of Philosophy* 68 (1971) 5–20.

15. See, e.g., Immanuel Kant, *Groundwork of the Metaphysics of Morals* (New York: Harper Torchbooks 1964). Other examples of formal principles of practical rationality are Thomas Nagel's principle that if a person has a subjective reason to promote an end, then anyone has an objective reason to promote that same end, in *The Possibility of Altruism* (Oxford: The Clarendon Press 1970), and John Rawls' principles of justice in *A Theory of Justice* (Cambridge, MA: Harvard University Press 1971) when they are viewed under the Kantian interpretation.

16. For the most detailed and plausible attempt that I know of to argue that it

would be irrational to act on principles that one could not will that everyone act on see Darwall, *Impartial Reason*, Ch. 14.

17. Nagel, *The Possibility of Altruism*, Chs. XI and XII.

18. One might wonder whether the theory really does satisfy all of these conditions. E.g., what is to be said in response to the kind of challenge to the objectivity of moral value raised by Nagel in 'The Absurd'? It may be that a moral life will appear to be valuable from the perspective of the rational nature of human beings. But, it might be argued, one can always step back and view this kind of life from another perspective. From that perspective it will appear to be arbitrary that human beings have a rational nature that leads them to take such a life to be valuable. Indeed, from this new perspective, a moral life may not appear to be valuable at all. Why doesn't this reopen the question of the objectivity of moral value?

I do not have the time to pursue this question in the detail that it deserves, but one or two things can be said at this time. The question we have been considering is what kind of life would be meaningful for human beings to engage in. Any answer to it would seem to have to take account of the conditions of human life, including whatever rational nature human beings happen to have. If from the point of view of that nature a certain life seems valuable, then that life will have a strong claim on being the kind of life that is valuable for human beings to live. Even if from another perspective it seems arbitrary that human beings have such a nature, it need not seem arbitrary that it is valuable for beings with such a nature to live a moral life. In the second place, if the theory I have sketched does provide an adequate basis for morality, then its adequacy will have to be acknowledged from any perspective that yields reliable judgments. If the theory is correct, then whatever perspective one adopts it will have to be true at that perspective that it

is valuable for human beings to live a moral life, even if it wouldn't be valuable for someone whose nature puts her at that perspective to live a similar life.

But is the theory correct? Why doesn't the fact that a moral life may not appear valuable when one adopts a different perspective undermine the correctness of the theory I have sketched? To raise this question is just to raise the possibility that the theory might not turn out to be a correct moral theory. Of course it might not. We have not seen all the arguments that could be given in support or in criticism of it. But by the same token, it might turn out to be a correct moral theory. If it is an open question whether this theory provides an adequate basis for morality, then it is an open question. To decide it one will have to look at the particular features of the theory to see just what can be said for and against it.

But doesn't this possibility show that we don't *know* whether the theory I have sketched provides an objective basis for morality? Perhaps it does. But this still doesn't show that morality doesn't have an objective basis. Nor does it show that in the absence of such knowledge it isn't reasonable to assume that morality does have an objective basis. This is an assumption that I think is reasonable. And it is all that is needed to take seriously the project of looking in detail at the theory I have sketched to see just what can be said on its behalf.

19. In putting forward this suggestion I am not claiming that the conception of morality I have outlined is the only one according to which a moral life would satisfy the conditions necessary for a meaningful life. Nor, as I have already indicated, am I claiming that a moral life is the only kind of life that can be meaningful. I will be happy if it is acknowledged that the theory I have sketched provides one way of seeing how a moral life can be a meaningful life.

20. This has been suggested both in discussion and by a referee.

21. This suggestion was also raised in discussion and by a referee. It might also be suggested that this shows that the formulation of the importance condition given in Section II is too weak. Instead one needs a more substantive account of what makes something important enough to contribute to the meaningfulness of life, including, perhaps, making a significant contribution to human well-being.

22. For a sustained attempt to argue that the kind of moral theory I have sketched can not adequately account for the moral value of acting on such personal attitudes see Lawrence A. Blum, *Friendship, Altruism and Morality* (London: Routledge & Kegan Paul 1980).

23. E.g., a person casting a play must choose between two candidates, one who is slightly better for the part, the other whom he knows will benefit more from being a member of the cast. Without knowing anything else, fairness suggests giving the part to the first candidate, compassion or concern suggests giving it to the second. It seems to me that on at least some occasions like this, considerations of compassion or concern should win out.

Presumably the kind of theory I have sketched would settle such a conflict by considering whether from the impersonal standpoint of a rational being one could choose that everyone act in one of these two ways rather than the other in these and all other similar circumstances. At first sight this might seem to tip the scales in favor of considerations of fairness, since the desire to treat people fairly is a much more direct instantiation of such an impersonal attitude than is compassion or concern. In an as yet unpublished paper, 'Impartialist Ethics and the Personal,' Stephen Darwall argues that there is no good reason for thinking that this is so. This seems to me to be correct. However, even if it is, it still doesn't follow that the kind of theory I have sketched attaches the proper weight to considerations like compassion or concern. To see whether it does or not still requires further investigation.

24. If the theory does fail in either of these two tasks, then I think that one will have to take seriously the suggestion that a stronger importance condition than that formulated in Section II needs to be satisfied before one can be assured that a moral life is a meaningful life.

34 / MICHAEL SLOTE

GOODS AND LIVES

The fact that goods occur at one time (of life) rather than another is generally held to make no difference to the overall goodness of lives or to the existence of reasons for action, and this rejection of 'time preference' can be found across a wide spectrum of moral theorists. But in this first chapter I shall argue that time preference is not the atypical or irrational phenomenon that so many otherwise divergent theorists assume and that our ordinary thinking quite naturally ascribes unequal importance to different periods of life.

The discussion will focus on some examples that have largely escaped the notice of those opposed to time preference, examples that I believe cannot be adequately explained without making some new conceptual distinctions about human good and using the philosophically rather neglected concept of 'the prime of life'. And the examples chosen will also enable us to question the equal importance of all time periods and the automatic transtemporal influence of reasons for action, without having to presuppose the sort of intrapersonal dissociation or disunity whose invidiousness has so largely motivated opposition to any sort of time preference. Our defence of time preference will be different, moreover, from what the most notable recent defender of the notion, Bernard Williams, has said on its behalf; and since the repudiation of temporal inequality seems to be an important underlying as-

sumption both of Utilitarianism and of such major anti-Utilitarians as Rawls and Nagel, it will also be important to see how our particular arguments against that assumption affect the various theories that have hitherto partly based themselves upon it. But first I would like to give some indication of the breadth and depth of its appeal.

I

Let us begin with the maximizers. Utilitarians seem to take the denial of time preference as a practically self-evident condition on any maximizing conception of human good or rational action. Sidgwick, for example, holds that the maximization of personal welfare over time pre-supposes the equal treatment of all the times in a person's life in much the same way that the maximization of social welfare (or the welfare of all sentient beings) requires us to accord equal weight to the welfare of every individual.[1] And for all their other disagreements, John Rawls follows the Utilitarians in presenting a maximizing conception of the goodness of single lives and of egoistically rational life-planning that treats all time periods in a single life equally: the timing of goods being important only as a means to maximizing individual well-being over time.[2] And he also argues (in a manner at least partially anticipated by Sidgwick)[3] that time preference involves 'not viewing all moments as equally parts of one's life'.[4] Of course, Rawls criticizes Utilitarianism for extending to society the (maximizing) principle of rational choice appropriate for one man.[5] He holds that the Utilitarian's conception of social (moral) choice mistakenly treats social groups as organic superindividuals, and that a proper sense of the distinctness of individuals within any social group entails a preference for his own non-maximizing principles of social justice. But he shares the Utilitarian maximizing conception of individual good and the rejection of time preference that, as we have noted, seems naturally to accompany it, and others influenced by Rawls and likewise opposed to Utilitarian moral theory have also insisted on the equal treatment of times within single lives. Thus Thomas Nagel in *The Possibility of Altruism* has attempted to show that all periods of an individual's life must play an equal role in the origination and transmission of reasons for action, and like Rawls (though more systematically) he attempts to derive the equality of different times from a proper metaphysical conception of them as forming the equally real parts of a single finite life.[6]

Moreover, the idea that periods in a single life are to be treated equally is not simply a presupposition or natural adjunct of the idea of maximization. For it can also be found among philosophers who explicitly doubt or deny the validity of maximization as a principle of rational choice or individual good. Thus Amartya Sen has recently pointed out that the tragedy of King Lear's fate is not thought to be effectively blunted by any facts about how fortunate he was in earlier years, and he has (tentatively) concluded that the fortunateness of a life cannot simply depend on how much good (or good-minus-evil) it contains.[7] Sen suggests that what is wrong with Lear's life is a lack of reasonable equality, with respect to goods and evils, between the different periods of that life. In the determination of intertemporal human good—the goodness of lives—he thinks the roughly equal intertemporal distribution of goods carries weight quite independently of good-maximizing considerations.

However, in saying all this, Sen is not questioning the maximizers' assumption of temporal equality, but rather giving and accepting a rather strong interpretation of that notion. Consider the parallel interpersonal case. A Utilitarian may claim to give the fullest valid expression to the idea of human equality by allowing each person to 'count for one' in determining what course of action or policy maximizes social (or overall human) welfare, but an advocate of an equal distribution of benefits and burdens in society will hold that his own emphasis on the independent value of equality gives a far better expression to what we cherish in the idea of interpersonal equality. The Utilitarian and the egalitarian may thus both claim to speak in the name of true and proper equality, and so can be thought of as presenting essentially competing conceptions (or expressions or interpretations) of a single underlying concept (or idea).[8] By the same token, intrapersonal maximizers may claim that indifference to when given satisfactions or goods occur in the process of calculating total welfare over time is the most proper expression of the idea of intrapersonal temporal equality, but an egalitarian might want to say that the idea is better expressed by placing an independent value on the intertemporal equality of goods within single lives. And although it is no part of our business here to adjudicate this dispute, I do want to emphasize that Sen's temporal egalitarianism seems to leave no more room for time preference than Sidgwick, Rawls, and Nagel do.

However, one may also oppose maximizing conceptions of rational choice and individual good through a more articulated conception of the value of intertemporal equality than Sen presents. Charles Fried rejects an egalitarianism of sheer temporal moments (or intervals) in favour of (what seems to be) an egalitarianism regarding the various stages or periods of the human life cycle. Childhood, youth, maturity, etc., have, he says, their own characteristic needs and projects (in addition to those that persist across such periods) and a rational plan for a good life involves not only a maximizing of goods realized but the giving of 'richness and realization to each period of life'.[9] Now the fact (so greatly emphasized by Fried) that time periods within single lives are plausibly carved out or articulated by natural and socially influenced facts about the typical human life cycle will turn out to be highly relevant to our own defence of the intrapersonal inequality of times, but Fried, it should be clear, makes no such use of the notion: like the other philosophers we have discussed, he seems to be suggesting that different (properly articulated) times of life are of (roughly) equal importance in determining the goodness of lives.

Rawls, Nagel, Sen, Fried, and even Sidgwick all lay stress on the need to test their views against reflective common-sense judgements of value and ideas of the self and human life,[10] and in rejecting time preference as irrational they seem to assume they are giving expression only to what is already enshrined in considered opinion about what makes lives fortunate and what gives people reasons for acting. But I believe and shall argue, on the contrary, that we typically and naturally think of some times of life as more important than others, and that this conclusion has important implications for our notions of personal good.

II

Human life seems, as I have said, to possess a natural, though socially influenced, development of different times or stages of life. Whether we speak, with Shakespeare, of 'seven ages of man' or, with Erikson,[11] of the eight stages of the 'life cycle', it seems plausible to suppose that a proper understanding of human life as human beings themselves see it requires a division into different periods that reflects not an indifferent mathematical conception of infinite successive moments but rather the definition and contour that common sense attributes to our lives by speaking, e.g., of youth, adulthood, and old age.

But I believe that such a division into 'times of life' tends to be accompanied, in most of us, by a sense of the greater importance or significance of certain times of life in comparison with others, and what I first want particularly to stress is the lesser seriousness with which we regard the successes and misfortunes of childhood (including adolescence) when considering, in the rough and ready way we sometimes do, how fortunate someone has been in life. I think we have a definite tendency to discount youthful misfortune or success that can be seen, for example, in what we think and say about someone who won all the prizes and captained all the teams in school, but whose later life seems dull or unfortunate by comparison. Hearing such things about people one knew in childhood, one may knowingly shake one's head: and what is peculiarly sad about such cases can be expressed, I think, in the thought that schoolboy (or schoolgirl) glories cannot compensate for (cannot begin to make up for) what happens later in life. But by the same token schoolboy misfortunes are also largely discounted. A statesman known to have led a very happy and successful adult life may be discovered to have had a miserable childhood, but unless we imagine that that embittered his adulthood in ways not immediately obvious from other biographical facts, I don't think our discovery will make us wonder whether we haven't been over hasty in supposing the man (or his life) to have been fortunate, enviable. Within a very wide range, the facts of childhood simply don't enter with any great weight into our estimation of the (relative) goodness of total lives.

In a way, our treatment of childhood (though, as we shall see, not exclusively of childhood) is interestingly similar to the way we regard what happens in dreams, Proust tells us (roughly) that we do not reckon the sufferings and pleasures of our dreams among the actual goods and evils of our lives.[12] And it would indeed seem that we have no tendency to consider someone's fortunateness or unfortunateness to be in any way a function of the quality of his dreams during his life. (We are not likely to withhold a judgement on how well someone has lived until we find out how he spent his nightly hours of sleep.) And just as dreams are discounted except as they affect (the waking portions of) our lives, what happens in childhood principally affects our view of total lives through the effects that childhood success or failure are supposed to have on mature individuals. Thus in cases where an unhappy schoolboy career is followed by (or, as we sometimes like to think, helps to bring about) happy mature years, we think of the later years as compensating for the childhood misery, even as wiping the slate clean, and I believe that Rawls, Sidgwick, and others who have assumed the equal status of all times of life have not taken this sort of common judgement sufficiently into account.

To make theoretical sense of the tendencies of thought we have just described and do so without having to attribute undue irrationality to common patterns of human thinking, we need to make some new distinctions. In order to see why, let us first consider whether our relative indifference to certain aspects of childhood cannot be plausibly understood in terms of the already familiar distinctions between rational and irrational desires and between a person's mere preferences (desires) and his values.[13] Can we, for example, explain our attitudes toward childhood on analogy with the unwilling drug addict or sadist who places no value on satisfying the cravings he finds himself subject to? The (or one kind of) unwilling addict would rather not have his (irrational) cravings; having them, he would rather not give in to them (satisfy them); and having satisfied them, he regrets having done so. And by the same token, an un-willing or reformed sadist may wish he had somehow failed to satisfy certain (former) sadistic impulses, because, again, he (now) finds them loathsome and irrational and places no *value* on satisfying them.[14]

Perhaps such examples give us every-

thing we need to understand the way we discount what happens in childhood. Perhaps children eagerly seek certain goals—membership of the school team, scout merit badges—and simply learn later, as adults, that such things are not worth pursuing, not really valuable. But competition for merit badges, school teams, high marks is quite characteristic of childhood and adolescence, and if we were really to press home the analogy with sadism and addiction, then we would have to claim that childhood was an irrational period of human life, characteristically fraught with the desire for and valuing of things one shouldn't value. We would have to say that the miseries, elations, and disappointments connected with success and failure in typical childhood aims were perverse and/or irrational in the way we commonly think of sadism or addiction.

All this would be utterly implausible. And that is no doubt the reason why philosophers like Rawls and Nagel, who make use of the distinction between rational and irrational desires (or between values and mere preferences) and recognize its application to examples like addiction or sadism, never use that distinction to differentiate the characteristic goals and strivings of childhood from those of other periods of human life. (Indeed to do so would involve them in what, as we shall see, they themselves would have to count as time preference.) Our problem, then, is to understand how we (adults) can discount typical childhood strivings, successes, and disappointments without being unfair to childhood in the way that the strict analogy with sadism and addiction would force us to be.

We think that the cravings of (unwilling) drug addicts make them irrational and becloud their judgement. They are momentarily weak or disabled; and there is, over time, something wrong with them and unfortunate about them. But we regard most schoolboy interests and goals in none of these ways, and although the reformed, cured, or temporarily clear-headed addict or sadist will typically repudiate and be repelled by his own actions and desires (and their attendant satisfactions), that is not our attitude to childhood. We may not take childhood's characteristic goals and disappointments very seriously, but neither is our attitude one of revulsion and repudiation. Instead, we are rather tolerant of schoolboy strivings and interests and find them appropriate to, and acceptable at, the period of life in which they characteristically occur. And this latter fact may actually offer a clue about how to distinguish the childhood goals we subsequently take so little seriously, from sheer irrationalities.

The desire for honour-roll marks and the like are appropriate to their time of life—to *some* time of life—in a way that addiction and sadism are not, so even if an adult doesn't take such desires seriously and discounts the value of their objects, he may still be able to say that those objects—honour-roll marks, captaincy of the basketball team—are valuable at or for the time of life when they occur. He may say, in other words, that such things have value for, or in, childhood, but not value *ueberhaupt*, i.e., not value from the perspective of human life as a whole.[15] And this would explain his *discounting yet accepting* attitude towards characteristic childhood successes and failures; it would enable us to understand why so many of us think such successes and failures make such a negligible contribution to the overall value or unfortunateness of a human life and yet find them appropriate to childhood and adolescence rather than, like sadism or addiction, a cause for despair or regret.

Moreover, the distinction between period-relative and overall human goods is useful not only in differentiating characteristic aspects of childhood from truly irrational phenomena, but in making some intuitive distinctions within childhood itself. A twelve-year-old who clings to his mother whenever company comes, may himself feel too old for such things and consequently ascribe no value to his success in clinging on various company occasions. And it seems plausible to liken the clinging to a kind of unwilling addiction and

say that, unlike getting good marks or being a team captain, the clinging has no value for the twelve-year-old, (even) at, or for, his own time of life. We are accustomed to the idea that goods (benefits, misfortunes, etc.) are often goods for particular individuals rather than free-floating and 'objective'. But the sentence before last suggests that our distinction between overall and period-relative goods requires in some cases a double relativity: not merely of goods to individuals, but of goods to individuals at times of life.[16] Such double relativity may not be familiar and, for that reason, its introduction must be properly motivated. But I hope the above discussion gives some indication of why efforts to formulate a plausible (and non-debunking) account of our actual attitudes towards childhood naturally reach out for the distinctions we have just introduced, in addition to the more familiar ones I have mentioned.[17]

We have thus far focused upon certain attitudes towards childhood and upon the idea of childhood-relative goods that they seem to imply, but I want to make room for the possibility that similar period-relativity may be helpful in understanding attitudes towards other times (periods) of life. For example, I have somewhere read that the Romans regarded the study of philosophy as a pursuit suitable for a young man, but not for a fully mature individual, and even if my particular readers are likely to disagree with this evaluation, it may be that in order to understand and best express the Roman perspective on philosophy, we must again speak of period-relative goods and attribute to them the view that philosophy has its appropriate place and value for a young man (for the period of young manhood), but is not to be taken fully seriously from a more mature perspective. Or, to take a less uncomfortable illustration, consider the (or a) common attitude taken to what happens during senescence or old age. Our view of a person— once a successful architect, academic, or politician—who while in retirement during his declining years concentrates on win-

ning senior citizen shuffleboard tournaments, may be similar to what we think of
childhood goals and strivings. His victories
will count negligibly or not at all towards
making his overall life seem happy or fortunate, because we tend not to take such
successes very seriously, but they may
none the less be taken as goods relative to
his particular time of life. (A senior citizen
may be fortunate overall to win if he in particular would otherwise become embittered or disconsolate, but that is another
matter, a matter of means and ends, and
we shall in any event find it sad that he
takes senior citizen shuffleboard so deadly
seriously.)

Of course, we can use slightly different
language in expressing our attitude from
what would be appropriate in speaking of
childhood. We may say, for instance, that
it is sad for a former architect or what-have-
you to be reduced to putting so much emphasis on shuffleboard tournaments, and
we would not similarly speak of a child's
being *reduced* to the desires that seem distinctive of childhood. But this need not
mean that we regard old-age strivings as
irrational in the manner of addictions.
Senescence itself may be sad and regrettable, but shuffleboard competitions can
none the less seem appropriate as a focus
of that declining time of life. They may be
the best thing one can do under the circumstances, whereas it is not usually
thought appropriate or best that someone
in the unfortunate situation of an addict
should keep satisfying his addictive cravings. So our talk of someone being 'reduced' to certain activities may indicate
only that the person in question is in a state
of decline relative to some earlier period,
and we can thus explain why we do not
use this locution of developing children,
while holding that senescent shuffleboard
victories are period-relative goods in the
sense of our earlier, childhood examples.[18]

I am by no means claiming that all, or
even most, of the satisfactions of senescence, or of childhood, are merely (period)
relative goods. But the examples we have
mentioned do suggest that some of the

principal goals, disappointments, successes, and satisfactions, characteristic of
certain life periods, have value only relative to those periods and make a rather
negligible contribution to what seems to
matter most in a total human life. On the
other hand, the period known as 'the prime
of life' is typically conceived as containing
precisely those goals, strivings, miseries,
and satisfactions, that are to be taken most
seriously in human life, and is thus largely
an exception to what we have been saying
about childhood and senescence.[19] Indeed,
the very expression 'prime of life' conveys
the implication that the failures and successes of other periods are inherently less
serious and less determinative of what
one's life has, for better or worse, been like.
And one might even say that the idea of
period-relative goods is the natural result
of superimposing our sense that there is a
prime of life on the relatively neutral framework of *periods* or *times* of life.[20]

On the other hand, one might try to
evade the time-period relativity of goods
by arguing that childhood (or senescent)
successes merely have very little (non-relative) value for life overall. But if children
spend so much time and effort pursuing
what are just very minor goods, then they
are like adults who expend great effort on
very unimportant goods or projects, e.g.,
like the author who (compulsively) spends
day and night searching galley proofs for
a single misprint that he knows to be trivial and not sense-affecting. (He may know
this through having gone over the proofs
of his tome earlier and having neglected to
remove a printing error he remembers to
have been trivial but cannot now place.)
And I think such a view makes children,
e.g., seem more irrational than they are
warrantedly held to be. Moreover, even if
we simply say that the characteristic goals
and strivings of youth and old age have
very little (overall) value—by comparison
with those of the prime of life—we seem
committed to a time preference for the period of adulthood.

Of course, children *do* have a narrower
perspective than adults; recognition of that

fact lies behind and helps to justify our adult willingness to make judgements about the status of childhood values. But it is the appropriateness of what children do within the naturally-given narrower perspective of their time of life that differentiates them from addicts and sadists and makes what is of negligible value for life overall a substantial good in relation to childhood. The idea of goods-relativity thus understandably takes a place *alongside* judgements of absolute (or overall) value, in attempts to discern the full complexity of human good.

III

When Rawls speaks of time preference, he has in mind the preference not only for what is strictly nearer or earlier in time but also for one or another *period* or *part* of human life; and his rejection of time preference thus leads him to treat the (rational) goals and preferences characteristic of each such period as equally serious and of equal value.[21] But we have seen that the very opposite of such an attitude is reflected in the way, e.g., childhood and extreme old age are commonly regarded, and since Rawls himself seeks (*ceteris paribus*) to be true to our ordinary considered judgements, his total rejection of any form of time preference may stand in need of qualification. Of course, what we have so far defended is not 'pure' time preference, if by that one means the favouring, say, of earlier or nearer times of life as such. Rather, it is a preference for the goals and interests characteristic of certain stages or periods of life rather than others, and these goals and interests are from a logical standpoint perhaps only contingently related to what comes earlier or later in time. So even if certain times of life in the ordinary sense count differently in determining the overall value of a life, one might still want to rule out as irrational any preference for the early or late (temporally near or far) as such.

I think, however, that even such pure time preference occupies a place in our thinking about the goodness of lives and can be found (ironically) not where Rawls is most intent on arguing against it, in any favouring of the temporally nearer or earlier, but rather in a precisely opposite preference for what comes later in life.[22] When a personal benefit or good occurs, may make a difference to how fortunate someone is (has been), quite independently of the effects of such timing in producing other good things and of the greater importance we attach to the distinctive goals and interests of certain life periods. And I believe, in particular, that what happens late in life is naturally and automatically invested with greater significance and weight in determining the goodness of lives. The point can be illustrated.

A given man may achieve political power and, once in power, do things of great value, after having been in the political wilderness throughout his earlier career. He may later die while still 'in harness' and fully possessed of his powers, at a decent old age. By contrast, another man may have a meteoric success in youth, attaining the same office as the first man and also achieving much good; but then lose power, while still young, never to regain it. Without hearing anything more, I think our natural, immediate reaction to these examples would be that the first man was the more fortunate, and this seems to suggest a time preference for goods that come late in life.

Now one might try to explain away these reactions to the above example by showing them to arise from something other than the time preference they seem to involve. For example, almost everyone thinks it better for a person to receive an (automatically) increasing salary over the years rather than an initially high but gradually decreasing one; and one might attempt to explain *this* preference as resulting, not from any sort of time preference, but (in the manner attempted by Rawls[23]) rather as due to the superiority of pleasures of anticipation over pleasures of memory. In other words, the industrial worker whose great benefits come later will simply have greater pleasures of anticipation than any pleasures of memory one would have in the case of decreasing salary. (Why Rawls assumes that good things are more likely to be remembered with pleasure and gratitude, than with bitterness at their loss, I do not know. See George Eliot's *Daniel Deronda* for a strong statement of the opposite view.) But however well this sort of (good-maximizing) explanation suits our preference for salary increments by seniority, it cannot adequately explain the typical initial reaction to the above political example. For the person who achieves and loses high office when he is still relatively young may well hope and have reason to expect to gain power again, whereas the politician who is in the political wilderness throughout his early and middle years may easily stop expecting to gain power. And in that case, the man who succeeds late may have *fewer* of the pleasures of anticipation or hope than the one who achieves early success, and our greater estimation of the former's career presumably cannot come from any assumption to the contrary. It seems, rather, to be a matter of sheer preference for goods that come later, of our assumption, even, that a good may itself be greater for coming late rather than early in life.[24]

Such 'pure' time preference is embodied not only in our natural and (I believe) persisting reactions to particular cases, but also in the very language with which we describe how well we think people have lived. We may say that later political success can 'compensate' or 'make up' for (someone's) years in the political wilderness; but it would be an abuse of language to describe early successes as 'compensating' or 'making up' for later failures or miseries. And lest someone reply that this is merely a fact of linguistic convention, can it not be said further that the very fact that we have expressions for the way later goods can counterbalance earlier evils, but none at all for the counterbalancing of later evils by earlier goods, is a rather good indication of our common belief in the greater intrinsic importance (value or disvalue) of what comes later in life?[25]

In the light of the above, it may also at this point be worth reconsidering the example of King Lear as Sen describes it. Sen treats the example as evidence that we do not think of the goodness of lives solely in terms of maximizing criteria, but rather require good lives to embody some sort of intertemporal equality of goods. But our discussion of time preference makes another interpretation possible. The badness or tragic quality of King Lear's life may be more a function of how badly it *ends* than of any inequality among its various periods. And this possibility can seem especially plausible when one considers how untragic a life that reversed the history of King Lear would seem. For the relative fortunateness of a life in which early misfortune was followed by a long and happy old age cannot be explained by Sen's considerations of equality: as with our earlier political example, we need to bring in time preference in order to do it justice.

We may now also be in a position more fully to account for our tendency to devalue what happens in childhood and adolescence. That tendency may be partly accounted for by the above-discussed lesser seriousness with which we regard childhood plans and interests, but some of it may be due to the separate fact that what happens early in life can be compensated for by what happens later. Both 'time of life' time preference and a purer sort of time preference may be involved. And this now more complicated picture of our attitudes towards childhood may be reinforced by the following further considerations relating to old age.

We tend to think that someone who suffers from bereavement or disease in old age is more to be pitied than someone similarly miserable in childhood (alone), but this opinion cannot entirely be due to the differential seriousness or importance of the goals and preferences of childhood and old age, since it seems in no way to depend on assuming that the person who suffers in old age is not senescent (senile). Instead, the idea seems to be that nothing can compensate for sufferings at the end of life, and that thought expresses the sort of 'pure' time preference we have just been considering. On the other hand, both the sorts of time preference we have mentioned appear to be involved in other attitudes towards old age: e.g., in the common assumption that it is better for an older person to die in harness, fully possessed of his powers, than to have a longer life of (forced) retirement subject to an increasing diminution of his powers.[26] For the latter assumption seems simultaneously to express both our preference for the prime of life and the importance we place on a life's ending well. At this point, however, it is time for us to see how such double-edged time preference affects the views of some of the philosophers referred to above.

IV

As I mentioned earlier, Rawls believes that Utilitarianism can be viewed as adopting 'for society as a whole the [correct] principle of rational choice for one man [i.e. for the rational egoist]' through a mistaken conflation of all individuals into a single (super)person.[27] This 'diagnosis' has recently come under attack for its assumption that Utilitarianism makes use of, and has a distinctive need for, the metaphysics of social organicism. Derek Parfit (following Sidgwick) has pointed out that Utilitarian ethical theories are far more characteristically found with (underlaid by) atomistic/associationalist views of the individual, of the sort so frequently advocated by empiricists.[28] But if our earlier defence of time preference has any validity, then Rawls's diagnosis can also be faulted for its assumption that the Utilitarian is right to make the goodness of single lives depend in a time-indifferent way on how much good (or good-minus-evil) they contain.[29]

On the other hand, Parfit argues forcefully that radically atomistic views of individual identity would (relatively) favour Utilitarianism over deontological social moralities like Rawls's, and it may well

turn out that such views are also incompatible with what we have said in favour of time preference (though we shall later have reason to defend ourselves against the precisely opposite charge that time preference fails to respect the unity of single lives). But since it is hardly clear what approach to individual identity is most likely to prove fruitful in the long run, Rawls's positive argument for his two principles of justice may in the end carry force despite a dual failure in his account of where Utilitarianism, as an ideal type, goes wrong.[30]

We have so far been concentrating on the sorts of judgements concerning individual good that are sometimes made when we consider the lives of others or stand back from our own lives and attempt to view them in a detached way. But what we have said in this connection may also be relevant to a proper understanding of the reasons for action people have in the midst of their lives. And in particular we shall see that it raises problems for the temporally egalitarian conception of reasons for action put forward by Thomas Nagel in *The Possibility of Altruism*.

According to Nagel, a proper appreciation of the equal status (equal reality) of all the time of a given person's life entails a conception of such reasons as essentially tenseless and (so?) operating across (all) the times of that life. If, as in Nagel's own example, I shall have reason to speak Italian at some future time, that gives me (some) reason now to prepare for that eventuality, e.g., by studying Italian. And if I do not study Italian and am unable to speak it when I need to, then I shall even later have reason to regret that I didn't study the language and was unable to speak at the appropriate time.[31] On Nagel's view, anyone who denies such things lacks a conception of himself as an individual all the times of whose life are equally real parts of a single life. But Nagel is also perfectly willing to allow that someone may at a given time think he has reason to do something and yet be mistaken. An alcoholic, for example, may have reason to place a time lock on a drinks cabinet in order to take precautions against a 'later self' who will mistakenly think he has reason to open the drinks cabinet. What Nagel does not allow is that genuine later reasons for action should give rise to no earlier reason to facilitate their realization or that one should ever have no reason to regret or be glad about what one did in response to earlier reasons for action. A person with a proper sense of his life's unity over time cannot be indifferent to what he acknowledges to be a genuine reason (as opposed to a mere desire or preference) existing at some other time in his life.

In making these claims, Nagel explicitly appeals to our own sense of our lives, and what he says about the Italian-speaking example seems hard to deny; for the person who grants he will have reason to speak Italian yet thinks that gives him no reason whatever to study the language seems abnormally 'dissociated' from his own future. But if one casts one's net a bit wider, I believe one finds examples that do not sustain Nagel's general thesis. Even in 'normal' lives, there are cases where reasons do not translate across times, and some of these have in fact already been mentioned. We tend not to regret childhood failures in the way that, years later, we regret the failures of our earlier adulthood, because of our tendency to discount the characteristic goals and interests of childhood; and an adult's lack of regret, say, for his failure to become a school team captain or make the honour roll is not a sign of abnormal dissociation, but rather a perfectly ordinary and understandable way of viewing things.

I believe that Nagel's only avenue of response, at this point, would be to assimilate our indifference to our own childhood to the lack of regret that might be felt by an unwilling alcoholic who failed to get a drink on a given occasion (though such a person might actually feel relieved, even elated, at missing an opportunity to drink). But earlier we saw the implausibility of such an analogy between childhood goals and irrational cravings, and we cannot therefore explain our lack of regret (gladness) about childhood failures (successes)

by saying that these occurred in connection with desires we even then had no reason to pursue (and reason even to resist?). Rather the reverse, our earlier conclusion that childhood goals and interests represent childhood-relative goods suggests that those goals and interests give rise to childhood-relative reasons for action, to reasons that exist in childhood but leave no 'trace' in appropriate regret or satisfaction later on. In other words, if (many of) the things children seek are not seen as goods from the large perspective of life as a whole, then it is understandable that these things should not be the subject of regret and gladness later in life; but since the satisfaction of childhood goals and interests really has childhood-relative value, it cannot be treated like the satisfaction of (non-reason-giving) irrational cravings or sadistic impulses. Rather, what is good for children in childhood gives rise to childhood-reasons to act, to reasons children have while they are still children. But these reasons do not translate into later reasons for regret and satisfaction, because of the strictly period-relative values they represent. (Our way of telling disappointed children 'someday you'll laugh at all this' expresses, hyperbolically, the lukewarmness adults tend to feel about childhood failures and successes at the same time that it unhelpfully, and somewhat cruelly, ignores the period-relative reasons a child may have for being disappointed.)

The same points, furthermore, can be made about old age or senescence. If shuffleboard is a significant good only in (relative to) old age, then a person may in old age have reason to seek victory in senior citizen shuffleboard competitions and yet lack any reason to practise shuffleboard in his earlier years. What seems abnormal in Nagel's Italian-speaking example may here be entirely understandable. The idea of time-relative goods thus naturally leads us to question Nagel's rejection of time-dependent, or time-relative, reasons for action and his thesis that the reasons of every time are equally able to transmit their force to other times of life.

Mine, however, is not the first attempt to contest Nagel's conclusions about the action of reasons across time. Bernard Williams has recently argued that reasons for action and feeling exist essentially from the perspective of the (moving) present, so that the fact that, if one lives long enough, one will later have reason, e.g., to compete at shuffleboard may give one no present reason to practise shuffleboard (unless one has a current desire to provide for a contented old age).[32] And in the same way Williams can hold that our lukewarmness towards schoolboy successes and disappointments simply reflects the fact that most schoolboy goals fall outside the scope of our present (adult) interests and purposes.

Williams's criticisms of Nagel are essentially different from those offered here because of their reliance on a temporal perspectivalism that makes the present into the fulcrum of all reasons for action and feeling. But I see no reason to believe that Williams' approach is incompatible with our own: and it is possible that they represent two equally valid ways of questioning Nagel's general thesis about the transmission of reasons. On the other hand, Williams's emphasis on the present commits him to at least one conclusion on which our own earlier arguments appear to be neutral. Consider the case of a happy-go-lucky apolitical artist or writer who lacks all plans and ambitions for the future, but who believes that the increasingly fascist political climate of her own country is likely to radicalize her into an anti-fascist political activist who does valuable things of a sort she now admires only from afar. On Nagel's view, such a person has reason in advance to prepare for her later political activity, but Williams presumably will hold that she does not. Our own view, by contrast, seems entirely neutral on this question; for it cannot, I assume, be said that the woman's future political activity represents an inferior or time-relative value, so our previous discussion provides no way to argue *against* the transmission of reasons for action from that later time; and

yet since we have said nothing about how *overall life goods* occurring at particular times translate into reasons for feeling and acting at other times, we may well wonder whether the woman has reason to prepare for her predictable (but presently unintended) subsequent activities.

For the moment, at least, I have no idea how to resolve this very delicate issue. But if it turned out that the woman does have reason to prepare, then Nagel would have the better of this particular disagreement with Williams and the latter's perspectivalism of the present would be damaged as a general thesis. Then, and perhaps only then, would we have reason to reject Williams's arguments against Nagel and rely exclusively on those developed here. On the other hand, even if we accept Williams's assumptions and conclusions, our previous discussion can account for phenomena Williams leaves untouched, because of its emphasis on the character of certain goods. It explains, for example, why certain periods seem more important than others in determining the overall goodness of lives, whereas Williams's view of reasons gives us no insight into this phenomenon (or into the above-discussed phenomena of pure time preference), because of his insistence on the separateness of goods and reasons for action. So although Williams's account and mine may turn out to be mutually reinforcing, they have their own separate tasks to perform.

However, the position defended in this first chapter may also help us to correct a misconception that I believe is common to Sidgwick, Rawls, Nagel, *and* Williams. All four philosophers appear to assume a dichotomy between, on the one hand, taking all the times of one's life as equal in status and as equally concerning one, and on the other, giving special importance to the present (or some different, indexically-specified time).[33] But this may be a false dichotomy if time preference can be established in the above manner; for, as I have already been at pains to point out, our previous arguments have attributed no special status to the moving present or to any other indexically-designated time of life.

V

Perhaps the main impetus behind the rejection of time preference has been the view that temporal equality is necessary to any proper conception of the unity of one's own (or any single) life. How then, finally, can the present discussion defend itself against the charge that, by giving unequal importance to different times or time-periods, it forces one to regard human lives as less unified than they actually are?

Consider, to begin with, the pure preference for what happens later in life that we defended above. Such preference cannot, I think, be criticized on the sole grounds of failing to treat earlier and later periods as parts of a single life, but perhaps the criticism will be that it fails to treat these periods as equally *real* (parts of a single life). In that case, however, the critic must hold that treating times as unequally important (to the goodness of lives) involves treating them as unequally real, and on the face of it, this assumption has little to recommend it. The analogue, in the case of individuals, would be to maintain that a hereditary aristocracy that treated some people as inherently more important, or higher, than others was committed to the lesser reality of the latter, and both these parallel assumptions seem uncomfortably similar to the ancient but presumably now discredited view that reality admits of degrees and is proportional to goodness or perfection.[34]

Indeed, something more positive can perhaps be said to defend pure time preference from the charge of failing to appreciate the equal reality of different times of life. Someone who understands the character of his own life must have some sort of view of its different periods, but must also be aware of its finitude. But this fact of finitude has important repercussions for our attitudes towards the different epochs of a single life. Older people sometimes envy the young for having so much of their lives left to live, and the young, in turn, often feel sorry for older people because they have so little time remaining. Having a substantial amount of time left is thus often thought to be of positive value, and judgements about how fortunate a given person is at a given time seem to depend not only on what is happening to him and what he is doing at that time, but on our estimation of how much time the person can reasonably count on in the future.[35] (There is thus something ironic about very old people who are still actively engaged in careers, for their undiminished powers seem to mock the second-order inability of those powers long to sustain themselves— compare the pseudo-rejuvenation of those about to die of starvation.) In that case, our preference for later happiness and success may in some way reflect a desire that the later parts of a life should receive some compensation for the fact that time is running out. The greater importance attributed to later periods may thus represent the idea of a larger overall equality that emerges when the different periods of life are seen against the background of non-existence and death. And when one sees pure time preference as a kind of balancing of the goods contained in a life against the structural (dis)advantages of different times of life, the criticism that it disregards the equal reality of different times of life, or the unity of life, may simply fall away. If we lived forever, our (detached) judgements about what makes lives good would perhaps put no weight on the distinction between earlier and later periods. But the fact is that life is finite, and Nagel himself stresses that finitude as one of the main features of a conception of reasons for action whose principal virtue is said to be its adequacy to the unity of life, its ability to treat life as more than a 'series of episodes'.[36] I agree with Nagel that the unity of life must be seen against the background of non-existence in order to be properly understood; but what I have said just above suggests none the less that far from entailing Nagel's temporal egalitarianism, such an understanding of life's unity may actually be favourable to pure time preference.

However, we should also consider

whether our defence of lukewarmness to the characteristic goals and interests of certain periods of life may not underestimate life's unity by allowing people to be invidiously dissociated from certain real parts of their lives. But how such dissociation can be invidious if it is also typical and widespread is not easy to understand. If the idea is supposed to be that life is more unified than people realize, than their attitudes imply, what happens to the ideal of justifying metaphysical and moral conceptions partly on the basis of normal human self-understanding, an idea Rawls, Nagel, *et al.*, themselves invoke? But perhaps the worry that in the present discussion, human life is somehow being disassembled before our eyes, can best be met by pointing out an important kind of unity that our ideas allow to individual lives. For I believe those ideas ascribe (or can be extended so as to ascribe) to human lives a unity analogous to the (satisfying) unity attributable to the development and decay of organisms.

Consider how ordinary people and biologists tend to think of plants and animals over time. Within the life cycle of a given organism a distinction is typically drawn between periods of development and periods of decay, and this distinction is partly marked by treating a certain period of maturity as representing the fullest development of the organism and other periods as leading 'up to', or 'down from', it. In keeping with these distinctions, there is also a tendency to think of organisms as being most fully what they are (what they have it in them to be) during maturity, a tendency perhaps most clearly exemplified in the tradition of making general reference to organisms by their adult names rather than by names appropriate to other stages of their life cycle.[37] (We speak of the parts of a tree's life, not of a seed's or sapling's life; of the development and decline, or old age, of a horse, but not of a colt.) These various habits of thought and nomenclature imply a bias in favour of the mature life of organisms that rather parallels what we have been saying here about the prime of human life.[38] But if such bias is compatible with,

even characteristic of, the unity (unified identity over time) attributable to organisms, then our own emphasis on the differential importance of different life periods is compatible with a notion of life's unity modelled on the unity that organisms possess through time, and I can see no reason to believe that such a unity is anything less than what we should expect, or want, from human life.

On the other hand, a biologically-modelled conception of life's unity need not overestimate or oversimplify that unity (e.g.) by presupposing the 'Simple View' of identity discussed by Parfit and attributable to Butler, Chisholm, and others. For the biological model does not say that identity through time requires the existence of something that undergoes no alteration; and although someone holding the Simple View will (according to Parfit)[39] be impressed by the fact that 'all the parts of a person's life are as much parts of his life', anyone who claims, with us, that some parts of a person's life are more important than others, is surely *not* going to be *impressed* by such a fact—even if he in some sense accepts it.

I do not claim to have said very much here about the nature of the unity-through-time of humans or of organisms generally, only to have defended the compatibility of what I have said about human life with a plausible notion of the unity of such lives that needs working out in detail.[40] And given the prevalence in Aristotle's thought of the organismic model of identity through time, it is not in the end very surprising that one can find anticipations of our present defence of time preference, and of its higher estimation of the goals and judgements of mature individuals, in the *Nicomachean Ethics*.[41]

Notes

1. *The Methods of Ethics*, London: Macmillan, 1907, seventh edition, pp. 381 f.

2. See *A Theory of Justice*, Cambridge: Harvard University Press, 1971, secs. 45, 64.

3. Op. cit. pp. 418 f.

4. Op. cit., p. 295.

5. Ibid., pp. 26 f.

6. *The Possibility of Altruism*, Oxford: Clarendon Press, 1970, Ch. 8 (esp. p. 60).

7. 'Utilitarianism and Welfarism', *Journal of Philosophy* LXXVI, 1979, 470 f. Sen abstracts from literary-critical considerations that might suggest that Lear, through suffering, attained something better at the end of his life than anything in his previous life, that Lear's life ended better than it began.

8. The above exposition benefits from ideas of Rawls (op. cit., sec. 1) and of Ronald Dworkin (*Taking Rights Seriously*, Cambridge: Harvard, 1978, esp. p. 180).

9. See *An Anatomy of Values*, Cambridge, Harvard, 1970, pp. 170–6.

10. See Rawls, op. cit., p. 19 f. and elsewhere; Nagel, op. cit., pp. 80, 126, 144 f. (though contrast p. 82); Sen, op. cit., pp. 470 f.; Fried, op. cit., Ch. 10, *passim*; and Sidgwick, op. cit., Book III, Chs. XI and XIII.

11. See *Childhood and Society*, N.Y.: Norton, 1963, 2nd ed., pp. 271 ff.

12. *Cities of the Plain*, N.Y.: Random House, 1970, p. 272.

13. Cf. Rawls, op. cit., pp. 416 ff.; Nagel, op. cit., pp. 40 ff., and Gary Watson, 'Free Agency', *Journal of Philosophy* LXXII, 1975, 205–20.

14. I believe I here disagree with what Phillip Bricker ('Prudence', *Journal of Philosophy* LXXVII, 1980, p. 383) says about similar cases.

15. Talk about what is good in, or from the perspective of, childhood is not reducible to the notion of being *thought* good by children, because such a reduction would, once again, fail to distinguish childhood goals from irrational addictions. We really require another argument place in order to describe (the good of) those goals—see below. It is also worth pointing out how the notion of childhood-relative goods gives rise to other locutions (some of which we shall be using in what follows). For example, what is good only in childhood is naturally described as being good *for children* (as opposed to being good for persons, for the persons who were such children).

16. Nagel, op. cit., argues against the possibility of independent person-relative reasons for actions, but in other writings seems to want to allow for the possibility of person-relative (subjective) goods and reasons for action. See, e.g., *Moral Questions*, Cambridge: C.U.P., 1979, pp. 2, 132 ff., 203.

17. When St. Paul speaks of putting aside childish things, he also seems to allow that understanding and speaking as a child are all right in childhood. Our notion of the childish thus seems to contain an ambiguity, or bipolarity, between the childish as what is irrational-in-the-manner-of-a child and the childish as what is appropriate to children only. This is close to the distinction we have been urging above in connection with childhood vs. addiction, and it supports the idea of period-relative goods for reasons already mentioned.

18. Incidentally, we do not regard childhood strivings and goals as appropriate merely because we regard them as means to what we take more seriously in adult life. Often we don't know—have no particular theory about—whether a given appropriate-seeming childhood activity will further adult values.

19. 'Prime of life' works better for what I have in mind than either 'adulthood' or 'maturity', which do not clearly enough exclude senescence.

20. Following up the analogy with dreams, could we not perhaps say that certain satisfactions in dreams are goods relative to those dreams or to what might be called one's dream life (on analogy with one's sex life)?

21. Op. cit., pp. 420 f., for example. He seems to assume, with Fried, that the value of

an activity may be assessed 'relative to its own period'. But despite the coincidence of terminology, this involves not the period-relativity of goods defended above, but rather the 'democratic' notion that the differing goals of each period give rise to overall (non-relative) life goods occurring within those periods.

Incidentally, even though the person who regards what happens in childhood as less determinative of the overall goodness of a life, may have this attitude on the basis of certain purely contingent features of childhood, in particular, its characteristic goals and strivings; this attitude may still count as a form of (impure) *time* preference. After all, someone who likes France better than Spain has what may properly be called a place preference, yet that preference is not independent of the contingent amenities of those two places.

22. Pure time preference for what comes later in life is defended by J. N. Findlay (*Values and Intentions*, London: Allen and Unwin, 1961, pp. 235 ff.) on the basis of arguments somewhat different from those offered here.

23. Op. cit., p. 421.

24. Perhaps the preference for what comes late (or last) makes sense not only for total lives, but for careers within lives. Muhammad Ali is still a relatively young man, but wouldn't some people have preferred to see him end his boxing career while still heavyweight champion, the way Rocky Marciano did?

25. Some people become embittered through early unsuccess and don't allow later success to mellow them, refusing, e.g., to see it as compensating for earlier failure. But we think it is irrational of someone if he can't or won't let later success make up for what went earlier, and the latter judgement again shows our preference for what comes later. Incidentally, given that Rawls is unequivocally opposed to time preference, I find it hard to know what to make of the sentence beginning at line 16 of page 421 of *A Theory of Justice*.

26. A point also made by Fried, op. cit.

27. Rawls, op. cit., pp. 26 f.

28. See 'Later Selves and Moral Principles', in A. Montefiore, ed., *Philosophy and Personal Relations*, London: Routledge and Kegan Paul, 1973, pp. 137–69. Cf. Sidgwick, op. cit., pp. 415 ff.

29. Rawls assumes that individual good and rational choice are intimately connected. See op. cit., pp. 417–22, e.g. We shall have occasion to doubt such a connection in Chapter 5, below.

30. However, for doubts as to whether Rawls's argument for the two principles is really compatible with 'atomistic' theories of the individual, see Samuel Scheffler's 'Moral Independence and the Original Position', *Philosophical Studies* 35, 1979, 397–403.

31. See Nagel, op. cit., Ch. 8.

32. 'Persons, Character and Morality', in A. Rorty, ed., *The Identities of Persons*, University of California Press, 1976, esp. pp. 208 f., 216.

33. See Sidgwick, op. cit., pp. 381 f.; Rawls, op. cit., pp. 293 ff, 420 f.; Nagel, *The Possibility of Altruism*, pp. 60 f., 101; and Williams, op. cit., p. 209.

34. I do not see how these assumptions are established by anything Nagel says in *The Possibility of Altruism*—see, especially, p. 79 n.

35. Such temporal values are no more inherently suspect than the value we attribute, e.g., to have a certain surgical operation over and done with.

36. See Nagel, *Altruism*, pp. 38 f., 60, 73.

37. Cf. J. H. Woodger, 'On Biological Transformations', in Le Gros Clark and P. Medawar, eds., *Growth and Form* (essays presented to D'Arcy Thompson), Oxford: 1945, p. 95; and David Wiggins, *Sameness and Substance*, Oxford: Blackwell, 1980, p. 64.

38. In keeping with what is said about the mature period of organisms, we have a tendency to think that people must attain

(forge) an identity rather than always having one. (The prime of life presumably *begins* when identity has been attained.) Cf. Wiggins, op. cit., p. 167; and Erikson, loc. cit.

39. Op. cit., p. 141.

40. For the interesting beginnings of such theory about the unity of lives and the unity-through-time of organisms, see Wiggins, op. cit., *passim*. Wiggins relies heavily on Aristotelian ideas about identity over time.

41. See Book I, Chs. 3 and 9, for example.

Bibliography on Contemporary Ethical Theory
Thomas L. Carson and Paul K. Moser

I. General

Arrington, Robert. *Rationalism, Realism, and Relativism*. Ithaca: Cornell University Press, 1989.

Attfield, Robin. *A Theory of Value and Obligation*. London: Croom Helm, 1987.

Baier, Kurt. *The Moral Point of View*. Ithaca: Cornell University Press, 1958.

Baron, Marcia. *Kantian Ethics Almost Without Apology*. Ithaca: Cornell University Press, 1995.

Blanshard, Brand. *Reason and Goodness*. London: G. Allen, 1961.

Blum, Lawrence. *Friendship, Altruism, and Morality*. London: Routledge & Kegan Paul, 1980.

Bond, E. J. *Reason and Value*. Cambridge: Cambridge University Press, 1983.

Bradley, F. H. *Ethical Studies*, 2d ed. Oxford: Oxford University Press, 1927.

Brandt, Richard. "The Definition of an 'Ideal Observer' in Ethics." *Philosophy and Phenomenological Research* 15 (1954): 407–13.

———. "Some Comments on Professor Firth's Reply." *Philosophy and Phenomenological Research* 15 (1954): 422–423.

———. *Ethical Theory*. Englewood Cliffs, N.J.: Prentice-Hall, 1959.

———. *A Theory of the Good and the Right*. Oxford: Oxford University Press, 1979.

———. *Morality Utilitarianism, and Rights*. Cambridge: Cambridge University Press, 1992.

Brentano, Franz. *The Origin of Our Knowledge of Right and Wrong*, Translated by Roderick Chisholm and Elizabeth Schneewind. New York: Humanities Press, 1969.

———. *The Foundation and Construction of Ethics*. Translated by Elizabeth Schneewind. New York: Humanities Press, 1973.

Brink, David. *Moral Realism and the Foundations of Ethics*. Cambridge: Cambridge University Press, 1989.

Broad, C. D. *Five Types of Ethical Theory*. London: Routledge & Kegan Paul, 1930.

———. *Broad's Critical Essays in Moral Philosophy*. New York: Humanities Press, 1971.

Butchvarov, Panayot. *Skepticism in Ethics*. Bloomington: Indiana University Press, 1989.

Carritt, E. F. *The Theory of Morals*. London: Oxford University Press, 1928.

Carson, Thomas. *The Status of Morality*. Dordrecht: Reidel, 1984.

Chisholm, Roderick. *Brentano and Intrinsic Value*. Cambridge: Cambridge University Press, 1986.

Copp, David. *Morality, Normativity and Society*. Oxford: Oxford University Press, 1995.

Copp, David, and David Zimmerman, eds. *Morality, Reason, and Truth*. Totowa, N.J.: Rowman and Allanheld, 1985.

Dancy, Jonathan. *Moral Reasons*. Oxford: Blackwell, 1993.

Darwall, Stephen L. *Impartial Reason*. Ithaca: Cornell University Press, 1983.

Darwall, Stephen L., Allan Gibbard, and Peter Railton. "Toward *Fin de siècle* Ethics: Some Trends." *Philosophical Review* 101 (1992): 115–89.

Dewey, John. *Human Nature and Conduct*. New York: Holt, 1922.

———. *The Theory of Valuation*. Chicago: University of Chicago Press, 1939.

Dewey, John, and James Tufts. *Ethics*. New York: Holt, 1932.

Donagan, Alan. *The Theory of Morality*. Chicago: University of Chicago Press, 1977.

Edwards, Paul. *The Logic of Moral Discourse*. New York: Free Press, 1955.

Ewing, A. C. *The Definition of the Good*. New York: Macmillan, 1947.

———. *Ethics*. New York: Macmillan, 1953.

———. *Second Thoughts on Moral Philosophy*. London: Routledge, 1959.

Falk, W. D. *Ought, Reasons, and Morality*. Ithaca: Cornell University Press, 1986.

Feinberg, Joel, ed. *Moral Concepts*. New York: Oxford University Press, 1970.

Findlay, J. N. *Language, Mind, and Value*. London: Unwin Allen, 1963.

————. *Values and Intentions*. London: Unwin Allen, 1963.

————. *Axiological Ethics*. New York: St. Martin's Press, 1970.

————. *Meinong's Theory of Objects and Values*. Oxford: Oxford University Press, 1983.

Finnis, John. *Natural Law and Natural Rights*. Oxford: Oxford University Press, 1980.

Firth, Roderick. "Ethical Absolutism and the Ideal Observer." *Philosophy and Phenomenological Research* 12 (1952): 317–45.

————. "A Reply to Professor Brandt." *Philosophy and Phenomenological Research* 15 (1954): 414–21.

Foot, Philippa. *Virtues and Vices*. Berkeley: University of California Press, 1978.

Frankena, William K. *Ethics*. Englewood Cliffs, N.J.: Prentice-Hall, 1963.

————. *Perspectives on Morality*. Notre Dame: University of Notre Dame Press, 1976.

Fried, Charles. *An Anatomy of Values*. Cambridge: Harvard Univerity Press, 1970.

————. *Right and Wrong*. Cambridge: Harvard University Press, 1978.

Gaita, Raimond. *Good and Evil: An Absolute Conception*. London: Macmillan, 1991.

Gaus, Gerald. *Value and Justification*. Cambridge: Cambridge University Press, 1990.

Gauthier, David. *Morals by Agreement*. Oxford: Oxford University Press, 1986.

Gensler, Harry. *Formal Ethics*. London: Routledge, 1996.

Gert, Bernard. *Morality*. Oxford: Oxford University Press, 1988.

Gewirth, Allan. *Reason and Morality*. Chicago: University of Chicago Press, 1978.

Gibbard, Alan. *Wise Feelings and Art Choices*. Harvard: Harvard University Press, 1990.

Glover, Jonathan. *What Sort of People Should There Be?* Harmondsworth: Penguin, 1984.

Green, T. H. *Prolegomena to Ethics*, 5th ed. Oxford: Clarendon Press, 1907.

Griffin, James. *Well-Being*. Oxford: Oxford University Press, 1986.

Hall, Everett W. *What is Value?* New York: Humanities Press, 1952.

Hare, R. M. *The Language of Morals*. Oxford: Oxford University Press, 1952.

————. *Freedom and Reason*. Oxford: Oxford University Press, 1963.

————. *Moral Thinking*. Oxford: Oxford University Press, 1981.

————. *Essays in Ethical Theory*. Oxford: Oxford University Press, 1989.

Harman, Gilbert. *The Nature of Morality*. Oxford: Oxford University Press, 1977.

Harrison, Jonathan. *Our Knowledge of Right and Wrong*. New York: Humanities Press, 1971.

Hartmann, Nicolai. *Ethics*. 3 vols. Translated by Stanton Coit. New York: Macmillan, 1932.

Hospers, John. *Human Conduct*. New York: Harcourt, Brace & World, 1961.

Hospers, John, and Wilfrid Sellars, eds. *Readings in Ethical Theory*, 2d ed. Englewood Cliffs, N.J. Prentice-Hall, 1970.

Hudson, W. D. *Modern Moral Philosophy*. Garden City, N.Y.: Doubleday, 1970.

Hurka, Thomas. *Perfectionism*. Oxford: Oxford University Press, 1993.

Hurley, S. L. *Natural Reasons*. Oxford: Oxford University Press, 1989.

Joseph. H. W. B. *Some Problems of Ethics*. Oxford: Clarendon Press, 1931.

Kekes, John. *Moral Tradition and Individuality*. Princeton: Princeton University Press, 1989.

Köhler, Wolfgang. *The Place of Value in a World of Fact*. New York: Liveright, 1938.

Korsgaard, Christine. *The Standpoint of Practical Reason*. New York: Garland, 1990.

————. *The Sources of Normativity*. Cambridge: Cambridge University Press, 1996.

Ladd, John. *The Structure of a Moral Code*. Cambridge: Harvard University Press, 1957.

Larmore, Charles. *Patterns of Moral Complexity*. Cambridge: Cambridge University Press, 1987.

Lemos, Noah. *Intrinsic Value*. Cambridge: Cambridge University Press, 1994.

Lewis, Clarence I. *An Analysis of Knowledge and Valuation*. LaSalle, Ill.: Open Court, 1946.

————. *Values and Imperatives*. Stanford: Stanford University Press, 1969.

MacIntyre, Alasdair, *After Virtue*. Notre Dame: Notre Dame University Press, 1981.

————. *Whose Justice? Which Rationality?* Notre Dame: Notre Dame University Press, 1989.

————. *Three Rival Versions of Moral Enquiry*. Notre Dame: Notre Dame University Press, 1990.

Mackie, J. L. *Ethics*. Middlesex: Penguin, 1978.

Mandelbaum, Maurice. *The Phenomenology of Moral Experience*. New York: Free Press, 1955.

Mayo, Bernard. *Ethics and the Moral Life*. New York: St. Martin's, 1958.

————. *The Philosophy of Right and Wrong*. London: Routledge & Kegan Paul, 1986.

McCloskey, H.J. *Meta-Ethics and Normative Ethics*. The Hague: Martinus Nijhoff, 1969.

McTaggart, John. *The Nature of Existence*, vol. 2. Cambridge: Cambridge University Press, 1927.

Meinong, Alexis. *Zur Grundleyung der allegemeinen Werttheorie*. Graz, 1932.

Miller, Richard. *Moral Differences*. Princeton: Princeton University Press, 1992.

Moore, George Edward. *Principia Ethica*. Cambridge: Cambridge University Press, 1903.

———. *Ethics*. London: Oxford University Press, 1911.

———. "A Reply to My Critics." In *The Philosophy of G. E. Moore*, edited by P. A. Schilpp, pp. 535–677. La Salle: Open Court, 1968.

Moser, Paul K. *Philosophy After Objectivity*. New York: Oxford University Press, 1993.

Nagel, Thomas. *The Possibility of Altruism*. Oxford: Oxford University Press, 1970.

———. *Mortal Questions*. Cambridge: Cambridge University Press, 1979.

———. *Equality and Partiality*. Oxford: Oxford University Press, 1991.

Narveson, Jan. *Morality and Utility*. Baltimore: Johns Hopkins University Press, 1967.

Nowell-Smith, P. H. *Ethics*. Baltimore: Pelican Books, 1954.

Nussbaum, Martha. *The Fragility of Goodness*. Cambridge: Cambridge University Press, 1986.

———. *The Therapy of Desire*. Princeton: Princeton University Press, 1994.

Parfit, Derek. *Reasons and Persons*. Oxford: Oxford University Press, 1984.

Paul, Ellen Frankel, Fred Miller, Jr., and Jeffrey Paul, eds. *The Good Life and the Human Good*. Cambridge University Press, 1992.

Pepper, Stephen. *The Sources of Value*. Berkeley: University of California Press, 1958.

Perry, Ralph Barton. *General Theory of Value*. Cambridge, Mass.: Harvard University Press, 1926.

———. *Realms of Value*. Cambridge, Mass.: Harvard University Press, 1954.

Philips, Michael. *Between Universalism and Skepticism*. Oxford: Oxford University Press, 1994.

Prichard, H. A. *Moral Obligation and Duty and Interest*. Oxford: Oxford University Press, 1968.

Raphael, D.D. *The Moral Sense*. London: Oxford University Press, 1947.

———. *Moral Philosophy*, 2d ed. Oxford: Oxford University Press, 1994.

———. *Moral Judgment*, New York: Macmillan, 1955.

Rashdall, Hastings. *The Theory of Good and Evil*. Oxford: Clarendon Press, 1928.

Rawls, John. *A Theory of Justice*. Cambridge, Mass.: Harvard University Press, 1971.

Rescher, Nicholas. *Introduction to Value Theory*. Englewood Cliffs, N.J.: Prentice-Hall, 1969.

Ross, David. *The Right and the Good*. Oxford: Clarendon Press, 1930.

———. *The Foundations of Ethics*. Oxford: Clarendon Press, 1939.

Schlick, Moritz. *The Problems of Ethics*. Englewood Cliffs, N.J.: Prentice-Hall, 1939.

Scheler, Max. *Formalism in Ethics and a Non-Formal Ethics of Values*. Translated by Manfred Frings and Roger Funk. Evanston, Ill.: Northwestern University Press, 1973.

Schneewind, J. B. *Sidgwick's Ethics and Victorian Moral Philosophy*. Oxford: Oxford University Press, 1977.

Sharp, F. C. *Good Will and Ill Will*. Chicago: University of Chicago Press, 1950.

Sidgwick, Henry. *The Methods of Ethics*, 7th ed. London: Macmillan, 1901.

Singer, Marcus. *Generalization in Ethics*. New York: Random House, 1962.

Slote, Michael. *Goods and Virtues*. Oxford: Oxford University Press, 1983.

Smart, J. J. C. and Bernard Williams. *Utilitarianism: For and Against*. Cambridge: Cambridge University Press, 1973.

Stace, Walter. *The Concept of Morals*. New York: Macmillan, 1937.

Stevenson, Charles L. *Ethics and Language*. New Haven: Yale University Press, 1944.

———. *Facts and Values*. New Haven: Yale University Press, 1963.

Stocker, Michael. *Plural and Conflicting Values*. Oxford: Oxford University Press, 1990.

Taylor, Paul. *Normative Discourse*. Englewood Cliffs, N.J.: Prentice-Hall, 1961.

Taylor, Richard. *Good and Evil*. New York: Macmillan, 1970.

Toulmin, Steven. *Reason and Ethics*. Cambridge: Cambridge University Press, 1970.

Von Wright, George H. *Norm and Action*. London: Routledge, 1963.

———. *The Varieties of Goodness*. London: Routledge, 1963.

Warnock, G. J. *The Object of Morality*. London: Methuen, 1971.

Westermarck, Edward A. *Origin and Development of the Moral Ideas*. London: Macmillan, 1906.

Williams, Bernard. *Morality*. New York: Harper and Row, 1972.

———. *Moral Luck*. Cambridge: Cambridge University Press, 1981.

———. *Ethics and the Limits of Philosophy*. Cambridge, Mass.: Harvard University Press, 1985.

———. *Making Sense of Humanity*. Cambridge: Cambridge University Press, 1995.

II. Concepts of Goodness

A. Theories of Meaning

Ayer, A. J. *Language, Truth and Logic*, 2d ed. London: Victor Gollancz, 1946.

———. "On the Analysis of Moral Judgments." In A. J. Ayer, *Philosophical Essays*, pp. 231–49. London: Macmillan.

Baylis, Charles. "Grading, Values, and Choice." *Mind* 67 (1958): 485–501.

Boyd, Richard N. "How to Be a Moral Realist," In *Essays on Moral Realism*, edited by Geoffrey Sayre-McCord, pp. 181–228. Ithaca: Cornell University Press, 1988.

Brandt, Richard. "The Emotive Theory of Ethics." *Philosophical Review* 59 (1950): 305–18.

———. "The Status of Empirical Assertion Theories in Ethics." *Mind* 61 (1952): 458–79.

———. "Moral Valuation." *Ethics* 56 (1946): 106–21.

Broad, C. D. "Is 'Goodness' the Name of a Simple Non-natural Quality?" In Broad, *Broad's Critical Essays in Moral Philosophy*, pp. 106–23. New York: Humanities Press, 1971.

———. "Some Reflections on Moral Sense Theories in Ethics." In Broad, *Broad's Critical Essays in Moral Philosophy*, pp. 188–222. New York: Humanities Press, 1971.

Castañeda, Hector-Neri. "Ethics and Logic: Stevensonian Emotivism Revisited." *Journal of Philosophy* 64 (1967): 671–83.

Davidson, Donald. *Essays on Actions and Events*. Oxford: Oxford University Press, 1980.

Ewing, A. C. "A Suggested Non-Naturalistic Analysis of Good." *Mind* 48 (1939): 1–22.

Foot, Philippa. "Moral Arguments." In Philippa Foot, *Virtues and Vices*, pp. 96–109. Berkeley: University of California Press, 1978.

———. "Moral Beliefs." In Philippa Foot, *Virtues and Vices*, pp. 110–131. Berkeley: University of California Press, 1978.

Frankena, William K. "The Naturalistic Fallacy." *Mind* 48 (1939): 464–77.

———. "Ewing's Case Against Naturalistic Theories of Value." *Philosophical Review* 57 (1948): 481–92.

———. "Arguments for Non-naturalism About Intrinsic Value." *Philosophical Studies* 1 (1950): 56–60.

Gallie, W. B. "Essentially Contested Concepts." *Proceedings of the Aristotelian Society* 56 (1956): 167–98.

Gardiner. P. L. "On Assenting to a Moral Principle." *Proceedings of the Aristotelian Society* 55 (1954–55): 23–44.

Gauthier, David P. "Moore's Naturalistic Fallacy." *American Philosophical Quarterly* 4 (1967): 315–20.

Gibbard, Allan. "An Expresivist Theory of Moral Discourse." *Ethics* 96 (1986): 472–85.

Hall, Everett W. "A Categorical Analysis of Value." *Philosophy of Science* 14 (1947): 333–44.

———. "Stevenson on Disagreement in Attitude." *Ethics* 58 (1947): 51–56.

Hare, R. M. "Universalizability." *Proceedings of the Aristotelian Society* 55 (1954–55): 295–312.

Hay, William H. "Stevenson and Ethical Analysis." *Philosophical Review* 56 (1947): 422–30.

Hume, David. *Treatise of Human Nature*, vols. I and II. London: John Noon 1739; vol. III, London: Thomas Longman, 1740.

Lemmon, E. J., and P. H. Nowell-Smith. "Escapism: The Logical Basis of Ethics." *Mind* 69 (1960): 289–300.

Lyons, David. "Mill's Theory of Morality." Nous 10 (1976): 101–20.

Marcus, Ruth Barcan. "Moral Dilemmas and Consistency." *Journal of Philosophy* 77 (1980): 121–36.

John McDowell. "Wittgenstein on Following a Rule." *Synthese* 58 (1984): 325–63.

Montefiore, Alan. "The Meaning of 'Good' and the Act of Commendation." *Philosophical Quarterly* 17 (1967): 115–29.

Quine, W. V. O. *Word and Object*. Cambridge, Mass.: MIT Press, 1960.

Raiffa, Howard. *Decision Analysis*. Reading, Mass.: Addison-Wesley, 1968.

Railton, Peter. "Facts and Values." *Philosophical Topics* 14 (1986a): 5–31.

———. "Moral Realism." *Philosophical Review*. 95 (1986b): 163–207.

Robinson, Richard. "The Emotive Theory of Ethics." *Proceedings of the Aristotelian Society, Supplementary Volume,* 22 (1948): 79–106.

Ryle, Gilbert. *The Concept of Mind.* London: Hutchison, 1949.

Sabini, John, and Maury Silver. *Moralities of Everyday Life.* Oxford: Oxford University Press, 1982.

Stevenson, Charles L. "The Emotive Meaning of Ethical Terms." In Charles L. Stevenson, *Facts and Values,* pp. 10–31. New Haven: Yale University Press, 1963.

———. "Moore's Arguments against Certain Forms of Ethical Naturalism." In Charles L. Stevenson, *Facts and Values,* pp. 117–37. New Haven: Yale University Press, 1963.

Strawson, P. F. "Ethical Intuitionism." *Philosophy* 24 (1949): 23–33.

Sturgeon Nicholas L. "Gibbard on Moral Judgment and Norms." *Ethics* 96 (1985): 22–33.

Tomas, Vincent. "Ethical Disagreements and the Emotive Theory of Values." *Mind* 60 (1951): 205–23.

Urmson, J. O. *The Emotive Theory of Ethics.* Oxford: Oxford University Press, 1968.

Van Fraassen, Bas. "Values and the Heart's Command." *Journal of Philosophy* 70 (1973): 5–19.

Wellman, Carl. "Emotivism and Ethical Objectivity." *American Philosophical Quarterly* 5 (1968): 90–99.

[See also the following items from the general bibliography: Brentano, *The Origin of Our Knowledge of Right and Wrong* and *The Foundation and Construction of Ethics*; Carson, *The Status of Morality*; Ewing, *The Definition of the Good*; Foot, *Virtues and Vices*; Gibbard, *Wise Choices and Apt Feelings*; Hare, *The Language of Morals, Freedom and Reason, Moral Thinking,* and *Essays in Ethical Theory*; Mackie, *Ethics*; Moore, *Principia Ethica* and *Ethics*; Ross, *The Right and the Good* and *The Foundations of Ethics*; and Stevenson, *Ethics and Language*.]

B. The Concept of Intrinsic Value

Baylis, Charles. "Intrinsic Goodness." *Philosophy and Phenomenological Research* 13 (1952): 15–27.

Beardsley, Monroe. "Intrinsic Value." *Philosophy and Phenomenological Reseach* 26 (1965): 1–17.

Chisholm, Roderick. "Intrinsic Value." In *Values and Morals,* edited by A. I. Goldman and J. Kim, pp. 121–130. Dordrecht: Reidel, 1978.

———. "Defining Intrinsic Value." *Analysis* 41 (1981): 99–100.

———. "The Defeat of Good and Evil." In *The Problem of Evil,* edited by Marilyn Adams and Robert Adams, pp. 53–68. Oxford: Oxford University Press, 1990.

Chisholm, Roderick, and Ernest Sosa. "On the Logic of `Intrinsically Better.'" *American Philosophical Quarterly* 3 (1966): 244–49.

Harman, Gilbert. "Toward a Theory of Intrinsic Value." *Journal of Philosophy* 64 (1967): 792–804.

Korsgaard, Christine. "Two Distinctions in Goodness." *Philosophical Review* 92 (1983): 169–97.

Lemos, Noah. "Higher Goods and the Myth of Tithonus." *Journal of Philosophy* 90 (1993): 482–96.

Moore, G. E. "The Conception of Intinsic Value." In G. E. Moore, *Philosophical Studies,* pp. 253–275. London: Routledge & Kegan Paul, 1922.

Quinn, Warren. "Theories of Intrinsic Value." *American Philosophical Quarterly* 11 (1974): 123–32.

Zimmerman, Michael. "Evaluatively Incomplete States of Affairs." *Philosophical Studies* 43 (1983): 211–24.

[In addition see the following items listed in the general bibliography: Chisholm, *Brentano and Intrinsic Value*; Lemos, *Intrinsic Value*; and Moore, *Ethics* and *Principia Ethica*.]

III. What Things are Good?

A. Hedonism and Happiness

Alston, William. "Pleasure." In Paul Edwards, ed., *The Encyclopedia of Philosophy,* vol. 6., pp. 341–347. New York: Macmillan, 1967.

Austin, Jean. "Pleasure and Happiness." *Philosophy* 43 (1968): 51–62.

Benditt, Theodore. "Happiness." *Philosophical Studies* 25 (1974): 1–20.

Berger, Fred. *Happiness, Justice and Freedom: The Moral and Political Philosophy of John Stuart Mill.* Berkeley: University of California Press, 1984.

Blake, R. M. "Why Not Hedonism?: A Protest." *Ethics* 37 (1926): 1–18.

Brandt, Richard. "Two Concepts of Utility." In *The Limits of Utilitarianism,* edited by Harlan Miller and William Williams, pp. 169–185. Minneapolis: University of Minnesota Press, 1982.

———. "Fairness to Happiness." *Social Theory and Practice* 15 (1989): 33–58.

Campbell, Richmond. "The Pursuit of Happiness." *The Personalist,* 54 (1973): 325–39.

Carson, Thomas L. "Happiness, Contentment, and the Good Life." *Pacific Philosophical Quarterly* 62 (1981): 70–84.

Chandler, Hugh. "Hedonism." *American Philosophical Quarterly* 12 (1975): 223–33.

Cowan, J. L. *Pleasure and Pain.* New York: St. Martin's Press, 1968.

———. "Why Not Happiness?" *Philosophical Studies* 56 (1989): 135–61.

Donner, Wendy. *The Liberal Self.* Ithaca: Cornell University Press, 1991.

Duncker, Karl. "Pleasure, Emotion, and Striving." *Philosophy and Phenomenological Research* 1 (1940): 391–430.

Edwards, Rem. *Pleasures and Pains.* Ithaca: Cornell University Press, 1979.

Gosling, J. C. B. *Pleasure and Desire.* Oxford: Oxford University Press, 1969.

Hall, Everett W. "The 'Proof' of Utility in Bentham and Mill." *Ethics* 60 (1949): 1–18.

Jones, Hardy. "Mill's Argument for the Principle of Utility." *Philosophy and Phenomenological Research* 38 (1978): 338–54.

Kekes, John. "Happiness." *Mind* 91 (1982): 358–76.

Kenny, Anthony. "Happiness." *Procedings of the Aristotelian Society* 66 (1965–66): 93–102.

Kraut, Richard. "Two Conceptions of Happiness." *Philosophical Review* 88 (1979): 167–97.

Kretzmann, Norman. "Desire as Proof of Desirability." *Philosophical Quarterly* 8 (1958): 246–58.

Marshall, John. "The Proof of Utility and Equity in Mill's *Utilitarianism.*" *Canadian Journal of Philosophy* 3 (1973): 13–26.

McFall, Lynne. *Happiness.* New York: Peter Lang, 1989.

McNaughton, R. M. "A Metrical Concept of Happiness." *Philosophy and Phenomenological Research* 14 (1953): 172–83.

Montague, Roger. "Happiness." *Proceedings of the Aristotelian Society* 68 (1966): 87–102.

Nozick, Robert. *Anarchy, State, and Utopia.* New York: Basic Books, 1974.

Penelhum, Terence. "The Logic of Pleasure." *Philosophy and Phenomenological Research* 17 (1956–57): 488–503.

Perry, David. *The Concept of Pleasure.* The Hague: Mouton, 1967.

Quinn, Warren. "Pleasure Disposition or Episode." *Philosophy and Phenomenological Research* 28 (1967–68): 578–86.

Raphael, D. D. "Mill's Proof of the Principle of Utility." *Utilitas* 6 (1994): 55–65.

Rashdall, Hastings. "Can There Be a Sum of Pleasures?" *Mind* 8 (1899): 357–82.

Russell, Bertrand. *The Conquest of Happiness.* London: Unwin and Allen, 1930.

Ryle, Gilbert. "Pleasure." *Proceedings of the Aristotelian Society,* Supplementary Vol. 28 (1954): 135–46.

———. "Pleasure." In Gilbert Ryle, *Dilemmas,* pp. 54–67. Cambridge: Cambridge University Press, 1954.

Schneewind, J. B. *Sidgwick's Ethics and Victorian Moral Philosophy.* Oxford: Oxford University Press, 1977.

Skorupski, John. *John Stuart Mill.* London: Routledge, 1989.

Sumner, Wayne. "Welfare, Happiness, and Pleasure." *Utilitas* 4 (1992): 199–223.

Tartarkiewicz, W. *Analysis of Happiness.* The Hague: Nijhoff, 1976.

Tefler, Elizabeth. *Happiness.* London: Macmillan, 1980.

Thomas, D. Lloyd. "Happiness." *Philosophical Quarterly* 18 (1968): 87–113.

Wallace, James D. "Pleasure as an End of Action." *American Philosophical Quarterly* 3 (1966): 312–16.

West, Henry. "Mill's 'Proof' of Utility." In *The Limits of Utilitarianism,* edited by Harlan Miller and William Williams, pp. 23–34. Minneapolis: University of Minnesota Press, 1982.

Wilson, John. "Happiness." *Analysis* 29 (1968): 13–21.

Zimmerman, Michael. "On the Intrinsic Value of States of Pleasure." *Philosophy and Phenomenological Research* 41 (1980–81): 26–45.
[In addition, see the following items from the general bibliography: Bond, *Reason and Value*; Broad, *Five Types of Ethical Theory*; Moore, *Principia Ethica*; Narveson, *Morality and Utility*; Rashdall, *The Theory of Good and Evil*; Ross, *The Right and the Good* and *The Foundations of Ethics*; Sidgwick, *The Methods of Ethics*; and Smart and Williams, *Utilitarianism: For and Against*.]

B. Desire-Satisfaction Theory

Brandt, Richard. "Rationality, Egoism, and Morality." *Journal of Philosophy* 69 (1972): 681–97.
———. "Overvold on Self-Interest and Self-Sacrifice." In *Rationality, Morality, and Self-Interest: Essays Honoring Mark Carl Overvold*, edited by John Heil, pp. 221–32. Lanhan, Md.: Rowman Littlefield, 1993.
Harsanyi, John. *Essays on Ethics, Social Behavior, and Scientific Explanation*. Dordrecht: Reidel, 1976.
Kagan, Shelly. "The Limits of Well-Being." In *The Good Life and the Human Good*, edited by Ellen Frankel Paul, Fred Miller Jr., and Jeffrey Paul, pp. 149–68. Cambridge University Press, 1992.
Kraut, Richard. "Desire and the Human Good." *Proceedings and Addresses of the American Philosophical Association* 68 (1994): 39–54.
Overvold, Mark. "Self-Interest, Self-Sacrifice, and the Satisfaction of Desires." Ph.D. diss., University of Michigan, 1976.
———. "Self-Interest and the Concept of Self-Sacrifice." *Canadian Journal of Philosophy* 10 (1980): 105–18.
———. "Self-Interest and Getting What You Want." In *The Limits of Utilitarianism*, edited by Harlan Miller and William Williams, pp. 186–94. Minneapolis: University of Minnesota Press, 1982.
———. "Morality, Self-Interest, and Reasons for Being Moral." *Philosophy and Phenomenological Research* 44 (1984): 493–507.
Rosati, Connie. "Persons, Perspectives, and Full Information Accounts of the Good." *Ethics* 105 (1995): 296–325.
———. "Internalism and the Good for a Person." *Ethics* 106 (1996): 297–326.
Scanlon, Thomas. "Value, Desire, and the Quality of Life." In *The Quality of Life*, edited by Martha Nussbaum and Amartya Sen, pp. 185–200. Oxford: Oxford University Press, 1993.
Schwartz, Thomas. "Human Welfare: What It Is Not." In *The Limits of Utilitarianism*, edited by Harlan Miller and William Williams, pp. 195–206. Minneapolis: University of Minnesota Press, 1982.
———. "Von Wright's Theory of Human Welfare: A Critique." In *The Philosophy of Georg Henrick Von Wright*, edited by P. A. Schilpp and L. E. Hahn, pp. 217–323. La Salle: Open Court, 1990.
Shope, Robert. "The Conditional Fallacy In Contemporary Philosophy." *Journal of Philosophy* 75 (1978): 397–413.
Sturgeon, Nicholas. "Brandt's Moral Empiricism." *Philosophical Review* 91 (1982): 389–422.
Sumner, Wayne. *Welfare, Happiness, and Ethics*. Oxford: Oxford University Press, 1996.
Velleman, J. David. "Brandt's Definition of 'Good'" *Philosophical Review* 97 (1988): 353–82.
[In addition, see the following items from the general bibliography: Bond, *Reason and Value*; Brandt, *A Theory of the Good and the Right*; Gauthier, *Morals by Agreement*; Griffin, *Well-Being*; Hare, *Moral Thinking*; Parfit, *Reasons and Persons*; Perry, *General Theory of Value*; Rawls, *A Theory of Justice*; and von Wright, *Varieties of Goodness*.

C. Aristotelian and Other Objectivist Theories of Value

Ackrill, J. L. "Aristotle on *Eudaimonia*." In *Essays on Aristotle's Ethics*, edited by Amelie Rorty, pp. 15–33. Berkeley: University of California Press, 1980.

Annas, Julia. *The Morality of Happiness*. Oxford: Oxford University Press, 1993.
Broadie, Sarah. *Ethics with Aristotle*. Oxford: Oxford University Press, 1991.
Cooper, John. *Reason and Human Good in Aristotle*. Cambridge: Harvard University Press, 1975.
————. "Contemplation and Happiness: A Reconsideration." *Synthese* 72 (1987): 187–216.
Hardie, H. F. R. "The Final Good in Aristotle's *Ethics*." In *Aristotle: A Collection of Critical Essays*, edited by J. M. E. Moravcsik, pp. 297–322. Notre Dame: Notre Dame University Press, 1968.
————. *Aristotle's Ethical Theory*, 2d ed. Oxford: Oxford University Press, 1980.
Korsgaard, Christine. "Aristotle and Kant on Source of Value." *Ethics* 96 (1986): 486–505.
Kraut, Richard. *Aristotle on the Human Good*. Princeton: Princeton University Press, 1989.
Norton, David. *Personal Destinies: A Philosophy of Ethical Individualism*. Princeton: Princeton University Press, 1976.
Nielsen, Kai. "Alienation and Self-Realization." *Philosophy* 48 (1973): 21–33.
Nozick, Robert. *Philosophical Explanations*. Cambridge, Mass.: Harvard University Press, 1981.
————. *The Examined Life*. New York: Simon and Schuster, 1989.
Nussbuam, Martha. "Nature, Function, and Capability: Aristotle on Political Distribution." *Oxford Studies in Ancient Philosophy*, Supplementary Volume, edited by Julia Annas and Robert Grimm. Oxford: Clarendon Press, 1988.
————. "Aristotle on Human Nature and the Foundations of Ethics." In *World, Mind and Ethics: Essays on the Ethical Philosophy of Bernard Williams*, edited by J. E. J. Altham and Ross Harrison, pp. 86–131. Cambridge: Cambridge University Press, 1995.
Reeve, C. D. C. *Practices of Reason: Aristotle's Nicomachean Ethics*. Oxford: Oxford University Press, 1992.
Roche, Timothy. "*Ergon* and *Eudaimonia* in Nicomachean Ethics I." *Journal of the History of Philosophy* 26 (1988): 175–94.
Rorty, Amelie, ed. *Essays on Aristotle's Ethics*. Berkeley: University of California Press, 1980.
Silber, John. "The Copernican Revolution in Ethics: The Good Reexamined." *Kant-Studien* 51 (1959): 85–101.
————. "Kant's Conception of the Highest Good as Immanent and Transcendent." *Philosophical Review* 68 (1959): 469–92.
————. "The Importance of the Highest Good in Kant's Ethics." *Ethics* 73 (1962–63): 179–97.
Whiting, Jennifer. "Human Nature and Intellectualism in Aristotle." *Archive fur Geschichte der Philosophie* 68 (1986): 70–95.
[In addition, see the following items from the general bibliography: Attfield, *A Theory of Value and Obligation*; Bradley, *Ethical Studies*; Brandt, *Ethical Theory*; Brentano, *The Foundation and Construction of Ethics* and *The Origin of Our Knowledge of Right and Wrong*; Brink, *Realism and the Foundations of Ethics*; Chisholm, *Brentano and Intrinsic Value*; Ewing, *The Definition of Good*; Findlay, *Axiological Ethics*; Finnis, *Natural Law and Natural Rights*; Frankena, *Ethics*; Green, *Prolegomena to Ethics*; Hurka, *Perfectionism*; McTaggart, *The Nature of Existence*; Moore, *Principia Ethica*; Parfit, *Reasons and Persons*; Rashdall, *The Theory of Good and Evil*; Ross, *The Right and The Good* and *The Foundations of Ethics*; Scheler, *Formalism in Ethics and a Non-Formal Ethics of Values*; and Williams, *Morality*.]

IV. Virtues and Ethics

A. The Virtues and the Concept of Virtue

Adams, Robert. "Saints." *Journal of Philosophy* 81 (1984): 392–401.
Becker, Lawrence. *Reciprocity*. London: Routledge, 1986.
Blum, Lawrence. "Compassion." In *Explaining Emotions*, edited by A. O. Rorty, Berkeley: University of California Press, 1980.
Driver, Julia. "The Virtues of Ignorance." *Journal of Philosophy* 86 (1989): 373–84.
Fletcher, George. *Loyalty*. New York: Oxford University Press, 1993.
Foot, Philippa. "Virtues and Vices." In Philippa Foot, *Virtues and Vices*, pp. 1–18. Berkeley: University of California Press, 1978.

Geach, Peter. *The Virtues*. Cambridge: Cambridge University Press, 1977.
Hampton, Jean, and Jeffrie Murphy. *Forgiveness and Mercy*. Cambridge: Cambridge University Press, 1988.
Hunt, Lester. "Generosity." *American Philosophical Quarterly* 12 (1975): 235–44.
———. *Nietzsche and the Origin of Virtue*. New York: Routledge, 1991.
Hurka, Thomas. "Virtue as Loving the Good." *Social Philosophy and Policy* 9 (1992): 149–68.
Kruschwitz, Robert and Robert Roberts, eds. *The Virtues*. Belmont: Wadsworth, 1986.
McDowell, John. "Virtue and Reason." *Monist* 62 (1979): 331–50.
Pence, Gregory. "Recent Work on Virtues." *American Philosophical Quarterly* 21 (1984): 281–97.
Roberts, Robert. "Will Power and the Virtues." *The Philosophical Review* 93 (1984): 227–48.
———. "Forgiveness." *American Philosophical Quarterly* 32 (1995): 289–306.
Sherman, Nancy. *The Fabric of Character: Aristotle's Theory of Virtue*. Oxford: Oxford University Press, 1989.
Slote, Michael. *Goods and Virtues*. Oxford: Oxford University Press, 1983.
Trianosky, Gregory. "Rightly Ordered Appetites: How to Live Morally and Live Well." *American Philosophical Quarterly* 25 (1988): 1–12.
Urmson, J. O. "Saints and Heroes." In *Moral Concepts*, edited by Joel Feinberg, pp. 60–73. Oxford: Oxford University Press, 1969.
———. "Aristotle's Doctrine of the Mean." *American Philosophical Quarterly* 10 (1973): 223–30.
Wallace, James. *Virtues and Vices*. Ithaca: Cornell University Press, 1978.
Walton, Douglas. *Courage*. Berkeley: University of California Press, 1986.
Wolf, Susan. "Moral Saints." *Journal of Philosophy* 79 (1982): 419–39.

B. Virtue Ethics

Baier, Annette. *Postures of the Mind*. Minneapolis: University of Minnesota Press, 1985.
———. *Moral Predjudices*. Cambridge, Mass.: Harvard University Press, 1994.
Baron, Marcia. "The Alleged Moral Repugnance of Acting from Duty." *Journal of Philosophy* 81 (1984): 197–220.
———. "The Ethics of Duty/Ethics of Virtue Debate and Its Relevance to Educational Theory." *Educational Theory* 35 (1985): 135–49.
———. "Varieties of Ethics of Virtue." *American Philosophical Quarterly* 22 (1985): 47–54.
Becker, Lawrence. "The Neglect of Virtue." *Ethics* 85 (1975): 110–22.
Bennett, Jonathan. "The Conscience of Huckleberry Finn." *Philosophy* 49 (1974): 123–34.
Frankena, William. "Prichard and the Ethics of Virtue: Notes on a Footnote." *The Monist* 54 (1970): 1–17.
Henson, Richard. "What Kant Might Have Said: Moral Worth and the Overdetermination of Dutiful Action." *Philosophical Review* 88 (1979): 39–54.
Herman, Barbara. "On the Value of Acting from the Motive of Duty." *Philosophical Review* 90 (1981): 359–82.
Lemos, Noah. "High-Minded Egoism and the Problem of Priggishness." *Mind* 93 (1984): 542–58.
Louden, Robert. "On Some Vices of Virtue Ethics." *American Philosophical Quarterly* 21 (1984): 227–36.
———. *Morality and Moral Theory*. Oxford: Oxford University Press, 1992.
Pincoffs, Edmund. *Quandaries and Virtues*. Lawrence, Kans.: University Press of Kansas, 1986.
Ross, David. "The Nature of Morally Good Action." *Proceedings of the Aristotelian Society* 29 (1928–29).
Slote, Michael. *From Morality to Virtue*. Oxford: Oxford University Press, 1992.
Trianosky, Greg. "Supererogation, Wrongdoing and Vice: The Autonomy of an Ethics of Virtue." *Journal of Philosophy* 83 (1986): 26–40.

C. Moral Psychology

Davidson, Donald. "How Is Weakness of Will Possible?" In *Moral Concepts*, edited by Joel Feinberg, pp. 93–113. Oxford: Oxford University Press, 1969.

Deigh, John. "Shame and Self-Esteem: A Critique." *Ethics* 93 (1983): 225–45.

———. *The Sources of Moral Agency: Essays in Moral Psychology and Freudian Theory*. Cambridge: Cambridge University Press, 1996.

———. ed. *Ethics and Personality*. Chicago: University of Chicago Press, 1992.

Fingarette, Herbert. *Self-Deception*. London: Humanities Press, 1969.

Flanagan, Owen, and Amelie Rorty, eds. *Identity, Character and Morality: Essays in Moral Psychology*. Cambridge, Mass.: MIT Press, 1990.

Greenspan, Patricia. *Emotions and Reasons*. New York: Routledge, 1988.

May, Larry, Marylin Friedman, and Andrew Clark, eds. *Mind and Morals: Essays on Ethics and Cognitive Science*. Cambridge, Mass: MIT Press, 1996.

Mele, Alfred. *Irrationality: An Essay on Akrasia, Self-Deception, and Self Control*. Oxford: Oxford University Press, 1987.

Mercer, C. M. *Sympathy and Ethics*. Oxford: Oxford University Press, 1972.

Morris, Herbert. *On Guilt and Innocence: Essays in Legal Philosophy and Moral Psychology*. Berkeley: University of California Press, 1976.

Murdoch, Iris. *The Sovereignty of Good*. New York: Schocken Books, 1971.

Oakley, Justin. *Morality and the Emotions*. London: Routledge, 1992.

Roberts, Robert. "What an Emotion Is: A Sketch." *Philosophical Review* 97 (1988): 183–210.

Scheler, Max. *The Nature of Sympathy*. Translated by Peter Heath. Hamden: Archon Books, 1972.

———. *Ressentiment*. Translated by William Holdheim. New York: Schocken Books, 1973.

Shoeman, Ferdinand. *Responsibility, Character and the Emotions: New Essays in Moral Psychology*. Cambridge: Cambridge University Press, 1987.

Smith, Michael. "The Humean Theory of Motivation." *Mind* 96 (1987): 36–61.

Stocker, Michael. "Desiring the Bad: An Essay in Moral Psychology." *Journal of Philosophy* 76 (1979): 738–53.

———. "The Schizophrenia of Modern Ethical Theories." *Journal of Philosophy* 14 (1976): 453–66.

Strawson, Peter. "Freedom and Resentment." In Peter Strawson, *Freedom and Resentment*, pp. 1–25. London: Methuen, 1974.

Taylor, Charles. "What Is Human Agency?" In Charles Taylor, *Human Agency and Language: Philosophical Papers I*, pp. 15–44. Cambridge: Cambridge University Press, 1985.

Taylor, Gabriele. *Pride, Shame, and Guilt*. Oxford: Oxford University Press, 1985.

Tefler, Elizabeth. "Self-Respect." *Philosophical Quarterly* 18 (1968): 114–21.

Thomas, Laurence. *Living Morally: A Psychology of Moral Character*. Philadelphia: Temple University Press, 1989.

———. *Vessels of Evil: American Slavery and the Holocaust*. Philadelphia: Temple University Press, 1992.

Wren, Thomas. *Caring About Morality: Philosophical Perspectives in Moral Psychology*. Cambridge, Mass.: MIT Press, 1991.

———. ed. *The Moral Domain: Essays in the Ongoing Discussion Between Philosophy and the Social Sciences*. Cambridge, Mass.: MIT Press, 1990.

[Also see the following items from the general bibliography: Blum, *Friendship, Altruism, and Morality*; Foot, *Virtues and Vices*; MacIntyre, *After Virtue*; Nussbaum, *The Therapy of Desire* and *The Fragility of Goodness*; Rawls, *A Theory of Justice* (Part III); and Von Wright, *The Varieties of Goodness*.]

V. Realism and Anti-Realism

Blackburn, Simon. "Moral Relativism." In *Morality and Moral Reasoning*, edited by John Casey, pp. 101–124. London: Methuen, 1971.

———. "Rule-Following and Moral Realisms." In *Wittgenstein: To Follow a Rule*, edited by Steven Holtzman and Christopher M. Leich, pp. 163–87. London: Routledge & Kegan Paul, 1981.

———. *Spreading the Word*. New York: Oxford University Press, 1984.

———. "Errors and the Phenomenology of Value." In *Morality and Objectivity*, edited by Ted Honderich, pp. 1–22. London: Routledge and Kegan Paul, 1985.

————. *Essays in Quasi-Realism*. Oxford: Oxford University Press, 1993.

Brink, David O. "Moral Realism and the Sceptical Arguments from Disagreement and Queerness." *Australasian Journal of Philosophy* 62 (1984): 111–25.

Copp, David. "Explanation and Justification in Ethics." *Ethics* 100 (1990): 237–58.

Haldane, John and Crispin Wright, eds. *Reality, Representation, and Projection*. Oxford: Oxford University Press, 1993.

Horgan, Terrance, and Mark Timmons. "New Wave Moral Realism Meets Moral Twin Earth." *Journal of Philosophical Research* 16 (1991): 447–65.

————. "Troubles for New Wave Moral Semantics: 'The Open Question Argument' Revived." *Philosophical Papers* 3 (1992): 153–75.

————. "Troubles on Moral Twin Earth: Moral Queerness Revived." *Synthese* 92 (1992): 221–60.

Klagge, James. "An Alleged Difficulty Concerning Moral Properties." *Mind* 93 (1984): 370–80.

Lovibond, Sabina. *Realism and Imagination in Ethics*. Minneapolis: University of Minnesota Press, 1983.

Mackie, J. L. "The Refutation of Morals." *Australasian Journal of Philosophy* 26 (1946): 77–90.

McDowell, John. "Values and Secondary Qualities." In *Morality and Objectivity*, edited by Ted Honderick, pp. 110–29. London: Routledge & Kegan Paul, 1985).

Miller, Richard. "Ways of Moral Learning." *Philosophical Review* 94 (1985): 507–56.

Moser, Paul. *Philosophy After Objectivity*. Oxford: Oxford University Press, 1993.

Platts, Mark. *Ways of Meaning*. Routledge and Kegan Paul, 1979.

————. "Moral Reality and the End of Desire." In *Reference, Truth, and Meaning*, edited by Mark Platts, pp. 69–82. London: Routledge and Kegan Paul, 1981.

Putnam, Hilary. *Reason, Truth, and History*. New York: Cambridge University Press, 1981.

————. *Realism and Reason, Philosophical Papers, Volume III*. Cambridge: Cambridge University Press, 1983.

————. *Realism with a Human Face*. Cambridge, Mass.: Harvard University Press, 1990.

Quinn, Warren. "Moral and Other Realisms: Some Initial Difficulties." In *Values and Morals*, edited by A. I. Goldman and J. Kim, pp. 257–63. Dordrecht: Reidel, 1978.

Railton, Peter. "Moral Realism." *Philosophical Review* 95 (1986): 163–207.

Rawls, John. "Kantian Constructivism in Moral Theory." *Journal of Philosophy* 77 (1980): 515–72.

————. "Justice as Fairness: Political Not Metaphysical." *Philosophy and Public Affairs* 14 (1985): 223–51.

Sayre-McCord, Geoffrey, ed. *Essays on Moral Realism*. Ithaca: Cornell University Press, 1988.

Sturgeon, Nicolas. "Moral Explanations." In *Morality, Reason, and Truth*, edited by David Copp and David Zimmerman, pp. 49–78. Totowa, N. J.: Roman & Allanheld, 1985.

————. "What Difference Does It Make Whether Moral Realism Is True?" *Southern Journal of Philosophy* 24 Supplement (1986): 115–41.

Tolhurst, William. "The Argument from Moral Disagreement." *Ethics* 97 (1987): 610–21.

Wiggins, David. *Needs, Values, and Truth*, 2d ed. Oxford: Blackwell's, 1991.

Wright, Crispin. *Truth and Objectivity*. Cambridge, Mass.: Harvard University Press, 1992.

————. *Realism, Meaning and Truth*, 2d ed. Oxford: Blackwell's, 1993.

[In addition, see the following items from the general bibliography: Arrington, *Rationalism, Realism, and Relativism*; Brink, *Moral Realism and the Foundations of Ethics*; Gauthier, *Morals by Agreement*; Harman, *The Nature of Morality*; Hurley, *Natural Reasons*; and Mackie, *Ethics*.]

VI. Value and Obligation

A. Consequentialism and Value

Adams, Robert. "Motive Utiltiarianism." *Journal of Philosophy* 73 (1976): 467–81.

Bennett, Jonathan. "Whatever the Consequences." *Analysis* 26 (1965–66): 83–102.

Brandt, Richard. "The Real and Alleged Problems of Utilitarianism." *Hastings Center Report* 13 (1983): 37–43.

———. "Fairness to Indirect Optimific Theories in Ethics." In Richard Brandt, *Morality, Utilitarianism, and Rights*, pp. 137–57. Cambridge: Cambridge University Press, 1992.

———. "Some Merits of One Form of Utilitarianism." In Richard Brandt, *Morality, Utilitarianism, and Rights*, pp. 111–36. Cambridge: Cambridge University Press, 1992.

Braybrooke, David. "The Choice Between Utilitarianisms." *American Philosophical Quarterly* 4 (1967): 28–38.

Brink, David. "Utilitarian Morality and the Personal Point of View." *Journal of Philosophy* 83 (1986): 417–38.

Brock, Dan. "Recent Work in Utilitarianism." *American Philosophical Quarterly* 10 (1973): 241–76.

Ewing, A. C. "Utilitarianism." *Ethics* 58 (1947): 100–11.

Feldman, Fred. *Doing the Best We Can*. Dordrecht: Reidel, 1986.

Frankena, William K. "Obligation and Value in the Ethics of G. E. Moore." In *The Philosophy of G. E. Moore*, edited by P. A. Schlipp, pp. 93–110. Evanston, Ill.: Northwestern University Press, 1942.

Gibbard, Allan. "Inchoately Utilitarian Common Sense." In *The Limits of Utilitarianism*, edited by Harlan Miller and William Williams, pp. 71–85. Minneapolis: University of Minnesota Press, 1982.

Harrod, R. F. "Utilitarianism Revised." *Mind* 45 (1936): 137–56.

Henson, Richard. "Utilitarianism and the Wrongness of Killing." *Philosohical Review* 80 (1971): 320–37.

Hodgson, D. H. *Consequences of Utilitarianism*. Oxford: Clarendon Press, 1967.

Hooker, Brad. "Rule Consequentialism," *Mind* 99 (1990): 67–77.

———. "Compromising With Convention." *American Philosophical Quarterly* 31 (1994): 311–17.

———. "Rule-Consequentialism, Incoherence, Fairness." *Proceedings of the Aristotelian Society* 95 (1994–95): 19–35.

Kagan, Shelly. *The Limits of Morality*. Oxford: Oxford University Press, 1989.

Lyons, David. *Forms and Limits of Utilitarianism*. Oxford: Oxford University Press, 1965.

Miller, Harlan and William Williams, eds. *The Limits of Utilitarianism*. Minneapolis: University of Minnesota Press, 1982.

Rawls, John. "Two Concepts of Rules." *Philosophical Review* 64 (1955): 3–32.

Regan, Donald. *Utilitarianism and Cooperation*. Oxford: Oxford University Press, 1980.

Scheffler, Samuel. *The Rejection of Consequentialism*. Oxford: Oxford University Press, 1982.

———. *Consequentialism and Its Critics*. Oxford: Oxford University Press, 1988.

Sen, Amartya. "Utilitarianism and Welfarism." *Journal of Philosophy* 76 (1979): 463–89.

Sen, Amartya, and Bernard Williams, eds. *Utilitarianism and Beyond*. Cambridge: Cambridge University Press, 1982.

Slote, Michael. *Common Sense Morality and Consequentialism*. London: Routledge & Kegan Paul, 1985.

[In addition see the following items from the general bibliography: Brandt, *A Theory of the Good and the Right*; Ewing, *The Definition of Good*; Griffin, *Well-Being*; Hare, *Moral Thinking*; Hurka, *Perfectionism*; Moore, *Principia Ethica* and *Ethics*; Parfit, *Reasons and Persons*; Schneewind, *Victorian Ethics and Sidgwick's Moral Philosophy*; Sidgwick, *The Methods of Ethics*; Smart and Williams, *Utilitarianism: For and Against*.]

B. Non-Consequentialist Theories

Dworkin, Ronald. *Taking Rights Seriously*. Cambridge, Mass.: Harvard University Press, 1977.

Emmet, Dorothy. *Rules, Roles, and Relations*. Boston: Beacon, 1975.

Garnett, A. Campbell. "Conscience and Conscientiousness." In *Moral Concepts*, edited by Joel Feinberg, pp. 80–92. New York: Oxford University Press, 1969.

Korsgaard, Christine. "The Right to Lie: Kant on Dealing With Evil." *Philosophy & Public Affairs* 15 (1986): 325–49.

Melden, A. I. *Rights and Persons*. Berkeley: University of California Press, 1977.

Nagel, Thomas. *The View From Nowhere*. New York: Oxford University Press, 1986.

Nozick, Robert. "Moral Complications and Moral Structures." *Natural Law Forum* 13 (1968): 1–50.

————. *Anarchy, State and Utopia*. New York: Basic Books, 1974.

Scanlon, Thomas. "Contractualism and Utilitarianism." In *Utilitarianism and Beyond*, edited by Amartya Sen and Bernard Williams, pp. 103–28. Cambridge: Cambridge University Press, 1982.

Taurek, John. "Should the Numbers Count?" *Philosophy and Public Affairs* 6 (1977): 293–316.

Thomson, Judith. "Killing, Letting Die, and The Trolley Problem." *The Monist* 59 (1976): 204–17.

[In addition, see the following items from the general bibliography: Bradley, *Ethical Studies*; Donagan, *The Theory of Morality*; Fried, *An Anatomy of Values* and *Right and Wrong*; Rawls, *A Theory of Justice*; Ross, *The Right and the Good* and *The Foundations of Ethics*; Smart and Williams, *Utilitarianism: For and Against*.]

C. The Divine Command Theory

Adams, Robert. "Autonomy and Theological Ethics." In Robert Adams, *The Virtue of Faith*, pp. 123–27. Oxford: Oxford University Press, 1987.

————. "Divine Command Metaethics Modified Again." In Robert Adams, *The Virtue of Faith*, pp. 128–43. Oxford: Oxford University Press, 1987.

————. "A Modified Divine Command Theory of Ethical Wrongness." In Robert Adams, *The Virtue of Faith*, pp. 97–127. Oxford: Oxford University Press, 1987.

————. "Moral Arguments for Theistic Belief." In Robert Adams, *The Virtue of Faith*, pp. 144–63. Oxford: Oxford University Press, 1987.

Chandler, John. "Divine Command Theories and the Appeal to Love." *American Philosophical Quarterly* 22 (1985): 231–39.

Ewing, A. C. "The Autonomy of Ethics." In *Prospects for Metaphysics*, edited by Ian Ramsey, pp. 33–49. London: Allen & Unwin, 1961.

Helm, Paul, ed. *Divine Commands and Morality*. Oxford: Oxford University Press, 1981.

Idziak, Janine, ed. *Divine Command Morality: Historical and Contemporary Readings*. New York: Edwin Mellen Press, 1979.

Mann, William. "Modality, Morality and God." *Nous* 23 (1989): 83–99.

Mouw, Richard. *The God Who Commands* Notre Dame: Notre Dame University Press, 1990.

Nielsen, Kai. *Ethics Without God*. Buffalo: Prometheus Books, 1973.

Outka, Gene and Reeder, John, eds. *Religion and Morality*. New York: Anchor Books, 1973.

Quinn, Philip. *Divine Commands and Moral Requirements*. Oxford: Clarendon Press, 1978.

————. "The Recent Revival of Divine Command Ethics." *Philosophy and Phenomenological Research* 50 (1990): 345–65.

Wierenga, Edward. "A Defensible Divine Command Theory." *Nous* 17 (1983): 387–407.

VII. Reason and Ethics

Bambrough, Renford. *Moral Scepticism and Moral Knowledge*. New York: Humanities Press, 1979.

Becker, Lawrence. *On Justifying Moral Judgments*. New York: Humanities Press, 1973.

Brandt, Richard. "The Concept of Rational Action." *Social Theory and Practice* 9 (1983): 143–64.

Bratman, Michael. *Intention, Plans, and Practical Reason*. Cambridge: Harvard University Press, 1987.

Carson, Thomas, and Paul Moser. "Relativism and Normative Nonrealism: Basing Morality on Rationality," *Metaphilosophy* 27 (1996): 277–95.

Daniels, Norman. "Wide Reflective Equilibrium and Theory Acceptance in Ethics." *Journal of Philosophy* 76 (1979): 256–82.

————. "Reflective Equilibrium and Archimedian Points." *Canadian Journal of Philosophy* 10 (1980): 83–103.

————. "Some Methods of Ethics and Linguistics." *Philosophical Studies* 37 (1980): 21–36.

Depaul, Michael. *Balance and Refinement: Beyond Coherence Methods of Moral Inquiry*. New York: Routledge, 1993.

Elster, Jon. *Ulysses and the Sirens*. Cambridge: Cambridge University Press, 1979.

————. *Sour Grapes*. Cambridge: Cambridge University Press, 1983.

———. *Solomonic Judgments*. Cambridge: Cambridge University Press, 1989.

Feigl, Herbert. "Validation and Vindication An Analysis of the Nature and Limits of Ethical Arguments." In *Readings in Ethical Theory*, edited by John Hospers and Wilfrid Sellars, pp. 667–80. New York: Appelton-Century-Crofts, 1952.

Frankena, William. "Concepts of Rational Action in the History of Ethics." *Social Theory and Practice* 9 (1983): 165–97.

Gauthier, David. "Morality and Advantage." *Philosophical Review* 76 (1967): 460–75.

Gensler, Harry. "Ethics Is Based on Rationality." *Journal of Value Inquiry* 20 (1986): 251–64.

Gert, Bernard. "Rationality, Human Nature, and Lists." *Ethics* 100 (1990): 279–300.

Griffiths, A. Phillips. "Justifying Moral Principles." *Proceedings of the Aristotelian Society* 58 (1957–8): 103–24.

Hudson, W. D., ed. *The Is/Ought Question*. London: Macmillan, 1969.

Kagan, Shelly. "The Additive Fallacy." *Ethics* 99 (1988): 5–31.

Kneale, William. "Objectivity in Morals." In *Readings in Ethical Theory*, edited by John Hospers and Wilfrid Sellars, pp. 681–97. New York: Appelton-Century-Crofts, 1952.

Moser, Paul, ed. *Rationality in Action*. Cambridge: Cambridge University Press, 1990.

Nozick, Robert. *The Nature of Rationality*. Princeton: Princeton University Press, 1995.

Pollock, John. "A Theory of Moral Reasoning." *Ethics* 96 (1986): 506–23.

Rawls, John. "Outline of a Decision Procedure for Ethics." *Philosophical Review* 66 (1957): 177–97.

Sencerz, Stefan. "Moral Intuitions and Justication in Ethics." *Philosophical Studeies* 50 (1986): 77–95.

Slote, Michael. *Beyond Optimizing*. Cambridge: Harvard University Press, 1989.

Williams, D. D. "Ethics as Pure Postulate." In *Readings in Ethical Theory*, edited by John Hospers and Wilfrid Sellars, pp. 656–66. New York: Appelton-Century-Crofts, 1952.

[In addition, see the following items from the general bibliography: Brandt, *A Theory of the Right and the Good* and *Morality, Utilitarianism, and Rights*; Darwall, *Impartial Reason*; Gauthier, *Morals by Agreement*; Gensler, *Formal Ethics*; and Gert, *Morality*.]

VIII. Meaning and Value of Life

Baier, Kurt. "The Meaning of Life." In *The Meaning of Life*, edited by Steven Sanders and David Cheney, pp. 47–63. Englewood Cliffs, N.J.: Prentice-Hall, 1980.

Dahl, Norman. "Morality and the Meaning of Life: Some First Thoughts." *Canadian Journal of Philosophy* 17 (1987): 1–22.

Feldman, Fred. *Confrontations With the Reaper*. New York: Oxford University Press, 1992.

Hare, R. M. "Nothing Matters." In *Meaning of Life*, edited by Steven Sanders and David Cheney, pp. 97–103. Englewood Cliffs, N.J.: Prentice-Hall, 1980.

Kamm, Frances. *Death and Whom to Save from It*. New York: Oxford University Press, 1993.

Klemke, E. D, ed. *The Meaning of Life*. New York: Oxford University Press, 1981.

Ladd, John. *Ethical Issues Relating to Life and Death*. New York, Oxford University Press.

McMahan, Jeff. "The Evil of Death." *Ethics* 99 (1988): 32–61.

Nagel, Thomas. "Death." *Nous* 4 (1970): 73–80.

———. "The Absurd." In Nagel, *Mortal Questions*. Cambridge: Cambridge University Press, 1979.

———. *The View From Nowhere*. New York: Oxford University Press, 1986.

Nozick, Robert. *The Examined Life*. New York: Simon and Schuster, 1989.

Sanders, Steven and David Cheney, eds. *The Meaning of Life*. Englewood Cliffs, N.J.: Prentice-Hall, 1980.

Silverstein, Harry. "The Evil of Death." *Journal of Philosophy* 77 (1980): 401–24.

Slote, Michael. "Goods and Lives." In Michael Slote, *Goods and Virtues*, pp. 9–37. Oxford: Oxford University Press, 1983.

Tolstoy, Leo. *My Confession*. Translated by Leo Weiner. London: J. M. Dent & Sons, 1905.

Velleman, J. David. "Well-Being and Time." *Pacific Philosophical Quarterly* 72 (1991): 48–77

Wiggins, David. "Truth, Invention, and the Meaning of Life." In *Essays on Moral Realism*, edited by Geoffrey Sayre-McCord, pp. 127–69. Ithaca: Cornell University Press.

Wolff, Susan. "Hapiness and Meaning: Two Aspects of the Good Life." *Social Philosophy and Policy* (forthcoming).

IX. Relativism and Pluralism

A. Relativism

Brandt, Richard. *Hopi Ethics*. Chicago: Unversity of Chicago Press, 1954.
————. "Ethical Relativism." In *The Encyclopedia of Philosophy*, vol. 3, edited by Paul Edwards, pp. 75–78. New York: Macmillan, 1967.
Carson, Thomas. "Relativism and Nihilism." *Philosophia* 15 (1985): 1–23.
Coburn, Robert. "Morality, Truth and Relativism." *Ethics* 92 (1982): 661–69.
Cooper, Neil. *The Diversity of Moral Thinking*. Oxford: Oxford Univeristy Press, 1981.
Duncker, K. "Ethical Relativity." *Mind* 48 (1939): 39–53.
Harman, Gilbert. "Moral Relativism Defended." *Philosophical Review* 84 (1975): 3–22.
————. "What is Moral Relativism?" In *Values and Morals*, edited by A. I. Goldman and J. Kim, pp. 143–62. Dordrecht: D. Reidel, 1978.
Henson, R. G. "Ethical Relativism and a Paradox About Meaning." *Philosophical Quarterly* 11 (1961): 245–55.
Kluckhohn, Clyde. "Ethical Relativity." *Journal of Philosophy* 52 (1955): 663–77.
Krausz, Michael, and Jack Meiland, eds. *Relativism: Cognitive and Moral*. Notre Dame: University of Notre Dame Press, 1982.
Krausz, Michael, ed. *Relativism: Interpretation and Confrontation*. Notre Dame: University of Notre Dame Press, 1989.
Ladd, John, ed. *Ethical Relativism*. Belmont: Wadsworth, 1973.
Lyons, David. "Ethical Relativism and the Problem of Incoherence." *Ethics* 86 (1976): 107–21.
Nielsen, Kai. "Ethical Relativism and the Facts of Cultural Relativity." In *Understanding Moral Philosophy*, edited by James Rachels, pp. 14–26. Encino, Calif.: Dickenson, 1976.
Nussbaum, Martha. "Non-Relative Virtues." In *The Quality of Life*, edited by Martha Nussbaum and Amartya Sen, pp. 242–69. Oxford: Oxford University Press, 1993.
Olafson, Frederick. "Meta-Ethics and the Moral Life." *Philosophical Review* 65 (1956): 159–78.
Popper, Karl R. *The Open Society and Its Enemies*, 5th ed. Princeton: Princeton University Press, 1971.
Postow, B.C. "Dishonest Relativism." *Analysis* 39 (1979): 45–48.
Rachels, James. *The Elements of Moral Philosophy*. New York: Random House, 1986.
Taylor, Paul W. "Four Types of Ethical Relativism." *Philosophical Review* 63 (1954): 500–16.
————. "Social Science and Ethical Relativism." *Journal of Philosophy* 55 (1958): 32–44.
Wellman, Carl. "The Ethical Implications of Cultural Relativity." *Journal of Philosophy* 55 (1963): 169–85.
Westermarck, Edward. *Ethical Relativity*. Westport, Conn.: Greenwood, 1970.
Wong, David. *Moral Relativity*. Berkeley: University of California Press, 1984.
[In addition, see the following items from the general bibliography: Arrington, *Rationality, Realism, and Relativism*; Brandt, *Ethical Theory*; Firth, "Ethical Absolutism and the Ideal Observer"; Ladd, *The Structure of a Moral Code*; and Westermarck, *Origin and Development of Moral Ideas*.]

B. Pluralism

Allinson, Robert, ed. *Understanding the Chinese Mind*. Oxford: Oxford University Press, 1989.
Antony, L. and C. Witt, eds. *A Mind of One's Own*. Boulder, Co.: Westview, 1993.
Appiah, Kwame. "Racism and Moral Pollution." *Philosophical Forum* 18 (1986–87): 185–202.
————. *In My Father's House*. Oxford: Oxford University Press, 1992.

————. "Identity, Authenticity, Survivial: Multicultural Societies and Social Reproduction." In *Multiculturalism,* edited by Amy Gutman, pp. 149–63. Princeton: Princeton University Press, 1994.

Baier, Annette. "What Do Women Want in a Moral Theory?" *Nous* 19 (1985): 53–63.

Calhoun, Cheshire. "Justice, Care, Gender Bias." *Journal of Philosophy* 85 (1988): 451–63.

Card, Claudia. *Feminist Ethics.* Lawrence, Kans.: University Press of Kansas, 1991.

Cole, Eve Browning and Susan Coultrap-McQuin, eds. *Explorations in Feminist Ethics.* Bloomington, Ind.: Indiana University Press, 1992.

Cox, Philip. "The Disputation of Hate: Speech Codes, Pluralism, and Academic Freedoms." *Social Theory and Practice* 21 (1995): 113–44.

Frazer, Elizabeth, Jennifer Hornsby, and Sabina Lovibond, eds. *Ethics: A Feminist Reader.* Oxford: Blackwell, 1992.

Friedman, Marilyn. "Multicultural Education and Feminist Ethics." *Hypatia* 10 (1995): 56–68.

Gilligan, Carol. *In a Different Voice.* Cambridge, Mass.: Harvard University Press.

————. *Mapping the Moral Domain.* Cambridge, Mass.: Harvard University Press, 1988.

Gutman, Amy, ed. *Multiculturalism.* Princeton: Princeton University Press, 1994.

————. "The Challenge of Multiculturalism and Political Ethics." *Philosophy & Public Affairs* 22 (1993): 171–206.

Haney, Eleonor Humes. "What Is Feminist Ethics: A Proposal for Continuing Discussion." *Journal of Religious Ethics* 8 (1980): 115–24.

Held, Virginia. "Feminist Transformations of Moral Theory." *Philosophy and Phenomenological Research* 50, Supplement (1990): 321–44.

Hoff-Sommers, Christina. *Who Stole Feminism?: How Women Have Betrayed Women.* New York: Simon and Schuster, 1994.

Manning, Rita C. *Speaking from the Heart: A Feminist Perspective on Ethics.* Lanham, Md.: Rowman & Littlefield, 1992.

Noddings, Nel. *Caring: A Feminine Approach to Ethics and Moral Education.* Berkeley: University of California Press, 1984.

Pittman, John, and Marx Wartofsky, eds. *African-American Perspectives and Philosophical Traditions.* London: Routledge, 1996.

Serequeberhan, Tsenay. *The Hermeneutics of African Philosophy.* London: Routledge, 1994.

Simon, Robert L. *Neutrality and the Academic Ethic.* Lanham, Md.: Rowman & Littlefield, 1994.

Taylor, Charles. *Multiculturalism: Examining the Politics of Recognition.* Princeton: Princeton University Press, 1994.

————. "Cross-Purposes: The Liberal-Communitarian Debate." From Charles Taylor, *Philosophical Arguments,* pp. 181–203. Cambridge, Mass.: Harvard University Press, 1995.

Tronto, Joan. *Moral Boundaries: A Political Argument for an Ethic of Care.* New York: Routledge, 1993.

Ward, Julie, ed. *Feminism and Ancient Philosophy.* London: Routledge, 1996.

Wiredu, Kwasi. "How Not to Compare African Thought With Western Thought." In *African Philosophy, an Introduction,* edited by Richard Wright, pp. 166–84. Washington, D.C.: University Press of America, 1979.

————. *Philosophy and an African Culture.* London: Cambridge University Press, 1980.

Wong, David. "On Flourishing and Finding One's Identity in Community." *Midwest Studies in Philosophy* 13 (1988): 324–41.

————. "Coping with Moral Conflict and Ambiguity," *Ethics* 102 (1992): 763–84.

INDEX